Nick at Nite's
C L A S S I C
TV
C O M P A N I O N

The All Nite, Every Nite Guide to
Better Living Through Television

EDITED BY TOM HILL

A FIRESIDE BOOK Published by Simon & Schuster New York London Toronto Sydney Tokyo Singapore

FIRESIDE
Rockefeller Center
1230 Avenue of the Americas
New York, NY 10020

Designed by Bonni Leon-Berman

Manufactured in the United States of America

1   3   5   7   9   10   8   6   4   2

Library of Congress Cataloging-in-Publication Data

Nick at Nite's classic TV companion : the all nite, every nite guide to
better living through television / edited by Tom Hill.
                    p.   cm.
                "Fireside book."
    1. Television comedies—United States—Plots, themes, etc.
        I. Hill, Tom.   II. Title: Classic TV companion
PN1992.8.C66N5   1996   95-52331
791.45'617—dc20   CIP

ISBN 0-684-81593-1

Contents

Acknowledgments

I would like to personally thank all the writers who screened and labored, wrote and cross-referenced, counted *Hi, Bob*'s and cataloged quotations for long hours, more for the love of Classic TV than any other reason. You're all brilliant. There were also many others whose work, support, and inspiration made this book possible.

Thanks to everyone in Nick at Nite's On-Air Promotion Department—where it all began and where it all happens. And special thanks to Rick Groel, Dina Anchelowitz, Jeremy Lipkin, Joe Boyd, Linda Walsh, Olivia Milonas, Rick Orlando, and Mr. Dennis Shinners.

To the 1995 summer interns, Kevin Cordero and his people, the Nick at Nite tape librarians, and the Museum of Television and Radio. To Cindy Gitter, Sheila Curry, Marilyn Abraham, Louise Gikow, and Erica Pass.

To Rich Cronin, Larry Jones, Catherine Ward, Jocelyn Jones, and Darlene Levy.

To Herb Scannell, Cyma Zarghami, Tom Harbeck, Diane Robina, David Vogler, Jim Burns, Paul Ward, and Gerry Laybourne.

To the founding fathers: Bob Mittenthal, Dave Potorti, Jim Levi, Will McRobb, Scott Webb, Steve Grieder, Andy Struse, and Chris Viscardi—and founding mothers Debby Beece, Betty Cohen, Nina Silvestri, and Eleo Hensleigh.

And to my wife, Alison, and our children, Deke and Frederica, who gave Daddy a turn on the computer now and then.

Foreword

by Dick Van Dyke, chairman of Nick at Nite

Watching TV just got easier—and better.

With this book by your side, and Nick at Nite on your set, you'll be able to enjoy Classic TV with new depth. As chairman, it's my pleasure to welcome you to this indispensable collection—the first book dedicated to Our Television Heritage, as only Nick at Nite can deliver it. It's chock-full of details, fun backstage stories, and unique observations, along with the occasional reckless opinion.

The gang has really done their homework. All those episodes! Before Nick at Nite came along, I remember how difficult it was to find so many of these shows; they were all buried as filler. When Nick at Nite first acquired *The Dick Van Dyke Show,* I was tickled just to be able to see it again. Carl Reiner had been busy trying to tape all the episodes, and all of a sudden it became easy. Once in a while he would call me up and ask me if I remember a specific episode. Not long after the show started on Nick at Nite, I was watching an episode that I had almost no recollection of . . . and laughing! Carl called and said he had the same reaction. It was the episode in which Alan Brady is doing a Broadway show and asks Rob to ghostwrite it and punch up the jokes. It had a farcical feel, and it was a little more sophisticated than the average episode, but very good. I guess if I had had this book back then, I could have looked up the episode in a matter of moments and known I was watching number 124, "Baby Fat."

I'm delighted Nick at Nite has rallied the Classic TV troops to put together this book. I hope it will prove a valuable resource for you—I know I'm keeping mine right by the TV, right here next to the remote . . . now, where the heck is that remote? Oh, well. Enjoy!

Yours in TV Land,

Dick Van Dyke

$\mathcal{I}$ntroduction

Finally, a book that's as good as watching television!

Yes, it's taken years of research, months of compilation, days of choosing a snappy title, but we at Nick at Nite are proud to present our very first book. We're not exaggerating when we call this volume a labor of love. For years we've pondered, proposed, designed, and redesigned this publication. What was the most important book Nick at Nite could do? What book would best serve fans of Classic TV?

In the end, we settled for nothing less than a complete viewer's guide to every episode of every show on Nick at Nite. Some of you may be disappointed—where is *Mister Ed? Donna Reed? Dragnet?* We love those shows, too, but we had to draw the line somewhere, and those shows can no longer be seen on Nick at Nite. The work of thoroughly cataloging the episodes of those series still awaits us.

In the meantime, the present volume is our effort to serve you, our viewers, with every bit of relevant information that could enhance your viewing experience—to offer Better Living through Television.

The features in the pages ahead are largely self-explanatory. We tried to provide all the information that would enhance your viewing of Nick at Nite's Classic TV lineup. There are lists of guest stars, running observations, scholarly comment, parallel plots, and much more.

This book is organized in what we hope will be the most useful fashion. The episodes of each show are listed in numerical order, generally the same order in which they are aired on Nick at Nite, so you should be able to find specific episodes by keeping track of where we are in the series. The only major exceptions are Christmas episodes, which are held out of the regular rotation until December.

We have included every show that currently airs on Nick at Nite, but our programming plans are constantly changing, so we apologize in advance if your favorite show is not included.

I've made every effort to be accurate, but there are undoubtedly errors, for which I take full responsibility. If you find some mistakes, let me know so that I'll be able to correct them in future editions and in our own records. See the Afterword for the address.

I hope you enjoy the book as much as we enjoyed putting it together! Happy viewing!

Tom Hill

Bewitched

One of the most adored, imaginative situation comedies from the 1960s more often than not left its viewers bewitched, bothered, and bewildered as a lovely sorceress named Samantha navigated her way through marriage to an ordinary and bemused mortal.
—David Story, *America on the Rerun*

Bewitched is not about cleaning the house with a magic wave . . . or zapping up the toast . . . or flying around the living room. It's about a very difficult relationship. And I think people pick up on this. They know there's something else going on besides the magic.
—Elizabeth Montgomery

But it was Sam's show. As played by Elizabeth Montgomery, she was one of the most appealing characters ever conjured up on prime time. Montgomery was one of TV's first "foxes," a nonthreatening but genuinely sexy woman. It was her allure, not her bag of tricks, that really made the show bewitching.
—John Javna, *Cult TV*

Headliner Elizabeth Montgomery . . . brings a sensual, yet dignified, quality to Samantha, as she demonstrates that witches have problems just like everybody else. Agnes Moorehead is regal as the never forgiving mother-in-law who is mortified that a mortal has made off with her daughter.
—Castleman and Podrazik, *Harry and Wally's Favorite TV Shows*

Bewitched was fantasy with its feet firmly planted in reality, in which two myths collided—the myth of witchcraft and the myth of the suburban idyll. Lucy and Ricky took reality and bent it out of shape to fit a special fantasy. Samantha and Darrin took fantasy and bent it into shape to fit a certain reality.
—Rick Mitz, *The Great TV Sitcom Book*

What really made *Bewitched* unique? The series is the definitive fantasy sitcom because its special premise never outshone its characters. Its stories never tampered with the internal logic of its own imaginative realm. The dialogue was masterfully structured to give life to its characters—there was no mistaking Darrin for Larry Tate or Samantha for Endora.
—Herbie J. Pilato, *The Bewitched Book*

Bewitched

on Nick At Nite

When Nick at Nite first aired *Bewitched* in September of 1989—the original black-and-white episodes only—it was with a simple promise: *Bewitched,* in the original broadcast order!

You don't start reading *Moby Dick* at page 273, and you don't fast-forward through *Citizen Kane,* so why start watching a classic series in the middle? That's why we showed the episodes in the original order of its run. Moreover, while the color episodes have been continually seen in syndication, the first seventy-four black-and-white episodes had not been seen in over a decade.

So Nick at Nite began providing not just TV but "Tinka-tinka-TV!," creating the Bewitched Answerman who fielded such tough questions as "If Samantha is so powerful, how come she doesn't do something about Darrin's looks?" and the philosophical query "Could Samantha create a boulder so heavy she herself could not lift it?"

When Nick at Nite's contract came up, a significant outcry emanated from viewers. A small group even picketed Nick at Nite's offices, among them fans dressed as Endora and Samantha. Nevertheless, *Bewitched* left Nick at Nite after only two short years.

Then came June 6, 1994—a momentous date. Not only is it Samantha's birthday, but it's also the date on which *Bewitched* became the first show that ever left Nick at Nite's schedule—

and returned! In "The Magic Hour," Jeannie and Samantha went head to head in a cosmic battle to answer the question "Whose powers are greater?" Some 1.4 million call-in votes were registered. On June 25, the winner was announced: Samantha won with 58 percent of the vote, but both shows went on to be featured in the 1994 Block Party Summer's nightly marathons, *Bewitched* BeWednesdays and *Jeannie* Thursdays. That summer, an episode of *Bewitched* scored a 3.1 in the ratings, a new high for Nick at Nite, and a particularly impressive performance for a show that was made some twenty-five years before.

Cast

(Black-and-White Episodes)

Samantha Stephens: Elizabeth Montgomery
Darrin Stephens: Dick York
Endora: Agnes Moorehead
Gladys Kravitz: Alice Pearce
Abner Kravitz: George Tobias
Aunt Clara: Marion Lorne
Uncle Arthur: Paul Lynde
Maurice: Maurice Evans
Larry Tate: David White
Louise Tate: Irene Vernon
Serena: Elizabeth Montgomery
Tabitha: Heidi and Laura Gentry as an infant; Tamar and Julie Young as a baby;
Erin and Diane Murphy as a child

The later Tabithas appeared only in color episodes. Also, Dick Sargent took over the role of Darrin, Sandra Gould that of Gladys, and Kasey Rogers that of Louise. However, none of these changes took place during the broadcast of the original seventy-four black-and-white episodes.

EPISODE 1

"I, Darrin, Take this Witch"

Writer: Sol Saks
Director: William Asher
Cast
Dave: Gene Blakely
Doctor: Lindsay Workman
Bartender: Paul Barselow
Sheila: Nancy Kovack

Boy meets girl, boy marries girl, boy has no idea girl is a witch—that is, until the honeymoon, when Samantha decides to tell Darrin the truth. After some soul-searching and a few stiff drinks, Darrin announces to Sam that he is prepared to accept her strange background, and she in turn vows to give up witchcraft. But when Darrin's ex-girlfriend Sheila makes Samantha look like a rube at a pretentious dinner party, Sam can't resist taking a bit of magic revenge.

For the Record: Darrin, skeptical about Sam's claim that she's a witch, tells her about his aunt, who think's she's a lighthouse: "Every time it rains, she insists on climbing on the garage roof to warn the sailors." This aunt becomes a recurring point of reference in episodes that explore insanity.

EPISODE 2

"Be It Ever So Mortgaged"

Writer: Barbara Avedon
Director: William Asher

Much to Endora's dismay, her daughter is determined to lead a plodding mortal existence. Still, Sam isn't above a little mother-daughter witch-play. When Endora accompanies her to inspect the house Darrin is planning to buy, the two have some fun rearranging the place. Neighbor Gladys Kravitz, spying from her window, is baffled by the spontaneous appearance of shrubbery and furniture. She shrieks her report to her husband, Abner, who begs her to take her medicine.

For the Record: Endora reads *Harpies Bizarre* magazine.

EPISODE 3

"It Shouldn't Happen to a Dog"

Writer: Jerry Davis
Director: William Asher
Cast
Babs Livingston: Grace Lee Whitney
Dr. Jason: Monroe Arnold
First Policeman: Karl Lukas
Rex Barker: Jack Warden

Darrin's prospective client, a baby food manufacturer named Rex Barker, attends a dinner party at the Stephenses' house and lustfully chases Sam. When the amorous client traps Sam in the gazebo, she turns him into a yapping poodle. When Sam tells Darrin what happened, he becomes angry and worries only about losing the account. But after Sam changes Mr. Barker back, Darrin finds the formerly canine client on top of

his wife and hits him—and not with a rolled-up newspaper, either.

Classic Guest Star: Grace Lee Whitney is best known as Yeoman Janice Rand on *Star Trek*.

Our Television Heritage: Have you ever watched *Bewitched* and had the weird feeling that you'd seen the episode, but at the same time that you hadn't? There's an earthly explanation.

Bewitched switched to color after the initial seventy-four episodes that can be viewed on Nick at Nite. Having made the switch, the show's producers felt free to reuse the scripts from the (superior) black-and-white era. This episode, in fact, was rewritten and remade twice! Herbie J. Pilato's definitive work, *The Bewitched Book*, provides a complete rundown of the entire series and explains which shows were partial or complete remakes.

EPISODE 4

"Mother Meets What's-His-Name"

Writer: Danny Arnold
Director: William Asher
Cast
Shirley Clyde: Hollis Irving
June Foster: Alice Backes
Phone Repairman: John Copage

Gladys Kravitz, who has been noticing strange goings-on in the Stephens house, leads the neighborhood welcoming committee in an investigative house call. The ladies, who bring their children along, soon find the kids tied up in an upstairs bedroom—Endora's handiwork. While the mothers try to figure out who tied up the third child, Darrin scolds his new mother-in-law for her behavior. Endora is tempted to resolve this first confrontation by turning Darrin into an artichoke, but refrains.

Classic Quote

BOY: Are you a good witch or a bad witch?
ENDORA: *Comme ci, comme ça.*

EPISODE 5

"Help, Help, Don't Save Me"

Writer: Danny Arnold
Director: William Asher
Cast
Caldwell: Charlie Ruggles

Darrin is suffering from a creative block. But when Sam comes up with some dynamite ideas for the Caldwell soup campaign, he suspects her of producing them magically and refuses to use them. After a major league fight, Darrin apologizes and then thinks up the soup slogan that will make him a Madison Avenue legend.

EPISODE 6

"Little Pitchers Have Big Fears"

Writer: Barbara Avedon
Director: William Asher
Cast
Coach Gribben: Byron Keith
Marshall Burns: Jimmy Mathers
Mrs. Burns: June Lockhart
Brush Salesman: Art Lewis
Umpire: Joe Brooks
Floyd Kravitz: Joel Davison
Player: Gregor Vigen

Sam befriends Marshall Burns, a ten-year-old neighbor whose overprotective mother outlaws everything from other children ("they're carriers") to juice ("too acidic"). To help boost his confidence, Sam encourages Marshall to participate in junior league baseball—and *somehow* his initially lame pitches become impossibly tricky curveballs. Sam's interference infuriates Marshall's mother ("Stay away from my little boy or I'll report you both to the authorities!") and upsets Darrin, but both have a change of heart when Marshall's enhanced self-esteem enables him to belt 'em out of the ballpark—*sans* witchcraft.

Epicurean Theme: To celebrate Marshall's victory, Sam offers to "twitch up a banquet" of dishes, which are repeatedly mentioned in the series as paragons of exotic cuisine: "Chateaubriand, coq au vin, you name it!"

Classic Guest Stars: Jimmy Mathers, who plays Marshall Burns, is the brother (and strikingly similar-looking, too) of *Leave it to Beaver*'s Jerry Mathers. June Lockhart, who plays his control-freak mother, was Ruth Martin on *Lassie*, as well as Maureen Robinson on *Lost in Space* and Dr. Janet Craig on *Petticoat Junction.*

EPISODE 7

"Witches Are Out"

Writer: Bernard Slade
Director: William Asher
Cast
Bertha: Reta Shaw
Mary: Madge Blake
Foreign Legion Officer: Jacques Roux
Brinkman: Shelley Berman

When Darrin's client wants to advertise his Halloween candy with images of ugly, frightening witches, Samantha takes a stand against bigotry. A Very Special *Bewitched.*

Classic Quote
SAMANTHA: I remember when I was a child, Mother and I used to have to leave the country so we wouldn't have to look at those ugly masks.

Classic Scene: When Samantha rallies her fellow witches in protest, they magically produce picket signs with slogans such as "Unfair to Witches!" and "Witches are People Too!"—all except Aunt Clara's, which reads "Vote for Coolidge."

Parallel Plot: See episode 43 for further study of holiday anti-witch sentiment.

Classic Guest Star: Shelley Berman, here in the role of Darrin's candy client, was one of the most popular stand-up comedians of the fifties and early sixties. He also made an appearance in episode 4 of *The Mary Tyler Moore Show*.

Madge Blake was occasionally seen on *Leave It To Beaver* as Larry Mondello's mother, but is best known as *Batman*'s Aunt Harriet.

For the Record: This is the first *Bewitched* episode of several written by Bernard Slade, who went on to write for *The Partridge Family* and *Welcome Back, Kotter* among others. He went on to pen the hit Broadway play *Same Time, Next Year.*

EPISODE 8
"Girl Reporter"

Writers: Paul David and John L. Greene
Director: William Asher
Cast
Liza Randall: Cheryl Holdridge
Marvin Grogan (Monster): Roger Ewing
Mr. Austen: Alex Gerry

Darrin must resist the advances of a coquettish junior college coed who interviews him for her thesis. Meanwhile, Samantha must feed the student's fiancé two kinds of pie while he's waiting to break Darrin in half.

EPISODE 9
"Witch or Wife?"

Writer: Bernard Slade
Director: William Asher
Cast
Stewardess: Raquel Welch
Waiter: Peter Camlin
Woman on Plane: Rowena Burack

To cure Sam's boredom while Darrin wrestles with deadlines, Endora suggests a quick lunch in Paris. Against her better judgment, Sam agrees, on the condition that they fly back before Darrin gets home. All goes smoothly until, by chance, they encounter Larry and Louise, who just can't wait to call and tell Darrin who they ran into!

Classic Cameo: An on-board aircraft scene features full back and partial side views, but not the full face of American sex symbol Raquel Welch, who offers Darrin his in-flight meal.

EPISODE 10
"Just One Happy Family"

Writers: Fred Freeman and Lawrence J. Cohen
Director: William Asher
Cast
Customer Number One: Thomas Anthony
Customer Number Two: Charlie Dugdale

Endora prepares Samantha for a visit from her father, Maurice. True to Endora's warnings, Maurice is less than pleased to learn that his daughter has married one of *them*—a mortal, that is. He dematerializes Darrin until Samantha begs for mercy.

EPISODE 11

"It Takes One to Know One"

Writer: Jack Sher
Director: William Asher
Cast
Janine: Lisa Seagram
Photographer: Robert Cleaves

The beautiful "spokesmodel" Darrin hired for the Jasmine perfume campaign has the hots for him. Sam, initially jealous, realizes the little witch really is a witch—sent by Endora to test Darrin's fidelity. After turning Darrin into a fish (natch), Sam chases away the hired hit and takes her faithful husband home in a glass of water.

Parallel Plot: See episode 21.

Classic Quote
ENDORA (on Darrin's supposedly roving eye): "Well, he's only human. Isn't that the excuse they're always using—'I'm only human'?"

EPISODE 12

"And Something Makes Three"

Writer: Danny Arnold
Director: William Asher
Cast
Little Witch Number One: Maureen McCormick

Looking for that swimming pool she's sure was there earlier, Gladys snoops around the Stephenses' property tapping for hollow spots. Meanwhile, Louise finds out she's pregnant and immediately tells Samantha, who accompanies her to the obstetrician's office. Larry, who's in the same building to have a tooth filled, sees the two women in the waiting room and thinks Samantha is expecting. He can't wait to tell Darrin—*that lucky son of a gun!*

Parallel Plot: For more conclusion-jumping and misapplication of the term "son of a gun," see episode 31.

Classic Cameo: Pre-*Brady* Maureen McCormick makes her first appearance on this series as one of the witch tykes Darrin imagines in a daydream about his and Sam's offspring.

EPISODE 13

"Love Is Blind"

Writer: Roland Wolpert
Director: William Asher
Cast
Susan: Chris Noel
Minister: Ralph Barnard
Kermit: Adam West
Gertrude: Kit Smythe

Sam persuades Darrin to set up his ad colleague Kermit with her forgettable friend Gertrude, and the two hit it off. Darrin, convinced his bachelor buddy has fallen for a witch, tries to thwart their romance by summoning up Kermit's old girlfriends. But love prevails, and the happy couple end up exchanging vows. And Gertrude turns out to be a mortal, to boot.

Classic Sponsorship Risk: Here's one for the Bible-belt affiliates: Sam actually freezes proceedings in the House of God for a private aside with Darrin.

Classic Guest Star: Holy debut! A pre-*Batman* Adam West makes his first TV appearance as reformed ladies' man Kermit. West went on to become a commercial spokesman for Nick at Nite, going on the air to put a chicken in a football helmet and tell America "I like Nick at Nite's shows, I like their style. I guess what I'm trying to say is that for me, Adam West, Nick at Nite is Big TV Pleasure."

EPISODE 14

"Samantha Meets the Folks"

Writer: Bernard Slade
Director: William Asher
Cast
Aunt Clara: Marion Lorne
Phyllis Stephens: Mabel Albertson
Frank Stephens: Robert F. Simon

When Darrin's parents come for their first visit, Samantha's apparent domestic prowess leaves Phyllis feeling inferior. Aunt Clara, anxious to make Sam look good, adds to the problem by conjuring up an exotic dinner complete with coq au vin. But Sam confesses she never had a hand in the feast and in fact isn't much of a cook at all, and Phyllis's motherly confidence is restored.

Epicurean Theme: As established in episode 6, coq au vin is the height of gustatory delight.

EPISODE 15

"A Vision of Sugar Plums"

Writer: Herman Groves
Director: Alan Rafkin
Cast
Tommy: Kevin Tate
Mrs. Grange: Sara Seegar
Mr. Johnson: Bill Daily
Mrs. Johnson: Berry Johnson
Santa: Cecil Kellaway
Michael: Billy Mumy

The Kravtizes and the Stephenses take home orphans for Christmas, and Darrin and Sam end up with Michael the problem child, who doesn't believe in Saint Nick. To help change his mind Darrin dresses up as Santa, but the kid sees right through the fake beard and belly. So Sam flies Michael and Darrin off to the North Pole, where a private interview with the whiskered one brings about a life-changing epiphany. The orphan's new Christmas spirit and improved attitude win over a childless couple, who adopt him on the spot.

Classic Guest Stars: *Lost in Space* juvenile protagonist Billy Mumy makes his first of two appearances. Also watch for Sara Seegar, who was Gale Gordon's Mrs. Wilson on *Dennis the Menace.* But best of all, look for the pre-Roger, pre-Howard Bill Daily.

EPISODE 16

"It's Magic"

Writers: Tom Waldman and Frank Waldman
Director: Sidney Miller
Cast
Roxie Ames: Virginia Martin
Norman the Waiter: Cliff Norton
June Foster: Alice Backes
Shirley Clyde: Hollis Irving
Floor Manager: Jimmy Murphy
Dr. Harry Clarke: Warren Parker
Master of Ceremonies: Eddie Ryder
Zeno: Walter Burke

Samantha is appointed chairman of entertainment for the hospital benefit, and she blows her whole fifty-dollar wad on a two-bit magician who can only make vodka disappear. Meanwhile, Gladys takes a turn at the kissing booth. Now, this scenario calls for witchcraft!

EPISODE 17

"A Is for Aardvark"

Writer: Earl Barrett
Director: Ida Lupino

Darrin sprains his ankle and is bedridden. Tired of running up and down the stairs to bring her husband sandwiches, Sam gives him some temporary powers. And guess what? Darrin thinks he might like witchcraft, after all. But life soon becomes too easy, and Darrin comes to see that fur coats and early retirement mean nothing when you haven't worked for them. He returns to the daily mortal struggle with a new understanding of its rich rewards.

Favorite: Of William Asher, who considered this episode the quintessential *Bewitched* story because it dealt with the show's fundamental theme. This episode explained why any witch in her right mind would embrace the tedium of the natural world and have to set the table with her hands or, say, walk somewhere.

EPISODE 18

"The Cat's Meow"

Writers: Richard and Mary Sale
Director: David McDearmon
Cast
Captain Kelly: George Ives
Kujo: Clarence Lung
Margaret Marshall: Martha Hyer
Charlie Godfrey: Harry Holcombe

Margaret Marshall (a.k.a. "the Iron Tigress"), a prospective client who has the hots for Darrin, insists that he fly to Chicago to help her with her cosmetics campaign. In order to land the account, Darrin must wriggle out of his and Sam's six-month anniversary celebration to meet Margaret on her yacht. Darrin, certain that Sam is on board in the form of a watchful cat, nervously fends off Margaret's advances. When he returns home with the cat and finds Sam waiting, he learns that his wife trusts him and that she is not a cat.

EPISODE 19

"A Nice Little Dinner Party"

Writer: Bernard Slade
Director: Sherman Marks
Cast
Conductor: Lindsay Workman
Captain: David Garner
Copilot: Hap Holmwood
Darrin's Mother: Mabel Albertson
Darrin's Father: Robert F. Simon

Darrin's parents meet Endora for the first time, and Endora's flirtatious ways make Darrin's father, Frank, feel young again. Banter leads to theater plans; his wife, Phyllis, gets jealous; and Frank ends up sleeping on the couch. Soon he's off on a world tour, and Phyllis is headed home to her mother in Phoenix, but witchcraft saves the day. Thanks to Sam and Endora—who caused this mess, after all—Darrin's parents wind up together at Angel Falls, where Frank popped the question years before.

Parallel Plot: See episode 32.

EPISODE 20

"Your Witch Is Showing"

Writer: Joanna Lee
Director: Joseph Pevney
Cast
Mr. Wolfe: Alex Gerry
Secretary: Peggy Lipton
Gideon Whitsett: Jonathan Daly

Endora, peeved that Darrin won't let Samantha accompany her to Cousin Mario's wedding in Egypt, predicts trouble for her son-in-law. The very next day Larry assigns to Darrin a brown-nosing assistant named Gideon Whitsett. As Darrin is beset by hiccups and fits of clumsiness before an important client, the seemingly earnest protégé takes every opportunity to show him up. When Darrin remembers Endora's prediction, he becomes convinced that Gideon is a warlock she has sent to snag his job. But Samantha casts a spell to reveal what Gideon really is—a duplicitous mortal headed right back to pencil-sharpening.

Classic Guest Star: This is the TV debut of Peggy Lipton of *The Mod Squad* and *Twin Peaks*.

EPISODE 21

"Ling Ling"

Writer: Jerry Davis
Director: David McDearmon
Cast
Ling Ling: Greta Chi
Wally Ames: Jeremy Slate

Darrin and Larry are having trouble finding the right face for the Jewel of the East campaign. Just when they're about to throw in the towel, Samantha changes a cat into an Asian siren named Ling Ling . . . and a supermodel is born. All's well until Wally Ames, the campaign photographer, begins dating Ling Ling. Alarmed at the inter-species romance, Samantha gets creative with some catnip, leading Ling Ling to show her true stripes.

Classic Quote
SAM *(covering for Ling Ling's odd table manners)*: Everyone feel free to eat your soup in the traditional way, with a spoon . . . or in the true native manner, as Ling Ling is doing. *(To Darrin)* Lap up your soup, darling, before it gets cold.

Parallel Plot: See episode 61 for animals turned into humans. See episode 11 for spokesmodels of supernatural origin.

EPISODE 22

"Eye of the Beholder"

Writer: Herman Groves
Director: William Asher
Cast
Dave: Gene Blakely
Mr. Bodkin: Peter Brocco
Officer Kern: Mark Tapscott
Bartender: Paul Barselow
Doctor: Lindsay Workman
Henry: Carter Deltaven
Agatha: Georgia Schmidt
Eddy: Stephen Whittaker
Kimme: Cindy Eilbacher
Miss Blanding: Sharon DeBord

Annoyed at Sam for devoting her time to Darrin instead of to her mother's lessons on witch heritage, Endora decides to stir up trouble. When she superimposes Sam's likeness on a portrait entitled *Maid of Salem, 1612*, Darrin sees it, as Endora intended, and discovers that his bride ages a little too well. Troubled by the prospect of becoming old and infirm while his wife remains forever nubile, Darrin goes off to do some serious thinking.

Parallel Plots: Each time he goes off to reconsider his life, Darrin seeks counsel from the same support circle: Dave (Gene Blakely), a doctor (Lindsay Workman), and a bartender (Paul Barselow). This combination of cast members is usually an indication that Darrin is suffering from marital doubts or low self-esteem, as in episodes 1 and 33.

EPISODE 23

"Red Light, Green Light"

Writer: Roland Wolpert
Director: David McDearmon
Cast
Dave: Gene Blakely
Mayor: Dan Tobin
Mayor's Chauffeur: Vic Tayback
Policeman: Robert Dorman

Led by Dave, the residents of Morning Glory Circle agitate to get a traffic signal installed at their dangerous intersection. Darrin creates an ad, Gladys bakes cookies, and Sam uses witchcraft to persuade the mayor. Meanwhile, Endora tries to help by contributing a multinational assortment of traffic lights (and a graceful English bobby).

Classic Guest Star: Vic Tayback is better known for his role as Mel, the surly but lovable short-order cook on *Alice*.

Parallel Plot: See episode 34 for more about the influence of witchcraft on local politics.

EPISODE 24

"Which Witch Is Which?"

Writer: Earl Barrett
Director: William D. Russell
Cast
Saleswoman: Monty Margetts
Elderly Gentleman: Donald Foster
Bob Frazer: Ron Randall

When Sam can't make a dress-fitting appointment, Endora offers to turn into her daughter's double and go in her place. While masquerading as Sam, Endora picks up author Bob Fraser, who's in the store for a book signing, and remains in his company through a montage of date scenes. Gladys sees the two together and thinks Samantha's having an affair. Meanwhile, the smitten writer turns out to be a friend of Darrin's, and he can't wait for his old buddy to meet his sassy new girlfriend.

Classic Quote

GLADYS: How would you like it if I invited one of *my* boyfriends to dinner?
ABNER: Fine. Just make sure he can play pinochle.

EPISODE 25

"Pleasure O'Reilly"

Writer: Ken Englund
Director: William D. Russell
Cast
Thor "Thunderbolt" Swenson: Ken Scott
Moving Man: Norman Burton
Police Sergeant: William Woodson
Pleasure O'Reilly: Kipp Hamilton

Sexy beauty pageant winner Pleasure O'Reilly moves in next door and has Darrin tripping over his tongue. When her jealous ex-beau, an offensive fullback named Thor, tracks her to the neighborhood, Darrin helps Pleasure hide. An encounter with Sam leads Thor to believe Darrin is Pleasure's new boyfriend, but Sam protects her husband by turning him into an old lady. Thor's next suspect is Abner, and the crazy mix-up lands Gladys, Thor, and Abner on the front page as a celebrity love triangle.

Classic Quote

THOR: Do you have Pleasure in this house?
ABNER: Not too often, but occasionally.

EPISODE 26

"Driving Is the Only Way to Fly"

Writer: Richard Baer
Director: William Asher
Cast
Basil Koenig: Paul Bryar
Harold: Paul Lynde

After a driving lesson with Darrin almost ends in divorce, Sam decides to try a professional. The fly-by-night driving school assigns her an instructor so nervous he nibbles on wafer-size tranquilizers and screams "Selfish!" instead of using the horn. After Endora's prankish behavior rattles him even further, Sam saves her teacher from being fired and enrolls him in a basket-weaving course to build his confidence.

Classic Guest Star: This is the first episode featuring Paul Lynde, beloved comedian and center square occupant on *Hollywood Squares*. Lynde later plays the recurring role of practical joker Uncle Arthur (see episode 41).

EPISODE 27

"There's No Witch like an Old Witch"

Writers: Ted Sherdeman and Jane Klove
Director: William Asher
Cast
Judge Virgil Winner: Gilbert Green
Bertha: Reta Shaw
Agnes Bain: Karen Norris
Beatrice Caldwell: Peg Shirley
Jimmy Caldwell: Brian Nash
Gary Bain: Michael Blake
Louise Bain: Vicki Malkin
Beulah: Nina Roman
Shirley: Penny Kunard

Clara, whose off-kilter witchcraft makes her feel old and useless, regains confidence by performing simple yet delightful tricks while baby-sitting. But when the neighborhood mothers decide that the town's hottest sitter is a deluded freak, they request a court order to keep her away from their children. Little do they know it's their doorknobs that are in danger.

EPISODE 28

"Open-the-Door Witchcraft"

Writer: Ruth Brooks Flippen
Director: William Asher
Cast
Noel: Hal Bokar
Max: Baynes Barron
Salesman: Eddie Hanley

Gladys spies Sam using her powers to open the garage door, but Abner assures her the door is electric. To cover for Sam, Darrin is forced to buy a real remote control instead of that great new fishing rod he's had his eye on. What's worse, the darned thing doesn't even work right. When radio signals from overhead planes cause it to open and close, Darrin accuses Sam of using witchcraft again. He orders her to put her nose "out to pasture," but wishes he hadn't when they end up locked in the garage because of a passing jet.

EPISODE 29

"Abner Kadabra"

Writers: Lawrence J. Cohen and Fred Freeman
Director: William Asher

When Gladys sees "moving pictures" at the Stephenses' house, Samantha makes her think that she has special psychic gifts. Dizzy with power, Gladys sets out to accomplish supernatural feats—until Samantha lets her believe that she has turned her dear Abner into a pile of dust.

EPISODE 30

"George the Warlock"

Writer: Ken Englund
Director: William Asher
Cast
Miss Thatcher: Sharon DeBord
Porterfield: Lauren Gilbert
Warlock George: Christopher George
Danger O'Reilly: Beverly Adams

While Darrin spends his free time next door helping Pleasure O'Reilly's baby sister, Danger, Samantha spends hers playing solitaire. Endora, seizing another chance to split the two up, sends a suave warlock named George to woo Samantha. The envoy arrives in the form of a postmodern raven who not only quoth "Nevermore" but also whistles the show's theme song.

Classic Quote

GEORGE: I'm a warlock.

DANGER: Well, so . . . It's a free country, isn't it? And everyone has the right to go to the church of their choice.

EPISODE 31

"That Was My Wife"

Writer: Bernard Slade
Director: William Asher
Cast
Ellen: Warrene Ott

Darrin and Sam plan a spicy encounter in the city to keep the magic alive. When Larry overhears that Darrin has hotel reservations and later sees him with a wig-clad Samantha, he thinks his employee is having an affair. That son of a gun!

Parallel Plots: Gladys takes a page out of Samantha's book and dons a wig to get Abner's attention. For more of Gladys in hairpieces, see episode 32. Also see episode 12.

Classic Quote

SAMANTHA *(on Larry's reaction):* I'm not sure I like his attitude. It's entirely too . . . French.

EPISODE 32

"Illegal Separation"

Writer: Richard Baer
Director: William Asher
Cast
Salesman: Dick Balduzzi

After a domestic squabble, Gladys locks Abner out of the house. When he shows up at their door in his pajamas, Sam and Darrin have no choice but to put him up for the night. Or at least they think it's for the night. When Abner wears his welcome to the bone, Darrin loosens his policy on witchcraft and asks Sam to step in with a little magic marriage counseling. Sam goes with the old bring-'em-back-to-the-day-they-got-engaged approach.

Parallel Plot: This same marital remedy worked for Darrin's parents in episode 19.

Classic Scene: Check out Gladys as she attempts to woo Abner back, fruitlessly sashaying about in a series of fetching costumes. Va-va-voom!

EPISODE 33

"Change of Face"

Writer: Bernard Slade
Director: William Asher
Cast
Gene Blakely
Paul Barselow
Marilyn Harold
Dick Wilson

While Darrin sleeps, Sam and Endora play Mr. Potatohead with his face by making a few improvements. When Darrin wakes with a straightened nose and a handlebar mustache, he learns what they were up to and becomes insecure about his looks.

Classic Guest Star: Dick Wilson, better known as bathroom-tissue icon Mr. Whipple, makes his first *Bewitched* appearance. For more Dick Wilson, see episodes 44 and 57.

EPISODE 34

"Remember the Main"

Writer: Mort R. Lewis
Director: William D. Russell
Cast
Ed Wright: Edward Mallory
John C. Cavanaugh: Byron Morrow
Charles Turner: Stuart Nisbet
Merrill Sedgewick: Justin Smith

Election fever sweeps Morning Glory Circle, and Sam and Darrin become campaign managers for a city council candidate. Endora's witchcraft helps bring his corrupt opponent's dirty dealings to light.

Classic Quote

CLARA *(after the candidate's rousing speech):* It's the greatest thing I've seen since the Lincoln-Douglas debates!

EPISODE 35

"Eat at Mario's"

Writer: Richard Baer
Director: William Asher
Cast
Vendor: Phil Arnold
Master of Ceremonies: Michael Quinn
Baldwin: Alan Hewitt
Mario: Vito Scotti

Sam and Endora lunch at this marvelous little Italian place that isn't doing too well, and they decide to help out its proud owner. (Yes, that would be Mario.) Sam zaps him up a full-page newspaper ad, dwarfing the one for a competing pizza chain. Of course, the pizza magnate happens to be Darrin's client, and boy, is he mad!

Classic Guest Star: Veteran character actor Vito Scotti made numerous appearances on *The Dick Van Dyke Show* and *Get Smart.*

EPISODE 36

"Cousin Edgar"

Teleplay: Paul Wayne
Story: John L. Green and Paul David
Director: E. W. Swackhamer
Cast
Cousin Edgar: Arte Johnson
Mr. Shelley: Charles Irving
Fred Froug: Roy Stuart

Edgar, the mute family elf, meets Darrin for the first time. Resentment, obviously couched in some Freudian or Greek mythological complex, compels Edgar to make life miserable for his cousin Sam's new husband.

Classic Guest Star: Arte Johnson was *Laugh-In's* dependable "Very interesting!" man. See also *Dick Van Dyke* episode 143.

EPISODE 37

"Alias Darrin Stephens"

Writer: Richard Baer
Director: William Asher
Cast
First Attendant: Orville Sherman

When Aunt Clara drops by the house with anniversary gifts, Darrin ends up being turned into a chimp and, worse, hugged by Gladys Kravitz. Sam finally cheers him up by telling her she's pregnant.

EPISODE 38

"A Very Special Delivery"

Writer: Howard Leeds
Director: William Asher
Cast
Dave: Gene Blakely
Man in Bar: Dort Clark
Bartender: Paul Barselow
Doctor: Henry Hunter
Reporter Number One: Jon Kowal
Reporter Number Two: Cliff Fields
Darrin's Secretary: Sharon DeBord
Mr. Martin: John Graham
Phil: Richard Vath

At first Darrin makes every effort to keep Sam, who's expecting, off her feet. But then Larry declares that an active mommy is a healthy mommy and counsels him to stop doing things for Sam. Darrin makes the mistake of trying out Larry's advice in front of Endora, who knows just the thing to make him more considerate of his pregnant wife. Suddenly Darrin is queasy, emotional, and willing to fight to the death for a pickle.

For the Record: Darrin's condition—which actually does afflict some husbands of pregnant women—is known colloquially as a sympathetic pregnancy and scientifically as couvade syndrome.

EPISODE 39

"We're in for a Bad Spell"

Writer: Bernard Slade
Director: Howard Morris
Cast
Mr. Abercrombie: Bartlett Robinson
Detective: Richard X. Slattery
Albert Harding: Arthur Peterson
Mr. Peterson: William Tregoe
Adam: William Redfield

When Adam Newlarkin, Darrin's friend from Salem, gets attacked by a dinner salad, Sam and Clara figure out that there's an ancient curse on his family. According to the spell, Adam is destined to steal a large sum of money and be branded as a common thief. To help him avoid his fate, Sam and Darrin work together on a spell-breaker that requires them to get him wet, make him kiss a Dalmatian's snout, and trick him into riding a horse through a shopping mall shouting praise for witches.

EPISODE 40

"My Grandson the Warlock"

Writers: Ted Sherdeman and Jane Klove
Director: E. W. Swackhamer
Cast
Kendrick Huxham
Minnie Coffin

When Gladys sees Darrin and Samantha baby-sitting for Jonathan Tate, she leaps to the conclusion that they have a new baby. She immediately congratulates Maurice on the birth of his grandson, and confusion ensues.

EPISODE 41

"The Joker Is a Card"

Writer: Ron Friedman
Director: E. W. Swackhamer
Cast
Mr. Foster: Douglas Evans

Merry prankster Uncle Arthur fools Darrin into thinking he can cast spells on Endora with an incantation, a cowbell, and a kazoo. Later, Darrin, Endora, and Sam get revenge by tricking Arthur into believing the ritual actually works.

Classic Performance: This is Paul Lynde's first appearance as Uncle Arthur.

EPISODE 42

"Take Two Aspirins"

Writer: Bernard Slade
Director: William Asher
Cast
Mr. Norton: Lauren Gilbert
Woman on the Street: Maudie Prickett
Police Sergeant: Larry Mann
Policeman: Ray Hastings
Mr. Trigby: Philip Coolidge

After coming in contact with a black Peruvian rose—once cultivated to drive the witches out of Peru—Sam breaks out in green spots and finds her witchcraft out of whack. Darrin buys porpoise milk and bat wings at a witch supply store, but has trouble getting the other antibiotics, which aren't available over the counter.

Classic Quote
GLADYS *(to Abner)*: I bet she's got some strange disease and we could catch it! You want to wake up with something strange?

EPISODE 43

"Trick or Treat"

Writers: Lawrence J. Cohen and Fred Freeman
Director: E. W. Swackhamer
Cast
Jack Rogers: Jack Collins
Mrs. Rogers: Barbara Drew
Endora (as a girl): Maureen McCormick

Samantha and Darrin plan to have the Tates and client, Jack Rogers, a costume-manufacturer, over on Halloween. Endora, incensed that her daughter would celebrate a holiday that vilifies witches, wreaks revenge by showing up as a little trick-or-treater and casting a spell on Darrin. When he turns into a werewolf, the delighted guests think he's swept up in the spirit of Halloween. But Endora had better remove that spell before her hirsute son-in-law does something he regrets.

Classic Guest Star: Maureen McCormick makes her second appearance, this time as li'l Endora.

Classic Quote
ENDORA: You're having a party? On Halloween? . . . I never thought I'd see a daughter of mine condoning bigotry."

Classic Moral: This episode gives considerable weight to the ongoing subtext of the series: prejudice. The Stephenses are horrified when they receive an anonymous package—sent by Larry, it turns out—of holiday decorations depicting scary, wart-ridden witches. Later on, after Endora hexes Darrin, Samantha berates her mother for living up to the very witch stereotype she so disdains.

Parallel Plot: See episode 7.

EPISODE 44

"Very Informal Dress"

Writers: Paul David and John L. Green
Director: William Asher
Cast
Charles Barlow: Max Showalter
Montague: Dick Wilson
Judge Cresetti: Hardie Albright
Policeman Number One: Dick Balduzzi
Policeman Number Two: Gene Darfler

Aunt Clara whips up outfits for Sam and Darrin to wear at a party for a client. The clothes look nice, but they don't stay on for very long. While Clara's designs start to disappear off their wearers' backs, the hydrant she moved away from Darrin's parking spot slides back into place. Darrin ends up fleeing in his intimate apparel from a ticket-happy cop.

Classic Guest Star: Dick Wilson, famous for pleading, "Please don't squeeze the Charmin," channels Mr. Whipple's negative energy into a fine performance as Montague, Darrin's boozy cellmate.

EPISODE 45

"And Then I Wrote . . ."

Writer: Paul Wayne
Director: E. W. Swackhamer
Cast
Captain Corcoran: Chet Stratton
Indian: Tom Nardini
Violet: Eileen O'Neill
Dr. Passmore: Olan Soule
Nurse: Joanie Larson
Vaudevillian Number One: Bill Dunyan
Vaudevillian Number Two: Skeets Minton

Sam gets stuck writing the pageant for a centennial celebration of the end of the Civil War. When Darrin criticizes her first draft, Sam conjures up a few key characters to help her create a more richly textured script. Gladys, spying an Indian, a Victorian lass, and a confederate officer in the Stephenses' living room, finally seeks psychiatric help.

EPISODE 46

"Junior Executive"

Writer: Bernard Slade
Director: Howard Morris
Cast
Mr. Harding: Oliver McGowan
Matronly Lady: Helen Winston
Boy Number One: John Reilly
Boy Number Two: Rory Stevens
Secretary: Sharon DeBord
Darrin (as a boy): Billy Mumy

For some reason, Sam has never seen a picture of Darrin as a boy. To show her what he looked like, Endora turns Darrin into a ten-year-old. This transformation puts him in touch with his inner child and inspires him with the perfect slogan for a toy campaign. And no, he doesn't think of it while dancing on heat-sensitive piano keys with Robert Loggia.

EPISODE 47

"Aunt Clara's Old Flame"

Writer: Bernard Slade
Director: William Asher
Cast
Hedley Partridge: Charlie Ruggles

It's embarrassing enough that Clara's tricks are failing her in front of the other witches: she's been losing altitude on long flights, and she got *caught* stealing a doorknob from Buckingham

Palace. But to make matters worse, her old beau's in town, and she can't bear for him to see her like this. After Sam goes to the trouble of assisting Clara with her witchcraft, Clara's suitor admits that *his* spells ain't what they used to be, either.

EPISODE 48

"A Strange Little Visitor"

Writers: Paul David and John L. Greene
Director: E. W. Swackhamer
Cast
James Doohan
Craig Hunely

Sam baby-sits for a ten-year-old warlock named Merle, who promises not to do any magic in front of Darrin. But when Darrin needs to be saved from a burglar, Merle learns that sometimes promises are made to be broken.

EPISODE 49

"My Boss the Teddy Bear"

Writer: Bernard Slade
Director: William Asher
Cast
Mr. Harper: Jack Collins
Receptionist: Jill Foster
Mr. Bertram: Henry Hunter
Toy Clark: Lon Bentley
Diane: Lael Jackson

Darrin, thinking that Endora has turned Larry into a teddy bear, acts really goofy in front of a client.

Classic Guest Star: Jack Collins, who plays Mr. Harper of Harper's Honey in this episode, appears in other episodes as various clients of McMann and Tate, including a costume manufacturer in episode 43 and a baby-food tycoon in episodes 66 and 67.

EPISODE 50

"Speak the Truth"

Writers: Paul David and John L. Greene
Director: William Asher
Cast
Elizabeth Fraser
Diana Chesney
Charles Lane

Endora outfits Darrin's office with a statue that makes people tell the truth. She soon finds out that while the truth often hurts, it can sometimes get your son-in-law a raise. Oh, well.

Parallel Plots: Lucy has to tell the truth for a day in episode 72; Bob Hartley tries to tell nothing but the truth in episode 56, "Brutally Yours, Bob Hartley." Finally, the very last episode of the *Bewitched* color series was a remake of this episode.

EPISODE 51

"A Vision of Sugar Plums"

More like "A Vision of Last Year's Christmas Special," this is simply episode 15, recut with a new beginning, but we feel it's our duty to provide all the information that explains why the episodes are numbered the way they are.

EPISODE 52

"Magic Cabin"

Writer: Paul Wayne
Director: William Asher
Cast
Charles MacBain: Peter Duryea
Alice MacBain: Beryl Hammond

Larry sends Darrin and Sam off for a relaxing weekend at his mountain cabin, which they find in a shambles. After Sam uses her you-know-what to fix it up, two young newlyweds wander in and declare the place their dream cottage. They surprise Larry with a generous bid.

EPISODE 53

"Maid to Order"

Writer: Richard Baer
Director: William Asher
Cast
Mrs. Luftwaffe: Elvia Allman
Naomi: Alice Ghostley

Sam's surreptitious help in the kitchen allows Naomi, the Stephenses' inept maid, to turn out a splendid dinner party. When Louise asks to borrow Naomi for her dinner party, Sam—who isn't invited—must assist from outside the Tates' window. Later, when Naomi tallies her debt for broken dishes, she reveals a gift for accounting. Darrin promises to find a place for her at the office.

Classic Guest Star: Alice Ghostley made such an impression as bumbling mortal maid Naomi that the producers later brought her back as bumbling witch-maid Esmerelda.

Epicurean Theme: Surprisingly, the meal is not coq au vin.

EPISODE 54

"And Then There Were Three"

Writer: Bernard Slade
Director: William Asher
Cast
Dave: Gene Blakely
Manager: Joseph Nell
Fred: Bobby Byles
Dr. Anton: Mason Curry
Student Nurse: Celeste Varnall
Nurse Kelton: Eve Arden

Sam finally has that baby. When Endora offers to age the infant a bit to see what she'll look like all grown up, Darrin declines. But then Serena, Sam's dark-haired doppelgänger-cousin shows up, Darrin thinks Endora has worked her witchcraft on the newborn, after all. After a series of chase scenes punctuated by pleas of "Come to Daddy," everything is cleared up. Realizing Endora's innocence, Darrin honors her wish to name the baby Tabitha.

Classic Quote
SERENA *(to Sam):* I'd like to leave a little plaything for the baby. I thought a centaur would be nice.

Classic Guest Star: Eve Arden is probably least known as that lady on the P.A. system in the movie *Grease.* She was also *Our Miss Brooks* and Eve Hubbard on *The Mothers-in-Law.*

For the Record: This is the first Serena episode. Though later billed with the pseudonym "Pandora Spocks," Elizabeth Montgomerys goes uncredited here as Sam's look-alike relative. The baby seen as Tabitha gets an "and introducing" mention.

EPISODE 55

"My Baby the Tycoon"

Writer: Richard Baer
Director: William Asher
Cast
Julius: Jack Fletcher

The Kravtizes give Tabitha one share of stock in Poughkeepsie Woolens, which hasn't moved in twenty years, and the next day it goes through the roof. When Tabitha picks profitable stocks by pointing randomly at the business page, Darrin becomes convinced that she has already developed witch powers. The Kravtizes, sensing a sure thing, invest in one of Tabitha's picks and lose their entire nest egg. Too bad they weren't around to take track-betting tips from the human horse in episode 61.

EPISODE 56

"Samantha Meets the Folks"

Again. This is a recut version of episode 14.

EPISODE 57

"Fastest Gun on Madison Avenue"

Writer: Lee Erwin
Director: William Asher
Cast
Kovacks's Manager: Herbie Faye
Kovacks: Roger Torrey
Tommy Carter: Rockne Tarkington
Bartender: Herb Vigran
Drunk: Dick Wilson

When the Stephenses dine out, Darrin ends up in an altercation with a large drunk who has been harrassing Sam. She comes to Darrin's aid by twitching her nose, and the big drunk ends up out cold. Of course, he also turns out to be prizefighter Joe Kovacks, and the morning's headlines tout Darrin as the next heavyweight champ. Kovacks demands that Darrin save his image by fighting him and taking a dive, but the setup goes awry—and guess who gets KO'd again?

Classic Guest Stars: Mr. Whipple strikes again! Dick Wilson logs another cameo as the belligerent drunk.

Herb Vigran appeared as various foes of Superman on the eponymous TV series.

EPISODE 58

"The Dancing Bear"

Writer: James Henerson
Director: William Asher
Cast
Hockstedder: Arthur Julian
Mrs. Stephens: Mabel Albertson
Mr. Stephens: Robert F. Simon

When the elder Stephenses give their new granddaughter, Tabitha, a stuffed bear identical to the one that Endora gave her, Endora decides to give her gift an athletic advantage. Casting a spell on her bear, she turns it into a plush hoofer that dances whenever Tabitha's name is spoken. Darrin convinces his baffled parents that he inserted a mechanism in the bear to make it dance ("You know how I like to tinker"), and his deluded father prepares to make a fortune in the toy market.

For the Record: James Henerson, who scripted this episode, later defected to *I Dream of Jeannie,* where he wrote many classic episodes.

EPISODE 59

"Double Date"

Writer: Paul Wayne
Director: William Asher
Cast
Turgen: Irwin Charone
Secretary: Jill Foster
Joyce: Kathee Francis

Darrin finally becomes a partner at McMann and Tate. Actually, he becomes Tate: Endora grants her son-in-law three wishes for his birthday, but she neglects to tell him she has done so. He wastes the first two wishes on inconsequential whims—the elevator he's waiting for comes really fast; that curvy number in the lobby finds herself half naked—and gets himself into a pickle with the third. That's right, he gets to be Larry for a day.

Classic Scene: Sam's rescue spell works just in time to save her husband from the plight of sleeping with Louise. Of course, the real Larry walks in the front door to find Darrin, wearing *his* pajamas, poised to kiss *his* wife . . . with Sam watching. Very Bob and Carol and Ted and Alice.

EPISODE 60

"The Dressmaker"

Writer: Lee Erwin
Director: William Asher
Cast
Doris: Barbara Morrison
J. T. Glenden: Harry Holcombe
Ethel: Arlen Stuart
Brigette: Janine Grandel
Aubert: Dick Gautier

Samantha is hard at work sewing a dress to wear to dinner with J. T. Glenden, an important client of Darrin's. Endora, noticing that the sorry garment looks like something for a "hard-times party," whisks Samantha off to Paris for an inspiring peek at the showroom of a couturier named Aubert. Back home, Sam magically copies one of the designs—and looks so good in it that she gets roped into reproducing it for Glenden's wife and sister-in-law and for Gladys Kravitz. Meanwhile, Darrin's newest client turns out to be none other than Aubert, who is outraged to find three homely American ladies sporting his unreleased designs. Observing American custom, he sues.

Classic Performance: Watch for Gladys Kravitz's star turn as a runway model in the episode's denouement.

Classic Guest Star: Dick Gautier, who plays the fashion designer, is not related to Jean-Paul Gaultier, the fashion designer. He is, however, the actor who played Hymie the robot on *Get Smart*. That said, real-life fashion designer Isaac Mizrahi cites this episode as one of his favorites.

EPISODE 61

"The Horse's Mouth"

Writers: Paul David and John L. Greene
Cast
Gus Walters: Robert Sorrells
Jack Spindler: Sidney Clute
Dolly: Patty Regan

Sam finds a runaway racehorse named Dallyrand in the backyard and turns it into a woman so as to improve communication. Darrin objects to this transformation, but Sam argues that it's a very special opportunity to *really* get to know a horse. They then take her to the racetrack and exploit her for inside information.

Parallel Plot: The horse-lady, now known as Dolly, reveals her equine origins with requests like "Never mind the coffee, I'll just take the sugar, in lumps, if you've got 'em." See episode 21, "Ling Ling," for more zoologically humorous dinner-guest behavior.

EPISODE 62

"Baby's First Paragraph"

Writer: James Henerson
Director: William Asher
Cast
First Reporter: John Newton
Second Reporter: Don Hammer
Postman: Robert De Coy
Clete Roberts

When the baby-sitter cancels, Sam reluctantly agrees to leave Tabitha with Endora, who promises to hold the witchcraft. But Gladys Kravitz comes by with her baby nephew and boasts unbearably about his accomplishments, so Endora shuts her up by making Tabitha talk. Gladys alerts the press, and the Stephenses come home to find that their newborn is a tabloid sensation. Endora finally clears things up by admitting she's a vaudevillian ventriloquist.

Classic Quote
DARRIN *(to Sam):* You *didn't* leave Tabitha alone with that broom jockey!

Classic Performance: Alone with her granddaughter, Endora reads her a witchcentric adaptation of "Hansel and Gretel." The revisionist version features a kindly witch and two gluttonous youngsters who vandalize her pretty house.

EPISODE 63

"The Leprechaun"

Writers: Paul David and John L. Green
Director: William Asher
Cast
Fogerly: Jess Kirkpatrick
Mr. Robinson: Parley Baer
Brian O'Brian: Henry Jones

Darrin, peeved to find a leprechaun in the house, learns that the fella is one of his own relatives, not one of Sam's. The leprechaun, Brian O'Brian, has come to the States to reclaim his lost pot of gold, which is hidden in the authentic Irish fireplace of a greedy tycoon. Sorcery, trespassing, and rich Celtic lore all come together in the resolution of this special holiday episode.

EPISODE 64

"Double Split"

Writer: Howard Leeds
Director: Jerry Davis
Cast
Miss Kabaker: Julie Gregg
Kabaker: Martin Ashe
Desk Clerk: Ivan Bonar

At a party, the snotty daughter of Darrin's client aims a series of backhanded insults at Sam. Without using her hands, Sam aims an hors d'oeuvre at the woman's face. Her rash behavior almost costs the company the client and causes a rift between Darrin and Larry. The two admen magically end up in bed together and exchange apologies.

Parallel Plot: Miss Kabaker's string of snide comments eerily mirrors the insult technique demonstrated by Darrin's ex-girlfriend, Sheila, in episode 1. The two women both remark on Sam's weight and dress, only warming up to ask her if she's acquainted with Dr. Hafter, who does beautiful nose work.

EPISODE 65

"Disappearing Samantha"

Writers: Paul David and John L. Green
Director: William Asher
Cast
Robert Andrews: Foster Brooks
Osgood Rightmire: Bernard Fox
Beverly Wilson: Nina Wayne

The Stephenses and the Tates attend a lecture given by self-proclaimed witch expert Osgood Rightmire, who angers Sam when he claims that witches do not exist. When he invites any so-called witches to prove their validity by striking him down, Sam can't resist the challenge. Rightmire strikes back, reciting an incantation that causes Sam to appear and disappear involuntarily. Now if only someone could get Rightmire to repeat that spell so that Endora could reverse it. The great Osgood refuses, but promises they can all find it in his book—when it comes out, that is.

Classic Guest Stars: This is Bernard Fox's first appearance in this series. Fox, formerly known for his role as Colonel Crittenden on *Hogan's Heroes*, later plays the recurring role of Dr. Bombay.
Foster Brooks was a wisecracking drunk on the Dean Martin roasts, as well as a regular on *Hollywood Squares*.

EPISODE 66

"Follow that Witch," Part One

Writer: Bernard Slade
Diector: William Asher
Cast
George Barkley: Steve Franken
Charlie Leach: Robert Strauss
Charmain Leach: Virginia Martin

Just as Robbins Baby Food is about to hire Darrin's services, Mr. Robbins's weasely assistant, George Barkley, decides to make sure Darrin's lifestyle is in keeping with the company's wholesome image. Behind Mr. Robbins's back, Barkley hires private detective Charlie Leach to tail Darrin. The professional snoop happens upon Samantha's secret, and the Stephenses' happy world threatens to crumble around them in the cliff-hanger of this two-part story.

Classic Guest Star: Steve Franken played the inimitable Chatsworth Osbourne Jr. on *Dobie Gillis*. The Osbourne family motto was "Never touch the capital."

EPISODE 67

"Follow that Witch," Part Two

Writer: Bernard Slade
Director: William Asher
Cast
Harriet: Mary Grace Canfield
Mr. Robbins: Jack Collins
Betty: Jill Foster
Mrs. Granite: Renie Riano
Mrs. Perkins: Judy Pace
George Barkley: Steve Franken
Charlie Leach: Robert Strauss
Charmain Leach: Virginia Martin

P.I. Charlie Leach threatens to reveal Sam's witchery unless she makes him rich, rich, rich! In the hope of saving Darrin's account, Sam refurnishes Leach's apartment with tasteful period pieces and gives him a brand-new car. Later, Barkley admits he had Darrin followed. Compelled by Sam's magic, he also blurts out his ambitious plan to steal the boss's job. In the exciting conclusion of this two-part thriller, Barkley gets fired, Darrin gets hired, and Leach's luxuriously appointed digs self-destruct.

Classic Encore: Virginia Martin, who plays lousy detective Charlie Leach's unsupportive and plaintive wife, Charmain, is the same actress who portrays lousy magician Zeno's unsupportive and plaintive girlfriend, Roxie, in episode 16.

Classic Guest Star: Harriet, Gladys Kravitz's sister, is played by Mary Grace Canfield, who would go on to play Ralph Monroe on *Green Acres*.

EPISODE 68

"A Bum's Rap"

Writer: Herman Groves
Director: Jerry Davis
Cast
Harriet: Mary Grace Canfield
Horace: Cliff Hall
William: Herbie Faye

Two ex-vaudevillian con men are making the rounds at Morning Glory Circle, and they try their luck at the Stephens house. When one of them rings the doorbell, Samantha mistakes him for Darrin's visiting uncle and invites him in. Going along with the mix-up, the impostor enjoys Sam's hospitality—then helps his partner loot the house. Out of respect for vaudeville, Sam lets them keep the stuff.

EPISODE 69

"Divided He Falls"

Writer: Paul Wayne
Director: R. Robert Rosenbaum
Cast
Sanford Stern: Frank Maxwell
Francie: Joy Harmon
Joe the Diver: Jerry Catron
Girl: Susan Barett

When Darrin is torn between work responsibilities and plans for a vacation with Sam, Endora solves his quandary by allowing him to be in two places at once. She divides her son-in-law into two equally repellent personae: a drone with excess initiative and a party animal with a Ph.D. in pleasure. Mr. Responsible stays and nearly kills a client with endlessly boring strategies, and Dr. Fun drives Sam nuts in Miami.

Our Television Heritage: This episode represented arguably Dick York's single finest performance as an actor, as he played both parts of his personality with his usual nervous energy and impeccable comic timing. When Dick Sargent replaced York in 1970, the very first episode he made, "Samantha's Better Halves," was a remake of this episode.

EPISODE 70

"Man's Best Friend"

Writer: Bernard Slade
Director: Jerry Davis
Cast
Harriet: Mary Grace Canfield
Rodney's Mother: Barbara Morrison
Rodney: Richard Dreyfuss

Just as Samantha is about to celebrate one whole month free of witchcraft and witchy company, Rodney, an exasperating warlock from her childhood, shows up and tries to woo her. When she refuses to run away with him, he turns himself into a shaggy dog and wins Darrin's affections. Behind Darrin's back, Rodney launches Operation Split-Up by answering the door in a robe and slippers to convince Harriet Kravitz that Sam is indulging in some daytime hanky-panky. Finally Rodney's mother comes to claim her son, who changes back only when he's threatened with a flea-and-tic bath.

Classic Guest Star: This episode marked the TV debut of Richard Dreyfuss. In high school, Dreyfuss was a friend of Michael Burns, the child actor who grew up to play Blue Boy in the well-known first episode of the color *Dragnet*. Burns later retired from acting and became a professor of European history at Mount Holyoke College as well as the author of a scholarly book about the Dreyfus Affair. Coincidence? Maybe.

EPISODE 71

"The Catnapper"

Writer: Howard Leeds
Director: R. Robert Rosenbaum
Cast
Toni Devlin: Marion Thompson
Charlie Leach: Robert Strauss
Charmain Leach: Virginia Martin

Endora and Sam see Darrin and Toni Devlin, an attractive client, lunching together. Convinced that Darrin has an early case of the seven-year itch, Endora turns Toni into a cat and then skips town. Blackmailing P.I. Charlie Leach, who's been lurking around the house again, witnesses Toni's transformation, kidnaps the feline CEO, and holds her for ransom. Sam turns him into a mouse, gets the cat back, and tracks down Endora in Tibet to make her break the spell.

For the Record: After all the talk about fallacious stereotypes, Sam actually flies in a black witch outfit, complete with cape.

EPISODE 72

"What Every Young Man Should Know"

Writers: Paul David and John L. Greene
Director: Jerry Davis

Samantha wonders whether Darrin would have proposed if he had known about her heritage beforehand. To answer the question, Endora sends her daughter back in time for a look at the alternate course of events, which—surprise!—lead to the same blissful destiny. How 'bout that.

EPISODE 73

"The Girl with the Golden Nose"

Writers: Syd Zelinka and Paul Wayne
Director: R. Robert Rosenbaum
Cast
Mr. Waterhouse: Oliver McGowan
Dave: Gene Blakely
Betty: Alice Backes
Butler: Owen McGiveney

Darrin begins to suspect that Samantha's witchcraft is behind his professional success. Determined to dump an account he thinks Sam helped him get, he tries to scare the conservative client with a swingin' hepcat act.

EPISODE 74

"Prodigy"

Writers: Fred Freeman and Lawrence J. Cohen
Director: Howard Morris
Cast
Cabdriver: Lennie Brenen
Louis: Jack Weston

Gladys's cousin Louis, a gifted violinist, hasn't performed since age nine, when his knickers fell down during a concert at Carnegie Hall. While "between engagements," he mooches on the Kravitzes while Gladys extols his genius and Abner insists he's a freeloading zero. To boost his confidence, Sam arranges for Louis to play at a benefit and uses her magic to help him overcome his stage fright. His brilliant performance leads to a TV appearance, during which he accidentally drops his pants again.

Classic Kravitz: As Abner winds up to hit Louis, Gladys throws herself in his path and points at her chin, shrieking, "You want to hit someone? Hit. Hit, hit, hit!"

The Bob Newhart Show

In part, what made the old Newhart show click was the contrast between the mumbly, polite Newhart and his scrapping ensemble, who represented a wide assortment of urban kinks and neuroses.

—Jay Wolcott, *New York*, November 22, 1982

Bob and his extended family accepted absurdity as the natural order of things . . . and somehow all of this strange behavior was anchored in utterly believable characters . . . witty, sincere people who daily faced the irrational realities of everyday life.

—Vince Waldron, *Classic Sitcoms*

Strange thing about Bob . . . he works small but gets those big laughs. They come more out of attitudes than lines.

—David Davis, co-creator, *TV Guide*, January 20, 1973

We had so many good people—Suzanne Pleshette, Bill Daily, Marcia Wallace, Peter Bonerz, and the rest, and they all made it look too easy.

—Bob Newhart, *New York Times*, December 26, 1982

Playing off the daffiness of the supporting characters with his flat, halting manner, Newhart captured the befuddlement of a mediocre man in a changing, loony world. This is the first sitcom to grapple with the increasing self-absorption of American culture.

—Gerard Jones, *Honey, I'm Home*

Casting Newhart as a shrink was inspired, because, for that job, he was supposed to sit, listen, and react. . . . One reason *The Bob Newhart Show* wears so well is that the excellent scripts are filled with a wide variety of humor: simple wordplay, running gags, clever setups, and even occasional slapstick. In addition, Newhart wisely steps back at times and lets all the characters have a chance to be funny. This is truly an ensemble comedy.

—Castleman and Podrazik, *Harry and Wally's Favorite TV Shows*

On paper, all sitcoms look alike: the wacky neighbor, the bumbling husband, the sensible wife, the man-hungry secretary, the nutty clients. . . . But somehow *The Bob Newhart Show* took an unexpected turn and created human beings, not beanbrains, and people whom, season after season after season after season after season after season (six of them in all), we grew to care about. *Care* about. Not the way we tuned in to *Bilko* or the *Beaver,* but a different way: to visit our buddies.

—Rick Mitz, *The Great TV Sitcom Book*

The Bob Newhart Show

on Nick at Nite

Who better to help launch this show than Nick at Nite's own television psycho-analyst, Dr Will Miller. In September of 1993, Miller hosted an entire week in which every single episode of the series was played, a week we called "Better Living through Bob." Call-ins, studio audiences, and others turned to Dr. Will for advice and counsel concerning their feelings about Bob and his team. One woman felt herself falling in love with Mr. Carlin, felt she could change him. Dr. Will helped her realize that she was deluded.

The Bob Newhart Show then entered the regular lineup. Viewers learned that "Bob knows . . . tennis. Bob knows . . . racing. Bob knows . . . clowns. Just view it." They were also informed that just by watching, they were automatically enrolled in the Bob Newhart School of Deadpan Comedy. At the end of that year, an episode of the show finished number one in Nick at Nite's Classic TV Countdown, and Bill Daily was on hand to accept the laurels.

The subsequent acquisition of *I Dream of Jeannie,* along with modern film technology, al-lowed a Classic TV fantasy to come true as Nick at Nite presented "Roger and Howard: Together at Last." Roger Healey and Howard Borden had never actually met until this very spe-cial event in July of 1995. Each had nothing but praise for the other.

Cast

Dr. Robert Anthony Hartley: Bob Newhart
Emily Joyce Hartley (*née* Harrison): Suzanne Pleshette
Howard Mark Borden: Bill Daily
Dr. Jerry Merle Robinson: Peter Bonerz
Carol Kester-Bondurant: Marcia Wallace
Elliot Carlin: Jack Riley
Ellen Marie Hartley: Pat Finley
Larry Bondurant: Will Mackenzie
Cliff "The Peeper" Murdoch: Tom Poston
Corinne Murdoch: Jean Palmerton
Howie Borden Jr.: Moosie Drier
Margaret Hoover: Patricia Smith
Debbie Flett: Shirley O'Hara

EPISODE 1

"Fly the Unfriendly Skies"

Writers: David Davis and Lorenzo Music
Director: Jay Sandrich

Cast

Margaret Hoover: Patricia Smith
Lillian Bakerman: Florida Friebus
Victor Gianelli: Noam Pitlik
Stewardess: Penny Marshall

It's a psychologist's field day as Bob faces a festival of phobias both in and out of the office. Howard has a fear of speaking in front of groups, Jerry is afraid of being bitten by his patients, and—most important—Emily has a major fear of flying, which Bob discovers for the first time in this episode. As it happens, Bob is treating his Fear of Flying therapy group by taking them to New York on Pathfinder Flight 21. Bob invites Emily to come along, in spite of the fact that, years ago, she made a plane turn around before it took off for Ann Arbor, Michigan. She wouldn't dare deplane in front of the group, would she? The effort ends in a tearful failure for Emily . . . so why can't Bob stop laughing?

Hartley Homily: Throughout the series, Bob offers sage (though sometimes strange) counsel to his patients and friends. Bob's timeless truisms are such a series staple that Mr. Carlin refers to them in episode 98 as "Hartley's homilies." In this episode, the philosophical shrink says, "When you love somebody, it's all right to tell them they're being stupid."

"Hi, Bob"-Ometer
Keeping track for those of you who are playing along at home, there are three "Hi, Bob" greetings in this episode—from Emily, Howard, and Jerry.

Classic Quote
BOB: Would you like a glass of chicken, Howard?

Classic Guest Star: Penny Marshall was Oscar Madison's secretary, Myrna Turner, on *The Odd Couple*. Then she really made her dream come true when she starred for seven and a half years as Laverne DeFazio on *Laverne and Shirley*.

For the Record: Notice that this show has a unique opening sequence in which Bob has a phone conversation with a patient before the theme music begins and he starts his nightly journey home to Emily. As a matter of fact, "Home to Emily" is the title of the show's theme song, which was written by show co-creator, Lorenzo Music, and his wife, Henrietta. Only episode 19 has a similar opening.

Florida Friebus begins her recurring role as Lillian Bakerman, the seemingly sweet supermarket checker. From 1959 to 1963, Friebus played Winnie Gillis, mother of the troublesome title character in *The Many Loves of Dobie Gillis*.

EPISODE 2

"Tracy Grammar School, I'll Lick You Yet"

Writers: Carl Gottlieb and George Yanok
Director: Jay Sandrich
Cast
Margaret Hoover: Patricia Smith
Dr. Bernie Tupperman: Larry Gelman
Deputy Chief Barnsdale: King Moody
Student: Tony Dickson
Student: Mia Bendixson

Bob begins his series-long struggle to justify his job. Grown-ups never seem to understand why he places such importance on listening. For Emily's class of third graders, the struggle to understand a psychologist is complicated by the fact that the word "has twelve letters in it and it's spelled funny." Plus, Bob doesn't have a uniform like the other guest speakers: Jerry, Howard, the fireman, and even the minister. For whatever reason, Bob feels he must be validated by the class, so he goes back determined to win them over and beat the fire drill.

"Hi, Bob"-Ometer
Just one in this episode, from Jerry. That's four and counting for the series.

Classic Quote
BOB *(to the third graders):* How many of you know yourselves . . . really *know* yourselves?

Classic Guest Star: King Moody makes the first of two appearances; his second is as a patient in episode 14. He's better known as KAOS henchman Shtarker on *Get Smart,* and—even weirder—he's best known as the original Ronald McDonald.

For the Record: Larry Gelman makes his first appearance as Dr. Bernard Tupperman. The overanxious urologist has his office and lab on the seventh floor of the Rimpau Medical Arts Building, near Bob and Jerry's offices. Throughout the series, Tupperman's urology lab and the samples therein provide a steady stream of humorous possibilities for Carol and the other doctors. Gelman also had a recurring role as Vinnie, one of Oscar's poker pals, on *The Odd Couple*.

Parallel Plot: Notice the conspicuous parallel between this episode and the "Father of the Week" episode of *The Dick Van Dyke Show*. Both Ritchie Petrie and Emily Hartley fear that Rob and Bob will be rejected.

EPISODE 3

"Tennis, Emily?"

Writers: David Davis and Lorenzo Music
Director: Alan Rafkin
Cast
Stan Conners: Peter Brown
Cheryl Sherwood: Barbara Barnett
Marci Windersol: Pay Lysinger

Emily's summer boredom leads her to the tennis court, where she takes lessons from pro Stan Conners, who never fails to make women's heads turn. He's convinced that Emily has fallen under his spell as well. As he divulges Emily's desire to Bob, he serves the psychologist this backhanded slam: "Bob, you have no idea what it's like to be incredibly good-looking." When all is said and done, the final score is Stan, 15; Bob, love.

Hartley Homily: "Working during a vacation from work is not a vacation from work."

"Hi, Bob"-Ometer
One, from Emily. Five for the series.

For the Record: It's implied that Bob Hartley lost his virginity at age nineteen.

EPISODE 4

"Mom, I L-L-Love You"

Writers: Dick Clair and Jenna McMahon
Director: Alan Rafkin
Cast
Eleanor Hartley: Martha Scott
Margaret Hoover: Patricia Smith
Mrs. Walker: Marilyn Child

A psychologist who can't tell his mother he loves her? Oedipus wasn't this complex! After all, it was Bob's talkative mom who gave him the "listening practice" that prepared him for his job. Only by dredging up memories of his childhood pets—a duck, a turtle, and especially his dog Freckles—is Bob finally able to bring himself to say it . . . well, sort of, anyway.

"Hi, Bob"-Ometer
One, from Jerry. Six for the series.

Classic Scene: There's a great elevator bit in this episode, in which Mrs. Walker hands Bob's hand-kerchief out to him just as the doors close. As the elevator drops, the hankie slides down between the doors and Bob struggles to grab it before it disappears.

For the Record: This is the only episode in which Mother Hartley's first name is Eleanor. Hereafter she is known as Martha. We won't meet Bob's father, Herb, until episode 59.

EPISODE 5

"Good Night, Nancy"

Writer: Susan Silver
Director: Jay Sandrich
Cast
Nancy Brock: Penny Fuller
Chuck Brock: Richard Schaal
Margaret Hoover: Patricia Smith
Dick: James B. Sikking
Judy: Anna Aries
Waiter: Jack Bernardi

With this episode, we begin to unravel the long string of love affairs that led Bob to Emily. Throughout the series, it becomes apparent that the stammering psychologist broke a lot of hearts before he and Emily tied the knot. In this case, however, it was Bob who got dumped—on his twenty-fifth birthday—by college sweetheart Nancy Brock. Now, it's fifteen years later, and Nancy's back in Chicago with a burning desire to see her old flame, "Bobby."

"Hi, Bob"-Ometer
None! The count still stands at six for the series.

Classic Quote
NANCY *(to Bob):* [Chuck] told me that if I had lunch with you today, he'd take his two-wood and drive your head four hundred yards.

Classic Guest Stars: Richard Schaal's knack for playing a sincere but self-absorbed sap would serve him well later on as a guest star in the MTM-produced comedies. Schaal made several appearances on *The Mary Tyler Moore Show* and eventually landed the regular role of photographer Leo Heatherton on *Phyllis*.

For the Record: Bob claims that, right before he married Emily, he dropped a girlfriend named Naomi. However, in episode 66, Hartley the Heartbreaker says that he dropped Gloria Webster to marry Emily.

EPISODE 6

"Come Live with Me"

Writer: Jerry Mayer
Director: Alan Rafkin
Cast
Roger Dixon: Eugene Troobnik
Emil Peterson: John Fiedler
Ronnie: Ric Carrott
Waiter: Jack Bernardi

Carol falls hard for Roger, the guy who sells Bob his office Kleenex. Bob smells trouble when he learns that Roger is already married. As we come to find out, Carol already knows about Roger's wife, and she truly believes that he's going to divorce Dolores. Unfortunately for Carol, Bob

sticks his nose in and helps Dolores and Roger reconcile. Sadly, when the time comes to break Carol's heart, even the Kleenex salesman can't soften the blow.

"Hi, Bob"-Ometer
Two, from Carol. Eight for the series.

For the Record: This is the first appearance of Bob's hilariously henpecked patient, Emil Peterson, played to perfection by John Fiedler.

EPISODE 7

"Father Knows Worst"

Writers: Tom Patchett and Jay Tarses
Director: Alan Rafkin
Cast
Lois Borden: Alice Borden
Waitress: Janice Carroll
Lady Patient: Kit Smythe

This is the first of many episodes in which Howard is perplexed by the complexities of parenting. By the terms of his divorce settlement, he gets his son, Howie, only "four days a month . . . to undo what Lois does the other twenty-seven." Certainly Howard's heart is in the right place, and he *does* think like an eight-year-old. So why does Howie want to spend all of his time with Jerry? Lois shows up to offer some insight, and ultimately it's Howard who ends up learning a lesson. Thank goodness there's banana cream pie on hand to soothe everyone's nerves.

"Hi, Bob"-Ometer
Four, all from Howard. Twelve for the series.

Classic Quote
HOWARD *(with a cotton candy wet spot):* I don't want my son to see me stained.

Classic Scene: Bob and Emily have a beautifully choreographed tag-team conversation with Howard while they rush to get ready for work.

For the Record: This is the first episode written by Tom Patchett and Jay Tarses, the prolific producers who met while working at the Armstrong Cork Company in Lancaster, Pennsylvania. The duo performed a stand-up comedy act before turning their talent to top-notch TV writing.

This is also the first and only episode in which we see Lois Borden, Howard's ex-wife.

EPISODE 8

"Don't Go to Bed Mad"

Writer: Gene Thompson
Director: Alan Rafkin

It's an all-out, all-night war of words between Bob and Emily, but the Hartleys once vowed they would never go to bed mad. At issue: Monday Night Football and a lap full of banana cream pie. Emily wants Bob to stop watching the prime-time pigskin because, as she puts it, "I don't feel like spending my Monday nights with you and Howard Cosell." But Bob stands by his couch-potato convictions—plus he can't get past that pie on his pants! At the dawn's early light, the battle finally ends in a truce. The terms of the Hartley Treaty are not revealed in this episode; in episode 18, however, Bob tells Jerry that he won the right to watch football by promising to let Emily buy new furniture.

"Hi, Bob"-Ometer
One, from Howard, bringing the series count to thirteen.

Classic Quote
BOB *(to Emily, when he notices a war movie on TV):* Wanna take a break and watch somebody else fight?

Our Television Heritage: The popularity of ABC's *Monday Night Football* was a relatively new phenomenon when this show was made. Cosell and company went on the air for the very first Monday night game on September 21, 1970.

EPISODE 9

"P-i-l-o-t"

Writers: David Davis and Lorenzo Music
Director: Jay Sandrich
Cast
Joan Radford: Louise Lasser
Margaret Hoover: Patricia Smith
Arthur Hoover: William Redfield
Jack Hoover: M. Emmet Walsh
Myrna Hoover: Helen Page Camp
Scottie Hoover: Ted Foulkes
Eric Hoover: Robert Foulkes
Mike Mitchell: Ron Masak

This is the *real* first episode of the series, the 1971 pilot film that looked totally out of place when dropped in as the show's ninth episode (for more on that, see below). After three years of marriage, Bob and Emily ponder the pressing question that would plague them throughout the series: are they ready to be parents? Both of them want a child so badly they consider adopting, on the recommendation of friend (and former orphan) Jerry Robinson. Maybe the Hartleys are lucky the adoption agency doesn't have any infants "in stock," because it's clear that Bob's real desire is to build their baby "from the kit."

"Hi, Bob"-Ometer
Two, from Mike Mitchell and Jerry. Fifteen for the series.

Classic Quote

BOB: There are a lot of good reasons for adopting a child, but having something to say at a party isn't one of them.

Classic Guest Star: In real life, Louise Lasser was Woody Allen's first wife, but she made her own mark in TV comedy by playing the title role in the satirical soap *Mary Hartman, Mary Hartman*. She also did several hilarious turns as Alex Reiger's ex-wife, Phyllis, on *Taxi*.

A Change of Hartley

These may not be the Hartleys we have come to know and love—their bedroom looks too bright, and Emily doesn't seem bright enough—but this pilot episode establishes Bob and Emily's warm and witty relationship. In a *TV Guide* interview, co-creator Lorenzo Music described the basic joke of the series: "the psychologist who is a whiz at dealing with other people's frailties, foibles, hangups, but not so hot at dealing with his own." Bob Newhart told *Rolling Stone* he made very few demands but did insist that Bob Hartley "be a psychologist, not a psychiatrist. Psychiatrists tend to deal with more serious problems. There was *that* demand, and no children . . . because I didn't want it to be a show about 'how stupid Daddy is, but we love him so much, let's get him out of the trouble he's gotten himself into.'"

Although David Davis and Lorenzo Music's basic premise remained true, Bob and Emily's lives had changed quite a bit by the time this fledgling pilot film took off as a topflight series. For instance, their apartment number, 523, used to be a condominium, number 426, and Bob was the chairman of the building. In his book *Classic Sitcoms*, Music explained, "We thought we needed other interests for Bob at home, so we made him manager of a condominium."

Howard Borden is nowhere to be found in this episode so obtrusive-neighbor duties are left to Arthur Hoover, played by William Redfield, who would return to the series in episode 90 as Howard's brother, Gordon. It's obvious that Arthur's wife, Margaret, the mother of two with another on the way, was originally intended to be a larger part of the Hartleys' life; however, the relationship was never developed and was dropped after the eleventh episode.

Finally notice that in this episode Emily is a teacher at Gorman Elementary instead of Tracy Grammar School.

EPISODE 10

"Anything Happen While I Was Gone?"

Writer: Martin Cohan
Director: Jay Sandrich
Cast
Cynthia Fremont: Elaine Giftos
Margaret Hoover: Patricia Smith

This is the first but not the last time we'll watch Jerry lose sight of himself for the sake of a beautiful woman. In this case, it's Cynthia, a headstrong hygienist, who's the object of the dentist's desire. He's known her for all of nine and a half days, but she wows him with the way she says "Your impression compound is hardening."

"Hi, Bob"-Ometer

Two, from Howard and Emily. Seventeen for the series.

Classic Quote

BOB *(at the bachelor party):* Take off your coat and be prepared to spit and swear a lot.

For the Record: It takes Bob Hartley exactly twenty-seven minutes to get from his home to the office.

EPISODE 11

"I Want to Be Alone"

Writer: Jerry Mayer
Director: Alan Rafkin
Cast
Margaret Hoover: Patricia Smith
Mrs. Prince: Helen Page Camp
Mrs. Brandell: Nora Marlowe
Mr. Warner: Alan Hewitt
Dr. Arnold: Bernie Kopell
Bellman: Archie Hahn

Bob goes out of his button-down mind as he tires of absorbing everyone else's problems. He says his head feels pressurized, like a deep-sea diver's helmet. When his depression sinks to new depths, he tells Emily he's going to get away from it all, including her, by moving into the Aberdeen Hotel. Howard is afraid his quasi-parents are heading for divorce, but Bob returns to apartment 523 after immersing himself in silence and self-analysis.

"Hi, Bob"-Ometer

Three, from Margaret Hoover, Howard, and Dr. Arnold. Twenty for the series.

Classic Guest Star: Bernie Kopell had a regular role on *That Girl,* but is better known for his role as KAOS mastermind Conrad Siegfried on *Get Smart* and as Dr. Adam Bricker on *The Love Boat.*

For the Record: This episode marks the final appearance of Patricia Smith as neighbor Margaret Hoover.

Keep an eye out for more of veteran actress Nora Marlowe. She turns up again in episode 29 as one of Bob's patients and in episode 86 as Emily's secretary. Her name is misspelled "Morlow" in the end credits of this episode.

EPISODE 12

"Bob and Emily and Howard and Carol and Jerry"

Writer: Charlotte Brown
Director: Peter Baldwin
Cast
Mrs. Walker: Marilyn Child
Bartender: Pat Morita
Waitress: Shizuko Hoshi
Man: James Hong

Throughout the run of the series, Emily is a notorious matchmaker, despite Bob's objections. This time she tries to play Cupid between Carol and Howard. However, just as the nutty navigator thinks he's found the way to her heart, Carol realizes they aren't meant to be a couple. As they share a bathroom kiss and then soar off to Ohio, there seems to be a little bit of hope for them—but not much.

"Hi, Bob"-Ometer
Five—three from Howard, one from Jerry, and one from Carol. The series total rises to twenty-five.

Classic Quote
HOWARD *(to Carol):* I thought you were gonna be sweaty tonight.

Classic Guest Star: Pat Morita went on to *Happy Days,* where he made his classic TV mark as Arnold Takahashi, head honcho and hash slinger at Fonzie's favorite hangout. More recently, Morita starred in the Karate Kid movies.

For the Record: Two important facts are revealed: that Bob and Emily met on a blind date and that Bob lives twenty miles from his office.
Take a close look at the Hartleys' guest bathroom. This is the only episode in which you'll ever see it.

EPISODE 13

"I Owe It All to You . . . but Not That Much"

Writer: Martin Cohan
Director: Alan Rafkin

Jerry is getting free professional help from Bob, but Dr. Hartley quickly grows impatient with his patient and just wants Jerry back as a best friend. The doc and the dentist sort it all out at Jerry's bash, which is such a bomb that even Howard's party wings can't save it!

"Hi, Bob"-Ometer
One, from Howard. Twenty-six for the series.

EPISODE 14

"His Busiest Season"

Writers: David Davis and Lorenzo Music
Director: Peter Baldwin
Cast
Barry Gorman: Harvey J. Goldenberg
Lillian Bakerman: Florida Friebus
Michelle Nardo: Renée Lippin
Ken Willet: King Moody

Christmas Day is approaching, and Bob decides to give the gift of group therapy to his depressed friends and patients. However, apparently misery doesn't love company at Christmas time, because the Hartleys' holiday party turns into another turkey. The guests can agree on only one thing: they're having a terrible time! But just as Jerry arrives, wearing his Yuletide pants, spirits are raised and the group sings a rousing carol.

"Hi, Bob"-Ometer
Two, both from Howard. Twenty-eight for the series.

For the Record: Bob Hartley's shoe size is 8B.

Bob's Uncle Harry and Aunt May are mentioned, but we don't actually see them until episode 17.

This marks our first meeting with Michelle Nardo, a recurring patient who primarily suffers from a dysfunctional relationship with her father. (It's highly possible that she is related to Elaine Nardo from *Taxi*.) Except for Michelle and Mrs. Bakerman, this episode's patients were never heard from again, including the Woody Allenesque Barry Gorman.

The closing credits ran over the cast singing "Deck the Halls," instead of the show's traditional ending—theme music accompanying various shots from the episode. Notice the wreath that forms around the MTM kitten at the end.

EPISODE 15

"Let's Get Away from It, Almost"

Writers: Tom Patchett and Jay Tarses
Director: Jay Sandrich
Cast
Hal Miller: Chuck McCann
Connie Miller: Joyce Van Patten
The Manager: Allen Garfield
Sanford Hettie: Danny Rees
Don: Joe Kier
Marv: John Meloch
Dave: Rudolph Schmelka

It's time for the Hartleys to take a well-deserved vacation, but when they head for the peace and quiet of a ski lodge, it's all downhill from there! The weather is unseasonably warm, so there's no snow on the ground, and there are hardly any other guests—except for Hal and Connie Miller, who share a bathroom with Bob and Emily. Hal's got a broken leg and a broken

marriage, and he asks Dr. Hartley for help in mending the marriage.

Hartley Homily: "Tell her you care about her, you want to please her, you think she's the greatest, and you love her."

"Hi, Bob"-Ometer
One, from Howard. Twenty-nine for the series.

Classic Scene: The ski lodge's restaurant revue, featuring creamed chicken in a basket, a juggling chef, and—fresh from Green Bay—the ever-popular Oom-Pah-Pahs.

For the Record: This is the first of two times this same story is told in the series. The second time is episode 133, in which Bob interrupts a Caribbean cruise to counsel another loud-mouthed, chauvinistic husband. The first version of the plot is the better of the two.

EPISODE 16

"The Crash of Twenty-Nine Years Old"

Writer: Charlotte Brown
Director: Alan Rafkin
Cast
Michelle Nardo: Renée Lippin
Lillian Bakerman: Florida Friebus
Victor Gianelli: Noam Pitlik
Paul Sanders: Jack Bender
Mr. Keeney: Dan Barrows
Mary Ellen: Jill Jaress

Twenty-nine-year-old Carol Kester may be great at her job, but her job grates on her nerves throughout the entire series. Her quest for a new career is heartbreakingly hilarious and is the subject of some of the show's best episodes. Here, thanks to Emily's advice, Carol quits her position as the seventh-floor secretary. Bob struggles to be supportive as Carol gets hired by an employment agency, misses her old job, and then comes to get it back.

"Hi, Bob"-Ometer

Two, from Howard and Carol. Thirty-one for the series.

Classic Quote

EMILY: Women all over the world are questioning their roles in life . . . the importance of their jobs. BOB: Not all women. Some women haven't had lunch with *you* yet.

EPISODE 17

"The Man with the Golden Wrist"

Writer: Bill Idelson
Director: Alan Rafkin
Cast
Dr. Bernie Tupperman: Larry Gelman
Wendy Rivers: Mimi Torchin
Mr. Carolla: Michael Lerner
Aunt May: Joan Tompkins

For Bob's fortieth birthday, Emily gives him a very expensive Pierre Giordeaux gold watch. How expensive? Let's just say that, since he was a child, Bob has measured monetary things in terms of ice cream cones, and when he finds out the watch cost $1,300, he feels as if he's "been run over by a Good Humor truck!" Another party scene goes awry as Bob's friends and relatives get the lowdown on Emily's extravagant gift.

"Hi, Bob"-Ometer

Three, from Carol, Jerry, and Howard. Thirty-four for the series.

Classic Quote

Watch inscription: "To Bob, the most wonderful husband in the world. I love you, love you, love you, Switzerland."

For the Record: This is the first script by writer-producer Bill Idelson, who also penned episodes of *The Dick Van Dyle Show* and *The Odd Couple*. Idelson is also known for his recurring appearances on *The Dick Van Dyke Show* as Sally Rogers's reticent boyfriend, Herman Glimsher.

EPISODE 18

"The Two Loves of Dr. Hartley"

Writer: Gene Thompson
Director: George Tyne
Cast
Mrs. Walker: Emmaline Henry

The irresistible psychologist adds to his string of broken hearts when one of his patients, Mrs. Walker, falls in love with him. Bob, while flattered, handles the situation delicately—he doesn't want to drive Mrs. Walker back to her food obsession. She's determined to have either Bob or a Twinkie.

"Hi, Bob"-Ometer

One, from Howard. Thirty-five for the series.

Classic Quote

EMILY *(to Bob):* When a grown woman wants to clap your erasers, that's a little different.

Classic Guest Star: Emmaline Henry played Amanda Bellows on *I Dream of Jeannie.*

EPISODE 19

"Not with My Sister You Don't"

Writer: Frank Buxton
Director: Alan Rafkin

Cast

Debbie Borden: Heather Menzies
Mr. Dabney: Mel Stewart

Bachelor Borden tries to tone down his swinging lifestyle during a week-long visit by his sister, Debbie. But she's not as innocent as big brother Borden believes, and Howie finds out the truth when Debbie dates Jerry—thanks to Emily the matchmaker. Howard's overprotective instincts give him yet another reason to act silly.

"Hi, Bob"-Ometer

Three, all from Howard. Thirty-eight for the series.

Classic Guest Star: Mel Stewart is Bob's angry patient, Mr. Dabney. Some of Stewart's hostility might have been left over from his two seasons of playing angry Henry Jefferson on *All in the Family.*

EPISODE 20

"A Home Is Not Necessarily a House"

Writers: David Davis and Lorenzo Music
Director: Peter Baldwin

Cast

Shirley Wolfson: Jenna McMahon
Roy West: Dick Clair
Betty the Stewardess: Betty Palivoda

The Hartleys seriously consider moving when Emily spots her dream home in the suburbs. The house is in the Marvella District and has hardwood floors, beamed ceilings, and a breakfast nook. A pushy agent from the Bullseye Real Estate Agency gets Bob to make a bid, but Bob almost instantly regrets it.

"Hi, Bob"-Ometer

Three, two from Carol and one from Howard. Forty-one for the series.

Classic Quote

BOB: Emily, it's hard to love a closet.

Classic Cameos: MTM writers Dick Clair and Jenna McMahon, who wrote episode 4, make a succcessful bid at portraying competing real estate agents Shirley Wolfson and Roy West.

For the Record: This is the last of the five exceptional scripts written by show creators and executive producers, David Davis and Lorenzo Music. Davis went on to help in the creation and production of *Taxi.* Music enjoyed a successful voice-over career, lending his distinct drone to such characters as Carlton the Doorman on *Rhoda* and as the caustic cartoon cat Garfield.

EPISODE 21

"Emily, I'm Home—Emily?"

Writer: Martin Cohan
Director: Rick Edelstein

Cast

Professor Trainer: Edward Winter
Mrs. Warren: Jessica Meyerson
Dr. Bernie Tupperman: Larry Gelman
Marina: Alma Beltran
Mary Ellen: Jill Jaress

Bob and Emily want two very different things: Bob just wants to watch the Bulls play the Lakers on TV while Emily wants to make a very important career move by accepting the position of full-time administrative advisor to the board of education. Selfishly, the somewhat chauvinistic shrink thinks Emily should be at home to greet him whenever he calls out "Honey, I'm home!"—which he does three times in this episode. But Emily stands by her decision to take the job and gets him to see it her way. Their "liberal marriage," as Bob calls it, is preserved.

"Hi, Bob"-Ometer
Three, two from Howard and one from Bernie Tupperman. Forty-four for the series.

Classic Scene: Because Bob Newhart is a master of minimalism, he gets big laughs whenever he does a rare bit of physical comedy. In this episode, he scores a big audience reaction as he frantically flails about in a desperate attempt to uncap a bottle of beer in the bedroom.

EPISODE 22
"You Can't Win 'Em All"

Writer: Bill Idelson
Director: Jerry London
Cast
Moose Washburn: Vern E. Rowe
Phil Bender: Jim Watkins
Dr. Bernie Tupperman: Larry Gelman
Ernie Atkins: Roy West

Bob is treating Cubs pitcher Phil Bender, who credits the therapy with helping him win games. Success with Bender brings to Bob both citywide fame and, unfortunately, a true loser wants the same treatment Phil's getting. The loser is Moose Washburn, the washed-up and often-traded Cubs catcher who has a .183 batting average. When Bob takes a swing at treating Moose, he starts taking the Cubs' losses personally. Much to Bob's relief, Washburn is eventually traded to a Japanese expansion team for a shortstop, a third baseman, and a Datsun.

"Hi, Bob"-Ometer
Two, both from Howard. Forty-six for the series.

Classic Quote
JERRY *(to Dr. Tupperman):* There's not a lot of people who are gonna brag about their urologist.

EPISODE 23
"Bum Voyage"

Writers: Austin and Irma Kalish
Director: Martin Cohan
Cast
Victor Gianelli: Noam Pitlik
Michelle Nardo: Renée Lippin
Lillian Bakerman: Florida Friebus
Emil Peterson: John Fiedler
Halstein the Steward: Archie Hahn
Strange Man: Pat McCormick

Emily is disappointed when Bob is reluctant to set sail on their sixty-three-day cruise. He has a sinking feeling that his therapy group's too dependent for him to be away for so long, but he is buoyed by the group's assurance they'll be fine. In the end, the Hartleys, Jerry, Carol, Howard, and Bob's patients all wind up in the same boat—literally. The stateroom scene is such a conspicuous nod to the movie *A Night at the Opera* that Howard announces: "The first one to make a Marx Brothers joke gets it!"

"Hi, Bob"-Ometer
One, from Jerry. Forty-seven for the series.

Classic Quote
BOB *(to Emily):* I'm not saying we're not going. And I'm not saying we're going. The chances are that we're gonna go—but you can never tell.

MICHELLE *(to Bob):* We've got enough guilt about feeling guilty about giving you guilt.

Classic Cameo: TV writer and stand-up comic Pat McCormick makes a peculiar appearance as the cruise guest who towers above the crowd.

EPISODE 24

"Who's Been Sleeping on My Couch?"

Writer: Jerry Mayer
Director: Alan Rafkin
Cast
Michelle Nardo: Renée Lippin
Mr. Atlee the Guard: Herbie Faye

The mystery begins when Bob discovers that his office couch contains some strange items: cracker crumbs, a comb with brown hair in it, and a copy of *The Feminine Mystique.* Who's been secretly snoozing on his sofa? The culprit is Jerry, whose love life has taken yet another nosedive. Bob tries to help the dejected dentist, but it's Carol who really comes to the rescue.

"Hi, Bob"-Ometer
One, from Carol. Forty-eight for the series.

Classic Quote
JERRY: Have you ever been thrown over for a twenty-two-year-old guy?
CAROL: As a matter of fact, yes.

For the Record: This was the last episode of the show's first season.

EPISODE 25

"Last TV Show"

Writer: Charlotte Brown
Director: Jay Sandrich
Cast
Michelle Nardo: Renée Lippin
Victor Gianelli: Noam Pitlik
Lillian Bakerman: Florida Friebus
Emil Peterson: John Fiedler
Floor Manager: Don Dandridge

No one understands why Bob is reluctant to accept an invitation to hold a session with his group to be broadcast live on a PBS show called *Psychology in Action.* His patients convince him that they should do it, but from the moment the TV announcer introduces him as Robert *Hartman,* it becomes clear that Bob should have trusted his original instincts. Stage fright paralyzes the group for the entire hour, leaving Bob with fifty-six minutes to fill. In deadpan desperation, the stammering psychologist treats the viewing audience to a myriad of unexciting memories from his youth—singing soprano in a boys' choir, spending his summers on Uncle Ned's farm, and working in the college library.

"Hi, Bob"-Ometer
One, from Howard. Forty-nine for the series.

EPISODE 26

"Motel"

Writers: Tom Patchett and Jay Tarses
Director: Jay Sandrich
Cast
Janine: Zohra Lampert
Angela: Barbara Brownell
Maintenance Man: Richard D. Hurst

Bob and Jerry can't score tickets to the Bears-Packers game, so they rush off to a Peoria motel to catch the game on TV. Not long after they've settled into room 535, Jerry changes their game plan. He meets Janine and Angela, makes a pass at Angela, and takes off with her to check the reception on the TV in the girls' motel room. Bob is left behind to awkwardly fumble through the rest of the night alone with Janine.

"Hi, Bob"-Ometer
Two, both from Howard. Fifty-one for the series.

Classic Scene: Bob arrives at the motel restaurant, where he learns that Jerry's been lying to Janine and Angela. According to Jerry's story, he's a movie director named Lloyd and Bob's a race car driver named Dave, a.k.a. "Mr. Guts." As Bob unravels the deceptive dentist's string of lies, Jerry tries changing his occupation to U.S. senator.

EPISODE 27

"Backlash"

Writer: Susan Silver
Director: George Tyne
Cast
Mr. Trevesco: Michael Conrad

Emily anxiously awaits the Hartleys' trip to Acapulco. It's more than just a chance to get away; according to their doctor, it's also the perfect time for Bob and Emily to conceive. But before they can soar off to the sand and sun, Bob suffers a serious back injury that leaves him bedridden in Chicago. With the vacation, and the conception, on hold, Emily hardly tries to hide her frustration over Bob's ill-timed bout with lumbago. The result is some of the series' most petulant pillow talk.

"Hi, Bob"-Ometer
None! The series total stalls at fifty-one.

Classic Quote
BOB *(bent over in pain, to Emily):* I want you to stay by my side to make sure no one throws a saddle on me.

Classic Guest Star: Michael Conrad makes his first of two appearances as Mr. Trevesco (look for him again in episode 48). Conrad also did noteworthy guest shots on *The Dick Van Dyke Show* and *All in the Family* before becoming Sergeant Phil Esterhaus, the huge cop with a huge heart, on *Hill Street Blues.*

Classic Scene: Bob does another of his rare bits of physical comedy as he hangs on to the towering Mr. Trevesco, who thinks the shrink is administering a therapeutic hug.

Parallel Plot: There's a strong resemblance between this pain-in-the-back episode and "The Brave and the Backache," *The Dick Van Dyke Show* (episode 82). Both Bob Hartley and Rob Petrie add insult to their injuries by trying to hide their anguish from their wives. Neither hunched-over husband gets much support, lumbar or otherwise.

EPISODE 28

"Somebody Down Here Likes Me"

Writer: Peter Meyerson
Director: Jerry London
Cast
Reverend Dan Bradford: John McMartin

Bob has hell to pay after Emily pays $350 for an antique Bible, including the solid oak stand, at a church auction. Things go bad when Bob tries to return the good book to the good church and meets good Reverend Bradford, who's bedeviled by his secret desire to stop being good (he's seen *Last Tango in Paris*). The repressed reverend admits he wants Bob's professional help: "I can't get through to God on this one, Dr. Hartley. That's why I came to you." As a result of therapy, Reverend Bardford decides to quit his congregation and run for mayor in his hometown.

Hartley Homily: "Don't quit even if your orange crate breaks!"

"Hi, Bob"-Ometer
Two, from Howard and Jerry. That's fifty-three for the series.

EPISODE 29

"Emily in for Carol"

Writer: Jerry Mayer
Director: Alan Rafkin
Cast
Dr. Phil Newman: Howard Platt
Dr. Bernie Tupperman: Larry Gelman
Miss Brennan: Teri Garr
Joan Rossi: Rhoda Gemignani
Mrs. Manning: Nora Marlowe

Because Carol decides to roam to Rome for three weeks, the doctors are desperately seeking a temp to replace her—and they aren't having much luck! When some suggest that Emily fill in, Dr. Hartley is immediately resistant. Only the threat of Tippy Tupperman and her ambulance-like voice can move Bob to consider the Emily option. When she's offered the job, it's Emily's turn to be resistant, but Bob talks her into it. Needless to say, they both should've gone with their gut feelings. In a unique marital moment, Bob is forced to fire his wife.

"Hi, Bob"-Ometer
Zero. Still at fifty-three for the series.

Classic Guest Star: Teri Garr makes the first of her two appearances as Miss Brennan (she's Dr. Walburn's secretary in episode 47). Garr made her mark in the big screen comedies *Young Frankenstein, Mr. Mom, and Tootsie*. Perhaps she's better known for her numerous guest spots with Johnny Carson and David Letterman.

Parallel Plot: This is another case of déjà vu Van Dyke, as the plot parallels the plight of the Petries in "My Part-Time Wife," an excellent episode of *The Dick Van Dyke Show*. The only real difference is that Emily is reluctant to work with Bob, whereas Laura looked forward to the prospect of being on the job with Rob.

For the Record: The reason for Howard's divorce is revealed. It seems that, after he and Lois were married, she worked as a stewardess on the same 747 that Howard navigated. He became jealous when passengers started hitting on his wife. As Howard puts it, "The skies were a little too friendly."

EPISODE 30

"Have You Met Miss Dietz?"

Writer: Bill Idelson
Director: George Tyne
Cast
Marilyn Dietz: Mariette Hartley
Mr. Brown: David Fresco

When old friend—and recent divorcée—Marilyn Dietz moves into the Hartleys' building, Emily begins her matchmaking maneuvers, introducing Miss Deitz to both Howard and Jerry. The guys fall hard for her, but they both want to be her one and only. At Marilyn's painting party, the riled Romeos begin a painting battle that ends with Bob the most colorful casualty.

"Hi, Bob"-Ometer
Three, two from Howard and one from Marilyn Dietz. Fifty-six for the series.

Classic Quote
HOWARD: You can't have two guys feeding the same cat without somebody getting hurt.

For the Record: Although Marilyn moves into apartment 325 to be "just three floors away from a good friend and a good shrink," she is never seen or heard from again. She does, however, get mentioned in episodes 34 and 40.

EPISODE 31

"Old Man Rivers"

Writer: Martin Cohan
Director: Martin Cohan
Cast
Dr. Bernie Tupperman: Larry Gelman
Dr. Scott Rivers: Jeff Corey
Young Doctor: Don Fenwick
Nurse: Monty Margetts

When Carol says she's going in for surgery, Bob's surprised to discover she's getting a tattoo of a monarch butterfly removed from her derriere. In a somewhat shocking turn of events, both Howard and Jerry seem to be familiar with Carol's backside butterfly. It's never explained how they know, but for possible explanations, see episodes 12 and 24.

In recovery, Carol tells her friends that the tattoo's gone and so is her heart—she's lost it to her doctor, Scott Rivers, a much older man. How much older? As Jerry puts it, "She's robbing the wheelchair." Just as Carol's about to let the ribbing ruin the romance, she realizes that love doesn't recognize age.

"Hi, Bob"-Ometer
One, from Howard. Fifty-seven for the series.

EPISODE 32

"Mr. Emily Hartley"

Writer: Charlotte Brown
Director: Jerry London
Cast
Dr. Ralph Hodiak: Bill Quinn
David Robbins: Tom Patchett
Waiter: Jay Tarses
Hostess: Claudette Nevins
Young Boy: Perry Casteliano

Suddenly Bob and Emily find themselves in a mixed marriage. First of all, he's a psychologist and she's become a psychometrist, qualifying her to administer IQ tests. Next, they discover that she's a genius and he's not. Of course the second revelation bothers Bob much more than the first. The mind games come to a head at the High IQ Club dance as Bob is subjected to the prejudice of stranger, yet greater, minds than his own.

"Hi, Bob"-Ometer
None. The series total stands at fifty-seven.

Classic Cameos: Writer-producers Tom Patchett and Jay Tarses make their first cameo appearances (both pop up again in later episodes). Here Patchett plays the party's pseudo-intellectual guest who has the unique ability to say everything backwards. Tarses is the tuxedo-clad guy from whom Bob takes comfort—that is, until he realizes he's talking to a "dumb" waiter.

For the Record: Emily's IQ is 151, Bob's is 129 ("almost gifted"), and Jerry's IQ is 136.

EPISODE 33

"Mutiny on the Hartley"

Writers: Tom Patchett and Jay Tarses
Director: Peter Baldwin
Cast
Lillian Bakerman: Florida Friebus
Victor Gianelli: Noam Pitlik
Michelle Nardo: Renée Lippin
Emil Peterson: John Fiedler
Mr. Nenn the Plumber: Henry Corden

When Skyline Management Corporation, owners of the Hartleys' apartment building, raise the monthly rent by fifty dollars, Bob is forced to raise his therapy rates. When the patients refuse to pay "Dr. Rip-Off's" higher rate, they try holding their own session at Mrs. Bakerman's house.

"Hi, Bob"-Ometer
Zero. Still at fifty-seven for the series.

For the Record: Noam Pitlik makes his final appearance as Victor Gianelli, the therapy group grouch who refuses to put up with Peterson's whining. After Pitlik left this series, he moved behind the scenes to work as a principal director for *Barney Miller* and, later, *Taxi*. Meanwhile, Mr. Gianelli, played by Daniel J. Travanti, is seen once more, in episode 50, before meeting his untimely—and unforgettable—demise in episode 75.

EPISODE 34

"I'm Okay, You're Okay, So What's Wrong?"

Writer: Earl Barret
Director: George Tyne
Cast
Dr. A. J. Webster: Katherine Helmond

After days of snow and self-examination, Emily is in a funk so deep that even moving the furniture can't fix it. She's tired of her life and bored with Bob, who's become far too predictable. (Even Carol knows what Bob will wear to work every day.) So the Hartleys seek marriage counseling from Bob's colleague, Dr. Webster.

"Hi, Bob"-Ometer
One, from Howard. Fifty-eight for the series.

Classic Quote
BOB *(to Jerry):* Emily's afraid to fly. I'm sure she's not going to enjoy plummeting!

Classic Guest Star: Katherine Helmond plays a psychologist here. She would later gain fame for her abnormal and offbeat roles in *Soap* and *Who's the Boss?*

For the Record: We learn of yet another girlfriend from Bob's romantic past. It's Francis Keck, whom he dated from the seventh grade to the tenth.

EPISODE 35

"Fit, Fat, and Forty-One"

Writers: Bill Idelson and Harvey Miller
Director: Peter Baldwin
Cast
Dr. Klein: Bruce Kirby
Nurse Burke: Samantha Harpur
Olga: Lilyan Chauvin
Mel the Repairman: Bob Ridgely
Second Repairman: Ron Glass

As his forty-first birthday approaches, Bob begins fighting the battle of the bulge. Emily calls his belly "happy fat," but Dr. Klein seriously wants Bob to shed at least eight pounds. Emily provides incentive by giving him a suit that's two sizes too small. Eventually Bob finds the willpower to become ten pounds lighter—the same weight he was on his honeymoon.

"Hi, Bob"-Ometer
Two, both from Howard. Sixty for the series.

Classic Guest Star: Ron Glass later starred as Detective Ron Harris on *Barney Miller*.

EPISODE 36

"Blues for Mr. Borden"

Writers: Tom Patchett and Jay Tarses
Director: Jerry London
Cast
Mr. Billings: Julius Harris

Emily thinks she sees romance rekindling between Howard and his ex-wife, Lois. Howard thinks so, too. But they're both wrong. In fact, Lois *is* in love but it's with a guy Howie Junior calls Uncle Mickey—a pilot, no less.

"Hi, Bob"-Ometer
Three, from Howard, Howie Junior, and Jerry. Sixty-three for the series.

"Sit, Whitey!"

The subplot of episode 36 contains a classic gag that has become a sort of legend by apparently being passed along as a true story. The "legend" begins when Bob is treating Mr. Billings, an insurance salesman who is conspicuously proud of his African-American heritage. He leads around a gigantic Great Dane that he's named Whitey, even though the dog is black. Jerry doesn't know anything about Billings, so when the black man walks up to the dentist and barks the command, "Sit, Whitey!" Jerry thinks it's directed at him and immediately plops himself down on Carol's desk.

It seems folks began telling this tale as though Jerry's experience had actually happened to their own friends or relatives. Variations of the story even began popping up in newspapers across the country. The various versions are chronicled in *The Choking Doberman and Other "New" Urban Legends*, by Jan Harold Brunvand. According to the author, the phenomenon raises "the question whether a TV sitcom might have given rise to an urban legend, or conversely, whether one of Newhart's writers might have based a script on a story he had heard." Bob Newhart doesn't remember which came first, but in a letter to Brunvand, he did recall the scene as "one of the largest laughs we ever got."

EPISODE 37

"My Wife Belongs to Daddy"

Writer: Jerry Mayer
Director: Jerry London
Cast
Cornelius "Junior" Harrison: John Randolph
Aggie Harrison: Ann Rutherford
Michelle Nardo: Renée Lippin
Mr. Devereaux: Byron Morrow
Milt: Dick Wilson
Alfredo the Waiter: Alberto Morin
George the Maître d': Luis DeCordova
Second Maître d': Tony Brande

When Emily's parents come to Chicago for a surprise visit, Bob has trouble living in the shadow of her larger-than-life father. Junior Harrison is a gregarious good ol' boy who runs a successful small business and can even get better Bears tickets than Bob can.

"Hi, Bob"-Ometer
One, from Howard. That's sixty-four for the series.

For the Record: This is the first time we meet Mr. and Mrs. Harrison, who return in later episodes. In fact, these are the only members of Emily's family we ever see, despite the fact that, in episodes 18 and 90, Emily refers to a younger sister.

EPISODE 38

"T. S Elliot"

Writers: Gerry Renert and Jeff Wilhelm
Director: Peter Baldwin

Cast

Debbie Flett: Shirley O'Hara
Mr. Miller: Robert Riesel
Hostess: Shizuko Hoshi

Elliot Carlin needs a date for the annual real estate banquet (the year before, his escort was a pink angora sweater). He gets up the nerve to ask Carol, and she surprises him by accepting! When the date is a qualified success, Mr. Carlin rushes things by asking her to become Mrs. Carlin. He has their whole future mapped out, from their children to their cemetery plots. Overwhelmed, Carol says, "I don't mind dating him. I just don't want to lie down next to him through eternity."

"Hi, Bob"-Ometer
Three, from Howard, Jerry, and Carol. The series total shoots up to sixty-seven.

For the Record: *Alert:* Notice that Bob's office number has changed to 751 from the 715 it has been in the first thirty-seven episodes. For more insight into the office door debate, see episode 48.

Classic Guest Star: This is the first of Shirley O'Hara's three classic turns as Debbie Flett, an absentminded receptionist from the Freedman Fill-In Agency. She proves to be one of Bob's best foils as she insists on calling him Dr. Ryan. She returns to the reception desk in episodes 55 and 102.

EPISODE 39

"I'm Dreaming of a Slight Christmas"

Writers: Tom Patchett and Jay Tarses
Director: Peter Baldwin

Cast

Emil Peterson: John Fiedler
Dr. Bernie Tupperman: Larry Gelman
Dr. Ralph Tetzi: Gene Blakely

It's another crummy Christmas for Bob and Emily. It all starts when Bob gives Mr. Peterson the ultimate gift: a clean bill of mental health. According to him, Emil is cured! But Mr. Peterson doesn't agree, and his subsequent anxiety attack brings Bob back to his office on Christmas Eve. Heavy snow and a power outage nearly strand Bob at the Rimpau Building, but he braves the blizzard and a dead car battery to get home for the holiday. Unfortunately, the experience leaves him too tired for much holiday cheer. As he dozes off, Emily says, "Merry Christmas, Bob. We'll get 'em next year."

"Hi, Bob"-Ometer
Two, from Jerry. That's sixty-nine for the series.

For the Record: Look for another unconventional Christmas-episode ending as the credits roll over Bob and Emily on the couch. Also, as in episode 14, the MTM kitten gets encircled by a holiday wreath.

EPISODE 40

"Oh, Brother"

Writer: Martin Cohan
Director: Peter Baldwin
Cast
Dr. Greg Robinson: Raul Julia
Joan Rossi: Rhoda Gemignani

Perhaps because he's never known the whereabouts of his biological family, Jerry is extremely protective of his adoptive family. So when his brother Greg, who is also a former orphan, comes to Chicago, Jerry rolls out the red carpet. Greg arrives, and since love is blind, Jerry has trouble seeing how obnoxious and uncaring his younger brother really is. Jerry's unqualified devotion is aptly likened to that of Sammy Davis Jr. around Frank Sinatra, but his eyes are eventually opened when Greg sets up shop as a competing dentist on the seventh floor of the Rimpau Building. Jerry put his little brother through dental school, and now Greg pays him back by stealing his patients away. Of course, if any two people can build a bridge between them, it's a couple of dentists . . . and they do.

Hartley Homily: "You can't solve anything by writing things on walls."

"Hi, Bob"-Ometer
One, from Howard. Seventy for the series.

Classic Guest Star: The late Raul Julia was best known as an accomplished and acclaimed film actor. His big-screen credits range from dramatic fare like *Kiss of the Spider Woman* to his popular portrayal of Gomez in the Addams Family movies.

EPISODE 41

"The Modernization of Emily"

Writer: Charlotte Brown
Director: Peter Baldwin
Cast
Lillian Bakerman: Florida Friebus
Rosalie Shaeffer: Sharon Gless
Roy Parker: Bill Miller
Miss Carmichael: Erica Hagen
Man in Market: J. J. Barry

Emily resumes her bittersweet struggle to find happiness within the confines of her reality, which is that she's growing older and she doesn't have the most conspicuously romantic husband in the world. It's the Hartleys' fifth wedding anniversary, and Emily is counting on Bob's gift to remind her that she's still vital and attractive. Unfortunately a thirty-two-speed "blenderizer" doesn't do the trick. So she resorts to a mini-midlife crisis, which has her buying hip clothes at the House of Tacky. In a party scene that's more painfully real than comical, Emily's friends are gathered around her to witness the woeful moment when she realizes she's been making a fool of herself.

Hartley Homily: "You've gotta be what you are."

"Hi, Bob"-Ometer
One, from Howard. Seventy-one for the series.

Classic Guest Star: Sharon Gless makes a brief appearance as Howard's date, Rosalie. After having appeared as a secretary on the series *Switch*, which starred Robert Wagner and Eddie Albert, Gless garnered rave reviews and a couple of Emmy awards in the mid-1980s for her arresting portrayal of Detective Chris Cagney on *Cagney and Lacey*.

Parallel Plot: This is reminiscent of *The Dick Van Dyke Show* episode entitled "My Blonde-Haired Brunette" (episode 9), in which Laura Petrie endures a comparable crisis. In fact, Bob Hartley notes that, in the past, Emily has tried to add some excitement to their marriage by dyeing her hair blond.

EPISODE 42

"The Jobless Corps"

Writers: Tom Patchett and Jay Tarses
Director: Peter Baldwin
Cast
Ed Herd: Oliver Clark
Craig Plager: Howard Hesseman
Edgar Vickers: Lucian Scott
Shirley Ullman: Millie Slavin

When Howard gets fired from his job as a navigator, he loses his direction in life and starts to spend even more time in the Hartleys' apartment.

Hartley Homily: "There's a lot more to life than being employed."

"Hi, Bob"-Ometer
One, from Howard. Seventy-two for the series.

Classic Guest Star: Howard Hesseman did several guest turns as Mr. Plager before 1978, when he began "living on the air in Cincinnati," as Dr. Johnny Fever on *WKRP in Cincinnati*.

For the Record: Three of Dr. Hartley's new patients later became "irregulars" on the show: Ed Herd, an apologetic nerd who's determined to excel in door-to-door sales despite his fear of people; Craig Plager, a frustrated TV writer who can't get the networks to buy his concepts, which include *The Nazi Hour*, *Darn That Pope*, and *Cockpit Capers*; Edgar Vickers, a sour but successful businessman who built up a substantial family-owned company only to be ousted by his own son.

EPISODE 43

"Clink Shrink"

Writers: Paul B. Lichtman and Howard Storm
Director: Peter Bonerz
Cast
Miles Lascoe: Henry Winkler
Spike Coolidge: Russ Grieve
Mr. Schwab: Len Lessor

Dr. Hartley tries to rehabilitate the criminal mind of mild-mannered Miles Lascoe, who's been serving time in prison for armed robbery.

"Hi, Bob"-Ometer
None. The count stands at seventy-two for the series.

Classic Quote
BOB: It's tough being cooped up in the stir with a bull in the tower with his piece trained on you all the time.

Classic Guest Star: Aaaaaaaayyyyy! Henry Winkler plays a real criminal here, but he became a national icon as Arthur "The Fonz" Fonzarelli, the hood with a heart, on *Happy Days*.

For the Record: This is the first of the twenty-nine episodes directed by Peter Bonerz.

Kennedy and Lincoln, Move Over

Abe Lincoln may have had a secretary named Kennedy while John F. Kennedy had a secretary named Lincoln, but consider the eerie parallels between Classic TV's two Roberts: Bob Hartley, of *Newhart,* and Rob Petrie, of *The Dick Van Dyke Show.*

Bob and Rob, both former servicemen, hail from Illinois, where they graduated from college. Both are married to bright and beautiful brunettes, Emily Hartley and Laura Petrie, who are notorious for their ill-fated matchmaking. Notice that the wives' first names are both five letters long. Coincidence?

And what about Bob's and Rob's best friends, Dr. Robinson and Dr. Helper—both named Jerry, both dentists, and both played by actors who began directing in the shows' second seasons. A case of mere happenstance?

And don't forget Carol Kester and Sally Rogers—both names eleven letters long—wisecracking women who can out-type their bosses and outrun the nearest single man.

How could Bob and Rob just happen to find themselves in so many similar situations? Submitted below for your perusal is a list of episodes with parallel plots. Watch, compare, judge for yourself, and don't forget that Rob and Laura were often compared to JFK and Jackie!

The Bob Newhart Show	The Dick Van Dyke Show
2 "Tracy Grammar School, I'll Lick You Yet"	23 "Father of the Week"
27 "Backlash"	82 "The Brave and the Backache"
29 "Emily in for Carol"	84 "My Part-Time Wife"
41 "The Modernization of Emily"	9 "My Blond-Haired Brunette"
65 "Think Smartly—Vote Hartley"	144 "The Making of a Councilman"
81 "Who Is Mr. X?"	48 "Ray Murdock's X-Ray"
85 "The Article"	95 "My Two Show-Offs and Me"
104 "A Crime Most Foul"	141 "Who Stole My Watch?"
114 "The Heartbreak Kidd"	46 "The Foul-Weather Girl"
123 "A Jackie Story"	151 "Talk to the Snail"
128 "You're Fired, Mr. Chips"	30 "The Return of Happy Spangler"
129 "Shallow Throat"	74 "The Sound of the Trumpets of Conscience Falls Deafly on a Brain That Holds Its Ears"

EPISODE 44

"Mind Your Own Business"

Writers: Tom Patchett and Jay Tarses
Director: Alan Rafkin
Cast
Jeff Boggs: Ron Rifkin
Dee Dee: Katherine Dunfee
Harry the Delivery Man: Lou Cutell

Bob wonders why he always finds himself strapped for money while Jerry can afford to buy a yacht. Jerry says his affluence is the result of having his cash handled by Jeff Boggs, a business manager. Bob gives Jeff a try but finds it tough to live on his fifty-dollar-a-week allowance. Worse yet, asking Jeff for more money makes Bob feel "like a duck."

"Hi, Bob"-Ometer
Two, from Carol and Jerry. Seventy-four for the series.

For the Record: Until now Bob's office number has remained 751 ever since it mysteriously changed in episode 38, but throughout this episode, it's back to being 715. In the next three episodes, however, it changes back to 751. Then, in episode 48, something even stranger occurs.
Bob Hartley's Social Security number is 352-22-7439.

EPISODE 45

"A Love Story"

Writer: Martin Cohan
Director: Peter Bonerz
Cast
Martha Hartley: Martha Scott
Aunt Jessica: Patti Jerome
Michelle Nardo: Renée Lippin
Lady in Elevator: Dorothy Love

Bob's thirty-two-year-old sister, Ellen, is engaged to a guy who's not right for her. That's where our hero, Howard, comes in. Thirty seconds after being introduced to Ellen, Howard proclaims, "Bob, I love her." Bob thinks Howard's crazy, Emily thinks Howard should pursue it, and Ellen thinks Howard's a pretty sweet guy. On the eve of her wedding, Ellen comes to his apartment to tell him his persistence has paid off. He's won her heart, so she's calling off the ceremony!

"Hi, Bob"-Ometer
Two, from Ellen and Howard. Seventy-six for the series.

Classic Quote
HOWARD *(talking about Ellen):* I heard Bob had a sister, but I didn't know how much. . . . I love her mind. I love her soul. I love her guts.

Classic Scene: Two things would remain constant in Howard and Ellen's relationship: (1) their song is always "As Time Goes By," and (2) Howard is always ironing before any crucial development. Both elements come together in this episode's classic scene, in which Howard and Ellen embrace in a *Casablanca* kiss. Steam from the iron engulfs them and "As Time Goes By" plays in the background.

For the Record: After this first appearance as Ellen Hartley, Pat Finley returns to the role throughout the third and fourth seasons of the series.

To get a look at John Emil Tobin, the guy Ellen gave up for Howard, see episode 64.

EPISODE 46

"By the Way . . . You're Fired"

Writers: Barbara Gallagher and Sybil Adelman
Director: Peter Baldwin
Cast
Don Livingston, a.k.a. Don Fezler: Richard Schaal
Dr. Phil Newman: Howard Platt
Dr. Bernie Tupperman: Larry Gelman
Dr. Ralph Tetzi: Gene Blakely
Mary Ellen: Jill Jaress
Man with Hat: Dick Wilson

Carol is obsessed with her new beau, Don, an aspiring poet who makes a living by writing articles for *Pharmaceuticals Illustrated*. Unfortunately, Carol's romantic preoccupation is distracting her from her work and inconveniencing the doctors, whose plaintive cries for assistance are going unheard. When Carol brings Don (and his painful feet) to Howard's fortieth birthday party, Jerry chooses that inopportune occasion to fire Carol (you know it's a bad party when one of your guests gets fired). Naturally, the red-haired receptionist is rehired when the seventh-floor physicians realize they would rather have a swooning secretary than none at all.

"Hi, Bob"-Ometer
One, from Jerry. Seventy-seven for the series.

Classic Quote
BOB (*relaying Don's latest revelation*): Life is like a merry-go-round; they both have horses.

For the Record: When Richard Schaal returns as Don Livingston, the master of metaphors, in episode 58, his name is changed to Don Fezler.

EPISODE 47

"Confessions of an Orthodontist"

Writers: Tom Patchett and Jay Tarses
Director: Peter Baldwin
Cast
Miss Brennan: Teri Garr
Dr. Frank Walburn: Roger Perry

When Dr. Hartley substitutes for one of his colleagues, he's shocked to discover that his first patient is none other than Jerry Robinson! It seems Jerry's been talking to Dr. Walburn about a true love that must remain unrequited. The object of his affections? Emily Hartley! If that's not enough of a soap opera, it gets even sudsier when Emily and Jerry confront the issue. The orthodontist has to brace himself when he learns that, of course, Emily only loves him as a friend.

"Hi, Bob"-Ometer
Three, from Carol, Jerry, and Howard. Eighty for the series.

For the Record: Dr. Frank Walburn (incorrectly listed in the end credits as "Frank Walker") is never quite the same after this episode. That's because this is the only time he's portrayed by Roger Perry. Look for a different actor, Phillip R. Allen, to fill Doc Walburn's shoes in episodes 68 and 82.

EPISODE 48

"A Matter of Principal"

Writers: Ray Jessel and Arnie Kogen
Director: Don Bustany
Cast
Mr. Trevesco: Michael Conrad
Lisa: Tara Talboy
Mr. Brimskill: Milton Selzer

She may appear to be Tracy Grammar School's sweet and unassuming third-grade teacher, but when someone pushes Emily Hartley, she pushes back. In a dispute with Principal Brimskill, Bob's "footloose little vixen" quits her job. But the headstrong Mrs. Hartley can't get all the way out of her classroom before her concern for the children, and for a couple of hamsters, brings her back to the blackboard.

Hartley Homily: "If you leave little problems alone, they become big problems, and before you know it, you're wacko!"

"Hi, Bob"-Ometer
Two, from Howard and Jerry. Eighty-two for the series.

For the Record: This final episode of the second season is the first and only installment directed by Don Bustany, who stepped away from his usual post as the show's camera coordinator.

The Office Door Debate

This classic sitcom has used comic reversals to such perfection that it has you expecting the unexpected. Episode 48, however, contains a switcheroo that's so confounding it's been known to break up families and dissolve friendships. More on that in a moment.

First, an examination of the event. In this episode, Dr. Hartley holds two sessions with Mr. Trevesco. Pay attention to the first session. The scene begins with a conventional establishing shot, zooming in to Bob's office door, which reads: "Robert Hartley Ph.D.," with "Psychologist" below. Above those words is the office number: 715. We dissolve into Bob's office, where Mr. Trevesco is ending his session. After thirty-five seconds of dialogue, Dr. Hartley and Mr. Trevesco walk out of Bob's office and we see that *(gasp!)* the number has somehow changed to 751. Though this is not the first time Bob's office number has changed, it *is* the most remarkable because it happened *during* the episode. (Previous switches occured between episodes 37 and 38, 43 and 44, and 44 and 45.) It's a numbers game that just doesn't add up. Who would switch the digits on Bob's door? And why?

This is like any other socially significant unanswerable question: everyone has an answer in which he or she believes very strongly. Some viewers have even joined factions made up of adamant believers. For instance, there are the Peeperians, who are convinced that Bob's college buddy Cliff "The Peeper" Murdoch is playing a practical joke on his old pal. Television historians have been quick to point out, however, that Bob isn't reunited with the Peeper until episode 73.

Members of another faction, the Carolians, contend that Dr. Hartley's receptionist, Carol Kester, must be treating herself to a few liquid lunches and coming back tipsy to the office. According to the Carolians, the intoxicated secretary has been accidentally knocking the numbers off the door and then fumbling to reapply them.

Meanwhile, the Pragmatists remind us that this is a TV show and that the transposed integers are probably the result of an honest mistake by a stagehand. Don't listen to the Pragmatists. They're no fun.

Though the great Office Door Debate has sometimes bred deep dissension among families and friends, everybody agrees that episode 48's sudden switch is one of TV Land's greatest mysteries.

By the way, throughout the next ninety-four episodes, the office number remains 751.

EPISODE 49

"Big Brother Is Watching"

Writer: Charlotte Brown
Director: Robert Moore

Bob's younger sister, Ellen, is grown up and has a mind of her own, but you wouldn't know it from the way she's being treated: Emily's trying to tell her where to live, Howard's trying to get her to live with him, and Bob's trying to keep from breaking Howard's legs. It becomes apparent that Ellen desperately needs to declare her independence when she strikes out on her own to find a job, a home, and a haven from her big brother and the rest of the busybodies. Self-sufficiency suits her well as she finds an apartment she can call her own.

"Hi, Bob"-Ometer

Seven, two apiece from Howard, Jerry, and Ellen, and one from Emily. This episode has the distinction of having the most "Hi, Bob" greetings. The series total shoots up to eighty-nine.

Classic Quote

HOWARD (*talking about Ellen*): Isn't she beautiful when she's humiliated?

For the Record: Carol Kester lives at 2601 Grace Avenue, apartment 2J.

Also, notice that this episode's opening title sequence includes shots of Emily coming home from her job at Tracy Grammar School. In the series' original opening, it was only Bob who braved the masses and mass transit of Chicago to get home, where Emily waited dutifully. In this updated version, Bob and Emily arrive at the apartment almost simultaneously. The change is a nice acknowledgment of the equal importance of both careers.

Also, at the very end, listen for the MTM kitten to bark intead of meow. That's the menacing snarl of Lobo, the dog sound effect from Carol's security system.

EPISODE 50

"The Battle of the Groups"

Writers: Tom Patchett and Jay Tarses
Director: Alan Rafkin

Cast

Michelle Nardo: Renée Lippin
Emil Peterson: John Fiedler
Victor Gianelli: Daniel J. Travanti
Ed Herd: Oliver Clark
Craig Plager: Howard Hesseman
Edgar Vickers: Lucian Scott
Shirley Ullman: Mille Slavin
Mrs. Havlicek: Lenore Woodward

Dr. Hartley makes the mistake of taking two separate therapy groups on a wilderness weekend marathon session. Trouble is inevitable when the only thing the groups have in common is Mr. Carlin.

"Hi, Bob"-Ometer
Three, from Howard twice and Ellen once. Ninety-two for the series.

The Boston Celtics
Mrs. Havlicek is the first of at least four women characters named for members of the Boston Celtics. For others, see episodes 52, 55, and 60.

Classic Quote
BOB: Therapy isn't exactly a stick. If you want to think of it as one, I try to give all of my patients the same end of it.

Classic Guest Star: This is the first and only time that Daniel J. Travanti fills in as patient Victor Gianelli, originally portrayed by Noam Pitlik. Travanti—whose name is misspelled "Travanty" in the end credits—went on to win accolades and a pair of Emmys for his performance as Captain Frank Furillo on *Hill Street Blues.*

EPISODE 51

"The Great Rimpau Medical Arts Co-Op Experiment"

Writers: Coleman Mitchell and Geoffrey Neigher
Director: George Tyne

Cast

Dr. Phil Newman: Howard Platt
Dr. Bernie Tupperman: Larry Gelman
Dr. Sharon Rudell: Julie Payne
Dr. Stan Whelan: Tom Lacy
Mrs. Loomis: Merie Earle

Jerry, having misconstrued Bob's words, sets off an ill-fated seventh-floor experiment that Bernie Tupperman calls Bob's "creation . . . concept . . . master plan!" The idea is that all of the physicians should treat each other for free. Abuses abound as the doctors take advantage of one another.

"Hi, Bob"-Ometer
One, from Howard. Ninety-three for the series.

Classic Quote
BOB *(in need of electricity):* I don't know why America has to be ashamed of its outlets!

For the Record: Merie Earle makes the first of her three appearances as the feisty Mrs. Loomis, who is Tippy Tupperman's great-aunt. In episode 67, she returns in a dual role as Mrs. Loomis and her twin sister, Bernice. By the time Bob meets up with Mrs. Loomis in episode 87, she's a *former* patient who has trouble remembering Dr. Hartley.

EPISODE 52

"The Separation Story"

Writers: Tom Patchett and Jay Tarses
Story: Bob Garland
Director: Peter Bonerz

Cast

Mr. Kuberski: Carl Gottlieb
Mrs. Heinsohn: Katherine Ish
Mr. Doheny: Bryan O'Byrne
Bellboy: Richard Stahl

There's no time for pillow talk. Bob and Emily are living hectic and harried lives. Bob suggests that Emily move into a college dorm to be close to school and that he take up residency at the Regency Hotel to be close to work. The Hartleys' "separation" is the cause of much concern among their friends. But there's no need to worry, because eventually Bob and Emily see the error of their wayward ways, and as Carol puts it, "Doris and Rock are back together."

The Boston Celtics
Mrs. Heinsohn would be Tommy's mother, we suppose.

"Hi, Bob"-Ometer
Two, from Howard and Jerry. Ninety-five for the series.

Classic Cameo: Though he pops up here as an inflatable furniture salesman, Carl Gottlieb also contributed to the series by co-writing episode 2.

EPISODE 53

"Sorry, Wrong Mother"

Writer: Charlotte Brown
Director: Jay Sandrich

Cast

Michelle Nardo: Renée Lippin
Dave: John Ritter
Phil: Steve Dolan

The fact that Howard loves Ellen doesn't mean Howie has to—and apparently he doesn't. Howard makes matters worse by blaming Ellen for not trying hard enough. When a trip to Uncle Yummy's ice-cream parlor—heaven for children, hell for Bob—can't create a bond between Howie and Ellen, it's time for Dr. Hartley to play child psychologist and find out what's up with the obstinate boy. Bob discovers that Howard's love for Aunt Ellen has thrown Howie Junior another curveball he can't seem to hit. Admirably, Ellen refuses to buy Howie's affections and instead opts for earning his respect, which she does—much to Howard's surprise.

"Hi, Bob"-Ometer
One, from Howard. Ninety-six for the series.

Classic Scene: Uncle Yummy's is the setting for one of the most unforgettably funny scenes of the series. The ice-cream parlor's policy is that every frozen dessert is a *special* frozen dessert—the goopier and fudgier the better! Faced with such menu offerings as Piggly Wiggly Giggly Glop and Jolly Jumper Jelly Jamboree, Bob makes the mistake of ordering a solo scoop of chocolate ice cream. He pays for the unimaginative selection when the Uncle Yummy spotlight is trained on him and a pair of waiters sing out: "Single scooper! Single scooper! This man is a party-pooper!!"

Classic Guest Star: As Dave the waiter, John Ritter displays his wonderful comic timing, which was completely wasted on the hit comedy *Three's Company.*

EPISODE 54

"The Gray Flannel Shrink"

Writer: Jerry Mayer
Director: Peter Bonerz
Cast
Mr. Charlie Colton: John Anderson
Wes Greenfield: Edward Winter
Paul Hollander: Jerry Fogel
Susan Wick: Mary Robin Redd
Ed Herd: Oliver Clark

A former patient offers Bob big bucks to become the staff psychologist at Loggers Casualty, a company that insures lumberjacks against injuries. In addition to a substantial salary, Dr. Hartley is also offered a chauffeured Mercedes and a "modern yet rustic" eighteenth-floor office in Loggers Towers. So it is that the stammering psychologist takes a swing at improving the mental state of the corporate world. Counseling members of the management team keeps Bob very busy, since everyone at Loggers has an ax to grind. Just as Bob starts making real progress with his new patients, he gets fired for helping blindly dedicated employees realize there's life beyond Loggers.

Hartley Homily: "Just because something is perfect, that's no reason to look into it."

"Hi, Bob"-Ometer
Two, from Mr. Colton and Howard. Ninety-eight for the series.

Classic Quote
LOGGERS CASUALTY MOTTO: We gotta insure these guys.

For the Record: Death-projections expert Susan Wick predicts that Bob Hartley's time will be up when he's seventy-seven years old.

Look for guest star Jerry Fogel to do another guest turn in episode 138, in which he plays the stuttering host of a kiddie show.

EPISODE 55

"Dr. Ryan's Express"

Writers: Tom Patchett and Jay Tarses
Director: Alan Rafkin
Cast
Debbie Flett: Shirley O'Hara
Edgar Vickers: Lucian Scott
Mrs. Della Vella: Paula Victor
Mrs. Chaney: Maxine Stuart

Bob and Jerry are once again in desperate need of a temporary receptionist. Unfortunately, Bob's worst fill-in fears are realized when absentminded Debbie Flett returns to the desk. As in episode 38, the senior secretary mishandles assignments and persists in calling Bob "Dr. Ryan."

The Boston Celtics
Mrs. Chaney would be Don's mom.

"Hi, Bob"-Ometer
One, from Jerry. Ninety-nine for the series.

For the Record: In episode 38, Debbie says she's a former White House secretary. In this episode, we discover that she worked for the FDR administration. Do you suppose she referred to Roosevelt as "President Ryan"?

EPISODE 56

"Brutally Yours, Bob Hartley"

Writer: John Rappaport
Director: Alan Rafkin
Cast
Ed Hoffman: Lawrence Pressman
Janet Hoffman: Rose Gregorio
Michelle Nardo: Renée Lippin

"Honesty is the only basis for a true relationship." So says Dr. Hartley, who decides that honesty is not only the best policy but also the best therapy. After he prescribes it for Michelle and Mr. Carlin, he takes his own advice and applies complete and total truthfulness to every aspect of his life. The results are truly disastrous.

"Hi, Bob"-Ometer

Four, from Howard twice and from Ed Hoffman and Jerry once. That's 103 for the series.

Classic Quote

EMILY *(reproaching Bob):* I'm glad you're not involved in shock therapy. You probably would have stuck their fingers in the toaster.

EPISODE 57

"Ship of Shrinks"

Writers: Coleman Mitchell and Geoffrey Neigher
Director: Alan Rafkin
Cast
Dr. Murray Kalisher: Jerome Guardino
Madelyn Kalisher: Delores Sutton
Dr. Rimmer: Bobby Ramsen
Milt the Delivery Boy: David L. Lander

Dr. Hartley's bursting with pride because he's contributed a chapter to a new book about psychology entitled *The Big Couch.* However, when the book is published, Bob finds that his twenty-page contribution has been cut down to two pages. Though somewhat daunted, he and Emily still intend to take advantage of the editor's offer to fly the contributors to Hawaii. Ellen and Howard want to tag along, but Howard sours their plans by obsessively reminiscing about his Hawaiian honeymoon with Lois, his ex-wife. When Ellen refuses to go, Howard is depressed and disoriented but still determined to navigate the planeload of psychologists to Hawaii. This gives Dr. Hartley a chance to impress his colleagues and co-authors by offering Howard some sound in-flight counseling.

Hartley Homily: "Superstition is one thing, but when it leads to dictatorial behavior, it's counterproductive and harmful to a healthy relationship."

"Hi, Bob"-Ometer

Two, from Madelyn Kalisher and Dr. Murray Kalisher. That's 105 for the series.

Classic Quote

BOB *(to Howard):* You can't keep Ellen chained up. You've gotta let her run . . . let her bury her bones.

Classic Guest Star: David L. Lander was Andrew "Squiggy" Squigman, Lenny's best buddy on *Laverne and Shirley.*

For the Record: Dr. Rimmer is the first of the six supporting roles that make Bobby Ramsen the show's most valuable stock player. Be on the lookout for Bobby in the following roles: Morty, the always hungry photographer (episode 85); Johnny Carson Jr., the oddball bartender (105 and 120); Mickey Melnick, the comedy-school teacher (127); and Mr. Gerber, the Hartleys' outlandish landlord (142).

EPISODE 58

"Life Is a Hamburger"

Writer: Jerry Mayer
Director: George Tyne
Cast
Don Fezler, a.k.a. Don Livingston:
Richard Schaal
Judge Fleming: John J. Fox
Mrs. Fleming: Meg Wyllie
Ricky Rasmussen: Bobby Eilbacher
Waitress: Dawna Shove

Carol's boyfriend, Don, is back, and although his last name has mysteriously changed from Livingston (episode 46) to Fezler, he's still the same guy, with sore feet and a growing list of life metaphors—life is a loaf of bread . . . a jetliner . . . a hamburger. Even though her friends seem to like Don less and less, Carol appears to love him more than ever. In fact, she plans to marry the sultan of similies. Miss Kester doesn't *really* love Don, however. She just desperately wants to be a missus and a mother, and she's not getting any younger. Carol sees the truth only after she has turned to Jerry for a night of meaningless passion. Consequently, she finds herself having to gently let down two beaux: "the guy with the feet" and "the guy with the nose."

"Hi, Bob"-Ometer

One, from Jerry. That's 106 for the series.

Classic Quote

DON: Life is a hamburger. Fry some of the fat away, take a couple bites, and it's gone.

EPISODE 59

"An American Family"

Writer: Charlotte Brown
Director: Peter Bonerz
Cast
Martha Hartley: Martha Scott
Herb Hartley: Barnard Hughes
Cornelius "Junior" Harrison: John Randolph
Aggie Harrison: Ann Rutherford

It's the holiday season, so how come no one's happy at the Hartley home? The trouble starts when Emily's parents come from Seattle for a surprise visit. The intrusion ruins Martha Hartley's best-laid plans for a quaint, traditional Thanksgiving dinner. To make matters worse, Junior Harrison has plans for a huge feast, featuring a thirty-five-pound turkey.

"Hi, Bob"-Ometer

Two, from Junior and Jerry. That's 108 for the series.

Classic Scene: There's not one word of dialogue—the comedy is all visual—as Howard struggles to put away groceries without stepping on the freshly waxed floor. Finally, the navigator finds himself on top of the kitchen counter, tossing the food into the refrigerator.

For the Record: This is the first time we meet Bob's dad, Herb Hartley, played by prolific character actor Barnard Hughes.

Mr. and Mrs. Hartley seem certain they have only two "wonderful children," Bob and Ellen, despite the fact that in episodes 9 and 36 Bob claimed to have a younger brother.

Notice that, in the dinner scene, Suzanne Pleshette is wearing the same dress she wore in the show's opening credit sequence for the first two seasons.

EPISODE 60

"We Love You . . . Good-bye"

Writer: Charlotte Brown
Director: Peter Bonerz
Cast
Michelle Nardo: Renée Lippin
Joan Rossi: Rhoda Gemignani
Adele Sinclair: Ann Weldon
Ingrid Bjorn-Bjork: Inge Maria
Mrs. Cowens: Joan Tompkins

Dr. Hartley's such a hero to his women's support group that one member tells him, "We don't think of you as a man—you're better than that!" But Emily knows the truth about Bob, and when she tells all at the group's next meeting, the patients turn on Dr. Hartley—who should be used to such behavior by now.

The Boston Celtics
Mrs. Cowens would be Dave's mom.

"Hi, Bob"-Ometer
Two, from Emily and Howard. That's 110 for the series.

EPISODE 61

"Jerry Robinson Crusoe"

Writer: Erik Tarloff
Director: Alan Rafkin
Cast
Courtney Simpson: Gail Strickland

It's been ten years since Jerry's seen Courtney Simpson, a former girlfriend who became a marine biologist and began traveling the world. When she shows up looking more beautiful than ever, Jerry vows to give up his mundane life and become Courtney's fellow free spirit, following her to the next exotic locale, which is Tahiti. In the face of mounting evidence to the contrary, Bob insists there's no way his best friend's really going to Tahiti. But Jerry does go . . . only to come back a month later, after Courtney moves on to Uganda.

"Hi, Bob"-Ometer
One, from Jerry. That's 111 for the series.

Classic Quotes
JERRY: It's the real me, the new me, the free me, the me I used to be before I became the me I was.

JERRY: Bob, in Chicago a man can't follow the sun.
BOB: Jerry, in Tahiti, a man can't follow the White Sox.

Classic Scene: In a running gag, it's established that Elliot Carlin is profoundly affected by the movies he sees. After he sees *The Exorcist*, for example, he thinks he's possessed by the devil. In this classic scene, Dr. Hartley helps Mr. Carlin decide which film to see next—*The Boys in the Band* or *Planet of the Apes*. Bob recommends the latter just as Elliot gets on the elevator, his back to the camera. When he turns toward us, the power of suggestion already appears to have transformed him: his face, with its expanded cheeks and deeply furrowed brow, is unmistakably simian.

For the Record: Actress Gail Strickland reprises her role as Courtney Simpson when she returns in episode 91.

EPISODE 62

"Serve for Daylight"

Writer: Jerry Mayer
Director: Alan Rafkin
Cast
Dr. Phil Newman: Howard Platt
Dr. Bernie Tupperman: Larry Gelman
Dr. Tammy Ziegler: Paula Shaw

It's time for the Urology Research Clinic's annual mixed doubles tennis tournament, and Dr. Tupperman's rounding up seventh-floor participants. The male doctors are eager to be paired up with Betty Jo Burkus, who made Phil Newman the champion last year. Unfortunately for Dr. Hartley, when the partners are randomly selected, Jerry gets Betty Jo, and Bob has to settle for, uh-oh, Emily! Mrs. Hartley has been taking tennis lessons (remember episode 3?), but she'd have to be Billie Jean King to please her victory-hungry husband. Of course, she double-faults thirty-four times, the Hartleys are eliminated in two straight sets, and Bob's a sore loser.

"Hi, Bob"-Ometer
Two, from Carol and Jerry, making the total 113 for the series.

EPISODE 63:

"Home Is Where the Hurt Is"

Writers: Tom Patchett and Jay Tarses
Director: Alan Rafkin
Cast
Eddie the Mailman: Bill Quinn

As Bob and Emily prepare to attend a Christmas Eve concert, Carol shows up to explain why she didn't go home for the holidays. Totally oblivious to the fact that the Hartleys are missing their concert, Carol rambles on through the night until she achieves an emotional breakthrough at 4:00 A.M. She calls her dad and takes off for Collinsville, leaving Bob and Emily in a sleepy stupor.

"Hi, Bob"-Ometer
None. Still at 113 for the series.

EPISODE 64

"Tobin's Back in Town"

Writer: Michael Zinberg
Director: Peter Bonerz
Cast
John Emil Tobin: Fred Willard
Dottie the Barmaid: Catherine Bacon
Leo the Private Detective: Russ Grieve

In episode 45, when Ellen realized she loved Howard Borden, she broke off her engagement to John Tobin. Now Tobin is coming from Cleveland to reclaim her heart, and Howard's so threatened he's taken to ironing. Ellen's sure she doesn't want John back, but after witnessing Howard's childish behavior, she begins to have serious doubts about him as well. Howard and Ellen do stay together, but their relationship undergoes a serious strain that foreshadows their eventual separation in episode 90.

"Hi, Bob"-Ometer
Zero. The count remains stalled at 113.

Classic Scene: In an effort to intimidate Ellen's former fiancé, Howard reinvents himself in the airport bar. It's not bad enough that in his uniform, scarf, and sunglasses he looks like Snoopy; he also has his airline dramatically page him. "Captain Howard Borden, we have an emergency only *you* can solve!"

Classic Guest Star: In the role of the arrogant and self-absorbed John Tobin, Fred Willard was already showing the early signs of developing the thick-headed Jerry Hubbard character that would make him a cult hero. Hubbard was the shamelessly ingratiating co-host of the satirical talk show *Fernwood 2-Night*.

EPISODE 65

"Think Smartly—Vote Hartley"

Writers: Coleman Mitchell and Geoffrey Neigher
Director: Bob Finkel
Cast
Rex Pottinger: George Wyner
Rita Montez: Lillian Garrett
Dr. Dalton: Quinn Redeker

Emily and many of her co-workers at Tracy Grammar School are incensed about Dr. Dalton's apparent lack of responsibility in his role as school board chairman. They want change, and Bob's their man! He initially turns down their nomination but, after Jerry describes Bob as the perfect candidate—"low-key, yet forceful . . . unobtrusive and yet dynamic . . . youthful exuberance coupled with fatherly wisdom"—Bob starts to believe he could win.

"Hi, Bob"-Ometer
One, from Emily, making it 114 for the series.

Classic Quote
BOB *(rehearsing his campaign speech):* The need for an effective school board is a need that has long been needed.

Classic Guest Star: George Wyner makes the first of two appearances as Vice Principal Rex Pottinger; he returns in episode 71. Seven years

later, in 1982, Wyner began his stint as Assistant D.A. Irwin Bernstein on *Hill Street Blues*.

For the Record: Bob Hartley's bid to be elected is similar to Rob Petrie's campaign in "The Making of a Councilman" episode of *The Dick Van Dyke Show*. Bob and Rob are both reluctant candidates who develop delusions of grandeur, only to have them crushed by men better suited to the positions.

EPISODE 66

"The Way We Weren't"

Writer: Roger Beatty
Director: James Burrows
Cast
Jennifer Evans: Casey Connors
Dennis Budmur: Joseph Sicari
Ralph: David Knapp
Pilot: Wayne Tippit
Copilot: Gary Krawford

What Emily doesn't know *does* hurt her—when she finds out that Bob broke up with someone named Gloria Webster just one week before he married Emily. Bob has kept his former fiancée a secret for years, but when Gloria plans a visit to Chicago, Emily discovers the details of Bob's clandestine romance.

"Hi, Bob"-Ometer
One, from Howard, making the count 115 for the series.

For the Record: This is the first episode directed by James Burrows, who began as an apprentice on *The Mary Tyler Moore Show* and went on to become one of television's most sought-after directors. Burrows, son of legendary Broadway and radio writer Abe Burrows, was directing in a little Florida theater in 1974 when MTM president Grant Tinker offered to help him learn the art of television direction. According to Grant Tinker's autobiography, *Tinker in Television,* there was one point, while Burrows was observing production of *The Bob Newhart Show,* at which Newhart "told the show's producers, 'Get that guy out of here. He makes me nervous.'" But Burrows continued to learn his craft at MTM and eventually directed eleven episodes of Newhart's show. (Look for him to make a Classic Cameo appearance in episode 113.) Over the years, Burrows has kept his streak of quality projects alive by being the principal director of *Taxi* and also of *Cheers,* which he co-created. His more recent projects include the top hits *Frasier* and *Friends.*

EPISODE 67

"A Pound of Flesh"

Writer: Jerry Mayer
Director: Alan Rafkin
Cast
Mrs. Loomis: Merie Earle
Bernice: Merie Earle
Mr. Berry: Dick Wilson

When Bob refuses to lend him money to buy a motorcycle, Jerry borrows $1,600 from Howard, who is led to believe that he and Jerry will be equal partners in the ownership of the chopper. From the very beginning of their ill-fated alliance, Jerry is in the driver's seat—and he refuses to get out.

Hartley Homily: "When you start putting a price tag on friendships, you find out your friendships aren't worth a nickel."

"Hi, Bob"-Ometer
Two, from Emily and Howard, making the count 117 for the series.

Classic Quote
BOB: Only a fool would endanger a friendship by getting mad at a friend because that friend had sense enough not to loan money to a friend.

EPISODE 68

"My Business Is Shrinking"

Writers: Arnie Kogen and Ray Jessel
Director: Alan Rafkin
Cast
Dr. Frank Walburn: Phillip R. Allen
Congressman Jerome Shetland: Ray Stewart
Wayne "Hilton" Jefferson: Ron McIlwain
Mrs. Engelhart: Mary Jo Catlett
Jay: Jay Kogen
Midge: Timothy Blake

A lot has happened to super-successful psychologist Dr. Frank Walburn since last we saw him (in episode 47, featuring Roger Perry in the role). He's written a best-selling book, *Fires of the Mind,* which is being made into a movie entitled *Blazing Brains.* While Frank's star is rising, however, Bob's business has gotten slower. The stammering psychologist wonders why he's having so much trouble turning up patients, especially since, as Howard puts it, "this is the golden age of craziness." Dr. Hartley seeks support by joining one of Dr. Walburn's therapy groups. When Bob is exposed to Frank's impatient and ineffective style, he regains his confidence, and his business again becomes brisk.

"Hi, Bob"-Ometer
Two, from Emily and Dr. Frank Walburn. That's 119 for the series.

For the Record: When Emily tells Bob to watch *Tonight* because Sir Laurence Olivier is being interviewed by guest host Don Rickles, it's a friendly poke at the caustic comedian, who's been Bob Newhart's best buddy for years. Rickles once told *TV Guide* that Newhart is "Mr. Mid-America in a crowd, Charlie Everybody, the American flag with a ribbon tied around him. . . . I remember the first time I embraced him. It was like holding on to an ice cake. . . . We have a helluva time together." Look for the ultimate Rickles reference in episode 127, in which an elderly woman imitates him.

EPISODE 69

"The New Look"

Writers: Gordon and Lynne Farr
Director: Peter Bonerz
Cast
Ed Herd: Oliver Clark
Maury: Cliff Norton
Dorothy: Marcia Lewis

Emily has grand plans for redecorating the Hartley home. While Bob is out of town, she replaces all of their old furniture with costly antiques in such a hodgepodge of styles that they don't create the "warm and eclectic" room Emily promised. When Bob comes home, he sums up his reaction in two words: "Holy smoke!"

"Hi, Bob"-Ometer
Two, from Ellen and Howard, making the count 121 for the series.

EPISODE 70

"Bob Hits the Ceiling"

Writer: Phil Davis
Director: Jay Sandrich
Cast
Diane Nugent: Cynthia Harris
Frank Nugent: Mike Henry
The Plumber: Al Stellone

Bob reluctantly agrees to help one of Emily's co-workers, Diane Nugent, with her marital problems. When Bob's expert advice persuades Diane to walk out on Frank, she seeks refuge in the Hartleys' apartment.

"Hi, Bob"-Ometer
One, from Emily. That's 122 for the series.

Classic Quote
BOB *(to Frank):* I love you.
FRANK: I'm gonna cave your face in.

For the Record: This is the last of the ten episodes directed by Jay Sandrich, MTM's foremost director of classic situation comedy. Back in 1965, Sandrich had worked as a producer on *Get Smart.* He then became the principal director of *The Mary Tyler Moore Show* in 1970. He is credited with revolutionizing the way in which sitcoms are shot. According to Grant Tinker, the founder of MTM, Sandrich "knows better than anyone what it takes to turn out superior television." In the mid-1980s, Sandrich set the tone for another long-running hit by directing the first two seasons of *The Cosby Show.*

EPISODE 71

"Emily Hits the Ceiling"

Writer: Jerry Mayer
Director: James Burrows
Cast
Rex "Flipper" Pottinger: George Wyner
"Band-Aid" Pottinger: Susan Davis
Rita "Shingle" Montez: Lillian Garrett
"Spitball": Tom Newman
Craig Plager: Howard Hesseman

Tracy Grammar School's vice principal, Rex Pottinger, has had a lifelong dream of starting his own summer camp for kids. When Emily offers to help make her boss's dream come true, they make preliminary plans for Camp Thundercloud, where the motto will be "*Nomoka keenata!*" ("Welcome aboard my canoe!") When assignments and nicknames are doled out to the teachers and friends who will serve as counselors, Bob's name is conspicuously missing from the list of participants. Emily's disappointed since, after all, even Howard "Iron Bow" Borden will be there to teach archery. Finally Bob figures out a way to go—just as "Flipper" Pottinger faces up to the fact that the camp is short on funds and unfeasible.

"Hi, Bob"-Ometer

Two, from Jerry and Howard. The series count is now 124.

EPISODE 72

"The Ceiling Hits Bob"

Writers: Tom Patchett and Jay Tarses
Director: Alan Rafkin
Cast
Edgar Vickers: Lucian Scott
Eddie the Mailman: Bill Quinn
Bud Brey: Jess Nadelman
The Waiter: Don Nagel

Bob is floored when he sees that his office ceiling has caved in, all over his desk and couch. With the building maintenance department in no rush to fix it, Dr. Hartley begins holding therapy sessions in his home. Unfortunately for Bob, his patients aren't the only ones who want to bend his ear: Carol's in a quandary over a job offer from the Landover Chemical Company; Howard's been promoted from navigator to copilot, which means he'll be transferred to New York City; Ellen is distraught when Howard assumes she'll marry him and move with him to the Big Apple; and Jerry wants Bob to hire his date to fill Carol's position. When they all pressure him for advice, the psychologist snaps and demands to know whom he's supposed to turn to in a crisis. Having made his point, he tells Carol to stay (she'll get a raise); he advises Ellen not to marry Howard, who gets to stay in Chicago anyway; and he informs Jerry there will be no need to fill Carol's position, since she's still in it. Of course, Dr. Hartley's own dilemma remains unresolved: his office is condemned and he's forced to operate out of the elevator.

"Hi, Bob"-Ometer

Four, from Carol, Howard, Jerry, and Eddie the Mailman. That's 128 for the series.

For the Record: This is the final installment of the series' third season.

EPISODE 73

"The Longest Good-bye"

Writers: Tom Patchett and Jay Tarses
Director: James Burrows

For the first time, Bob is reunited with his old college buddy, Cliff "The Peeper" Murdoch. Cliff has come to convince the Chicago Cereal Company to include his latest invention in their boxes of cereal. When the Peeper has trouble getting anyone to listen to his sales pitch, he moves in with the Hartleys for a night, which drags out to a week! Bob doesn't mind, because he loves his prank-playing pal unconditionally, but Emily thinks Cliff, whom she never calls the Peeper, is taking advantage of them. Before Bob is forced to put the Peeper on the spot, Cliff announces that he's leaving, although his invention remains unsold. But not to worry—the Peeper shall return.

"Hi, Bob"-Ometer
Three—Howard twice and Emily once—making 131 for the series.

Classic Quote
CLIFF: The Peeper is here to see the Mooner.
CAROL: And the blue fish swims in muddy waters.

Classic Scene: Undoubtedly one of the best moments in the series occurs when Bob and Cliff reprise their "Sonny Boy" number from their fraternity show. Bob's sitting on Cliff's knee when Jerry enters and plops down on the other knee to join in the song.

Classic Guest Star: In this episode, veteran comic Tom Poston makes the first of his five appearances on the Peeper. In 1959 he won an Emmy for his role as the befuddled everyman on *The Steve Allen Show.* In the late seventies Poston joined the cast of *Mork and Mindy* as grouchy neighbor Franklin Bickley. Then, in 1982, he was

reunited with Bob Newhart for the eight-year run of *Newhart*, in which Poston played George Utley, a dim-witted handyman. By the way, *Newhart* was set in Vermont, which was George Utley's home state and, coincidentally, the state from which the Peeper hailed.

EPISODE 74

"Here's Looking at You, Kid"

Writers: Gordon and Lynne Farr
Director: Peter Bonerz
Cast
Fred Goring: Richard Balin
Trumpet Player: Vern E. Rowe
Harvey the Waiter: Don Nagel

As the Hartleys celebrate their sixth anniversary, Howard officially proposes to Ellen. She says yes, but almost instantly regrets it. After consulting Emily on the adjustments and compromises common to every marriage, Ellen decides she's not ready. She goes to Howard's apartment, where, of course, he's ironing and listening to "As Time Goes By." When Ellen breaks off the engagement, Howard pretends to take it in stride—as Bogey would. In one of the show's rare bittersweet endings, Howard says good-bye to Ellen with a "Here's looking at you, kid," then sadly returns to his ironing board.

"Hi, Bob"-Ometer
One, from Carol. That's 132 for the series.

Classic Quote
EMILY *(remembering the exact words of Bob's proposal):* Dearest Emily, we've been together for over a year now, and I'm very fond of you, and I'd like us to spend the rest of our lives together. Will you be my wife?

BOB *(remembering the exact words of his mother's chewing rhyme):* Thirty-two times keeps your tummy from danger. Then you can stay up and listen to *The Lone Ranger*.

Classic Scene: It's petty pillow talk at its best in the bedroom scene, where Bob complains about the way Emily cuts her sandwiches, and she refuses to let him chew his food thirty-two times. Just another example of why the Hartleys are such a genuine sitcom couple.

EPISODE 75

"Death of a Fruitman"

Writers: Tom Patchett and Jay Tarses
Director: Peter Bonerz
Cast
Lillian Bakerman: Florida Friebus
Michelle Nardo: Renée Lippin
Emil Peterson: John Fiedler

The patients in Dr. Hartley's therapy group are fed up with one of their fellow members, Victor Gianelli, who is always late and always abusive, especially to Mr. Peterson. They want Gianelli kicked out of the group. Bob is giving their request serious consideration when they receive word that Mr. Gianelli has met a peculiar demise: he was crushed to death by a wayward load of zucchini. (Who knew that selling produce could be such a dangerous business?) Suddenly the members of the group have nothing but fond memories of the former couch grouch.

"Hi, Bob"-Ometer
One, from Howard, making the series total 133.

Classic Quote
PETERSON: You helped us all in every way.
CARLIN: You got inside our head.
MICHELLE: And that is why we'd like to say—
CAROL: Mr. Gianelli's dead!

For the Record: This episode was the first of the fourth season and ushers in a fresh title sequence. As opposed to merely featuring Bob and Emily Hartley, it features all of the regular characters except Mr. Carlin. Also, whereas the two previous openings depicted Bob and Emily at the *end* of the workday, this sequence finds the Hartleys just beginning their day, leaving their apartment (and Howard) behind. Next, various shots of Bob, making his way through the city, are scattered over a bright orange Chicago background. Finally he gets to the office, where Jerry and Carol are talking just outside the elevator doors. Bob walks by and grabs a coffee cup out of Carol's hand, but by the time he reaches his office door, he realizes the mug is empty. The new "title visualization" is credited to writer-producer-director Michael Zinberg.

EPISODE 76

"Change Is Gonna Do Me Good"

Writers: Gordon and Lynne Farr
Director: John Erman
Cast
Box Boy: Brian Byers

In order for Bob to enjoy a task, he must have a ritual for accomplishing it. For instance, when he pays the household bills, he has to follow a strict bill-paying regimen, complete with uniform and rubber thumb. Emily thinks the anal-retentive psychologist needs to unclench and be more flexible—like her. The debate results in a role reversal that finds Bob doing the grocery shopping while Emily hurriedly writes the checks for their monthly payments. No lessons are learned, however, since, even as a shopper, Bob is still a stickler with a ritual, and twelve of Emily's checks bounce.

"Hi, Bob"-Ometer
One, from Howard. That's 134 for the series.

EPISODE 77

"The Heavyweights"

Writers: Tom Patchett and Jay Tarses
Director: Bob Claver
Cast
Leonard DePaolo: Cliff Osmond
Michelle Nardo: Renée Lippin
Dr. Bernie Tupperman: Larry Gelman
Louise Gross: Marcia Lewis

When Bob conducts a support group meeting for "people of the hefty persuasion," he uses Carol as a role model for the group. She was overweight when she began working on the seventh floor, but even back then she was on a diet and ultimately lost 116 pounds. When Carol addresses the group, the most obnoxious member, Leonard DePaolo, asks her out. Carol doesn't want to go, but to avoid looking like a hypocrite, she accepts the invitation. The date is such a complete disaster that Carol is forced to tell the loathsome Leonard that he's repugnant—not because he's a fat person but because he's a fat*head*.

"Hi, Bob"-Ometer
Three, from Howard, Jerry, and Bernie Tupperman, making a total of 137 for the series.

EPISODE 78

"Carol's Wedding"

Writers: Gordon and Lynne Farr
Director: Michael Zinberg
Cast
Larry Bondurant: Will Mackenzie
Judge W. H. Tanner: Robert Casper
Old Gentleman: Pat Cranshaw
First Moving Man: Vince Milana
Second Moving Man: Rick Mancini

Carol has had enough of Emily's attempts to play matchmaker. She tells Bob, "No offense, but Emily fixed me up about ten times, and her taste in men is the pits." Just as the single secretary vows "no more blind dates," Mrs. Hartley comes up with one more. This time it's Larry Bondurant, the brother of one of Emily's friends. Carol breaks her vow, goes out with Larry, and (after only one date) starts making plans for an immediate wedding at City Hall. Her friends are skeptical of her matrimonial plans, and they don't want to see her get stranded in a deserted aisle. Just when it seems Larry's a no-show for the nuptials, Carol's luck is altered, and the groom shows up for a speedy ceremony. Who cares if Larry left her ring in Cincinnati? Carol Kester is just overjoyed to be Mrs. Kester-Bondurant.

"Hi, Bob"-Ometer
One, from Howard. That's 138 for the series.

Classic Quote
EMILY: Howard, a parakeet is not a very good wedding present.
HOWARD: Why not?
EMILY: Well, it's not very personal.
HOWARD: I'll have it engraved.

For the Record: After this brief appearance as Larry Bondurant, guest star Will Mackenzie would return in six more episodes. Mackenzie is another actor-turned-director, who helmed episode 110 of this series before going on to direct episodes of *WKRP in Cincinnati* and *Newhart*.

EPISODE 79

"Shrinks across the Sea"

Writers: Phil Doran and Douglas Arango
Director: Bob Claver
Cast
Dr. Alan Durocher: Rene Auberjonois
Louise: Françoise Ruggieri
Cabdriver Artie Berkowitz: Richard Foronjy

As part of a psychologists' exchange program, the Hartleys play host to an arrogant French analyst, Dr. Durocher, and his companion, Louise. Initially, the two appear to be married, but eventually it is revealed that Louise is actually Dr. Durocher's mistress. It's a culture shock for Bob and Emily when they're exposed to the cheating couple's cavalier approach to fidelity, but Dr. Durocher truly believes that "the jealous heart is a passionate heart!"

"Hi, Bob"-Ometer
Three—two from Carol and one from Jerry. The series count is now 141.

Classic Guest Star: Though Rene Auberjonois portrays a mere human here, he costars as Odo, the shape-changing security guard on *Star Trek: Deep Space Nine.*

EPISODE 80

"What's It All About, Albert?"

Writer: Phil Davis
Director: Michael Zinberg
Cast
Dr. Eugene Albert: Keenan Wynn
Webb Franklyn: Tom Fitzsimmons
David: Bobby Eilbacher

In his ongoing and incessant search for meaning in his work, Dr. Hartley returns to the hallowed halls of Loyola University, where he discovers that his mentor has come to the conclusion that psychology is "a crock"—a revelation that hardly comforts Dr. Hartley. Convinced there's no worth to his work, Bob decides to emulate the movie *Born Free* by casting off his patients to search for real solutions to their phobias and anxieties. Ironically, it's Dr. Hartley's number one patient, Mr. Carlin, who talks him through the crisis and keeps him in business.

"Hi, Bob"-Ometer
Two, from Carol and Howard, making a total of 143 for the series.

Classic Quote
DR. ALBERT: I screamed before it was fashionable.

Classic Guest Star: Here the late Keenan Wynn is daffy and delightful as Dr. Albert, but much of Wynn's other television work was in the golden age of the dramatic anthology. He often appeared in *The U.S. Steel Hour* and *Playhouse 90,* in which he costarred in the TV classic "Requiem for a Heavyweight."

For the Record: In this episode Dr. Hartley refers to Dr. Albert as his greatest educational influence, but in episode 128, Bob says his mentor and favorite Loyola professor was Dr. Dreeben, played by another accomplished actor, Ralph Bellamy.

EPISODE 81

"Who Is Mr. X?"

Writer: Bruce Kane
Director: Peter Bonerz
Cast
Ruth Corley: Jennifer Warren
Emil Peterson: John Fiedler
Congressman Emmet Avery: Alan Manson
Sister Mary Catherine: Claudette Duffy

After being asked to discuss psychology on *The Ruth Corley Show,* Dr. Hartley is feeling pretty cocky. The feeling fades quickly, though, when Bob finds out Mrs. Corley is a barracuda with a clipboard. When she corners Bob with tough questions, he blurts out that he once treated an elected official. The slip sets off a media frenzy, with the press clamoring to know the identity of the "loony legislator."

"Hi, Bob"-Ometer
Four, from Jerry, Carol, Howard, and Congressman Avery. The series count rapidly rises to 147.

Classic Quote
RUTH CORLEY *(introducing Bob):* It's been said that today's psychologist is nothing more than a con man, a snake-oil salesman, flimflamming innocent people, peddling cures for everything from nail-biting to a lousy love life—and I agree! We'll ask Dr. Hartley to defend himself after these messages.

Classic Scene: Seemingly sweet talk-show host Ruth Corley turns ferocious and suddenly rips Dr. Hartley, leaving him stunned and stammering.

When the interview ends and Ruth expresses her pleasure, Bob tells her, "You would've enjoyed Pearl Harbor."

For the Record: In the same way a befuddled Bob betrays Mr. X on the air, Rob Petrie betrays his wife in the *Dick Van Dyke Show* episode entitled "Ray Murdock's X-Ray." Television appearances are almost always disastrous for both the Hartleys and the Petries.

EPISODE 82

"Seemed like a Good Idea at the Time"

Writers: Tom Patchett and Jay Tarses
Director: Richard Kinon
Cast
Dr. Frank Walburn: Phillip R. Allen
Kelly: Linda Sublette
Gene the Janitor: Titos Vandis

Celebrity psychologist Dr. Frank Walburn suggests that he and Dr. Hartley combine their practices to form "a psychological corporation." After discussing this proposal with Emily, Bob agrees to the merger, and, you guessed it, quickly regrets his decision.

Hartley Homily: "I just tell my patients to get in touch with their feelings after every meal."

"Hi, Bob"-Ometer
Three, from Carol, Kelly, and Dr. Walburn, bringing the series total to 150.

Classic Quote
BOB: Run out and get a bottle of champagne.
CAROL: What year?
BOB: Right now!

For the Record: This episode has an unusual stylized format. The scene titles (i.e. "The Deal," "The Decision," etc.) and jazz piano rags are patterned after "The Sting," the 1973 film starring Robert Redford and Paul Newman.

EPISODE 83

"Over the River and through the Woods"

Writer: Bruce Kane
Director: James Burrows
Cast
Elaine: Janet Meshad
Delivery Guy: David Himes

This episode can be summed up in four words: "Moo goo gai pan." Now for the longer version: When Emily leaves for Seattle to spend Thanksgiving with her family, Bob expects to be alone for the holiday. But then Jerry and Mr. Carlin invite themselves over to keep Bob company. Jerry shows up with a jug full of vodka and cider, while Mr. Carlin, of course, brings his sarcasm and a bottle of cheap wine. Just when you think the party can't get any more depressing, an unhappy Howard enters—he's missing his son because "Howie's in Maui." Once the guys hit rock bottom (and the bottom of Jerry's jug), the party starts to pick up. When Howard suggests they order Chinese food, Bob makes the call. In a drunken haze, he orders $93.80 worth of take-out, including twelve quarts of moo goo gai pan! Emily surprises Bob by coming home early, and after getting a good look at the liquor shop quartet, she nurses them back to sobriety.

"Hi, Bob"-Ometer
Three, from Howard, Carol, and Emily. That's 153 for the series.

Classic Quote
MR. CARLIN: You know you're at a bad party when Elliot Carlin is the happiest man in the room.

EPISODE 84

"Fathers and Sons and Mothers"

Writer: Arnold Kane
Director: James Burrows
Cast
Martha Hartley: Martha Scott
Edgar T. Vickers: Lucian Scott
Edgar T. Vickers Jr.: William Daniels

Bob's parents are having their house painted, inside and out. Of course, avid angler Herb Hartley takes off fishing, leaving Martha to search for a place to stay. Bob reluctantly welcomes her into his home, but her constant sniping quickly reminds him of why he was reluctant. As in episode 4, when he couldn't tell his mother he loved her, Bob is incapable of asking her to treat him like an adult.

"Hi, Bob"-Ometer
One, from Jerry, bringing the series count to 154.

Classic Guest Star: William Daniels gives an outstanding performance as cutthroat businessman and insensitive son Edgar T. Vickers Jr. In the mid-1980s, Daniels made his mark on classic TV with his Emmy-winning portrayal of Dr. Mark Craig on *St. Elsewhere*. More recently he played an irascible teacher on *Boy Meets World*.

For the Record: Bob Hartley's height is five feet ten.

EPISODE 85

"The Article"

Writer: Erik Tarloff
Director: Michael Zinberg

Cast

Dr. Phil Newman: Howard Platt
Dr. Bernie Tupperman: Larry Gelman
Dr. Sarah Harris: Ellen Weston
Gail Bronson: Kristina Holland
Morty the Photographer: Bobby Ramsen
Plumber Roland Sneed: Jack O'Leary

When Bob agrees to let Ellen write an article about life on the seventh floor of the Rimpau Medical Arts Building, he doesn't foresee the lengths to which his colleagues will go to outdo each other.

"Hi, Bob"-Ometer
One, from Morty. The total is now 155 for the series.

Parallel Plot: Too bad Rob Petrie couldn't warn Bob Hartley about the danger of giving one's co-workers access to the press. Rob learned that lesson when he, Buddy, and Sally let their egos run wild in *The Dick Van Dyke Show* episode 95 entitled "My Two Show-Offs and Me."

EPISODE 86

"A Matter of Vice Principal"

Writers: Gordon and Lynne Farr
Director: Peter Bonerz

Cast

Ed Hoffman: Lawrence Pressman
Janet Hoffman: Frances Lee McCain
Gail Bronson: Kristina Holland
Billy Foster: Poindexter
Joanie: Nora Marlowe
Lou the Bun Man: Martin Garner

Now that Rex Pottinger has quit his job and gone to Hawaii, Tracy Grammar School needs a new vice principal, and Emily is hoping the job will go to her friend and co-worker, Ed Hoffman (remember him from episode 56?). Although Ed feigns insecurity, he and his wife, Janet, are actually counting on the promotion, and they've got big plans for the extra money. Consequently, Emily finds herself in an extremely awkward position when, much to her surprise, *she* is chosen as the new vice principal.

"Hi, Bob"-Ometer
Three, from Ed Hoffman, Janet Hoffman, and Gail Bronson, making the total 158 for the series.

Classic Quote
EMILY: How would you like having me as your boss?
BOB: I do.

EPISODE 87

"Bob Has to Have His Tonsils Out, So He Spends Christmas Eve in the Hospital"

Writers: Tom Patchett and Jay Tarses
Director: James Burrows
Cast
Mrs. Loomis: Merie Earle
Dr. Bickwell: Graham Jarvis

Given their holiday history, it's a wonder the Hartleys and their friends still look forward to Christmas, but they do. This time, Bob is dejected because he has to have his tonsils removed on Christmas Eve.

"Hi, Bob"-Ometer
Two, from Jerry and Carol. That's 160 for the series.

Classic Quote
BOB: Everybody knows that the wise men arrived in Bethlehem before the Rose Bowl game.

For the Record: Of the show's six Christmas episodes, this is the only one in which the MTM kitten logo isn't encircled by a colorful wreath.

EPISODE 88

"No Sale"

Writer: Michael Zinberg
Director: Eddie Ryder
Cast
Mr. Arbogast: Malcolm Atterbury

Because of his amazing ability to make money in real estate, Elliot Carlin is known as "Mr. Buy and Sell," top salesman for twelve years in a row. Yet Bob is still reluctant to help bankroll Elliot's latest plan, which will turn a condemned tenement building into a row of town houses. After Bob is goaded into investing $5,000, he and Emily take a tour of the run-down dwelling. That's when they meet Mr. Arbogast, an apparent derelict who appears to live in the shambles. When the Hartleys jump to the conclusion that Mr. Arbogast is so poor he has to eat cat food, they become uneasy with the idea of having to evict him. They pull out of Carlin's real estate deal— only to discover that Mr. Arbogast is actually the wealthy wheeler-dealer who sold Elliot the building.

"Hi, Bob"-Ometer
Three, from Emily, Howard, and Carol, bringing the series total to 163.

For the Record: This is the only installment of *The Bob Newhart Show* that concludes without the familiar shot of the MTM kitten in the logo. The traditional meow is heard, but the featured feline is the cat from this episode.

EPISODE 89

"Carol at 6:01"

Writers: Gordon and Lynne Farr
Director: Peter Bonerz
Cast
Larry Bondurant: Will Mackenzie
Lillian Bakerman: Florida Friebus

There was a time when Carol went to great lengths to attract the attention of a man. Now that she has attention, she doesn't want it. Her husband, Larry, is a doter who won't let her have a minute to herself.

Hartley Homily: "Carol is like a good steak, and you're trying to smother her with ketchup."

"Hi, Bob"-Ometer
Zero. Still at 163 for the series.

EPISODE 90

"Warden Gordon Borden"

Writers: Gordon and Lynne Farr
Director: James Burrows
Cast
Gordon Borden: William Redfield

In Episode 82 Howard's brother, game warden Gordon Borden, stopped by on his way to Jordan, but he was only mentioned and never seen. This time Gordon's visit is longer, giving Howard a chance to reminisce about all of the things his sibling has stolen from him through the years. Now the game warden has set his sights on Ellen, who, although she broke off her engagement with Howard, remains romantically involved with him. When it appears she's going to be torn between two Bordens, she surprises them both by announcing that she's accepted a newspaper job in Cleveland. Ellen doesn't mind leaving Gordon, but as time goes by, she's sure to miss Howard and his ironing board. Oh, yeah, Howard also gets a call from his other brother, Norman Borden the Mormon doorman!

"Hi, Bob"-Ometer

Four—two from Howard and one each from Ellen and Gordon, making 167 for the series.

Classic Quote

BOB: The last thing Ellen's going to do is drop Howard for Gordon. That's like trading a whoopee cushion for an exploding cigar.

For the Record: This is the last of Pat Finley's fifteen appearances as Ellen Hartley, Bob's sweet and sensible sister and Howard's true love.

If actor William Redfield looks familiar, you're probably remembering him from the series pilot (episode 9), in which he portrayed the Hartleys' overbearing neighbor, Arthur Hoover.

EPISODE 91

"My Boy Guillermo"

Writer: Sy Rosen
Director: Alan Myerson
Cast
Courtney Simpson: Gail Strickland
Richie: Matthew Laborteaux

Dr. Robinson's former flame, Courtney Simpson (episode 61), is back from her world travels, and she wants to marry Jerry. It seems she plans on adopting an eight-year-old Spanish boy named Guillermo, and she'd like Jerry to be the dad in her "immediate" family. He is elated, especially about being a father for a fellow orphan. But his joy is short-lived when Courtney learns that the adoption agency has given Guillermo to a Spanish family. Jerry bemoans the loss of the son he never met, and without Guillermo in the picture, Courtney doesn't want to hang around. She goes back to Bolivia, and the dentist stands alone.

"Hi, Bob"-Ometer

Two, from Courtney and Howard. That's 169 for the series.

Classic Scene: As he shows off his gas-station magic kit to Bob and Emily, Howard tries to do a card trick his grandma taught him. He asks Bob to pick a card, look at it, and put it back. Then he takes the entire deck and hurls it against the wall, scattering cards everywhere. After the appropriate beat, he deadpans, "It didn't work."

EPISODE 92

"Duke of Dunk"

Writers: Douglas Arango and Phil Doran
Director: Peter Bonerz
Cast
Dwayne Granger: Anthony Costello

Bob attempts to fill a tall order by counseling a hotshot pro basketball star, Dwayne "Duke of Dunk" Granger, who has no interest in being a team player. When Bob finally gets the star to be one of the "beans" instead of a "hot dog," his teammates are forced to play catch-up, compensating for their star player's new unselfish approach. By the end, Bob is treating the entire Chicago Sun Spots squad in his fear-of-winning support group.

Hartley Homily: "A hot dog needs a bun to be picked up with. It might also need some ketchup, some sauerkraut. In order to win, a hot dog needs a team, just like you need a team."

"Hi, Bob"-Ometer
Two, from Emily and Howard, making the count 171 for the series.

EPISODE 93

"Guaranteed Not to Shrink"

Writer: Sy Rosen
Director: James Burrows
Cast
Larry Bondurant: Will Mackenzie
Mr. Firman: Paul Bryar
Mrs. Firman: Claudia Bryar

Carol's still searching for a life beyond her reception desk. Consequently, she enrolls in night classes at Bob's alma mater, Loyola University, and decides to be a psychology major, just like you-know-who.

"Hi, Bob"-Ometer
Three, from Larry, Emily, and Howard. That's 174 for the series.

Classic Quote
BOB: You're not so tall. You're compact. . . . Well, not compact. But, you know, you have a nice . . . bulk.
EMILY: Like our furniture?

EPISODE 94

"Birth of a Salesman"

Writer: Sy Rosen
Director: John C. Chulay
Cast
Ed Herd: Oliver Clark

When Bob persuades Ed Herd to be more assertive, the unsuccessful salesman starts sticking his head in his customers' doors, although Bob had told him to use his foot. Nevertheless, when his face winds up bandaged and bruised, the new self-assured Mr. Herd decides to sue Dr. Hartley for forcing him to be forceful. Bob feels betrayed since, in the past, he has purchased appliances from Herd in an effort to bolster his confidence. Ironically, when Herd does decide to drop the charges, he worries that Dr. Hartley will be disappointed in him for backing down.

"Hi, Bob"-Ometer
Three, from Emily, Jerry, and Howard. The count is now 177 for the series.

For the Record: The ever-apologetic Mr. Herd says he's sorry twelve times in this episode.

EPISODE 95

"The Boy Next Door"

Writer: Hugh H. Wilson
Director: Peter Bonerz
Cast
Mitzi Margolis: Brooke Adams
Mrs. Walker: Amzie Strickland

When Howie Junior decides to live with his dad, he sees less of his father than ever before. Howard's busy flight schedule keeps him out of town, and that keeps "Aunt Emily" and "Uncle Bob" busy watching Howie.

"Hi, Bob"-Ometer
One, from Howie Junior. That's 178 for the series.

Classic Quote
HOWARD: All you can do is try. It's all any parent can do.
BOB: I'm not a parent, Howard. I'm the next-door neighbor.
HOWARD: Well, then, you'll just have to try harder.

For the Record: This is the first of three scripts written by Hugh Wilson, who went on to create the sitcoms *WKRP in Cincinnati* and *Frank's Place*. Wilson met executive producers Tom Patchett and Jay Tarses when the three of them were simultaneously employed by the Armstrong Cork Company in Lancaster, Pennsylvania.

Mrs. Walker's name is incorrectly listed as "Walhauser" in the end credits.

EPISODE 96

"Peeper—Two"

Writers: Tom Patchett and Jay Tarses
Director: Michael Zinberg
Cast
Rosemary: Veronica Hamel
Sharon: Sally Stark
Paula: Barbara Ellen Levene

Just when you thought it was safe to open your sock drawer, the ultimate purveyor of pranks, the Peeper, is back for another sudden, and extended, stay at the Hartleys. He's come from Montpelier, Vermont, where his wife of twenty-two years, Marie, has just left him for the milkman.

"Hi, Bob"-Ometer
Four, from Jerry, Rosemary, Howard, and Carol, bringing the count to 182.

Classic Guest Star: In this episode she tries to warm up to Bob at the piano bar, but actress Veronica Hamel became a star by playing cold-as-ice public defender Joyce Davenport on *Hill Street Blues*.

For the Record: When Dr. Hartley realizes someone has painted the lobby walls ultra-bright orange, he says, "Get 'em out of here!" It must've worked, because in the next installment the walls are back to blue.

This is the final episode of the show's fourth season, but it's also the last of the twenty remarkable scripts that were contributed by executive producers Jay Tarses and Tom Patchett. You can still spot the two writers in upcoming Classic Cameos, however: Tarses in episode 97 and Patchett in 115. They have since gone on to create several other TV shows, including the memorable *Buffalo Bill* with Dabney Coleman, Bob Newhart's all-time favorite sitcom, according to his list of favorites in *The Bob Book*.

EPISODE 97

"Enter Mrs. Peeper"

Writers: Gordon and Lynne Farr
Director: Michael Zinberg
Cast
Corinne Murdoch: Jean Palmerton
Messenger: Charles Thomas Murphy
Waiter: Jay Tarses

Bouncing back after his failed marriage, the Peeper shows up at the Hartley home with good news for a change: he's happily remarried to a Montpelier librarian named Corinne, whom he brings along to meet Bob and Emily. Bob doesn't like the effect Corinne is having on the Peeper, who's actually starting to act like an adult, much to Bob's dismay and Emily's delight. As usual, the perceptive Peeper recognizes Bob's jealousy and resolves the rift by revealing that he wasn't too crazy about Emily, either, when Bob first married her.

"Hi, Bob"-Ometer
Three, from Jerry, the Peeper, and Carol. That's 185 for the series.

Classic Quote
BOB: That's the great thing about the Peeper. You know it's gonna happen, but you don't know when.
EMILY: Kinda like death?

Classic Cameo: Jay Tarses plays the sage server who advises Bob to stop embellishing his past.

For the Record: Jean Palmerton reprises her role as Mrs. Murdoch in two more episodes (105 and 120).

EPISODE 98

"Caged Fury"

Writers: Gordon and Lynne Farr
Director: Michael Zinberg

This is perhaps the best episode of the series. It's July 1976, and the Hartleys plan to celebrate America's bicentennial by attending a costume party in Howard's apartment. Of course, with Howard as host, Bob and Emily are ultimately responsible for bringing all of the supplies, which they attempt to retrieve from their basement storage locker. But in an unguarded moment, they accidentally lock themselves in, with no hope of being discovered until Howard comes looking for them—*if* Howard comes looking for them. As time passes, Bob and Emily alternate between arguments and acts of affection. Meanwhile, up at the costume party, all of the guests, except Mr. Carlin, are dressed in similar Uncle Sam suits. Eventually, they find the caged Hartleys and grant them their freedom on Independence Day.

Hartley Homily: "Even the humblest person makes awesome progress, though their pace be like a snail."

"Hi, Bob"-Ometer
One, from Howard. The series total is now 186.

Classic Quote
EMILY *(trapped):* Do you ever wish we had kids?
BOB *(also trapped):* Right now I wish we had a kid who was a human mole!

EPISODE 99

"Some of My Best Friends Are . . ."

Writers: Patricia Jones and Donald Reiker
Director: James Burrows
Cast
Craig Plager: Howard Hesseman
Michelle Nardo: Renée Lippin
Lillian Bakerman: Florida Friebus
Emil Peterson: John Fiedler

For the sake of rejuvenation, Dr. Hartley decides to bring a new member into his central therapy group, which consists of Mr. Carlin, Mr. Peterson, Mrs. Bakerman, and Michelle Nardo. Peterson warns Bob that they don't want "anyone who will disrupt the harmony of our little family." When Bob brings in Craig Plager, all seems fine—that is, until they come to the slow realization that Mr. Plager is gay.

"Hi, Bob"-Ometer
Two, both from Howard. That's 188 for the series.

EPISODE 100

"Still Crazy After All These Years"

Writer: Hugh Wilson
Director: Alan Myerson
Cast
Dr. Ned Podbillion: Leonard Stone

This episode is "fine and dandy." Just as the Hartleys consider weaning Howard away from his complete dependence upon them, one of Bob's colleagues, Dr. Podbillion, comes up with a radical therapy method that will completely transform the personality of the patient. Howard chooses to undergo the Podbillion Process while Bob and Emily are away on a dude ranch vacation. They return to find Howard a changed man, very sophisticated and totally self-sufficient. All is not "fine and dandy," however, because the Hartleys realize they miss the old Howard. They successfully bring him back to his former Howardness by tempting him with free food.

Hartley Homily: "You can take the joy out of the man, but you can't take the man out of the joy."

"Hi, Bob"-Ometer
One, from Howard, making a total of 189 for the series.

Classic Quote
BOB: Howard, you've got a full deck. It's just that sometimes you like to pass the deal.

EPISODE 101

"The Great Rent Strike"

Writer: David Lloyd
Director: John C. Chulay

When Bob complains to Mr. Carlin about his awful landlord and unbearable living conditions, the real estate wizard vows to come to the rescue, using his renowned acumen. But Bob gets more than he bargained for when Mr. Carlin buys the building and becomes the new landlord.

"Hi, Bob"-Ometer
One, from Howard. It's now 190 for the series.

Classic Quote
BOB *(calling another tenant):* Hello, this is Bob Hartley in apartment 523. Are you and your husband as hot as we are?

Classic Scene: To get relief from the hot apartment, Bob steps out onto the terrace for a blast of winter air and accidentally locks himself out. With no one inside to let him back in, Bob scrawls "HELP" in the frost on the window.

EPISODE 102
"Et Tu, Carol"

Writer: Gary David Goldberg
Director: Alan Myerson
Cast
Dr. Phil Newman: Howard Platt
Dr. Bernie Tupperman: Larry Gelman
Debbie Flett: Shirley O'Hara

Carol threatens to quit. Nothing new about that, but when Bob offers her the option of staying and working for only two of the seventh-floor physicians, she chooses Dr. Robinson and Dr. Tupperman! As though being betrayed by a friend isn't enough, Dr. Hartley suffers a worse fate at the hands of the Freedman Fill-In Agency. Yes, they've sent over Bob's secretarial nemesis, the forgetful Debbie Flett! Fortunately for both "Dr. Ryan" and "Big Red," Carol quickly decides to come back to Bob, whom she didn't choose initially because he always fights her battles for her.

"Hi, Bob"-Ometer
Two, both from Emily. That's 192 for the series.

For the Record: This is the first of three scripts written by Gary David Goldberg, who went on to create the 1980s hit *Family Ties.*

EPISODE 103
"Send This Boy to Camp"

Writer: David Lloyd
Director: Michael Zinberg
Cast
Mr. Perlmutter: Sorrell Brooke
Phil Dorigo: Michael LeClair
Wally Carson: Tierre Turner
Man at Elevator: Fil Formicola

Just as Jerry's looking for a way to help orphans, Bob is regretting that he never went to summer camp. That's why the two of them decide to get a couple of boys from Jerry's former orphanage and take them on the adventure of a lifetime. The teens, Phil and Wally, are supposedly twins, but Phil is blond, white, and talkative, and Wally isn't. In fact, Wally chooses to remain mute, letting Phil do the talking for both of them. The trip takes a wrong turn when Bob doesn't call ahead to reserve a campsite and the next available space is in Green Bay, Wisconsin. Determined to forge ahead, however, the pseudo-pioneers set up camp in a city parking lot. By the faint light of the Wrigley Building, Wally finally breaks his silence and sings a chorus of "The Happy Wanderer."

"Hi, Bob"-Ometer
One, from Carol, bringing the count to 193 for the series.

Classic Quote
HOWARD: Are you done with Howie's shorts?
EMILY *(who's sewing in name tags):* Well, I would be if his name were shorter.
HOWARD: My name is Borden. Why would I name him Howie Shorter?

EPISODE 104

"A Crime Most Foul"

Writer: Sy Rosen
Director: John C. Chulay

Cast

Ed Herd: Oliver Clark
Lillian Bakerman: Florida Friebus
Emil Peterson: John Fiedler

Bob is so proud of his new $420 tape recorder—three speeds, automatic counter, lifetime battery, extra-long microphone cord—that, when it mysteriously disappears, he finds it very easy to believe it was stolen. Everyone is a suspect, including his patients, his friends, his wife, and even his mother! Only after he has accused and offended everyone close to him does Bob remember that he inadvertently covered the recorder with his coat.

"Hi, Bob"-Ometer
Zero. Still at 193 for the series.

EPISODE 105

"The Slammer"

Writers: Gordon and Lynne Farr
Director: Michael Zinberg

Cast

Corinne Murdoch: Jean Palmerton
Johnny Carson Jr.: Bobby Ramsen
Kim: Kim O'Brien
Darva: Lucy Lee Flippin
Detective: David Himes
Man: Rhodes Reason

In an effort to recapture the glory of their days at Loyola University, Bob and the Peeper head off to their old college hangout, Runyan's Beanery,

A Peeper by Any Other Name . . .

Jeepers creepers, why can't Howard say "Peeper"? Whenever Bob's college buddy comes to visit, Howard finds new ways to mangle his nickname. In this episode alone, the neighborly navigator refers to Cliff as "the Weeper" and "the Creeper."

Below is a complete list of the names Howard has called the Peeper, followed by a list of the names he could have used:

Howard's Names

The Sneaker
The Honker
The Tweeter
The Snipper
The Winker
The Weeper
The Creeper
The Leaper

Names Howard Missed

The Clapper
The Bleeper
The Leaker
The Rapper
The Minesweeper
The Stinker
The Bee Keeper
The Little-Bo-Peeper
The-Take-A-Flying-Leaper
Glen

which is a very faint version of its former self. To make matters worse, the lonely alumni get arrested for vice violations after a misunderstanding with two female undercover officers. Afraid that Emily and Corinne won't believe the truth, Bob and the Peeper sit in their jail cell, hoping for another way out. The prankster and the shrink are let out of the clink when the false charges are dropped on a technicality.

"Hi, Bob"-Ometer

Two, from Howard and Corinne. It's now 195 for the series.

For the Record: Like Bob Hartley, Bob Newhart graduated from Loyola University. Unlike Dr. Hartley, however, Newhart earned a bachelor's degree in commerce.

In this episode, stock player Bobby Ramsen docs his first turn as bizarre bartender Johnny Carson Jr. You'll see Johnny again when Bob and the Peeper down some drinks in episode 120.

EPISODE 106

"Jerry's Retirement"

Writer: Hugh Wilson
Director: Alan Myerson
Cast
Cornelius "Junior" Harrison: John Randolph
Shorty Vance: Howard Morris

Jerry has always dreamed of retiring before the age of forty. Now, thanks to a lucrative real estate deal, he's reached his goal at thirty-eight. Bob thinks it's ridiculous to stop working at such a young age, but Jerry does it anyway. Immediately he goes on a buying binge, acquiring expensive clothes, a Ferrari, and a yacht. Meanwhile, Emily's dad, Junior, has also recently retired. He and his fishing partner, Shorty, are in Chicago, us-

ing the Hartley home as a fishing lodge, where they make big plans that never come to fruition. Shorty seems to think that true retirement means being as inactive as humanly possible. So when Jerry meets up with fellow retirees Junior and Shorty, his fast-paced lifestyle slows down to a snail's pace. He takes up whittling and starts talking in a slow, Mark Twain-ish drawl. When Bob makes one more attempt to motivate him, Jerry just dozes off. Finally, the young old-timer leaves for Europe in search of the world's best "sharp stick."

"Hi, Bob"-Ometer

Five: two from Howard, and one apiece from Shorty, Jerry, and Carol. The total is now 200 for the series.

Classic Guest Star: To his role as Shorty Vance, versatile veteran comic Howard Morris brings an impressive list of classic TV credits. He was a regular on Sid Caesar's *Your Show of Shows* before he created memorable Mayberry moments in his recurring role as Ernest T. Bass on *The Andy Griffith Show*. Morris also directed several episodes of *The Dick Van Dyke Show* and *Bewitched*.

For the Record: This is the first half of a two-parter. For the surprising outcome of Jerry's retirement and trip to Europe, don't miss episode 107!

A "Hi, Bob" Hallmark

Within the tag of this episode, there is a true television landmark—the 200th "Hi Bob" of the series! That's not counting "Hey, Bob," "Oh, Bob," or even "Why, Bob?" It has to be those two little words "Hi" and "Bob," directly adjacent to one another, with the "Hi" always coming first.

In celebration of episode 106's "Hi, Bob" hallmark, here are some salutatory statistics: In the entire series, there are 256 "Hi, Bob" greetings, with 118 attributed to Howard Borden, who is the undisputed "Hi, Bob" king! You may be surprised Emily isn't on top of the "Hi, Bob" heap but she only logged seventeen such greetings. She usually opted for the endearing "Hi, Honey" or "Hi, Dear." Together, Jerry Robinson and Carol Kester-Bondurant account for seventy-seven (with forty-one from Jerry and thirty-six from Carol), and forty-three other "Hi, Bob" greetings are assigned to guest stars or minor characters. The ultimate "Hi Bob" can be found in episode 115, in which Bob himself says it.

With seven of the salutations, episode 49 has the distinction of having the highest "Hi, Bob" count.

Finally, you may be surprised to learn that an amazing twenty-two episodes don't include any "Hi, Bob"s at all. It makes you wonder how much fun the legendary college drinking game—chug whenever someone says "Hi, Bob"—really was.

EPISODE 107

"Here's to You, Mrs. Robinson"

Writers: Gordon and Lynne Farr
Director: James Burrows
Cast
Jerry's Mother: Lucy Landau
Mr. Robinson: Fred D. Scott
Young Man: Steve Anderson

Jerry comes back from Europe with a renewed commitment to finding his natural parents. He uses the rest of his retirement money to fund a media blitz—complete with full-page newspaper ads, TV commercials, and a $5,000 reward. Unfortunately, his efforts appear to be in vain when the publicity doesn't turn up a single valid lead. Financially spent, Jerry returns to his practice on the seventh floor. Just as he's given up his familial dream, a charming British woman shows up claiming to be Jerry's mother. The doubting dentist says, "Get out of here, you old crone!" But when she correctly states that Jerry has a banana birthmark on his behind and two webbed toes, he knows she's really his mummy—at long last! It seems Jerry's real name is Miles Robertson, and he was separated from his parents during the Battle of Britain. His father—"a Yank in plumbing supplies"—was killed by a buzz bomb during the battle. When the authorities couldn't find Jerry's mother, they shipped him off to the Chicago orphanage. Somewhere along the way, his last name was changed from Robertson to Robinson. In a matter of minutes, Jerry's entire past is revealed to him, and he's overjoyed.

"Hi, Bob"-Ometer
Four, all from Howard. That's 204 for the series.

EPISODE 108

"Breaking Up Is Hard to Do"

Writer: Sy Rosen
Director: Peter Bonerz
Cast
Martha Hartley: Martha Scott
Brian McDermott: John Holland
Lillian Bakerman: Florida Friebus

Bob's parents surprise everybody by calling it quits after forty-seven years. Martha leaves Herb because he makes her feel insignificant; she says he just wants someone to "clean his fish and unsnarl his line." Bob has a hard enough time dealing with his parents' separation, but then his mom starts dating. Worst of all, she seems to be enjoying it!

Hartley Homily: "People are strangers until we talk to them. Then they're not strangers anymore."

"Hi, Bob"-Ometer
None. The count still stands at 204 for the series.

For the Record: Herb Hartley is mentioned many times but never appears in this episode. His side of the story is revealed in episode 109.

EPISODE 109

"Making Up Is the Thing to Do"

Writers: Gordon and Lynne Farr
Director: Harvey Medlinsky
Cast
Martha Hartley: Martha Scott
Herb Hartley: Barnard Hughes

Christmas can mean only one thing: another horrendous Hartley holiday party. This time Bob's estranged parents are putting a damper on the doings by arguing in front of the guests, who quickly look for a way out. Left alone with Herb and Martha, Bob and Emily feign their own argument in the hope of giving the parents a common cause. Naturally, Herb and Martha abandon their own sniping to help heal the rift between "the children." In the process, the elderly lovers reconcile. After his parents leave together, Bob and Emily are actually able to celebrate a truly happy holiday ending.

"Hi, Bob"-Ometer
Two, from Larry and Herb. The count is now 206 for the series.

For the Record: Although episode 87 broke the tradition, this installment resumes the Christmas custom of ending the holiday episodes with the MTM kitten encircled by a cheery wreath.

EPISODE 110

"Love Is the Blindest"

Writer: Gary David Goldberg
Director: Will Mackenzie
Cast
Andrea Duff: Mary Ann Chinn

Bob and Emily make the mistake of double dating with Mr. Carlin and his dim-witted secretary, Andrea. She believes every outlandish lie Elliot tells her about himself—for example, that he invented stuffed mushrooms, that he met Bob when they were both at the Green Bay Packers' training camp, and that he killed a man in Rio. Dr. Hartley insists that Mr. Carlin be honest with Andrea, because "there's a difference between little white lies and science fiction." So for the first time in thirteen years, Elliot acts on Bob's advice and tells Andrea the truth. Fearing that she'll break up with him first, he quickly follows the truth with a lie about having to fly back to his ranch in Tasmania. When he finally lets down his defenses and abandons his pretenses, he discovers that she does love the "real" Elliot Carlin. Could this actually be a happy conclusion for Carlin?

Hartley Homily: "Get the weeds of deceit out of the garden, and then real love can bloom."

"Hi, Bob"-Ometer
One, from Howard. That's 207 for the series.

For the Record: Will Mackenzie steps out of his role as Larry Bondurant to direct his first and only episode. Mackenzie also helmed the classic "Zen and the Art of Cab Driving," episode 57 of *Taxi*.

EPISODE 111

"The Ironwood Experience"

Writer: Phil Davis
Director: Peter Bonerz
Cast
Dr. Morgan: Max Showalter

Dr. Hartley is looking forward to giving a lecture at the Ironwood Institute, where he'll lead a sex workshop during a weekend retreat. He seems confident he can do the topic justice—that is, until he discovers the naked truth about Ironwood: it's a nudist colony, and he'll be addressing an audience of undressed individuals. He will have the option of being naked, too, but he won't get a lectern to hide behind—just a microphone. When the weekend is over, Bob happily comes home to Emily, who's waiting for a private lesson.

"Hi, Bob"-Ometer
Two, both from Howard. The count is now 209 for the series.

Classic Quote
JERRY *(to Bob):* What do *you* know about sex? You've been married eight years. Oh, I get it— those who can't, teach.

Classic Scene: Bob discovers that clothing is optional at Ironwood when he walks into Dr. Morgan's office and finds him naked (carefully seated behind a desk). Bob's reaction is topped only by his question to the doctor: "Don't you stick to your chair?"

EPISODE 112

"Of Mice and Men"

Writer: Bruce Kane
Director: Peter Bonerz
Cast
Emil Peterson: John Fiedler
Ed Herd: Oliver Clark
Flo: Betty Kean

Despite the fact that history has shown it to be a very bad move, Bob invites Emily to sit in with one of his therapy groups. Doesn't he remember the women's support group debacle in episode 60? Emily remembers, and she's reluctant to attend the session, but Bob talks her into it. This time the group is made up of men who can't relate to women: Mr. Carlin, Mr. Herd, and Mr. Peterson. Emily is there to supply them with a real female point of view. When she tries to contribute, however, Bob disregards her comments, causing a marital fight in front of the group. It's another case of "Physician, heal thyself!" as Dr. Hartley is forced to realize that he still has a lot to learn about what women really want.

Hartley Homily: "Just like dinner in a diner, a marriage can be bland. A man has to season his marriage with trust, spice it with honesty, and, of course, sweeten it with affection."

"Hi, Bob"-Ometer
Zero. The series total stalls at 209.

EPISODE 113
"Halls of Hartley"

Writer: Michael Zinberg
Director: James Burrows
Cast
Dr. Eleanor Doctor: Toresa Hughes
Dr. Franklin Pitt: Richard Libertini
Dr. Scranton: Addison Powell
Chuck Morgan: Craig Wasson
Maintenance Man: James Burrows

Fed up with life in the big city, Dr. Hartley applies for a faculty position at Pleasant Acres College in a small Iowa town, where the folks love to thresh and the crickets like to chirp. Not long after he arrives there for the job interview, Bob starts to miss the sights and sounds of the "City of the Big Shoulders," which he greets with open arms upon his return. He does get the job offer, but he promptly turns it down, because nothing can break up his rekindled love affair with Chicago.

"Hi, Bob"-Ometer
Three: two from Howard and one from Chuck Morgan, bringing the series count to 212.

Classic Quote
CHUCK *(a student, sizing up Bob):* You're built like a thresher: good arms, small head.

Classic Cameo: James Burrows, who directed the episode, also makes a brief appearance as the unsympathetic maintenance man who closes down both Rimpau Building elevators. This is the last time Burrows called the shots on this series, but a year later he began his four-year tenure as the principal director on *Taxi.* Then, in 1982, he co-created the hit comedy *Cheers,* for which he served as executive producer and principal director throughout its eleven-season run.

EPISODE 114
"The Heartbreak Kidd"

Writer: Sy Rosen
Director: Dick Martin
Cast
Veronica Kidd: Tovah Feldshuh

When Veronica, an attractive psychology student, is assigned to observe Dr. Hartley for a couple of months, she obviously likes what she sees. She hangs on his every word, which she finds brilliant and meaningful. Bob's ego feeds on the attention and praise, but needless to say, Emily isn't fond of Veronica's forward and flirtatious manner.

"Hi, Bob"-Ometer
Three, from Jerry, Carol, and Veronica Kidd. The count is 215 for the series.

For the Record: This is the first of eleven episodes directed by Newhart's pal, Dick Martin, who already had a hugely successful career as a stand-up comic and as co-host of *Rowan and Martin's Laugh-In* (1968–1973). In the early sixties Martin had a recurring role as Harry Conners on *The Lucy Show.*

Parallel Plot: In this episode, Bob and Emily Hartley find themselves in yet another marital predicament that parallels that of the Petries. In

The Dick Van Dyke Show episode 46 "The Foul-Weather Girl," Laura is similarly suspicious of a show business hopeful who keeps fawning over Rob and effectively flattering him.

EPISODE 115

"Death Be My Destiny"

Writer: Sy Rosen
Director: Michael Zinberg
Cast
Ed Herd: Oliver Clark
Dave Death: Tom Patchett
Lady on Elevator: Lieux Dressler

After narrowly escaping certain death down an elevator shaft, Bob becomes obsessed with his eventual demise. He refuses to ride the elevator for fear it will turn into a stairway to heaven. In a moment of pure irony, the always fearful Mr. Herd coaxes Dr. Hartley to confront his fear and ride the lift. Bob does it, but when the doors open back up, we realize that Bob, like the elevator, is only halfway healed.

"Hi, Bob"-Ometer

One—the ultimate "Hi, Bob" because it's said by Bob himself as he tells Emily about his death dream. The series count is now 216.

Classic Quote

BOB: I feel terrific. I'm on top of the world. I am strong. I am invincible.
JERRY: You are woman.

EPISODE 116

"Taxation without Celebration"

Writer: Sy Rosen
Director: Peter Bonerz
Cast
Chauffeur: Vince Martorano
Bellboy: Drew Michaels

Emily prepares to celebrate the Hartleys' seventh wedding anniversary on April 15, the day income taxes must be filed. But Bob's been procrastinating, and on April 14 he is still nowhere near ready to file his annual statement. So when Emily whisks him away on a surprise trip to San Francisco, he ruins the romance by frantically filing.

"Hi, Bob"-Ometer

Four—one apiece from Howard and Larry, and two from Carol. That's 220 for the series.

Classic Quote

BOB: I have to march in the annual Ickets Day Parade. I'm the Grand Icket.

EPISODE 117

"Desperate Sessions"

Writers: Michael Zinberg and Martin Davidson
Director: Dick Martin
Cast
Mel: Robert Pine
Sergeant Webber: Walker Edmiston
Police Officer: Ron Vernan
Bank Guard: Richard Dioguardi
Bank Teller: Andrea Adler

When a fellow bank customer makes friends with him in line, Bob has no idea the stranger is about to commit a crime. Then, as though witnessing a bank robbery isn't amazing enough, Bob discovers the likable larcenist, Mel, hiding out in his office.

Hartley Homily: "Forget about the leisure suits and the mood rings. Just be yourself and be happy with that."

"Hi, Bob"-Ometer
Four: from Carol three times and from Jerry once. That's 224 for the series.

Classic Quote
HOWARD: I've got some good news about the fried chicken.
CAROL: What?
HOWARD: The colonel has breasts!

EPISODE 118

"The Mentor"

Writer: Gary David Goldberg
Director: Michael Zinberg

The Bondurants can agree on one thing for sure: they both hate their dead-end jobs. Everyone knows that Carol's life is a constant search for a more fulfilling career. Larry's dissatisfaction, however, comes as a complete surprise to his friends. When the downtrodden travel agent says his job is going nowhere, Bob wonders if Larry has considered becoming his own boss. Bob lives to regret those words when Larry opens his own office—on the seventh floor! Carol and Emily transform the reception area into a Polynesian jungle, and while Bob and Jerry are forced to battle their way through the underbrush, Larry's customers are not. His business is bombing, and Bob doesn't know how to help. The answer eventually comes from a most unlikely source: Howard.

"Hi, Bob"-Ometer
None. The count stands at 224 for the series.

EPISODE 119

"Shrinking Violence"

Writer: Sy Rosen
Director: Peter Bonerz
Cast
Lillian Bakerman: Florida Friebus
Ed Herd: Oliver Clark
Marvin: Bob Ridgely
Receptionist: Marsha Kramer

Just as Dr. Hartley is trying to get Mr. Carlin to redirect his anger, Emily is stomping mad about the shoddy treatment she's been getting from a mechanic named Marvin. Bob says there's no sense in Emily going ape over the grease monkey if she's not willing to confront him. When she still wimps out, Bob takes matters into his own hands and goes to the garage, where Marvin punches Bob in the eye. In the end, Dr. Hartley wishes he had controlled his anger, and Mr. Carlin gives up trying to control his.

Hartley Homily: "There's an obvious difference between being angry and making an idiot out of yourself."

"Hi, Bob"-Ometer

Three, from Howard twice and from Marvin once. That's 227 for the series.

Classic Quote

MRS. BAKERMAN: It's a wonderful day. The sun is beaming, the breeze is murmuring, and the flowers are pushing their dainty heads toward the heavens.
MR. CARLIN: Why don't you push your dainty head through a wall?

EPISODE 120

"You're Having My Hartley"

Writers: Gordon and Lynne Farr
Director: Peter Bonerz
Cast
Johnny Carson Jr.: Bobby Ramsen

Can it be that Bob and Emily are soon going to hear the pitter-patter of a baby Hartley's feet? It appears so, when Emily announces that she's pregnant. As it turns out, so is Carol. All of the men—Bob, Jerry, Howard, and the Peeper—are driven to tears of joy at the thought of cute little itty-bitty bundles of joy. But just as Bob starts to wonder if fatherhood might be a nightmare, he finds out that the whole thing is just a dream . . . except for Carol, who really *is* pregnant.

"Hi, Bob"-Ometer

One, from Howard, taking the series count to 228.

Classic Quote

BOB: It's the end of an era, end of my youth. . . . Where does the time go?
CLIFF: Cleveland.

EPISODE 121

"Bob's Change of Life"

Writers: Glen Charles and Les Charles
Director: Peter Bonerz
Cast
Martha Hartley: Martha Scott
George Simmons: Charles Thomas Murphy

Big changes are in store for Bob Hartley. His book is about to be published, he's moving into a new apartment, and his father wants to sell the house in which Bob grew up. Bob, who's hardly known as an unpredictable chameleon, isn't sure how he should feel about the unavoidable up-heaval.

"Hi, Bob"-Ometer

Four: three from Howard and one from Jerry. That's 232 for the series.

Classic Quote

BOB: The number seven pizza has anchovies on it, but it's still the same pizza underneath.

For the Record: This is the first of three episodes written by brothers Glen and Les Charles, who had already written scripts for *The Mary Tyler Moore Show* and *M*A*S*H*. From 1978 to 1982, they were part of the cadre of *Taxi* writers and producers. During that time, the brothers worked extensively with director James Burrows, and in the fall of 1982 the trio launched the mega-hit comedy *Cheers*, which ran for eleven seasons.

EPISODE 122

"Ex-Con Job"

Writer: Ziggy Steinberg
Director: Michael Zinberg

Cast

Arthur Tatum: Taurean Blacque
Steve Kopelson: Allen Case
Al Brolio: Ric Mancini
Richard Hawkins: Wyatt Johnson
Reuben Ortiz: Bert Rosario
The Hammer: H. B. Haggerty
The Man: Greg Lewis

Bob goes behind bars to counsel a collection of "rehabilitated" convicts, who will soon be released. Dr. Hartley becomes quickly frustrated, however, when the group's ringleader, Arthur Tatum, continues to mock Bob's attempts to offer real help. When Bob suggests that they continue to meet as a group after their release, Arthur and the others just scoff. Once on the outside, however, Arthur pays the Hartleys a welcome visit, which soon turns into an unwelcome holdup.

"Hi, Bob"-Ometer

One, from Howard, making the total 233 for the series.

Classic Quote

BOB: I'm gonna boogie for a ride on your soul train.

Classic Scene: When Arthur attempts to rob the Hartleys, he has them stand with their hands up against the wall. Suddenly, Howard bursts in and quickly assesses the situation—he's witnessing a "hold up," that is, Bob and Emily are obviously struggling to "hold up" the wall of their apartment! He rushes over, past Arthur, and joins in the fight to fortify the falling wall.

"Hill Street Bob"

If it seems strangely ironic to see Taurcan Blacque in the role of holdup man Arthur Tatum, you're probably remembering him from his role on the other side of the law. He was Detective Neal Washington on *Hill Street Blues*. Actually, Blacque's not alone in his connection to both *The Bob Newhart Show* and television's all-time greatest police drama. A lot of *Hill Street* regulars logged time walking the Bob beat.

Before he won Emmys for his portrayal of calm, cool, and effective Captain Frank Furillo, Daniel J. Travanti did a one-time-only guest turn, in episode 50, as grumpy patient and ill-fated fruitman Victor Gianelli.

On *Hill Street Blues*, Captain Furillo's love interest was the ambitious and beautiful public defender Joyce Davenport, played by Veronica Hamel. Hamel had a smaller romantic role on *The Bob Newhart Show* when she appeared in episode 96 as Rosemary, an aggressive piano bar patron who falls prey to Bob's irresistible charms.

Though the late Michael Conrad won a pair of Emmys for turning Sergeant Phil Esterhaus into the lustful heart of Hill Street Station, he'll also be remembered as Mr. Trevesco, the patient who injured Bob's back in episode 27 and then claimed to have spotted UFOs in episode 48.

With his bravado and misplaced machismo, Lieutenant Howard Hunter would have made a fascinating psychological study for Bob Hartley. When James B. Sikking, who portrayed Hunter, appeared in episode 5 of *The Bob Newhart Show*, however, it was as Dick, a stranger whom Bob mistook for the husband of an old girlfriend.

As Rex Pottinger, the vice principal of Tracy Grammar School in episodes 65 and 71, actor George Wyner played a somewhat screwy school administrator who, at one point, asked to be called Flipper. It was very unlike the dramatic fare Wyner would serve up as Assistant District Attorney Irwin Bernstein on *Hill Street Blues*.

Travanti, Hamel, Conrad, Sikking, Blacque, and Wyner—six *Hill Street* stars who make up the "Hill Street Bob" roll call, which always ends with the same seven words: "And, hey, let's be sane out there."

EPISODE 123

"A Jackie Story"

Writer: Lloyd Garver
Director: Michael Zinberg

Cast

Jackie Windsor: Hope Alexander-Willis
Danny James: Sam Kwasman
Waiter: Roger Etienne
Girl Number One: Sondra Theodore
Girl Number Two: Jordan Michaels

When Jerry starts dating Carol's friend—the beautiful Jackie Windsor, a professional model—he tries to anticipate their inevitable breakup by dumping her first. Emily eventually brings Jerry to his senses, and after Jerry apologizes to Jackie, he gets a rare second chance.

"Hi, Bob"-Ometer

None. The count holds at 233 for the series.

Classic Scene: This episode includes one of the show's funniest subplots. Dr. Hartley's new patient, Danny James, is a schizophrenic ventriloquist who lets his dummy, Frank, do all the talking. Danny's concerned because Frank wants to break up the act and go solo. "I'm holding him back," explains Danny. The dummy asks Bob to leave the room so he can talk to Danny alone, and Dr. Hartley obliges; then that funny moment gets topped when Danny comes out of the office and says the dummy would like to talk to Bob alone. Newhart's understated style plays perfectly against this ludicrous situation.

EPISODE 124

"Who Was That Masked Man?"

Writers: Glen Charles and Les Charles
Director: Dick Martin

Cast

Emil Peterson: John Fiedler
Lillian Bakerman: Florida Friebus
Doris Peterson: Toni Lamond
Cop: Larry Goldman

While Bob dreads an upcoming costume party, Emil Peterson looks forward to a future without his nagging wife, Doris. This time she went too far when she called him a "spineless, gutless, wishy-washy pansy-face." After Peterson decides to leave Doris, he celebrates his liberation with libation in great quantities, shared with his new best buddy and roommate, Mr. Carlin! Once Carlin sobers up, however, he makes Emil move out, pushing a petrified Peterson over the edge. When he heads for the nearest ledge and threatens to jump, Dr. Hartley is called upon to save the day. Appropriately, Bob arrives in a Zorro outfit, straight from the costume party. As the masked psychologist climbs out to help Emil, Mrs. Peterson shows up and joins them on the ledge. Dr. Zorro helps the Petersons come to grips with their problems without losing their grip on the building. After the Petersons reach a reconciliation and leave the ledge, our hero strikes a striking pose.

"Hi, Bob"-Ometer

The dry spell continues for the second episode in a row! Still at 233 for the series.

Classic Quote

MRS. PETERSON *(to Mr. Peterson, who's on the ledge):* Emil, let's go home and make up . . . if you know what I mean.
MR. CARLIN: Peterson, jump while you've got the chance!

EPISODE 125

"Carlin's New Suit"

Writer: Andrew Smith
Director: Dick Martin
Cast
Billy: Sparky Marcus
Earl Stanley Plummer: Mark Lenard
Leslie Greely: Loni Anderson
Bum: Pat Cranshaw

As a wealthy real estate tycoon, Elliot Carlin is vulnerable to the scams of swindlers. One such schemer is Leslie Greely, who files a phony paternity suit against Elliot.

"Hi, Bob"-Ometer

Three: two from Howard and one from Carol. That's 236 for the series.

Classic Guest Stars: Here actress Loni Anderson plays a woman who tries to take advantage of Mr. Carlin, but from 1978 to 1982 she took care of Mr. Carlson in her role as receptionist Jennifer Marlowe on *WKRP in Cincinnati*. Incidentally, on *WKRP*, Anderson costarred with Howard Hesseman as Dr. Johnny Fever. Hesseman also played Dr. Hartley's patient, Craig Plager, the homosexual TV writer.

Child actor Sparky Marcus made his mark on cult TV with his recurring role as junior evangelist Jimmy Joe Jeeter on the soap satire *Mary Hartman, Mary Hartman*.

EPISODE 126

"A Day in the Life"

Writers: Kathy Donnell and Madelyn Dimaggio Wagner
Director: Dick Martin
Cast
Mr. Swerdlow: Bud Kenneally
Mrs. Swerdlow: Joan Kenneally
Tom Swerdlow: Rob Kenneally
Becky Swerdlow: Pam Kenneally
Mel: Richard Stahl
Steward: Michael Boyle

Bob accepts a challenge from the Peeper, who calls in the morning and dares his college chum to be in New Orleans by that night. Since Bob isn't known for his spontaneity, it's a struggle for him to clear his schedule of appointments on such short notice. Throughout the episode, the time of day appears on-screen as a means of marking Dr.

Hartley's progress as he struggles toward his day-end deadline. When the Hartleys *do* make it to the airport, the Peeper calls to tell Bob not to bother coming, because he's not really in New Orleans—it's all a practical joke. After all he's gone through, Bob says they're going anyway and storms off to the plane. In a surprise twist, Emily tells the Peeper, "It worked like a charm. I owe you one!"

"Hi, Bob"-Ometer
Zero. The count stands at 236 for the series.

EPISODE 127

"My Son the Comedian"

Writer: David Lloyd
Director: Dick Martin
Cast
Mickey Melnick: Bobby Ramsen
Minnie Farber: Elizabeth Kerr
Jackie Whitefeather: Johnny West

Howie Borden Jr. may be an outstanding kid, but does he have what it takes to be a stand-up comic? He thinks so, and so does Mickey Melnick, a teacher at a comedy school who wants to take the boy on the road.

For the Record: That's Elizabeth Kerr as Minnie Farber, the elderly comedienne who wants to emulate the comic stylings of Don Rickles. You may remember Kerr in her role as Cora Hudson, Mindy's energetic grandmother on *Mork & Mindy*.
Meanwhile, the show's most valuable stock player, Bobby Ramsen, turns in another first-rate comedy performance, this time as the slick but simple Mickey Melnick.

"Hi, Bob"-Ometer
Three, all from Howard. That's 239 for the series.

EPISODE 128

"You're Fired, Mr. Chips"

Writer: Lloyd Garver
Director: Peter Bonerz
Cast
Dr. Alan Dreeben: Ralph Bellamy
Emil Peterson: John Fiedler
Lillian Bakerman: Florida Friebus
Dr. Thompson: Richard Roat
Dr. Ellis: Howard Witt

As it happens, Bob has posted a job opening for an assistant psychologist at the same time that his favorite college professor, Dr. Alan Dreeben, has recently been forced into retirement. So when Dr. Dreeben applies for the job, how can Dr. Hartley say no? Bob decides to employ the experienced instructor, but he almost instantly regrets the decision, because Dr. Dreeben treats the patients like errant students who can simply be brought back in line with a lecture instead of a therapy session. Consequently, Bob is forced to fire one of his heroes. Dr. Dreeben gives the firing a B-plus.

Hartley Homily: "Just because a woman loves another man, that doesn't mean she still doesn't like you—although it is a definite possibility."

"Hi, Bob"-Ometer
One, from Howard, bringing the count to 240 for the series.

Classic Guest Star: The late Ralph Bellamy played the role of Dr. Alan Dreeben more like straight drama than comedy, which makes the professor seem all the more authentic. A serious portrayal may have been more natural for Bellamy, since most of his TV credits are rooted in drama—from the gritty detective fare of *Man against Crime* to his wealth of work in dramatic anthologies such as *The U.S. Steel Hour* and *Goodyear Playhouse*.

Parallel Plot: When Bob Hartley hires his mentor, one is reminded of Rob Petrie's ill-fated job offer to the veteran comedy writer who gave him his first break. Like Bob, Rob is forced to fire a man he admires in episode 30 of *The Dick Van Dyke Show* entitled "The Return of Happy Spangler."

EPISODE 129

"Shallow Throat"

Writer: Earl Pomerantz
Director: Dick Martin
Cast
Mr. Twillmer: Richard Libertini
Sergeant O'Conner: Frank Maxwell
Williams: J. Jay Saunders
Denise: Lorrie Gia
Terry: Julienne Wells
Felon: Alan Haufrect

If a patient tells Dr. Hartley something, no matter how shocking, he's obligated to keep it to himself. That tenet is put to the test when an unusually mum man, Mr. Twillmer, suddenly spills his guts and confesses that he's embezzled $150,000 from his company over the past twenty-five years.

"Hi, Bob"-Ometer
Two, both from Howard. That's 242 for the series.

EPISODE 130

"A Girl in Her Twenties"

Writer: Laura Levine
Director: Peter Bonerz
Cast
Grace Dubois: Mildred Natwick
Nora Dubois: Sondra Currie
Dr. Malcolm: Macon McCalman
The Man: J. J. Johnson

With Bob off promoting his book, Emily and Howard are curious about the woman living on the other side, in apartment 2082. A little neighborly nosiness reveals that the mysterious tenant is Grace Dubois, an elderly woman who, as Emily puts it, "is still living in 1920." Grace's niece, Nora, wants to admit her to Sunset Haven, a rest home. Howard and Emily will not hear of it, however. They help Grace prove she's competent to stay put.

"Hi, Bob"-Ometer
Zero. Still at 242 for the series.

Classic Guest Star: Emily and Howard do all of the investigating in this episode, but, in the early 1970s, guest star Mildred Natwick played senior sleuth Gwen Snoop in *The Snoop Sisters*. Natwick won an Emmy for that role in 1974.

For the Record: This is the first of the five final-season episodes in which Bob Newhart made only cameo appearances. When he somewhat reluctantly agreed to return for a sixth season, it was with the stipulation that he not be required to appear in all twenty-two episodes. Consequently, the writers created story lines in which Bob Hartley goes off to promote his book, which is said to be selling well, "considering it's not about sharks, diets, or sex." The other installments of *The Bob Newhart Show* that include very little Bob Newhart are "Grizzly Emily" (134), "Emily

Carlin, Emily Carlin" (137), "It Didn't Happen One Night" (139), and "Crisis in Edukation" (141).

EPISODE 131

"Grand Delusion"

Writer: Lloyd Garver
Director: Dick Martin
Cast
Linda/Bianca: Morgan Fairchild
Mr. Marcus: F. William Parker
Maître d': Michael Evans

As the Hartleys enjoy an anniversary meal, they imagine what their lives might have been like if they had married someone else. Emily is the first to fantasize. She still sees herself married to a psychiatrist-author, but it's Howard Borden! Does Emily have a secret desire for her friend and neighbor? Of course not, because, while she imagines herself married to Howard, her fantasy man is still Bob, who is now her navigator neighbor. "Emily Borden" and Bob enjoy a passionate, conspicuous affair. When it's Bob's turn to fantasize, he imagines himself as a world-renowned superpsychologist. Bianca, his beautiful girlfriend, desperately wants to marry him, but he simply doesn't hear bells with Bianca. It's not until he takes Bianca out to dinner and he meets their waitress, Emily, that he finally hears the clanging bells of true love. As the Hartleys come back to reality, two things are conspicuously the same in their separate fantasies: (1) both dream of being humbly catered to by Jerry, as Gerald the manservant, and (2) they still see themselves in each other's arms. Ten years after their wedding, they still hear bells.

"Hi, Bob"-Ometer
None. The series total remains on hold at 242.

Classic Quote
JERRY *(as Gerald the manservant):* Good evening, Master Borden. Shall I draw a bath for you?
HOWARD: No, thank you. I can recognize it when I see it.

Classic Guest Star: Morgan Fairchild appears here as Dr. Hartley's fantasy fair maiden, who fawns over the fabulous psychologist—only to have Bob toss her aside in favor of Emily. In the 1980s, Fairchild became an expert at similarly melodramatic situations when she starred in a string of prime-time soaps, including *Flamingo Road, Paper Dolls,* and *Falcon Crest.*

For the Record: Time flies for the Hartleys in the sixth season of the show. Only fifteen episodes back (116), they celebrated their seventh anniversary. As this installment begins, it's their tenth. With three years having gone by, one has to wonder what ever became of Carol's pregnancy, which was announced in episode 120.

This is the only fantasy sequence in the series.

EPISODE 132

"'Twas the Pie before Christmas"

Writer: Phil Davis
Director: Dick Martin
Cast
Lillian Bakerman: Florida Friebus
Emil Peterson: John Fiedler
Saul "Santa" Lebowitz: Ben Freedman
Pieman: Rik Pierce

The Hartleys celebrate another Christmas with their time-honored tradition of arguing, backstabbing, and pie-throwing.

"Hi, Bob"-Ometer
Two, from Jerry and Howard. That's 244 for the series.

Classic Quote
EMILY: You have always been a sucker for the runt of the litter, the skinny little waif that no one else wants.
BOB: That's what my mother said at our wedding.
EMILY: Yours, too?

For the Record: For the fifth time in the series, a holiday episode ends with a Christmas wreath encircling the MTM kitten.

EPISODE 133
"Freudian Ship"

Writer: Earl Pomerantz
Director: Peter Bonerz
Cast
Vern Hackler: John Crawford
Clara Hackler: Jeff Donnell
Graham: Robert Phelps
First Scavenger: Timothy Himes
Second Scavenger: Claudette Duffy
Third Scavenger: Jack Scalici

The Hartleys take a ten-day Caribbean cruise to get away from it all, but, as in episode 15 ("Let's Get Away from It, Almost"), Dr. Hartley can't escape his work, because dysfunctional relationships are everywhere. This time, it's the Hacklers' marriage that's on the rocks. Fellow passengers Vern and Clara Hackler have become strangers to each other after twenty-eight years of wedded blahs, and Clara can't take it anymore. She lets Vern know by dumping a bowl of soup in his lap. Bob later meets up with Vern in the ship's bar, and after four boilermakers the besotted psychologist persuades Vern to reacquaint himself with the wonderful things about Clara. The

Hacklers are reunited as Bob recovers from his drunken stupor.

"Hi, Bob"-Ometer
One, from Graham, brings the count to 245 for the series.

For the Record: The complete list of items on the cruise ship's scavenger hunt: one red sock, a peppermint stick, a carrot, an empty fountain pen, a picture of Myrna Loy, a pink teddy bear, an Italian flag, a spear, and a catcher's mask.

EPISODE 134
"Grizzly Emily"

Writer: Laura Levine
Director: Peter Bonerz
Cast
Herb Hartley: Barnard Hughes

Since Bob is in Kansas City promoting his book, Herb Hartley plans a weekend fishing trip with Emily, Howard, and Jerry. Emily awaits the trip with bated breath because she's expecting it to be like her childhood fishing trips with her father. Herb, however, expects Emily to spend her time cleaning the cabin and cooking what the men catch. The in-laws clash, and neither is willing to give until a bear scare brings them together.

"Hi, Bob"-Ometer
None. The count still stands at 245 for the series.

Classic Quote
HERB: Isn't it nice to get up here where you can hear yourself think:
HOWARD: I don't hear anything.

For an interesting parallel quote, see *Taxi* episode 53.

EPISODE 135

"Son of Ex-Con Job"

Writer: Emily Purdum Marshall
Director: Michael Zinberg
Cast
Arthur Tatum: Taurean Blacque
Steve Kopelson: Allen Case
Al Brolio: Ric Mancini
Richard Hawkins: Wyatt Johnson
Reuben Ortiz: Bert Rosario

Dr. Hartley's support group for former prisoners, which first convened in episode 122, consists of five ex-cons who have remained very close since their release. Just as Bob is trying to wean them away from one another, they decide to go into business together and open a barbershop. Bob is wary and worried. His fears appear to be justified when he visits the shop and finds only two barber chairs for the five partners to work. Finally he convinces the ex-cons that they must divide if they really want to conquer the world.

Hartley Homily: "Friendship is a wonderful thing, but it's not a living."

"Hi, Bob"-Ometer
Two, from Carol and from Steve Kopelson. That's 247 for the series.

EPISODE 136

"Group on a Hot Tin Roof"

Writer: Andrew Smith
Director: Michael Zinberg
Cast
Craig Plager: Howard Hesseman
Lillian Bakerman: Florida Friebus
Emil Peterson: John Fiedler
Bakerman Character: Amzie Strickland
Peterson Character: Lou Cutell
Carlin Character: Jerry Define
Bill "Major Hartman" Morgan: Frank Ashmore
Tommy: Ty Wilson
Girl: Mary Ellen Olsen

Terrible television writer Craig Plager continues to come up with truly awful TV show concepts—for example, *Police Barber*, *Vermin Kingdom*, and a telethon for chapped lips. Then, with support from the members of his therapy group, Plager becomes a playwright, penning a wartime drama entitled *All Noisy on the Western Front*. When Dr. Hartley and his patients attend a rehearsal, they're amazed at how familiar the characters seem.

"Hi, Bob"-Ometer
Two, from Jerry and Howard. The count is now 249 for the series.

Classic Quote
CAROL *(sarcastically):* Jer, you have such a way with children.
JERRY: It's a gift.
CAROL: Return it.

EPISODE 137

"Emily Carlin, Emily Carlin"

Writer: Laura Levine
Director: Peter Bonerz
Cast
Peggy Ann Marble: Karen Ericson
Burt Harrison: Michael Alldredge
Jack Evans: Woody Skaggs
Bonnie: Carole Shelyne Barry

As Mr. Carlin's twentieth high school reunion approaches, he's nervous about living up to some of the lies he's been telling his former classmates. The most unforgivable untruth is that Emily is his wife and the mother of his three children—oh, yeah, and she's a former Playboy centerfold, too. When Carlin asks Emily to make his fabrication appear to be a reality, she flatly refuses. But after a phone call with Bob, who's out on the book tour, Emily decides to help Mr. Carlin look like a winner in front of the classmates who used to ridicule him, espccially one named Peggy Ann Marble. In high school, Elliot had such a crush on Peggy Ann that he used to kiss her locker. When they arrive at the reunion, Mr. Carlin is pleased to see that his "wife" and his life are impressing everyone—including Peggy Ann, who's still single. When he makes a conspicuous play for her, it infuriates his "wife," Emily, who walks out, divorcing herself from the whole affair.

"Hi, Bob"-Ometer
Zero. The series count stalls at 249.

EPISODE 138

"Easy for You to Say"

Writer: Andrew Smith
Director: Dick Martin
Cast
Paul R. "Ralph Alfalfa" Billingham: Jerry Fogel
Lillian Bakerman: Florida Friebus
Emil Peterson: John Fiedler
First Kid: J. R. Miller
Second Kid: K. C. Martel

Bob has the challenge of trying to help kiddy show host, Ralph Alfalfa, with his stuttering problem. Presently his show, *Fun on the Farm*, is only on the radio, where no one can see the distraction techniques he employs to stop the stuttering.

"Hi, Bob"-Ometer
Two, both from Howard. That's 251 for the series.

For the Record: This is the second appearance by actor Jerry Fogel, who had a smaller role in episode 54. You may also remember Fogel as Bill Donahue, Ken Reeves's brother-in-law, on *The White Shadow*.

When Carol practices for her scuba-diving classes, she appears to have gone off the deep end, but this is not the first time she's signed up for classes to expand her horizons; it's just one more step in her series-long search for knowledge. So far, for instance, she has taken tap-dancing lessons (episode 41) and gourmet cooking classes (episode 49), and of course she indulged her short-lived desire to be a shrink like Bob (episode 93).

EPISODE 139

"It Didn't Happen One Night"

Writer: Laura Levine
Director: Dick Martin
Cast
Steve Darnell: David Hedison
The Man: Russell Shannon

With Bob in Cincinnati promoting his book, Emily is home alone when she's visited by her handsome former boyfriend, Steve Darnell. Bob's friends worry about what will happen, because, after all, "Emily's only human, you know." She's embarrassed by, and angry about, their obvious suspicions—that is, until Steve surprises her with a kiss! Emily is quick to put Steve in his place. As for the undercover "Bob Squad," she tells them—as well as a restaurant full of people—that Bob might not look like a matinee idol to them, but to her, he's beautiful.

"Hi, Bob"-Ometer
Zero. The series count remains at 251.

Classic Quote
CAROL: Think how awful it would be if anything ever came between Bob and Emily.
HOWARD: What a terrible thought. Who's gonna get custody of me?

EPISODE 140

"Carol Ankles for Indie-Prod"

Writer: Lloyd Garver
Director: Mark Tinker
Cast
Gary Johnson: John Terry Bell
Miss Pringle: Madeleine Fisher
Mr. Stevens: Neil Flanagan
Angry Man Number One: Joe George
Angry Man Number Two: Mert Rich

Carol's search for a fulfilling career hits an all-time low when she quits the seventh floor to work as Mr. Carlin's receptionist. She hopes to learn all about the real estate business, but she soon discovers that working for the cynical slumlord is more tedious and menial than her old job. A surprise is in store for her when she tries to return to her former job: Bob tells her she can't come back!

"Hi, Bob"-Ometer
Three: one from Howard and two from Carol, for a series count of 254.

Classic Scene: Dr. Hartley's new patient, Mr. Stevens, is a clown—literally. The beleaguered buffoon reclines on Bob's couch while wearing his clown outfit, complete with big rubber nose and baggy pants. He's very concerned that no one's taking him seriously. As Mr. Stevens laments his laughable life, he honks the horn on his pants, and Dr. Hartley can barely stifle a snicker. Only after the clown is gone does Bob let loose a howl.

EPISODE 141

"Crisis in Edukation"

Writer: Earl Pomerantz
Director: Peter Bonerz
Cast
Principal Phil Bannister: Edward Andrews
Sal Petrone: Robert Costanzo
Wanda Moss: Patricia Stevens
Ms. Hunsinger: Jan Fisher
Mr. Kreever: Bill Zukert
Miss Nightingale: Delores Albin
Billy: Brian Miller

There's turmoil at Tracy Grammar School! The reading scores are at an all-time low, and Principal Bannister is afraid that the parents will make him the scapegoat. So he takes off to fish in Montana, leaving the problem and the parents in the hands of the vice principal, Emily Hartley.

"Hi, Bob"-Ometer
Zero. The series total sits at 254.

For the Record: On and off throughout the series Jerry and Howard have battled over which of them is truly Bob Hartley's best friend. In this episode they challenge each other to name Bob's likes and dislikes. Emily also tries to name them, but none of the three people closest to Bob have the right responses.

Here are the answers Bob gives in the hotel telephone scene:

Favorite color: green
Favorite meal: roast duck
Favorite song: the theme from *The High and the Mighty*
Biggest pet peeve: people who talk out loud in the theater

EPISODE 142

"Happy Trails to You"

Writers: Glen Charles, Les Charles, and Lloyd Garver
Directors: Michael Zinberg and Peter Bonerz
Cast
Lillian Bakerman: Florida Friebus
Emil Peterson: John Fiedler
Dr. James Wyler: Bill Quinn
Mr. Gerber: Bobby Ramsen

In this episode, the series finale, the characters go through some significant changes. First of all, Dr. Hartley has accepted a job as a professor at a small college in Oregon. That means Emily has to resign from Tracy Grammar School and Howard won't have the Hartleys to rely on anymore. When the neighborly navigator finally comprehends what's happening, he passes out. Meanwhile, Dr. Hartley's patients have no desire to be passed along to a new psychologist. Mr. Carlin tries to get Bob to stay by promising, "I'll buy you a college!" Then, on the day Bob turns his patients over to Dr. James Wyler, Mr. Carlin enters wearing a dress. He's hoping Bob's conscience won't allow him to leave, but his efforts are to no avail. Bob and Emily are definitely going to Oregon. First, however, they have the tough task of saying good-bye to good friends Jerry Robinson, Carol Kester-Bondurant, and Howard Borden. Before the episode's final scene, Emily says that if she starts to feel too sad, she's going to sing "Oklahoma." So when the friends start to exchange sentiments such as "I'm gonna miss you" and "I love you guys," Emily tries to hide her emotions by singing. As the six seasons of the series come to a close, the friends join in a rousing chorus: "You're doing fine, Oklahoma! Oklahoma! O-k-l-a-h-o-m-a! Oklahoma! O.K.!"

"Hi, Bob"-Ometer

Two, both from Howard. The grand total of "Hi, Bob" greetings is 256.

Classic Quote

CAROL: Come on, Jerry, let's go to lunch.
JERRY: Who's buying?
CAROL: Why don't we go dutch? Me at one table and you in Holland.

Classic Scene: In his sixth appearance of the series, character actor Bobby Ramsen turns in his best performance yet, as Mr. Gerber, the Hartleys' unreasonable landlord.

For the Record: Bill Quinn plays Dr. Wyler, the psychologist who takes over Bob's practice. Quinn played a know-it-all newspaper columnist in episode 32 and made two appearances as Eddie the Mailman, in episodes 63 and 72.

Notice that the end credits run over a shot of the cast in their final curtain call.

Always in Our Hartleys

During the six years (1972–1978) *The Bob Newhart Show* ran on CBS, the series never received the attention and acclaim it so clearly deserved (not one Emmy!). After the sixth and final season, Bob Newhart decided to call it quits. He told *TV Guide* that the show was "still doing well enough. But I got very disturbed about the trends in TV. . . . The kiddie audience seemed to be taking over the tube. . . . I felt my type of low-key comedy—aimed at intelligent adults—was finished. So I just told MTM and CBS I wasn't coming back for the seventh season. We were not canceled. I left on my own."

When *The Bob Newhart Show* stopped production in 1978, the series and its wonderful cast of characters did not disappear from television. Instead, they've taken on a second life, replete with character development and more classic moments. Here is a rundown of the tributes to this underrated but unforgettable series:

- *Taxi,* fall 1982. Marcia Wallace appears in an episode entitled "The Schloogel Show," in which Latka and Simka have set their friends up with the blind dates of their lives. As it turns out, Jim Ignatowski's all-time favorite comedy is *The Bob Newhart Show,* so the matchmakers get him a date with Marcia Wallace, who appears as herself. The date doesn't go well because Jim insists on constantly talking about the show. For instance, he asks Marcia to re-create Carol's laugh from the Christmas show in which she filled the water cooler with eggnog (episode 14). Then Jim says he's written lyrics to the show's theme song, and he insists on singing them. Jim's lyrics: "Here comes Bob and Carol / His wife Emily really likes him / He has five people in his group. . . ."
- *Newhart,* fall 1988. Bob Newhart's second long-running sitcom was set at the Stratford Inn in Vermont. He played innkeeper Dick Louden, who was also a how-to author and a talk show host. Throughout this series, there were regular reminders of the first series, such as Tom (the Peeper)

Poston's appearance as handyman George Utley and Will (Larry Bondurant) Mackenzie's directorship of a number of episodes. Early in the 1988 season there was another *Newhart* nod to the original series. In the episode entitled "I Married Dick," Joanna, Dick's wife, persuades Dick to attend marriage counseling. When he does, one of the therapist's other patients is played by Jack (Mr. Carlin) Riley.

- *Newhart,* winter 1990. In "Good Neighbor Sam," Bill (Howard Borden) Daily guest stars as Sam Leary, a bothersome Stratford Inn guest. Dick becomes downright unneighborly when Sam moves in next door.

- *Newhart,* May 1990. A moment of pure Classic TV history occurs when, after eight seasons as Dick Louden, Bob Newhart turns the entire second series into a figment of Bob Hartley's subconscious. The episode, appropriately titled "The Last Newhart," finds Dick refusing to go along with the rest of the town by selling the Stratford Inn to Japanese investors, who go ahead and build around him anyway, so that the inn becomes a hazard on the fourteenth fairway of the Tagadachiville Hotel and Country Club golf course. Dick remains defiant right up until the moment he gets conked by a wayward golf ball. As the innkeeper sinks to the ground, the scene dissolves to a familiar shot of Bob and Emily in bed. After sitting up in bed, Bob Hartley says, "You wouldn't believe the dream I had." Emily disregards the entire thing by telling Bob he can no longer have Japanese food before bed. Fittingly, *Entertainment Weekly* named *Newhart*'s final episode as "the most inspired finale in TV history," adding that the brilliant dream sequence manages to wrap "two terrific comedies into one surrealistic bundle." *EW* quotes Newhart as saying, "The minute the [studio] audience saw the set from the old show, they caught on right away. We had to wait a really long time to say our lines because the applause went on and on."

- *19th Anniversary Special,* fall 1991. This reunion special reunited the original cast for an actual episode of the show, thirteen years later. Everyone is in character as the show picks up at the point when Bob woke up from his dream. Apparently, episode 142 of the show was a dream as well, because, as this new episode begins, Dr. and Mrs. Hartley have not moved to Oregon. They're still in Chicago, and Bob still works out of office number 751. After the "Hi, Bob" montage at the beginning, there are three "Hi, Bob" greetings in this episode. The rest of the dialogue essentially serves to introduce classic clips.

- *Murphy Brown,* winter 1994. In the "Anything But Cured" episode, Carol Kester-Bondurant becomes the latest (and greatest) in the string of secretaries who have tried to serve tough news anchor Murphy Brown. Carol, who is Secretary Number 66, has apparently left Dr. Hartley for the umpteenth time in search of a better career opportunity, and unlike Murphy's other secretaries, Carol is actually satisfying her hard-to-please boss. But of course Dr. Hartley is desperate without her, and in a cameo appearance, Bob Newhart suddenly shows up to retrieve his receptionist. For Murphy, however, the secretary search goes on.

- *Saturday Night Live*, winter 1995. Host Bob Newhart appears as guest psychologist Dr. Robert Hartley, who's been summoned to help a dysfunctional talk show family on *Ricki Lake*. After the show's end credits, Suzanne Pleshette reprises her role as Emily Hartley in another bedroom scene. This time Bob awakens from a nightmare in which he tells her that he dreamed he was hosting *Saturday Night Live*, to which Emily responds by saying she didn't even know *SNL* was still on the air. A classic homage finale to the original homage finale of *Newhart*.

The Dick Van Dyke Show

It's a loser. A sure loser. You've got material that's already failed once. A star who's made a number of pilots before—none of which have sold. And you've got Morey Amsterdam and Rose Marie—two stars from radio! This show cannot make it. And I cannot let you do it.
—An agent of the William Morris Agency to Sheldon Leonard, from Vince Waldron,
The Official Dick Van Dyke Show Book

The humor comes from the juxtaposition of believable people and absurd events, and as an added dividend, it keeps the situations . . . fresh.
—José M. Ferrer III, *Life* magazine

The Dick Van Dyke Show was very special. Not because it was funnier more regularly than most but because it was lovingly crafted every week of its long life with honest, painstaking craftsmanship.
—Frank Penn, *Ottawa Citizen*, March 30, 1966

Whenever asked what I consider my best effort of all the things I've ever done in show business, I answer, unhesitatingly, *The Dick Van Dyke Show.*
—Carl Reiner

New audiences continue to delight in what more seasoned viewers have known for years: *The Dick Van Dyke Show* is classic comedy, and therefore, timeless.
—Ginny Weissman and Coyne Steven Sanders,
The Dick Van Dyke Show: Anatomy of a Classic

Today it still plays as a nearly flawless combination of superb writing and performing . . . the quality of the series remains consistently high throughout. As a result, it's definitely worth following *The Dick Van Dyke Show* from beginning to end.
—Castleman and Podrazik, *Harry and Wally's Favorite TV Shows*

[*The Dick Van Dyke Show*] argued that the new America offered solutions not just to the drones of the middle class and the rural poor but to urban sophisticates as well. Ultimately it modernized the image of the sitcom family and gave it an explicitly Kennedyesque glamour.
—Gerard Jones, *Honey, I'm Home*

In the space of only five years, Carl Reiner and his company of actors, writers, and fellow producers . . . succeeded in creating a work of such consistent intelligence and invention that it would set a new standard for quality television—a standard that still serves as a benchmark for prime-time comedy to this day.
—Vince Waldron, *The Official Dick Van Dyke Show Book*

The Dick Van Dyke Show

on Nick at Nite

The Dick Van Dyke Show premiered on Nick at Nite in September 1991, with eight episodes called "The Dick Van Dyke Collection." In February of 1992 a week-long marathon presented the show according to themes such as Flashbacks Night and "Oh, Rob" Night.

Shortly afterward an official announcement was made: Dick Van Dyke would be the chairman of Nick at Nite, as together we launched our effort to continue preserving America's precious television heritage. The chairman then went on the air to spread the word about our mission. In one memorable spot, he asked the American public to consider their television heritage when considering names for their pets—or even their newborns. One young couple, by way of example, proudly claimed to have named their new baby Agarn.

In February of 1993 the chairman hosted his five favorite episodes, with newly filmed segments that included guests Larry Mathews, Frank Adamo, and Kathleen Freeman. The famous walnut scene, among others, was re-created (see episode 51 for details).

The Dick Van Dyke Show was also frequently featured in the Very Very Nick at Nite collections. "Very Very Jerry," for example, included all four of Jerry Van Dyke's appearances. Two other programming events were noteworthy: "Carl on Camera," which featured a collection of Carl Reiner's acting performances, and "Head of the Family," which was an airing of the original pilot episode, starring Carl Reiner as Rob Petrie.

Sponsored by Nick at Nite in 1993, Dick Van Dyke was given the long overdue recognition of having his star placed in Hollywood Boulevard.

The most recent Nick at Nite on-air promotion for *The Dick Van Dyke Show* featured new lyrics for the theme song, which helped explain the opening. The ninth draft of those lyrics (the tenth is the one you hear on the air) went as follows:

Dick . . . Van . . . Dyke is Robert Petrie,

Who comes home,

Hugs Laura,

And accidentally trips across that thing.

But sometimes he doesn't do that,

Because they

Changed it.

Instead, he skirts it with a nifty step.

And then there's a third version.

He sidesteps

It suavely

But ironically he stumbles on his toe.

And when Rob

Shakes hands with Buddy and Sally

The episode title comes up (obscuring Ritchie)

And notice Rob shakes Buddy's hand again!

The end.

Cast

Rob Petrie: Dick Van Dyke
Laura Petrie: Mary Tyler Moore
Ritchie Petrie: Larry Mathews
Buddy Sorrell: Morey Amsterdam
Sally Rogers: Rose Marie
Mel Cooley: Richard Deacon
Millie Helper: Ann Morgan Guilbert
Jerry Helper: Jerry Paris

EPISODE 1

"The Sick Boy and the Sitter"

Writer: Carl Reiner
Director: Sheldon Leonard
Cast
Sam: Michael Keith
Janie: Mary Lee Dearing
Dr. Miller: Stacey Keach
Dotty: Barbara Eiler

Ritchie isn't sick, but Laura's intuition tells her he might be *getting* sick. After all, he didn't eat his cupcake. In order to get to an important party at Alan Brady's posh penthouse apartment, Rob has to persuade a reluctant Laura to leave Ritchie with the baby-sitter. In fact, he finally has to pick her up and carry her out of the house.

Stacey Keach the elder—not his son, who played Mike Hammer—has a cameo role as Dr. Miller, but his scene has been edited out of the show as it is currently seen in syndication.

Keep your eyes peeled for one of the rare visits to Ritchie's bedroom.

Classic Quote
LAURA: The alphabet is *not* stupid. You have to learn it if you want to write television shows like daddy does.

Classic Performance: At the party, Rob, Buddy, and Sally are called upon to entertain, providing an opportunity for us to see Rob's drunk act, hear Sally sing, listen to Buddy play the cello, and enjoy Rob, Buddy, and Sally's rendition of "Hello, Hello," a Morey Amsterdam composition.

For the Record: The total cost of this, the recast pilot episode, was under $50,000. The episode was filmed several months before regular production began. Note the many differences, including:

Laura's hairstyle, the design of the kitchen, and Rob's odd makeup, with thick mascara and pancake.

EPISODE 2

"The Meerschatz Pipe"

Writer: Carl Reiner
Director: Sheldon Leonard
Cast
Elevator Operator: Jon Silo

Rob's battle with low self-esteem begins when Buddy Sorrell shows off the rare pipe that Alan Brady has given him. Then Sally Rogers, the human joke machine and bow-wearing husband hunter, knocks out a killer script for *The Alan Brady Show* while Rob is out sick. The self-doubting head writer begins to wonder if the others really need him.

For the Record: This episode marked the first time Alan Brady's voice was heard.

EPISODE 3

"Jealousy!"

Writer: Carl Reiner
Director: Sheldon Leonard
Cast
Valerie Blake: Joan Staley

Rob is working long hours with the beautiful Valerie Blake as that week's guest on the show. Look for the classic scene when he comes home late and takes his shoes to bed with him, and listen for the slow, mournful version of the show's theme music that accompanies that scene.

For the Record: Jerry and Millie Helper make their first appearance, and Millie's fast-talking character is fully formed and in high gear: "Jerry, you're just awful. He's just awful. Isn't he just awful?"

This is the last episode directed by Sheldon Leonard, who retreated to a less hands-on role as executive producer. Dick Van Dyke recalls that Leonard would stop by the set and look on, shake his head, and say simply, "The otters at play."

This is also the very first time Mel replies to Buddy's wisecracks with his classic: "Yicchh."

EPISODE 4

"Sally and the Lab Technician"

Writer: Carl Reiner
Director: John Rich
Cast
Thomas: Eddie Firestone
Delivery Boy: Jamie Farr

In the first of many episodes centered on Sally's ill-fated romances, Laura plays matchmaker, inviting her quiet cousin Thomas, a pharmacist, to dinner with Rob's fellow joke writer. Sally starts with "Hi, I'm Sally Rogers. Are you still single?" and keeps up the rapid-fire wisecracks all night long. Alas, Thomas seems overwhelmed, and the next day a melancholy Sally regrets her nervous joking, because she really liked him.

Classic Guest Star: Jamie Farr, best known as Corporal Klinger on M*A*S*H, makes the first of his four appearances as the delivery boy. While delivering Buddy's prune danish, he makes comments like "Now, that's funny! Why don't you put jokes like that in the show, instead of that junk?"

EPISODE 5

"Washington vs. the Bunny"

Writer: Carl Reiner
Director: John Rich
Cast
Bill: Jesse White
Delivery Boy: Jamie Farr

In an episode that explores the tension between the demands of work and home, Alan—through Mel and a phone call—insists that Rob make a business trip that will force him to miss Ritchie's performance as a bunny in the school play.

Classic Performance: Look for the first and perhaps best dream sequence in this series as Rob's unconscious wrestles with his dilemma. The scene, reminiscent of early German Expressionist films, shows Laura in a bunny suit, pulling the strings that manipulate Rob, a helpless marionette. "Dance! Dance!" she calls, until a mechanical looking Mel, wielding giant scissors, cuts Rob loose.

Classic Quote

ROB: I've seen every one of Ritchie's performances.
LAURA: No, you haven't. You didn't see him when he played Hamlet.

The Adamo Watch
Frank Adamo, Dick Van Dyke's personal assistant and frequent extra, appears as one of the passengers on the airplane with Rob. This is his first on-camera appearance. See episode 17 for more about Adamo.

EPISODE 6

"Oh, How We Met on the Night That We Danced"

Writer: Carl Reiner
Director: John Rich
Cast
Sol Pomeroy: Marty Ingels
Marcia Rochelle: Nancy James
Mark: Glenn Turnbull
Ellen Helper: Jennifer Gillespie
Dancing Girl: Pat Tribble

The first of many classic flashback episodes transports Rob and Laura back to the night they met, when they danced on-stage together to the tune "You Wonderful You" and when in the process he broke her foot.

For the Record: Laura's maiden name in this episode is Meeker. At the time, Mary Tyler Moore was married to Richard Meeker. After they were divorced, Laura's maiden name was quietly changed to Meehan.

Classic Guest Star: Marty Ingels, a familiar character actor who played Fenster in "I'm Dickens, He's Fenster," and was later married to Shirley Jones of *The Partridge Family*.

EPISODE 7

"The Unwelcome House Guest"

Writer: Carl Reiner
Director: Robert Butler

Rob is saddled with Buddy's dog for the weekend. Ritchie is terrified and insists that the dog is, in fact, a wolf. Rob's efforts to keep the dog quiet at night include reconstructing Ritchie's old crib.

There is no credit for the animal who played the dog.

For the Record: Carl Reiner said he wrote this episode for his family dog: "I had a big German Shepherd, Rinny, who just sat there looking at me, so I said 'Okay, Rinny, I'll write you a show.'"

Parallel Plot: See episode 130, "Ugliest Dog in the World"

EPISODE 8

"Harrison B. Harding of Camp Crowder, Mo."

Writer: Carl Reiner
Director: John Rich
Cast
Policeman: Peter Leeds
Harrison B. Harding: Allan Melvin
Evelyn Harding: June Dayton

"I don't think you remember me, Sarge" says Harrison, who claims to be Rob's old army buddy. And indeed Rob doesn't, but he fakes it. When the Hardings come to dinner, however, he begins to think he may be playing host to a con man.

For the Record: Trying to prove himself, Harding says he knows that the first time Rob and Laura danced together was to "You Wonderful You." But we all knew that, from having watched the flashback in episode 6.

Classic Guest Stars: Dough-faced Allan Melvin played Corporal Henshaw on *Sergeant Bilko* and was later to become Sam the Butcher, Alice's romantic interest, on *The Brady Bunch*.

EPISODE 9

"My Blonde-Haired Brunette"

Writer: Carl Reiner
Director: John Rich
Cast
Druggist: Benny Rubin

Has the magic gone out of the Petries' marriage? A bad weekend, plus a series of coincidences, convinces Laura that it has. Then, with a little prodding from Millie, she is convinced that going blond might just be the answer. This was the first star turn for Mary Tyler Moore, whose performance throughout was stunning.

Classic Quote
ROB: Honey, you can stop crying, I'm eating my eggs!

For the Record: This episode, shot ninth in sequence, was chosen as the second show to air.

EPISODE 10

"Forty-Four Tickets"

Writer: Carl Reiner
Director: John Rich
Cast
Mrs. Billings: Eleanor Audley
Nice Old Lady: Opal Euard
Shabby Man: Joe Devlin
Policeman: Paul Bryar

Good old friendly Rob invites the whole PTA to come and see *The Alan Brady Show,* but forgets about it until just before showtime, when he's forced to try to procure tickets from scalpers.

Army Buddies: The Complete List

Allan Melvin was a semi-regular as Rob's army buddy, though the show's writers couldn't seem to settle on his name. He started as Harrison B. Harding, but he later became Sam (47), Sam Pomeroy (85), Sam Pomerantz (131), Sol Pomerantz (137) and finally, just Sol (147). And Melvin wasn't Rob's only army buddy. That group would have to include Sam Pomerantz, played by Henry Calvin (54), and Sol Pomeroy, played by Marty Ingels (6, 16). For good measure, Melvin also played two other roles on the series, as a guard (103) and as a gun salesman (158).

The following are all of Rob's army buddies from Camp Crowder:

Harrison B. Harding (8)

Frank "Sticks" Mandalay (118)

Mark Mullen (6)

Leslie Murkell (155)

Sam Pomerantz (131)

Sol Pomerantz (137)

Sol Pomeroy (6, 16)

Sam Pomeroy (47, 85)

Buzzy Potter (118)

Sam (47)

Sol (147)

Bernie Stern (137)

Unnamed soldier (played by Frank Adamo) (85)

Captain Warwick (137)

Neil Schenk (maybe?) (108)

Also, Ray Kellogg played Rob's captain (47) and his corporal (34), than lost a painting to Rob's higher auction bid (65) and eventually became a police officer (74).

One final note: Joe Coogan, as in "the Life and Loves of Joe Coogan," episode 80, was named after one of Carl Reiner's real-life army buddies.

Here are eight other names that could have been Rob's army buddies but weren't:

Sam Pomeroy

Sal Pomeroy

Sal Pomerantz

Sol Pomerantz

Ron Pomerantz

Sid Pomerantz

Sid Pomeroy

Max Patkin

The Adamo Watch

Frank Adamo makes another uncredited appearance as an usher.

EPISODE 11

"To Tell or Not to Tell"

Writer: David Adler
Director: John Rich
Cast
Delivery Boy: Jamie Farr

Laura decides to resume her career as a dancer by filling in for a hoofer on *The Alan Brady Show*. Unfortunately, the stint doesn't last long. Whatever else it proves, though, this episode clearly highlights the fact that Mary Tyler Moore can definitely dance.

Classic Guest Star: Jamie Farr makes his third appearance in this series. Watch and see why he never really caught on.

For the Record: David Adler was the pen name for writer Frank Tarloff, who had been blacklisted for refusing to cooperate with Senator Joseph McCarthy's House Un-American Activities Committee. He wrote for many of Sheldon Leonard's shows under this pseudonym.

EPISODE 12

"Sally Is a Girl"

Writer: David Adler
Director: John Rich
Cast
Delivery Boy: Jamie Farr
Pickles Sorrell: Barbara Perry
Ted Harris: Paul Tripp

The old conclusion-jumping trick. Rob decides to take Laura's advice and stops treating Sally like one of the boys. His new charming and respectful manner toward her makes Buddy and Mel jump to the unlikely conclusion that something's going on between them.

Classic Guest Stars: This was Jamie Farr's fourth and final appearance on the show and the first appearance of Pickles Sorrell, played by Barbara Perry. Paul Tripp was best known as Mr. I. Magination, host of the popular children's television show of the 1950s.

EPISODE 13

"Empress Carlotta's Necklace"

Writer: Carl Reiner
Director: James Komack
Cast
Pa Petrie: Will Wright
Ma Petrie: Carol Veasie
Maxwell Cooley: Gavin MacLeod

"Sit down, your loveliness, because in about twelve seconds you're going to give out the biggest 'Oh, Rob' that you ever gave out in your life," says Rob the night before he proudly presents Laura with a necklace so monstrous and ugly that she can only say, "Oh, Rob!" The rest of the episode consists of Laura's efforts to find a way to tell him what she really thinks of Empress Carlotta's taste.

Classic Quote
BUDDY: This guy'll laugh at anything. Watch. . . . Shoehorn!

Classic Guest Star: Gavin MacLeod played Murray Slaughter on *The Mary Tyler Moore Show* and Captain Merrill Stubing on *The Love Boat*.

Parallel Plot: See episode 145, "The Curse of the Petrie People," which also focused on ugly jewelry.

For the Record: James Komack, director, actor, writer, went on to create a number of successful sitcoms, including *Welcome Back, Kotter*, *The Courtship of Eddie's Father*, and *Chico and the Man.*

EPISODE 14

"Buddy, Can You Spare a Job"

Writer: Walter Kempley
Director: James Komack
Cast
Jackie Brewster: Len Weinrib

Buddy Sorrell quits *The Alan Brady Show* and takes another job. When it doesn't work out, Rob and Sally have to scramble to bring him back.

Our Television Heritage: Shecky Greene was originally cast as Jackie Brewster, but he had to withdraw for personal reasons.

For the Record: This was the last show with the original bongo-driven arrangement of the theme music. Hereafter, the more familiar theme that had been used at the end was moved to the opening sequence.

EPISODE 15

"Who Owes Who What?"

Writer: Carl Reiner
Director: John Rich

Rob tries fruitlessly to hint to Buddy that he has forgotten about a loan Rob had made him. In the end, as so often happens, real life becomes comedy fodder for *The Alan Brady Show*.

For the Record: The voice of the flight announcer is Carl Reiner's.

EPISODE 16

"Sol and the Sponsor"

Writer: Walter Kempley
Director: John Rich
Cast
Sol Pomeroy: Marty Ingels
Arlene Johnson: Patti Regan
Henry Bermont: Roy Roberts
Martha Bermont: Isabel Randolph

Fine performances keep this standard plot lively as one of Rob's old army buddies intrudes on an important dinner party the Petries are hosting for one of the sponsors of *The Alan Brady Show*.

EPISODE 17

"The Curious Thing about Women"

Writer: David Adler
Director: John Rich
Cast
Delivery Man: Frank Adamo

One of Nick at Nite's most-requested episodes, this includes great office banter as Rob, Buddy, and Sally collaborate on creating a sketch. Unfortunately the sketch is based on an ongoing argument at home about Laura's opening Rob's mail, and when it is performed on national television, Laura is peeved. But as events will prove, she hasn't learned her lesson.

Classic Quote

BUDDY: That's the problem with real life—no punch lines.

For the Record: Carl Reiner wasn't crazy about the ending of this episode, and he had a point. After seeing the sketch on TV, would Laura really continue her behavior?

The Adamo Watch

Frank Adamo, who delivers a fateful package in this episode, was given his first lines and earned his first show credit.

EPISODE 18

"Punch Thy Neighbor"

Writer: Carl Reiner
Director: John Rich
Cast
Singing Messenger: Frank Adamo
Freddie Helper: Peter Oliphant
Vinnie: Jerry Hausner

This is a Rob-and-Jerry showcase piece, much like "A Man's Teeth Are Not His Own," episode 43, and "The Ballad of the Betty Lou," number 72. The opinionated-bigmouth aspect of Jerry Helper's character takes the wheel here, and his public criticism of *The Alan Brady Show* gets under Rob's skin.

The Adamo Watch

Frank Adamo delivers Jerry's singing telegram.

Frank Adamo

Frank Adamo began his show business career as Dick Van Dyke's personal assistant when Van Dyke was doing the musical *Bye Bye Birdie* on Broadway. On *The Dick Van Dyke Show* he remained Van Dyke's assistant and also served as his stand-in. He also served as a frequent walk-on and bit player.

Here at Nick at Nite, soon after *The Dick Van Dyke Show* began its run, we ran a promotional spot encouraging viewers to try to spot Frank Adamo. Then one day the phone rang in the on-air promotion department. It was Frank, calling to say thanks. He had seen the spot and was amused, even touched, by the attention.

After the show, Frank went on to work for Mary Tyler Moore during the run of her series. Eventually he more or less retired to New Jersey, where he worked as a volunteer in a hospital. Nick at Nite lured Frank back in front of the cameras for one more cameo, serving as a delivery man for Dick Van Dyke in the "Chairman's Choice" event, which aired the chairman's five favorite episodes with new introductions.

Frank's larger roles included that of the poet H. Fieldston Thorley in episode 55; a turn as an actor in episode 101; and a performance as the deliverer of a memorable singing telegram in episode 18.

EPISODE 19

"Where Did I Come From?"

Writer: Carl Reiner
Director: John Rich
Cast
Cabbie: Bill Braver
Willie: Herbie Faye
Laundry Man: Jerry Hausner

Young Ritchie Petrie asks the title question, leading Rob and Laura to recall the hectic days just before his birth. The episode features Van Dyke's classic scene as he lies in bed, hat at the ready, waiting for Laura to say, "It's that time." In the end, it turns out that all Ritchie really wanted to know was where he was born. And that answer is simple: New Rochelle.

Classic Performance: One of the show's biggest live laughs came when Buddy was persuaded to hand over his pants.

For the Record: Ann Morgan Guilbert was pregnant throughout the first season. In most episodes, her condition was disguised with wardrobe. In this one, her pregnancy was perfectly suited to the flashback scenes.

Favorite: Of Dick Van Dyke's—that is, one of his five favorite episodes. This is also director John Rich's top all-time favorite.

EPISODE 20

"The Boarder Incident"

Writers: Norm Liebmann and Ed Haas
Director: John Rich

Pickles is out of town, so this time the Petries get not only Buddy's dog but also Buddy himself for the weekend. The unwelcome guests quickly wear out their welcome.

Dick Van Dyke's Five Favorite Episodes

One of Dick Van Dyke's first duties as chairman of Nick at Nite was to host the "Chairman's Choice" programming special, which consisted of his five favorite episodes. The evening featured visits from Larry Mathews, Frank Adamo, and Kathleen Freeman, who played the cantankerous maid in "Never Bathe on Saturday," plus a re-creation of the famous walnut scene from "It May Look Like a Walnut."

Here are five episodes the chairman chose as his personal favorites:

"Where Did I Come From?" (episode 19)
"It May Seem Like a Walnut" (51)
"That's My Boy (64)
"I'd Rather Be Bald Than Have No Head at All" (93)
"Never Bathe on Saturday" (121)

EPISODE 21

"A Word a Day"

Writer: Jack Raymond
Director: John Rich
Cast
Reverend Kirk: William Schallert
Mrs. Kirk: Lia Waggner

Ritchie comes home with a fresh new word in his vocabulary, but don't bother to listen closely, because it's apparently one of the words you don't hear—or didn't used to hear—on TV. Rob is appalled, but his effort to root out the corrupting influence makes for a classic moment at the front door of 148 Bonnie Meadow Lane.

This scene foreshadows the parallel scene in episode 128, "That's My Boy."

Classic Guest Star: William Schallert is known around Nick at Nite as the hardest working man in TV Land because of his many regular and guest-starring roles. Among other parts, he played Dobie Gillis's teacher, Patty Lane's father, and the admiral on *Get Smart*, and he was a guest on every show from *Perry Mason* to *The Bionic Woman*. Here he makes a guest appearance as the Reverend Mr. Kirk. His TV wife, Lia Waggner, was also his real-life wife.

EPISODE 22

"The Talented Neighborhood"

Writer: Carl Reiner
Director: John Rich
Cast
Ellen Helper: Anne Marie Hediger
Cynthia: Ilana Dowding
Florian: Barry Van Dyke
Frankie: Christian Van Dyke
Mrs. Kendall: Doris Singleton
Kenneth Kendall: Jack Davis
Philip Mathias: Barry Livingston
Martin Mathias: Michael Davis
Annie Mathias: Kathleen Green
Mr. Mathias: Ken Lynch

A casual call for talented kids for *The Alan Brady Show* quickly turns the Petries' living room into audition central. Among the moppets are two young Van Dykes (Dick's son and daughter) and Barry Livingston, who played Ernie on *My Three Sons*.

Classic Performances: One kid sings opera, and the "winner" is the flamenco dancer who performs a whole number.

EPISODE 23

"Father of the Week"

Writers: Arnold and Lois Peyser
Director: John Rich
Cast
Floyd Harper: Patrick Thompson
Mrs. Given: Isabel Randolph
Allan: Allan Fiedler
Candy: Cornell Chulay

Rob is Father of the Week for Ritchie's class, but only because all of the other fathers have already received the honor. Petrie *fils*, it seems, is a little unsure about what Petrie *père* does for a living. Rob faces the ultimate challenge—going face-to-face with a classroom full of first graders to explain comedy writing. After a slow start, Rob puts on a classic pantomime performance that salvages his paternal pride.

For the Record: This script was drawn in part from the pilot episode (see below).

EPISODE 24

"The Twizzle"

Writer: Carl Reiner
Director: John Rich
Cast
Randy Twizzle: Jerry Lanning
Counter Boy: Tony Stag
Mr. Eisenhower: Jack Albertson
Freddie Blassie: Himself

The script for this episode was conceived as a vehicle for Jerry Lanning. . . . Jerry who? As it turned out, this episode wasn't much of a vehicle. Sally does discover Randy Twizzle, though, and she brings the entire *The Alan Brady Show* gang down to a bowling alley to see his performance.

The Pilot: "Head of the Family"

Carl Reiner originally wrote the thirteen episodes of *The Dick Van Dyke Show* as a vehicle for himself. He was then known primarily as a comic actor, second banana to Sid Caesar on *Your Show of Shows*.

The pilot episode, "Head of the Family," was filmed in late 1958. It aired once on CBS in the summer of 1960 and was not seen again until Nick at Nite showed it as a part of Our Television Heritage in 1992.

The cast of this episode was made up of Carl Reiner as Rob Petrie, Barbara Britton as Laura, Gary Morgan as Ritchie, Sylvia Miles as Sally, and Morty Gunty as Buddy. Alan Brady, who was then known as Alan Sturdy, was played by Jack Wakefield.

This episode is well crafted and funny, but the characterizations are vastly different from those of the familiar series. Carl Reiner is aggressive and fast-talking, with no sign of Van Dyke's self-doubt or comic stumbling. Barbara Britton is a clever, glamorous wife, more like Donna Reed than the beautiful but very real Laura created by Mary Tyler Moore. Gary Morgan is a loudmouthed brat, completely different from the nicely underplayed Ritchie of Larry Mathews. And Sylvia Miles and Morty Gunty, though interesting, bear no resemblance to the Sally and Buddy we know today.

Luckily, Sheldon Leonard got hold of the pilot long after it was initially rejected and recognized that the script was wonderful and that recasting could save the show. His only problem was how to tell Carl Reiner that he had miscast himself. But he did it.

Favorite: Of almost no one. Carl Reiner notes that this is one of the cast's single least favorite episodes. But it's really not that bad.

EPISODE 25

"One Angry Man"

Writers: Leo Solomon and Ben Gershman
Director: John Rich
Cast
Marla Hendrix: Sue Ann Langdon
Mr. Berger: Dabbs Greer
Mr. Mason: Lee Bergere
Bailiff: Doodles Weaver
First Juror: Herb Vigran
Second Juror: Herbie Faye
Third Juror: Patsy Kelly
Judge: Howard Wendell

A light spoof of *Twelve Angry Men* takes Rob into the jury room, where he finds himself swayed by the logic of the beautiful blond defendant.

EPISODE 26

"Where You Been, Fassbinder?"

Writer: John Whedon
Director: John Rich
Cast
Pickles Sorrell: Barbara Perry
Leo Fassbinder: George Neise

Sally meets Mr. Right, an insurance salesman named Leo Fassbinder, falls in love, gets married, and is written out of the show. Just kidding. Fassbinder turns out to be yet another failed romance.

For the Record: This is Barbara Perry's second and final turn as Pickles.

EPISODE 27

"The Bad Old Days"

Writers: Norm Liebmann and Ed Haas
Director: John Rich

Stop me if you've heard this one, but the guys at the office are talking, and Buddy convinces Rob that he, like many other American men, is being lorded over by his wife. Rob decides that Buddy is right, and he longs for the good old days—until the fantasy sequence.

Classic Performance: This is the show with the "Gay Nineties" costumes. Enough said.

Favorite: Not of Dick Van Dyke. He considered it one of the worst in the series. Most viewers will agree that it *is* pretty lame.

EPISODE 28

"I Am My Brother's Keeper"

Writer: Carl Reiner
Director: John Rich
Cast
Stacey Petrie: Jerry Van Dyke

When Rob's bashful brother, Stacey, walks into the room with a loud "Burford!" Rob's fears are confirmed. His brother is fast asleep, and Stacey doesn't just sleepwalk; he also sleep-jokes, sleep–plays banjo, and sleep-entertains like no one else. This is the first half of a two-part story.

This episode was based on the real-life fact that young Jerry Van Dyke was a legendary sleep walker.

Classic Quote
ROB: There's not much demand for a sleeping comedian.

For the Record: Jerry Van Dyke was the first actor to be credited as a guest star on this series.

EPISODE 29

"The Sleeping Brother"

Writer: Carl Reiner
Director: John Rich
Cast
Alan Brady: Carl Reiner
Stacey Petrie: Jerry Van Dyke

How can Stacey successfully audition for *The Alan Brady Show*, when he can perform only while he is fast asleep? This is the second of a two-part episode.

For the Record: At Stacey's audition, Alan Brady, played by writer-producer Carl Reiner, appears for the very first time, but he's shot from behind so that his face is never revealed.

Classic Performances: Buddy plays the cello and tells jokes in this episode. Sally sings "Crying Out My Heart for You," and Rob and Laura do a quick rendition of "Mountain Greenery." These performances serve as a warm-up for Stacey's big audition.

EPISODE 30

"The Return of Happy Spangler"

Writer: Carl Reiner
Director: John Rich
Cast
Happy Spangler: J. C. Flippen

Rob does his best to help an old radio comedy writer try to make a comeback. This episode is a must-see for the classic physical-comedy lecture in which Rob explains why pain is funny.

The Adamo Watch
Frank Adamo plays the other customer in the store.

For the Record: This was the last episode of the first season. The series was not yet a success in the ratings; at this point, it was languishing in eightieth place. In fact, the show was essentially canceled after the first season and was saved only by the intense lobbying efforts of Sheldon Leonard.

Awards: Despite the low ratings, Carl Reiner won the 1962–1963 Emmy for comedy writing, and John Rich was nominated for Best Director.

EPISODE 31

"Never Name a Duck"

Writer: Carl Reiner
Director: John Rich
Cast
Miss Singleton: Jane Dulo
Miss Glasser: Geraldine Wall
Mr. Fletcher: Jerry Hausner
Veterinarian's Assistant: Frank Adamo

Laura is upset when Rob brings home two baby ducks, but they soon become beloved pets. When one dies and the other languishes, Ritchie must face the harsh realities of life and death.

This episode presents another rare opportunity to see Ritchie's bedroom, where he was so often sent. Rob visits his son there to have a heart-to-heart.

Classic Performance: Watch frequent bit player Jerry Hausner's tug-of-war with an extremely recalcitrant kangaroo, and notice that the director has to resort to a film editing trick to make the scene work.

Classic Quote
ROB: Ducks love ducks much more than they love people.

The Adamo Watch
Luckily for Frank, he got to play the veterinarian's assistant, leaving the kangaroo wrestling to fellow bit player Jerry Hausner.

EPISODE 32

"The Two Faces of Rob"

Writers: Sheldon Keller and Howard Merrill
Director: John Rich

"Dolce farniente," says Rob in a thick Italian accent on the phone to Laura. His point is that a wife can't always recognize a husband. But his little stunt backfires, and she responds to his flirtation. Who's zooming who is never entirely clear, even as the credits roll.

For the Record: After the filming of this episode, the cast stayed late to shoot the immortal ottoman-trip opening sequence with the sidestep variation. The third version—the sidestep followed by the caught toe—was filmed later.

The Trip Heard 'Round the World

It may be surprising, but Rob Petrie's trip over the ottoman is actually only the second most famous fall in television history. However, the ski jumper who demonstrated "the agony of defeat" in the opening of *Wide World of Sports* is no longer on the air, while Rob continues to tumble every night on Nick at Nite. One can reasonably expect Classic TV's greatest pratfall to eventually supersede that of the skier.

On the other hand, to be perfectly accurate, Rob does not trip in every episode, as casual viewers may think. In fact, there were four different opening sequences to the show. The last three were made to keep viewers on their toes: would he fall or wouldn't he? The four sequences are as follows:

1. Photographs and a hot drum mix theme song. No tripping and falling at all. Airs on the first fourteen episodes.
2. Rob trips and does a full flip onto the floor, then shakes hands all around.
3. Rob heads toward the ottoman, but catches himself and sidesteps it successfully, smoothly, and with evident pride.
4. Rob heads toward the ottoman, catches himself, sidesteps it smoothly, but then catches his toe on the rug and almost falls. In this variation, he shakes Buddy's hand twice.

EPISODE 33

"Bank Book 6565696"

Writers: Ray Allen Saffian and Harvey Bullock
Director: John Rich

When Rob discovers that Laura has a secret nest egg, he jumps to the wrong conclusion, doesn't get the birthday gift he's been hinting at (a new projector), finally discovers the truth, and gets hit with a pillow.

Our Television Heritage: The new projector was a fitting choice for home movie buff Dick Van Dyke. The actor became the producer-director of films starring his kids. Today Van Dyke is still at it, but he's now up-to-date, tinkering with video editing as a hobby.

Classic Quote
ROB: Just think, at this very moment the mighty Niagara is harnessed to mighty generators, its power racing over 400 miles of copper wire . . . just to heat our toaster.

EPISODE 34

"The Attempted Marriage"

Writer: Carl Reiner
Director: John Rich
Cast
Doctor: Sandy Kenyon
Orderly: Ray Kellogg
Chaplain: Dabbs Greer

This is one of the memorable flashback-romance episodes written by Carl Reiner. Rob recalls the farce that was his wedding day.

Classic Quote
ROB (*looking under the hood of his stalled Jeep*): Yup, there it is. A motor.

EPISODE 35

"Hustling the Hustler"

Writer: Carl Reiner
Director: John Rich
Cast
Blackie Sorrell: Phil Leeds

Buddy's no-good brother Blackie arrives, but Buddy can't be found, so Rob sociably offers to take Blackie home. "You know we can't offer you much, except some home cooking, some fresh suburban air, maybe a home movie or two." They have a swell time, until they get to the pool table, where Rob falls victim to a classic hustle.

Classic Quotes
LAURA (*describing Rob*): You've heard of Minnesota Fats? This is Illinois Skinny.

BUDDY: I told you he's not your type.
SALLY: Is he single?
BUDDY: Yes.
SALLY: He's my type.

For the Record: Laura is in a hurry to end her pool game with Rob because she wants to watch *The Maltese Falcon* on television.

Mary Tyler Moore outhustled everyone by making the final trick shot all by herself. A billiards professional was standing by ready to perform the trick for an insert shot, but it wasn't necessary.

EPISODE 36

"What's in a Middle Name?"

Writer: Carl Reiner
Director: John Rich

Cast

Mr. Meehan: Carl Benton Reid
Mrs. Meehan: Geraldine Wall
Grandpa Petrie: Cyril Delevanti
Sam Petrie: J. Pat O'Malley
Clara Petrie: Isabel Randolph

The day comes when Ritchie discovers that his middle name is Rosebud. Rob's explanation makes this one of the most often requested episodes in the series. The classic flashback takes us back to the naming of young Ritchie and, by the way, also includes the moment when Laura tells Sally, and then Rob, that "the rabbit died."

For the Record: The names that "must" be used are Robert, Oscar, Samuel, Edward, Benjamin, Ulysses, and David.

EPISODE 37

"My Husband Is Not a Drunk"

Writer: Carl Reiner
Director: John Rich

Cast

Glen Jameson: Charles Aidman
Mr. Boland: Roy Roberts

This episode features one of the all-time classic physical performances by Dick Van Dyke. It begins when Rob's hypnotist friend entertains the Helpers, the Petries, Buddy, and Sally by hypnotizing them one by one. But a coincidence and Rob's susceptibility leave him with a posthypnotic suggestion that makes him act drunk every time he hears a bell ring and sober up at the next ring. When the phone rings in *The Alan Brady Show* staff writers' room, the fun begins.

Game

Match the hypnotized behavior with the hypnotizee.

Laura	Becomes Abraham Lincoln
Rob	Cannot be hypnotized, but fakes it
Buddy	Becomes the person he admires most—himself
Jerry	Becomes a screaming teeny-bopper
Millie	Acts drunk at the sound of a bell

EPISODE 38

"Like a Sister"

Writer: Carl Reiner
Director: Hal Cooper
Cast
Ric Vallone: Vic Damone

First Rob is worried about Sally's crush on Ric Vallone; then Vic Damone—guest-starring as himself, more or less—woos Sally right back.

EPISODE 39

"The Night the Roof Fell In"

Writer: John Whedon
Director: Hal Cooper
Cast
Freddie Helper: Peter Oliphant

Like Akira Kurosawa's classic 1950 film *Rashomon,* this episode presents the same events retold from three different perspectives, exploring the nature of subjective experience, history, and reality. The three perspectives are those of Rob, Laura, and a pair of aquarium fish. The event: a marital spat after a hard day.

Classic Quote
ROB: I love that ottoman!

EPISODE 40

"The Secret Life of Buddy and Sally"

Writer: Lee Erwin
Director: Coby Ruskin
Cast
Waiter: Phil Arnold

Buddy and Sally's mysterious behavior leads Rob to suspect that they're secretly writing for another show—or worse—but as Laura says, "Buddy and Sally? Buddy's a married man!"

Classic Performances: Buddy and Sally do an act as "Gilbert and Solomon." Buddy plays the cello and does shtick, Sally sings "Come Rain or Come Shine," and Rob and Laura do a song-and-dance number under the names Lester and Esther Bushwhacker.

For the Record: The events of the second act take place at Herbie's Hiawatha Lodge.

EPISODE 41

"A Bird in the Head Hurts"

Writer: Carl Reiner
Director: John Rich
Cast
Game Warden: Cliff Norton

A giant woodpecker is attacking Ritchie's head. Needless to say, this is one of the most memorable episodes in the series.

Our Television Heritage: Surprisingly, this episode's story was based on reality. In fact, many of the stories used in the series were based on true-life experiences of the writers, the performers, or others. In this instance, the son of Carl Reiner's neighbor was confronted by a woodpecker who wanted to nest in his hair. If that's not enough cribbing from real life, the advice given to Laura in the show is exactly the same as that offered by a real ASPCA official: "Let him wear a pith helmet."

EPISODE 42

"Gesundheit, Darling"

Writer: Carl Reiner
Director: John Rich
Cast
Allergist: Sandy Kenyon

Once *The Brady Bunch* uses a plot, it forever changes the way we perceive that plot, even if that interpretation came after another, older show's version. Thus it is difficult to judge this episode, in which Rob becomes convinced that he is allergic to Laura. For what it's worth, Dick Van Dyke's performance is far more convincing than Eve Plumb's in the corresponding *Brady* episode—though hers did offer a compelling pathos.

EPISODE 43

"A Man's Teeth Are Not His Own"

Writer: Carl Reiner
Director: John Rich

Rob breaks a tooth on a chicken salad sandwich. When he has it fixed by "another dentist," whose work is particularly excellent, he fears that Jerry will be jealous.

Classic Performances: Right before he bites into the chicken salad, Rob performs a great bit of physical comedy as a pianist with a scratch in the middle of his back. In fact, Dick Van Dyke is truly an accomplished pianist.

EPISODE 44

"Somebody Has to Play Cleopatra"

Writer: Martin A. Ragaway
Director: John Rich
Cast
Mrs. Billings: Eleanor Audley
Harry Rogers: Bob Crane
Mrs. Rogers: Shirley Mitchell

Suburban angst, as none of the husbands want his wife to be cast as the femme fatale of the Nile.

Classic Guest Star: Bob Crane was of course best known as Hogan in *Hogan's Heroes*.

EPISODE 45

"The Cat Burglar"

Writer: Carl Reiner
Director: John Rich
Cast
Policeman: Barney Philips
Photographer: Johnny Silver

The Petrie living room is mysteriously emptied by a burglar, furniture and all. This episode includes the memorable jewelry box scene.

EPISODE 46

"The Foul Weather Girl"

Writer: Carl Reiner
Director: John Rich
Cast
Jane Leighton: Joan O'Brien

A singing weather girl from Rob's hometown wants to get a leg up on a career in New York City. Her "appeal" to Rob makes Laura jealous.

EPISODE 47

"Will You Two Be My Wife?"

Writer: Carl Reiner
Director: John Rich
Cast
Dorothy: Barbara Bain
Sam: Allan Melvin
Captain: Ray Kellogg
Mother: Elizabeth Harrower

This episode features another flashback to army days, when Rob must break off his "engagement" to his hometown sweetheart, having since fallen for a certain USO dancer we all know and love.

Classic Guest Star: Barbara Bain went on to play Cinnamon on *Mission Impossible.*

EPISODE 48

"Ray Murdock's X-Ray"

Writer: Carl Reiner
Director: Jerry Paris
Cast
Ray Murdock: Gene Lyons

Rob goes on a talk show and, in an effort to be entertaining, manages to make it seem that Laura is the inspiration for all of the ridiculous domestic situations depicted on *The Alan Brady Show*. She comes off as a nut, and Rob ends up deep in the doghouse.

For the Record: This is the directorial debut of dentist-neighbor Jerry Paris.

Parallel Plot: See episode 128, "Coast-to-Coast Bigmouth." The lesson is that talk shows are trouble.

EPISODE 49

"I Was a Teenage Head Writer"

Writers: Sheldon Keller and Howard Merrill
Director: Jerry Paris
Cast
Anatole: Phil Arnold
Herman Glimsher: Bill Idelson
Pickles Sorrell: Joan Shawlee

Rob stands up to Alan Brady, but Buddy and Sally seem to abandon Rob behind his back. The situation leads Rob to flash back to his first day on the job, when he was brought in from Illinois as head writer over the hard-edged, urban, and experienced Buddy and Sally.

Classic Performance: As the three writers put together a script for Alan, Rob proposes and then performs a piece in which he becomes a personified automobile. Buddy and Sally pretend they don't like it, but it's a good one.

Classic Quote
BUDDY *(describing Mel):* Here's the only guy I know who can walk into a barbershop and say, "Give me a shave and . . . a shave."

Classic Guest Star: This is the first appearance of Bill Idelson as Herman Glimsher. Idelson was primarily a writer: his first script for this show was episode 56, "The Square Triangle." He went on to write frequently for *The Andy Griffith Show* and was a writer and producer for *The Bob Newhart Show*.

EPISODE 50

"My Husband Is a Check Grabber"

Writer: Carl Reiner
Director: Jerry Paris

According to Carl Reiner, his own marriage was the basis for this story, in which Laura attempts to stop Rob from always picking up the tab.

EPISODE 51

"It May Look Like a Walnut!"

Writer: Carl Reiner
Director: Jerry Paris
Cast
Twilo-ite: Danny Thomas

This is probably the most memorable, and definitely one of the most requested, episodes of the entire series. The "Walnut" story line takes Rob through a nightmarish sci-fi-inspired journey be-

You Might Have Thought It Was a Walnut!

When Dick Van Dyke hosted the "Chairman's Choice" event, during which his five favorite episodes were presented on Nick at Nite, writers Hillary Rollins and Steve Weiner decided to re-create the scene in which the walnuts pour out of the closet. The chairman was willing, so the production crew went to work, buying 600 pounds of walnuts and rigging the set's closet door. The plan was to shoot the scene twice, once at the end of the day and once the next morning. The time necessary to re-set the closet meant that the shot had to be shot in one of those two takes.

When the moment came to shoot it, the room was alive with anticipation. Dick read his lines: "Where should I put all these tapes? The closet! That's it—perfect." Then he carried an armful of tapes to the closet where he tried to open the door, but it wouldn't budge.

"The weight of the walnuts had jammed the door closed," recalled producer Nina Silvestri. "He couldn't turn the handle."

After tape was cut, the assistant director went out and tried to turn the handle. He did it, and immediately the door opened a quarter of an inch. That was enough. The walnuts prevented the door from being closed. After some hasty deliberations, the director decided to shoot the scene for possible use after editing—in a medium shot so that the camera would not reveal the two lucky production assistants who were lying on the floor holding the door closed until Dick was ready to open it. That strategy worked, more or less, and the two human doorstops survived the deluge.

The next day, after some re-rigging, the door worked like a charm, pouring a true flood of walnuts across the office. The original plan was for Morey Amsterdam, instead of Mary, to pour out with the walnuts. Perhaps it's just as well that Morey couldn't make it, though. With all the other production snafus, he might never have made it out alive.

yond the limits of the imagination. And of course it includes the classic moment where a very fetching Laura Petrie slides out head first of an entire closet full of walnuts.

Classic Guest: Danny Thomas, one of the show's producers, guest stars as a Twilo-ite.

Classic Quote
LAURA: So everybody ends up looking like Danny Thomas, and that's the end of the story. Fine. Good night.

For the Record: This was the first time the episode's title was shown as part of the opening credit sequence.

EPISODE 52

"Don't Trip over That Mountain"

Writer: Carl Reiner
Director: Coby Ruskin
Cast
Nurse: Jean Allison
Doctor: Ray Kellogg

See Rob ski! Ski, Rob, ski! Pride cometh before a fall. Women's intuition notifies Laura that Rob is going to hurt himself badly on his weekend skiing trip with Jerry. Rob assures her that no such thing will happen, but in a four-person pile-up involving a mountain goat, Rob sprains his entire body.

Classic Quotes
LAURA: Millie, when he left here, he was pretty angry. He might break a leg just to cause me pain.
MILLIE: Laura, Rob loves you! He'd rather cut off an arm than break a leg to cause you pain!

EPISODE 53

"Give Me Your Walls!"

Writer: Carl Reiner
Director: Jerry Paris
Cast
Vito Giotto: Vito Scotti

Rob accidentally marks up the living room wall with ink. He tries to clean it off but ends up smearing it and making more of a mess. Then he tries to paint over it, but he runs out of paint. The Petries hire Vito Giotto—the master painter of Rome, Florence, and Brooklyn—to paint the wall. After five days Vito has still not painted the wall. Rob and Laura begin to suspect that Vito is purposely staying longer so that he can charge them an obscene amount of money for the job, but Vito finally paints the wall and charges the Petries a reasonable rate. As a bonus, he comes back to the Petries' home and puts on a show for Ritchie and his little pals.

EPISODE 54

"The Sam Pomerantz Scandals"

Writer: Carl Reiner
Director: Claudio Guzman
Cast
Sam Pomerantz: Henry Calvin
Danny Brewster: Len Weinrib
Pickles Sorrell: Joan Shawlee

This is one of the musical shows. Sally sings "I Wanna Be Around," Buddy does shtick, and Rob and Laura hoof their way through "Carolina in the Morning."

Classic Performance: Dick Van Dyke's memorable Stan Laurel impersonation is a loving homage to his boyhood idol, who later became his friend.

For the Record: Claudio Guzman directed just this one episode of *Dick Van Dyke*, but he directed almost all of the episodes of *I Dream of Jeannie*.

EPISODE 55

"I'm No Henry Walden"

Writer: Carl Reiner
Story: Ray Brenner and Jack Guss
Director: Jerry Paris
Cast
Mrs. Huntington: Doris Packer
Miss Evelyn: Rosane Berard
Mrs. Fellows: Betty Lou Gerson
H. Fieldstone Thorley: Frank Adamo
Yale Sampson: Carl Reiner
Henry Walden: Everett Sloane

Rob is invited to mingle with the literati, but he feels uncomfortable until he finds a kindred spirit.

Carl Reiner makes his second acting appearance on the series, but this is the first time he shows his face (see episode 29). He plays a pretentious intellectual who says things that "seem vague but are in reality meaningless."

Classic Quote
ROB: Television writers marry the prettiest girls.

The Adamo Watch
The poet Thorley was one of Frank Adamo's most substantial roles.

EPISODE 56

"The Square Triangle"

Writer: Bill Idelson
Director: Jerry Paris
Cast
Jacques Savon: Jacques Bergerac

Rob and Laura are less than delighted when French singing star Jacques Savon comes to New York. It seems he was part of a strange chapter in their lives: Rob and Laura both think that they broke up his marriage. When Sally uncovers the truth, Jacques explains why he has never set the record straight.

Classic Quote
JACQUES: Laura is a happily married woman. But she is a woman. Every woman have some secret memory, a memory that keeps her heart young and her soul warm on cold nights. It is so?
SALLY: It is so.

Parallel Plot: This basic story bears an uncanny resemblance to an episode of *Alfred Hitchcock Presents* entitled "The Legacy." In that episode, a handsome, aristocratic playboy romances a somewhat plain and somewhat older married woman. When she rejects him—though it "keeps her heart young" to feel desired and makes her husband appreciate her and feel that he has won her again—the playboy commits suicide by driving his car off a cliff. What the woman and her husband don't know is that the playboy was completely broke, that he was after the wife's money, and that the car crash was an accident. The detective debates telling the couple the truth but decides "He had given them a precious legacy. Who was I to rob them of it?" Here's the truly incredible part of the story. The part of the doomed playboy was played by none other than Jacques Bergerac.

EPISODE 57

"Racy Tracy Ratigan"

Writers: Ronald Alexander and Carl
Reiner
Director: Sheldon Leonard
Cast
Tracy Ratigan: Richard Dawson

If you've never seen Richard Dawson's bird
calls, you've never seen this episode. But bird
calls are just the beginning, as the lascivious
Ratigan sets his sights on—who else?—Laura.

Classic Guest Star: Richard Dawson, before he
began kissing strangers nightly on *Family Feud*,
played the wisecracking and safe-cracking
Newkirk of *Hogan's Heroes*.

EPISODE 58

"Divorce"

Writer: Carl Reiner
Director: Jerry Paris
Cast
Pickles Sorrell: Joan Shawlee
Bartender: Charles Cantor
Girl: Marian Collier

When Buddy finds a bunch of canceled checks
made out to a Floyd B. Bariscale, he thinks that
Pickles is having an affair. Rob becomes involved
when Buddy announces that he's going to divorce
Pickles.

Classic Quote
ROB *(to Buddy, who just took sleeping pills):* I want
you to go back to bed, and don't take any more
Dozey Doodles! . . . Yes, you can have a cupcake.

For the Record: Carl Reiner is the TV defense
lawyer in an uncredited voice-over, and Sheldon
Leonard is the voice of Floyd B. Bariscale.

This episode marks the final on-camera appearance of Buddy's wife, Pickles.

EPISODE 59

"It's a Shame She Married Me"

Writers: Sheldon Keller and Howard
Merrill
Director: James Niver
Cast
Jim Darling: Robert Vaughn
Edward: Frank Adamo

Richard Dawson has only been gone for one
episode, and already the green-eyed monster is
raising its ugly head again, this time in the form of
the more threatening Robert Vaughn. Poor old Rob
just can't keep up with the handsome charmer.

The Adamo Watch
Edward is the role Frank Adamo was born to play.

Classic Guest Star: Robert Vaughn's most
prominent role in TV Land was as Napoleon Solo,
one of the men from U.N.C.L.E.

EPISODE 60

"A Surprise Is a Surprise Is a Surprise"

Writer: Carl Reiner
Director: Jerry Paris

Laura has gone through elaborate precautions
to make sure that Rob doesn't find out about the
surprise party she is planning to throw for him.
But Rob finds out anyway.

Parallel Plot: See *The Mary Tyler Moore Show,* episode 87, "Happy Birthday, Lou," for another unsuccessful surprise party thrown by Mary-Laura.

EPISODE 61

"Jilting the Jilter"

Writer: Ronald Alexander
Director: Jerry Paris
Cast
Fred White: Guy Marks

Poor Sally. Here's another ill-fated romance—this time with a Lothario who is after her only for her jokes.

EPISODE 62

"When a Bowling Pin Talks, Listen"

Writer: Martin A. Ragaway
Director: Jerry Paris
Cast
Willie: Herbie Faye
Barber: Jon Silo

Rob is all out of ideas when Ritchie suggests a funny idea—a talking bowling pin! Rob loves it and writes it up. Alan loves it and performs it. Then they find out that Ritchie didn't think it up: he saw Uncle Spunky do it on a kiddie show. Spunky, the original talking bowling pin, calls Alan Brady with accusations of plagiarism. Alan saves the day with some fast-talking diplomacy.

For the Record: This was the last episode shown in the second season. By this time the show had climbed out of its first-season ratings slump to be the number 9 show overall. It never again fell out of the top 20.

Awards: Two weeks after this episode aired, *The Dick Van Dyke Show* dominated the Emmy Awards. The show won as Best Program in the field of humor, Carl Reiner took home the comedy writing award, and John Rich walked away with the comedy directing award. Dick Van Dyke, Mary Tyler Moore, and Rose Marie were nominated.

EPISODE 63

"All About Eavesdropping"

Writers: Sheldon Keller and Howard Merrill
Director: Stanley Cherry

In the midst of getting ready for a dinner party at the Helpers', Rob and Laura accidentally overhear their neighbors' conversation through Ritchie's toy intercom. Then, unfortunately, they can't resist listening to more and more. Among other things, the Helpers describe the Petries as selfish, insincere, and competitive. Rob and Laura are miffed, but they attend the dinner party nonetheless, ruining it with their dour attitude. At night's end, they "accidentally" turn on the intercom again and hear their neighbors being sympathetic and kind, so they realize how wrong they were. A late night apology, a few words of explanation, a look or two, and all's well.

For the Record: Laura really did leave the mustard out of her recipe for peanut butter and avocado dip.

Also, the end of one of Buddy's punch lines is obscured by a huge torrent of laughter. What he says, as best we can tell, is "I haven't had laughs like this since the Saint Valentine's massacre."

Classic Performance: Buddy and Sally sing a soulful snippet of "Go Tell Aunt Rhody."

Our Television Heritage: This episode is the perfect example of what makes this show so much better than most other sitcoms. Even when the show begins with a typical sitcom premise, the writers transcend the material by providing brilliant ideas and clever lines that somehow make all the events seem plausible.

EPISODE 64

"That's My Boy"

Writers: Bill Persky and Sam Denoff
Director: John Rich
Cast
Nurse: Amzie Strickland
Mr. Peters: Greg Morris
Mrs. Peters: Mimi Dillard

This episode elicited the longest laugh by the studio audience in the whole series. (That's according to most sources, but see episode 90.) The story is a flashback to the days after Rob and Laura bring the infant Ritchie home from the hospital. Rob becomes convinced that they have brought home the wrong baby. To straighten everything out, he invites over the couple whose baby he believes was switched with theirs. The longest laugh begins the minute he answers the door. Much of the laughter was actually edited from the show, as you can tell by the reaction shot of Laura, which the producers used to cover the transition.

For the Record: This was a smashing debut for Persky and Denoff, who became the show's most regular writers, aside from the indefatigable Carl Reiner.

Favorite: Of almost everyone, including Dick Van Dyke, John Rich, and the authors of *The Dick Van Dyke Show: Anatomy of a Classic,* in which you can find the entire script for the episode.

EPISODE 65

"The Masterpiece"

Writers: Sam Denoff and Bill Persky
Director: John Rich
Cast
Mr. Holdecker: Howard Morris
Auctioneer: Alan Reed
Woman: Amzie Strickland
Man: Ray Kellogg

Rob is having a good laugh joking with Buddy about a funny sketch they could do about auctions, and in the meantime he's inadvertently bidding wildly on some unusual objects. He tries to back out of it but returns home with two objets d'art that turn out to be rather interesting items.

The Adamo Watch
Frank Adamo appears in the auction crowd.

Classic Guest Stars: Howard Morris was a writer-performer with Carl Reiner on *Your Show of Shows.*
Alan Reed provided the voice of Fred Flintstone.

EPISODE 66

"Laura's Little Lie"

Writers: Carl Reiner and Howard Merrill
Director: John Rich
Cast
Ed Rubin: Charles Aidman

Laura is acting very strange. She's nervous and evasive every time their insurance agent, Ed Rubin, calls. She disappears for a whole evening. Her evasive behavior continues throughout the episode until finally she confesses, revealing a truth long hidden from Rob. She lied about her age when they were married. She was only seventeen—too young to be working as a USO show girl—and worried that Rob would have second thoughts about marrying someone so young.

For the Record: This is not, strictly speaking, a two-parter episode, but it leads directly to the events of the next episode.

EPISODE 67

"Very Old Shoes, Very Old Rice"

Writer: Carl Reiner
Director: John Rich
Cast
Old Man: Burt Mustin
Young Man: Frank Adamo
Judge: Russell Collins
Old Woman: Madge Blake

The Petries discover they are not legally married—Laura's "little lie" on the license invalidates the contract—so they plan to elope. Eventually, they renew their marriage vows even though they're in the middle of a tempestuous argument.

Classic Guest Star: Madge Blake was Batman's Aunt Harriet in the Adam West television series.

The Adamo Watch
Frank Adamo plays the Young Man with his usual verve.

EPISODE 68

"Uncle George"

Writer: Bill Idelson
Director: Jerry Paris
Cast
Herman Glimsher: Bill Idelson
Uncle George: Denver Pyle
Mrs. Glimsher: Elvia Allman

Old rough-and-ready Uncle George comes to visit, but he's not just sight-seeing—he's on the lookout for a woman to be his bride. It doesn't take long for him to set his sights on eternal bachelorette Sally Rogers.

For the Record: Writer-actor Bill Idelson makes his second appearance in this episode.

EPISODE 69

"Too Many Stars"

Writers: Sheldon Keller and Howard Merrill
Director: Jerry Paris
Cast
Carmelita Lebost: Sylvia Lewis
Mrs. Billings: Eleanor Audley
Delivery Man: Jerry Hausner
Howard Lebost: Eddie Ryder

Rob gets talked into directing the fund-raiser for Ritchie's school, as usual, and is bombarded with "talent." Perhaps the most memorable of all is the unlikely ventriloquism act performed by Mel Cooley and his very bald dummy.

EPISODE 70

"Who and Where Was Antonio Stradivarius?"

Writer: Carl Reiner
Director: Jerry Paris
Cast
Hostess: Betty Lou Gerson
Aunt Mildred: Amzie Strickland
Uncle Edward: Hal Peary
Graciella: Sallie Jones
Host: Chet Stratton

Rob finds himself at a party in a strange town, swaying to the bossa nova with a breathless young woman who adores him. Meanwhile, Laura is at home, panic-stricken, wondering if he's "lying in an alleyway, calling my name."

EPISODE 71

"Big Max Calvada"

Writers: Bill Persky and Sam Denoff
Director: Jerry Paris
Cast
Max Calvada: Sheldon Leonard
Bernard: Art Batanides
Kenneth Dexter: Jack Larson
Clarisse Calvada: Sue Casey
Mr. Parker: Tiny Brauer
Waiter: Johnny Silver

Big Max Calvada is a mobster whose nephew, Kenneth, wants to be a comedian. Max wants his nephew to have the best writers, and Max is used to getting what he wants.

For the Record: Max's manner of speaking is apparently a spoof of sociology major Sheldon Leonard's unique blend of a Bronx accent and professorial verbiage. As Max says of *The Alan Brady Show*, "It's neither too esoteric nor too mundane."

Big Max, of course, took his name from the show's production company. The name Calvada is composed of the *Ca* in *Ca*rl Reiner, the *l* in Sheldon *L*eonard, the *va* in *Va*n Dyke, and the *da* in *Da*nny Thomas.

Classic Guest Star: The Jack Larsen in this episode is clearly not *the* Jack Larsen who was *Superman*'s Jimmy Olsen.

EPISODE 72

"The Ballad of the Betty Lou"

Writer: Martin A. Ragaway
Director: Howard Morris
Cast
Sailor: Danny Scholl

Jerry and Rob hear the Siren's call and head for the open seas, the spray of brine, and the misery of co-owning a boat.

Favorite: Of Jerry Paris, who in this episode stepped forward into the acting spotlight.

EPISODE 73

"Turtles, Ties, and Toreadors"

Writer: John Whedon
Director: Jerry Paris
Cast
Maria: Miriam Colon
Taxi Driver: Tiny Brauer
Immigration Officer: Alan Dexter

Overworked Laura is finally provided with some help when Rob employs a maid . . . who can't speak a word of English. Neither Rob nor Laura has enough gumption to fire her.

For the Record: The family portrait of the Petries on the turtleshell was drawn by accomplished sketch artist Dick Van Dyke.

EPISODE 74

"The Sound of the Trumpets of Conscience Falls Deafly on a Brain That Holds Its Ears . . . or Something Like That!"

Writers: Bill Persky and Sam Denoff
Director: Jerry Paris
Cast
Witness: Frank Adamo
Patrolman Nelson: Bernie Hamilton
Lieutenant Yarnell: Ken Lynch
Man: Edward Homes
Hoodlum: Alan Dexter
Officer: Ray Kellogg

When the FBI shows up, Rob can't resist playing G-man. When he goes to small claims court, he wants to be Perry Mason. In this episode, he's embroiled in crime again, this time as a witness—maybe—of two perpetrators running from the scene of an infraction.

The Adamo Watch
Frank speaks up in this episode, thus earning a credit.

EPISODE 75

"The Third One from the Left"

Writer: John Whedon
Director: Jerry Paris
Cast
Joan Delroy: Cheryl Holderidge
Ernie: Jimmy Murphy

Before they were through, the show played out nearly every variation of jealousy. In episode 3 Laura is jealous of a starlet; in number 46 she's jealous of the weather girl. In 131 Rob is jealous of a rival suitor, in 59 he's jealous of Robert Vaughn, and in 80 he's jealous of an ex-beau of Laura's who is now a priest. The Helpers are jealous of the Petries' new neighbors in episode 156, and Rob is afraid that Jerry will be jealous when he sees another dentist in number 43. And in this episode a lovely young dancer from *The Alan Brady Show* falls head over heels for Rob. Laura doesn't care. All right, actually, she's jealous.

EPISODE 76

"*The Alan Brady Show Presents*"

Writers: Sam Denoff and Bill Persky
Director: Jerry Paris
Cast
Girl: Cornell Chulay
Boy: Brendan Freeman

They're serving *corn* on Christmas. Alan turns over *The Alan Brady Show* to his staff and their families to put on a Christmas Spectacular. This corny Christmas special includes Sally singing "Santa, Send Me a Fella," Rob and Laura as tap-dancing Santas, and Ritchie singing "The Little Drummer Boy" (not even close to David Bowie's version). The show concludes with Rob, Laura, Buddy, Sally, Mel, and the rest of the cast singing a few bars of *The Dick Van Dyke Show* theme song with the trip-over-the-ottoman sound effect included.

For the Record: Carl Reiner wasn't excited about doing this episode because he thought they wouldn't be able to replay it during summer reruns. He only reconsidered it when he realized that the holiday episode could be used every Christmas from then on. This was one of the very few episodes that was not filmed before a live audience, because of the complicated costume and set changes. The songs were written by Persky and Denhoff.

Classic Cameo: Cornell Chulay was the daughter of assistant director John Chulay. (See episode 78 for details.)

EPISODE 77

"My Husband Is the Best One"

Writer: Martin A. Ragaway
Director: Jerry Paris
Cast
Diane Mosby: Valerie Yerke
Alan Brady: Carl Reiner
Waiter: Frank Adamo

Rob is to be interviewed over dinner, and Laura joins him, only to throw in some rather impolitic comments, which make Rob persona non grata back at *The Alan Brady Show.*

The Adamo Watch
Frank goes to work as a waiter in this episode.

Awards: This show won the 1963 Writers Guild Award as Best Episodic Comedy script.

EPISODE 78

"Happy Birthday and Too Many More"

Writers: Bill Persky and Sam Denoff
Director: Jerry Paris
Cast
First Boy: Michael Chulay
First Girl: Cornell Chulay
Second Boy: Brendan Freeman
Third Boy: Tony Paris
Delivery Man: Johnny Silver

The Petries throw a birthday party for Ritchie, and a torrent of screaming tykes nearly destroys them.

Our Television Heritage: This episode is not considered one of the show's best. One reason may be that the assassination of President Kennedy called a halt to the third day of rehearsals. After considering canceling the week, the staff decided to proceed, but the cast and crew filmed the episode without a live audience, assuming that a crowd would be in no mood for laughter.

For the Record: The Chulay family had an interesting and varied history in Classic TV. John Chulay was the assistant director of the series; Michael and Cornell, who appear in this episode, were his children. John also worked on *The Mary Tyler Moore Show,* where another son, Benjamin Chulay, appeared as the very recognizable blond extra often seen working in the back of the newsroom. Benjamin had occasional lines as Pete the newsboy—things like "Mail's in!" Today he works behind the scenes as a film editor, most recently for *Melrose Place.*

EPISODE 79

"The Lady and the Tiger and the Lawyer"

Writer: Garry Marshall and Jerry Belson
Director: Jerry Paris
Cast
Donna Palmer: Lyla Graham
Arthur Stanwyck: Anthony Eisley

It's the old competing cupids story. A handsome bachelor moves in next door, and Rob tries to hook him up with Sally, while Laura tries to get him interested in her cousin Donna.

For the Record: The outrageous caricature of Mel Cooley seen in this episode was drawn by Dick Van Dyke.

Writer Garry Marshall went on to produce many hit shows, including *The Odd Couple* and *Happy Days*.

EPISODE 80

"The Life and Loves of Joe Coogan"

Writer: Carl Reiner
Director: Jerry Paris
Cast
Joe Coogan: Michael Forest
Waiter: Johnny Silver

At a country club, Laura runs into Joe Coogan, a former beau, who is now a priest. Rob is—yes, indeed—jealous.

Favorite: Of Carl Reiner, who recalled spending hours crafting the poem Laura overhears.

EPISODE 81

"A Nice Friendly Game of Cards"

Writer: Ernest Chambers
Director: Howard Morris
Cast
Beth Gregory: Shirley Mitchell
Lou Gregory: Ed Platt

Rob is caught using marked cards during a friendly game of cards. Of course, he wasn't actually *using* them, but he finds it impossible to explain that to Lou Gregory.

Classic Guest Star: Ed Platt played the Chief on *Get Smart*.

EPISODE 82

"The Brave and the Backache"

Writers: Sheldon Keller and Howard Merrill
Director: Jerry Paris
Cast
Tony Daniels: Ken Berry
Dr. Philip Nevins: Ross Elliot

Laura's trying to get Rob to take her away for the weekend—just the two of them—but at the last moment Rob throws out his back. Or does he? Is this a psychosomatic manifestation of some deep-seated resentment of his wife? Rob turns to his fellow commuter Phil, the psychiatrist, to plumb the depths of his subconscious and discover the true meaning of Lake Sissimanunu.

Classic Guest Star: Ken Berry played Captain Parmenter on *F Troop*.

EPISODE 83

"The Pen Is Mightier than the Mouth"

Writers: Bill Persky and Sam Denoff
Director: Jerry Paris
Cast
Bernie Quinn: Herb Vigran
Dave: Johnny Silver
Stevie Parsons: Dick Patterson

Sally is a star! Her appearances on *The Stevie Parsons* (read: Johnny Carson) *Show* take her away from her duties at *The Alan Brady Show*, leaving Buddy and Rob to fend for themselves. The chemistry is all wrong without her, and they can't get anything done. This is essentially the first of a two-part episode.

EPISODE 84

"My Part-Time Wife"

Writers: Bill Persky and Sam Denoff
Director: Jerry Paris
Cast
Jackie: Jackie Joseph

Laura finally gets her wish and lands the job filling in at Rob's office as typist while Sally is off starring on *The Stevie Parsons Show*. But Rob can't deal with having her around; he feels like a little boy at parents' day, with his mom peering over his shoulder. In another classic sobbing speech, much like the one in "My Blonde-Haired Brunette" (episode 9), Laura tells him off.

EPISODE 85

"Honeymoons Are for the Lucky"

Writer: Carl Reiner
Director: Jerry Paris
Cast
Mr. Campbell: Johnny Silver
Sam Pomeroy: Allan Melvin
Captain Lebost: Peter Hobbs
Mrs. Campbell: Kathleen Freeman

Perhaps the first "Oh, Rob"—chronologically speaking—occurs in this flashback to Rob and Laura's ill-fated and G-rated honeymoon. The story, based on Carl Reiner's own honeymoon misadventures, begins as Rob begs for a special exception to the ban on passes out of his army camp. Unable to get out legitimately, he goes AWOL disguised as a woman, heading toward his first encounter with Kathleen Freeman.

The Adamo Watch
In this episode Frank Adamo plays a soldier who gives Millie the setup line, "Hi, honey, whadda ya know?"

EPISODE 86

"How to Spank a Star"

Writers: Nathaniel Curtis and Bill Idelson
Director: Jerry Paris
Cast
Paula Marshall: Lola Albright

One of Rob's favorite stars, the beautiful Paula Marshall is the guest star on *The Alan Brady Show*, but she threatens to refuse to do the show unless Rob produces it. Winsome Paula has Rob rewriting the whole show before he realizes she's walking all over him. He then tells Paula he will not change the script at all and threatens legal action when she says she'll walk out. She backs down and does the show with the original script.

Classic Guest Star: Lola Albright's best-known TV role was that of Edie Hart, the nightclub singer on *Peter Gunn*.

EPISODE 87

"The Plots Thicken"

Writers: Carl Reiner, Bill Persky, and Sam Denoff
Director: Jerry Paris
Cast
Mrs. Meehan: Geraldine Wall
Mr. Meehan: Carl Benton Reid
Sam Petrie: J. Pat O'Malley
Clara Petrie: Isabel Randolph

This is a plot plot. The in-laws compete to include Rob and Laura in their family burial plans.

Awards: This was the first episode in which all three principal writers shared credit. The three together won the 1963–1964 Emmy award for Comedy Writing on a series.

EPISODE 88

"Scratch My Car and Die"

Writer: John Whedon
Director: Howard Morris

Rob is in love . . . with his new car. Laura scratches it—or at least she's in the car when someone else scratches it. Then she tries to hide the disaster.

EPISODE 89

"The Return of Edwin Carp"

Writer: Carl Reiner
Director: Howard Morris
Cast
Arlene Harris: Herself
Bert Gordan: Himself
Edwin Carp: Richard Haydn

Rob has a big idea for the show: bringing back classic radio acts. Arlene Harris and Bert the Mad Russian are easy, but it turns out that Edwin Carp can't perform his famous fish imitations without the aid of elderberry wine to soothe his severe stage fright. Well now, he has sworn never again to become a slave to the grape, but Rob forces him to go on and he succeeds—sober—in reciting a poem glorifying the pedal extremities.

Feet

by scoutmaster Allan

You need feet to stand up straight with.
You need feet to kick your friends.
You need feet to keep your socks on.
And keep your legs from fraying at the ends.
You need feet to stand on tippy-toe
Or to dance the hootchy-koo.
Yes, the whole world needs feet for something,
And I need feet to run away from you.

EPISODE 90

"October Eve"

Writers: Bill Persky and Sam Denoff
Director: Jerry Paris
Cast
Serge Carpetna: Carl Reiner
Man: Howard Wendell
Woman: Genevieve Griffin

Years ago Laura tried to get a painting of herself done as a gift to Rob. She posed fully clothed, but the young Greenwich Village artist, Serge Carpetna, painted her quite naked. (No, you never see the painting.) She refused to accept the painting, but now it has resurfaced because the artist has become well known.

Classic Performance: Film editor Bud Molin asserts that, contrary to what other people have said, the audience laugh at Rob's "stove take" was actually even longer than the laugh at the finale of episode 64, "That's My Boy."

Favorite: Of writers Bill Persky and Sam Denoff.

EPISODE 91

"Dear Mrs. Petrie, Your Husband Is in Jail"

Writers: Jerry Belson and Garry Marshall
Director: Jerry Paris
Cast
Benny Joey: Herkie Styles
Maureen Core: Barbara Stuart
Alberta Schweitzer: Jackie Joseph
Nick: Johnny Silver
Arnold: Art Batanides
Policeman: Henry Scott

Rob faces a long, lonely weekend without Laura, and after a hilarious soliloquy at home, he heads out to spend the evening with an old army buddy. He ends up rolling the dice in a backstage craps game, which ultimately lands him in the clink.

EPISODE 92

"My Neighbor's Husband's Other Life"

Writers: Carl Reiner, Bill Persky, and Sam Denoff
Director: Jerry Paris
Cast
Waiter: Johnny Silver

Uh-oh. Rob and Laura see their neighbor Jerry out at dinner with a beautiful woman. They jump to the obvious conclusion and find themselves in a dilemma.

EPISODE 93

"I'd Rather Be Bald Than Have No Head At All"

Writers: Bill Persky and Sam Denoff
Director: Jerry Paris
Cast
Irwin: Ned Glass

This bizarre-dream episode begins when Rob becomes convinced that he is going bald. The story line came from real life: Van Dyke was worried about his hairline. Naturally, mostly hairless producer Carl Reiner had little sympathy, and helped create this memorable episode.

Classic Scene: This show features the classical surreal image of Rob with a literal head of lettuce—or maybe it's cabbage.

Classic Quote
LAURA: Tastes good and is good for you!

EPISODE 94

"Teacher's Petrie"

Writers: Jerry Belson and Garry Marshall
Director: Jerry Paris
Cast
Mr. Caldwell: Bernie Fox
Miss Prinder: Cheerio Meredith

Laura is taking writing classes, but when her teacher says she shows promise, Rob makes the very big mistake of suspecting that it is not her writing talent that has made this fellow pay attention to his wife. Naturally, Laura's self-esteem takes a beating.

For the Record: This was the final show to air during the third season.

Awards: The third season was the show's peak Emmy windfall. The series won as best comedy, and Dick Van Dyke and Mary Tyler Moore both won for their performances. Jerry Paris won for directing, and the team of Reiner, Persky, and Denoff accepted an Emmy for writing.

EPISODE 95

"My Two Showoffs and Me"

Writers: Sheldon Keller and Howard Merrill
Director: Jerry Paris
Cast
Lorraine Gilman: Doris Singleton

He knows it's a bad idea, and he knows exactly what will happen, but Rob gets roped into letting a magazine journalist sit in while the show's writers weave their magic. Buddy, Sally, and Rob take turns behaving badly, claiming credit for every good idea, presenting old ideas just to get laughs, and undercutting one another. Rob gets defensive and begins to posture academically about the psychology of television viewers.

EPISODE 96

"My Mother Can Beat Up My Father"

Writers: Bill Persky and Sam Denoff
Director: Jerry Paris
Cast
Miss Taylor: Imelda de Martin
Drunk: Paul Gilbert
Ed Wilson: Tom Avera
Vinnie: Lou Cutell
Tony Daniels: Ken Berry

Rob tells the story from his hospital room, where he is in traction after wrestling a stuffed chimp. It begins when an obnoxious drunk punches Rob, only to be thrown to the floor, thanks to some judo moves Laura picked up in the USO. Rob's pride is wounded, then pummeled beyond recognition when the whole story shows up in a gossip column the next day.

Classic Guest Star: Ken Berry makes his second appearance in the series, this time in the role of the choreographer. He went on to play Captain Parmenter in *F Troop* and Sam Jones in *Mayberry, R.F.D.*

EPISODE 97

"The Ghost of A. Chantz"

Writers: Bill Persky and Sam Denoff
Director: Jerry Paris
Cast
Mr. Little: Maurice Brenner
Man: Milton Parsons
Cameraman: Edward McCready

The gang heads out to the woods for some rest and relaxation, only to find that their cabin is haunted. Go ahead, laugh! But then they start to disappear one by one. . . . This unusual episode, with its parody of *Candid Camera*, has proven to be a durable favorite with Nick at Nite fans, always ranking high on the requestometer.

EPISODE 98

"The Lady and the Baby-Sitter"

Writers: Bill Persky and Sam Denoff
Director: Jerry Paris
Cast
Man: Frank Adamo
Roger McChesney: Eddie Hodges

The Petries' baby-sitter, Roger McChesney, has a crush on Laura. When Laura tries to find out who Roger's dream girl is, she has no luck. Laura persuades Rob to give Roger some lessons in love. Roger takes Rob's advice and writes Laura a letter about his "fruital" love for her.

Our Television Heritage: In this episode the dairy-loving Petries offer the lactose-tolerant Roger milk five times. A total of six glasses of milk are actually consumed—five by Roger and one by Rob—and milk is mentioned twelve times during the episode. Watch for the scene in which Laura and Roger discuss his crush: Roger takes a sip of his milk after each speech. There's a whole lotta sippin' goin' on.

Classic Quote
ROB: Chocolate cake is milk-cake.

For the Record: Rob was known as Rapid Robert, the Devil of Danville High. His mother tells Laura he got the epithet because he had so many girlfriends, but he really earned it because, as a pitcher, he had a great fastball.

The Adamo Watch
Frank Adamo takes on the challenging role of Man and can be seen looking supercilious in the library.

EPISODE 99

"The Vigilante Ripped My Sports Coat"

Writer: Carl Reiner
Director: Peter Baldwin

The all-time biggest Petrie-Helper feud occurs in this episode. Jerry has joined with the other neighbors to forcibly attack one man's crabgrass. Rob thinks it's trespassing, vandalism, and anarchy. The argument might have blown over, but a dinner invitation is misplaced, then mailed too late, setting up a comedy of errors that culminates in an Italian restaurant, where steam is hissing out of the ears of Rob, Millie, Jerry, and even Laura.

Classic Performance: This is a must-see episode for fans of the Mel-Buddy battles. The archnemeses really go at it, no holds barred.

EPISODE 100

"The Man from Emperor"

Writers: Carl Reiner, Bill Persky, and Sam Denoff
Director: Jerry Paris
Cast
Drew Patton: Lee Phillips
Slave Girl: Gloria Neil
Coffee Girl: Nadia Sanders
Florence: Sally Carter
Miss Finland: Tracy Butler
Masseur: Abdullah Abbas

This episode is a parody of *Playboy* and Hugh Hefner. Rob is offered a job as a humor consultant and pays a memorable visit to the offices of *Emperor* magazine. And the secretary? Man, can she type!

Classic Cameo: Abdullah Abbas also appears in episode 126.

EPISODE 101

"Romance, Roses, and Rye Bread"

Writers: Jerry Belson and Garry Marshall
Director: Jerry Paris
Cast
Bert Monker: Sid Melton
Usherette: Jeri Lou James
Actor: Frank Adamo

Sally is romanced by a secret admirer—Burt Monker, the owner of Monker's Delicatessen. As desperate as Sally is for a husband, she decides that the fact that two people are lonely doesn't mean they will be happy together.

Classic Quote
ROB: Well, I guess I'll call Laura and tell her to start dinner without me.
BUDDY: I'd better call Pickles and tell her to start fighting without me.

Classic Guest Star: Sid Melton played Alf Monroe on *Green Acres*.

The Adamo Watch
This is another of Frank's more substantial roles, as the not-really-an-actor actor plays an actor.

EPISODE 102

"4 1/2"

Writers: Jerry Belson and Garry Marshall
Director: Jerry Paris
Cast
Lyle Delp: Don Rickles

Trapped in an elevator with Don Rickles while you're pregnant? That nightmare comes true for Laura as she and Rob are stalled with Lyle Delp, a criminal who's holding them up.

EPISODE 103

"The Alan Brady Show Goes to Jail"

Writers: Bill Persky and Sam Denoff
Director: Jerry Paris
Cast
Lyle Delp: Don Rickles
Boxer Morrison: Robert Strauss
Harry Tinker: Arthur Batanides
Warden Jackson: Ken Lynch
Guard Jenkins: Allan Melvin
Ira: Vincent Barbi

While entertaining in a prison, Rob is mistaken for one of the inmates. He gets locked up with the other prisoners, who force him to tap dance and sing "Camptown Races."

For the Record: Alan Brady's name was accidentally misspelled with two *l*'s in this episode's title.

EPISODE 104

"Three Letters from One Wife"

Writers: Bill Persky and Sam Denoff
Director: Jerry Paris
Cast
Alan Brady: Carl Reiner
Miss Thomas: Valerie Yerke

By persuading Alan to do a cultural documentary program, Rob risks his job, because Alan threatens to fire him if the show is not a success. Millie comes up with a surefire plan to help Rob by writing fourteen letters from fourteen different people, praising the show and its talented writer. Unfortunately, the station preempts Alan's segment with a developing news story. Millie then frantically shows up at the Petries' home to tell Laura that she already mailed the letters.

For the Record: This was the first full frontal appearance of Alan Brady.

EPISODE 105

"It Wouldn't Hurt Them to Give Us a Raise"

Writers: Jay Burton and Ernest Chambers
Director: Peter Baldwin
Cast
Douglas Wesley: Roger C. Carmel

When they decide to demand higher salaries, Rob, Sally, and Buddy find themselves lost in the maze of corporate finance.

Classic Quote
MEL: Alan said that instead of the jokes that you wrote for him, he'd like something funny for the end of the show.
BUDDY: Why don't you just stand there and squint?

EPISODE 106

"Pink Pill and Purple Parents"

Writers: Jerry Belson and Garry Marshall
Director: Al Rafkin
Cast
Clara Petrie: Isabel Randolph
Sam Petrie: Tom Tully

Laura takes a couple of pills supplied by Millie to help calm her nerves as she prepares to meet her in-laws for the first time. The pills render her completely loopy.

For the Record: Mary Tyler Moore turns the tables on Dick Van Dyke by turning in an outlandish and hilarious physical-comedy performance.

EPISODE 107

"The Death of the Party"

Writers: Bill Persky and Sam Denoff
Director: Al Rafkin
Cast
Uncle Harold: Willard Waterman
Cousin Margaret: Jane Dulo
Cousin Grace: Patty Regan
Paul: Pitt Herbert
Frank: Frank Adamo

She told him so! Rob goes out for an early morning round of golf, and sure enough, he comes down sick on the night of a long-planned party. Reluctant to admit that Laura was right, he gamely suffers through the party, sneezing, shaking with chills, and generally being a slug. He makes it most of the way, but a game of charades does him in.

Classic Quote
ROB: The twenty-four-hour virus is not as painful as the two-week cold shoulder.

Our Television Heritage: Maybe I'm crazy, but watch the end credits of this one. Is the entire frame wiggling all around? Maybe I'm seeing things.

The Adamo Watch
Laura says, during a game of charades, "You sure the rest of you wouldn't like to play? How 'bout you, Frank?" To which Frank Adamo in old-fashioned clothes dolefully responds by shaking his head.

For the Record: In the ill-fated golf game, Rob shoots a 99, Jerry a 104. And Rob's charade is "The Canterbury Tales."

EPISODE 108

"Stretch Petrie vs. Kid Schenk"

Writers: Jerry Belson and Garry Marshall
Director: Jerry Paris
Cast
Neil Schenk: Jack Carter
Head Waiter: Albert Carrier
Bill Sampson: Peter Hobbs
First Model: Judy Taylor
Second Model: Lynn Borden
Messenger: Frank Adamo

Neil "Kid" Schenk, an opportunistic childhood chum of Rob's, comes around looking for a job in return for a favor he did for "Stretch" years ago: he got Rob his first job.

Our Television Heritage: Rob briefly imitates Art Carney's classic TV character, Ed Norton of *The Honeymooners*.

The Adamo Watch
Jack-of-all-trades Frank plays a messenger.

EPISODE 109

"The Impractical Joke"

Writers: Bill Persky and Sam Denoff
Director: Jerry Paris
Cast
Phil Franklin: Lennie Weinrib
William Handlebuck: Alvy Moore
Guest: Johnny Silver

As a prank, Buddy and some friends call Rob from a party and make him do a bunch of crazy things with his phone, such as unscrewing the earpiece and mouthpiece and talking into the metal disks. Buddy eventually confesses that he's a part of the joke, and Rob swears to get revenge. Buddy suspects a visit from an agent of the Internal Revenue Service as retaliation from Rob, but he's very, very wrong.

Classic Guest Star: Alvy Moore played Hank Kimball in *Green Acres.* This is the first of his two appearances on this series; the other is in episode 114.

EPISODE 110

"Brother, Can You Spare $2,500?"

Writers: Jerry Belson and Garry Marshall
Director: Jerry Paris
Cast
Harry Keen: Herbie Faye
First Bum: Gene Baylos
Second Bum: Tiny Brauer
Warren: Brian Nash
Cop: Larry Blake

After writing and rewriting for eleven hours, Rob comes home from the office only to realize that he left the script in Grand Central Station. The next morning he goes back to Grand Central to find the script, but has no luck. Just as Rob, Sally, and Buddy are about to give up and write a new one, Rob receives a phone call from a bum who is holding the script. Rob can't stress enough to the bum how valuable the script is to him, leading the bum to come up with a brilliant idea—holding the script ransom for $2,500.

EPISODE 111

"Stacey Petrie," Part One

Writer: Carl Reiner
Director: Jerry Paris
Cast
Stacey Petrie: Jerry Van Dyke
Dr. Lemler: Howard Wendell

Rob's brother, Stacey, arrives at the Petries' home with big news: he's finished with the army, he's moving to New York, he's opening a club in Greenwich Village called the Coffee Pot, and he's getting married. *Married?* Turns out Stacey has been writing to a girl named Julie for years, posing as a guy named James Garner, a drummer she met long ago. Stacey wants to ask Julie to marry him, but he's afraid of how she'll react to the real him. Besides, he's extremely shy. Rob sets up a date between Sally and Stacey, figuring it will help Stacey build up confidence. Stacey shows up at Sally's with a banjo on his knee, and the clumsy chaos begins.

EPISODE 112

"Stacey Petrie," Part Two

Writers: Carl Reiner, Bill Persky, and
Sam Denoff
Director: Jerry Paris
Cast
Stacey Petrie: Jerry Van Dyke
Julie Kincaid: Jane Wald
Tinker: Kendrick Huxham
Lou Temple: Herbie Faye
Willie Cooke: Carl Reiner

Stacey has gotten slapped by Julie for pretending to be James Garner, which leaves him an emotional wreck. On opening night at the Coffee Pot, Rob and Laura comfort Stacey. As the show is about to begin, Julie walks in and tells the distressed Stacey that she wants to give their relationship a chance. Delighted by the turn of events, Mr. Banjo puts on one heck of a performance, and everyone is ecstatic.

EPISODE 113

"The Redcoats Are Coming"

Writers: Bill Persky and Sam Denoff
Director: Jerry Paris
Cast
Ernie: Chad Stuart
Freddie: Jeremy Clyde
Richard Karp: Bill Beckley
Phoebe: Mollie Howerton
Janie: Wendy Wilson
Estelle: Ellie Sommers
Margie: Trudi Ames

Ernie and Freddie, the latest rock and roll sensation from England, are set to appear on *The Alan Brady Show*, but need a place to stay that no one would think of so that they can get some peace and quiet away from screaming teenaged girls. Rob refuses, but not for long, and soon enough he has two teen heartthrobs in his spare bedroom.

For the Record: Real-life folk rockers Chad and Jeremy brought their own brand of British invasion to Hollywood: appearing not only here, but also on *The Patty Duke Show, Batman,* and the western series *Laredo.*

Our Television Heritage: Listen for Rob's empathetic thoughts about how Clark Kent must have felt about being Superman.

EPISODE 114

"Boy Number One Versus Boy Number Two"

Writer: Martin Ragaway
Director: Jerry Paris
Cast
Freddie Helper: Peter Oliphant
Announcer: Colin Male

Ritchie and Freddie go dimple-to-dimple when they try out for a TV commercial. Millie and Laura, despite themselves, turn into typical stage mothers.

EPISODE 115

"The Case of the Pillow"

Writers: Bill Persky and Sam Denoff
Director: Howard Morris
Cast
Bailiff: Joel Fluellen
Wiley: Alvy Moore
Judge: Ed Begley
Man: Frank Adamo

Rob turns into Perry Mason, may it please the court, when he goes to small claims court because his pillows smell like ducks. "Isn't it true? Isn't it true?"

For the Record: It's worth noting that the bailiff in this episode is played by Joel Fluellen, but in Judge Wapner's *People's Court* Doug *Llewellyn* is not bailiff, Rusty is. Or maybe it's not worth noting, but there you go.

Classic Guest Star: Alvy Moore played the memorable Hank Kimball on *Green Acres*. This was his second *Dick Van Dyke Show* appearance.

The Adamo Watch
Which "man" is he? Watch and decide for yourself.

Our Television Heritage: This episode is based on an experience of writer Bill Persky. There is no record of whether Persky was granted relief by the court.

EPISODE 116

"Young Man with a Shoehorn"

Writers: Jerry Belson and Garry Marshall
Director: Jerry Paris
Cast
Sexy Girl: Larue Farlow
Lou Sorrell: Lou Jacobi
Sid: Milton Frome
Laughing Woman: Amzie Strickland
Customer: Jane Dulo

Buddy is singing Mel's praises, calling him "a prince among men." Why? Because Mel brings tidings of great bucks—a big bonus for some writing Alan Brady is using on a network special. Buddy and Rob invest their money in Uncle Lou Sorrell's shoe store, but after they alienate the star

salesman, they end up spending a Saturday afternoon as amateur shoe clerks.

Classic Quote
ROB: The whole world needs underwear.

EPISODE 117

"Girls Will Be Boys"

Writers: Jerry Belson and Garry Marshall
Director: Jerry Paris
Cast
Doris Darwell: Doris Singleton
Ogden Darwell: Bernard Fox
Priscilla Darwell: Tracy Stratford

Ritchie comes home from school with a black eye. When Laura asks Ritchie who beat him up, he responds, "Priscilla Darwell!" Rob and Laura try to reason with Mr. and Mrs. Darwell, but they don't believe their daughter hit Ritchie. Rob and Laura decide to give Ritchie permission to hit Priscilla back. Ritchie comes home and reports that Priscilla hit him in the throat, so he kissed her. Why did Ritchie kiss her? Because every day Priscilla has threatened Ritchie, "kiss me, or I'll hit ya." When Ritchie kissed her, she told him he kisses "dopey"—but at last he's off the hook.

Classic Guest Star: Bernard Fox went on to play Dr. Bombay on the color episodes of *Bewitched.*

EPISODE 118

"Bupkis"

Writers: Bill Persky and Sam Denoff
Director: Lee Phillips
Cast
Buzzy Potter: Robert Hall
Secretary: Patty Regan
Songwriter: Tim Herbert
Mr. Doldan: Charlie Dugdale
Frank "Sticks" Mandalay: Greg Morris

There's a new hit song on the radio called "Bupkis." Not only does Rob like it, but he wrote it—years ago. It seems an old army buddy has taken the liberty of publishing their old songs without sharing the credit.

Our Television Heritage: Rob is in the office and calls himself a jerk, which leads to the following dialogue that recalls many previous episodes:

BUDDY: The first time you said you were a jerk, you broke your tooth biting into a soft chicken sandwich [episode 43], and then another time you were hypnotized and every time a bell rang you acted like you were drunk [37].
SALLY: What about the time you ended up in the hospital after you wrestled with a stuffed monkey [96]?
ROB: What about when I left my only copy of the script in Grand Central Station [110]?
BUDDY: Yeah! And what about—
ROB: That's enough. I think we've proven what I am.

EPISODE 119

"Your Home Sweet Home Is My Home"

Writers: Howard Ostroff and Joan Darling
Director: Lee Phillips
Cast
Bert Steele: Eddie Ryder
Jack Parkly: Stanley Adams

This episode is a flashback to when the Petries and the Helpers tried to buy the same house in New Rochelle. At one point Laura suggests moving to Aloha Street in a Hawaiian-theme housing complex, to which Rob responds, "I don't know, honey. Our New England furniture in a Hawaiian house? I'd feel like a missionary."

EPISODE 120

"Not Now, Anthony Stone"

Writer: Joseph C. Cavella
Director: Jerry Paris
Cast
Anthony Stone: Richard Angarola
Delivery Man: Frank Adamo
Waiter: Bob Hoffman

Sally meets her new boyfriend, Anthony Stone, while on a Caribbean vacation. He's tall, rich, and handsome, but Sally refuses to discuss him. Rob and Buddy are curious, so they begin to investigate who this Tony really is. Sally confesses to Laura at lunch that she doesn't want anyone to know about Tony because he's a mortician and she's afraid of how people will react. Meanwhile, Rob and Buddy call Tony's home and find that he's married.

The Adamo Watch
Frank Adamo returns to his roots as a delivery man–messenger in this episode.

EPISODE 121

"Never Bathe on Saturday"

Writer: Carl Reiner
Director: Jerry Paris
Cast
Bellboy: Bill Idelson
Maid: Kathleen Freeman
Waiter: Johnny Silver
Detective: Bernard Fox
Engineer: Arthur Malet

While on a second honeymoon with Rob, Laura gets her toe stuck in the bathtub spout while "playing with the drip." Getting her out becomes a comedy of errors culminating when Rob—wearing a painted mustache and holding hotel security at bay—shoots the lock off the door.

Our Television Heritage: Unlike many series, *The Dick Van Dyke Show* seemed to gain steam after only its first hundred episodes. This episode kicks off a string of four great episodes, and still to come are such classics as number 128.

Awards: The script for this episode was nominated for an Emmy in 1964–1965.

EPISODE 122

"100 Terrible Hours"

Writers: Bill Persky and Sam Denoff
Director: Theodore J. Flicker
Cast
Alan Brady: Carl Reiner
Waring: Dabbs Greer
William Van Buren: Fred Clark
Arley Chambers: Howard Wendell
Photographer: Johnny Silver
Dr. Gage: Harry Stanton
Dr. Adamo: Frank Adamo

This story is a flashback to the time just before Rob's interview with Alan Brady, when he pulled a publicity stunt by hosting a radio show for one hundred straight hours.

The Adamo Watch
Who else could have played the role of Dr. Adamo?

EPISODE 123

"A Show of Hands"

Writer: Joseph C. Cavella
Director: Theodore J. Flicker
Cast
Roger Johnson: Joel Fluellen
Joe Clark: Henry Scott
Delivery Man: Herkie Styles

While Rob is being forced to take Alan Brady's place at an awards dinner, Laura is making Ritchie a "thundercloud" costume. As a result of a series of surprisingly typical sitcom events, Rob's hands and Laura's are indelibly dyed black. Watch Laura's face when she realizes that the awards dinner is being held by the CIU—the Committee for Interracial Understanding.

Classic Quote
BUDDY: You know why they named him Mel? Because they couldn't spell "bleagch!"

The Adamo Watch
Frank Adamo can be seen briefly, sitting on the far right in the front row during the first few moments of the dinner.

EPISODE 124
"Baby Fat"

Writers: Jerry Belson and Garry Marshall
Director: Jerry Paris
Cast
Alan Brady: Carl Reiner
Lionel Dann: Sandy Kenyon
H. W. Yates: Strother Martin
Buck Brown: Richard Erdman

Rob shows surprising gumption in this episode—considering how spineless he is when facing Alan Brady in later episodes, such as the one in which Mel is fired—as he helps Alan out by doing some punch-up writing for a play. At first Rob does the work out of fear, but as Alan tries to hide Rob's identity, introducing him to others as his tailor, Rob starts to bristle.

Favorite: Of Carl Reiner, who felt this was one of his best acting turns on the show, and of Vince Waldron, author of *The Official Dick Van Dyke Show Book,* who says it "easily ranks among the show's very best—if most frequently overlooked—efforts."

EPISODE 125
"Br-room, Br-room"

Writers: Dale McRaven and Carl Kleinschmitt
Director: Jerry Paris
Cast
Counter Man: Johnny Silver
Jolly: Jimmy Murphy
Mouse: Bob Random
Gus: Carl Reindel
Doris: Linda Marshall
Policeman: Sandy Kenyon

In a minor midlife crisis, Rob gives in to temptation and buys himself a motorcycle. Sally presents him with a "Robby Baby" leather jacket, and Rob is all set to be arrested as a joyriding gang member.

For the Record: The second "Calvada" in-joke appears on a billboard during the exterior sequence.

Awards: This script won the Writers Guild award for Best Episodic Comedy of 1965.

EPISODE 126
"There's No Sale like Wholesale"

Writers: Jerry Belson and Garry Marshall
Director: Jerry Paris
Cast
Nunzio Vallani: Lou Krugman
Opal Levinger: Jane Dulo
Emil: Peter Brocco
Mr. Garnett: A. G. Vitanza
Angelo: Abdulla Abbas

Rob and Laura are celebrating the "No Holiday in Particular Holiday." Once a year, for no reason, they buy each other a nice gift. This year Laura wants a South American nutrient-dyed raccoon fur coat that costs $500. Buddy offers to get the coat for Rob wholesale, which he does, but Laura has to pick it up in Forest Hills, Long Island, and pretend that she is Nunzio Vallani's wife. She carries off the deception, but when she gets the coat home, she finds that it's way too big and the wrong style. Rob tells Buddy, and Buddy angrily snatches the coat, vowing to settle things once and for all. He comes back with the right size and right style, and Laura is overjoyed. Rob asks Buddy how he did it. He fesses up to buying the coat retail—at full price.

For the Record: This was the final show to air as part of the fourth season.

Awards: By now Emmy Awards for this series were old news, but they were nonetheless appreciated. The show won one, Dick Van Dyke won a performer's award, and Carl Reiner was nominated for the script "Never Bathe on Saturday."

EPISODE 127

"A Farewell to Writing"

Writers: Fred Freeman and Lawrence J. Cohen
Director: Jerry Paris
Cast
Horace: Guy Raymond

Rob sets out to rise above mundane sketch writing and become an "author," but when he faces that great task, he develops a bad case of writer's block.

For the Record: Ann Morgan Guilbert met guest star Guy Raymond for the first time during the filming of this episode. After falling out of touch, the two later met again and were married.

Carl Reiner himself has taken time out from his film and television work to write novels (see Box, below).

Carl Reiner: Author

In 1995, Carl Reiner published his latest novel, *Continue Laughing*. His first novel, *Enter Laughing*, was written during the same period when he was writing the first thirteen episodes of *The Dick Van Dyke Show*. The introduction to that novel follows:

The young man that you will meet in this book decides to become an actor in the seventeenth year of his life. I too decided to become an actor at the same tender age. The reasons I became an actor have never been clear to me and until they do become clear I shall never attempt to write an autobiography. The young man in this book knows why he is becoming an actor. It was easy for him to find out. I invented him and I told him why.

In other words, David Kokolovitz is a fictitious character. I strongly believe that I am not. All the characters described in this novel are not real. Only their fears, anxieties, hopes and other emotions are—at least I hope they will seem so to the reader.

Carl Reiner. Fire Island, August 11, 1957

EPISODE 128

"Coast-to-Coast Big Mouth"

Writers: Bill Persky and Sam Denoff
Director: Jerry Paris
Cast
Alan Brady: Carl Reiner
Johnny Patrick: Dick Curtis

In one of the best-loved episodes in the series, Laura gets tricked by a fast-talking TV host and blurts out that Alan Brady wears a toupee. This had not been public information, and given Brady's temper, Rob fears for his very job. Fearfully, Laura sets out to undo the damage by calling on Brady. He proceeds to bawl her out, but in the end, decides to forgive and forget—almost.

Our Television Heritage: A snippet of this episode—the beginning of the classic scene in which Alan Brady tells his toupees that they are all out of work—was recently seen on the big screen in the Robin Williams vehicle *Mrs. Doubtfire.* The children in the film insist to their new nanny that they *always* get to watch *The Dick Van Dyke Show.* The film is more or less an over-produced sitcom itself, climaxing with the hoary formula of the main character hopping between two tables at a restaurant. All in all, you're better off watching Alan Brady and Laura Petrie.

Favorite: Of writers Persky and Denoff.

Award: This was an Emmy winning script.

Parallel Plot: See episode 48, "Ray Murdock's X-Ray."

EPISODE 129

"Uhny Uftz"

Writers: Dale McRaven and Carl Kleinschmitt
Director: Jerry Paris
Cast
Hugo: Karl Lukas
Lady: Madge Blake
Dr. Phil Ridley: Ross Elliott
Karl: John Mylong

When the writers have to work late, Sally yawns, Buddy can only manage his lamest Mel-insult ever ("Mel, you're very bald"), and Rob sees a flying saucer. The problem is that the answer to Rob's question, "Am I Crazy?" is "No, you're in a sitcom." As far as sci-fi episodes, this is no "Walnut."

For the Record: The sound of the water cooler burping was provided by vocal maestro Carl Reiner. The name of the pill Rob takes to stay awake is Nervy Dervy.

Classic Guest Stars: Madge Blake, who played Batman's aunt Harriet, does an amusing walk-on as a nutty lady. Ross Elliott returns as Phil, the psychiatrist with whom Rob takes the train, although Phil now has a different last name—it was Nevins in episode 82.

EPISODE 130

"The Ugliest Dog in the World"

Writers: Bill Persky and Sam Denoff
Director: Lee Philips
Cast
Rex Spaulding: Billy De Wolfe
Mrs. Spaulding: Florence Halop
Mr. Berkowitz: George Tyne
Mack: Michael Conrad
Customer: Barbara Dodd

Rob and Laura do their darndest to find a permanent home for an ugly mutt from the dog pound.

Awards: This script was nominated for an Emmy but lost to another Persky-Denoff script, "Coast-to-Coast Big Mouth," episode 128. The dynamic writing duo was responsible for two of the three scripts nominated in 1965–1966; the third was "Mr. Big," the very first episode of *Get Smart*, written by Buck Henry and Mel Brooks.

Parallel Plot: See episode 7, "The Unwelcome House Guest."

EPISODE 131

"No Rice at My Wedding"

Writers: Jerry Belson and Garry Marshall
Director: Lee Philips
Cast
Humphrey Dundee: Johnny Silver
Sam Pomerantz: Allan Melvin
Clark Rice: Van Williams
Heckler: Bert Remsen

Two plot staples of the show, the flashback and jealousy, come together when the Petries recall how Rob nearly lost Laura to Clark Rice in their courtship days back at Camp Crowder.

Classic Guest Star: Van Williams was the star of TV's *The Green Hornet*.

EPISODE 132

"Draw Me a Pear"

Writers: Art Baer and Ben Joelson
Director: Jerry Paris
Cast
Valerie Ware: Ina Balin
Agnes: Jody Gilbert
Doris: Dorothy Neumann
Missy: Jackie Joseph
Sebastian: Frank Adamo

Rob and Laura enroll together in an art class, and the beautiful instructor, Valerie Ware, has designs on Rob. She schemes to change the day and time of the art class, making it impossible for Rob to attend but possible for her to offer him private lessons.

For the Record: The caricature of Laura Petrie was drawn by Dick Van Dyke.

The Adamo Watch
As Sebastian, Frank Adamo plays another student.

EPISODE 133

"The Great Petrie Fortune"

Writers: Ernest Chambers and Jay Burton
Director: Jerry Paris

Cast

Hezekiah: Dick Van Dyke
Luthuella: Elvia Allman
Alfred: Herb Vigran
Rebecca: Amzie Strickland
Ezra: Howard Wendell
Leland Ferguson: Dan Tobin
Ike Balinger: Tiny Brauer
Mr. Harlow: Forrest Lewis

Uncle Hezekiah, one of Rob's aged relatives, dies and bequeaths to his favorite nephew an old desk and a mysterious film of a song-and-dance act that seems to be some sort of clue. Eventually, Rob and Laura unravel the mystery.

Parallel Plot: Dick Van Dyke played a similar dual role in *Mary Poppins,* starring as Bert, the spry chimneysweep, but also taking on the role of the ancient banker.

EPISODE 134

"Odd but True"

Writers: Jerry Belson and Garry Marshall
Director: Jerry Paris

Cast

Potato Man: David Fresco
Lady: Hope Summers
Upside-Down Man: Bert May
Tetlow: James Millhollin

While Rob is napping, Freddie Helper and Ritchie play connect-the-dots on his bare back and notice that his freckles form an almost perfect outline of the Liberty Bell. Millie persuades them to submit this strange fact to a believe-it-or-not outfit, where they meet some very strange people.

EPISODE 135

"Viva Petrie"

Writer: John Whedon
Director: Jerry Paris

Cast

Manuel: Joby Baker
Doctor: Jack Bernardi

Remember Maria, the maid from episode 73? Well, a so-called friend of hers named Manuel, a bullfighter, arrives at the Petries' home, paints half of the garage, fails to kill a spider, cooks a mean paella, and breaks Rob's rib during a mock bullfight. The entire plot is more or less an excuse to get Rob into a matador outfit for some physical comedy—especially the classic picador scene.

EPISODE 136

"Go Tell the Birds and the Bees"

Writer: Rick Mittleman
Director: Jerry Paris

Cast

Dr. Gormsley: Peter Hobbs
Miss Reshovsky: Alberta Nelson

Where do babies come from? It's simple. "When a mommy and a daddy want a baby, they put a silver dollar under their pillow before they go to sleep. When it's gone, that means Mr. Cabbage has visited. He takes it to Esmeralda, the Queen Tomato, and in front of the other vegetables (three broccolis and a radish), Esmeralda plants the seed and says Starlight, star bright, we're gonna grow a baby tonight." When Ritchie spins a few fantastic stories for his friends, his parents wind up in the school psychologist's office; then Rob is forced to tell his son where babies really come from. If you don't know, tune in!

EPISODE 137

"Body and Sol"

Writers: Dale McRaven and Carl Kleinschmitt
Director: Jerry Paris
Cast
Sol Pomerantz: Allan Melvin
Referee: Garry Marshall
Bernie Stern: Michael Conrad
Norma: Barbara Dodd
Captain Worwick: Ed Peck
Boom Boom Bailey: Paul Stader

In this flashback episode, Rob's dilemma is whether to picnic with his girl, Laura, or—as "Pitter Patter"—to fight for his outfit's honor against Boom Boom Bailey. The boxing scenes are sadly unrealistic when compared to Tony Danza's fights on *Taxi*—especially the final blow to Boom Boom's appendix. However, Rob's duck walk is a classic piece of physical comedy.

Classic Guest Star: The late Michael Conrad may now be best known for his Emmy-winning performance as Sergeant Esterhaus on *Hill Street Blues*.

Classic Cameo: Writer Garry Marshall appears briefly as the referee.

EPISODE 138

"See Rob Write, Write Rob, Write"

Writers: Lawrence J. Cohen and Fred Freeman
Director: Jerry Paris
Cast
Lenny Burns: John McGiver
Kid: Casey Morgan
Secretary: Barbara Dodd

Laura decides to write a children's story, with high hopes of getting it published. She and Rob then become literary rivals when Rob tries to offer her his professional help.

EPISODE 139

"You're Under Arrest"

Writer: Joseph C. Cavella
Director: Jerry Paris
Cast
Man: Tiny Brauer
Norton: Philip Pine
Cox: Sandy Kenyon
Policeman: Ed McCready
Taxey: Johnny Silver
Mrs. Fieldhouse: Bella Bruck
Bartender: Lee Krieger

After a major tiff with Laura, Rob goes out to cool off. His evening quickly gets complicated when the police accuse Rob of taking part in a barroom brawl in which an elderly lady was struck. Unfortunately, Rob's alibi is highly suspect.

Classic Quote
ROB *(to Laura, who is feigning sleep):* Honey, you're up. You've got a swinging lamp and a hot television set.

EPISODE 140

"Fifty-Two Forty-Five or Work"

Writer: Rick Mittleman
Director: Jerry Paris
Cast
Johnson: Al Ward
Dawn McCracken: Reta Shaw
Truck Driver: John Chulay
Herbie Finkel: John Hausner
Brumley: Dabbs Greer
Joe Galardi: James Frawley

In a flashback, Rob remembers the time when *The Alan Brady Show* was on hiatus for the summer and he was forced to take a job writing copy for an electronics catalog to support himself and his pregnant wife.

Classic Cameo: Assistant Director John Chulay steps in as the truck driver. For the whole Chulay story, see episode 78.

EPISODE 141

"Who Stole My Watch?"

Writer: Joseph Bonaduce
Director: Jerry Paris
Cast
Mr. Evans: Milton Frome

Rob's watch is missing, and he suspects his friends. Naturally, they aren't too happy with this lack of trust. The result is the usual hemming and hawing, accusations and shock, and relatively happy ending.

For the Record: Carl Reiner was off making a movie, and this was the one show shot in his absence that he thought was a mistake. He just didn't believe that Rob could genuinely suspect his friends. It does seem that the premise has become a hackneyed sitcom plot device.

EPISODE 142

"Bad Reception in Albany"

Writers: Jerry Belson and Garry Marshall
Director: Jerry Paris
Cast
Forrest Gilley: Tom D'Andrea
Bartender: Bert Remsen
Fred: Joseph Mell
Sam: John Haymer
Wendell: Robert Nichols
Sugar: Chanin Hale
Chambermaid: Bella Bruck
Edabeth: Lorraine Bendix
Organist: Joyce Wellington
Lou: Tiny Brauer

Rob and Laura go to Albany to attend a wedding. In accordance with Alan Brady's orders, Rob must first watch a televised fashion show to scout out possible new talent for the show. But the TV set in his room breaks, forcing him to go on a wild-goose chase in search of a functioning TV set in the hotel.

EPISODE 143

"I Do Not Choose to Run"

Writers: Dale McRaven and Carl Kleinschmitt
Director: Jerry Paris
Cast
Bill Schermerhorn: Arte Johnson
Voter: Peter Brocco
Doug: George Tyne
Mr. Howard: Philip Ober
John Gerber: Howard Wendell

Rob gets talked into running for city council in this first episode of a two-part story.

Classic Guest Star: Arte Johnson is perhaps best known for saying "Very interesting . . . but stupid" on *Rowan and Martin's Laugh-in.*

EPISODE 144

"The Making of a Councilman"

Writers: Dale McRaven and Carl Kleinschmitt
Director: Jerry Paris
Cast
Lincoln Goodheart: Wally Cox
Martha Goodheart: Lia Waggner
Doug: George Tyne
Mrs. Birdwell: Margaret Muse
First Lady: Kay Stewart
Second Lady: Holly Harris
Third Lady: Marilyn Hare
Herb: Arthur Adams
Samantha: Lorna Thayer
Duke: Remo Pisani
Booth: James Henaghan Jr.

Rob campaigns successfully for a seat on the city council, but he's racked with guilt when he sees that his charisma and considerably greater height are preventing people from seeing that his opponent is eminently more qualified to fill the office.

Classic Guest Stars: Wally Cox was the star of the popular early sitcom *Mr. Peepers.*

Lia Waggner played William Schallert's wife when they guest-starred in episode 21.

EPISODE 145

"The Curse of the People"

Writers: Dale McRaven and Carl Kleinschmitt
Director: Jerry Paris
Cast
Sam: Tom Tully
Clara: Isabel Randolph
Jeweler: Leon Belasco

The heirloom pin, a garish facsimile of the map of the United States, is handed down to Laura, who promptly drops it in the garbage disposal—the subconscious at work.

Parallel Plot: See episode 13, "Empress Carlotta's Necklace."

EPISODE 146

"The Bottom of Mel Cooley's Heart"

Writer: John Whedon
Director: Jerry Paris
Cast
Alan Brady: Carl Reiner

Mel is having a rough time with Alan Brady, and Rob, Buddy, and Sally think he should learn to stand up to his boss. To build up his courage, they take Mel to lunch, during which Buddy tries to resist throwing out stray insults. Mel summons courage all right, but from a bottle, and when he returns to the office, he tells Alan exactly what he thinks and is promptly fired. Then Rob and the others have to get Mel his job back.

EPISODE 147

"Remember the Alimony"

Writers: Dale McRaven and Carl Kleinschmitt
Director: Jerry Paris
Cast
Sol: Allan Melvin
Bernie: Lee Krieger
Gonzales: Don Diamond
Juan: Bernie Kopell
Maxine: Shelah Hackett

During a rained-out cookout, Rob and Laura recount the story of how they ended up getting a divorce—or at least acquiring the unexecuted papers—during a three-day vacation in Mexico.

Classic Guest Star: Bernie Kopell, as Juan, tries to sell them the divorce, having gone to the trouble of writing it up.

EPISODE 148

"Dear Sally Rogers"

Writer: Ronald Axe
Director: Richard Erdman
Cast
Herman Glimsher: Bill Idelson
Stevie Parsons: Dick Schaal
Announcer: Bert Remsen

Remember "The Piña Colada Song"? Well, perhaps the songwriter was thinking of this episode, in which Sally advertises for a husband on *The Stevie Parsons Show*. She does it just for laughs, but she receives bundles of proposals, including one from the mysterious Box 7030, which turns out to belong to Herman Glimsher.

Classic Guest Star: Dick Schaal is the same Richard Schaal who played Chuckles the Clown on *The Mary Tyler Moore Show* and went on to play Dr. Sandler on *Trapper John, M.D.* He plays Stevie Parsons in the style of Johnny Carson, though without slavishly imitating him. Interestingly, Johnny Carson was originally considered for the role of Rob Petrie.

EPISODE 149

"Buddy Sorrell— Man and Boy"

Writers: Ben Joelson and Art Baer
Director: Richard Erdman
Cast
Dorothy: Pippa Scott
Cantor: Arthur Ross Jones
Leon: Ed Peck
David: Sheldon Golub

It may be hard to believe until you've seen it, but this is a sentimental Buddy episode. The wisecracking joke scribe is hiding something from his fellow writers, and they fear the worst—that he's having an affair. Poor Pickles. But Buddy isn't carrying a torch—he's carrying a Torah.

EPISODE 150

"Long Night's Journey into Day"

Writers: Jerry Belson and Garry Marshall
Director: Jerry Paris
Cast
Artie: Ogden Talbot

Rob and Jerry are away on a fishing trip, leaving Laura, Millie, and a Mynah bird alone for the weekend. Listening to every little sound in the dark of night, they give themselves a serious case of the heebie jeebies.

For the Record: As originally conceived, this story would have left Laura completely alone, but it seemed too strange to leave her there talking to animals and thin air, so Millie was brought in to give her a little company. The voice of the Mynah bird was provided by Carl Reiner.

Favorite: Of Ann Morgan Guilbert.

EPISODE 151

"Talk to the Snail"

Writers: Jerry Belson and Garry Marshall
Director: Jerry Paris
Cast
Claude Wilbur: Paul Winchell
Alan Brady: Carl Reiner
Doug Bedlork: Henry Gibson

Rob jumps to the conclusion that Alan Brady is going to cut him loose, so he looks for work and ends up holding a classic interview with an obnoxious snail, an interview that takes Rob almost to the point of beating up a puppet.

Classic Guest Stars: Henry Gibson, Arte Johnson, and Richard Dawson were the *Dick Van Dyke Show* guests who all went on to appear as regulars on *Laugh-in*.

Paul Winchell, best known for his own show, *Paul Winchell and Jerry Mahoney,* also guest-starred on *The Lucy Show.* Winchell was also an amateur medical inventor who patented an artificial human heart. Winchell later provided the voice of Dastardly in the cartoon show *Dastardly and Muttley.*

EPISODE 152

"A Day in the Life of Alan Brady"

Writer: Joseph Bonaduce
Director: Jerry Paris
Cast
Alan Brady: Carl Reiner
Blanche: Joyce Jameson
Hi: Lou Wills

This episode is classic Alan Brady. When the Petries plan to throw an anniversary party for the Helpers, Alan insists that Rob change the date of the party so that he and a film crew can come over and shoot his documentary. The result? The Helpers' anniversary party stars their "good friend" Alan Brady.

Classic Cameo: Assistant director John Chulay appears as a cameraman.

EPISODE 153

"Obnoxious, Offensive, Egomaniac, Etc."

Writers: Dale McRaven and Carl Kleinschmitt
Director: Jerry Paris
Cast
Alan Brady: Carl Reiner
Mac: Forrest Lewis

Rob and his writers scribble insults throughout a script for *The Alan Brady Show*. Usually they give him the version with the insults edited out, but this time they hand in the slanderous original. In trying to retrieve the script before Alan sees it, they break into his office and eventually his house.

EPISODE 154

"The Man from My Uncle"

Writers: Jerry Belson and Garry Marshall
Director: Jerry Paris
Cast
Mr. Girard: Steve Goney
Harry Bond: Godfrey Cambridge
Mr. Phillips: Biff Elliott

The FBI sets up a surveillance post in the house, and Agent Bond moves into Ritchie's room. Rob, of course, is not so secretly delighted to be participating in this secret agent stuff, accidentally snapping an infrared photo and threatening T.H.R.U.S.H.—a rare TV Land reference—over what he thinks is an inoperative walkie-talkie.

EPISODE 155

"You Ought to Be in Pictures"

Writer: Jack Winter
Director: Jerry Paris
Cast
Leslie Merkle: Michael Constantine
Lucianna: Jayne Massey
Headwaiter: Frank Adamo

Rob jumps at the opportunity to get in front of the camera, playing a writer in a film directed by his army buddy Leslie Merkle, maker of low-budget "art" films. Rob's bad acting makes for a classic scene, especially when his fingers get caught in his leading lady's hair.

Awards: This script earned the 1966 Writers Guild Award for Best Episodic Comedy.

The Adamo Watch
Frank Adamo has apparently been promoted since episode 77, in which he was just waiter.

EPISODE 156

"Love Thy Other Neighbor"

Writers: Dale McRaven and Carl Kleinschmitt
Director: Jerry Paris
Cast
Mary Jane Stagg: Sue Taylor
Fred Stagg: Joby Baker
Actor: Carl Reiner

The Staggs, two old friends of the Petries, move in next door. When Rob and Laura spend all of their free time with the Staggs, Millie and Jerry become jealous.

EPISODE 157

"The Last Chapter"

Writers: Carl Reiner, Bill Persky, and
Sam Denoff
Directors: Jerry Paris and John Rich
Cast
Alan Brady: Carl Reiner

Even this "best of" compilation episode was done with more panache than other clip shows. In a TV Land wink to reality, Rob writes his autobiography, recalling many funny moments past, and then Alan Brady decides to buy the rights and turn the book into a television series. If they had only made one more episode, we could really have come full circle, watching Rob, Laura, Buddy, and Sally watching themselves being played by other people in "The Sick Boy and the Sitter."

For the Record: This episode includes scenes from episode 34 "The Attempted Marriage," episode 19 "Where Did I Come From," and episode 64 "That's My Boy."

EPISODE 158

"The Gunslinger"

Writers: Bill Persky and Sam Denoff
Director: Jerry Paris
Cast
Alan Brady: Carl Reiner
Gun Salesman: Allan Melvin

While worrying over a Wild West sketch for Alan Brady, Rob is anesthetized for some dental work and has a whopper of a fantasy, in which the whole gang is transported into *High Noon* territory. Like the "Walnut" episode, this show is a rare melding of high concept and good writing.

For the Record: Writers Bill Persky, Sam Denoff, Jerry Belson, and Garry Marshall all put in cameos in the bar sequence in this episode. Persky and Denoff are the skeptical-looking cowboys in the beginning of the episode, Marshall is the bartender, and Belson is the poker player who gets shot by Rob.

I Dream of Jeannie

Larry Hagman and Barbara Eden play their roles perfectly, obviously having fun with the silly premise and the many opportunities for well-timed comic denials, deadpans (following one of Jeannie's stunts), and unexpected pratfalls (Hagman is surprisingly good at those). Perennial sidekick Bill Daily fits right into the mix, bringing his patented style of professional competence hidden behind nervous confusion.
—Castleman and Podrazik, *Harry and Wally's Favorite TV Shows*

The special effects are excellent and could win one of those coveted Emmy Awards.
—*Variety,* September 22, 1965

Jeannie has a delightful streak of just plain mischievousness—and this, combined with her legerdemain, not only makes life miserable for all men (Tony, Roger, Dr. Bellows)—but also makes *I Dream of Jeannie* bearable for the rest of us.
—Cleveland Amory, *TV Guide,* March 12, 1966

Jeannie is a TV success story.
—*The National Observer,* July 19, 1965

I Dream of Jeannie premiered in 1965 and has been going strong in repeat ever since it left the network in 1970.
—Susan Kings, *TV Times,* 1991

I Dream of Jeannie

on Nick at Nite

The controversy had raged for years. Finally the time had come to lay the debate to rest. Nick at Nite put the question to America: Whose powers are greater—Jeannie's or Samantha's?

I Dream of Jeannie premiered on Nick at Nite on June 6, 1994, head to head with *Bewitched*, its greatest rival. In that month, 1.4 million phone-in votes were cast, and in the end, Jeannie had lost by a margin of 58 to 42 percent. But the debate was not laid to rest. Jeannie's supporters rushed to her defense. Industry trendsetter *TV Guide* went so far as to state in its "Jeers" section,

> *To you 810,938 Nick at Nite viewers who think Samantha has more power than Jeannie. In a viewers' poll to decide which sitcom's sprite packed the most mystic muscle—Bewitched or I Dream of Jeannie—the Nick-at-nuts picked simpy Samantha by about 200,000 votes. Are you crazy? Sam didn't even have enough wattage to keep the same Darrin for the run of her show. She also received frequent paranormal assists from Endora and her TV coven. Meanwhile, bottled beauty Jeannie not only kept Major Nelson in a trance for five seasons, she wed him, kept her evil sister in check, and did it all with nothing but her crossed arms. We think Tabitha was stuffing the ballot box.*

Jeannie survived her initial setback on Nick at Nite and has become one of the network's most-watched shows. On the air, Nick at Nite's resident psychologist, Dr. Will Miller, speculated about the subconscious effect the absent belly button may have on us as viewers, while eagle-eyed members of the Nick at Nite squad found at least two instances in which the navel accidentally does show—despite the famous edict from the network that it should never be seen. Further, Nick at Nite's Jeannie's Diner song parody explained the show to new viewers, and Nick's researchers were the first to isolate and study the Major Nelson howl. In 1995, Major Healey appeared on Nick at Nite with Howard Borden of *The Bob Newhart Show.* The two men hosted an evening of their favorite episodes. Earlier that year *The Jeannie Movie* (episodes 77, 78, 79, and 80 shown consecutively) aired to great critical and viewer praise. Before long, Jeannie may in fact call for another vote.

Cast

Jeannie: Barbara Eden
Captain Anthony Nelson: Larry Hagman
Captain Roger Healey: Bill Daily
Dr. Alfred Bellows: Hayden Rorke
Amanda Bellows: Emmaline Henry
General Stone: Philip Ober
General Peterson: Barton MacLane
General Schaeffer: Vinton Hayworth
Jeannie's sister Jeannie: Barbara Eden

SERIES REGULARS

Jeannie's Mother: Florence Sundstrom
Hajii: Abraham Sofaer

EPISODE 1

"The Lady in the Bottle"

Writer: Sidney Sheldon
Director: Gene Nelson
Cast
Second Garbage Man: Joe Higgins
First Garbage Man: Richard Reeves
Melissa: Karen Sharpe
Husband: Warren Kemmerling
Wife: Patricia Scott
Lieutenant Pete Conway, USNR: Don Dubbins
Commander: Baynes Barron

The first episode in this series finds Captain Tony Nelson, an astronaut, stranded on a desert island, where he inadvertently frees a beautiful genie from a bottle. After being imprisoned for two thousand years, the grateful Jeannie is eager to please her handsome new master and insinuate herself into his life. The problem is, Tony must hide her from his fiancée, General Stone's daughter. The general—along with the suspicious Dr. Bellows, and pretty much everyone else—thinks the captain's brains have been scrambled, causing him to imagine Jeannie, "the classic fantasy."

Our Television Heritage: Larry Hagman was not the producer's first choice for Tony Nelson. He was second in line after Darren McGavin. McGavin eventually did get to work with Bill Daily, however, in the situation comedy *Small & Frye,* in which McGavin played private investigator Nick Small and Daily played Dr. Hanratty, head of the police labs.

EPISODE 2

"My Hero"

Writer: Sidney Sheldon
Director: Gene Nelson

Cast

Ali: Richard Kiel
Turhan: Peter Brocco
Jeannie's Father: Henry Corden
Princess Fatima: Pamela Curran
Woman: Magda Harout
Auctioneer: Jon Arvan
Bidder: Jeno Mate

Jeannie comes home from the market upset because a man hit her. She takes the angry Tony back to the market, not in Cocoa Beach but in ancient Persia. And Ali, who hit her two thousand years ago, is an enormous brute. In perilous Persia, Tony is chased, sold as a slave, imprisoned, whipped, almost neutered, and shackled. And what's more, he's to be married to Jeannie.

Classic Guest Star: Richard Kiel who played Jaws, the heavy in two of the James Bond movies, stars in this episode as the humongous Ali. He is the first in a long line of menacing Persian giants that will include Ted "Lurch" Cassidy (in episodes 79 and 81).

EPISODE 3

"Guess What Happened on the Way to the Moon?"

Writers: Tom Waldman and Frank Waldman
Director: Alan Rafkin

Cast

Orderly: Ron Brown
Crewman: Tom Anthony

In preparation for a flight to the moon, Tony and his pal Roger play a harsh survival game—a week in the desert with nothing but their wits and a quart of water each. Jeannie sneaks along to help her master, ruining the exercise, but not before Tony takes a bite from his walkie-talkie and Roger eats a boot.

Classic Cameo: Ron Brown later became the chairman of the Democratic Party. Just kidding.

EPISODE 4

"Jeannie and the Marriage Caper"

Writers: Tom Waldman and Frank Waldman
Director: Alan Rafkin

Cast

Grover Caldwell: John Hudson
Kato: Mako
Astronaut Cartwright: Sal Ponti
Melissa: Karen Sharpe

Tony's fiancée Melissa—a dark-haired witch whose vibrations, according to Jeannie, are all wrong—is a headstrong woman with some very definite opinions with which she feels the frazzled Tony must fall in line. Jeannie is genuinely concerned that her adorable master is making a big mistake. Melissa's cute and all, but she *is* pushy.

And when she and her father, General Stone, make decisions for Tony—such as changing his best man from Roger to an old family friend and making the honeymoon destination Honolulu instead of Jamaica, Tony himself begins to doubt the wisdom of the union. But only Jeannie can save the day. . . .

For the Record: Jeannie's sister is the worst cook in the Middle East.

EPISODE 5

"G.I. Jeannie"

Writer: William Davenport
Director: Alan Rafkin
Cast
Colonel Joe Fenton: Edmon Ryan
Lieutenant Snyder: Peg Shirley
Major Margaret Fiefield: Jane Dulo
Sergeant Pete Morgan: Bob DoQui
Corporal Lola Burns: Eileen O'Neill

Though their relationship is platonic, Jeannie can't help feeling jealous when Tony gets a gorgeous new secretary. She joins the Women's Air Force in an effort to get that position—and to keep an eye on Tony. Without using her magic powers, however, she's qualified only to bring the air force to its knees.

EPISODE 6

"Jeannie and the Murder Caper"

Writers: David Braverman and Bob Marcus
Director: Gene Nelson
Cast
General Fletcher: Lindsay Workman
Colonel Brady: Richard Webb
Mrs. Flaherty: Sandra Gould
Carson: Robert Dornan
Albert: Roy Taguchi
Young Woman: Victoria Carroll
P. J. Ferguson: David Brian
Nina Ferguson: Sharon Farrell

Tony is chosen to show off NASA to P. J. Ferguson, president of the largest aerospace firm in the country. As a bonus, Ferguson has brought with him his attractive daughter, Nina, who seems to have a crush on Tony. Later, on P. J.'s yacht, Nina plots to snag Tony, not for himself but for the firm. Jeannie blinks on board to be with Tony, but he promptly sends her home. When P. J. and Nina witness this occurrence, they jump to the conclusion that he pushed Jeannie overboard.

EPISODE 7

"Anybody Here Seen Jeannie?"

Writer: Arnold Horwitt
Director: Gene Nelson
Cast
Lieutenant George Webb: Dabney Coleman
Walter: Davis Roberts
Newscaster: Ed Stoddard

Tony will be the first American to walk in space . . . *if* Dr. Bellows deems him healthy.

There's something strange about the young captain, though, and the doctor is determined to find out what it is. Jeannie fears for Tony, engaging in such a dangerous mission. She sabotages his tests by making him run too fast on a treadmill, tampering with his heart rate, and making him extremely ticklish. Not surprisingly, the doctor is even more baffled.

Classic Guest Star: Dabney Coleman, of the cult series *Buffalo Bill,* among other projects, plays one of Tony's fellow astronauts.

For the Record: Though the statistical systems used to measure this variable are somewhat crude, we believe that the average number of times per episode—with a standard deviation of plus or minus 2—Tony says *Jeannie* is 22.

EPISODE 8
"Americanization of Jeannie"

Writer: Arnold Horwitt
Director: Gene Nelson
Cast
Armand: Steven Geray
First Woman Shopper: Mittie Lawrence
Sam: Del Moore
Second Woman Shopper: Jewell Lain
Waiter: Jacques Roux
Third Woman Shopper: Yvonne White
Driver: Bobby Johnson
Sadelia: Tania Lemani

Jeannie wants to be the perfect modern American woman—independent, self-reliant, and unpredictable. That way Tony won't take her for granted anymore. She decides that she will do no more magic tricks. Tony will do all the conjuring from now on—with his credit card.

For the Record: Tony and Jeannie go out on their first date in this episode.

EPISODE 9
"The Moving Finger"

Writers: Harry Essex and Jerry Seelen
Director: Gene Nelson
Cast
Rita Mitchell: Nancy Kovack
Ronnie: Jim Begg
Jason Huberts: David McLean
Assistant Director: Arthur Romans
Henry Tracy: Woodrow Parfrey
Bellboy: Stephen Whittaker
Sammy: Dick Balduzzi
Crane Driver: Joe Brooks

Tony has a new mission as a consultant on an astronaut film in Hollywood. Never one to be left behind, Jeannie mails herself to her master. Then, jealous that he is going on a lunch date with a glamorous movie star, she deduces that if she were a movie star, Tony would take *her* on a lunch date. She lands a screen test and does surprisingly well, only to discover that genies don't show up on film.

Jeannie Logical?
If Jeannie can nod herself through time and space, why does she have to use the U.S. Postal Service to get to Hollywood?

EPISODE 10

"Djinn and Water"

Writer: Mary C. McCall Jr.
Director: Gene Nelson
Cast
Bilejik: J. Carroll Naish

Tony's latest project is learning how to turn seawater into fresh water. The ever-helpful Jeannie conjures up her scurrilous great-grandfather, Bilejik (beh-lay'-jzek), who will reveal the secret—if the price is right. Tony's hand are full, between bargaining with Bilejik, keeping Bilejik from trying to swipe things, avoiding the snooping Dr. Bellows, and trying not to get run over by a car controlled by Jeannie.

EPISODE 11

"Whatever Became of Baby Custer?"

Writers: Austin and Irma Kalish
Director: Gene Nelson
Cast
Major Jamison: Herbert Voland
Policeman: Arthur Adams
Mrs. Jamison: Grace Albertson
Custer: Billy Mumy

Tony and Jeannie relax in the sun, levitating five feet above the patio. Unfortunately for them, Custer, the kid next door, bursts in on them, then tells his parents. Major Jamison, annoyed with his son's wild imagination, brings the boy to Dr. Bellows, who eagerly agrees to help Custer, especially once he learns that Tony Nelson is involved. Custer and Dr. Bellows harass Tony to the point of near exhaustion, and when Custer fails to show up at home, the major accuses Jeannie of making him disappear. Meanwhile, eight-year-old Custer is certain that Jeannie is a genie, prompting Dr. Bellows to put more pressure on Tony.

Classic Guest Star: In answer to the title question, actor Billy Mumy, who played Custer, was in *Lost in Space*. In fact, when this episode first aired, Mumy, as Will Robinson, and the rest were also on the air.

EPISODE 12

"Where'd You Go-Go?"

Writers: Austin and Irma Kalish
Director: Gene Nelson
Cast
Sergeant: Don Mitchell
Maître d': Bruno Della Santina
Diane: Elizabeth MacRae

Feeling unappreciated when Diane, an old flame of Tony's, stops by, Jeannie embarrasses him by yanking a chair out from under him and trying to whack Diane's head with a golf club. Then she gets a better idea: she'll date Roger to make Tony jealous. The plan works . . . a little too well. Tony's jealous all right, but meanwhile, Roger becomes completely enamored of Jeannie.

EPISODE 13

"Russian Roulette"

Writers: Arthur Alsberg and Bob Fisher
Director: E. W. Swackhamer
Cast
Posnovsky: Richard Gilden
Sonia: Arlene Martel
Sergeant: John Beck
Airline Pilot: George DeNormand
Russian: David Azar
Girl: Lael Jackson
General Barkley: Paul Reed

Jeannie agrees not to date others if Tony will agree to the same. But when she hears that Tony's to escort Sonia, a pretty Russian cosmonaut, she hides out in her bottle in Roger's coat. Later, Roger finds the bottle and gives it to Sonia. When she realizes the bottle is magic, she has no intention of giving it up. Tony pretends to return the romantic overtures of the sexy, slang-spouting Soviet in an effort to reclaim Jeannie.

EPISODE 14

"What House Across the Street?"

Writers: Arthur Alsberg and Bob Fisher
Director: Theodor Flicker
Cast
Mama: Lurene Tuttle
Minister: Walter Woolf King
General Hadley: Jack Collins
Mr. Prescott: Oliver McGowan
Mrs. Prescott: Avis Scott

Jeannie desperately wants to marry Tony. He does love her—just not enough to shake his bachelor habits. She summons her mother, who suggests she propose to Roger to provoke Tony's jealousy.

Classic Scene: Jeannie tries to impress Roger by blinking up perfect parents. "Perfect" to Jeannie means the kind you see in TV commercials, and the two she creates speak in bizarre commercial-speak. Oh, and they live in the perfect house—right on the vacant lot owned by none other than Dr. Bellows.

Parallel Plot: Let's face it. The writers of *Cheers* lifted the whole Sam and Diane shtick straight from the Tony-Jeannie scrapbook.

EPISODE 15

"Too Many Tonys"

Writer: Arnold Horwitt
Director: E. W. Swackhamer
Cast
Chaplain: Henry Hunter

Dr. Bellows tests the performance and stability of married and unmarried astronauts, arriving at one conclusion: Tony Nelson needs a wife. In response, Jeannie blinks up a voraciously romantic Tony. After meeting Jeannie and the duplicate Tony, the pleasantly surprised Bellows sets a wedding date for the following Sunday. Of course, the real Tony must now deal with the phony Tony, the happy doctor, a jilted Roger, and a marriage he doesn't want.

EPISODE 16

"Get Me to Mecca on Time"

Writers: James Allardice and Tom Adair
Director: E. W. Swackhamer
Cast
Achmed: Jamie Farr
American Husband: Owen Cunningham
First Policeman: Joseph Gillgoff
American Wife: Alice Reinhart
Englishman: Foster Brooks
Diane: Lael Jackson

Jeannie's not feeling well—she's tired, weak, unable to muster spells, and slowly disappearing! It's the Day of the Ram, and the only cure for her condition is for genie and master to make a pilgrimage to Mecca. More problems arise when Jeannie and Tony arrive in Mecca and find that the sacred spot they're searching for lies inside the walls of a closed modern building—the First National Bank of Mecca.

Classic Guest Star: Jamie Farr, who played Corporal Kingler on *M*A*S*H*, appears as a fast-talkin' Arabian wheeler-dealer.

EPISODE 17

"Richest Astronaut in the World"

Teleplay: Sidney Sheldon
Story: William Davenport
Director: E. W. Swackhamer
Cast
Italian Maid: Nadine Nardi
Maid: Gerry Lock
Helga: Britt Semand
French Maid: Danielle Beausejour

Roger accidentally summons Jeannie from her bottle, and when he regains consciousness after passing out, he finds that he is now her master. Overcome with greed, Roger takes full advantage of the genie's powers. And Tony, overcome with desperation to get her back, drops hints to Dr. Bellows about how wealthy Roger is, creating suspicion that Roger may be selling top secret information to other countries.

For the Record: Yes, you read it right—there is a character in this episode called French Maid.

EPISODE 18

"Is There an Extra Jeannie in the House?"

Writer: Charles Tannen
Director: Hal Cooper
Cast
Arnie: Bernard Fox
Sheila Bellows: Judy Carne
Myrt: Emmaline Henry

Roger abuses his genie privileges by staying out until 3:00 A.M. on a hot date. He exhausts Jeannie, angers Tony, and lands in trouble with his date's irate uncle, Dr. Bellows. More problems arise for the hapless Healey when Bellows plans to send him away for a month and Tony forbids Jeannie to help him.

For the Record: In this episode, we learn that Tony's phone number is 783-3369.

Classic Guest Stars: Judy Carne would later become the Sock-It-to-Me Girl on *Laugh-In*. She returned to this show to play herself in episode 106.

Emmaline Henry later played the recurring character of Mrs. Bellows, Dr. Bellows's wife.

British actor Bernard Fox spun plenty of his own magic as Dr. Bombay, the wacky warlock on *Bewitched*.

EPISODE 19

"Never Try to Outsmart a Jeannie"

Writer: Martin A. Ragaway
Director: Herb Wallerstein
Cast
Clerk: Peter Brocco
Danny: Orville Sherman
Mollie: Ila Briton
Ethel: Lenore Kingston

Jeannie attempts every trick in the book to accompany Tony on a three-week cruise to Rome. Travel by ocean is just too dangerous—after all, that's how she ended up stranded on the island. Besides, it would be very romantic to go as a woman instead of crammed into her bottle. Tony sets the rules, though, telling her she can join him only if she obtains a passport without using her magic—no easy feat for a two-thousand-year-old Babylonian.

Jeannie-Logical?
Yeah, but how hard would it really be—even without magic—to whip up some fake documents and get a passport?

EPISODE 20

"My Master, the Doctor"

Writer: Sidney Sheldon
Director: Hal Cooper
Cast
Susan: Maureen McCormick
Big Charlie: Peter Leeds
Stranger: Julio Medina
Julia: Jane Dulo
First Nurse: Elaine Nelson
Intern: Don Larson
Second Nurse: Carol O'Leary

Tony, forgetting how annoyingly literal Jeannie can be, blurts out his secret wish to become a doctor. He's then stunned to realize that's he's suddenly been transported to an operating room where he's about to perform an appendectomy. Of course, he's no more stunned than his patient, Roger, who doesn't want to die at his friend's hands.

Classic Guest Star: Maureen McCormick played Marcia, Marcia, Marcia on *The Brady Bunch*.

EPISODE 21

"Jeannie and the Kidnap Caper"

Writer: Sidney Sheldon
Director: Hal Cooper
Cast
Chan: James Hong
Wong: Richard Loo
Princess: Linda Ho

With Jeannie constantly waiting on him, life for Tony has become too cushy. He makes her solemnly swear not to help him anymore—no matter what. So it's tough luck, Charlie, when he's captured by Communist Chinese spies who threaten to kill him. Meanwhile, Dr. Bellows, receiving updates from a frantic Roger on Tony's predicament, is convinced he's finally cornered the kooky captains concocting a caper.

EPISODE 22

"How Lucky Can You Get?"

Writer: Sidney Sheldon
Director: Claudio Guzman
Cast
Mr. Phillips: Ted De Corsia
Blackjack Dealer: Buddy Lewis
Croupier: Tim Herbert
Pit Boss: Paul Hahn

The two newly promoted majors are heading for Reno, and Roger wants to know why Jeannie can't come to fix the games. Tony, of course, says, "No way." Roger sneaks her with him anyway, and, boy, is he excited about making some big bucks. In Reno, Roger loses several games, even with Jeannie's help, until he realizes that she doesn't know how to play. He gives Tony money to play for him, and Tony starts winning big with every roll of the dice. Everyone is happy—except the security guard, who hauls Tony away on suspicion of cheating when he rolls double sevens.

For the Record: This historic episode marks the promotion of both Tony and Roger from captain to major.

Roger's air force serial number is AF69244296 (the same number backwards or forward).

EPISODE 23

"Watch the Birdie"

Writer: Sidney Sheldon
Director: Hal Cooper
Cast
Admiral Tugwell: Ray Teal
Golf Pro: Jerry Barber
Commander Davis: Herbert Anderson
Captain Baxter: Gene Boland

After seeing Tony drive a ball 500 yards, General Peterson demands that Tony be his golf partner in an important game against Admiral Tugwell. Problem is, Tony can't play golf at all; Jeannie made that ball soar. Now the big dilemma is whether to let Jeannie help him play, which would be cheating, or risk a court-martial if she doesn't. Watch for Tony to use his golf club as a pool cue while his ball's in the drinking fountain.

Classic Guest Stars: This episode features Dennis the Menace's dad, Herbert Anderson, and golf pro Jerry Barber as—appropriately—a golf pro. For more on Barber and golf, see *I Love Lucy*, episode 96.

Jeannie-Logical?
Is the fact that "it would be cheating" really a sufficient reason to make the golfing decision as complicated as it is?

EPISODE 24

"Permanent House Guest"

Writer: Sidney Sheldon
Director: Hal Cooper
Cast
General Koster: Martin Ashe
Pedro: Romo Vincent
Commander Hastings: Jack Davis
Agnes: Kate Murtagh

Unsatisfied with the answer to his question "Why is there an elephant in your bedroom?" Dr. Bellows moves in with Tony to put an end to his shenanigans and to test his sanity once and for all. Jeannie's got a few tricks up her sleeve, though, to get rid of the unwanted house guest, such as conjuring up Tony's long-suffering "house maid" Patricia—in reality a fat, slovenly Parisian named Pedro, who speaks with Jeannie's voice.

EPISODE 25

"Bigger Than a Bread Box"

Writer: Sidney Sheldon
Director: Claudio Guzman
Cast
Aunt Sue: Alice Dudley
Hakim: Joseph Abdullah
Mrs. Bates: Natalie Leeb
Uncle Jeff: Lincoln Demyan
Madame Zolta: Jorja Curtright

Roger hasn't been around much lately to borrow Jeannie for one of his crazy schemes, and he piques Tony's curiosity when he claims he's got something better than Jeannie—namely the fortune-teller Madame Zolta. Certain she's a con artist, Tony agrees to participate in a séance with her to contact his deceased Uncle Jeff and Aunt Sue, knowing full well he doesn't have an Uncle Jeff or Aunt Sue. Dr. Bellows joins the group to see what the fuss is all about. And with Jeannie's help, the fortune teller "summons" a lot more than she bargained for.

Classic Cameo: Test-pilot hero and STP pitchman Chuck Yeager makes an uncredited appearance in an early scene.

EPISODE 26

"My Master, the Great Rembrandt"

Writer: Sidney Sheldon
Director: Claudio Guzman
Cast
Dean Geller: Booth Colman
Van Weesen: Jonathan Hole
Pierre Millay: E. J. Andre

Tony paints a copy of a Rembrandt for an Air Force benefit auction. Unbeknownst to him, Jeannie changes it into the original so that her master's work will sell like the Old Master's. Two art experts engage in a $300,000 bidding war when they suspect that it's the real thing, and the ever-suspicious Dr. Bellows flies in the world's foremost art expert after warning Tony that if the painting *is* an original, he's guilty of grand larceny. Of course, if he actually painted it, he's guilty of art forgery.

EPISODE 27

"My Master the Thief"

Teleplay: Sidney Sheldon
Story: Sidney Sheldon and Robert Kaufman
Director: Claudio Guzman
Cast
Alice: Kathee Francis

At a museum, Jeannie pilfers a pair of slippers from a Bukistan exhibit, claiming they were stolen from her two thousand years ago. The Bukistani government will treat the incident as a prelude to war if the slippers are not returned within twenty-four hours. Unless Tony can wrest the slippers away from the stubborn genie, he'll face the wrath of Dr. Bellows—and life in prison.

Classic Performance: Dr. Bellows eats a shoe box for General Peterson.

EPISODE 28

"This Is Murder"

Writer: Sidney Sheldon
Director: Hal Cooper
Cast
Announcer: Ivan Bonar
Turhan: Vic Tayback
Princess Tarjii: Gila Golan

Tony doesn't have to worry about Jeannie being jealous when he escorts a sultan's beautiful daughter, whose family cheated her ancestor out of his business, his camels, and his wives—he just has to stop Jeannie from killing her! To distract Jeannie for the duration of the princess's visit, Tony requests a ski chalet in the Caribbean, a pineapple plantation in Alaska, and a yacht in the Gobi Desert.

This episode explores the darker side of own-ing a genie, as Jeannie, recognizing the ruse, turns Tony into a puppy, a skunk, and ultimately a parakeet.

Classic Guest Star: Vic Tayback, who played Mel on *Alice*, makes a brief appearance as Turhan.

EPISODE 29

"My Master the Magician"

Writer: Sidney Sheldon
Director: Hal Cooper
Cast
Nestor: Chet Stratton
Cleaning Man: William Benedict
Sergeant: Don Mitchell
Specialty Act: Chester Hayes

This episode is devoted to Dr. Bellows's persis-tent claims that something is desperately strange about Tony Nelson. First he catches Jeannie and a banquet of food in Tony's office late one night. Then he finds Tony floating in a chair in his house—and demands that Tony sign a note admit-ting as much. Finally he commands Tony to per-form a magic act and float, and if he doesn't, he'll have to explain the signed confession. Either way, Tony's in a lot of trouble.

EPISODE 30

"I'll Never Forget What's-Her-Name"

Writer: Sidney Sheldon
Director: Hal Cooper
Cast
Miss Gordon: Greta Lenetska

Tony gets conked on the head by a vase, which causes amnesia—but only about Jeannie's iden-tity. He falls in love with her, mistaking her for his aunt's visiting friend, Miss Gordon. Roger believes Tony's subconscious mind has blocked her out because it has trouble accepting her, and when Tony proposes marriage to her, Roger knows he has to tell him her true identity. But Jeannie isn't willing to give up Tony's new romantic interest in her, so she removes Roger from the picture—to the South Pole, for starters.

Parallel Plot: Amnesia is, of course, TV Land's most popular neurological disorder. See also *Dick Van Dyke*, episode 70, and *The Munsters*, episode 47. *I Dream of Jeannie* used it twice! See episode 69 for the other case of this affliction.

EPISODE 31

"Happy Anniversary"

Writer: Sidney Sheldon
Director: Claudio Guzman
Cast
Operator: Arthur C. Romans
Sergeant: Donald Mitchell
Blue Djinn: Michael Ansara

It's the first anniversary of Tony's discovery of Jeannie, and she wants to spend a romantic day on the deserted isle. Tony, however, has forgotten the anniversary and is scheduled to go into orbit that morning. The miffed genie causes the astronaut to crash-land on the island. Once there, he rubs a bottle, thinking it houses Jeannie. But he accidentally unleashes the Blue Djinn, the evil genie who imprisoned Jeannie two thousand years ago, and who vows to kill whoever frees him.

For the Record: The second seasons opens in glorious color with the new cartoon opener and theme that everyone has come to know and love.

Our Television Heritage: The word "djinni," or "djinn" (sounds like "gin"), is derived from the Arabic "jinniy," meaning a spirit capable of assuming human form and wielding supernatural influence over men. But the English word "genie," derived from the French, is ultimately from the Latin "genius," meaning guardian spirit. The name Jeannie is the Scottish version of *Jane*, which in turn is the feminine form of John.

Classic Guest Star: Michael Ansara makes the first of three appearances on the series (he's also in episodes 76 and 125). At the time the episodes were filmed, he was married, in real life, to Barbara Eden.

Jeannie-Logical?
Genies can't kill the person who frees them; that's just not the way it works!

EPISODE 32

"Always on Sunday"

Writer: Sidney Sheldon
Director: Hal Cooper
Cast
Eddie: Bob Hoffman
Pancho Segura: Himself

Tony's been working too hard, so Jeannie turns the day into Sunday. To teach him relaxation, she sends him on a safari, then to play tennis. Finally, to further make her point, she stops the calendar completely. Jeannie ignores Tony's request to change his life back to normal. In a series of events that reflects sheer insanity, the borderline psychotic Tony confronts Dr. Bellows with the news that every day is Sunday.

Classic Guest Star: Pancho Segura was inducted into the professional tennis Hall of Fame in 1984.

Parallel Plot: The movie *Groundhog Day*, starring Bill Murray, has a similar plot.

EPISODE 33

"My Master the Rich Tycoon"

Writer: Sidney Sheldon
Director: Claudio Guzman
Cast
Harry Huggins: Paul Lynde

After Harry Huggins criticizes Tony's simple interior decor, a miffed Jeannie blinks up a Renoir, a Louis XIV desk, a safe filled with money, and other luxuries. Huggins *is* impressed, particularly since he's with the IRS. He threatens to have an assessor come over in the morning to check the value of the items and to throw Tony in jail as the leader of an international smuggling ring. And just so Tony doesn't try any funny stuff, the snide revenue agent announces he's going to spend the night.

Classic Guest Star: Center-square quipster Paul Lynde, of *The Hollywood Squares*, make the first of his three guest appearances on this series.

EPISODE 34

"My Master the Rainmaker"

Writer: Sidney Sheldon
Director: Claudio Guzman
Cast
Ali Habeeb: Romo Vincent
Corporal Sam: Robert F. Lyons
Sergeant Ben Roberts: Steve Ihnat

With Jeannie's powers, no feat is too big, and no task too small. No weather pattern is too wild for her to tame. So when she and Tony plan a picnic on a rainy day, Jeannie simply makes the weather sunny, reminding Tony of his snow-filled youth back in Wisconsin. To please her master, Jeannie blinks, causing snow to fall over Tony's house—just as Dr. Bellows drops by for a visit. Tony explains that the snow is part of a top-secret experiment, and the doctor is impressed. After the news spreads through NASA that Tony can control the weather, a sergeant begs him to help his brother, a farmer who desperately needs rain. For once Tony agrees that Jeannie's powers could be used for some good. She blinks up a storm for Sergeant Roberts's brother, and everyone is happy . . . until the sergeant returns with the news that the rain hasn't let up and his brother's farm has washed away.

EPISODE 35

"My Wild-Eyed Master"

Writer: Sidney Sheldon
Director: Hal Cooper
Cast
Miss Gordon: Jean Marie
Senator: Howard Wendell

Tony won't be going on the next Apollo mission because he failed an eye test due to eye strain from working too hard. Roger suggests he utilize Jeannie's power, but Tony knows only too well that her help always leads to disaster. Jeannie just can't stand seeing her master so morose, however, and after setting Roger on fire to learn why, she vows that Tony's eyes will work better than anyone else's. And she isn't kidding—during his next test, Tony sees through Dr. Bellows's clothes and then sees through the walls to a conference going on in the next room.

EPISODE 36

"What's New, Poodle Dog?"

Writer: Sidney Sheldon
Director: Hal Cooper
Cast
Mr. Wimple: Dick Wilson
Mrs. Anderson: Hazel Shermet
Mr. Asher: Norm Burton
Keith Asher: Kevin Tate

Roger comes by to finish an important report with Tony and tells Jeannie that he wants Tony to double-date with him and a couple of beauty-pageant contestants. Sure that Tony will find a pageant contestant prettier than she is, she turns Roger into a little poodle to shut him up. Tony finds the situation amusing, until he learns that the dog catcher has taken Roger away. Tony runs off to the pound to save his friend, but he doesn't know what kind of dog Roger is. Once he finds him, he runs into more trouble when Dr. Bellows catches the dog helping Tony to finish the report—one bark for yes, two for no.

Classic Quote
ROGER: Boy, I've heard of insecure genies in my life, but you're ridiculous.

Classic Guest Star: Dick Wilson, a character actor on various sitcoms (see *Bewitched,* episodes 33, 44, and 57), gained fame as Mr. Whipple, who chastised anyone who dared to squeeze the Charmin.

EPISODE 37

"Fastest Gun in the East"

Writer: Sidney Sheldon
Director: Hal Cooper
Cast
Horace: Whit Bissell
First Man: Richard Reeves
Eddie: Eddie Firestone
Bull: Hoyt Axton
Al: Fred Krone
Georgia: Stephanie Hill
Josh: Bud Perkins

As Tony watches a TV western, he unthinkingly wishes he lived back in those days. Sure enough, he suddenly finds he's marshal of Gopher Junction in the Old West. Almost immediately he's challenged to a gunfight in a saloon, where Jeannie's having a ball working as a barmaid. With her help, Tony does some fancy shootin'.

Classic Guest Star: Country singer-songwriter Hoyt Axton wrote the song "Joy to the World," which Three Dog Night turned into a major hit; his mother wrote the song "Heartbreak Hotel."

EPISODE 38

"How to Be a Genie in Ten Easy Lessons"

Writer: Sidney Sheldon
Director: Hal Cooper

Tony is at his wit's end with Jeannie. She's an incompetent, inexperienced genie, and she's driving him crazy. He plans to give her a copy of *The Arabian Nights' Entertainments* to study, but in a rare moment of insight, Roger warns him that the book will just lead to more trouble. Tony makes Jeannie swear she'll learn to do whatever the book says, unaware that the book describes how to make a master submit through torture and foul play.

EPISODE 39

"Who Needs a Green-Eyed Jeannie?"

Writer: Sidney Sheldon
Director: Hal Cooper
Cast
Two-Gun Richard: Ted DeCorsin
Joan Sheldon: Joan Patrick
Otto: Orville Sherman

Jeannie imprisons Tony in a metal cage after catching him trying to sneak out to see someone named "Charlie Suzy," a man whose name makes Jeannie thinks he is a girl. Roger tries to help, but Jeannie sends him to the top of the Empire State Building. After she realizes she was wrong, Jeannie vows never to doubt Tony again. However, it turns out the whole thing *was* a trick, set up so Tony could really go out with an old flame. Stay with us, now: Jeannie finds out about the scheme and turns the girl into a chimp. That being the final straw, Tony packs up to move out. Seeing that he is truly upset, Jeannie promises not to get involved and sends him back to the beginning of the date. What Tony doesn't know, however, is that his date is the wife of an escaped mobster who plans to kill them both.

For the Record: This episode established a new U.S. indoor record for the most plot turns jammed into a half-hour sitcom. The previous record had been held by an episode of *Car 54, Where Are You?* entitled "What Happened to Thursday?"

Classic Quote
DR. BELLOWS: Major, what are you doing in your pajamas in a jail cell in your living room?

Jeannie-Logical?
The fact that Jeannie can send Tony back in time suggests that she could use similar methods to resolve almost all of the sticky situations they get into. But of course the show would be rather dull.

EPISODE 40

"The Girl Who Never Had a Birthday," Part One

Writer: Sidney Sheldon
Director: Claudio Guzman

Jeannie informs Tony that she's never had a birthday party because no one knows when she was born. All she knows is that Neptune was in Scorpio on the day of her birth. Tony wants to rectify that situation, promising her the biggest birthday party ever, on Cocoa Beach. He enlists ERIC (Electronic Rapid Input Computer), a $5 million NASA computer, to compute Jeannie's birthday with the limited information she has. ERIC figures it out, but Dr. Bellows catches Tony and Roger playing with the computer and rips the date from Tony's hands before he can read it. Jeannie goes into a depression, and slowly begins to fade away.

EPISODE 41

"The Girl Who Never Had a Birthday," Part Two

Writer: Sidney Sheldon
Director: Claudio Guzman
Cast
Cleopatra: Diane Stanton
Sigmund Freud: Larry Gelman
Henry VIII: Jack Fife
Shakespeare: Martin Ashe
Marie Antoinette: Siri
Ben Franklin: Bart Greene
Man: Kenneth Washington

Jeannie is still fading, and she has no powers. In another attempt to discover Jeannie's birth date, Roger taps into ERIC again while Tony occupies the doctor's attention. Roger retrieves Jeannie's birth date, which makes her happy and helps her regain her powers, but Roger is shipped off to Alaska before he discloses the date. Tony appeases Jeannie by throwing a party for just the two of them, and by telling her she's "the most wonderful genie a master ever had." To liven up the party, Jeannie blinks up some of her friends, including Sigmund Freud.

Classic Guest Star: Look fast for Larry Gelman as Freud. Gelman later played Tupperman, the urologist on *The Bob Newhart Show.*

EPISODE 42

"How Do You Beat Superman?"

Writer: Sidney Sheldon
Director: Claudio Guzman
Cast
Jump Master: Julius Johnson
Radio Announcer: Fred Hessler
Tony Millionaire: Mike Road

Tony's too wrapped up in football to notice Jeannie or to take her on a picnic, so she invents a handsome, rich, successful, and suave perfect man named Tony Millionaire. Tony laughs it off, claiming he's not the jealous type. But when Jeannie informs him that, after only a couple of dates, she's engaged to marry Mr. Millionaire, Tony realizes he's lost the best girl he ever knew. After a pep talk from General Peterson—"The first rule in love or war is an all-out frontal attack"—Tony prepares to fight for the woman he loves.

EPISODE 43

"My Master the Great Caruso"

Writer: Sidney Sheldon
Director: Hal Cooper
Cast
General Brill: Arthur Peterson
Hennessy: Frank De Vol

Jeannie wants Tony to win the trophy at the NASA Talent Show, which will be televised to 30 million people, so, as a warm-up, she makes him sing in an amazing, glass-shattering tenor voice, which of course Dr. Bellows overhears. Tony makes Jeannie promise never to change his voice again, but soon word gets out around the base about his amazing voice, and everyone expects Tony to win the talent contest. The problem is, Jeannie can't break her promise to her master.

For the Record: In this episode Jeannie finally learns her birth date from Roger—after trapping him in an iron maiden. It's April 1.

Classic Guest Star: Frank De Vol was the dour orchestra leader Happy Kyne on *Fernwood 2-Night*. He also composed many classic TV theme songs, including the theme from *My Three Sons*.

Jeannie-Logical?
If Jeannie really can't break a promise the plots of many other episodes could not have happened, and Tony could very simply avoid any future disasters.

EPISODE 44

"The World's Greatest Lover"

Writer: Sidney Sheldon
Director: Hal Cooper
Cast
Evelyn: Julie Gregg
Morgan: John Milford

When Roger declines a double date with Tony and Jeannie, she suspects he's having trouble getting a date. She fixes things so that he'll never have that problem again—by making him the most desirable man in the world. His phone begins to ring off the hook, he gets no work done, and there aren't enough days in the year for him to satisfy the surge of newly smitten Roger-fanatics. Roger spreads himself pretty thin and finds himself in a bit of trouble, especially when Dr. Bellows's wife falls head over heels for him.

For the Record: This episode marks the introduction of the recurring character of Amanda Bellows, played by Emmaline Henry. Amanda's efforts to catch Tony Nelson in one of his strange predicaments make her husband's efforts seem paltry by comparison.

EPISODE 45

"Jeannie Breaks the Bank"

Writer: Sidney Sheldon
Director: Hal Cooper
Cast
Melnick: Tom Palmer
Widow: Queenie Leonard
Peterfy: Lindsay Workman
Sven: Torben Meyer

In order to buy a sailboat with Roger, Tony needs a loan from the Bank of Cocoa Beach. Jeannie's skeptical about banks, since the ones she's familiar with cut off the ears of those who can't repay their loans. The snooty bank officer is about to reject Tony's loan application for lack of collateral until Jeannie blinks $3 million into his account. Then the banker wants to give Tony anything he wants. As he leaves the bank, the loan officer discusses him with another employee, and who should overhear the conversation but Dr. Bellows? "This time," he claims, "Major Nelson won't get away with it."

Parallel Plot: Rob Petrie and Jerry Helper buy a boat together in episode 72 in *The Dick Van Dyke Show*.

EPISODE 46

"My Master the Author"

Writer: Sidney Sheldon
Director: Richard Goode
Cast
Mother: Mary Foran
Gina: Kimberly Beck
Richard: Butch Patrick

To get Jeannie off his back, Tony suggests she write a book. The prospect of penning a parenting book excites Jeannie, so aftr blinking up a pair of nerdy glasses, some paper, and a typewriter, she's set to go. When she finishes her book, *How to be a Fantastic Mother,* however, she puts Tony's name on it, figuring no one will read it anyway. Of course the book becomes a best-seller. Because it's illegal for an astronaut to publish anything without first getting clearance from NASA, Dr. Bellows devises a surefire way to prove that Tony couldn't possibly have written it: he makes Tony tame his nephew Richard, the most incorrigible child on earth, in just one evening.

Classic Quote
QUESTION POSED TO TONY: Would you explain your theory about breast-feeding?

Classic Guest Star: Butch Patrick, who plays the little monster Richard in this episode, had experience as a real Munster when he was Eddie in *The Munsters.*

Our Television Heritage: After writing this episode, Sidney Sheldon thought to himself, You know, I'll bet I could write a pretty good book. . . . Well, that may not be exactly how it happened, but one way or another, Sheldon, who had also created *The Patty Duke Show,* changed careers after creating this show and became the author of best-selling novels.

EPISODE 47

"The Greatest Invention in the World"

Writer: Sidney Sheldon
Director: Hal Cooper
Cast
Colonel Harris: William Bakewell
Groucho Marx: Himself

After all this time and Roger's begging, Tony finally caves in and allows Roger one wish from Jeannie. In his excitement, Roger spills coffee on Tony's dress shirt and blurts out that he wished he hadn't done that, thus blowing his one wish. Jeannie fixes the stain, and later Tony and Roger realize that she's rendered the shirt totally indestructible. Dr. Bellows bursts in and notices the shirt's amazing properties, so Tony and Roger claim that a can of fly spray is the shirt's secret protective formula. The doctor takes the fake miracle spray to General Peterson and ruins three of the general's uniforms. The perturbed commander in chief, fed up with the doctor's nonsense, decides to send him to Iceland, where he can annoy the Eskimos, leaving it up to Tony to save Dr. Bellows from another one of Jeannie's messes.

Classic Guest Star: The one and only Groucho Marx makes a brief appearance as himself. Harpo Marx appeared in episode 124 of *I Love Lucy.*

EPISODE 48

"My Master the Spy"

Writer: Sidney Sheldon
Director: Hal Cooper
Cast
General Alton: Byron Morrow
Aide: Davis Roberts
Professor Karr: Noah Keen
French Waiter: Larry Hall
General Jacques: Guy De Vestal
Chuck: Fred Krone
Lou: Benny Rubin
Joe: Charles Horvath

Jeannie talks Tony into going to Chez Moustache, a chic Parisian restaurant, by sending his double to a top-secret meeting at NASA. But what she doesn't count on is a French general seeing Tony in Paris and calling Dr. Bellows about it. The doctor arrives at only one conclusion: Operation Galaxy is being sabotaged, and Tony Nelson is a spy.

EPISODE 49

"You Can't Arrest Me . . ."

Writer: Sidney Sheldon
Director: Hal Cooper
Cast
Judge Hennessey: Herb Vigran
Zane: Billy M. Greene
Police Officer Don Anderson: Alan Hewitt

Tony reneges on his promise to take Jeannie for a ride, so she decides to go by herself, but she drives through a red light while going the wrong way down a one-way street. After causing a traffic jam, she innocently offers a policeman anything he wants if he'll let her go and not upset Major Nelson. The cop impounds the car.

Later, Jeannie tricks Tony into giving her driving lessons, but she makes the same mistake again. This time the cop has it in for Tony. Tony goes to the cop's house to apologize, unaware that his every word is being recorded on film and when he says he'll get the cop's nephew a model rocket, the angry cop accuses him of bribery. In court, it's up to Jeannie to set things straight.

Classic Quote:
COP: It's a one-way street.
JEANNIE: I was only going one way.

EPISODE 50

"One of Our Bottles Is Missing"

Writer: Sidney Sheldon
Director: Hal Cooper
Cast
Salvatori: Frank Puglia
Gino: Richard Lapp

While inspecting Tony's house, Amanda Bellows sees Jeannie's bottle and simply must have it. She takes it to be copied, and a peeved, homeless Jeannie takes Tony's room, shrinking him down and making him sleep in a desk drawer. The next morning, Jeannie goes to the bottle maker's shop and happily jumps into her bottle, then waits for Tony to pick her up. He does, but when she doesn't appear, the obvious mix-up occurs and Mrs. Bellows ends up with the genuine bottle—and Jeannie. Tony tries to convince Roger that when Dr. and Mrs. Bellows go out that evening, the two astronauts have to break in and retrieve Jeannie before Amanda accidentally summons her. But it's tough getting through to Roger: "Roger, what's the first thing Mrs. Bellows is going to do when she gets home?" Roger's reply: "Take off her girdle."

Classic Quote
DR. BELLOWS: Amanda, we're going to be late. That's very neurotic of you.

For the Record: One of Jeannie's all-time favorite games is the ancient sport of hubato (Ping-Pong).

EPISODE 51

"My Master the Civilian"

Writer: Sidney Sheldon
Director: Hal Cooper
Cast
Greta: Nadia Sanders
Sue: Kathleen Hughes
Aggie: Carol Worthington
Ellen: Jane Zachary
Sally: Kathleen Freeman

When four generals and three senators suggest that Tony take a position as vice president of a booster rocket manufacturing company in Columbus, Ohio, it behooves him to comply. He's not very happy about it, though, and Roger's upset with Tony for not discussing it with him first. Even Dr. Bellows is planning to retire—after all, if Tony leaves, the doctor will have no more work to do. But when Roger and Jeannie view Tony's future through a magic machine and see that his new job involves golf, two beautiful secretaries, and a massage—and that's on his *worst* day—they connive to depict the future differently for Tony. They show him a cold, cramped, dripping office with two crabby, bitter secretaries and a hectic workload.

Classic Guest Star: Oft-seen TV Land inhabitant Kathleen Freeman makes a memorable appearance in this episode as one of the crabby secretaries. She can also be seen as a crabby character in episodes 85 and 121 of *The Dick Van Dyke Show.*

For the Record: Tony's interior decorating style reflects exquisite taste and culture. Chinese character paintings on the living room wall say "winter" and "summer."

EPISODE 52

"There Goes the Best Genie I Ever Had"

Writer: Sidney Sheldon
Director: Hal Cooper
Cast
Miss Atom Bomb: Virginia Ann Ford
Miss Galaxy: Willy Koopma
Male Guest: Ron Brown

When Jeannie serves Tony his breakfast in bed and wishes him a good time on a double date with Roger and two beauty-pageant contestants (those pageant contestants again!), it doesn't take a rocket scientist to figure out that something is up. But Tony is lucky. It's Hajii Day, during which all masters who are unhappy with their genies can send them back for good. Tony tells Roger he's thinking about doing just that with Jeannie—she's a sweet girl, but she's just too much trouble. Could this be the end for Jeannie? Will Tony get rid of the girl of his dreams . . . and ours?

EPISODE 53

"The Greatest Entertainer in the World"

Writer: Sidney Sheldon
Director: Claudio Guzman
Cast
Master of Ceremonies: Bob Melvin
Charles: James J. Waters
Man in Hotel: Murphy Bennett
Mack: George Rhodes
Sammy Davis Jr.: Himself

Roger needs someone to head the entertainment committee for the party celebrating General Peterson's tenth anniversary as a general, and after much pleading from Jeannie, Roger gives the job to Tony. Tony goes to Miami to enlist the talents of the general's favorite performer, Sammy Davis Jr. Davis's manager turns Tony away because he's got a big, big gig at the Copa on the same day as the party. Tony returns and bumps into the excited general, who says he saw Sammy perform on the day he received his first star and is thrilled about his upcoming appearance at the party. Only Jeannie can save Tony's hide, make the general happy, and place Sammy in two spots at once so he can sing, baby, sing.

Classic Guest Star: Get ready to tear the rug with Sammy's fabulicious renditions of "The Girl from Ipanema" and "Black Magic."

EPISODE 54

"The Incredible Shrinking Master"

Writer: Sidney Sheldon
Director: Claudio Guzman

Tony and Roger are in the garage working on miniaturizing parts for a missile. Jeannie, always quick to lend a hand, or a blink, shrinks one of the parts for the boys. Unfortunately, she shrinks Tony along with it. Roger carries his diminutive friend into the house, where he misplaces him. Just then Dr. Bellows barges in—simultaneously letting in a hungry tabby cat who's got his eye on Tony. Slapstick abounds in this classic episode as Tony matches wits with the ferocious, roaring pussy cat and battles obstacles such as his telephone and stereo. Watch for Roger holding Dr. Bellows's hand, so he won't step on the tiny Tony.

Classic Quote:
JEANNIE: In Atlantis, we always pinch the peaches.
STORE CLERK: Look, lady, this isn't Georgia.

For the Record: If you've been trying to reach Major Nelson at 783-3369 (episode 18), note that his number has been changed. The new number is 783-7099.

EPISODE 55

"My Master the Pirate"

Writer: Sidney Sheldon
Director: Claudio Guzman

Cast

George: Joseph Perry
Fred: William Bagdad
Lady Diane: Elaine Deuvy
Captain Fenwick: Digby Wolfe
Captain Kidd: Al Wyatt

Arrggghh . . . Thar's chills, spills, and swashbuckling thrills in this action-packed episode in which Jeannie transports Tony and herself back to the age of pirates on the Spanish Main. Typically, Tony finds himself face-to-face with the infamous Captain Kidd, who immediately tries to kill him. Jeannie just giggles and watches the fun. Tony proves his mettle by sidestepping the scurrilous pirate, causing him to fall overboard. His victory makes Tony the de facto captain of Kidd's ship, but the equally scurrilous first mate soon plots to kill the skinny new skipper and take control. Things get even more complicated when Tony discovers a prisoner belowdecks—the courageous Lady Diane Nelson, who is, as it turns out, Tony's great-great-great-great-grandmother. If Tony can't save her from her imminent plank-walking, he'll cease to exist. Holy *Back to the Future!*

EPISODE 56

"A Secretary Is Not a Toy"

Writer: Sidney Sheldon
Director: Claudio Guzman

Cast

First Officer: Donald Briscoe
Susie: Eileen O'Neill
Al: Jack Mills
Amos Lincoln: Bing Russell
Second Officer: Lincoln Tate
Miss Murphy: Ila Briton
Third Officer: David Loud

Roger blurts out in front of Jeannie that General Peterson's secretary is retiring. Instantly she applies for the position so she can make Tony a general—it's embarrassing to tell all the other genies that he's only a major. She insinuates herself into the general's office, using her powers to clean the place up, read his thoughts, and predict who's calling on the phone. He just *has* to hire her—and he does. After Tony's heart palpitations slow down, he demands that Jeannie go home. Of course she refuses to leave until he's made a general. That's when Dr. Bellows becomes suspicious of the new secretary and calls in the CIA to investigate.

EPISODE 57

"There Goes the Bride"

Writer: Sidney Sheldon
Director: Larry Hagman
Cast
Clerk: Jonathan Hole
Dr. Dawson: Jack Bailey
Minister: Bill Quinn
Dr. Benson: Charles Irving
Bellboy: Larry Hall
Sue: Shirley Borme

Jeannie, who still desperately wants to marry Tony, resorts to the Spell of Laha Laba, an ancient, dangerous, and extremely powerful incantation that has never been known to fail. After procuring the necessary talismans from Tony—a lock of hair, a piece of fingernail, and a small circle of fabric from his clothing—Jeannie follows the ancient instructions and recites the chant of Laha Laba: "O great space where spirits dwell, hear thee now my magic spell. Hair and nails and cloth of loom make [fill in first and last name of subject of spell; give middle initial if any] be my groom. Ere another change of tide make [fill in first and last name of person casting spell; give middle initial if any] be my master's bride."

Tony instantly desires to marry Jeannie. But Hajii appears, citing Genie Decree 720, Paragraph 6, Subhead 3, which states that it is forbidden for any genie to cast a love spell on her master. He warns Jeannie three times that only bad will come of it, but Jeannie ignores him. Consequently Tony is in for some painful experiences: every time Jeannie blinks, Tony breaks a bone. Jeannie recants: "Laha Laba, hear my shame. Return the spell from whence it came. Listen now and listen well. Take away my master's spell."

For the Record: So far as we know, neither Jeannie nor Tony has a middle name.

Also, this is the first of three episodes directed by Larry Hagman.

EPISODE 58

"My Master, Napoleon's Buddy"

Writer: Sidney Sheldon
Director: Claudio Guzman
Cast
Josephine: Danielle Demetz
General Pichegru: Booth Colman
Napoleon: Aram Katcher

Tony's to give a lecture on military strategy during the Napoleonic Wars, and he mentions to Jeannie that Napoleon is his personal hero. Before he can say "crêpe suzette," Tony's standing in front of the Little Corporal himself. But for once, Tony is delighted! He thinks this is the greatest thing Jeannie's ever done. Realizing that he can change history, Tony tells Napoleon about certain things he hasn't done yet, and the amused emperor takes him for a fortune-teller. But when Tony advises him against attacking Russia, Napoleon decides Tony's a spy and therefore he *should* attack Russia. Oh, yes, he also plans to send Tony to the guillotine.

For the Record: It is revealed in this episode that Napoleon had his hand tucked inside his coat because his wool uniforms were itchy.

EPISODE 59

"The Birds and the Bee Bit"

Writer: Allan Devon
Director: Larry Hagman
Cast
Jeannie Junior: Lorette Strome
Tony Junior: Jimmy Jarratt
Sally: Judy Rockley

When Tony finds a book entitled *The Care and Feeding of Genie* and reads that a genie loses all power after marrying a mortal, he instantly proposes to Jeannie. She's happy, but Roger warns her that if they get married and people find out she was a genie, Tony will be fired. With the help of Hajii, Jeannie and Roger take a look into Tony's future and see how happily married they are. All's well. But what if they have kids? Again they peek into the future, where they see that while Tony Junior is a normal boy, Jeannie Junior has the power to create as much havoc as her mother ever did. Jeannie plans on going through with the marriage nonetheless. Roger plans to save the day by warning Tony, but Jeannie shackles him to a dungeon wall.

For the Record: This is the second of the three episodes directed by Larry Hagman.

EPISODE 60

"My Master the Swinging Bachelor"

Writer: Sidney Sheldon
Director: Hal Cooper
Cast
Kathryn: Bridget Hanley
Mr. Fakeling: Woodrow Parfrey

Amanda Bellows snoops through her husband's files and finds that Tony has gained three pounds.

Since no bachelor ever gains weight, she and Dr. Bellows invite themselves over for dinner to discover what's up. Tony schemes to get rid of Jeannie so that he can invite a more "normal" date to dinner, but when Jeannie finds out, she sabotages the date's cooking and ruins the meal. She also inadvertently creates a cake that makes everyone revert to childhood—and they end up playing jacks and post office. Tony's got some explaining to do when Amanda has a piece of the cake analyzed the next day and makes a startling discovery: an unidentifiable ingredient in the cake is the cure for old age.

Jeannie-Logical?
Those wacky scientists. Curing the common cold is beyond them, but they can quickly identify a previously unheard of chemical and establish that it has a seemingly impossible power within a few hours? Who knew our nation's cake-analysis research had come so far?

EPISODE 61

"The Mod Party"

Writer: Peggy Chantler Dick
Director: Claudio Guzman
Cast
Captain Yardley: Dabney Coleman
First Girl: Hilarie Thompson
Saleslady: Cathleen Cordell
Porky: Hollis Morrison

Roger throws a wowie-zowie mod party, but first, to get out of Dr. Bellows's boring meeting, he and Tony tell the doc they're going hunting. Meanwhile, coincidentally enough, Amanda Bellows overhears Jeannie tell someone that Majors Healey and Nelson are having a mod party.

The many classic moments at this get-together include Roger playing the bass, Roger and Tony wearing Roman togas, Tony displaying his striped underwear, Dr. Bellows analyzing a hippie, and a hippie analyzing Amanda Bellows!

Classic Guest Stars: Dabney Coleman returns! And hippie girl Hilarie Thompson will soon be promoted to the role of General Schaeffer's hippie daughter Suzie.

EPISODE 62

"Fly Me to the Moon"

Writer: Robert Marcus
Director: Hal Cooper
Cast
General Whitfield: Parley Baer
Receptionist: Judy Page
Beautician: Howard Morton
Sam: Larry Storch

Under Dr. Bellows's supervision, Tony and Roger begin a special mission to send Sam, a chimp, into space. A bored Jeannie appears, and just for fun she turns Sam into a human being. Once Tony and Roger recover from their initial shock, they try to persuade Sam to become a chimp again and return to Dr. Bellows. But Sam, like any self-respecting monkey, only wants to smoke cigars and party. When Tony finally gets in touch with Jeannie, her cooperative blink misfires and changes Tony into a monkey instead. So Dr. Bellows prepares to send Tony the chimp into outer space.

Classic Guest Star: Larry Storch, one of the stars of *F Troop*, turns in a convincing performance as Sam the chimp.

Parley Baer also appeared in episode 63 of *Bewitched*.

Our Television Heritage: Could naming the chimp Sam have been a not-so-subtle dig at *Betwitched?* The two shows were highly competitive. The *Bewitched* staff always felt that the latecomer *Jeannie* had stolen their act and made it tawdrier. As if to reinforce this theory, *Jeannie*'s staff stole the special-effects supervisor away from *Bewitched*.

EPISODE 63

"Jeannie or the Tiger"

Writer: James Henerson
Director: Hal Cooper

It's been two hundred years since Jeannie's sister—who, like all her sisters, is also named Jeannie—has paid her a visit. When she does, she tricks her naive sister into her bottle and plans to steal Tony away. Roger comes by and discovers Jeannie trapped, but before he can help, the bad Jeannie blinks him to the North Pole. Then she takes Tony out for dinner and dancing all night in Brazil. Roger returns to warn Tony and is sent back to the frigid north. Tony finally figures out that this aggressive new Jeannie is not *his* Jeannie, and he tricks *her* into the bottle. But Roger returns again and, thinking Jeannie is Jeannie, releases Jeannie. They're both out! And a spectacular Jeannie vs. Jeannie battle ensues, with Tony as the grand prize.

For the Record: This is our first meeting with Jeannie's sultry and duplicitous dark-haired sister, played, of course, by Barbara Eden in a mesmerizing dual role.

EPISODE 64

"Second Greatest Con Artist in the World"

Writer: Allan Devon
Director: Claudio Guzman
Cast
Eddie: Hal Cooper
Second Reporter: Wayne Harada
Realtor: James Davis
Vanderhaven: Fred Clark
Manager: Yankee Chang
Copter Pilot: Herb Jeffries
First Reporter: Bert Darr
Charlie: Milton Berle

Milton Berle—Mr. Television—plays Charlie, a two-bit crook in Hawaii employed as the servant to the world's richest man, Mr. Vanderhaven. After seeing a photo of Jeannie wearing a genuine King Tut scarab pin worth half a million dollars, he comes up with a brilliant scheme to get Jeannie to give the scarab to him. Charlie convinces Jeannie that he is Mr. Vanderhaven and shows her his closed-off miracle beach, where diamonds get washed up onto the sand. He gives the beach to her in return for the scarab. When Tony tells her there are no diamonds in Hawaii, Jeannie admits, "I have really done it this time, have I not, master?" But as Tony has learned many times before, and as Charlie soon finds out, it's not wise to trick Jeannie.

Classic Cameo: *Jeannie* director Hal Cooper plays the dim-witted chauffeur, Eddie.

Classic Guest Star: Uncle Miltie defined television comedy in the early years. In the 1960s he appeared in dozens of Classic TV shows, including *The Lucy Show, Get Smart, F Troop,* and *Batman.*

For the Record: Yes, he does see Jeannie's photograph in the paper. Apparently, the fact that she cannot be photographed is somewhat negotiable, especially when it might help further the plot.

EPISODE 65

"My Turned-On Master"

Writer: Dennis Whitcomb
Director: Hal Cooper

In a truly classic episode, Jeannie promises to transfer her powers for twenty-four hours to someone else if Tony will let her come along to a big reception. Little does Tony know that he is the someone else. So when he says, "We're really up to our ears in paperwork," the figurative expression becomes a literal reality. Naturally, Tony knows it's somehow Jeannie's doing. But the real excitement begins when Dr. Bellows demands that Tony discuss his troubles. At that point Tony accidentally and unwittingly passes the powers on to Dr. Bellows!

Classic Cameo: Director Hal Cooper is on a roll, appearing in a second straight episode, this time in an unbilled cameo as a house painter.

Parallel Plot: *Bewitched* also came up with a memorable episode by utilizing the old transfer-the-powers trick. In episode 17, Darrin gets Sam's powers and goes a little nuts.

I Dream of Jeannie

EPISODE 66

"My Master the Weakling"

Writer: Ron Friedman
Director: Claudio Guzman
Cast
Orderly: David Soul
General Powlett: Harry Harvey Sr.
Officer: Robert Pickering
Kiski: Don Rickles
Jump Master: Carl Byrd

Maniacal physical trainer Commander "Killer" Kiski deems Tony and Roger weaklings and vows to teach them to survive—even if it kills them. After delivering lengthy verbal abuse, making them run ten miles, and putting them through three hours of special exercises, Kiski informs the exhausted majors that with the next day comes the *hard stuff*. Physical comedy abounds as the boys run uphill in jackets filled with 150 pounds of sand, and then Jeannie forces the stumbling, beaten, half-asleep duo to go dancing. Angered at Kiski for his cruelty, Jeannie changes his personality to that of his sweet old aunt Effie. The reformed officer brightens his tent with chintz, has the beleagured pair engage in painting bunnies, and enforces proper etiquette when they jump from a plane.

Classic Guest Stars: The foul-mouthed Kiski is played by the inimitable Don Rickles. Perhaps this episode was the inspiration for his later show, *C.P.O. Sharkey.*

Classic Cameo: Look sharp for a young Starskey-less Hutch: David Soul appears in a minor role.

EPISODE 67

"Jeannie, the Hip Hippie"

Writer: Christopher Golato
Director: Hal Cooper
Cast
Steve Davis: Phil Spector
The Boyce & Hart Group: Themselves

For his first vacation in years Tony plans a camping trip with Jeannie, only to learn that he must first help Amanda Bellows find a mod music group for her charity bazaar. Jeannie has a simple solution—she blinks in four young men and creates the moddest, hippest, fabbest group this side of the Beat—er, that is—the Monkees. Jeannie becomes so overwhelmed with the Boyce & Hart Group's success that she forgets all about Tony's trip and focuses on the group's upcoming tour.

Classic Guest Stars: Pop music producer Phil Spector plays himself, but is credited, oddly enough, as having played "Steve Davis."

Tommy Boyce and Bobby Hart were one of the top songwriting duos of the rock-and-roll era, penning, among other things, many of the Monkees' hits. The other two members of the Boyce & Hart Group are William Lewis and Steve O'Reilly.

In the scene in which Boyce & Hart come to audition for Spector, listen for an actual Boyce & Hart recording, "Love Everything," playing in the background in his office, apparently as an inside joke for rock aficionados.

EPISODE 68

"Everybody's a Movie Star"

Writer: Mark Rowane
Director: Claudio Guzman
Cast
Technician: Larry Vincent
Soundman: David Loud
Allen Kerr: Paul Lynde

When snobby Hollywood movie director Allen Kerr comes to Cocoa Beach to film a day in the life of an average astronaut, he sees potential in the handsome Tony, who, of course, wants nothing to do with his venture. Roger, however, sees an opportunity to make it big. Filming begins in Tony's home, and scene after scene is ruined by Roger. Kerr tells Dr. Bellows that Roger is king of the clods, but he wants to make Tony a star. Roger overhears this conversation and thinks they're talking about him. So when Roger shows up the next day with leather jacket, cigar, sunglasses, and inflated ego, someone has to tell him that he's the world's worst actor.

Classic Guest Star: This episode features another quality performance by Paul Lynde. His other two Jeannie appearances are in episodes 33 and 81.

Classic Quote
KERR: Why are all the little people always frustrating me?

Parallel Plot: In episode 20 of *Taxi*, guest star Martin Mull wants to make Alex a star of his movie, while everyone except Alex is clamoring to be in it.

Also worth comparing: Rob as the world's worst actor in episode 155 of *The Dick Van Dyke Show*, "You Ought to be in Pictures."

EPISODE 69

"Who Are You Calling a Genie?"

Writer: Marty Roth
Director: Hal Cooper
Cast
First Nurse: Corinne Camacho
Campbell: Arthur Adams
Dr. Breckinridge: Chet Stratton
Harley Z. Pool: Richard Deacon

While Jeannie is visiting NASA to annoy Tony with trivia, Dr. Bellows knocks her out with an enthusiastically opened door. From out of nowhere comes sleazy attorney Harley Z. Pool, claiming to represent Jeannie and demanding $3 million for the poor girl who's become a victim of space age technology. Tony and Roger race to the hospital to find that Jeannie has no recollection of who or, more importantly, *what* she is. Tony tries to convince her that she is a genie. When Dr. Bellows recognizes Jeannie, Tony tells her to blink him back to his house, but instead she turns him into a mouse that's heading for Mars on a space probe.

Parallel Plot: In this episode, the writers go to the amnesia well again. See episode 30 for Tony's case.

Classic Guest Star: Richard Deacon played Mel, the Buddy-hating producer of the *Alan Brady Show* on *The Dick Van Dyke Show.*

EPISODE 70

"Meet My Master's Mother"

Writer: Marlene Fanta Shyer
Director: Claudio Guzman
Cast
Mother: Spring Byington

Tony's loving but overprotective mother arrives unexpectedly from Bridgeport and is appalled at her son's bad haircut and at how thin he is. And at the dust in his house. And that the only thing in the fridge is ice. Seething, Jeannie feels personally insulted. After all, it's her responsibility to make sure her master is well fed, clean, and pampered, and no one, not even his mother, is going to tell her she is not doing her job well. Of course, Tony and Jeannie are in for an even bigger surprise when Mother announces that she'll stay on permanently since her son needs so much help.

Jeannie-Logical?

When Jeannie blinks sequined makeup onto Tony's mother's face, he explains that it was caused by "the atmospheric conditions combined with the creptactic light sequentials"—an explanation she readily accepts.

EPISODE 71

"Here Comes Bootsie Nightingale"

Writer: Paul West
Director: Hal Cooper
Cast
Bootsie Nightingale: Carol Wayne
Sam: Jesse White

Amanda Bellows asks for Tony's and Roger's help in preparing for a benefit ball at the hospital. They gladly agree to help, especially when they find out that Tony will escort the glamorous movie star Bootsie Nightingale. Meanwhile, Bootsie's manager plots the biggest publicity stunt of his career: at the ball, Bootsie will propose marriage to one of the astronauts. When Jeannie spies the blond bimbo all over her master, she transforms his voice into a mouselike squeak. Fickle Bootsie drops him and "falls in love" with Roger.

Classic Quote:

BOOTSIE: I just get chills thinking about all those planets you to go—Mars and Juniper . . .

EPISODE 72

"Tony's Wife"

Writer: Christopher Golato
Director: Claudio Guzman
Cast
Helen Wheeler: Shannon Farnon

Jeannie's sister warns her that she must leave Tony and stay in Baghdad for sixteen years becuase she was born under the sign of the Jinx and disaster will come to her master. When Tony complains of the bad luck he's been having, Jeannie is certain her sister is right. Loving and thoughtful to the very end, Jeannie does something that utterly confounds Tony: she fixes him up on a date.

EPISODE 73

"Jeannie and the Bank Robbery"

Teleplay: Seaman Jacobs, Fred Fox, and James Henerson
Story: Seaman Jacobs and Fred Fox
Director: Larry Hagman

Cast

Conway: Vince Howard
Mother: Sue Taylor
Mr. Walsingham: Allen Davis
Milton: Severn Darden
Bank Teller: Geoff Edwards
Girard: Mike Mazurki

With only three days to finish an important report, Tony needs no distractions. To get Jeannie out of his hair, he suggests she help someone else for a change. So she does just that. When she overhears two men talking in the park, she borrows Tony's car and helps them "get" money from the Cocoa Beach State Bank, whose mean bankers won't give them any money. Soon a police inspector visits Tony, wanting to know why his car was seen driving away from the scene of the robbery. So much for getting rid of distractions.

For the Record: This episode was the last of Larry Hagman's three directorial efforts on this series.

EPISODE 74

"My Son the Genie"

Writer: Bill Richmond
Director: Claudio Guzman

Cast

Pinter: Sheldon Allman
Photographer: Mousie Garner
Interviewer: Sal Ponti
Harold: Bob Denver

Jeannie prepares Tony to expect a visit, as every genie-in-training must spend one day with an experienced genie. That said, the klutzy apprentice genie comes bursting through the fireplace. He's Harold, the first son of Hajii himself, so no amount of yelling is going to get rid of him. And if that isn't enough, the president of the United States is coming to Tony's house to congratulate him on his latest space success, and Harold insists on cooking the dinner.

Classic Guest Star: Bob Denver secured his niche in TV land first as Maynard G. Krebs on *The Many Loves of Dobie Gillis* and then, of course, as the inimitable Gilligan on *Gilligan's Island*, but his guest-starring roles are few. Enjoy.

For the Record: Two guest characters named Harold and Pinter? Coincidence? Homage? One thing's for sure—the dialogue in the episode cannot be described as Pinteresque. The teleplay was written by Bill Richmond, who co-wrote the screenplays for such Jerry Lewis classics as *The Nutty Professor* and *The Ladies' Man*.

EPISODE 75

"Jeannie Goes to Honolulu"

Writer: Mark Rowane
Director: Claudio Guzman
Cast
Doris: Lee Saltonstall
The Aliis: Themselves
First Nightclub Patron: Natalie Leeb
Don Ho: Himself
Second Nightclub Patron: Frances Gordon
Eleanor: Brenda Benet

Tony and Roger trick Jeannie into believing they're going on a survival mission to North Pole, but they actually go to beautiful Hawaii. Once she finds out, Jeannie blinks her way to Waikiki Beach, where she humiliates Tony by draping him in a fur parka that he can't take off. (Of course Amanda and Dr. Bellows are there to witness this little stunt.) To get Jeannie off his back, Tony tells her that the pretty girl he's with is a princess whom he must protect from Robolkian the Deadly, who's really singing sensation Don Ho.

Classic Guest Star: Watch Hawaiian star Don Ho croon the Presleyesque "It Ain't No Picnic," then slide right into the mellow "Beautiful Days of My Youth," complete with MTV-style video of Ho walking through Hawaii with the young version of himself. Ho also guest-starred in the three-part *Brady Bunch* vacation epic.

Our Television Heritage: During the beach scenes, feel free to enjoy the sight of Larry Hagman's belly button along with the belly buttons of female extras. But note that Barbara Eden's banned navel remains under wraps in a one-piece maillot swimsuit.

EPISODE 76

"Battle of Waikiki"

Writer: Marty Roth
Director: Hal Cooper
Cast
Native: Theodore Nobriga
Customer: Pat Meible
General: Marc Towers
King Kamehameha: Michael Ansara

While sight-seeing in Hawaii, Tony is impressed with the history of King Kamehameha, and he wishes he could have met him. *Blink.* Jeannie makes the supreme Hawaiian monarch appear, and though she's skeptical about the strong, somewhat angry king, Tony wants him to stay and learn about modern civilization. Jeannie and Tony spend most of their time running after the king, who isn't too crazy about progress. He incites the locals to attack a luau (attended by Dr. Bellows and other top NASA brass) in an effort to win back the independence of the Hawaiian Islands.

Classic Cameo: Michael Ansara directed episode 138. He appears as Biff Jellico in episode 125.

EPISODE 77

"Genie, Genie, Who's Got the Genie?" Part One

Writer: James Henerson
Director: Claudio Guzman
Cast
Stewart: Dennis Cooney
Joe: Jack Donner
Bartender: Joseph Perry
The Professor: Edward Andrews
Congressman Widdicomb: Jack Smith
Charlie: Lou Antonio
Mike: Sidney Clute

Roger accidentally locks Jeannie in a safe filled with astronaut survival gear that's to be launched to the moon the following morning. Unable to get the combination code from an angry Dr. Bellows, Tony learns that no one else knows the code, and if anyone tries to get into the safe, it will explode. Desperate, Tony and Roger enlist the hired help of the Professor and Charlie, two professional safecrackers, but when the yeggs see how frantic the majors are, they decide to steal the safe for themselves, since whatever's inside must be of incredible value.

Jeannie-Logical?
When you're launching something into space, it's always a good idea to add a lot of unnecessary explosives as a security precaution, no?

And why can't Jeannie just blink her way out of that safe?

EPISODE 78

"Genie, Genie, Who's Got the Genie?" Part Two

Writer: James Henerson
Director: Claudio Guzman
Cast
Annie: Reta Shaw
Charles Fries: Ned Wertimer
Stewart: Dennis Cooney
The Professor: Edward Andrews
Miss Temple: Susan Howard
Charlie: Lou Antonio
Bartender: Joseph Perry

Follow the bouncing safe. Fortunately, Roger switches the Jeannie-filled safe with a dummy safe before the launch. Unfortunately, the Professor and Charlie steal the Jeannie-safe. They're too scared to risk being blown to itty bits, so they pawn it. Seeing the safe's markings, the pawnbroker calls NASA, but Dr. Bellows thinks the call is a prank, so the safe is sent to a scrap yard to be crushed. Believing they've lost Jeannie forever, Tony and Roger drown their sorrows in milk. Then the owner of the scrap yard calls NASA, and this time Dr. Bellows gets suspicious, which isn't too hard for him. Roger overhears the phone conversation and tells Tony, who runs to the scrap yard with flowers just in time for the doctor to witness him telling the safe he loves it.

EPISODE 79

"Genie, Genie, Who's Got the Genie?" Part Three

Writer: James Henerson
Director: Hal Cooper
Cast
Bronze Vendor: Al Dennis
Astronaut Arland: Mike Farrell
Silk Vendor: William Bagdad
Harem Girl: Debbie Wong
Habib: Ted Cassidy

Jeannie's wicked sister is only too happy to find Jeannie locked in a safe—now she can pursue Tony with no distractions. She switches work orders so Tony will be sent to the Middle East, and once she and the major arrive in Baghdad, the sneaky brunette makes short work of his resistance by shrinking him and trapping him in a birdcage. Roger goes to rescue Tony, and in no time he too is confined in the birdcage. But soon Habib, the wicked sister's gigantic master, arrives and is angry to find the astronauts in his harem tent. After a comical battle in which Tony inflicts more damage to himself than to Habib, he convinces the giant that his own genie brought them there, and Habib makes the wicked Jeannie send them back.

Classic Guest Stars: Mike Farrell, soon to play B. J. Hunnicut on *M*A*S*H*, appears briefly.
You will undoubtedly recognize Ted Cassidy as Lurch on *The Addams Family*. Watch the caged astronauts chirping and tweeting for him.

EPISODE 80

"Genie, Genie, Who's Got the Genie?" Part Four

Writer: James Henerson
Director: Hal Cooper
Cast
Dr. Wedermeyer: Benny Rubin
Joe: Ron Masak
Gas Station Attendant: William Fawcett

This is the exciting conclusion of this four-part story. After being trapped in the safe for four weeks, Jeannie informs Tony that if she remains locked up during a full moon, whoever frees her will be her new master. Dr. Bellows is having a specialist come from Washington with the code to open the safe. So while Roger tries to stall the specialist, Tony has to disguise the safe as an ice-cream cart, steal it from NASA, somehow open it, and hope that it doesn't blow up in his living room with Jeannie inside. Whew! What a conclusion!

EPISODE 81

"Please, Don't Feed the Astronauts"

Writer: Ron Friedman
Director: Hal Cooper
Cast
Commander Porter: Paul Lynde
Harem Girl: Sally Ann Richards
Nurse Lugosi: Hazel Shermet
Hamid: Ted Cassidy

Paul Lynde is back yet again, this time as snooty Commander Porter, who has a bone to pick with NASA. He vows to push Roger and Tony until they break on a five-day survival mission on Skull Island (didn't Don Rickles already do this?), where they will subsist on berries, bugs, and his expertise. Jeannie helps her master by conjuring up a nice big chicken—thirty feet tall. The commander, thinking he's hallucinating, wanders into a friendly native village, courtesy of Jeannie, complete with tents, women, and Jeannie's humongous cousin Hamid—who then plans to kill Porter for desecrating his harem.

Classic Quote:

HAMID: Now if you will excuse me, I must cut your friend to ribbons.

Classic Guest Star: This is Paul Lynde's third and final appearance on this series.

Our Television Heritage: The giant chicken has a grand tradition as a Classic TV concept. The earliest giant chicken is in a *Dobie Gillis* episode entitled "The Chicken from Outer Space."

EPISODE 82

"My Master the Ghostbreaker"

Writer: Christopher Golato
Director: Hal Cooper
Cast
Sir Widgin Willingham: Ronald Long
Chauncy: Leslie Randall
James Ashley: Jack Carter

A late great-uncle bequeaths to Tony a three-hundred-year-old mansion in England, and the estate representative invites Tony, Jeannie, and Roger to visit. Once there, they are greeted by a creepy butler and discover the mansion is an even creepier dump. All through the night the three are kept awake by ghoulish screams, rattling chains, demonic laughter, and other assorted bumps in the dark. Roger and Jeannie are terrified, certain the place is haunted. However, when an arrogant Brit comes by the next day claiming that they are

in *his* house, Tony believes there are no ghosts—just a big rat named Ashley.

Classic Quote:

TONY: Oh, Roger, what kind of a coward are you?
ROGER: I don't know. What kind of cowards are there?

Parallel Plot: Every *Scooby-Doo* ever made.

EPISODE 83

"Divorce, Genie Style"

Writer: James Henerson
Director: Hal Cooper
Cast
Mr. Murdock: Woodrow Parfrey

Tony reminisces about an evening spent at the Bellows home enjoying Amanda's fine cooking and wonderful housekeeping. A jealous Jeannie jumps to the conclusion that he finds her inferior because she resorts to blinking up whatever Tony wants. To prove otherwise, she summons Hajii to take her powers away and make her mortal. But when Amanda unexpectedly drops by and discovers the harem-costumed young woman trying to be a good housewife, sleeping on the couch, and calling Tony "master," she assumes that the two are married and angrily vows to help Jeannie get what she really needs—a divorce.

EPISODE 84

"My Double-Crossing Master"

Writer: Mark Rowane
Director: Hal Cooper

Upset about his most recent romantic disaster, Roger says he hates all women, that they can't be trusted. He bets Tony fifty dollars that if another guy came along, Jeannie would be disloyal to him. Tony, who doesn't believe all women are untrustworthy, especially not his loving Jeannie, disguises himself as a dashing British officer to test her loyalty. When Jeannie seems smitten and even lies about living with her old uncle, Tony is miffed. Meanwhile, Dr. Bellows, mistaking Tony for the English psychologist he's to meet with, wants to discuss the British breakthroughs in—appropriately enough—schizophrenia.

Parallel Plot: Episode 32 of *The Dick Van Dyke Show* is an elegant variation on the old disguised-to-see-if-she's-loyal plot.

EPISODE 85

"Have You Ever Had a Genie Hate You?"

Writer: Allan Devon
Director: Claudio Guzman
Cast
Gigi: Carole Williams
Spanish Girl: Jan Sherman

Jeannie calling Tony a son of a misbegotten jackal? Only after her devilish sister arrives bearing gifts: a white bottle of lazantium seed lotion to make Tony love his Jeannie forever, and a blue bottle to make her hate his enemies. Then the evil Jeannie switches the bottles on her naive sister, who soon begins to hate Tony with a passion hitherto unheard of. The mere sound of the poor confused master's voice drives her to fitful rages that make her do some pretty rotten things to him, like roasting him in the oven and placing his head in a guillotine. Roger absentmindedly splashes the other lotion on himself, and to his utter joy Tony's Jeannie falls madly in love with him, proclaiming that she is now *his* genie.

EPISODE 86

"Operation: First Couple on the Moon"

Writer: Arthur Julian
Director: Claudio Guzman
Cast
Dr. Swanson: Kay Reynolds
Turk: William Smith

Jeannie is none too happy about the possibility of Tony going to the moon with the ridiculously beautiful Dr. Swanson. Her devious sister Jeannie oh-so-graciously helps by rigging the physical tests so that Swanson will lose out to her! Unless the good Jeannie does something, her master is going to spend three months in a small isolation bubble with her Tony-hungry sister, who plans to skip the moon and head for Venus—a really swinging planet.

EPISODE 87

"Haven't I Seen Me Someplace Before?"

Writer: Marty Roth
Director: Claudio Guzman
Cast
Girl: Pat Delaney
Nurse Fromkis: B. B. Boland
Maître d': Steve Vincent

For Roger's birthday, Jeannie grants him one wish, and Roger blurts out that he would like to trade places with Tony, who's leading the Trailblazer Project. Sure enough, they switch bodies, and Roger—well, er, Tony—and Jeannie must find Tony—that is, Roger—so that Roger-Tony can rescind his birthday wish before Dr. Bellows—who is still Dr. Bellows—finds out about the switch.

Classic Quote:

TONY: Jeannie, what's Major Healey's reflection doing in my mirror?

Our Television Heritage: Who hasn't wanted to see Roger act like Tony and Tony act like Roger? Or wished to hear Roger's voice come out of Tony's mouth? This classic episode offers both a unique premise and a fascinating study of the two characters. Look for Larry Hagman doing his version of Bill Daily's trademark body language, including the nervous hands-on-chest maneuver.

EPISODE 88

"U.F.Oh Jeannie"

Writer: Marty Roth
Director: Hal Cooper
Cast
Paw: J. Pat O'Malley
Clem: William Bassett
Maw: Kathleen Freeman
Daisy Lou: Lisa Gaye

Tony and Roger test an experimental UFOish aircraft high in the Floridian sky. Jeannie pops in with peanut butter and jelly sandwiches for them to enjoy. Despite Roger's pleas—he's hungry—Tony orders her to go home, but her weight throws off the machine's calibration, forcing them to land far off course. When they leave the capsule, the two friends are accosted by a family of hillbillies, who, thinking they're Martians, plan to kill them.

Classic Quote:

MAW: Don't touch them or you'll be corntaminated too.

Classic Guest Stars: J. Pat O'Malley played Rob Petrie's father in various episodes, and Kathleen Freeman played the maid in the hotel in which Laura suffered her infamous toe-spout mishap (episode 121).

EPISODE 89

"Jeannie and the Wild Pipchicks"

Writer: James Henerson
Director: Claudio Guzman
Cast
Colonel Finch: Reta Shaw

Via flying carpet, Jeannie's mother sends her favorite candy, pipchicks. When Tony eats one of the delicious candies, he finds that it gives him superhuman strength. Dr. Bellows scarfs down a pipchick and, to his astonishment, lifts a 300-pound coffee machine. Dr. Bellows wants Tony to disclose the ingredients of the candy, as it could be the solution to the astronaut capsule food problem. Tony begs Jeannie's mother for the ingredients, but she's none too fond of him. Instead, she delivers a new batch of pipchicks, which contain a secret ingredient that releases inhibitions. Practically every character ingests one of these pipchicks, resulting in drug-induced chaos.

Classic Quote:

DR. BELLOWS: Cats don't shrink. They only *look* shrunk when they're wet.

EPISODE 90

"Tomorrow is Not Another Day"

Writer: Bruce Howard
Director: Hal Cooper
Cast
Commander Ross: Stewart Bradley
Sam: Roosevelt Grier
First Tout: Herbie Faye
Corporal: Xavier Nash
Second Tout: Johnny Silver

There's no morning paper today for Jeannie to give her master. Roger suggests she blink one up, mistakenly telling her the date is the seventeenth. Roger grabs the sports section and leaves before Tony realizes that the date is the sixteenth, which means Jeannie conjured the next day's paper. When they read the headline, "Astronaut Breaks Leg in Accident," Tony and Jeannie set out to find Roger and warn him that one of them will get hurt—*and* to stop him from using the paper to cheat at the racetrack.

Classic Scene: Jeannie, fearing for Tony's safety, uses her powers to make him run in slow motion.

Classic Quote:
ROGER: (Discussing the broken leg to come): Tony, I'd like to say it's me instead of you.
TONY: Thanks, Rog.
ROGER: But I can't. I hope it's you instead of me.

EPISODE 91

"Abdullah"

Writer: Marty Roth
Director: Claudio Guzman
Cast
Frank: Jack Riley
Woman in Park: Ila Britton
Maternity Nurse: Margie Hall
Burly Nurse: Jane Dulo
Sally: Sheryl Formberg

Jeannie is caring for her baby nephew for a week, and Tony's not too pleased. Little Abdullah keeps them up with his incessant crying, and Tony must hold the cute li'l Persian peanut all night long. The next morning, Jeannie leaves unexpectedly for the day, and Roger lies to Dr. Bellows, telling him Tony's sick. When the doctor finds that the exhausted Tony really is sick, that leaves the teeny genie in the uncertain hands of Mr. Bachelor himself—Roger.

Classic Guest Star: Jack Riley plays Mr. Carson, an expectant father with a name similar to that of Mr. Carlin, the abrasive neurotic he played on *The Bob Newhart Show.*

EPISODE 92

"The Used Car Salesman"

Writer: James Henerson
Director: Hal Cooper
Cast
Policeman: Henry Beckman
Homer: Bob Hastings
Carl Tucker: Carl Ballantine

On the way to a TV talk show interview, Jeannie bangs up Tony's car in an accident. She brings the damaged Thunderbird to a used car salesman who is about to televise live commercial breaks during the same talk show. He offers her a meager $400 for the car, assuring her that he's honest. If she catches him in a lie, he says, he'll tell the truth to the whole world. Well, she catches him in a lie, and he soon learns the hard way that he picked the wrong genie to mess with.

EPISODE 93

"Djinn Djinn, Go Home"

Writer: James Henerson
Director: Hal Cooper

A scruffy little dog appears at Tony's house, becomes invisible, and attacks Tony, ripping his uniform to shreds. Amanda Bellows drops by, and when she sees the now-visible dog, she thinks he's just too adorable and wants to keep him, even though Tony does his best to dissuade her. A delighted Jeannie explains that the dog is her beloved Djinn Djinn, and now Tony must deflate Amanda's interest in the magic dog. Jeannie explains that the pup attacks people in uniforms because the guards at the nearest palace back home were cruel to him—bad news for Tony, Roger, Dr. Bellows, General Peterson, and all of the uniformed personnel at NASA.

For the Record: This is the first of many stories dealing with Djinn Djinn, Jeannie's irascible but lovable pooch.

EPISODE 94

"The Strongest Man in the World"

Writer: Ray Singer
Director: Claudio Guzman

Cast

Jerry Quarry: Himself
Referee: Hollis Morrison
General Hamilton: Richard X. Slattery
Man: Slapsie Maxie Rosenbloom
General Gorman: Steve Roberts
Punk: Lee J. Lambert
Killer Culligan: Pepper Martin

It's the fight of the century for the heavyweight championships of the armed forces. In this corner, the challenger, weighing in at 190 pounds, is One-Punch Nelson, who is oblivious to the fact that his boxing talent is coming from Jeannie. Meanwhile, the champ, Killer Culligan, is 230 pounds of pure punching power. One-Punch is all alone and in serious trouble when his power source gets stuck in a locker. Let the slaughter—er, fight—begin. Ding, ding.

For the Record: In one of the funniest boxing scenes ever filmed, Tony Nelson endures a record number of blows to the head. Compare to Tony Danza's many realistic bouts in *Taxi* and Rob Petrie's ill-fated bout in episode 137 of *The Dick Van Dyke Show.*

Classic Guest Star: Just for the record, this is not the same Pepper Martin who played linebacker for the New York Giants in the late 1980s.

EPISODE 95

"Indispensable Jeannie"

Writer: James Henerson
Director: Claudio Guzman
Cast
Joe: Roger Garrett
Redhead: Bobbie Collins

What would happen if Tony Nelson and Roger Healey were to test their compatibility for one week by sharing a house that's genie-ized to respond to their every wish? Pure domestic chaos, that's what. See Tony live by his checklists. Learn Roger's porch light system for dates. Watch as the best friends drive each other absolutely crazy while attempting to convince Dr. Bellows that they're the perfect astronautical team.

EPISODE 96

"Jeannie and the Top Secret"

Writer: Searle Kramer
Director: Hal Cooper
Cast
Valerie: Sabrina Scharf
Passenger: Bruce Kirby
General Watson: Vinton Hayworth
General Lewis: Bill Quinn
Sergeant Marion: Joseph Perry
General Phillips: Tom Palmer
Stewardess: Valerie Hawkins

Happily celebrating his third anniversary with Jeannie, Tony has lots of fun planned for the day. Before they go, however, Dr. Bellows calls Tony to the base to inform him that, in a top secret mission, he must deliver a briefcase containing a secret film to Washington, D.C. Back home, he tells Jeannie he can't spend the day with her. That's bad enough, but when she also listens in on a phone call from Dr. Bellows and hears him re-minding Tony to meet Marion at the airport, she makes Tony's trip an in-flight disaster, nearly getting him court-martialed in the process.

Classic Guest Star: Vinton Hayworth makes his *Jeannie* debut as the irritable General Watson. He goes on to play the recurring character of irritable General Schaeffer, beginning in episode 99.

EPISODE 97

"How to Marry an Astronaut"

Writer: James Henerson
Director: Hal Cooper

Jeannie's wicked sister Jeannie returns, suggesting that she marry Roger so that Jeannie won't worry about her stealing Tony. She uses the opportunity to teach Jeannie a lesson in man-capturing. Jeannie's sister confronts Roger, who's terrified, after all the nasty tricks she's pulled in the past, but he quickly realizes the advantages of having his very own genie. She pops a button off his jacket and sews it back on, waits on him hand and foot, and even makes him dinner—all *sans* magic. Roger's so touched that he falls in love, even though the dinner she cooked tasted like shredded cardboard. Tony's convinced that Jeannie's sister is using Roger to get to him, but the others—even Dr. and Mrs. Bellows—think Tony's just jealous. Can Tony save his pal from embarrassment? Will Roger make a huge mistake, as usual? Will the wedding be ruined by . . . fog?

EPISODE 98

"Dr. Bellows Goes Sane"

Writer: James Henerson
Director: Richard Kinon
Cast
Sergeant Kroder: Paul Vaughn
Dr. Corbett: Joe Flynn

Dr. Bellows hands General Peterson a report detailing all of the strange events surrounding Tony Nelson. And finally, after nearly four years of patience, the general decides the doc has gone nuts and fires him. Tony gets wind of this and feels truly bad—after all, the doctor was telling the truth. Tony's given added incentive to help Dr. Bellows get his job back when Bellows is replaced by an aggressive new doctor who vows to get Tony's secrets through hypnotherapy and sodium pentathol—commonly known as truth serum!

Classic Guest Star: Joe Flynn is best known as the long-suffering captain on *McHale's Navy*.

EPISODE 99

"Jeannie, My Guru"

Writer: James Henerson
Director: Claudio Guzman
Cast
Harold: Michael Margotta
Suzie: Hilarie Thompson
Lewis & Clark Expedition members:
Themselves

This classic *Jeannie* episode introduces the abrasive General Schaeffer, Tony's new boss and neighbor, who regards hippies as a threat to national security. Tony picks up a hitchhiking beatnik, who happens to be Shaeffer's daughter, Suzy, and he plans to turn her in. Then Jeannie pops up in her harem garb and Suzy blackmails Tony: "How can you turn me in as a hippie when you're going with one?" There's trippy-hippie psychedelia to spare as Suzy uses Tony's pad for parties, and he must keep the general from seeing Harold, Suzy's fasting, out-of-his-mind boyfriend who's too whacked to stand up straight—and who's crashing at Tony's.

For the Record: The Lewis and Clark Expedition were part of the slim artist roster for Columbia Television's record label, Colgems (a hybrid of the names Columbia and Screen Gems). The only other artists on the label were the Monkees and Sajid Khan and the New Establishment. The leaders of the Lewis and Clark Expedition, Travis Lewis and Boomer Clarke (pseudonyms for Michael Martin Murphy and Owens Castleman) co-wrote the classic Monkees song "What Am I Doing Hangin' Round."

EPISODE 100

"The Case of My Vanishing Master," Part One

Writer: James Henerson
Director: Hal Cooper
Cast
Arabian Reverend: Benny Rubin
First Air Policeman: Joe LaGrasso
Second Air Policeman: Jerry Shane

Action and intrigue prevail as a security leak at NASA prompts Dr. Bellows to send Tony to a secret location to finish modifying the plans for the Apollo 12 capsule. Unbeknownst to him, a duplicate agent who's been surgically altered to look like him takes his place at the base and at home while Tony's away. Jeannie is confused at the odd way her master is behaving. He even offers to pay her for her cleaning services and volunteers to drive her home. And what do you suppose the fake Tony thinks of his harem girl and her unusual talents?

EPISODE 101

"The Case of My Vanishing Master," Part Two

Writer: James Henerson
Director: Hal Cooper
Cast
Arabian Reverend: Benny Rubin
First Air Policeman: Joe LaGrasso
Second Air Policeman: Jerry Shane

Tony's double at NASA, who is also an enemy agent, has plenty of bizarre information to report to Dr. Bellows, who delights at finally learning Major Nelson's secrets. Via a monitor in the doctor's office, the real Tony explains to Roger that the other Tony is a fake, and Roger in turn warns Jeannie. Enraged at discovering that someone has dared impersonate her wonderful, perfect, beautiful master, Jeannie disproves the duplicate's charges by acting like a Brooklynese maid in front of the doctor. She then proceeds to make the phony Tony's life a living nightmare.

EPISODE 102

"Ride 'Em, Astronaut"

Writer: James Henerson
Director: Claudio Guzman
Cast
Wild Bill Barrows: Mark Miller
Akins: John Myhers
Store Manager: Richard Erdman

Jeannie happens to be the one millionth customer to shop at Food City, becoming Queen of the Supermarket. Though she knows Tony won't be happy, Jeannie accepts her coronation. Among her prizes, she is also made Queen of the Cocoa Beach Rodeo. The problem is that the winner of the rodeo receives a date with the queen. Tony has to save Jeannie from the clutches of a lecherous Wild Bill Barrows, "the roughest, toughest, rootinest, tootinest wrang-tail buckaroo that ever roped a calf." Of course, the only way to do this is to enter the competition as the Pinto Kid.

Parallel Plot: Classic TV abounds with millionth customers. Cousin Oliver of the *Brady Bunch,* to cite just one example, was the millionth tourist to pass through the gates of a TV studio.

EPISODE 103

"Invisible House for Sale"

Writer: James Henerson
Director: Hal Cooper
Cast
Mr. Winkler: Harold Gould
Mrs. Winkler: Joan Tompkins
Charlie Merkle: Ed Peck

Jeannie shares a chopped yacus sandwich with Roger and complains that Tony never lets her help with household chores. Roger suggests selling the house and getting an apartment. That way he wouldn't have to do chores. Jeannie tries to suggest this to Tony just as Roger gives him a hot Persian pepper pickle, which burns his mouth. Thoroughly distracted, he blurts out to the insistent Jeannie to do whatever she wants, so she puts the house on the market. Tony and Roger, working on life-support systems for Apollo 12 with gung-ho Mr. Winkler, freak out when Mrs. Winkler tells her husband about the great deal she found on a house with a pool, tennis courts, a palatial dining room, and a veranda, at 1020 Palm Drive in Cocoa Beach—Tony's address.

Classic Quote

MRS. WINKLER: How many bedrooms does the house have?

JEANNIE: How many do you want?

For the Record: Tony's address, as mentioned here, is 1020 Palm Drive. In episode 84, however, it's 811 Palm.

Classic Guest Star: Harold Gould would later play Rhoda's dad on *Rhoda*.

EPISODE 104

"Jeannie, the Governor's Wife"

Writer: Christopher Golato
Director: Hal Cooper
Cast
Distinguished Man: Jack Smith
Mailman: Xavier Nash
Woman with Baby: Tommie Banks
Man at Rally: Mel Gallagher

Jeannie gets the idea that Tony should run for governor. Who could resist her master's handsome, honest face? Sensibly, Tony wants nothing to do with it. Nevertheless, Jeannie fills the house with campaign posters, placards, banners, pins—the whole kit and kaboodle. Jeannie's future-machine shows that Tony will win the election, and even Roger has to admit that Tony's got charisma, plus he likes the fact that he will become state treasurer if Tony wins. But when Roger turns his office into campaign headquarters and Jeannie blinks up a marching band, tons of constituents, and a party van, Dr. Bellows finally catches wind of the electioneering.

Our Television Heritage: We like to think it was this episode that first inspired astronaut John Glenn to enter the political arena. He went on to serve as a U.S. senator from Ohio.

Jeannie-Logical?

Jeannie's future-machine must be an innovation developed since episode 59, in which she had to keep calling up the increasingly irritable Hajii to get a glimpse of her future married life with Tony. Also, if Jeannie can see the future, surely she can see what will happen in episode 117. So why does she worry so much about her relationship with Tony?

EPISODE 105

"Is There a Doctor in the House?"

Writer: Christopher Golato
Director: Oscar Rudolph

Tony keeps nodding off. He sleeps while General Peterson talks to him, bumbles his way around NASA, and generally can't keep his eyes open. The general tells Dr. Bellows that if this continues, Tony will be taken off the moon mission. Nonetheless, Tony falls asleep and can't be roused. Jeannie seeks help from her mother—no big fan of Tony Nelson—and discovers that it's her mother who's behind the whole nasty trick to begin with. She demands that her mother return to set things straight, and she does. The only problem is that she also accidentally puts Dr. Bellows to sleep and falls in love with his virile, sleeping visage.

For the Record: Oscar Rudolph directed many episodes of *The Donna Reed Show*.

EPISODE 106

"The Biggest Star in Hollywood"

Writer: James Henerson
Director: Claudio Guzman
Cast
Judy Carne: Herself
Arte Johnson: Himself
Gary Owens: Himself
George H. Schlatter: Himself
Reynolds: Sid Melton
Salesgirl: Susan Howard

Gary Owens and George Schlatter, the producers of *Laugh-In*, spy Jeannie's image in a mirror—with Jeannie herself not present—a little stunt she prepared as a send-off for Tony, who's heading to Hollywood. The producers are so impressed with her little magic trick that they just have to get her onto the show. Seeing this as his big opportunity to become rich and famous, Roger tells them he's her manager, and yes, the Princess Armena will be on *Laugh-In*.

Classic Guest Star: Sid Melton played Alf Monroe on *Green Acres,* among many other roles.

Our Television Heritage: Because *Rowan and Martin's Laugh-In* was shot on videotape, Jeannie does not encounter the problem she faces in episodes 9 and 124, in which her image doesn't appear on film.

EPISODE 107

"Porcelain Puppy"

Writer: James Henerson
Director: Claudio Guzman
Cast
Mr. Farber: Woodrow Parfrey

While practicing a new spell for changing organic material into porcelain, Jeannie accidentally converts Tony's hat and his briefcase, which contains an important document. Art aficionado Amanda Bellows sees the newly created porcelain items and thinks Tony's pottery work is exceptional. To substantiate his story that *he* is the potter, Tony has Jeannie blink up some amateurish crockery, but she accidentally turns her dog, Djinn Djinn, into a porcelain statue, and she can't undo the spell. Amanda finds the statue and takes it to an art expert, who says it is a genuine relic of the Ming Dynasty worth a quarter of a million dollars. Don't worry, Djinn Djinn is restored to his true doggy form in the end.

Our Television Heritage: Two truisms of Classic TV are that modern art is a crock, and that art experts are fools. This episode establishes the latter point, episode 122 the former.

EPISODE 108

"Jeannie for the Defense"

Writer: Bruce Howard
Director: Hal Cooper
Cast
Norman Cashman: Dick Sargent
Thelma Crawford: Ann Morgan Guilbert
Judge Miller: J. Pat O'Malley
Edgar Crawford: Kay E. Kuter
Sam Farrow: William Bassett
Drunk: Bruce Howard
Policeman: William Bramley
Woman at phone booth: Elsie Baker

While on a fishing trip, Tony and Roger get a speeding ticket in Clarkston, a crooked backwoods town. To make matters worse, Tony accidentally nudges another car, giving the occupants an excuse to jump out screaming and writhing in feigned pain. Tony gets arrested, and only Jeannie can save him from the so-called victims, who are now swathed in bandages. Tony's bumpkin lawyer doesn't want to defend him, the biased judge has already made up his mind, and Roger proves to be such a bad witness that he damages Tony's case more than his opponents could ever hope to.

Classic Guest Stars: This star-studded episode features Samantha's second Darrin (Dick Sargent) plus Rob Petrie's neighbor Millie Helper (Ann Morgan Guilbert) and Rob's father (J. Pat O'Malley).

Classic Cameo: The writer of the episode wrote himself into this episode.

EPISODE 109

"Nobody Loves a Fat Astronaut"

Writer: Christopher Golato
Director: Claudio Guzman

Jeannie's deceitful sister appears once again to cause trouble and steal Tony away. This time she convinces Jeannie that a trip to the moon is just too dangerous for him—why, his chances of returning alive are only *vedj in vedjnadji* (Persian for "one in a thousand"). So, pretending to offer her help, she gives Tony hallucinations so that Dr. Bellows will deem him unfit for space travel. When that doesn't work, she makes Tony put on a little excess weight—just a paltry 150 pounds.

EPISODE 110

"Around the World in 80 Blinks"

Writer: James Henerson
Director: Claudio Guzman
Cast
Wingate: Richard Mulligan
Technician: Xavier Nash
Airman: Jerry Shane
Engineer: Sandy Harbin

While in lunar orbit with Roger and no-nonsense Commander Wingate, Tony suffers from a bad cold. Seeing this on TV, Jeannie blinks him down to his room for some rest. The problem is, Jeannie, who also has a cold, accidentally brings back Wingate instead of Tony. She tries again and gets Tony, but now she can't send either of them back up, and Dr. and Mrs. Bellows have come to the house to decorate for a welcome home party. Meanwhile, Roger orbits the moon alone. . . .

Classic Guest Star: Comic actor Richard Mulligan is best known for his roles on *Soap* and *Empty Nest.*

Jeannie-Logical?

If Jeannie can nod-boink a man down from the moon, how come she can't cure the common cold?

EPISODE 111

"Jeannie-Go-Round"

Writer: James Henerson
Director: Claudio Guzman
Cast
Bonnie Greer: Lainie Nelson
Betty: Karen Carlson
Dave Berry: Himself

Tony grudgingly agrees to double-date with Jeannie and Roger to the opening of the Cocoa Beach Cabana—to the delight of Jeannie's impish sister, who devises a fiendish plot to humiliate Jeannie and steal Tony for herself. First she fools Dr. Bellows into going, so that Tony won't be able to bring Jeannie. Then she traps Jeannie in her bottle and goes onstage disguised as her innocent sister to make Tony think Jeannie has totally flipped her lid. In a uproarious scene, the deceitful Jeannie sings a whacked-out 1960s song and embarrasses the pants off Tony, literally.

EPISODE 112

"Jeannie and the Secret Weapon"

Writer: Larry Markes
Director: Leo Garen
Cast
Mackhorter: Ron Masak
Jason: Sheldon Collins
Oglethorpe: Dick Schaal
Beattie: Jeff DeBennig

Tony and Roger are studying Dr. Oglethorpe's sketches on AGNES—the Anti-Gravity Nuclear Earth Station. Ever-helpful Jeannie suggests they make a scale model. When Tony explains that building a model would take months, she begs to differ. *Blink.* Dr. Bellows sees the new model, and Tony and Roger explain that it's just a toy, which puts them in deeper trouble, because if the plans are based on a toy . . . Of course the trouble gets deeper still when Jeannie gives the model to the son of a toy manufacturer, whose father believes this "toy" will make him millions. But wait, there's even deeper, deeper trouble—when Oglethorpe accuses Tony and Roger of selling AGNES to the toy maker for profit.

Classic Guest Star: Actor Dick (a.k.a. Richard) Schaal is no stranger to TV Land. He played Carol's footsore boyfriend on *The Bob Newhart Show,* he dated Mary Richards, and he played Chuckles the Clown on *The Mary Tyler Moore Show.*

EPISODE 113

"Blackmail Order Bride"

Writer: James Henerson
Director: Claudio Guzman
Cast
Farnum: George Furth
First Reporter: Damian London
Sue Ellen: Barbara Bostock
Second Reporter: Arthur Adams
Tony Junior: Teddy Quinn
Third Reporter: Syl Lamont
Joey: Kerry MacLane

When Tony won't divulge information about his private life at a press conference, ace reporter Farnum makes it his goal to get an exclusive on Major Nelson's personal life. Disguised as a plumber, he gets into Tony's house and hides tape recorders and cameras all around. What he finds—a harem girl who calls Tony "master"—is dirt of the juiciest kind. To coerce Tony into giving an interview, Farnum sends over a woman with screaming kids claiming to be Tony's neglected wife, creating a sticky situation for both NASA and Tony. Meanwhile, a distraught Jeannie, learning that Tony is married, heads for Reno, Persia, where genies go to get divorced from their masters.

For the Record: This is the second time that Jeannie has threatened to divorce Tony, and they still haven't gotten married.

EPISODE 114

"Jeannie at the Piano"

Writer: James Henerson
Director: Hal Cooper
Cast
Eddie: George Spell

Jeannie shows up at the officers' lounge to ask Tony what he wants for dinner. Tony freaks out and quickly pretends to play the little red piano there. Jeannie makes the piano magical so that he plays like Chopin. Everyone is so impressed that General Schaeffer sends him on a concert tour. Tony is forced to comply, because Jeannie can't alter the spell. Tony enjoys tickling the ivories all across America, but panic strikes at his Carnegie Hall debut, when General Schaeffer and Dr. Bellows replace the little red piano with a beautiful grand—and Jeannie gets locked in a file cabinet.

For the Record: Amazingly, in the credits for this episode, Bill Daily finally gets billing over Hayden Rorke. But don't fear, Doc Bellows fans, the credit arrangements flip-flop back and forth for the rest of the series.

Jeannie-Logical?
It's really no wonder that NASA has cost the taxpayers billions of dollars, what with senior-level officers going off on whimsical concert tours and buying grand pianos.

EPISODE 115

"Djinn Djinn, the Pied Piper"

Writer: James Henerson
Director: Claudio Guzman
Cast
Dockweiler: Dick Wilson

Jeannie accepts a collect call at Tony's office from her aunt Melama in Babylon, who has a gift for them. A package blinks in—surprise! It's Djinn Djinn. General Schaeffer meets the scruffy little genie-dog and, unlike Dr. Bellows, who remembers the uniform-ripping mutt all too well, finds him cute and wants him to meet his Great Dane, Jupiter, and compete in a dog show. At the park, it's nonstop slapstick as Djinn Djinn goes invisible, incites the general's huge dog, and takes Tony on the run of his life.

For the Record: Architects take notice of the stunning new exterior shots of NASA.

EPISODE 116

"Guess Who's Going to Be a Bride?" Part One

Writer: James Henerson
Director: Hal Cooper
Cast
Suleiman: Jackie Coogan
Osman: Brad Logan
Achmed: Mickey Morton
Hamid: Frank De Vol

Jeannie needs to find the perfect gift for Tony for their fifth anniversary. As if in response to this need, Jeannie's uncle plans to abdicate the throne of Basenji, making her the queen. She can give Tony a country for their anniversary, but if Tony's to be the new maharajah, her uncle must do a little investigating. Meanwhile, Tony's latest assignment is to escort the ambassador of Kasha around NASA. He mistakes Jeannie's uncle and his retinue for Kashians, a serious faux pas because Kasha is Basenji's most hated enemy. Jeannie's uncle demands that Tony avenge the honor of Basenji by killing the Kashian ambassador and marrying Jeannie. Tony loses his temper, saying he wouldn't marry Jeannie if she was the last genie on earth. Jeannie overhears and says good-bye forever.

EPISODE 117

"Guess Who's Going to Be a Bride?" Part Two

Writer: James Henerson
Director: Hal Cooper

Tony and Roger, who've been dropped from the space program for causing so much havoc with the Kashians, are sent to live in an igloo in the Aleutians. Tony tries to convince himself that he's better off without Jeannie, but, hey, who's he fooling? Meanwhile, in Basenji, Jeannie is told that the man who answers the Riddle of the Box shall marry her and those who can't will be beheaded. When Tony and Roger return to NASA, Tony reads about the forthcoming wedding in Basenji and admits to Roger that he loves Jeannie and always has. Besides, Jeannie's definitely the kind of girl worth losing your head over.

Classic Quote:
TONY: I wish you'd take your snowshoes off before you come into the igloo.
ROGER: They are off. My feet are swollen.

For the Record: This milestone-laden episode features momentous historic moments as Tony admits that he loves Jeannie, proposes to her, and introduces her to Dr. Bellows as his fiancée.

This is the proposal that sticks, but it's far from

the first. Tony proposed to Jeannie—for various reasons—in episodes 31, 57, and 59. Other close scrapes with marriage occurred in episodes 2, 15, and 97. In number 14 Jeannie proposed to Roger, and in episode 97 Roger proposed to Jeannie's sister.

EPISODE 118

"Jeannie's Beauty Cream"

Writer: Joanna Lee
Director: Hal Cooper
Cast
General Whetherby: Harold Gould
Airman: Jerry Shane
Lieutenant: Jim Begg
Young Tony: Eric Boler
The new Amanda: Laraine Stephens

Amanda Bellows mentions to Jeannie that the sun makes her face all leathery, so Jeannie gives her some genie cream. Amanda applies some, and her face is transformed into that of a hot young woman. "She makes Raquel Welch look like Everett Dirksen," proclaims Roger. After figuring out what happened, as well as cooling off the love-struck Roger, Tony has Jeannie concoct an anti-dote to change Amanda's face back. They take Amanda back to her house, where total craziness ensues as Dr. Bellows, not recognizing his wife, tries to hide her from—well, his wife—and Tony and Roger chase her around, trying to smear the antidotal cream on her face and hide her from Dr. Bellows. And they're *all* trying to hide from General Whetherby, who'll be dropping by at any minute.

EPISODE 119

"Jeannie and the Bachelor Party"

Writers: Dick Bensfield and Perry Grant
Director: Hal Cooper
Cast
Admiral: Richard McMurray
Guard: Wright Colbert Sr.
Party Girls: Francine York, Chanin Hale, Judy Sherven, Nancy Fisher, Judy Baldwin, Yvonne Shubert

Roger and Dr. Bellows conspire to throw a wild bachelor party for Tony. Of course, Roger is thinking of liquor, women, and dancing, while Dr. Bellows's idea of wild is poker, cigars, and foot-ball movies. They bully Tony into coming to a "se-cret meeting." Amanda and Jeannie, set to go to a movie, decide to invite General Schaeffer's wife, and when the general himself answers the phone, Amanda becomes suspicious about what her hus-band's up to. She offers Jeannie some premarital advice about men while they head for the party. Meanwhile, General Schaeffer, thinking he forgot about the meeting, calls all the top brass to rush down and attend. Well, the so-called meeting *is* under way—Tony, Roger, and Dr. Bellows are the only men in a room full of women—and unbe-knownst to the daunted Bellows, Roger has doc-tored the punch with booze.

EPISODE 120

"The Blood of Jeannie"

Writer: John L. Greene
Director: Claudio Guzman
Cast
Mr. Beamish: Ned Glass
Mrs. Horlick: Ruth McDevitt
Ormandy: Ivor Francis

Jeannie needs to have a blood test before she marries Tony, and she informs him that, luckily, genies have blood just like everyone else, with corpuscles, both red and . . . green. Tony scrambles to have Roger stand behind a screen and poke his arm through, so Dr. Bellows will take his blood, thinking it's Jeannie's. But earlier in the day, Roger was inoculated, so now the doctor thinks Jeannie is a walking disaster with typhoid, cholera, *and* yellow fever. Tony then devises a brilliant scheme—in a brilliant scene—to get the blood sample from the doctor himself.

For the Record: In this episode we learn that Jeannie tips the scales at 127 pounds.

EPISODE 121

"See You in C-U-B-A"

Writer: John McGreevey
Director: Hal Cooper
Cast
Pablo: John Myhers
Clerk: Howard Morton
José: Pedro Gonzales Gonzales
Tina: Farrah Fawcett

Making wedding plans is making Jeannie more zap-happy than ever—she positively wears Tony out with her blinks. Meanwhile, he's testing the experimental T-38 computerized jet on a flight to Puerto Rico. First she blinks him from the jet to the office to help with plans for a dinner party that night; then she blinks him back home. He begs for mercy, so she blinks him back . . . onto the nose of the jet as it lands—in Havana. He's captured by a Cuban militant, but then gets blinked back to a Cocoa Beach sporting goods store, where Jeannie is shopping with Amanda Bellows, who spots the supposedly airborne major. As if that isn't enough, Tony and Roger both get blinked to Cuba, and Tony gets recaptured.

For the Record: Anthony Nelson's air force serial number is AF4469108.

Classic Guest Stars: This episode showcases many TV Land stars: Howard Morton, who's appeared in several episodes of *I Dream of Jeannie;* Pedro Gonzales Gonzales, an unassuming unknown who rose to instant stardom when Groucho Marx took a liking to him on *You Bet Your Life;* and of course Farrah Fawcett, whose photograph would later grace the bedroom wall of nearly every fifteen-year-old boy in America.

EPISODE 122

"The Mad Home Wrecker"

Writer: Howard Ostroff
Director: Hal Cooper
Cast
Mr. Belber: Marvin Silbersher
Helasco: Michael Lipton
Airman: Robert Munk

If Jeannie and Tony are to live happily together forever, they're going to have to redecorate the house. But a wedding present from Jeannie's uncle, a bed of nails, is not what Tony had in mind. He begins a new wedding tradition of being honest about incoming presents—that is, until Dr.

and Mrs. Bellows bring them an Helasco original—a thoroughly repulsive gurgling, belching blob of modern art. And when they see how ostensibly pleased Tony and Jeannie are, they chip in, along with NASA, to redecorate the entire house, under the mod direction of Helasco himself.

Parallel Plot: Bad interior decoration provides plenty of comic mileage in Classic TV. It gives the set decorators a chance to stretch their wings a little and add to the comedy. Other great TV redecorations include Rhoda's work on Lou Grant's apartment on *The Mary Tyler Moore Show* (episode 37) and Emily's work on the Hartleys' apartment (69) and on Bob's office (82) on *The Bob Newhart Show.*

EPISODE 123

"Uncle a Go-Go"

Writer: Ron Friedman
Director: Russ Mayberry
Cast
Azmire: Ronald Long
Vasmir: Arthur Malet

Tony is in for some serious trouble when Jeannie's foppish, upper-crust uncle Azmire arrives to grant approval of the union and is confronted by another uncle, the crude, gambling, fun-loving Vasmir, who pops in for the same job. The uncles argue over whose job it is to investigate Tony, resorting to fisticuffs and inadvertently knocking Tony out cold. The two uncles disagree about everything but the fact that they dislike each other intensely *and* that Tony had better pass both of their inspections. Can Jeannie convince her concerned uncles that her wonderful master is both formally serious and spontaneously non-stuffy?

Classic Performance: Dr. Bellows, with a newspaper over his head, plays the ukulele and sings "I've Got a Lovely Bunch of Coconuts."

EPISODE 124

"The Wedding"

Writer: James Henerson
Director: Claudio Guzman
Cast
Henshaw: Cliff Norton
Second Photographer: Reginald Henderson
Reverend Weems: Jack Smith
Mr. Nelson: Hal Taggart
First Photographer: Harvey Fisher
Mrs. Nelson: June Jocclyn

Here it is, the event we've all been waiting for—no one more eagerly than Jeannie herself. We finally hear those immortal words, "Don't call me 'master,' call me Tony." If this classic must-see episode seems too good to be true, well, it does to Jeannie, too, and she spends so much time fantasizing about her dream wedding that she almost forgets to attend her real one. And what would a classic TV wedding be without some mishaps? For example, Tony, being a major public figure, must devise a way for Jeannie to avoid the photographers, since genies don't show up on film. Nevertheless, a wedding is always a happy event. See Amanda cry. See Amanda make Roger cry. See Jeannie's enchanting sleeveless gown. See Tony's parents for a very, very brief moment. But, most importantly, break out those hankies. After all, who doesn't cry at wedding episodes?

EPISODE 125

"My Sister the Home Wrecker"

Writer: James Henerson
Director: Claudio Guzman
Cast
Biff Jellico: Michael Ansara
Cindy: Farrah Fawcett

Jeannie's back. No, not *that* Jeannie—the other, dark-haired, troublemaking one. Jeannie's sister returns with a vengeance and a surefire plan to break up Jeannie's nascent marriage to Tony Nelson. When all of the women flock around the handsome, debonair, impossibly perfect astronaut Biff Jellico at a party, Jeannie's sister disguises herself as Jeannie and joins the crowd. But since Jeannie is supposed to be home waiting for Tony instead of at the party flirting and smooching with Biff, more than a few eyebrows are raised, particularly those of Roger, Dr. Bellows, and Amanda. Sparks really fly when Biff falls in love with the false Jeannie and decides to tell Tony about the affair.

Classic Guest Star: Farrah Fawcett reprises her role as Roger's girlfriend, but now her name is Cindy, whereas in episode 121 she was known as Tina.

EPISODE 126

"Jeannie the Matchmaker"

Writers: Don Richman and Bill Daily
Director: Claudio Guzman
Cast
Patricia: Janis Hanson
Laverne: Elaine Giftos

Roger's feeling neglected. Tony's hands are full with his new wife and his household chores and he just doesn't have time for his old buddy. As al-

ways, Jeannie has a solution. If Roger needs a perfect mate, what better place to get one than the Perfect Mate Computer Service? She quickly finds Laverne there, but unbenownst to her, at General Schaeffer's command, Tony fixes Roger up with Patricia, the general's visiting niece. Roger instantly likes her—she even uses his come-ons on him before he can use them on her. Competitive till the end, Jeannie arrives with Laverne and blinks a sleeping potion into Patricia's drink so that Laverne will have a better chance. Unfortunately, Laverne sips from the same drink. Now Roger's got two passed-out women on his hands, and just then General Schaeffer shows up to see how Roger and his niece are getting along.

For the Record: Double-duty player Bill Daily co-wrote and stars in this classic episode, which is chock-full of physical comedy.

EPISODE 127

"Never Put a Genie on a Budget"

Writer: Sidney Sheldon
Director: Oscar Rudolph
Cast
Gregorian: Noam Pitlik
Joan: Maggie Thrett
Lieutenant Morgan: Stafford Repp
Girl Hippie: Ellen Nance
Dick: Larry Bishop
Sheer Delight: Herself

Jeannie goes nuts charging clothes, so Tony decides to put her on a budget. In an act of rebellion, she turns the tables on him by becoming the most frugal, penny-pinching wife a husband could have. Of course, this behavior comes at a bad time—just when he's required to entertain a visiting Soviet cosmonaut. For dinner, Jeannie serves them each half a TV dinner, bread that's harder than brick, and half an apple for dessert. (And the Soviet thought things were bad in his country.) The cosmonaut even offers Tony money to help him get back on his feet. Things couldn't get much worse—that is, until Jeannie brings in two hippies as boarders.

Classic Guest Star: Apparently Sheer Delight's career peaked with this episode.

For the Record: For some inexplicable reason, no laugh track exists on this episode, allowing viewers an interesting opportunity to compare and contrast. The jokes and performances are on a par with those of most of the show's episodes, but for once you have to figure out where to laugh on your own. See how it feels.

EPISODE 128

"Please Don't Give My Jeannie No More Wine"

Writer: James Henerson
Director: Jon Anderson
Cast
Congressman Farragut: Alan Oppenheimer
Linda: Mary Grover

When Tony and Jeannie arrive at the Bellows home for dinner, Tony realizes he didn't bring any wine. Jeannie blinks up Imer's Delight, a Persian wine from 1591, "a very good year." Tony is a little apprehensive about the wine, but Dr. Bellows and Amanda find it absolutely delightful. That's great, but then they both become invisible. Wackiness ensues as Tony and Jeannie try to act normal and figure out a solution as they follow Dr. Bellows by watching his pipe. Keeping track of Amanda proves slightly more difficult—especially when she wants to play charades.

Parallel Plot: See Laura Petrie's charade in episode 63 of *The Dick Van Dyke Show,* "All About Eavesdropping."

EPISODE 129

"One of Our Hotels Is Growing"

Writer: Robert Rodgers
Director: Jerry Bernstein
Cast
Perkins: Marvin Kaplan
Fatheringay: Jimmy Cross
Montjoy: Ned Wertimer
Switchboard Operator: Fran Ryan

While in Los Angeles on vacation, the whole gang finds that Roger's hotel reservations didn't go through, so they have nowhere to stay—that is, until Jeannie adds a thirteenth floor to the building. In a series of quick changes and disguised faces they somehow keep the hotel staff at bay and keep Dr. Bellows and Amanda in their room, lest they go downstairs and mention what floor they're on.

Classic Quote:
TONY: Children grow, trees grow, but hotels just don't grow.

EPISODE 130

"The Solid Gold Jeannie"

Writer: Joanna Lee
Director: Jerry Bernstein
Cast
Wingate: Robert Hogan
First Crewman: Bill McKinney
Sally: Shirley Born
Second Crewman: Robert Gros
Heatherington: Jim Galante

After a successful moon trip, Tony, Roger, and Commander Wingate must spend three weeks in quarantine to ensure that they are free from space germs. But Jeannie, excited to see her master—er, husband—walks right through the dividing glass. Now she might be contaminated, too! She disguises herself as a six-inch gold trophy in order to spend the next three weeks with them. The real trouble comes after Tony's trophy-wife is dropped on her head. When she develops a headache she accidentally takes a sleeping pill, thinking it's aspirin. Now Tony and Roger must hide a full-size passed-out gold Jeannie.

For the Record: Robert Hogan takes over the role of Wingate from Richard Mulligan (episode 110).

EPISODE 131

"Mrs. Djinn Djinn"

Writers: Dick Bensfield and Perry Grant
Director: Russ Mayberry

Djinn Djinn, Jeannie's beloved magic pooch, is back, but he's not alone. He brings with him a female magic poodle and a surprise—he's going to be a father! Roger drops by, seeing a bassinet and pregnancy pills, and jumps to the natural conclusion. He spreads the word at NASA that Tony's going to be a dad. Tony and Jeannie try to explain that they aren't having a baby, but everyone's so excited that no one believes them.

Our Television Heritage: As a rule, pregnancy and conclusion-jumping go hand in hand in TV Land. In episode 4 of *The Munsters*, Herman and Grandpa jump to the conclusion that Lily is expecting, and in episode 12 of *Bewitched*, Larry jumps to the conclusion that Samantha's expecting, when it's really Louise!

For the Record: Jeannie's original outfit was banned by network censors, who infamously required that her bellybutton be covered. However, if you look very closely, you can glimpse the forbidden naval in this episode.

EPISODE 132

"Jeannie and the Curious Kid"

Writers: Perry Grant and Dick Bensfield
Director: Claudio Guzman
Cast
Melvin: Michael Barbera

Amanda and Dr. Bellows inform Tony that he's to baby-sit with their nephew Melvin for a day. Jeannie inadvertently comes out of her bottle right in front of the boy, and when he tells Dr. Bellows, the doctor blames Melvin's wayward imagination on too many comic books. But after seeing a few more unexplainable things, Melvin steals Jeannie's bottle with her in it and takes it back to the Bellowses' house, determined to expose the magical genie. He dumps Jeannie into a sherry bottle, and by the time Tony and Roger figure out what happened and rush over to steal the bottle back, it's late at night, and Jeannie has what is often known in Classic TV circles as Moo Goo Gai Pan syndrome—in other words, she's drunk.

EPISODE 133

"Jeannie, The Recording Secretary"

Writer: Sidney Sheldon
Director: Claudio Guzman
Cast
Mrs. Endicott: Joan Tompkins
Mrs. Ross: Norma Connolly
Mrs. Wilson: Elizabeth Lane

Jeannie is very nervous about attending her first meeting of the Officers' Wives Association. Things go so well, however, that she's voted the group's recording secretary. The women decide to present their first annual Good Husband Award, so they hold a secret contest to determine which officer is the most sympathetic. Jeannie just knows her wonderful husband will win, but to her disappointment, Tony will be spending the whole week of the contest with Roger in a capsule simulator testing a new astronaut sleeping pill. She should really just leave him alone to do his work. Then again, she could blink his comatose being into the house and make him get coffee and do dishes, manipulating his zombie body like a marionette, risking his career and sanity. . . . Well, for Jeannie, nothing ventured, nothing gained.

EPISODE 134

"Help, Help, a Shark"

Writer: James Henerson
Director: Claudio Guzman
Cast
General Fitzhugh: Jim Backus

Seven nerve-racking, ear-piercing, earth-shaking, Jeannie-inspired Major Nelson howls punctuate this classic scream-filled episode. Tony ruins General Schaeffer's pivotal pool shot against his longtime rival General Fitzhugh, dashing his dreams of making it to the National All-Military Pool Championships. To keep from being sent to the North Pole, Tony agrees to play the cocky General Fitzhugh in a rematch. With Jeannie watching and supplying her unique assistance, Tony is a sure bet to win the game. Then General Schaeffer will be avenged, Tony can stay in Florida, Roger will win some money, and everyone will be happy. There's only one minor glitch: General Fitzhugh refuses to play with Jeannie in the room. He believes that women and pool don't mix.

Classic Guest Star: Jim Backus, who played Thurston Howell on *Gilligan's Island,* is the top brass pool shark in this episode. He also guest-starred on *The Brady Bunch* as Mike's pool-playing boss. Can we safely assume that Backus is a fan of pool? Perhaps he even makes it a requirement of any guest appearance.

EPISODE 135

"Eternally Yours, Jeannie"

Writer: James Henerson
Director: Joseph Goodson
Cast
Bonnie: Damian Bodie
Officer: Wright Colbert
Moose: Denny Miller
WAF: Sally Ann Richards

Jeannie seethes with jealousy as she reads a scented letter addressed to "Major Bunky Nelson" from Tony's high school sweetheart. She flips through his old Fowler's Corner, Ohio, yearbook, *Ye Old Acorn,* and reads: "Dear Bunky, You are the coolest guy in A-12 homeroom, eternally yours, Bonnie" and sees his response which reads, "Love and smooches, Bonnie, from Bunky." Jeannie convinces herself that Tony still loves Bonnie. What to do? The answer is obvious—she blinks herself to the office as Bonnie to test his love. Too bad the real Bonnie decides to visit him at the same time.

EPISODE 136

"An Astronaut in Sheep's Clothing"

Writer: James Henerson
Director: Bruce Kessler
Cast
Commander Jay Russell: Don Dubbins

It's Tony's second year as a major and his six-month wedding anniversary with Jeannie. For a gift, Jeannie blinks him a drum major suit. He explains that he's tired of her always blinking things for him, and that anything she prepared by hand—no matter what—would mean more to him than something she blinked up. So, to prove that she can do it, she blinks in a Tibetan cashmere sheep, from which she plans to get wool and knit him a beautiful sweater for their anniversary dinner that evening.

Classic Guest Star: Don Dubbins appeared in the very first episode of this series as Lieutenant Pete Conway of the Naval Reserve. Now he's changed his name, moved to the air force, and received a promotion. Only in TV land.

EPISODE 137

"Hurricane Jeannie"

Writer: James Henerson
Director: Claudio Guzman

While a tremendous hurricane rages in Cocoa Beach, Tony, Dr. Bellows, and Roger have to sit it out at Tony's house for the night. When Tony is needed to talk down a pair of astronauts, he uses his phone—thanks to Jeannie—to contact Control. Dr. Bellows gets suspicious, since all the phones are supposed to be out. He gets even more suspicious that they're eating a hot dinner and drinking coffee when the electricity is out for miles around. Then Dr. Bellows comes downstairs in the middle of the night and sees Jeannie blink the two astronauts in from space so that her husband can finally get some sleep. There must be some logical explanation, right?

EPISODE 138

"One Jeannie Beats Four of a Kind"

Writers: Perry Grant and Dick Bensfield
Director: Michael Ansara
Cast
Martino: Herbert Rudley
Torpedo: Tony Giorgio
Provost Marshall Ross: William Wintersole
The Boss: Walter Burke

There's a cardshark con man at NASA. Dr. Bellows and General Schaeffer are suspicious when Tony clears up at the poker table, beating them, Roger, and an out-of-state senator. But unbeknownst to them, the so-called senator is really the con man, and he works for cigar-chomping Mr. Big. His strategy is to allow Tony to win so that he can win big the next time. To divert attention from Tony, Jeannie creates a magic chair that empowers its occupant to win at poker. Poor old unsuspecting Roger sits on the chair, leading the general and the doctor to suspect both Tony and Roger—and angering Mr. Big, who wants Roger dead.

For the Record: This episode is directed by actor Michael Ansara, who can be seen as Biff Jellico in episode 125.

EPISODE 139

"My Master the Chili King"

Writer: James Henerson
Director: Claudio Guzman
Cast
Arvel: Gabriel Dell
Master Sergeant: Lew Brown
Market Clerk: Dick Van Patten
Woman Shopper: Pearl Shear

Arvel, Tony's cousin twice removed, persuades Jeannie to invest $1,000 in his great recipe for Texas chili. He convinces her that Tony agreed to endorse it, and Jeannie is so excited that she blinks up hundreds of cans with his picture on them. She then distributes them to every grocery store in the area—and even to the NASA cafeteria. Which is all well and good, except that astronauts can't endorse products. . . .

Classic Guest Star: Dick Van Patten appeared as Friar Tuck in the cult short-run sitcom *When Things Were Rotten.* He also played the harried dad on *Eight is Enough.*

I Love Lucy

Lucille Ball's brand of humor transcends time and national boundaries. Turn on a TV in virtually any country in the world, and chances are you'll be able to see Lucy—knee-deep in grapes at an Italian vineyard, stuffing herself with chocolates as they stream down a conveyor belt, becoming drunker and drunker as she flubs take after take of a commercial for an elixir called Vitameatavegamin.

—Michael Winship, *Television*

It is so important to have what I like to call the enchanted sense of play. Many, many times you should think and react as a child in doing comedy. All the inhibitions and embarrassments disappear. We did some pretty crazy things in *I Love Lucy*, but we believed every minute of them. It's like getting drunk without taking a drink.

—Lucille Ball, *TV Guide*, 1959

Lucy and Ricky and Fred and Ethel are probably the most recognized neighbors in television history. . . . most of what made *I Love Lucy* special back then still applies today.

First and foremost, there is an excellent ensemble. While Lucy is clearly the lead character, the strength of Ricky, Fred, and Ethel helps to keep the stories from getting stale. . . .

The set pieces are another timeless strength, especially the physical shtick that centers around Lucy. Though *I Love Lucy* certainly did not invent the screwball comedy format (it thrived in feature films long before), few series have been as successful in transferring the form to television.

—Castleman and Podrazik, *Harry and Wally's Favorite TV Shows*

In about six months [Lucille Ball's] low-comedy antics, ranging from mild mugging to baggy pants clowning, have dethroned such veteran TV headliners as Milton Berle and Arthur Godfrey. . . . Her mobile, rubbery face reflects a limitless variety of emotions, from maniacal pleasure to sepulchral gloom. Even on a flickering, pallid TV screen, her wide-set saucer eyes beam with the massed candlepower of a lighthouse on a dark night.

—*Time,* May 26, 1952

If you sat down to watch all the TV shows Lucille Ball starred in, shown one after another without pause, you wouldn't get up again for ten days and 15 1/2 hours.

—Ed Weiner, *The TV Guide TV Book*

I Love Lucy

on Nick at Nite

When Nick at Nite first acquired the rights to air *I Love Lucy*, there was no question about what to do. The home of classic TV would give this classic among classics the treatment it deserved, with newly transferred prints and—best of all—with restored scenes that had been edited out of the show for syndication. The original episodes of *I Love Lucy* ran much longer than the sitcoms of later eras, so the syndicators made room for their commercials by taking the scissors to the show. Nick at Nite chose to sacrifice advertising and promotional time in order to give viewers Lucy as she had not been seen in thirty years: in clean prints, uncut, and back in prime time. Having restored as much as four minutes to some episodes, Nick at Nite, on average, delivered 18 percent more Lucy than syndicators ever had.

The first week, entitled "Nick at Nite Loves Lucy," showcased the twenty-five most memorable, most wonderful episodes. Since then *I Love Lucy* has held an honored place in Nick at Nite's schedule, has been featured weekly on Lucy Tuesdays during our summer-long Block Party marathons, and has gained legions of new fans.

Cast

Lucy Ricardo: Lucille Ball
Ricky Ricardo: Desi Arnaz
Fred Mertz: William Frawley
Ethel Mertz: Vivian Vance

SERIES REGULARS
Freddy Fillmore: Frank Nelson
Mrs. Trumbull: Elizabeth "Patty" Patterson
Little Ricky (Infant): James John Ganzer
Little Ricky (Baby): The Simmons Twins
Little Ricky (Toddler): Joseph and Michael Mayer
Little Ricky (Child): Keith Thibodeaux

The Writers and Directors

Unlike later situation comedies, *I Love Lucy*'s writing and directing were done by a team that seldom changed. The writers all worked together as a team. Rather than credit each show, here, in brief, are all the writers and directors for each season.

First Season (episodes 1–38)

Director: Marc Daniels
Writers: Jess Oppenheimer, Madelyn Pugh, and Bob Carroll, Jr.

Second, Third, and Fourth Season (episodes 39–127)

Director: William Asher
Writers: Jess Oppenheimer, Madelyn Pugh, and Bob Carroll, Jr.

Fifth Season (episodes 128–153)

Director: James V. Kern

Writers: Jess Oppenheimer, Madelyn Pugh, Bob Carroll, Jr., Bob Schiller, and Bob Weiskopf

Sixth Season (episodes 154–179)

Director: James V. Kern (154–166), William Asher (167–179)

Writers: Madelyn (Pugh) Martin, Bob Carroll, Jr., Bob Schiller, and Bob Weiskopf

Also, please note that in this chapter, unlike the others, we follow the original order in which the episodes were filmed. These are the episode numbers that are generally used in other references to *I Love Lucy*. This seemed like the most sensible approach to a show whose episode enumeration is full of confusing sidesteps. They air on Nick at Nite in the order they were originally broadcast. These variations are noted in the episodic notes that follow.

EPISODE 1

"Lucy Thinks Ricky Is Trying to Murder Her"

Cast
Jerry: Jerry Hausner

Between the murder mystery she's reading and Ethel's amateur attempts at fortune-telling, Lucy is convinced that she's not long for this world. Then, when she overhears a business call Ricky has with his agent, Jerry, about a replacement at the club, she thinks he's the one who's out to do her in.

Classic Cameo: Jerry Hausner, who plays Jerry, makes his first appearance in this episode.

Classic Quote
LUCY: I got a Mickey from Ricky!

For the Record: This very uneven episode was the first *I Love Lucy* ever filmed, though it originally aired later in the season, and it's infused with the manic energy of a cast and crew who don't yet quite know what they're doing. There are some brilliant comedy moments (Lucy bobbing and weaving to avoid Ricky's "attack") and some obvious gaffes (look for the very visible cable in the hallway outside the Ricardos' apartment).

EPISODE 2

"The Girls Want to Go to a Nightclub"

It's Ethel's and Fred's wedding anniversary, and the big question is where to celebrate? The girls want to go to a fancy nightclub, and the boys want to take in the fights. When Lucy and Ethel decide to go to the Copacabana without them, Ricky and Fred arrange to follow them with a couple of blind dates. The dates turn out to be—who else?—Lucy and Ethel done up as a pair of not-so-attractive hillbillies. When the smoke clears, all is well, and the couples celebrate the Mertzes' anniversary . . . at ringside.

Classic Performance: Ricky serenades his blind date with "Guadalajara."

Classic Quote

LUCY: Since we said "I do," there are so many things we don't.

For the Record: This was the second episode to be filmed, but it was thought to be more polished than the premiere episode, so it was the very first *I Love Lucy* to air.

EPISODE 3

"Be a Pal"

Cast

Hank: Richard J. Reeves
Charlie: Tony Michaels

Lucy thinks the magic is gone from her marriage and turns to Ethel who, as luck would have it, is reading *How to Keep the Honeymoon from Ending.* Following the book's advice, Lucy goes glam at breakfast, but gets no response from Ricky. She then tries to be one of the boys by joining the weekly poker game. Finally she attempts to re-create his happy childhood by redecorating the apartment with a heavy Cuban accent . . . including live chickens, mules, and Ethel in sombrero and mustache. To complete the picture, Lucy does it up as Carmen Miranda.

Classic Performance: Classic Lucy clowning as she sings along with Carmen Miranda to "Mama Yo Quiero."

Classic Guest Star: Richard J. Reeves appears as Hank in the first *I Love Lucy* cameo. He later plays a neighbor of the Ricardos, an electrician at the Tropicana Club, and an actor auditioning for Ricky's "Indian Show." Reeves also made frequent appearances on *The Adventures of Superman.*

EPISODE 4

"The Diet"

Cast

Pianist: Marco Rizo

Lucy weasels her way into Ricky's nightclub act for the very first time in this episode. Ricky promises that if she can lose twelve pounds (in four days!) and get into the costume, she can dance at the Tropicana Club. Lucy's willpower, determination, and crash diet ultimately pay off, and Lucille McGillicuddy does a turn on the dance floor with Ricky Ricardo.

Classic Performance: Lucy and Ricky dance a mean rumba to "Cuban Pete," one of Desi Arnaz's biggest hits. This dance number was a highlight of the couple's pre–*I Love Lucy* vaudeville tour.

Classic Cameo: Marco Rizo, Ricky's accompanist, is played by Marco Rizo, Desi's real-life accompanist.

For the Record: In this episode, Lucy fights with Butch, the Mertzes' dog, over a piece of steak. This is the only time we see Butch, and we never again even hear of Fred and Ethel having a pet.

EPISODE 5

"The Quiz Show"

Cast

Announcer: Lee Millar
Mrs. Peterson: Hazel Pierce
Harold: John Emery
Arnold: Phil Ober

Lucy goes on a radio show, hoping to win enough money to wipe out her household debts. The show, *Females Are Fabulous,* is hosted by Freddy Fillmore and operates on "the theory that any woman would make an idiot of herself in order to win a prize." All Lucy has to do is convince Ricky that her "long-lost first husband" has come back.

Classic Guest Stars: This is the first time out for Hazel Pierce who, along with Barbara Pepper, was one of the regular *I Love Lucy* bit players.

Frank Nelson, who plays Freddy Fillmore, among other characters throughout the series, knew Lucille Ball from her radio days.

For the Record: Phil Ober, who turns up, finally, as the long-lost hubby, was married to Vivian Vance at the time.

Our Television Heritage: The Fillmore-hosted game shows *Females Are Fabulous* and *Be a Good Neighbor* (episode 88) were loosely based on the real TV and radio show *Queen for a Day*, which featured women telling real-life sob stories in order to win a prize of their own devising.

EPISODE 6

"The Audition"

Cast
Boffo: Himself

Lucy wants to be in Ricky's show again . . . especially since a couple of talent scouts from TV are going to be at the Tropicana. As usual, Ricky does everything he can to keep her at home where he thinks she belongs. But she ends up at center stage, replacing Boffo the Clown. The TV scouts are so impressed that they offer her the contract, but she turns down a shot at fame to pursue her true calling as Mrs. Ricky Ricardo, happy housewife . . . at least for now.

Classic Performance: This is the first time on the show that Ricky performs "Babalu," Desi Arnaz's signature number.

Classic Cameo: The TV scouts are played by Jess Oppenheimer, who wrote and produced *I Love Lucy,* and Harry Ackerman, a CBS vice president.

Our Television Heritage: This episode is a revision of the pilot that was made to sell *I Love Lucy* to CBS. The professor routine, which shows off Lucille Ball's brilliant clowning skills to perfection, was part of the pair's earlier stage show. Look for Desi's obvious delight in his wife's comic sensibilities. He can barely keep himself from breaking up.

For the Record: This is one of the rare episodes in which Ethel does not appear.

EPISODE 7

"The Séance"

Cast
Mr. Merriweather: Jay Novello

Lucy and Ethel are in the middle of an astrology craze just when Ricky is trying to set up a deal with Mr. Merriweather, a theatrical producer. When it turns out that Mr. Merriweather is also a supernatural nut, Lucy sets up a séance with Madame Ethel Mertzola, a.k.a. "the medium Raya," in the hope of contacting his dear departed wife, Tillie.

Classic Guest Star: Jay Novello makes his first *I Love Lucy* appearance in this episode. He'll return to play two other roles: a man who wants to sublet the Ricardos' apartment, and Mario, the visitor from Italy.

Classic Quote
FRED: Well done, Medium Raya.

EPISODE 8

"Men Are Messy"

Cast

Kenny the Press Agent: Kenny Morgan
Jim the Photographer: Harry Shannon
Maggie: Hazel "Sunny" Boyne

Lucy, tired of cleaning up after her slob of a husband, comes up with a plan. She'll divide the apartment in two: Ricky can keep his half in disarray, and her half will be clean. When Ricky calls Lucy to warn her of a magazine photo shoot in the apartment, she decides to teach him a lesson. She turns the whole apartment into a backwoods hovel and herself into a toothless mountain Mama. The scheme backfires when—too late—Lucy learns the shoot is not for a musicians' publication but for *Life* magazine.

Classic Performance: Ricky does a charming rendition of "The Straw Hat Song" with Maggie, the Tropicana's cleaning lady.

Classic Cameo: In another instance of typecasting, Kenny Morgan was actually Desilu's press rep.

Classic Quote
RICKY: *(upon seeing the trashed apartment):* This is a regular pigpen.
LUCY: It ain't a regular one . . . but it'll do!

EPISODE 9

"Drafted"

Lucy reads a letter that orders Ricky to report to Fort Dix, and she's convinced he's been drafted, although he's really been tapped to perform for the troops. Then Ricky persuades Fred to help him with an old vaudeville routine, and Ethel thinks Fred has enlisted, too. Lucy and Ethel do what any loyal wives would do and start knitting socks for their "brave soldiers," at which point Ricky and Fred do some major conclusion-jumping.

Our Television Heritage: The guests that Lucy Ricardo invites to the men's going-away party—the Sedgwicks, the Orsattis, and others—were the names of Lucille Ball's real friends. Given the chance, she always liked to use the names of people and places she knew in real life.

EPISODE 10

"The Fur Coat"

Cast

Thief: Ben Weldon

Ricky brings home a beautiful, expensive fur coat that he's using in a number at the club. Lucy assumes it's her anniversary present from him, and she won't take it off . . . never, never, never. Now it's Ricky's turn to scheme. How can he get the fur back without letting Lucy know he forgot their anniversary?

Classic Quote
FRED: Lucy's attached to the coat, huh?
RICKY: I'm beginning to think the coat is attached to Lucy!

EPISODE 11

"Lucy Is Jealous of Girl Singer"

Cast
Rosemary: Helen Singer

A blind item in the daily paper's gossip column has Lucy nervous. Could Ricky really have an eye for Rosemary, the lead dancer at the Tropicana Club? "It's only publicity," says he. "We'll just see," says Lucy, even if it means busting into the chorus line for a bird's-eye view. And of course it does.

Classic Performance: Ricky does a rousing version of "El Cumbanchero" and dances with Rosemary to "Jezebel."

For the Record: This is the first episode that deals with Lucy's fear of losing Ricky to another woman. Also noteworthy is the fact that the title of the episode reflects an early draft of the script where Rosemary was a singer rather than a dancer.

EPISODE 12

"The Adagio"

Cast
Jean Valjean Raymand: Shepard Menken

Lucy's bitten by the show biz bug again—what, so soon?—and sets her sights on the French Apache dance number in Ricky's Paris revue. Working with famous French dance expert Fred Mertz proves a washout, so Ethel locates a real Frenchman. Ricky discovers the Frenchman and Lucy in mid-lesson and decides to fight a duel for his wife's honor.

EPISODE 13

"The Benefit"

Lucy convinces Ethel that she and Ricky are the perfect husband-and-wife act for the big benefit performance that Ethel's club is presenting. Now can Lucy convince Ricky? Of course, he eventually agrees, provided he can pick the song. Artistic differences almost prove disastrous for the duo, but as always, Lucy and the show must go on.

Classic Performance: Ricky and Lucy try out the song "Auf Wiedersehen," which has Lucy sounding like a trained seal. They later settle on "We'll Build a Bungalow," which they ultimately perform with all the charm and humor of a seasoned song-and-dance team.

Classic Quote
RICKY: *(setting his terms for picking the song):* Beggars can't be shoosers.
LUCY: Just make sure you shoose something that shows me off.

EPISODE 14

"The Amateur Hour"

Cast
Mrs. Hudson: Gail Bonney
Timmy Hudson: David Stollery
Jimmy Hudson: Sammy Ogg

Has Lucy finally gone off her trolly, or is the little boy she's minding able to vanish and reappear at will? Nah, she's not crazy. The little boy is actually Jimmy and Timmy, the identical twins from . . . Well, you get the picture. Is baby-sitting for big bucks worth all this trouble?

Classic Performance: Lucy and the boys sing "Ragtime Cowboy Joe." And with the help of a frog named Elmer, Ricky, and his conga drum, Lucy turns it into an impromptu Latin dance number.

For the Record: This is one of the very rare Fredless episodes.

EPISODE 15

"Lucy Plays Cupid"

Cast

Miss Lewis: Bea Benaderet
Mr. Ritter: Edward Everett Horton

Kindly Miss Lewis, Lucy and Ricky's neighbor, has eyes for Mr. Ritter, the grocer. All they need is a little matchmaking from Lucy, which of course Ricky has strictly forbidden. Well, that never stopped her before, and by the time you can say, "Lucy, I tole you so," the grocer thinks it's Lucy Ricardo who's interested in him.

Classic Guest Stars: Bea Benaderet had worked with Lucy for years in radio. She was the original choice to play the role of Ethel Mertz, but she had already made a commitment to the Burns and Allen TV show.
　　Edward Everett Horton was a well-known character actor from the thirties who appeared in many Fred Astaire–Ginger Roger movies. He later narrated the Fractured Fairy Tales segments on the Rocky and Bullwinkle show.

For the Record: The Mertzes do not appear in this episode.

EPISODE 16

"Lucy Fakes Illness"

Cast

Hal March: Himself

Lucy tries a new strategy to get into Ricky's nightclub act—fabricating a deep-seated nervous breakdown. After taking a crash course in abnormal psychology, she devises a complex complex: she impersonates Tallulah Bankhead, develops amnesia, and reverts to juvenile behavior. But Ricky learns of the scheme and gives her a strong dose of her own medicine.

Classic Cameo: Hal March makes his first appearance in *I Love Lucy,* playing Ricky's actor friend Hal March. He returns in episode 62 as lingerie salesman Eddie Grant.

For the Record: This is a wonderful example of Lucille Ball's great mimicry skills as she lampoons the great Taloo. This episode also marks the first time Lucy Ricardo exclaims "Eeeewwwww," a Lucy trademark referred to by the show's writers as "the spider take."

EPISODE 17

"Lucy Writes a Play"

Cast

Club chairwoman: Myra Marsh
Stage manager: Maury Thompson

Role reversal! Finally Ricky is the one who wants to be in the show. At first he refuses to have anything to do with Lucy's play "A Tree Grows in Havana," but on opening night he finds out that a Hollywood producer will be judging the performance. By then, of course, Fred Mertz has taken the lead, and the play has moved from its Cuban setting to a manor house somewhere in jolly old

England. That doesn't stop Ricky, of course. He joins in the action, hoping to make an impact on the Movietown bigwig.

Classic Cameo: Maury Thompson, who plays the stage manager, was an *I Love Lucy* script clerk.

EPISODE 18

"Breaking the Lease"

Cast
Bum: Bennett Green
Jam Session Guests: Hazel Pierce, Barbara Pepper

After a silly fight with the Mertzes, Lucy and Ricky decide to move out. The only hitch is the lease on the apartment, which building-owners Fred and Ethel will hold the Ricardos to. It's Ricky who comes up with the scheme this time—to break the lease, they'll become the worst tenants in the history of rentals.

Classic Performance: In the opening scene the four principals sing a chorus of "Sweet Sue" around the piano in the Ricardos' apartment. Later Ricky's orchestra blasts "El Cumbanchero" and "The Mexican Hat Dance" during an all-night jam session.

Classic Guest Star: This is the first episode in which Barbara Pepper appears as an extra. Pepper was one of Lucille Ball's oldest friends. In fact, she and Lucy had traveled from New York to Hollywood together in 1933 to be Goldwyn Girls. Barbara Pepper went on to play Doris Ziffel, Arnold the pig's mother, on *Green Acres*.

EPISODE 19

"The Ballet"

Cast
Madame Lamand: Mary Wickes
Comic: Frank Scannell

Once again Lucy is itching to get into Ricky's act—first as a ballerina and, when that doesn't pan out, as a burlesque comic. As luck would have it, Ricky actually calls on her to fill in for an ailing character, but Lucy mistakenly shows up onstage for the burlesque turn.

Classic Performance: Lucy demonstrates her inimitable slapstick sensibilities, not only in the ballet class scene, but also in the rehearsal with the burlesque comic as she learns the "Slowly I Turn" bit.

For the Record: *I Love Lucy* legend has it that Lucy improvised much of the clowning in the ballet scene because her foot accidentally got caught in the barre, but members of the production staff have said that Lucille Ball made it look accidental on purpose.

EPISODE 20

"The Young Fans"

Cast
Peggy: Janet Waldo
Arthur: Richard Crenna

A neighborhood girl develops a major crush on Ricky, so Lucy tries to interest her in a boy her own age named Arthur. He, of course, develops a yen for Lucy. To end the teenagers' infatuations, the Ricardos decide to play up the age differences . . . in a big way.

Classic Quote

PEGGY: Oh, Ricky is soooo sophisticated. He must be pushing twenty-five.

LUCY: Yeah, he's pushed it all the way to thirty.

Classic Guest Stars: Richard Crenna went on to costar in Desilu's second TV venture, *Our Miss Brooks*.

Janet Waldo later provided the voices of cartoon characters Judy Jetson, Penelope Pittstop and Josie of the Pussycats.

For the Record: This is another one of the rare Mertzless story lines.

EPISODE 21

"New Neighbors"

Cast

Tom O'Brien: Hayden Rorke
Mrs. O'Brien: K. T. Stevens
Police Sergeant: Allen Jenkins

Lucy and Ethel are dying to get a good look into their new neighbors' apartment. Ricky forbids Lucy to set foot in the O'Briens' flat, but that doesn't mean she can't go in on her hands and knees to get a good peek. When she overhears the couple rehearsing for a radio play, she thinks they're plotting to overthrow the government.

Classic Guest Stars: Actress K. T. Stevens was a close friend of Vivian Vance.

Hayden Rorke, of course, went on to costar as the suspicious Dr. Bellows in *I Dream of Jeannie*.

EPISODE 22

"Fred and Ethel Fight"

Cast

Soda Jerk: Hazel Pierce

While trying to patch up a tiff between the Mertzes, Lucy and Ricky start a battle of their own. Ricky moves out, and Lucy is distraught, but neither one wants to be the first to apologize. So this time Fred and Ethel offer the Ricardos advice on how to get back together . . . without saying "I'm sorry."

Classic Quote

FRED: She said my mother looks like a weasel!

LUCY: Ethel . . . apologize!

ETHEL: (to Fred) I'm sorry your mother looks like a weasel.

For the Record: This plot was based on a real life Lucy-Desi experience. They actually did patch up another couple's marital squabble, only to end up fighting themselves.

EPISODE 23

"The Mustache"

Cast

Mr. Murdoch: John Brown

Lucy loves the fact that Ricky is auditioning for a movie, but she hates the mustache he's growing to win the part. To prove her point, she acquires some facial hair of her own. The fake beard does the trick, and Ricky shaves, but then Lucy realizes she has attached the beard with Bulldog cement instead of spirit gum. How can she worm her way into Ricky's audition looking like one of the Smith Brothers?

Classic Performance:: Ricky belts out "I'll See You In C-u-b-a" for the movie producer.

For the Record: The press clippings Ricky shows are actually from Desi's early career on Broadway and in nightclubs.

This is the first time Ethel turns up in costume to sing and dance her way into the act.

EPISODE 24

"The Gossip"

Cast
Bill Foster: Richard J. Reeves
Milkman: Robert Jellison

Ricky criticizes Lucy and Ethel for "goss'pin'," and Lucy argues that men are just as gossipy as women. A bet follows: whoever gossips first will serve the other breakfast in bed for a month. In an attempt to make Lucy cave in, Ricky reveals a juicy tidbit about their neighbors, the Fosters, while pretending to talk in his sleep. Lucy can't resist telling Ethel, and the boys catch them spilling the dirt. Just when it seems that the girls have lost, it turns out that the rumor about the Fosters is true, and if it's the truth—according to well-known TV Land regulations—it isn't gossip.

Classic Cameo: Robert Jellison plays Bobby the bellhop at the hotel the Ricardos and Mertzes stay at during their Hollywood visit (beginning with episode 114).

For the Record: This is the first official "bet" episode for *I Love Lucy*. This device—Ricky making a bet with Lucy, or the boys betting the girls—is used frequently in the series.

Also, look for the blatant product placement by the show's sponsor, Philip Morris, in the drugstore scene.

EPISODE 25

"Pioneer Women"

Cast
Mrs. Pettebone: Florence Bates
Mrs. Pomerantz: Ruth Perrott

A discussion on how easy the girls have it leads to another bet. Can the foursome survive without any modern conveniences and live the way their grandparents did? Ethel churns butter, Lucy bakes bread, and Ricky rides a horse to the club. But how will their new—or rather old—lifestyle mesh with the standards of the scouts from the Society Matrons League who are investigating the girls for possible membership?

EPISODE 26

"The Marriage License"

Cast
Mr. Willoughby: Irving Bacon
Mrs. Willoughby: Elizabeth Patterson

Lucy discovers that Ricky's name is misspelled on their marriage license and decides that their marriage is null and void. She persuades him to redo the whole thing—proposal, ceremony, and all—just like the first time—"the one that didn't take."

Parallel Plot: For similar reasons Laura decides that she and Rob are not legally married in episode 66 of *The Dick Van Dyke Show*.

Classic Guest Stars: Irving Bacon, who plays Mr. Willoughby, returns later in the series to play Ethel's dad. Elizabeth "Patty" Patterson, of course, went on to play Mrs. Trumbull, Lucy's neighbor and handy baby-sitter for Little Ricky.

For the Record: The Ricardos' second wedding ceremony takes place at the Byram River Beagle Club, where Lucy and Desi's real wedding had taken place eleven years earlier.

EPISODE 27

"The Kleptomaniac"

Cast

Dr. Tom Robinson: Joseph Kearns

When Ricky becomes aware of large amounts of cash and assorted valuable items hidden around the house, he suspects Lucy of thievery. Of course she's actually organizing a club bazaar. Lucy, who can't believe Ricky could be so distrustful, decides to play the role of klepto . . . to the hilt.

Classic Performance: A classic *I Love Lucy* comedy moment occurs when Lucy tries to hide a chiming cuckoo clock from Ricky and Fred.

Classic Guest Star: Joseph Kearns, who turns up in this episode as a psychologist hired to help Lucy forgo her life of crime, went on to play the long-suffering Mr. Wilson in *Dennis the Menace*. Interestingly, his role in that series was later taken over by Gale Gordon, best known as Lucy's foil, Mr. Mooney, on *The Lucy Show*.

EPISODE 28

"Cuban Pals"

Cast

Carlos: Alberto Morin
Maria: Rita Convy
Renita Perez: Lita Baron

Lucy tries to win over Ricky's old friends from Cuba by insisting that he let "little Renita Perez"

dance with him at the Tropicana Club. When Lucy discovers that "little Renita" is not so little anymore, she does everything to keep the vixen away from her husband.

Classic Performance: Ricky sings and Renita dances to a sexy version of "The Lady in Red," another of Desi Arnaz's hit recordings before the series premiered.

EPISODE 29

"The Freezer"

Cast

Delivery Men: Frank Sully, Bennett Green
Butcher: Fred Aldrich
Customers: Kay Wiley, Barbara Pepper, Hazel Pierce

The girls buy an old freezer from one of Ethel's uncles, and, to save money, they order a side of beef . . . each. How much is a "side," you ask? Well, over 700 pounds of meat is delivered and can't be returned. After a disastrous scheme in which Lucy tries to steal customers from the local butcher shop, she and Ethel just concentrate on keeping Ricky and Fred from discovering the whole mess.

Classic Quote
LUCY: It's seventy-nine cents a pound.
CUSTOMER: How can you sell meat so cheap?
LUCY: I'm glad you asked that. We rope, we brand, we butcher. We do everything but eat it for you—seventy-nine cents a pound.

For the Record: Starting with this episode, Desi Arnaz receives a credit as the executive producer of the series.

EPISODE 30

"Lucy Does a TV Commercial"

Cast

Director: Ross Elliot
Joe: Jerry Hausner
Script Clerk: Maury Thompson

This is the famous Vitameatavegamin episode. Lucy wants to get into Ricky's act again. In this case, she's desperate to appear in the commercial that runs during the live TV show Ricky is doing. By exercising a lot of gumption—and a little treachery—she wins the part of the Vitameatavegamin girl, only to lose to the 23 percent alcohol content of the tonic. During the rehearsals for the commercial, she drinks so much of the product that she gets relaxed, then giddy, and finally incoherent.

Classic Cameos: For some reason, Jerry Hausner, who usually plays Ricky's agent, Jerry, turns up as Joe in this episode. Maury Thompson, the *I Love Lucy* script clerk, plays the script clerk in the commercial.

Classic Quote
LUCY: Hello, friends, I'm your Vitameatavegamin girl. Are you tired, run down, listless? Do you poop out at parties? Are you unpopular? The answer to all your problems is in this little bottle: Vitameatavegamin. Vitameatavegamin contains vitamins, meat, vegetables, and minerals. Yes, with Vitameatavegamin you can spoon your way to health. All you do is take a tablespoon after every meal. It's so tasty, too! Tastes just like candy. So why don't you join the thousands of happy, peppy people and get a great big bottle of Vitameatavegamin tomorrow. That's Vita-meata-vegamin!

Our Television Heritage: This is considered one of the all time best *I Love Lucy* episodes. Lucy's transition from sober to paralytic is a part of TV comedy history.

The search for the perfect liquid to use as Vitameatavegamin during rehearsals and filming led eventually to apple pectin, which had just the right consistency and a flavor Lucy liked.

EPISODE 31

"The Publicity Agent"

Cast

Reporter: Peter Leeds
Photographer: Bennett Green
Assassins: Richard J. Reeves, Gil Herman

When Ricky decides his career is in a slump and what he needs is good publicity, Lucy rises to the occasion. She transforms herself into a highly visible member of foreign royalty, the Maharincess of Franistan, who's so obsessed with a certain Cuban bandleader that she travels around the world for a private command performance.

Classic Performance: Ricky serenades the swooning Maharincess with "I Get Ideas."

Classic Quote
LUCY: I'm not a Maharincess, I'm a henna-rinsess.

EPISODE 32

"Lucy Gets Ricky on the Radio"

Cast
Office Boy: Bobby Ellis
Announcer: Roy Rowan

Lucy knows that she and Ricky will be successful on Freddy Fillmore's new radio quiz show *Mr. and Mrs. Quiz*—especially if she can get the questions ahead of time. The only snag is that the questions are changed right before show time.

Classic Guest Star: Frank Nelson is back as Freddy Fillmore.

EPISODE 33

"Lucy's Schedule"

Cast
Mr. Littlefield: Gale Gordon
Mrs. Littlefield: Edith Meiser

Ricky is nervous about asking for a promotion at the nightclub. When Lucy makes them an hour late for a business dinner with the club owner, Ricky is furious and puts her on a schedule to prove that he can certainly manage his wife. Now it's Lucy's turn to prove that a schedule is not going to turn her into a "trained seal."

Classic Guest Stars: Gale Gordon, who makes the first of his two appearances as Ricky's boss, Mr. Littlefield, would of course go on to play Mr. Mooney in *The Lucy Show*. Gordon, who had worked with Lucy on her radio series, was Lucy and Desi's first choice to play Fred Mertz, but unfortunately he was under an exclusive radio contract at the time.
　　Edith Meiser had appeared with Vivian Vance in the Broadway show *Let's Face It*.

EPISODE 34

"Ricky Thinks He's Going Bald"

Cast
Mr. Thurlow: Milton Parsons

Ricky is so self-conscious about his thinning hair that he's taken to wearing a hat indoors, so Lucy decides to do something about it. She surrounds him with truly bald men in an attempt to restore his confidence, but that effort is a flop. Lucy then gives Ricky some hair restoration treatments that she's sure will snap him out of his hair-related anxiety.

For the Record: The hair-treatment scene originally occurred in the first half of the episode. But the scene was so funny that the show was re-cut and re-shot so that this scene could become the climax of the second act and end the episode.

EPISODE 35

"Ricky Asks for a Raise"

Cast
Maurice: Maurice Marsac
Mr. Littlefield: Gale Gordon
Mrs. Littlefield: Edith Meiser

Lucy prods Ricky into asking Mr. Littlefield for a raise, and then she exaggerates the other job offers Ricky has received. Mr. Littlefield realizes he can't stand in Ricky's way, so he releases him from the Tropicana. Lucy—with some help from Fred, Ethel, and a trunk full of costumes—tries to prove what a mistake Mr. Littlefield has made.

For the Record: During the quick-change sequence at the Tropicana, look for a very fetching Fred Mertz done up in drag.

EPISODE 36

"The Anniversary Present"

Cast
Grace Foster: Gloria Blondell

With the Ricardos' eleventh anniversary almost here, why is Ricky acting so strangely? He's sneaking around the apartment building and spending an awful lot of time with Grace Foster, whose husband is conveniently out of town.

For the Record: This episode was written at the time of the Arnazes' eleventh anniversary.

EPISODE 37

"The Handcuffs"

Cast
Jerry: Paul Dubov
Mr. Walters: Will Wright
Emcee: Veola Vonn

Tired of never seeing Ricky, who even spends his nights off working, Lucy handcuffs herself to her husband with a pair of Fred's trick handcuffs for a laugh. The joke is on her, however, when the handcuffs turn out to be real, the key is missing, and Ricky is slated to sing in a big TV special.

Classic Performance: Ricky sings a peppery rendition of "In Santiago, Chili," accompanied by hand gestures from Lucy.

Classic Quote
LUCY: Well, you said you wanted to be joined to me forever!

EPISODE 38

"The Operetta"

Cast
Club President: Myra Marsh

Lucy has managed the finances of the Wednesday Afternoon Fine Arts League with the same skill she demonstrates in organizing her household accounts—and as a result, the league's treasury is completely empty. How will they do their annual show? Well, if Lucy and Ethel write it, and they postdate a check for the production costs, the show *could* go on. And it does—with a startling climax.

Classic Performance: Where to begin? Ethel finally gets the spotlight as she sings "I'm Lily of the Valley." Fred, as the Innkeeper, sings "The Inn on the River Out" with the ladies' chorus. Lucy wants to sing a rousing tune called "I Am Queen of the Gypsies," but no one will let her. And Ricky croons the romantic "I'll Be True to You, Lily."

For the Record: Original *I Love Lucy* director Marc Daniels ended his Lucy stint with this episode. He was replaced by William Asher, who stayed for the rest of the series, and went on to produce and direct *Bewitched*, starring his wife, Elizabeth Montgomery.

EPISODE 39

"Job Switching"

Cast
Mr. Snodgrass: Alvin Hurwitz
Factory Foreman: Elvia Allmann
Chocolate Dipper: Amanda Milligan

Once again, Ricky is exasperated by Lucy's chaotic household money management, and he tells her she'd behave differently if *she* had to make the money. She lets him know that running a house is no easy task, and to prove that point, she and Ethel decide that they'll be the breadwinners if their husbands will do the cooking and cleaning. The girls end up at a chocolate factory, where Ethel will be boxing chocolates, while Lucy talks her way into the dipping room: "They call me the big dipper."

Meanwhile, Ricky and Fred attempt housewifery with the best of intentions. During the first day, the fudge flies fast and furiously when Lucy comes to blows with the senior candy dipper. Ethel is reassigned after pinching each candy to see what it is, and they both end up in the wrapping department for the classic battle with the conveyor belt. At home, Fred and Ricky fare no better at mastering housekeeping, and the meal they are attempting to cook ends up all over the kitchen floor and ceiling.

Classic Guest Stars: Elvia Allmann does a splendid job as the no-nonsense factory foreman, and Amanda Milligan was a real-life candy dipper. She had no acting experience at all and was extremely timid when they rehearsed the chocolate fight. To make sure the battle looked real during filming, Lucy hauled off and slapped her a good one, and Amanda Milligan retaliated in earnest. This gave the fight the energy it needed.

Our Television Heritage: This episode, along with Vitameatavegamin, is probably the most popular *I Love Lucy* episode ever. Lucille Ball often referred to it as her favorite.

EPISODE 40

"The Saxophone"

Cast
Jule: Herb Vigran
Man in Closet: Charles Victor

Ricky is going out on the road with his band, and Lucy wants to come along. She tries valiantly to master the sax and auditions for an opening in the orchestra. When Ricky says no, Lucy decides to make him so jealous that he won't dare leave her at home.

Classic Performance: Lucy toots an anemic version of "Glowworm" on the saxophone.

Our Television Heritage: Lucy Ricardo says she learned to play the sax when she was in school in Celoron, New York. Lucille Ball actually did go to Celoron High School near Jamestown, New York, but she learned to play the saxophone during the week of rehearsals for this episode.

EPISODE 41

"Vacation from Marriage"

Lucy realizes that her marriage—and the Mertzes', too—is in a rut. To rejuvenate it, she and Ethel spend a week away from Ricky and Fred. The days crawl by, and pretty soon it's clear that the whole idea was a bust. How can they get back together without losing face?

Classic Quote
RICKY: You know, Fred, I miss Lucy.
FRED: I can top that. I miss Ethel.

EPISODE 42

"The Courtroom"

Cast

Judge: Moroni Olsen
Process Server: Harry Bartell
Bailiff: Robert B. Williams

Lucy and Ricky give the Mertzes a new TV set for their twenty-fifth wedding anniversary. Ricky and Fred argue about how to improve the set's reception and Ricky ends up connecting two wires that blow the new set up. To retaliate, Fred charges down to the Ricardos' and kicks in their set. The fiasco lands the two couples in court, where they all try to prove their innocence and the others' guilt.

For the Record: Only one year earlier, in episode 2, Fred and Ethel celebrated their eighteenth anniversary.

EPISODE 43

"Redecorating"

Cast

Mr. Jenkins: Hans Conried
Women on Phone: Margie Liszt, Florence Halop

Lucy gets tired of her old ratty furniture and enters one hundred postcards in the Home Show contest. Just knowing she's going to win, she refuses to leave the house because she needs to answer the phone when the Home Show calls. Ricky, who has tickets to a hit Broadway show, persuades Fred to call her and tell her she's won, so she'll leave the house and go to the theater. Thinking she's won, Lucy sells her old furnishings to a junk man. Ricky finds out and has to buy all the stuff back.

Classic Guest Stars: Hans Conried makes the first of two memorable *I Love Lucy* guest appearances in this episode. He'll return in episode 53 as Percy Livermore, elocution teacher. Conried is best known for his wonderful portrayal of Uncle Tonoose on Danny Thomas's show, *Make Room for Daddy,* a later Desilu production.

For the Record: Lucille Ball was tired of the existing Ricardo furniture, and that fact was the inspiration for this story line.

EPISODE 44

"Ricky Loses His Voice"

Cast

Mr. Chambers: Arthur Q. Bryan
Chorus Girls: Gertrude Astor, Hazel Pierce, Helen Williams, Barbara Pepper

What is Lucy to do? Ricky is sick in bed and his new boss, Mr. Chambers, is expecting a brand-new show to reopen the Tropicana Club. With a little help from Fred and Ethel, who just happen to have a musical revue up their sleeve, Lucy mounts a revival of the *1927 Follies* while Ricky recuperates. When he shows up on opening night, he's greeted by Lucy, Ethel, and Fred who've given themselves splashy musical numbers and a line of vintage chorines from the original production.

Classic Performance: The musical highlights of this episode include Ricky opening the *Follies* with "Sweet and Lovely," Fred and Ethel singing "Carolina in the Morning," and Lucy leading the chorus in "Has Anybody Seen My Gal?"

For the Record: The Tropicana set was enlarged and redecorated for this episode.

"Carolina in the Morning" was a song that Bill Frawley sang during his vaudeville days.

EPISODE 45

"Sales Resistance"

Cast

Harry Martin: Sheldon Leonard
Mrs. Simpson: Verna Felton

Lucy is putty in the hands of the Handy Dandy Company salesman. She spends $7.98 for the Kitchen Helper, a forerunner of the Veg-O-Matic, and when she tries to return it, she ends up buying a Handy Dandy vacuum cleaner. Ricky attributes this to the weakness of her sex, but Lucy will do anything to get rid of the vacuum—short of having the Handy Dandy rep come to take it away.

Classic Cameo: Sheldon Leonard, who later produced such TV hits as *The Dick Van Dyke Show*, appears as the smooth-talking Handy Dandy salesman.

For the Record: This was the first of five flashback episodes—shot out of chronology—that were put in the can to cover the time Lucille Ball needed to take off before and after the birth of Desi Junior. Rerunning episodes was not a consideration at the time. In order of airing this is episode 52.

Classic Performance: Ricky begins this flashback episode by singing "There's a Brand New Baby at Our House" to celebrate the arrival of Little Ricky.

EPISODE 46

"The Inferiority Complex"

Cast

Dr. Henry Molin: Gerald Mohr

Lucy is worried when no one wants to listen to her jokes or partner with her in bridge. When she ruins Ricky's breakfast, her fears grow worse, and she takes to her bed with a full-fledged complex. It's up to the Mertzes and Ricky to snap her out of it.

For the Record: In order of airing, this is episode 53.

EPISODE 47

"The Club Election"

Cast

Lillian Appleby: Doris Singleton
Mrs. Knickerbocker: Ida Moore
Marion Strong: Margie Liszt
Grace Munson: Hazel Pierce
Club President: Lurene Tuttle

It's election day for the Wednesday Afternoon Fine Arts League, and Lucy is determined to become an officer. When no nomination is forthcoming, she resorts to bribery to get herself into the running. Her competition? None other than Ethel Mertz. The ex–best friends wage an all-out war to get the winning vote.

Classic Performance: Ricky sings "Cuban Cabbie."

For the Record: Lucy's nemesis, Lillian Appleby, made her first appearance in this episode. Her first name was changed to Caroline after members of the *I Love Lucy* staff decided that Lillian and Lucy sounded too similar. In order of airing, this is episode 54.

EPISODE 48

"The Black Eye"

Lucy and Ricky take delight in reading aloud from a gruesome mystery. The Mertzes mistake a passage from the book for a real-life quarrel and are concerned. When Lucy suddenly turns up with a black eye (which she got accidentally when Ricky tossed her the book), their concern turns serious. Even though Lucy won't admit to any marital discord, Fred and Ethel decide it's up to them to get the Ricardos back together.

For the Record: In order of airing, this is episode 55.

EPISODE 49

"Lucy Changes Her Mind"

Cast
Waiter: Frank Nelson
Harry Henderson: Phil Arnold
Tom Henderson: John L. Hart

Ricky is tired of Lucy's indecisiveness and failure to follow through. After a disastrous evening out, during which she can't decide where to sit or what to eat, Ricky puts his foot down and demands that she finish everything she starts. Okay, if that's what Ricky wants, she'll do it. She'll even finish writing an old love letter from before they knew each other. And just to get his goat, she decides to deliver it in person.

Classic Guest Star: Frank Nelson turns up in a non–Freddy Fillmore role as the thickly bespectacled waiter whom Lucy tortures with her indecision.

For the Record: In order of airing, this is episode 56.

EPISODE 50

"Lucy Is Enceinte"

Cast
Maître d': William Hamel
Stagehand: Richard J. Reeves

Feeling a little run down, and putting on weight, Lucy goes to the doctor for a checkup. Instead of suggesting a liver shot or a tonic, the doctor tells her that she and Ricky are going to have a baby. She tries to tell Ricky and keeps getting interrupted, first by the well-meaning Mertzes and then by a chaotic rehearsal at the club. Finally, she tells Ricky . . . in the middle of his nightclub act.

Classic Performance: With Lucy on his arm, Ricky sings "We're Having a Baby."

Our Television Heritage: In order of airing, this is episode 45. Television history was made with this episode: this was the first time a real-life pregnancy was dealt with in a comedy show. The decision to let Lucy Ricardo have a baby was a monumental one which was arrived at only after discussing two other possibilities: going off the air until after the baby was born, and trying to hide Lucy's pregnancy.

Once CBS and the sponsor agreed to incorporate the pregnancy into the series, they laid down some ground rules: (1) every script dealing with the pregnancy would be approved by a priest, a rabbi, and a minister to make sure it would not offend anyone (okay, so a priest, a rabbi, and a minister are stuck on a desert island, when a . . . oh, never mind), (2) the word "pregnant" was verboten; "expectant" was the term to be used, and (3) Lucy Ricardo would not smoke cigarettes in any of the pregnancy stories. Despite all the fuss, Lucille and Desi were delighted, and all the happy emotion of the event is evident throughout this episode, especially in the final scene at the Tropicana.

EPISODE 51

"Pregnant Women Are Unpredictable"

Cast
Deliveryman: Bennett Green

Lucy is having trouble deciding on a name for the baby. Ricky will be happy with whatever Lucy chooses, and he continues to bring home gifts for the baby. Lucy then gets it into her head that Ricky doesn't care about her anymore, that he cares only about the baby. Is there a problem, or is it just her "'spectant" condition?

Classic Performance: Ricky sings and dances with his large and lovely wife to "Cheek to Cheek."

Classic Quote
LUCY: I want the names to be unique and euphonious.
RICKY: Okay. Unique if it's a boy, and Euphonious if it's a girl.

For the Record: In order of airing, this is episode 46.

If the word "pregnant" was banned in the episodes themselves, how could this episode be titled as it is? The episode titles were never shown as part of the airing of *I Love Lucy,* so it was not a problem. In fact, looking over the titles, it is apparent that very little effort went into the naming of episodes. They were considered a behind-the-scenes necessity, for production information only.

EPISODE 52

"Lucy's Show Biz Swan Song"

Cast
Jerry: Jerry Hausner
Pepito the Clown: Himself

Expecting or not, Lucy wants to be in the show, especially since Ricky has asked the Mertzes to audition. Lucy and Ethel try out with a soft-shoe number and are promptly nixed. The only opening left is in the barbershop quartet, and even Lucy wouldn't dare attempt those close harmonies . . . would she?

Classic Performance: The usual bedlam prevails at Ricky's club, with "Sweet Adeline" as the grand finale.

Classic Cameo: Pepito the Spanish clown does a turn in an audition sequence for the Tropicana.

For the Record: Pepito was a very close friend of the Arnazes. He coached their pre–*I Love Lucy* stage act and appeared in the pilot film they made to sell the show to CBS. In order of airing, this is episode 47.

EPISODE 53

"Lucy Hires an English Tutor"

Cast
Percy Livermore: Hans Conried

Lucy makes up her mind that her baby is going to speak proper English even if it kills her. And it almost does—when she gets Ricky, Fred, and Ethel to join her in taking English lessons from the very uptight Mr. Percy Livermore. When Ricky learns about the deal Lucy has made with the tutor, he takes the matter into his own hands.

Classic Guest Star: Hans Conried is back as the hilarious Mr. Livermore.

EPISODE 54

"Ricky Has Labor Pains"

Cast

Jerry: Jerry Hausner
Dr. Rabwin: Louis D. Merrill
Clubwoman: Hazel Pierce

With all the attention going to the expectant Lucy and the baby-to-be, Ricky is feeling a little neglected. Lucy persuades Fred to have a men-only "daddy shower" for Ricky to make him feel important. But when the men start calling it a stag party, Lucy has second thoughts and decides to keep an eye on the festivities.

For the Record: In order of airing, this is episode 49.

EPISODE 55

"Lucy Becomes a Sculptress"

Cast

William Abbott: Shepard Menken
Clerk: Leon Belasco
Mr. Harvey: Paul Harvey

Lucy wants her child to have a love of beauty and art, so she starts dabbling in sculpture. After she drops a bundle for clay and other supplies and persuades Fred to model for her, Ricky argues that she has no talent. It's art or bust, however, as Lucy is determined to prove him and the art world wrong by creating a lifelike self-study.

For the Record: In order of airing, this is episode 50.

EPISODE 56

"Lucy Goes to the Hospital"

Cast

Mr. Stanley: Charles Lane
Maître d': William Hamel
Policeman: Ralph Montgomery
Nurses: Adele Longmire, Peggy Rea, Barbara Pepper, Ruth Perrott, Hazel Pierce
Orderly: Bennett Green

"The time has come," says Ricky as he, Fred, and Ethel, calmly rehearse the moment when Lucy is to leave for the hospital. When the real thing occurs, all hell breaks loose, and the trio almost leave Lucy behind. Once at the hospital, all that's left for Ricky is the waiting game. Since Ricky is about to open a new show at the club and the doctor has said it could be hours before the baby is born, Ricky goes to work. In the middle of his big voodoo number, the call comes, and Ricky is off to the hospital to meet his new baby.

Our Television Heritage: This was another history-making episode, as America finally met Little Ricky. More people watched Little Ricky's birth than the televised inauguration of President Eisenhower. The day after the episode aired, *I Love Lucy* fans were elated to learn that Lucille Ball and Desi Arnaz had their blessed event at the same time as the Ricardos. A miracle? Not quite. The Arnazes knew the birth would be a cesarean, so they scheduled Little Ricky's birth to coincide with their own baby's due date.

For the Record: In order of airing, this is episode 51.

EPISODE 57

"No Children Allowed"

Cast
Little Ricky: The Simians Twins
Mrs. Trumbull: Elizabeth Patterson
Clubwomen: June Whitney, Charlotte Lawrence, Vivi Janiss, Peggy Rea, Margie Lizst, Kay Wiley

When Ethel stands up to old Mrs. Trumbull, a neighbor who complains about Little Ricky's crying, the Ricardos are sincerely grateful. But when Ethel tells the story to anyone who'll listen, Lucy gets a little impatient. Lucy finally snaps when Ethel recounts the story to the entire bridge club. Ethel, shocked at Lucy's ingratitude, storms out. And Lucy, appalled at Ethel's insensitivity, refuses to apologize.

Classic Guest Star: This is Elizabeth "Patty" Patterson's first appearance as Mrs. Trumbull, who later serves as an ever-present baby-sitter for Little Ricky Ricardo.

Our Television Heritage: This was the first episode filmed after the break Lucille Ball took for the birth of Desi Junior. The addition of the Mrs. Trumbull character was an important one. Not only was she available in the middle of any plot during which the Ricardos had to leave the apartment suddenly, but she also allowed for an often used line: "The baby's with Mrs. Trumbull." This convention freed them up for their shenanigans while still giving credence to them as wonderfully responsible parents.

EPISODE 58

"Lucy Hires a Maid"

Cast
Mrs. Porter: Verna Felton

Exhausted from caring for a newborn, Lucy hints to Ricky that she needs some help around the house. He agrees, and in walks Mrs. Porter. But instead of telling the maid what to do, Lucy ends up catering to her every whim. "Just get rid of her," suggests Ricky . . . but Lucy finds that easier said than done.

Classic Cameo: Verna Felton appeared earlier in the season as the woman on whom Lucy tried to unload the Handy Dandy vacuum cleaner.

Classic Quote
LUCY: What's your name?
MAID: Mrs. Porter.
LUCY: And what do I call you?
MAID: Mrs. Porter.

For the Record: In many of these episodes, the sound of Little Ricky crying was supplied by Jerry Hausner, who played Ricky's agent.

EPISODE 59

"The Indian Show"

Cast
Jerry: Jerry Hausner
Jaunita: Carol Richards
Actor: Richard K. Reeves

Ricky's staging a big new American Indian Show at the Tropicana, but he's not worried this time about Lucy wanting to be in it. Being a mother is her new career, and it's a full-time job. But when he hires the Mertzes, Lucy decides she *can* have it all—motherhood *and* a singing career.

The only problem is, what will she do with Little Ricky?

Classic Performance: Ricky, Fred, and Ethel ugh and war-whoop their way through "Pass that Peace Pipe," but the highlight of this episode is the beautiful "Waters of the Minnetonka," first sung by Ricky and Juanita, the club's resident chanteuse, and then massacred by Lucy.

Classic Quote

LUCY: Me heap sorry me smackum' on coco.

EPISODE 60

"Lucy's Last Birthday"

Cast

Jerry: Jerry Hausner
Mrs. Trumbull: Elizabeth Patterson
Maître d': William R. Hamel
Friends of the Friendless: Ransom Sherman, Byron Foulger, Barbara Pepper

This is another of the best-remembered *I Love Lucy* episodes. Everyone has forgotten Lucy's birthday: Ricky, Fred, Ethel—everyone. After Mrs. Trumbull makes a pathetic attempt to throw a party, Lucy goes for a walk and runs into a group of misfits who have banded together for mutual support. She joins the Friends of the Friendless and decides to teach her foregetful hubby a "lesson on the true meaning of friendship." She then marches the group to the Tropicana and discovers her surprise birthday party in progress.

Classic Performance: Ricky and the party guests sing the "I Love Lucy" theme to an exuberant Lucy Ricardo.

For the Record: This is the only time the lyrics to the show's theme song were ever sung on the series.

EPISODE 61

"The Ricardos Change Apartments"

Cast

Mrs. Benson: Norma Varden

With the new baby, the apartment seems very small and cramped. Lucy persuades her neighbor, Mrs. Benson, who's just married off her daughter, to swap her larger flat for the Ricardos' smaller one. Now if only she can persuade Ricky to shell out the additional twenty dollars a month.

For the Record: The new apartment, complete with a window in the living room and a room for Little Ricky, keeps Lucy content until the last season of the series, when she and Ricky decide to move to a country house in Connecticut.

EPISODE 62

"Lucy Is a Matchmaker"

Cast

Eddie Grant: Hal March
Man in Hotel: Phil Arnold

Lucy meets Eddie Grant, an attractive, unattached friend of the Mertzes, and decides he'd be perfect for Sylvia Collins, one of her unmarried girlfriends. When Sylvia can't make the date, Lucy shows up to let Eddie down easy. He jumps to the wrong conclusion and thinks Lucy's got an eye for him. What's more, he starts bragging to Fred and Ricky about "a married woman who's nuts about me."

EPISODE 63
"Lucy Wants New Furniture"

Lucy's tired of the furniture again. This time she buys a new living room set, using the old furniture as a deposit. Ricky finds out and locks up the new furniture down at the club until Lucy can pay for it out of her household allowance. No more "stravagances" for her; Lucy is determined to show Ricky she can save money. In fact, she'll make her new dress and give herself a home permanent. That'll show him!

Classic Quote

LUCY: *(after her home perm):* Waahh . . . I look like a chrysanthemum!

EPISODE 64
"The Camping Trip"

Cast
Jerry: Jerry Hausner
Clubwomen: Doris Singleton, June Whitney

Lucy decides that she and Ricky need to bond a little more closely. But when she announces that she'll be going on his annual camping trip with the boys, Ricky decides to teach her about the hardships of the great outdoors. They arrange a weekend trip to break her in, just the two of them—and Ethel, who secretly tags along to ensure that Lucy makes a good showing.

EPISODE 65
"Ricky's Life Story"

Cast
Dance coach: Louis A. Nicoletti

Life magazine does a big spread on Ricky and all but excludes Lucy from the piece (her elbow shows up in one photo). Why? Because Ricky has kept her out of show business, that's why! To teach her a lesson about the hardships of life in front of the footlights, he lets her do a big song-and-dance number in the new show. Lucy is thrilled, thinking the number has been designed to show her off, but when she learns it's been constructed to knock the show biz bug out of her, she sings a different tune.

Classic Performance: At the Tropicana, Ricky sings "Lady of Spain" and "The Loveliest Night of the Year" as Lucy sits calmly behind him—at least she's *supposed* to sit calmly. . . .

EPISODE 66
"Ricky and Fred Are TV Fiends"

Cast
Restaurant man: Larry Dobkin
Cop: Allen Jenkins
Sergeant: Frank Nelson

When Fred and Ricky are glued to the set watching the fights, Lucy and Ethel go out for a night on the town. Everywhere they go, they encounter men with their eyes glued to the same televised boxing match.

Classic Guest Stars: Look for Frank Nelson as the gruff desk sergeant who thinks he recognizes Lucy and Ethel as a pair of lady criminals. Nelson usually plays Freddy Fillmore.

EPISODE 67
"Never Do Business with Friends"

Cast
Mrs. Trumbull: Elizabeth Patterson
Joe: Herbert Vigran

Ricky's father said it best: "Never do business with friends or relations." Even so, after the Ricardos get a new washing machine, they sell their old one to Fred and Ethel. The next day the old machine gives up the ghost, and since the Mertzes haven't given Lucy and Ricky the check yet . . . just whose washer is it, anyway?

Classic Guest Stars: Herb Vigran, who plays Mrs. Trumbull's nephew, turned up earlier in *I Love Lucy* episode 40 and played a long series of bad guys on the *Adventures of Superman.*

For the Record: Wait a minute . . . Didn't Fred buy Ethel a Handy Dandy washer earlier this season? He did, but don't tell anyone.

EPISODE 68
"The Girls Go into Business"

Cast
Mrs. Hansen: Mabel Paige
Customers: Barbara Pepper, Kay Wiley
Cop: Emory Parnell

Lucy and Ethel know they could make a fortune in business if only the boys would let them. They buy a local dress shop and—surprise!—the only sales they make are to each other. Can they unload the shop before Ricky and Fred find out they've bought it?

Classic Quote
Deciding on a name for the shop, Ethel suggests "EtheLu's." Of course, Lucy objects to the second billing:
LUCY: We need [a name] that rolls off the tongue . . . like LucyEth's.
ETHEL: LucyEth's? Well, that certainly rolls off the tongue. You couldn't keep that on your tongue if you wanted to!

Our Television Heritage: This episode was filmed the night that Lucille Ball was waiting to hear if she would need to testify before the House Un-American Activities Committee about any possible involvement in the Communist Party in Hollywood in the 1930s. She was completely cleared, but even an accusation could have ruined her career and Desi's as well.

EPISODE 69
"Lucy and Ethel Buy the Same Dress"

Cast
Marion Strong: Shirley Mitchell
Caroline Appleby: Doris Singleton
Clubwomen: Ruth Perrott, Hazel Pierce

Ricky has declared that, no matter what, he won't perform in any more of Lucy's club's shows. And he means it—until Lucy tells him that someone else is going to emcee this year's show. The trick works, and Ricky asks to be involved. He even rehearses the song that Ethel and Lucy want to sing. It's Cole Porter's "Friendship," and it reflects the true nature of the girls' relationship, until they both buy the same evening gown to wear for the show.

Classic Performance: Along with the girls' "Friendship" number, Ricky sings "Vaya con Dios."

EPISODE 70

"Equal Rights"

Cast

Waiter: Lawrence Dobkin
Cops: Fred Aldrich, Louis A. Nicoletti
Station Cop: Richard J. Reeves

Lucy and Ethel decide they want to be treated as equals, and after an argument in a restaurant, Ricky and Fred do exactly that—they stick the girls with a bill for their share of the meal. Unable to pay, Lucy and Ethel retreat to the restaurant's kitchen sink to work off the bill—and to plot revenge on their mean-spirited husbands.

EPISODE 71

"Baby Pictures"

Cast

Caroline Appleby: Doris Singleton
Charlie Appleby: Hy Averback

The battle of the flashbulb erupts as the Ricardos and the Applebys jockey for position in the whose-baby-takes-the-cutest-picture competition. Since Ricky is up for a job at Charlie Appleby's TV station, the Ricardos hold back. But the next day, Lucy and Little Ricky ambush Caroline Appleby and little Stevie with an unannounced visit. After an outrageous exchange of insults, Ricky's TV chances are nil, unless Lucy can do something to make amends—and fast!

Classic Performance: Ricky delivers the Latin number "In Acapulco."

Classic Quote
LUCY: I just hope little Ricky doesn't pick up any of Stevie's bad habits.
CAROLINE: My Stevie doesn't have any bad habits.
LUCY: Well then, I hope he doesn't pick up any of his good habits—like scratching himself and peeling bananas with his feet.
CAROLINE: Well, I never . . .
LUCY: It's time for us to leave. . . . Where do you keep your child's cage?

EPISODE 72

"Lucy Tells the Truth"

Cast

Caroline Appleby: Doris Singleton
Marion Strong: Shirley Mitchell
Casting Director: Charles Lane
The Professor: Mario Siletti
Woman Who Sings like a Chicken: Dorothy Lloyd

Tonight's bet: can Lucy tell the absolute truth for twenty-four hours? She makes it through an afternoon of bridge with the girls, who strike while the iron is hot by asking her all kinds of personal questions. Later she confronts the Mertzes—Fred's a tightwad, and Ethel always looks tacky—and Ricky. Lucy insists it's Ricky's tremendous fear that keeps her out of show biz—fear that she'll give him a run for his money . . . and she can prove it.

Classic Guest Stars: Shirley Mitchell, who plays Marion Strong, comes into her own with a cackle to end all cackles.

Charles Lane makes one of several *I Love Lucy* cameos. He'll later appear as the Ricardo's business manager and a clerk in the Passport office.

And the lady who sings like a chicken . . . well, what can we say?

Parallel Plots: Darrin, among others, is forced to tell the truth in episode 50 of *Bewitched,* and Bob Hartley decides to be truthful in episode 56 of *The Bob Newhart Show,* "Brutally Yours, Bob Hartley."

Classic Quote

ETHEL: What do you really think of Marion's new hat?

LUCY: Marion, if you wanted a hat like that, you sure got a good one!

EPISODE 73

"The French Revue"

Cast

Robert DuBois: Alberto Morin
Stagehands: Richard J. Reeves, Fred Aldrich
Maître d': Louis A. Nicoletti

Ricky is staging an authentic French Revue at the Tropicana Club, and Lucy is determined to get into it. She arranges for French lessons and bones up on her Maurice Chevalier impression to give her an inside edge, but Ricky won't budge. Rest assured, however, that on opening night a certain redhead will be at center stage doing the cancan.

Our Television Heritage: Bad impressions of Maurice Chevalier abound as not only Lucy but also Fred and Ethel try to horn in on Ricky's nightclub act. Lucille Ball and Desi Arnaz were actually big Chevalier fans and tried to get him to do the show during the European trip episodes. He was unavailable, so Charles Boyer filled in.

EPISODE 74

"Redecorating the Mertzes' Apartment"

Ethel is so embarrassed by the state of her run-down flat that she refuses to have the club meet there. Trying to be a good friend, Lucy suggests a painting-and-wallpapering party, just to spruce things up a bit. And with the money they save doing the work themselves, they'll be able to re-upholster the furniture. What could be easier?

For the Record: Vivian Vance begins the episode singing to herself in her living room. She's actually singing "Lily of the Valley," Ethel's big number from the operetta in episode 38 of the season before.

EPISODE 75

"Too Many Cooks"

Cast

Mrs. Trumbull: Elizabeth Patterson
Cop: Allen Jenkins
Madame X: Alice Wills

The neighborhood is besieged by a string of robberies carried out by a mysterious woman wearing men's clothes. When Lucy is seen sneaking out of the Mertzes' apartment with one of Fred's suits, she's suspected of being the perpetrator of the crime wave. But what about Ethel? Lucy catches a glimpse of her outside on the fire escape wearing a man's overcoat. . . . Will the real Madame X please stand up?

EPISODE 76

"Changing the Boys' Wardrobe"

Cast

Zeb Allen: Oliver Blake
Jerry: Jerry Hausner
Photographer: Lee Millar
Award Presenter: Paul Power

Lucy and Ethel try to improve the boys' image by getting rid of their shabby old wardrobes. But the secondhand man sells the ragged clothes back to Ricky and Fred, who gloat in delight. Then the girls decide to teach them a lesson by fighting fire with fire.

EPISODE 77

"Lucy Has Her Eyes Examined"

Cast

Arthur "Kingcat" Walsh: Himself
Mr. Parker: Dayton Lummis
Eye Doctor: Shepard Menken

It's show time once again when Ricky brings home a producer who's casting for a college musical. The producer persuades Ricky to let Lucy and the Mertzes audition live at the Tropicana Club. Lucy rehearses a red-hot jitterbug routine, and her prospects look good—that is, until she takes a trip to the eye doctor right before the show.

Classic Performance: Besides Lucy's dance number, Fred and Ethel sing "Varsity Drag."

EPISODE 78

"Ricky's Old Girlfriend"

Cast

Carlota Romero: Rosa Turich
Jerry: Jerry Hausner
Dream Carlota: Lillian Molieri

In a playful mood, Ricky mentions an old flame of his, one that Lucy's never heard of before. It turns out the woman, Carlota Romero, is appearing in New York at the moment. Lucy gets extremely jealous and is sure that Ricky's going to be reunited with the woman. Lucy has Ricky's agent, Jerry, invite Carlota to the apartment for a showdown.

Classic Performance: Watch for a rare *I Love Lucy* dream sequence, in which Lucy Ricardo's happy home is ripped asunder by Carlota Romero, a sultry Cuban vixen.

Classic Cameo: Lillian Molieri has a wonderful cameo as the full-figured Carlota.

Classic Quote
LUCY (*upon meeting a very overweight Carlota*): Why, Carlota Romero . . . am I glad to see you!
CARLOTA: Am I what you were expecting?
LUCY: I wasn't expecting anyone so full of . . . so full of . . . well, so full!

For the Record: The list of former boyfriends that Lucy reels off in the opening scene—Billy, Jess, Jerry, Bob, Maury, Argyle, Bud, Wilbur, Karl, Martin, et cetera—was made up of the names of *I Love Lucy* staff members.

EPISODE 79

"Million Dollar Idea"

Cast

Dickie Davis: Frank Nelson

Lucy and Ethel go into business yet again, this time with Lucy's recipe for salad dressing, and they manage to get free advertising time on Charlie Appleby's TV station. Their first commercial is so successful that the orders start pouring in. There's only one hitch: because of a slight miscalculation in production costs, they're actually losing money on every jar they produce.

Classic Performance: It's a classic *I Love Lucy* comedy gem when Ethel and Lucy create the commercials first to sell Aunt Martha's Old Fashioned Salad Dressing and then to unsell it.

Classic Guest Stars: Frank Nelson reappears, this time as a different TV show host. Why didn't they just let him play Freddy Fillmore again?

EPISODE 80

"Ricky Minds the Baby"

Cast

Little Ricky: Joseph and Michael Mayer

After a gentle nudge from Lucy, Ricky decides to spend his whole vacation with Little Ricky. He'll take complete charge of caring for his son, doing everything from feeding and dressing him to playing with him. Lucy won't have to worry about a thing. The plan works like a charm—until Lucy gets a little bored and Ricky gets a little careless.

Classic Performance: Desi Arnaz shines in the scene in which Ricky acts out Little Red Riding Hood in "Espanish," to the delight of Little Ricky, not to mention Lucy and the Mertzes.

Our Television Heritage: Because this story line depended on the performances of the toddlers who played Little Ricky, this is the only episode that was filmed without a studio audience. The producers were afraid that audience reactions would confuse or frighten the babies and that the television audience wouldn't get a good show.

EPISODE 81

"The Charm School"

Cast

Bill Hall: Tyler McVey
Louann Hall: Vivi Janiss
Tom Williams: Maury Hill
Eve Whitney: Eve Whitney Maxwell
Phoebe Emerson: Natalie Schafer

After the boys go gaga for the sultry, sophisticated Eve Whitney one night at a get-together, Lucy and Ethel go running to Miss Emerson's Charm School for some remedial lessons. The results are so staggering that Ricky and Fred barely recognize them. When all is said and done, of course, they want their formerly frumpy wives back.

Classic Guest Star: Miss Emerson is charmingly played by Natalie Schafer, who went on to play Lovey Howell, the millionaire's wife, on *Gilligan's Island.*

EPISODE 82

"Sentimental Anniversary"

Cast

Party guests: Barbara Pepper, Hazel Pierce, Bennett Green

Lucy wants to celebrate her thirteenth wedding anniversary with a quiet, romantic dinner at home with Ricky, but the Mertzes have planned a surprise party with all the Ricardos' friends. Lucy fibs, saying that she and Ricky have to go to a business dinner with Rodgers and Hammerstein. The Ricardos pretend to leave but really hunker down for a candlelit dinner for two. The Mertzes let themselves in and start setting up for the party, forcing Lucy and Ricky to move champagne, candles, and all other signs of their intimate dinner to the hall closet.

EPISODE 83

"Fan Magazine Interview"

Cast

Eleanor Harris: Joan Banks
Jerry: Jerry Hausner
Minnie Finch: Kathryn Card
Minnie's Neighbors: Elvia Allman, Hazel "Sunny" Boyne

Eleanor Harris is interviewing Ricky for a magazine. She spends a day with him to see what an exciting life he really has. All is going well, with Lucy and the Mertzes joining in to make Ricky's life seem even more glamorous and exciting than it really is. Miss Harris eventually succeeds in making Lucy jealous of Ricky's female fans, so when Lucy finds a letter to someone named Minnie Finch in Ricky's tuxedo, she thinks he's two-timing her.

Classic Guest Star: Kathryn Card, who plays the unkempt Minnie Finch, will return later in the series to play Mrs. McGillicuddy, Lucy's mother.

For the Record: This was Jerry Hausner's last outing as Jerry, Ricky's agent. A technical problem during the filming of the show started an argument between Desi and him, which grew into an ugly scene in front of cast, crew, and studio audience. Hausner quit the show, never to return.

EPISODE 84

"Oil Wells"

Cast

Sam Johnson: Harry Cheshire
Nancy Johnson: Sandra Gould
Ken: Ken Christy

In their eternal effort to get rich quick, Lucy and Ethel persuade Ricky and Fred to invest in some oil wells that their new neighbors are selling. They do some imaginative speculating about how to spend the money they're bound to make, but then Lucy gets cold feet and thinks that they've been swindled. How can she get the money back?

Classic Guest Stars: If Mrs. Johnson looks familiar, it's because actress Sandra Gould went on to play the second Mrs. Kravitz in *Bewitched*.

EPISODE 85

"Ricky Loses His Temper"

Cast

Mrs. Mulford: Madge Blake
Morris Williams: Byron Kane
Ventriloquist: Max Terhune

Ricky hits the ceiling when Lucy brings home another new hat. She admits that she buys too many hats, but she boasts that at least she can control her temper. And so they make yet another bet: will Ricky blow his Cuban stack before Lucy gives in and purchases another "dilly of a hat"? That very day Lucy can't resist buying a lovely new cocktail hat, so her goal then becomes to make Ricky crack before the hat is delivered.

Classic Guest Star: Madge Blake, best remembered as Batman's aunt Harriet, worked with the Arnazes in their film, *The Long, Long Trailer*. She can be also seen in *I Love Lucy* (episode 85), *Dick Van Dyke* (67), and *Bewitched* (7).

EPISODE 86

"Home Movies"

Cast
Bennett Green: Stanley Farrar

Lucy and the Mertzes are sick of watching Ricky's home movies. In a huff, Ricky tells them they will never see another Ricky Ricardo production, not even "Tropical Rhythms," the television pilot he is about to make. Realizing that this could be their springboard to stardom, Lucy, Fred, and Ethel make a film of their own—a western musical—and splice it into Ricky's.

Classic Performance: Lucy and Ethel turn into cowpokes for "I'm an Old Cowhand," and Ricky sings the Spanish ballad "Vaya Con Dios."

For the Record: The TV producer in this episode is named Bennett Green, the actual name of Desi's stand-in, who was a frequent *I Love Lucy* bit player. (See episode 87, for example.)

EPISODE 87

"Bonus Bucks"

Cast
Laundryman: Tony Michaels
Grocery Boy: Don Garner
Laundry Checker: Frank Jacquet
Laundry Workers: Bennett Green, Patsy Moran
Newspaper Seller: John Frank

Like everyone else in New York City, Lucy and Ethel are examining every dollar bill they get their hands on, searching for one of the winning "Bonus Bucks" featured in a local newspaper contest. When one turns up, both Lucy and Ethel claim it as their own. In the spirit of true friendship, and after a struggle in which the bill is torn in half, the Ricardos and Mertzes decide to split the winnings. Ricky takes half of the bill and puts it in the pocket of his pajamas for safekeeping—but the pj's are promptly picked up by the laundry man. And so the chase begins. . . .

EPISODE 88

"Ricky's Hawaiian Vacation"

Lucy is determined to get herself and the Mertzes invited along on Ricky's upcoming tour to Hawaii. After a delightful audition of their Hawaiian Revue, which Ricky turns down—the last thing he needs to take to Hawaii is a Hawaiian act—Lucy, Fred, and Ethel plot to get on Freddy Fillmore's new show, *Be a Good Neighbor.* To win the trip that Fillmore is offering, Lucy has the Mertzes pose as a poor but honest couple whose lifelong dream is to take their ailing mother to Hawaii. All goes well enough, until Ricky gets wind of the scheme.

Classic Performance: On Freddy Fillmore's show, Ricky sings a medley of songs with food items in their titles, and Lucy gets pelted with the foods mentioned in the song. Other songs include "Honey," "Let's Have Another Cup of Coffee," and "I'm Putting All My Eggs in One Basket."

Classic Guest Star: This is the last appearance of Freddy Fillmore, but don't worry, there's more Frank Nelson to come.

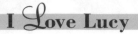
EPISODE 89

"Lucy Is Envious"

Cast

Cynthia Harcourt: Mary Jane Croft
Al Sparks: Herbert Vigran
Henry: Dick Elliot
Martha: Kay Wiley
Elevator Operator: Louis Nicoletti

Trying to impress Cynthia Harcourt, a rich friend from her school days, Lucy pledges money for a charity drive. The shock comes when her pledge of "five" is mistaken for $500. Rather than lose face, Lucy is determined to get the cash. Even it if means dressing up as an alien and kidnapping unsuspecting earthlings? Why not?

Classic Guest Star: Mary Jane Croft makes her first *I Love Lucy* outing as snooty Cynthia.

Classic Quote
LUCY (*as a Martian*): Itz a muumuu.

EPISODE 90

"Lucy Writes a Novel"

Cast

Mr. Dorrance: Pierre Watkin
Mel Eaton: Dayton Lummis
Messenger: Bennett Green

In order to fulfill her need for artistic expression—and to earn a lot of cash—Lucy sets out to write a best-seller. The tome involves some thinly disguised characters named Nicky Nicardo and Fred and Ethel Nurtz. The truth hurts . . . and so does Lucy's fiction, so when a publisher seems interested, Ricky and the Mertzes decide to take matters into their own hands.

EPISODE 91

"Lucy's Club Dance"

Cast

Caroline Appleby: Doris Singleton
Marion Strong: Shirley Mitchell

It's time once again to raise money for the Wednesday Afternoon Fine Arts League, so the members form an all-girl band to do so. They reluctantly let Lucy join as saxophonist, but only after she promises to talk Ricky into acting as musical director.

Classic Performance: The girls try to make their way through "Twelfth Street Rag."

EPISODE 92

"The Diner"

Cast

Mr. Watson: James Burke
Drunk: Fred Sherman
Delivery Boy: Don Garner
Patrons: Marco Rizo, Nick Escalante, Alberto Calderone, Joe Miller

Ricky's lost his taste for show biz and decides to try a different line of work, so he and Lucy join with the Mertzes in buying a diner. Fred and Ethel have some restaurant experience—they were once stranded in Indianapolis where they worked as short-order cooks—and Ricky has a celebrated name, so the diner is bound to be a success. And it is . . . until the Mertzes get tired of working at the hot griddle and demand to switch jobs with the Ricardos, who keep cool while greeting and seating customers.

EPISODE 93

"The Black Wig"

Cast

Roberta: Eve McVeagh
Doug: Douglas Evans
Waiter: Louis A. Nicoletti
Man: Bennett Green

In trying to convince Ricky that she should have her hair cut in the new Italian style, Lucy borrows a short black wig. Ricky plays along and acts as if he doesn't recognize her. Lucy is shocked when he flirts with her and promises to teach her to rumba. She accepts the date and asks him to bring a friend along for her girlfriend, who likes older men. Her plan is to show up with Ethel for the assignation . . . and then lower the boom.

Parallel Plot: Rob plays Italian lover to Laura, who plays along, in episode 32 of *The Dick Van Dyke Show.*

Classic Quote

WAITER: What did the men look like?
LUCY: Well, one is tall, dark, and handsome and speaks with an accent. and the other is . . . Well, the other is . . .
ETHEL: Let's face it, Lucy, there's only one way to describe Fred—short, fat, and bald.

Our Television Heritage: Desi offered to teach Lucy to rumba the very first time they met, during a rehearsal for the RKO film *Too Many Girls* in the early 1940s.

EPISODE 94

"Tennessee Ernie Visits"

Cast

Cousin Ernie: Tennessee Ernie Ford

Lucy gets a letter from her mother saying that her "dear friend's roommate's cousin's middle boy" is coming to New York to visit, and asking Lucy and Ricky to make him feel welcome. The boy is Cousin Ernie Ford from Bentfork, Tennessee, and he's come to New York with only a handful of change. He's planning to stay with the Ricardos indefinitely. Ernie makes "hisself to home" and tries to be helpful by doing things around the house—like taking the sand out of Ricky's maracas. Lucy tries everything to get him to leave, including turning herself into a wicked city woman and vamping for him.

Classic Performance: Cousin Ernie rouses the Ricardos at the crack of dawn with "The Wabash Cannonball."

EPISODE 95

"Tennessee Ernie Hangs On"

Cast

Cousin Ernie: Tennessee Ernie Ford
Show Host: Richard J. Reeves

He's still here, and now the Ricardos are desperate. When they plant a bus ticket to Bentfork in the hallway, Ernie finds it and gives it away. When Lucy concocts a story about how Ricky has lost his job and can no longer support him, Ernie collects food and money from the Ricardos' neighbors. Finally Ernie books them all on Millikan's Chicken Mash Hour, which will not only give Lucy and Ricky enough money to make ends meet for awhile, but will also let Ernie return to Tennessee with a clear conscience. Before you can say "I'll be ding-donged," the group is all gussied up and singing for Millikan.

Classic Performance: Ernie Ford et al. warble the countrified, "Y'all Come."

EPISODE 96

"The Golf Game"

Cast

Jimmy Demaret: Himself
Caddy: George Pirrone
Tournament Announcer: Louis A. Nicoletti

Lucy and Ethel are ready to hit the links with the boys, who've gone golf crazy. In order to discourage them, Ricky and Fred teach them the game with special rules devised to drive the girls nuts. Lucy and Ethel, in turn, teach these rules to real-life golf champ, Jimmy Demaret when they bump into him on the course.

Parallel Plot: Look for real-life pro golfer Jerry Barber in episode 23 of *I Dream of Jeannie*. Demaret won the Masters Tournament three times, in 1940, 1947, and 1950; Barber never won the green jacket, but in 1961 he won the PGA Championship, a title Demaret never earned.

EPISODE 97

"The Sublease"

Cast

Mrs. Hammond: Virginia Brissac
Mr. Beecher: Jay Novello

When Ricky books his band at a resort in Maine, Lucy and Little Ricky plan to go there with him. Before they leave, the Ricardos arrange to sublet their apartment for the summer to a quiet little man in need of peace and solitude. When Ricky's summer gig falls through, however, the timid sublessee refuses to give up the apartment.

Classic Guest Stars: Jay Novello returns in this episode for another comic gem in a small role as the neurotic Mr. Beecher. He'll be back as Mario, the visitor from Italy, in episode 158.

EPISODE 98

"Lucy Cries Wolf"

Cast

Mrs. DeVries: Beppy DeVries
Crooks: Fred Aldrich, Louis A. Nicoletti

Unimpressed by Ricky's promise to protect her, Lucy is determined to test his loyalty. She fabricates an emergency and waits for Ricky to rush home to her aid. When he sends the Mertzes instead of coming himself, Lucy concocts a scheme designed to teach him—and the Mertzes—a lesson.

EPISODE 99

"The Matchmaker"

Cast

Dorothy: Sarah Selby
Sam: Milton Frome
Messenger: Bennett Green

Lucy tries to paint a picture of happy married life for couple Dorothy and Sam, in the hope that Sam will finally pop the question. Everything goes wrong. The baby is fussy, the dinner gets ruined, and worst of all, Ricky gets mad and starts a fight. How can Lucy push two people into matrimony when her own marriage is such a tangle?

EPISODE 100

"The Business Manager"

Cast

Mr. Hickox: Charles Lane
Mrs. Trumbull: Elizabeth Patterson

Ricky decides that since a certain redhead cannot control the household finances, a business manager is required. Enter Mr. Hickox, who goes over Lucy's books and puts her on a very tight budget. With only five dollars in spending money for the month, Lucy works out a complex financial scheme in which she buys groceries for her neighbors, using Hickox's credit account, then keeps their cash. It's a perfect system, until Ricky finds a wad of bills and wants to know where Lucy got the money.

EPISODE 101

"Mr. and Mrs. TV Show"

Cast

Harvey Cromwell: John Litel
Mr. Taylor: Lee Millar

Sometimes dreams do come true. Ricky is signed to do a daily "at home" TV show for Phipps Department Store, and Lucy will be his costar. All is perfection, until Lucy finds out that a certain Cuban didn't want her to do the show at all. In fact, the sponsors forced Ricky to cast his wife. In retaliation, Lucy turns the dress rehearsal into a nightmare, just to teach Ricky a lesson, not knowing that the rehearsal is actually the live show.

Classic Quote

RICKY: Why, a Phipps Foam Mattress rocks you to sleep.
LUCY: You mean a Phipps Foam Mattress is like sleeping on rocks.

EPISODE 102

"Mertz and Kurtz"

Cast

Barney Kurtz: Charles Winninger
Little Barney: Stephen Whooten

Kurtz is Fred's old vaudeville partner, Barney, who is coming to visit. Jealous of his friend's continued success in show biz, Fred wants Barney to think that he's made a killing in the real estate business. To help out, Lucy pretends to be the Mertzes' maid. When the truth is revealed, it turns out that Barney isn't performing much at all these days; in fact, he's a cook in a restaurant. But don't worry, Ricky lets Barney do his act at the club so that he can impress his grandson. And Lucy, Fred, and Ethel join in!

Classic Performance: This episode offers viewers an entire musical revue called "On the Boardwalk" with songs including "By the Beautiful Sea" and "On the Boardwalk in Atlantic City."

EPISODE 103

"Ricky's Movie Offer"

Cast

Ben Benjamin: Frank Nelson
Pete: James Dobson
Mrs. Trumbull: Elizabeth Patterson

A big-time Hollywood scout comes to discuss a screen test with Ricky for the upcoming movie *Don Juan*. Lucy, realizing that Ricky's chance at stardom could be her big break as well, decides to make her move. After all, Mr. Benjamin said they're looking for a Marilyn Monroe type. Once the word is out, the Mertzes are also ready to horn in on the audition, along with Mrs. Trumbull and Pete the grocery boy.

Classic Guest Star: Frank Nelson is back!

For the Record: This is the beginning of the story line that will eventually take the *I Love Lucy* gang to Hollywood. It's a brilliant move that not only offers Lucy, Ricky, Fred, and Ethel many new comic situations, but also opens up countless guest star possibilities, breathing new life into the show after three seasons.

EPISODE 104

"Ricky's Screen Test"

Cast

Director: Clinton Sundberg
Assistant Director: Ray Kellogg
Boom Man: Louis A. Nicoletti
Clapstick Man: Alan Ray

Lucy is thrilled about Ricky's film opportunity until she learns that every glamorous leading lady in Hollywood is being considered for the female lead. Ricky reignites Lucy's enthusiasm by naming her as his partner in the screen test. "Hallelujah!" she thinks. It's her big break, at last. But how can she be discovered if Ricky won't give her equal time on camera during the short scene?

Classic Performances: Ricky sings "Canta Guitarra" as part of the movie tryout. More significantly, Lucy's desperate attempts to make an impact during Ricky's *Don Juan* screen test make for one of the best-remembered comic scenes in all of *I Love Lucy*.

EPISODE 105

"Lucy's Mother-in-Law"

Cast

Ricky's Mother: Mary Emery
Professor: Fortunio Bonanova
Assistant: Virginia Barbour
Party Guests: Pilar Arcos, Rodolfo Hoyos

Lucy's mother-in-law arrives for a visit, and Lucy is in a panic. She gets off to a bumpy start—burning dinners, scorching her best dress, and losing Ricky's mother in the subway, but Lucy is determined to make a good impression. She decides to learn to speak Spanish in time for a dinner party for Mrs. Ricardo's dear friends. With the help of minimicrophones and a hidden earpiece, she might just pull it off.

Classic Guest Star: Mary Emery makes the first of her two appearances as Ricky's sweet Cuban mother.

EPISODE 106

"Ethel's Birthday"

When Fred asks Lucy to buy a present for Ethel's birthday, Lucy decides on a chic pair of hostess pants. Ethel, thinking that Fred has bought them, ridicules the whole notion, making Lucy furious. A fight erupts, and it looks as if the girls will never make up, until watching a hit Broadway drama makes them see the error of their ways.

Classic Quote
LUCY: They're hostess pants. You wear them when you throw smart dinner parties.
ETHEL: I was wondering what to wear at all those smart dinner parties I throw.
LUCY (*holding up the pants*): I dunno, Ethel. I think they're nice. You get yourself a little off-the-

shoulder blouse, a big crushy belt, and ballet slippers, and you're all set.

ETHEL: For what . . . Halloween?

EPISODE 107
"Ricky's Contract"

Ricky is going crazy waiting to hear if he got the movie role in *Don Juan*, so Lucy and the Mertzes try fruitlessly to divert his attention. Finally Lucy tells him to go to rehearsal while she stays by the telephone and reports any news ASAP. When Ethel and Fred take over the phone watch, a message mistakenly gets written down that Ricky got the job, and before they can tell Lucy it's not true, she relays the good news to Ricky. How can they break it to the Cuban ham that Hollywood didn't call after all?

Classic Quote

LUCY: I'll just tell him the truth. I'll calmly say "Ricky, there's been a mistake. Fred mistakenly wrote the message down, Ethel accidentally left it by the phone . . . and I innocently called you at the club." Of course, I'll be holding Little Ricky when I tell him. He wouldn't dare hit a woman with a baby.

EPISODE 108
"Getting Ready"

With Ricky signed to a film contract, it's up to Lucy to decide how they should travel from New York to Hollywood—by train, bus, or plane. Finally she hits upon the perfect means of transport: they'll buy a car! After all, they'll need one in California, and it would be a shame to waste that big old empty back seat, so it's decided that Fred and Ethel will join them in their cross-country adventure. What kind of car will they buy? Well, Fred visits his friend who runs a used-car

lot and comes back with a Cadillac convertible . . . circa 1925!

EPISODE 109
"Lucy Learns to Drive"

Fred agrees to take the 1925 Caddy back to the dealer, and Ricky buys a new 1955 Pontiac convertible. Lucy persuades her husband to teach her to drive so she'll be able to pitch in as they travel west, but her first driving lesson turns Ricky into a gibbering mess. Undaunted, Lucy sets out to show Ethel what she has learned. The result? The Pontiac smashes into the Cadillac, and the two cars are locked together. To make matters worse, Lucy has failed to get the car insured.

Classic Quote

LUCY: How was I supposed to know we didn't have enough room to make a U-turn in the Holland Tunnel?

EPISODE 110
"California, Here We Come!"

Cast
Mrs. Trumbull: Elizabeth Patterson
Mrs. McGillicuddy: Kathryn Card

The departure to California is just one day away, and Lucy is sure that nothing else can possibly go wrong—until her mother shows up, having decided that a trip to Los Angeles is just what she needs. Ricky blows his stack, and for a while it looks as if no one will be going to Tinseltown. When all is said and done, however, the trip is on and everyone is going—the Ricardos and Mertzes by car, as planned, and Lucy's mom and Little Ricky later, by airplane. With a song in their hearts and on their lips, Lucy, Ricky, Ethel, and Fred leave the Big Apple for points west.

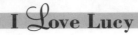

Classic Performance: As they drive over the George Washington Bridge, the adventurers belt out "California, Here I Come!"

Classic Guest Stars: Kathryn Card makes her debut as Mrs. McGillicuddy, garbling Ricky's name (Mickey Bacardi) for the very first time—long before Darrin's mother-in-law, Endora, began her infamous garbling of *his* name.

EPISODE 111
"First Stop"
Cast
George Skinner: Olin Howlin

The first day on the road has taken its toll on the Ricardos and Mertzes. Tired and hungry, they stop at a little country roadside place, where they find only an eccentric owner and some stale cheese sandwiches. After another hour on the road, they find themselves back at the same crummy joint, and they decide to spend the night. The only accommodation available is one shack located right next to the railroad tracks with a rump-sprung double bed and a pair of bunks. Well, it's only for one night—how bad could it be?

For the Record: This episode marked the first time that *I Love Lucy* scenes were shot on location rather than in the studio.

EPISODE 112
"Tennessee Bound"
Cast
Cousin Ernie: Tennessee Ernie Ford
Sheriff: Will Wright
Teensy and Weensy: The Borden Twins
Gas Station Man: Aaron Spelling

In Bentfork, Tennessee, Ricky is pulled over for driving 40 miles an hour in a 15 mph zone. When Lucy and the gang end up in the pokey for sassing the local sheriff, who should turn up to save the day but Cousin Ernie Ford? He's willing to marry one of the constable's hefty twin daughters if it'll get his New York "cousins" out of jail. But that plan backfires when Ernie proposes to the wrong daughter: the two of them are as "alike as two peas in a pod . . . or two watermelons in a patch." The sheriff gives the gang a choice: they can spend sixty days in prison or they can get his daughters into the movies. Ay-yi-yi!

Classic Performance: Teensy and Weensy give Ricky a taste of their talent by singing the snappy country tune "Ricochet Romance."

Classic Guest Stars: This is the last appearance of Tennessee Ernie Ford on *I Love Lucy*.

We know nothing about the Borden Twins, but everyone knows what became of Aaron Spelling—he became the father of *Beverly Hills 90210's* Tori Spelling.

Classic Quote

COUSIN ERNIE: I told the sheriff you'd haul the girls into Hollerwood. They're just dying to get into motion pictures . . . and they'd be perfect for the wide screen.

EPISODE 113

"Ethel's Hometown"

Cast
Will Potter: Irving Bacon

When the group stops in Albuquerque, Ethel's old stomping ground, the locals think Ethel's the one who's going to star in a big Hollywood film. Instead of setting the record straight, she plays the diva, granting interviews and giving a big benefit recital at the city's Little Theater. Lucy, Ricky, and Fred decide to help out with the performance and show Albuquerque just how talented Ethel really is.

Classic Performance: The spotlight is on Ethel Mae Potter as she sings "Shortnin' Bread" and the operatic "My Hero."

Classic Quote
ETHEL'S DAD: Y'know, little Ethel's big in Albuquerque.
FRED: Little Ethel's big all over.

Our Television Heritage: Vivian Vance was originally from Albuquerque, where she was a star performer at the Little Theater. The numbers that Ethel sings in this episode were songs that Vivian had sung to great acclaim in her early stage career.

For the Record: It is revealed that Ethel's beau in Albuquerque was Deke Hartley.

EPISODE 114

"L.A. at Last"

Cast
Bobby: Robert Jellison
Waiter: Harry Bartell
Mr. Sherman: Dayton Lummis
Secretary: Dani Sue Nolan
William Holden: Himself
Eve Arden: Herself

Well, they've arrived, and things certainly are looking good. They're staying in a beautiful hotel, Ricky's due to start filming at Metro, and there's a whole city full of movie stars for Lucy to hunt down. William Holden is the first; she runs into him at the Brown Derby, with disastrous results. And when Ricky brings him home to meet her, she panics—until she tries to disguise herself with a little reconstructive makeup.

Classic Guest Stars: Robert Jellison makes his first appearance as Bobby the bellboy, who assists Lucy throughout her Hollywood stay at the Beverly Palms Hotel.

William Holden and Eve Arden were the first movie stars to appear as themselves in *I Love Lucy*. They did it not only to plug their latest projects but also because they all wanted to appear on TV's top-rated show. At the time, Eve Arden was starring in *Our Miss Brooks*, another Desilu project.

Our Television Heritage: The Bill Holden episode, one of the funniest of all, was nominated for an Emmy Award. The final scene, in which Lucy disguises herself with a fake nose, is another of Lucy's best-remembered bits. TV legend has it that the nose going up in flames was unplanned, but if you look closely, you can see the wick that was built into the waxy nose putty.

EPISODE 115

"Don Juan and the Starlets"

Cast

Ross Elliot: Himself
Starlets: Dolores Donlon, Beverly E.
Thompson, Shirlee Tigge, Maggie
Magennis
Maid: Iva Shepard

Lucy is uneasy when the studio publicity downplays Ricky's happy married life and starts pairing him with a bevy of young beauties. And when she misses out on a fancy Hollywood premiere so he can attend with the aforementioned starlets, Lucy begins to suspect that Ricky is enjoying his newfound lifestyle a little too much.

EPISODE 116

"Lucy Gets into Pictures"

Cast

Bobby: Robert Jellison
Frank Williams: Lou Krugman
Stagehand: Louis A. Nicoletti

Everyone, including the Mertzes and even Bobby the bellboy, is landing a job in the movies—everyone, that is, except a certain redhead. After a valiant but vain attempt to get discovered at Schwab's Drugstore, Lucy finally gets a bit part in a movie at MGM after Ricky pulls some strings. She's to play a showgirl who gets shot in the middle of a splashy musical number. But when she flubs take after take, it seems that her film debut might get killed as well.

Classic Performance: Lucy, wearing a six-foot headpiece, parades down a staircase to the strains of "A Pretty Girl is like a Melody."

For the Record: The writers can't seem to make up their minds. Lucy refers to her friend as *Lillian* Appleby, even though her name has been *Caroline* since episode 69.

EPISODE 117

"The Fashion Show"

Cast

Don Loper: Himself
Amzie: Amzie Strickland
Sheila MacRae, Mrs. William Holden,
Mrs. Dean Martin, Mrs. Van Heflin, Mrs.
Forrest Tucker, Mrs. Alan Ladd, Mrs.
Richard Carlson: Themselves

The one thing Lucy needs, now that she's the wife of a big star, is a Don Loper original. She takes Ethel to the Don Loper Salon, pays $500 for a dress, and worms her way into a fashion show featuring some glamorous Hollywood wives. In order to stop Ricky from getting mad at her "'stravagance,'" she plans to get just enough of a sunburn to look pained, but not enough to really hurt her. The plan backfires when she falls asleep in the sun and ends up burned to a crisp, but the fashion show must go on and so does Lucy . . . in a form-fitting tweed suit.

Favorite: Of fashion designer Isaac Mizrahi.

Classic Cameo: Mrs. Forrest Tucker is indeed the wife of Forrest Tucker, best known in Classic TV circles as Sergeant O'Rourke on *F Troop*.

EPISODE 118

"The Hedda Hopper Story"

Cast
Hedda Hopper: Herself
Charlie Pomerantz: Hy Averback
Bobby: Robert Jellison
Mrs. McGillicuddy: Kathryn Card
Lifeguard: John Hart

Lucy's mom arrives in sunny L.A. with Little Ricky, and she immediately starts complicating things for the Ricardos. Meanwhile, Ricky has a new press agent who's trying to create enough publicity to get the Cuban star-to-be into the Hollywood gossip columns, especially Hedda Hopper's. Finally, it's decided to stage a poolside rescue so Ricky can play the hero. Now, where will they find a young woman to act the poor victim?

Our Television Heritage: Hedda Hopper, Hollywood's leading lady of the scandal sheets, was a powerful force in the movie world, making and breaking celebrities' careers with mentions in her column. She and Lucy had been friends since Lucy's movie days, and she always wrote flatteringly about the Arnazes.

EPISODE 119

"Don Juan Is Shelved"

Cast
Mrs. McGillicuddy: Kathryn Card
Bobby: Robert Jellison
Dore Schary: Phil Ober
Miss Ballantine: Jody Drew
Jim Stevens: John Hart

Can it be? Is *Don Juan* really to be canceled? The answer, sadly, is yes. But Lucy and the Mertzes try valiantly to make Dore Schary, the head of MGM, realize what a find he has in Ricky Ricardo—first by bombarding the studio with fan mail, then by finding someone to impersonate a big movie mogul who's interested in stealing the Cuban from Metro.

Classic Cameo: Phil Ober, who was married to Vivian Vance at the time, makes his second *I Love Lucy* appearance as Dore Schary.

For the Record: Dore Schary was scheduled to appear as himself but backed out at the last minute. Luckily, Phil Ober was able to step into the movie chief's shoes.

EPISODE 120

"Bullfight Dance"

Cast
Ross Elliot: Himself
Prop Man: Ray Kellogg

Lucy wants into the act again, this time in a benefit Ricky is hosting on TV. With a little blackmail, she gets her way, but when she can't handle the song Ricky has chosen for them to sing, Lucy finds herself reduced to a bit part in a novelty dance act, dressed as a bull. Never one to take things lying down, the redhead decides to make it a memorable dance routine, much to the surprise of matador Ricky Ricardo.

Classic Performance: After the Mertzes perform the familiar "Dear Old Donegal," Ricky and Lucy sing and dance to "Fernando the Matador."

For the Record: Ricky's Heart Fund benefit takes place at CBS Television City in a not-too-subtle plug for the network's new broadcast center.

EPISODE 121

"Hollywood Anniversary"

Cast

Mrs. McGillicuddy: Kathryn Card
Ross Elliot: Himself

Ricky, like every TV Land husband, has forgotten the date of his anniversary. He panics and tells Lucy that he knew all along—in fact, he's planned a big celebrity-studded party at the Mocambo. When Lucy finds out it's all a lie, she won't speak to him, and she refuses to attend his attempt at a make-amends party at the Hollywood nightspot. Will they reconcile before the big night?

Classic Performance: Ricky sings the sentimental "Anniversary Waltz" to his angry wife.

For the Record: The Ricardos' Mocambo celebration was based on the real life party Desi threw for Lucille Ball in honor of their thirteenth anniversary.

EPISODE 122

"The Star Upstairs"

Cast

Cornel Wilde: Himself
Bobby: Robert Jellison

Lucy's quest to meet all of the movie stars in Hollywood continues when she finds out that movie hunk Cornel Wilde is staying in the suite above her. She'll stop at nothing, even pretending to be a bellboy, to gain entry to Wilde's room and see the star up close and very, very personal.

Classic Guest Star: How many times do we have to tell you? Cornel Wilde!

EPISODE 123

"In Palm Springs"

Cast

Rock Hudson: Himself
Mrs. McGillicuddy: Kathryn Card

It's time for another vacation from marriage, this time to get away from each other's annoying little habits. Lucy and Ethel take Mrs. McGillicuddy to Palm Springs for a little break from the boys. Funny, though, after a day or two, those little habits don't seem to matter much, and the girls miss the guys something awful. Even an encounter with Rock Hudson, who happens to be staying at the same resort, only makes Lucy and Ethel miss Ricky and Fred even more.

Classic Guest Star: Hunka hunk Rock Hudson makes a charming and funny appearance as he tells the story of Adele Sliff, a script girl who tiffed with her hubby over his annoying habit of whistling.

For the Record: Adele Sliff was the name of an *I Love Lucy* script girl.

EPISODE 124

"Harpo Marx"

Cast

Harpo Marx: Himself
Caroline Appleby: Doris Singleton

Caroline is so pleased to have met Van Johnson that she decides to stay in Hollywood an extra day to see who else will turn up. Lucy and Ethel steal her glasses, without which Caroline is as blind as a bat, and the redhead impersonates as many stars as she dares—Jimmy Durante, Clark Gable, Gary Cooper, and others. Just when Lucy dons a Harpo Marx outfit, who should turn up but the real Harpo?

Classic Performances: Harpo Marx plays a lovely version of "Take Me Out to the Ball Game" on his harp. Better yet, Lucy and Harpo make classic TV magic by re-creating the mirror scene from the Marx Brothers' movie *Duck Soup*.

For the Record: In order of airing, this is episode 125.

EPISODE 125

"The Dancing Star"

Cast
Van Johnson: Himself
Caroline Appleby: Doris Singleton

Lucy's friend Caroline has arrived from New York on her way to Hawaii, and Lucy decides to exaggerate the glamour of her new Hollywood lifestyle. Thinking that Caroline will never discover the truth, she fibs, saying she'll be dancing with Van Johnson, who's appearing at the Hotel. When Caroline decides to witness the dancing duo, Lucy has to do some quick talking to persuade Van to let her be his partner.

Classic Performance: Lucy and Van Johnson dance to the lovely "How about You?"

Classic Guest Stars: Van Johnson, who was a dear friend of the Arnazes, stepped in for Ray Bolger, who played the Scarecrow in *The Wizard of Oz*, when Bolger couldn't fulfill the assignment.

Classic Quote
VAN JOHNSON (*to Lucy*): Excuse me, lady, but you're talking nutsy-cuckoo.

For the Record: In order of airing, this is episode 124.

EPISODE 126

"Ricky Needs an Agent"

Cast
Mr. Reilly: Parley Baer
Miss Klein: Helen Kleeb

Lucy is sick and tired of waiting for MGM to find her talented hubby a new movie role. In order to light a fire under studio honchos, she poses as Ricky's new agent and tries to illustrate how much in demand the Cuban entertainer really is. Not wanting to stand in his way, the studio decides to release Ricky from his contract and let him take the nonexistent offers. How will Lucy tell him she's gotten him fired from his shot at film stardom?

Parallel Plot: Surprisingly, Lucy hasn't learned the lesson of episode 38.

EPISODE 127

"The Tour"

Cast
Richard Widmark: Himself
Bus Driver: Benny Rubin
Women on Bus: Barbara Pepper, Audrey Betz
Maid: Juney Ellis

While taking a bus tour of the stars' homes in Beverly Hills, Lucy talks Ethel into helping her get a souvenir grapefruit from a tree in Richard Widmark's yard. Lucy gets stuck in the yard, which is enclosed by a giant wall, and must exit through the house. She gets trapped when Widmark returns home with none other than Ricky Ricardo, with whom he was having lunch.

Classic Guest Star: Richard Widmark appears and talks up his latest film, *A Prize of Gold*.

For the Record: The exterior shots showing Widmark's house are actually of the Desi Arnaz–Lucille Ball home on Roxbury Drive in Beverly Hills, which was surrounded by a high brick wall.

EPISODE 128

"Lucy Visits Grauman's"

Cast

Tourist couple: Gege Pearson, Hal Gerard
Cops: Ben Nunis, Clarence Straight

Lucy and the Mertzes are trying to take in all the sights before they return to New York, so they visit Grauman's Chinese Theatre. When they discover that John Wayne's cement block is wobbly, Lucy realizes that she has found the ultimate souvenir. That night, Lucy, Ethel, and Fred return with a crowbar and take the autographed block. When Ricky finds out, he demands they return it. The three agree, but the cement slab gets dropped accidentally and shatters into hundreds of pieces. To be continued . . .

EPISODE 129

"Lucy and John Wayne"

Cast

John Wayne: Himself
George: Ralph Volkie
Little Ricky: Mike Mayer

The missing cement block is now making the news, and Lucy and Ethel are wanted by the police, so Ricky calls up John Wayne and asks him to sign another slab. He agrees, and the plan is to sneak the new block back in place in time for the premiere of John Wayne's new movie, *Blood Alley*. But no matter how many times he signs the cement blocks, they keep getting ruined.

Classic Guest Stars: The Duke meets Lucy Ricardo for the first time in this episode, although John Wayne and Lucille Ball had been friends for years. John Wayne also appeared with Lucy on *The Lucy Show* several years later.

For the Record: These two John Wayne footprint episodes were the first scripts written by Bob Schiller and Bob Weiskopf, who joined the writing team in the fifth season and would continue to write for Lucille Ball on her post–*I Love Lucy* shows.

EPISODE 130

"Lucy and the Dummy"

Cast

Chip Jackson: Lee Millar

Even though Lucy has accepted for the two of them, Ricky refuses to perform at a studio party because he's made prior plans to go fishing. Lucy takes matters into her own hands and builds a Ricky dummy, using a realistic rubber head that the studio had made for makeup tests. The act, designed to show off her talent, goes wrong when the dummy gets attached to her elaborate Spanish veil. The audience hails Lucy Ricardo as a new comic genius. Will Lucy stay in Hollywood and seize her chance at stardom, or will she return to New York to be wife and mother?

Classic Performance: Lucy sings one of Ricky's trademark numbers, "I Get Ideas," during her solo song-and-dance turn at the studio party.

EPISODE 131

"Ricky Sells the Car"

Cast

Messenger: Bennett Green
Ticket Agent: Donald L. Brodie

Ricky sells the car for a neat profit and decides to buy train tickets back east. He forgets, however, that Fred and Ethel were attached to the back seat, literally. When only enough train tickets are delivered for the Ricardo family, the Mertzes get mad and buy a vintage Harley to bring them back to New York.

EPISODE 132

"The Great Train Robbery"

Cast

Conductor: Frank Nelson
Mrs. McGillicuddy: Kathryn Card
Jewelry Salesman: Lou Krugman
Jewel Thief: Harry Bartell

Everyone is safely aboard the Super Chief, so what could go wrong? Well . . . Lucy could leave her purse at the magazine stand on the platform, Ricky could almost get crushed retrieving it, Lucy could get involved with a gun-toting jewel thief, and *someone* could keep pulling the emergency cord, bringing the train to a screeching halt again and again. All this and more happens as the Ricardos and Mertzes head back to the Big Apple.

Classic Guest Stars: Frank Nelson is again on hand as the exasperated conductor who tries to get a certain redhead to stop pulling the emergency brake.

Classic Quote
LUCY: (*with a gleam in her eye*): I can see it now . . . *I Was a Woman . . . for the FBI.*

EPISODE 133

"The Homecoming"

Cast

Mrs. Trumbull: Elizabeth Patterson
Nancy Graham: Elvia Allman
Neighbors: Eve June Mayer, Roy Schallart, Charlotte Lawrence, Barbara Pepper, Bennett Green, Hazel Pierce

The Ricardos are happy to be back in New York, but why is everyone making such a fuss over Ricky? During an interview with reporter Nancy Graham, Lucy suddenly realizes that now that her hubby is a star, she must dedicate her life to him—and him alone—after all, he now belongs to the world. And Ricky, the Cuban ham, decides to play it up.

EPISODE 134

"The Ricardos Are Interviewed"

Cast

Johnny Clark: John Gallaudet
Edward Warren; Elliot Reid
TV Director: Monty Masters
Cameraman: Bennett Green

Ricky's new agent thinks it's time the Ricardos upgraded their image by moving into a plush new apartment. Fred and Ethel agree that moving would be the best thing for Ricky's career, so they pick a fight with their best friends so they'll have a reason to evict them. The fabricated fight turns real and eventually erupts during a live TV interview with Lucy, Ricky, Fred, and Ethel.

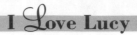

Classic Performance: At the interview, Ricky sings "Rancho Grande" with the help of the Mertzes and Lucy. During the song, they exchange barbs.

For the Record: The *Face to Face* program in this episode is based on the popular interview show *Person to Person*, which featured celebrities chatting in their own homes.

EPISODE 135
"Lucy Goes to the Rodeo"

Cast
Johnny Clark: John Gallaudet
Rattlesnake Jones: Dub Taylor
Announcer: Doye O'Dell

Due to a scheduling conflict involving a show at Madison Square Garden, Ricky can't perform at Fred's annual lodge show. Fred eventually invites Lucy and Ethel to join in as talent for the western-theme revue, but when Ricky discovers that his commitment is to perform for the rodeo that's playing the Garden, he has to beg Lucy and the Mertzes to help him out.

Classic Performance: Ricky—decked out in a ten gallon hat, cowboy guns, and holsters—sings "Texas Pete." The Mertzes belt out "Red River Valley." And then it's time for Lucille McGillicuddy and Her Western Bell Ringers to tinkle their way through "Down by the Old Mill Stream."

EPISODE 136
"Nursery School"

Cast
Dr. Gettleman: Olan E. Soule
Dr. Barnett: Howard Hoffman
Nurses: Iva Shepard, Maxine Semon
Orderlies: Alan Ray, Robert Brubaker

After a reprimand from Ricky, Lucy reluctantly takes Little Ricky to nursery school. He catches a cold, which eventually turns into tonsillitis. Faced with the idea of her baby staying in the hospital overnight and having an operation, Lucy is determined to buck the hospital's rules and stay in his room with him.

EPISODE 137
"Ricky's European Booking"

Cast
Mr. Feldman: Harry Antrim
Mr. Jamison: Barney Phillips
Mrs. Wolbert: Dorthea Wolbert
Hazal Pierce: Hazel Pierce

Ricky and the band are booked on an extensive European tour, for which Fred will act as band manager. Lucy and Ethel can go, too, if they can raise the bucks to cover their expenses—a paltry $3,000! The girls declare themselves a charity and organize a raffle to raise the funds.

Classic Performance: Ricky and a singing group, the Pied Pipers, are seen in the recording studio performing "Forever, Darling."

Classic Quote
LUCY: We'll call it . . . the Ladies Overseas Aid.
ETHEL: Can we do that?
LUCY: Well . . . we're ladies, we want to go overseas, and boy, do we need aid!

For the Record: *Forever, Darling* the second Lucy-Desi movie, was about to be released when this episode was shot.

EPISODE 138

"The Passports"

Cast
Helen Kaiser: Sheila Bromley
Sidney Kaiser: Robert Forrest
Dr. Peterson: Sam Hearn

In order to get a passport, Lucy needs a copy of her birth certificate. But the Jamestown Hall of Statistics has no record of her birth. Now she has to find two people to sign statements attesting to her being born. And the search begins. . . .

Classic Performance: Old Doc Peterson sings a rousing chorus of "Skip to My Loo."

EPISODE 139

"Staten Island Ferry"

Cast
Passport Clerk: Charles Lane
Ferry Attendant: Stanley Farrar

On the last day to get their passports for the trip, Fred is suddenly panicked. The thought of a long ocean crossing, given his history of seasickness, fills him with terror. Lucy swings into action and, armed with a hefty supply of seasick pills, takes Fred on a dry run aboard the Staten Island ferry. Fred does fine, but Lucy is a physical wreck, so she downs a handful of pills—which knock her out. Can she be revived in time to make it to the passport office?

Classic Guest Stars: Charles Lane returns to play the officious passport clerk, having previ-

ously played Mr. Hickox, the Ricardos' officious business manager in episode 100.

EPISODE 140

"Bon Voyage"

Cast
Mrs. McGillicuddy: Kathryn Card
Mrs. Trumbull: Elizabeth Patterson
Officer: Tyler McVey
Dock Agent: Ken Christy
Helicopter Dispatcher: Jack Albertson
Pilot: Frank Gerstle
Dockworker: Bennett Green

Moments before the USS *Constitution* is about to set sail, the warning call is heard: "All ashore who's going ashore!" But Lucy has to give Little Ricky, who's staying Stateside with his grandma, one more kiss. Wouldn't you know, Lucy is left standing on the pier and the ship sails without her. But don't worry . . . nothing will stop this red-head from sailing on her dream trip to Europe.

Classic Guest Star: Yes, that's a young Jack Albertson playing the helicopter dispatcher; he later starred in *Chico and the Man.*

Classic Cameo: Look for the bearded passenger standing next to Vivian Vance at the rail of the ship. It's *I Love Lucy* writer Bob Carroll Jr., making one of his infrequent cameo appearances.

EPISODE 141

"Second Honeymoon"

Cast

Social Director: Tyler McVey
Kenneth Hamilton: Harvey Grant
Passengers: Louis A. Nicoletti, Virginia
Barbour, Herbert Lytton, Paula Winslow

It's perfect sailing and so romantic that even the Mertzes are billing and cooing under the intoxicating influence of the soft sea air. Everyone is in a state of bliss, except Lucy, who is rendered husbandless due to Ricky's schedule (he's performing in exchange for free passage). If only she could get him alone . . .

Classic Performance: Ricky sings "Cielito Lindo" to Lucy, who is stuck in a porthole.

EPISODE 142

"Lucy Meets the Queen"

Cast

Bellboy: Sam Edwards
Man on the Street: Robert Shafter
Maid: Nancy Kulp
Dancers: Betty Scott, Patti Nestor

The happy foursome are tickled pink to be in jolly old England. The girls immediately do some serious sight-seeing; Lucy is desperate to catch a glimpse of Queen Elizabeth. When she discovers that Ricky and company are to be presented to the queen after a command performance, Lucy says, "Ricky, put me in the show" with so much feeling that he can't resist. Will Lucy really get to meet the queen? Only if she can master the complicated dance routine.

Classic Guest Star: Nancy Kulp, who went on to play Miss Hathaway in *The Beverly Hillbillies*,

plays a cockney maid with a very questionable accent.

EPISODE 143

"The Fox Hunt"

Cast

Sir Clive Richardson: Walter Kingsford
Angela Randall: Hilary Brooke
Groom: Trevor Ward

Lucy's dream of visiting an English manor house looks as if it might come true when she wheedles an invitation from old Sir Clive. The only problem is Sir Clive's daughter, actress Angela Randall, who seems to have her sights set on a certain Cuban bandleader.

EPISODE 144

"Lucy Goes to Scotland"

Cast

Mayor Ferguson: Larry Orenstein
Townspeople: John Gustafson, John Hynd, Robert E. Hamlin, Ann Ellen Walker, Norma Zimmer, Betty Noyes, Dick Byron, Chuck Schrouder, Betty Allen

The Ricardos are only a stone's throw away from the McGillicuddys' ancestral village of Kildoonan. When Ricky vetoes a side trip, Lucy has a vivid dream in which she returns to Kildoonan. As fate would have it, the town is under a curse, which will be lifted only when a McGillicuddy is fed to a two-headed dragon, which happens to look a lot like Fred and Ethel. Can the dashing Scotty MacTavish MacDougal MacCardo save the bonny lass?

Classic Performance: The dream sequence is a parody of the Broadway musical *Brigadoon*, and one member of the chorus is Norma Zimmer, who went on to become a featured performer on *The Lawrence Welk Show*.

EPISODE 145

"Paris at Last"

Cast

Counterfeiter: Lawrence Dobkin
Charpontier: Shepard Menken
Waiter: Maurice Marsac
Chef: Rolfe Sedan
Tour Guide: Fritz Feld
Cops: Trevor Ward, Ramsey Hall, John Mylong
Drunk: Vincent Padula
Tourist: Hazel Pierce

Ah, Paree! Lucy's in heaven, walking through the city known for great art and great food. She buys a painting destined to become a future masterpiece and eats snails for lunch at a sidewalk café. Unfortunately, she also innocently exchanges her U.S. currency for fake French money and ends up in a Parisian pokey.

Classic Performance: Another classic Lucy moment occurs as the redhead valiantly does battle with a plateful of escargots, then learns the proper usage of the snail clamp.

Classic Quote
LUCY: Hey, waiter, this food has snails in it!

EPISODE 146

"Lucy Meets Charles Boyer"

Cast

Charles Boyer: Himself
Waiter: Jack Chefe

Remembering the disastrous encounters between Lucy and certain movie stars in Hollywood, Ricky does everything he can to keep her away from romantic idol Charles Boyer, with whom Ricky is about to meet regarding some business. On Ricky's advice, Boyer pretends to be a down-and-out actor named Maurice Dubois, who just happens to look like the French star; Lucy ends up employing Dubois to teach Ricky a lesson in marital fidelity.

EPISODE 147

"Lucy Gets a Paris Gown"

Cast
Waiter: John Bleifer

Itching to own a pricey outfit from Paris designer Jacques Marcel despite Ricky's resistance, Lucy goes on a hunger strike. Seeing her grow pale and gaunt—no easy trick since Ethel is sneaking her masses of food—Ricky gives in and agrees to buy her a Marcel outfit. When he and Fred learn of the girls' dishonest ways, though, they come up with a scheme of their own to turn Lucy and Ethel into a pair of high-fashion don'ts.

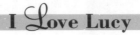

EPISODE 148

"Lucy in the Swiss Alps"

Cast
Swiss Bandleader: Torben Meyer

Ricky blows his top when tour scheduler Fred Mertz goofs and sends the bus carrying the band to Locarno instead of Lucerne. Taking advantage of this unexpected layoff, Lucy plans a hike in the Alps for the Ricardos and the Mertzes. After they make a wonderful ascent, a snowstorm crops up, and they seek refuge in a mountain cabin. With no supplies or food, they are wondering how long the blizzard will last when suddenly an avalanche traps them, and they can't escape. Is this the end of our favorite foursome? Don't bet on it.

Classic Quote
ETHEL: If I'm going to go, I want to go with a clear conscience. Fred, when we got married, I told you I was eighteen. I wasn't eighteen, I was nineteen. FRED: Honey bunch, I've got news for you. You were twenty-four.

EPISODE 149

"Lucy Gets Homesick in Italy"

Cast
Hotel Manager: Vincent Padula
Giuseppe: Bart Bradley
Woman: Ida Smeraldo
Mrs. McGillicuddy: Kathryn Card
Teresa: Kathleen Mazalo

The Ricardos and the Mertzes find themselves in a somewhat less than luxurious hotel in Florence, and Lucy is sad because it's Little Ricky's third birthday and she misses him terribly. After trying unsuccessfully to reach him by telephone, she meets a local street kid, Giuseppe, who tells her that it's his birthday, too! Well, that's all she needs. She and Ethel plan an international birthday party for Little Ricky and Giuseppe with gifts for all the local Italian kids.

Classic Guest Star: Bart Bradley, who plays Giuseppe, grew up to become Bart Braverman, a series regular on *Vega$*.

EPISODE 150

"Lucy's Italian Movie"

Cast
Vittorio Filippi: Franco Corsaro
Bellboy: Saviero LoMedico
Wine Stomper: Teresa Tirelli
Vineyard Boss: Ernesto Molinari
Grape Picker: Rosa Barbato

Lucy's dream has come true! She's been asked by an Italian film director, Vittorio Filippi, to be in his *currant* movie, *Bitter Grapes*. With filming slated to begin immediately, Lucy wastes no time in researching her role. She finds out where the local wine industry is located and gets out there pronto to soak up the local color. Unfortunately, she soaks up a little too much color.

Our Television Heritage: This episode, along with "Vitameatavegamin" and "The Candy Factory," is one of the best-remembered *I Love Lucy* shows. The image of Lucy and the short Italian woman doing battle in a vat of grapes is burned into the memories of countless fans of Classic TV. *I Love Lucy* legend has it that during the fight, Teresa Tirelli, the Italian woman, didn't know her own strength and nearly drowned Lucille Ball.

EPISODE 151

"Lucy's Bicycle Trip"

Cast

Farmer: Mario Siletti
French Guard: Francis Ravel
Italian Guards: Felix Romano, Henry dar Boggia

Impressed by the Europeans' favorite form of transportation, Lucy talks Ricky and the Mertzes into biking with her from Italy to the French Riviera city of Nice. After spending the night in a friendly farmer's barn, they reach the Italian-French border, where Lucy realizes her passport is in the luggage, which has been sent ahead to Nice. Eeuuhhhh! indeed.

EPISODE 152

"Lucy Goes to Monte Carlo"

Cast

Casino Manager: John Mylong
Gambler: Gordon Clark
Croupiers: Jacques Villon, Louis A. Nicoletti

Although Ricky has forbidden Lucy to go to the casino to gamble, she sees no reason not to eat at the restaurant located there. After dinner, while taking an innocent stroll through the casino with Ethel, Lucy discovers a single chip lying on the floor next to a roulette table. She tosses it onto the table, and, lo and behold, she wins. Despite her protests that she never intended to place the bet, she wins spin after spin of the roulette wheel until she walks away with a small fortune. She hides the money from Ricky, but he finds it and accuses Fred of embezzling. It only goes to prove that ill-gotten gold is no one's gain.

Classic Cameo: Look for the gambler wearing a fez. It's another appearance by *I Love Lucy* writer Bob Carroll Jr.

EPISODE 153

"Return Home from Europe"

Cast

Evelyn Bigby: Mary Jane Croft
Stewardess: Mildred Law
Customs Official: Frank Nelson
Airline Official: Ray Kellogg
Newsreel Interviewer: Bennett Green

Packing for the return flight to the States, Lucy has to decide what to do with all the souvenirs she's bought. She can ship most things, but the one item she has to take on the plane is a huge hunk of cheese she bought for her mother. Thinking that the airlines don't charge for babies, Lucy dresses the twenty-five-pound cheese as an infant. Ricky refuses to have anything to do with this scheme, and Lucy is forced to sit next to another mother traveling with her baby. Problems start when this nice but nosy woman is determined to get a look at Lucy's bundle of joy.

Classic Guest Stars: Mary Jane Croft is back for her second *I Love Lucy* outing before settling into her recurring role as Lucy's Connecticut neighbor, Betty Ramsey. Frank Nelson—you know him as Freddy Fillmore—will later return as Betty's husband, Ralph.

EPISODE 154

"Lucy and Bob Hope"

Cast

Bob Hope: Himself
Little Ricky: Keith Thibodeaux
Club Babalu Manager: Lou Krugman
Mr. Krausfeld: Peter Leeds
Spectators: Dick Elliot, Maxine Semon,
David Saber
Guard: Ralph Sanford
Hot Dog Vendor: Bennett Green

For all of the obvious reasons, Ricky doesn't tell Lucy that Bob Hope has agreed to appear at the opening of his new nightspot, Club Babalu. When she bumps into Hope at a Yankee game, Lucy swings into action to book him for the gala event and succeeds only in getting him knocked unconscious by a foul ball. All is forgiven, however, and somehow Lucy persuades Hope to talk Ricky into letting her join them in their act!

Classic Performance: Lucy and Ricky team up with Bob Hope for a baseball number called "Nobody Loves the Ump" and a special version of Hope's theme song, "Thanks for the Memories."

For the Record: This episode marks the debut of Keith Thibodeaux as Little Ricky. He would play the smallest Ricardo for the rest of the series and in all of the Lucy-Desi Comedy Hour specials. This episode also gave Ricky a promotion to nightclub owner, which would eventually free him up to move to the suburbs of Connecticut.

EPISODE 155

"Lucy Meets Orson Welles"

Cast

Orson Welles: Himself
Miss Hanna: Ellen Corby
Babalu Manager: Lou Krugman
Macy's Clerks: Ray Kellogg, Jack Rice
Customers: Fred Aldrich, Hazel Pierce,
Bennett Green

Ricky has booked Orson Welles for a benefit at Club Babalu, and he decides to send Lucy on a Florida vacation in order to get her out of the way. While she and Ethel are at Macy's buying vacation items, she runs into the great Orson Welles, who's signing autographs for his latest Shakespearean album release. Well, as we all know, it's been Lucy's lifelong dream to act a Shakespearean scene with Orson Welles (*what?*). Trouble is, Orson wants to do magic tricks. So what's a redhead to do?

Classic Guest Star: Ellen Corby, who went on to play John Boy's grandma on *The Waltons*, turns up as Lucy's high school drama teacher.

Our Television Heritage: Orson Welles, Hollywood's brilliant bad boy, was under contract to Desilu to develop some dramatic properties for them, but he proved much too troublesome for the Arnazes. He never followed through on the development deal and was very difficult to work with in his *I Love Lucy* assignment, so Desilu quickly dropped his contract.

EPISODE 156

"Little Ricky Gets Stage Fright"

Cast

Mr. Crawford: Howard McNear
Mrs. Van Fossen: Marjorie Bennett
Child Musicians: Laurie Blaine, Diana Van Fossen, Jeffrey Woodruff, Larry Gleason, Robert Norman, Buddy Noble, Earl Robie

It's time for Little Ricky's first drum recital, and everything is fine until Lucy and the Mertzes make him nervous about performing in public. It's up to Ricky to give his son a lesson in self-confidence, and it's Lucy's job to make sure he knows his parents are behind him—literally—onstage.

Classic Performance: Little Ricky and his Dixieland combo riff to the tune of "Five Foot Two, Eyes of Blue," with Lucy strumming a mean uke.

Classic Cameo: Look at Mr. Crawford closely, and you'll see Floyd the barber from *The Andy Griffith Show.* It's Howard McNear, who went on to be a Mayberry regular in the popular Desilu series.

EPISODE 157

"Little Ricky Learns to Play the Drums"

Cast

Mrs. Trumbull: Elizabeth Patterson

The apple doesn't fall very far from the tree, and when Little Ricky takes a shine to the toy snare drum that Ricky gives him, everyone is thrilled—that is, until he beats out the same annoying rhythm all day every day for four solid days. This manifestation of talent is enough to start a battle between the Ricardos and the Mertzes, who eventually threaten their tenants and ex–best friends with—what else?—eviction.

Our Television Heritage: Keith Thibodeaux was discovered by Ricky after an extensive search. Billed as the world's youngest professional drummer, he looked like a mini version of Desi Arnaz and could certainly handle the drumming. The only problem was his heavy Louisiana accent, which, after considerable coaching, approximated something close to neutral American flavor. Thibodeaux moved in with Lucille Ball and her family for the season's taping schedule so that he would feel more natural and comfortable with them.

For the Record: Didn't Little Ricky face stage fright in episode 156? And *now* he learns to play? Yes. This episode originally aired before 156, and why it is numbered 157 is just one of the unsolved mysteries of *I Love Lucy.*

EPISODE 158

"Visitor from Italy"

Cast

Mario: Jay Novello
Mr. Martinelli: Eduardo Ciannelli
Immigration Officer: James Flavin
Pizza Chef: Aldo Formica
Dominic: Peter Brocco
Waiter: Louis Nicoletti

When Italian visitor Mario comes to New York, he drops by to see the Ricardos and the Mertzes. It takes them a while to figure out just who he is: the singing gondolier they befriended in Venice, of course. He's come to see Dominic, his brother, who's staying with his sick friend Sam Francesco. When Lucy realizes that Dominic is actually in

San Francisco, she tries to figure out a way to get the money to send Mario to the West Coast.

Classic Guest Star: Jay Novello returns for his final *I Love Lucy* assignment as Mario Orsatti, the gondolier from Venice.

EPISODE 159

"Off to Florida"

Cast
Mrs. Grundy: Elsa Lanchester
Café Waiter: Strother Martin

Lucy and Ethel are supposed to join Ricky, Fred, and Little Ricky in Florida for a vacation (the boys have gone ahead to do some fishing), but Lucy can't find the train tickets. With no money and no way to contact the men, the girls decide to share a ride down to Florida. They hitch a ride with a Mrs. Grundy, who fits the description of Evelyn Holmby, a convicted murderer who's escaped from a New York prison. When the girls find a hatchet in Mrs. Grundy's trunk, they are sure she's America's most wanted woman, and they're determined to avoid becoming her next victims.

Classic Guest Stars: Character actress Elsa Lanchester, best known in films as the Bride of Frankenstein, gives a delightful performance as the watercress sandwich–munching Mrs. Grundy.

Classic Quote
LUCY: Could you pull over? I need to make a phone call.
MRS. GRUNDY: Who to?
LUCY: Uhm . . . my landlady. I just remembered I left the tub running.
MRS. GRUNDY (*indicating Ethel*): I thought you told me she was your landlady.
LUCY: Oh, yeah. (*To Ethel*) Hey, landlady . . . my tub is running over!

EPISODE 160

"Deep Sea Fishing"

Cast
Boat Captain: James Hayward
Bellboy: Billy McLean

While staying at the deluxe Eden Roc Hotel, Lucy and Ethel bet the boys that they can catch a bigger fish than their husbands can. Of course the $150 winnings from the bet will cover the bills from Lucy and Ethel's unmentioned shopping spree. To make sure that they snag the money, Lucy and Ethel buy a huge fish, which they'll pretend to have caught. Of course, they underestimate their sneaky mates, who've come up with the same exact plan. Suddenly there are two giant tunas floating between hotel rooms.

EPISODE 161

"Desert Island"

Cast
Claude Akins: Himself
Jil Jarmyn: Herself
Joi Lansing: Herself

Determined to keep the fellas from judging a bathing beauty contest, Lucy and Ethel plan a boat trip for the four of them—with only enough gas to get them out to sea, not to get them back. Unfortunately, the supply they've hidden for their eventual rescue gets left behind, and the boat really does get stranded. Eventually they drift to an island and meet up with some pretty scary natives.

Classic Guest Stars: Claude Akins, the bad guy of many movie westerns, went on to play TV's Sheriff Elroy P. Lobo in *B.J. and the Bear* and *Lobo*, and is now most visible as a pitchman for "Double-A—(*beep, beep*)—MCO," the transmission people.

EPISODE 162

"The Ricardos Visit Cuba"

Cast

Uncle Alberto: George Trevino
Cigar Store Owner: Nacho Galindo
Ricky's mother: Mary Emery
Cigar maker: Angelo Didio
Ricky's relatives: Lillian Molieri, Rodolfo
Hoyos Jr., Manuel Paris, Amapola
DelVando, Abel Franco
Stewardess: Barbara Logan
Emcee: Eddie LaBaron

The Ricardos and the Mertzes fly to Havana to meet all of Ricky's relatives. When Lucy tries to impress the head of the Ricardo family, feisty Uncle Alberto, she succeeds only in spilling punch on him, ruining his fancy cigars, and calling him a big fat pig *en español*. She tries desperately to win him over, and she finally succeeds when he sees what a terrific job she's done raising Little Ricky.

Classic Performance: In Havana's Casino Parisian, Ricky sings "I'm a Lucky Guy," and he and Little Ricky do a wonderful duet of the song "Babalu," to the delight of Ricky's relatives.

EPISODE 163

"Little Ricky's School Pageant"

Cast
Suzy: Candy Rogers Schoenberger

When Little Ricky is given the lead in the school play, Lucy impresses on him that the size of the role is not important; acting is all about co-operation. But when the Ricardos and Mertzes are given non-flashy supporting roles, there's a lot of griping all around—except from Ethel, who's

playing the fairy princess. Everyone eventually participates, and *The Enchanted Forest* turns out to be a smash hit.

EPISODE 164

"Lucy and the Loving Cup"

Cast

Johnny Longden: Himself
Hazel Longden: Herself
Cop: Robert Foulk
Train Passengers: Jesslyn Fax, Byron
Kane, Lester Dorr, Phil Tead, Sandra
Gould, Florence Ann Shawn
Bum: William L. Erwin

As a joke, Lucy puts a silver trophy on her head and then realizes that she can't get it off. Under a big hat and veil, Lucy and Ethel take the subway downtown to a silversmith, but somehow they get separated from each other. Can she remove the loving cup and get it to Ricky's Club Babalu in time for the presentation to jockey Johnny Longden?

Classic Quote

ETHEL: If we're taking the subway, I'd better change out of these blue jeans.
LUCY: Honestly, Ethel, with a loving cup stuck to my head, I hardly think anyone's going to notice your blue jeans.

EPISODE 165

"Little Ricky Gets a Dog"

Cast
Mr. Stewart: John Emery
Voice of the Dog: June Foray

Fred Mertz, landlord with a heart of gold, has looked the other way while Little Ricky kept goldfish, turtles, frogs, and parakeets in the apartment. But when he brings home a puppy, the No Pets clause must be enforced—that is, until Little Ricky names the dog Fred as a tribute to the grumpy Mr. Mertz. Suddenly the rules seem a little too harsh, and Fred and Ethel have to decide between the Ricardos and their little pooch or a disgruntled, animal-loathing tenant and his big monthly check.

Classic Cameo: Making an off-screen appearance as the voice of Little Ricky's puppy is June Foray, one of Hollywood's leading character voices. Her well-known vocal characterizations include Rocket J. Squirrel and Natasha, from *Rocky and His Friends*, and the little old lady who owns Tweety, from the Looney Tunes cartoons.

EPISODE 166

"Lucy and Superman"

Cast

Superman: George Reeves
Caroline Appleby: Doris Singleton
Charlie Appleby: George O'Hanlon
Martha: Madge Blake
Husband: Ralph Dumke
Stevie Appleby: Steven Kay

Little Ricky and Stevie Appleby are both planning birthday parties on the same day. Caroline has arranged all kinds of entertainment for her boy's bash. Not to be outdone, Lucy boldly announces that Superman will be coming to Little Ricky's party, forcing Caroline to reschedule Stevie's. When it looks as if the Man of Steel won't make it, Lucy decides to impersonate the superhero and plans to make a grand entrance from the apartment window ledge. Fortunately, the real Superman saves the day by showing up and thrilling all the kiddies. Meanwhile, Lucy's stuck on the ledge—and of course it looks like rain.

Classic Guest Stars: George Reeves plays Superman, the character he created in the TV series *The Adventures of Superman.*

Charlie Appleby is played by George O'Hanlon. Now, he might not look familiar, but if you close your eyes and listen, you'll hear the voice of George Jetson.

Madge Blake appears in this Superman episode; she went on to play Aunt Harriet in *Batman!*

EPISODE 167

"Lucy Wants to Move to the Country"

Cast

Mr. Spaulding: Frank Wilcox
Mrs. Spaulding: Eleanor Audley

Lucy is determined to raise her child in the fresh, clean air of the country. She even manages to convince Ricky that a move away from the dirty, dusty city is necessary. When he buys her a dream house in Connecticut she's ecstatic . . . until she realizes a move to the suburbs means a Mertzless life. The only way to get Ricky's $500 deposit back is to prove herself an undesirable purchaser. With the help of Fred and Ethel, Lucy shows just how undesirable a purchaser can be.

EPISODE 168

"Lucy Hates to Leave"

Cast

Mr. Taylor: Gene Reynolds
Mrs. Taylor: Mary Ellen Kaye

Despite a case of new homeowner jitters, the Ricardos are getting ready for their big move to Westport, Connecticut. Fred asks them if they can vacate the apartment four days earlier than scheduled so he can let the new tenants move in. They agree, of course, and spend the last few days in the Mertzes' cramped flat with Fred and Ethel—and all of their worldly possessions. Can close friends get a little too close? Well, it'll be tight living quarters for only four days . . . or will it?

EPISODE 169

"Lucy Misses the Mertzes"

Cast

Harry Munson: Tristram Coffin
Station Clerk: Jesse Kirkpatrick
Moving Man: Robert Bice
Delivery Man: Gary Gray

It's a tearful parting for the Ricardos and the Mertzes. They pledge eternal friendship as Lucy and Ricky leave East Sixty-eighth Street for their idyll in Connecticut. They unpack, settle into their new home, and realize that the one thing they need to do now is visit their old friends Fred and Ethel in the city. Funny thing, the Mertzes have the same idea and head to Westport to see Lucy and Ricky.

EPISODE 170

"Lucy Gets Chummy with the Neighbors"

Cast

Ralph Ramsey: Frank Nelson
Betty Ramsey: Mary Jane Croft
Bruce Ramsey: Ray Ferrell
Mr. Perry: Parley Baer

With $500 from Ricky, Lucy goes furniture shopping with her new friend Betty Ramsey. Mistaking stock numbers for prices, Lucy gets carried away to the tune of over $3,000. Ricky flips his lid and tells Lucy to return everything

immediately. This insults Betty Ramsey, who thinks that her taste is being questioned. What's a redhead to do? Return the furniture and lose a new best friend, or keep the furniture and find a new husband?

EPISODE 171

"Lucy Raises Chickens"

Cast

Betty Ramsey: Mary Jane Croft
Magazine Team: Mary Alan Hokenson, Tyler McVey

Country life turns out to be more expensive than Ricky imagined, and the Ricardos need to find a way to make a few extra bucks to cover their expenses. "What if we were to raise chickens?" says Lucy. "Why not?" says Ricky. All they need is someone who knows a little about poultry. Enter that well-known chicken expert Fred Mertz and his lovely country wife, Ethel. They've come to apply for the job, and before you can say "Wait a chicken-pickin' minute," the Ricardos and the Mertzes are in the egg business. The first order of business is to purchase five hundred baby chicks—future producers—which arrive before the coop is ready and make themselves at home in the Ricardos' living room.

For the Record: It was never even a consideration to separate the Ricardos and the Mertzes, and, all things considered, it only took a few Connecticut episodes to create the need in the *I Love Lucy* story line to move Fred and Ethel into the Ricardos' guest house.

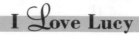

EPISODE 172

"Lucy Does the Tango"

Cast
Bruce Ramsey: Ray Ferrell

The five hundred chicks have been traded in for two hundred chickens. The only problem is, they're not laying. When Ricky threatens to pull the plug on the chicken enterprise, Lucy and Ethel decide to plant a few dozen eggs so the birds will get the idea. What happens next, as Lucy, with four dozen eggs hidden on her person, is required to rehearse a dramatic tango, which she and Ricky are slated to perform for the Westport PTA, has to be seen to be believed.

For the Record: The egg-breaking grand finale of the tango, and Lucy's subsequent reaction to it, provided the longest recorded laugh of any *I Love Lucy* episode. The audience response lasted for a full sixty-five seconds.

EPISODE 173

"Ragtime Band"

Lucy, eager to make points with the Westport Historical Society, promises to produce Ricky Ricardo as the entertainment at the annual fundraiser. He refuses, naturally, and she thinks she can substitute Little Ricky and still be true to her word. So with Little Ricky on drums, Lucy picks up her trusty old sax and persuades the Mertzes to join in the musical madness. Ricky has no choice but to bail them out, and he, of course, ends up performing at the benefit.

Classic Performance: Ricky Ricardo Jr and his combo struggle through "Sweet Sue" and "She'll Be Comin' 'Round the Mountain" while Ricky Senior and his combo do a calypso number called "Woman Smarter."

EPISODE 174

"Lucy's Night in Town"

Cast
Theater Manager: Joseph Kearns
Woman with Purse: Gladys Hurlbut
Couple in Box: Doris Packer, John Eldredge
Waiter: Louis A. Nicoletti

Lucy is all geared up for her first night on the town since moving to the country: the Ricardos and the Mertzes will have dinner at an elegant restaurant and then take in the biggest hit on Broadway, *The Most Happy Fella*. They bought the tickets six months ago and they're the best seats in the house. The only problem is that the tickets were for the matinee! Lucy discovers this slight problem moments before Ricky and Fred are to join Ethel and her at the restaurant. But maybe the situation is not all that bad. Maybe four seats for the evening performance will be available at the box office. Maybe . . . *not.*

Classic Guest Star: Joseph Kearns is back for his second *I Love Lucy* appearance as the theater manager.

For the Record: This whole episode served as a promotion for *The Most Happy Fella*, to which Desilu was a financial contributor. The show had opened on Broadway earlier that year.

EPISODE 175

"The Housewarming"

Cast
Betty Ramsey: Mary Jane Croft
Bruce Ramsey: Ray Ferrell

What's gotten into Ethel lately? Just because Lucy is spending time with Betty Ramsey, Mrs.

Mertz is all bent out of shape. Lucy tries to make amends by inviting Betty and Ethel to a get-to-know-each-other luncheon. Well, they do, and it turns out they grew up in the same hometown. Now *Lucy's* the one who feels left out. In fact, Ethel and Betty start spending so much time together that Lucy is desolate—until she jumps to the conclusion that the two girls are planning a housewarming party for the Ricardos.

Classic Quote

LUCY: Betty, once you get to know Ethel, you'll see she's more fun than a barrel of monkeys.
Ethel: Yes. Monkeys that don't get invited out of their barrels very often.

EPISODE 176

"Building a Barbecue"

To keep Ricky out of her hair, Lucy comes up with a project for his week-long vacation. As he and Fred set out to build an impressive brick barbecue, Lucy misplaces her wedding ring and is sure it got mixed into the cement used constructing the grill. That night the girls go out and take the barbecue apart one brick at a time, looking for the golden band—with no luck. Now Lucy not only has to explain what happened to the boys' handiwork, she also has to account for the loss of her ring.

EPISODE 177

"Country Club Dance"

Cast

Ralph Ramsey: Frank Nelson
Betty Ramsey: Mary Jane Croft
Diana Jordan: Barbara Eden
Harry Munson: Tristram Coffin
Grace Munson: Ruth Brady

Boys will be boys, especially at a dinner dance, when a sultry young lady appears. Ricky, Fred, and Ralph Ramsey pay a little too much attention to the Munsons' cousin Diana, and the girls are furious. Determined to win back their husbands' attention, they go all out to make themselves more glamorous, with new dresses, hairstyles, and perfume. When the boys do respond, it's too good to be true. In fact, Lucy becomes suspicious and decides the dirty dogs are up to something.

Classic Guest Stars: A sexy twenty-something Barbara Eden makes a splashy appearance as Diana, who casts a spell over the boys. Barbara Eden would go on casting spells, of course, in *I Dream of Jeannie.*

EPISODE 178

"Lucy Raises Tulips"

Cast

Betty Ramsey: Mary Jane Croft
Flower Judges: Peter Brocco, Eleanor Audley

Lucy and Betty Ramsey have a friendly competition going on when it comes to their flower gardens. Both are after first prize for Westport's Best Garden. But that competitive spirit starts to get a little unfriendly when Lucy loses control of the lawn mower and accidentally plows through Betty's tulip patch. What's a neighbor to do? How about replacing Betty's blooms with wax tulips from the village gift shop? Sounds like a good plan. . . .

EPISODE 179

"The Ricardos Dedicate a Statue"

Lucy has gotten everyone involved in the Westport Historical Society's Yankee Doodle Day. Ricky will dedicate a lifelike statue of a Minuteman crouched and ready for battle, Fred will be the town crier, and Ethel is putting up signs touting the festivities all over town. The only one not cooperating is Little Ricky's dog, Fred, who decides to run away the day before the big celebration. While Lucy is trying to find him, she forgets the statue is on a trailer hitched to the car, and she backs into a tree, destroying the statue. What will the fine citizens of Westport see when Ricky unveils the statue? Any bets?

Classic Cameos: Among the people gathered for the unveiling are two little kids standing with Little Ricky. They're actually little Lucie and Desi Junior, in the only appearance the Arnaz children ever made on *I Love Lucy*. Because this was the final episode of the series, their parents wanted them to be a part of the show.

Our Television Heritage: And so it ended. Although Desilu used the characters and the Westport house as a foundation for the thirteen Lucy-Desi comedy hour specials over the next three seasons, the day-to-day adventures of the Ricardos and the Mertzes came to an end with this episode.

The Mary Tyler Moore Show

We were lucky that our creative people were so tuned in to what was happening in the world. It wasn't that Jim Brooks and Allan Burns created *The Mary Tyler Moore Show* because they were interested in polemics for women's rights—it wasn't that kind of program. But they *were* interested in what was happening to women in our society, and like all good writers, they wrote about what was foremost in their minds.

—Mary Tyler Moore

If Edward R. Murrow was the past of television news and Walter Cronkite is its present, Ted Baxter is a portent of its future.

—Robert Sobel

It was a very good television show—the characters were well conceived, and the writing . . . not the stories so much, because you know, in twenty-two minutes of situation comedy, that isn't important. The words given those characters to speak to each other were better words than characters were getting on other shows.

—Grant Tinker

Nobody liked the scripts. The development people hated them. They didn't think they were funny. They couldn't understand them. They were used to a different kind of comedy.

—Allan Burns

Maybe the only reason we seemed political was that we were writing about a woman who had a job in the early seventies, and that kind of woman would herself have had to be politically aware. So if you're going to write truthfully about her, you include her political awareness. It was only that, and not—repeat: *not*—to get some point across.

—Stan Daniels

While *All in the Family* was making vast inroads into the public's thinking, with issues tackled directly, I think our show took the more difficult path and was more subtle. . . .

—Treva Silverman

It was sweet; it was honest; there was love all around, appreciation, very good ensemble work . . . it was seven years of life that went by so swiftly I don't even remember shaving. It was fantastic.

—Ed Asner

Probably the best way to appreciate *The Mary Tyler Moore Show* is to try to catch it at the beginning of its rerun cycle. Then you can see all the elements in place from the start and watch as both the writers and the performers help the characters to grow, reacting to situations like real people might. Along the way, you'll also be treated to clever dialogue, funny situations, superb timing, and an ensemble of performers that evolves into a wonderful surrogate family. In short, you might want to follow the series from beginning to end.

—Castleman and Podrazik, *Harry and Wally's Favorite TV Shows*

The *Mary Tyler Moore* Show

on Nick at Nite

Mary arrived on Nick at Nite in a week-long "Mary-Thon" in September 1992. Each evening Nick presented the best episodes from each of the show's seven seasons. As the first show aired in Minneapolis at a Nick at Nite–sponsored stunt, a thousand people gathered to throw their hats in the air.

Mary quickly laid claim to the ten o'clock slot, and soon back-to-back episodes were being broadcast every night. Special program events highlighted "The Happy Homemaker" (episodes featuring Betty White) and "Mother's Day with Ida Morgenstern" (episodes featuring Rhoda's mom).

In August 1994, Nick at Nite offered the first ever Mary Tyler Moore Merit Badge (no longer available, so don't write), earned by passing a difficult twenty-question test that required in-depth knowledge of the show. Almost 30,000 viewers took the test; 90 percent of them passed. That summer, to help promote Mary Mondays, Nick at Nite brought Ed Asner on-line in one of America Online's most popular events up to that time.

The Mary Tyler Moore Show is one of the network's true foundation shows, and it will be shown on Nick at Nite through the end of this millennium and beyond.

M

Cast

Mary Richards: Mary Tyler Moore
Lou Grant: Ed Asner
Ted Baxter: Ted Knight
Murray Slaughter: Gavin MacLeod
Rhoda Morgenstern: Valerie Harper
Phyllis Lindstrom: Cloris Leachman
Bess Linstrom: Lisa Gerritson
Gordy Howard: John Amos
Georgette Franklin Baxter: Georgia Engel
Sue Ann Nivens: Betty White
Marie Slaughter: Joyce Bulifant
Edie Grant: Priscilla Morrill
David Baxter: Robbie Rist

EPISODE 1

"Love Is All Around"

Writers: James L. Brooks and Allan
Burns
Director: Jay Sandrich
Cast
Angus Duncan
Dave Morich

In search of a fresh start, Mary Richards—thirty, unmarried, attractive . . . what's not to like?—moves to Minneapolis and lands a job at WJM-TV, a small local station. There she finds a young woman named Rhoda who has designs on her new apartment, and a boss who hates spunk, which Mary has in abundance. Will Mary overcome these obstacles and begin to "make it after all"?

Classic Quote
RHODA (*to Mary*): Hello . . . get out of my apartment.

For the Record: Filmed in June 1970, this is the episode that started it all. As all classic pilot episodes are supposed to do, it clearly establishes the relationships that will be developed in the years to come.

The rent on Mary's new apartment is $130 a month.

EPISODE 2

"Today I am a Ma'am"

Writer: Treva Silverman
Director: Jay Sandrich
Cast
Richard Schaal
Jack DeMave
Sheilah Wells
David Hayword

Fast friends already—hey, this is a sitcom, after all—Mare and Rho commiserate about being thirty and single. Letting desperation cloud their judgment, they invite two men over for dinner without realizing that one of them is married!

Classic Quote
RHODA: I've got to lose ten pounds by eight-thirty!

For the Record: Character actor Richard Schaal, who played Rhoda's date in this early episode, was married to Valerie Harper at the time.

EPISODE 3

"Bess, You Is My Daughter Now"

Writer: John D. F. Black
Director: Jay Sandrich

Is there nothing Mary can't do? After agreeing to baby-sit Phyllis's daughter, Bess, she throws away Phyllis's overly clinical child-care books and experiments with a radical new method of child-rearing—good old love and respect. Naturally, Bess decides she wants Mary to be her new mom. Phyllis bravely steps aside, even as her heart is breaking.

For the Record: Lisa Gerritsen makes her first appearance as Bess Lindstrom, Phyllis's surprisingly sensible daughter, a role she would continue to play for the next seven years, the last two on *Phyllis*, the spin-off series.

EPISODE 4

"Divorce Isn't Everything"

Writer: Treva Silverman
Director: Alan Rafkin
Cast
Dr. Walter Udall: Shelley Berman
Sparkie: Pat Finley
Dave Ketchum

Mary and Rhoda happily discover a club that offers a discount rate on a trip to Europe. A catch, you say? You bet there is: it's a club for divorced people. Think that stops Mare and Rho? Think again! Rhoda plays the schemer—the Lucy to Mary's Ethel, if you will.

Classic Guest Stars: Catskills comic Shelley Berman plays the hilariously crazy dentist who falls in love with Mary's teeth—establishing that Mary really could "turn the world on with her smile."

Pat Finley, who plays Sparkie in this episode, is better known for her stint as Ellen Hartley on *The Bob Newhart Show*.

David Ketchum, another familiar TV face, had the recurring role of Agent 13 on *Get Smart*.

EPISODE 5

"Keep Your Guard Up"

Writer: Steve Pritzker
Director: Alan Rafkin
Cast
John Schuck
Tim Brown

Mary meets good-natured, bumbling ex–football player Frank Carelli at the station. In her soon-to-be typical fashion, Mary champions this underdog, believing him to be perfect for the sportscaster position that is open. Naturally, Frank flops at his audition, but with Mary's help, he finds his true calling—working with children.

Classic Guest Star: John Schuck, a fine character actor, was the bumbling but loyal assistant to Rock Hudson on *McMillan and Wife* and the bumbling but loyal robotic police officer, Yoyo, on *Holmes and Yoyo.* He also, sadly, played Herman in the almost sacrilegiously ill-crafted revival, *The Munsters Today.*

EPISODE 6

"Support Your Local Mother"

Writers: James L. Brooks and Allan Burns
Director: Alan Rafkin
Cast
Ida Morgenstern: Nancy Walker

Ida Morgenstern, the mother of all Jewish mothers, comes to visit her estranged daughter Rhoda, but Rhoda doesn't want to see her because . . . well, Ida is Rhoda's mother. Guess who's caught in the middle of this ill-fated mother-and-child reunion? You get three guesses, and the first two don't count.

Classic Guest Star: This episode's importance in MTM history can be summed up in two words: Nancy Walker. Ms. Walker's first appearance as Ida laid the crucial groundwork for the ongoing mother-daughter relationship that would evolve into a cornerstone of the spin-off series *Rhoda.* Aside from her winning turn as Ida, Nancy Walker was a regular on *McMillan and Wife* and achieved true TV immortality as Rosie the waitress on countless Bounty—"the quicker picker-upper"—commercials.

For the Record: *Mary Tyler Moore* co-creator Allan Burns credits Grant Tinker, MTM president and Mary Tyler Moore's husband at the time, for getting this episode approved by CBS. The network initially objected to Rhoda's "harsh" treatment of her mother.

Awards: This episode earned Burns and his fellow writer and co-creator, James Brooks, an Emmy for Best Writing on a Comedy Series.

EPISODE 7

"Toulouse-Lautrec Is One of My Favorite Artists"

Writers: Lloyd Turner and Gordon Mitchell
Director: Jay Sandrich
Cast
Hamilton Camp
Robert Rothwell

Mary is smitten with a man she meets at the station, who happens to be sitting at a table. After Mary has agreed to go on a date with him, the man stands up, and Mary discovers that he is, uh, height-challenged. Will Mary get over her height prejudice and find happiness?

Classic Guest Star: Hamilton Camp, who plays Mary's diminutive date, was a guest on dozens of TV series. He also played a recurring character on the Ted Knight sitcom *Too Close for Comfort.*

Awards: Principal *Mary Tyler Moore* director Jay Sandrich won an Emmy as Best Director of a Comedy Series for this episode. Sandrich would direct seventeen of the first season's twenty-four episodes and over seventy percent of the show's 168 segments.

EPISODE 8

"The Snow Must Go On"

Writers: David Davis and Lorenzo Music
Director: Jay Sandrich

Minneapolis is hit with a terrible snowstorm on the evening WJM is scheduled to provide election-night coverage. Members of the staff, with Rhoda volunteering on the toteboard—are unable to report the returns, and they have to fill airtime—any way they can.

For the Record: "The Snow Must Go On" was the first episode written by David Davis and Lorenzo Music, who went on to create *The Bob Newhart Show.*

Our Television Heritage: Lorenzo Music used his real-life experiences as a snow-savvy Minnesota native to good advantage in this early episode. Music's voice would later become familiar to viewers of *Rhoda,* as he provided the voice of Carlton the Doorman.

EPISODE 9

"Bob and Rhoda and Teddy and Mary"

Writer: Bob Rodgers
Director: Peter Baldwin
Cast
Bob: Greg Mullavey
M.C.: Dick Patterson
Mr. Hartunian: Henry Corden

Teddy alert! This is the first episode that features the Teddy Awards, which are presented at a local TV awards dinner. In this show, Mary gets nominated for her first Teddy, but she's more concerned with Bob, an attractive man who has eyes for her. The problem? He's Rhoda's date!

Classic Guest Star: Greg Mullavey later played Mary Hartman's husband on *Mary Hartman, Mary Hartman.*

EPISODE 10

"Assistant Wanted, Female"

Writer: Treva Silverman
Director: Peter Baldwin

It's not enough that Phyllis bugs the heck out of Mary at home; now she gets hired as Mary's assistant, too. For the gang at WJM, it's hate at first sight as they struggle to deal with the obnoxious Phyllis.

Classic Performance: John Amos's winning performance as Gordy Howard, WJM's wry weatherman, no doubt solidified his status as a recurring character in the early years of the show. Amos, of course, went on to star in the hit sitcom *Good Times* and earned a well-deserved Emmy nomination for playing the adult Kunta Kinte in *Roots.*

For the Record: This episode marks the first appearance of Gordy, and his presence is used to good comic effect, as Phyllis mistakes the affable weatherman for the sportscaster, simply because of his race and athletic build.

EPISODE 11

"1040 or Fight"

Writers: David Davis and Lorenzo Music
Director: Jay Sandrich
Cast
IRS Agent: Paul Sand

In another "weird date" episode, Mary is dating a sweet, unassuming auditor for the IRS. His attraction to Mary complicates matters when he has to audit Mary's taxes.

Classic Guest Star: Paul Sand made a career out of playing nervous, nebbishy types in dozens of TV appearances. He also starred in a short-lived series from the MTM production company, *Paul Sand in Friends and Lovers*, which costarred Penny Marshall.

EPISODE 12

"Anchorman Overboard"

Writer: Lorenzo Music
Director: Jay Sandrich
Cast
Bob Fiore
Clock Man: Bob Duggan

Phyllis wants Ted . . . to speak to an organization for which she's the program chairperson. She asks Mary to recruit him as a guest speaker, and, against her better judgment, Mary complies. Ted's disastrous performance makes Mare wish she'd trust her better judgment more often.

For the Record: Throughout the series, there was a suggestion that Phyllis had a crush on Ted, and this early episode lends credence to that supposition.

EPISODE 13

"He's All Yours"

Writer: Bob Rodgers
Director: Jay Sandrich
Cast
Allan Stevens: Wes Stern

Lou Grant asks Mary to look after Allen Stevens, a fresh-faced new WJM cameraman. Although Allen is younger than Mary, he constantly puts the moves on her. Just when she's had enough, she finds out that Allen is Lou's nephew. She grits her teeth and endures more of Allen's overtures, but Lou finds out and douses his nephew's flame for good.

Classic Quote
LOU (*To Allen*): I think of this girl here as if she were my own daughter, and that means she's your cousin—you get my meaning?

Classic Guest Star: Wes Stern went on to costar with teen heartthrob Bobby Sherman in *Getting Together*, a series that was piloted as an episode of *The Partridge Family*.

EPISODE 14

"Christmas and the Hard-Luck Kid"

Writers: James L. Brooks and Allan Burns
Director: Jay Sandrich
Cast
Ned Wertimer

The first Christmas episode finds Mary at WJM, trying to bring joy to a joyless bunch stuck working on Christmas Day. Talk about your thankless jobs.

EPISODE 15

"Howard's Girl"

Writer: Treva Silverman
Director: Jay Sandrich
Cast
Henry Jones
Richard Schaal
Mary Jackson

Mary, who's always enjoyed an active social life, begins dating her former boyfriend's brother Paul, but her relationship with Paul's parents is far closer. Actually, it's too close—she can't get away from them.

Classic Guest Star: Venerable character actor Henry Jones, who specialized in playing lovable curmudgeons, delivered in spades in this episode. He became a full-fledged member of the MTM team when he landed the role of Judge Dexter in *Phyllis* several years later.

EPISODE 16

"Party Is Such Sweet Sorrow"

Writer: Martin Cohan
Director: Bruce Bilson
Cast
Dick Clair

It's only midway into the first season, and Mary's already looking for greener pastures. She finds them at another station in town, which has offered her a better job. She accepts, but changes her mind after her farewell party, where her co-workers show her how much they love and need her.

EPISODE 17

"Just a Lunch"

Writers: James L. Brooks and Allan Burns
Director: Bruce Bilson
Cast
Monte Markham

Mary's latest boyfriend is a dashing foreign correspondent. He's charming, he's gorgeous, he's . . . married! When Mare finds out, she continues to go out with him. *Quel scandale!*

Classic Guest Star: Veteran TV actor Monte Markham has appeared in countless series and movies. He even had the formidable task of trying to fill Raymond Burr's shoes in *The New Perry Mason* in 1972; he lasted exactly half a season in that role.

For the Record: Bubbly actress Joyce Bulifant makes her first appearance as Marie Slaughter, beloved spouse of Murray. In real life, Bulifant married director William Asher after his divorce from Elizabeth Montgomery.

EPISODE 18

"Second-Story Story"

Writer: Steve Pritzker
Director: Jay Sandrich
Cast
Vic Tayback
Burt Mustin
Bob Dishy

Is no one safe in Minneapolis anymore? Mary is burglarized two days in a row, and she's so shaken up that her friends take matters into their own hands and try to capture the felon themselves. Hilarity ensues.

Classic Guest Star: Vic Tayback achieved lasting fame in TV history as Mel of Mel's Diner in the long-running hit series *Alice*.

Elderly Burt Mustin played the suitor, and later the husband, of Mother Dexter on *Phyllis*.

EPISODE 19

"We Closed in Minneapolis"

Writers: Kenny Solms and Gail Parent
Director: Jay Sandrich

The spotlight is on Murray: a play he's written is to be produced locally. In an example of Murray's infamous bad luck, Ted Baxter is cast in the lead. Does this play stand even the slightest chance of being a hit?

For the Record: This is the first episode to feature Murray in the main plot, and it establishes the tone with which he's treated in future shows. Although Murray is a very competent newswriter, he's not creatively fulfilled. The ill-fated production of his play shows how hapless Murray is in trying to achieve his goals, even though he's

supported by the love of two good women—his devoted wife, Marie, and his loyal co-worker, Mary.

EPISODE 20

"Hi!"

Writer: Treva Silverman
Director: Jay Sandrich
Cast
Mrs. Khune: Pat Carroll
Bruce Kirby
Robert Cooper
Arthur Adelson

Mary's in the hospital to have one tonsil removed, and she has to share a room with Mrs. Khune, a grumpy middle-aged woman laid up with a broken leg and an ulcer. Talk about your oil-and-water mixes! Not one to leave well enough alone, Mary's determined to cheer up her grouchy roomie.

EPISODE 21

"The Boss Isn't Coming for Dinner"

Writers: David Davis and Lorenzo Music
Director: Jay Sandrich
Cast
Waiter: Paul Micale

There's trouble in paradise, as Lou tells Mary that he's having marital problems with his wife, Edie. Mary, it seems, is the last one to know, and she probably wouldn't have been told, except that the Grants are invited to her apartment for dinner. Mary's natural instincts land her right in the middle of their business, even as Lou resists Mary's meddling.

Our Television Heritage: This pivotal first-season episode foreshadows the divorce of Lou and Edie Grant. Their problems in this show stem from Edie's desire to further her education, but we'll see in future episodes that this rift is merely a symptom of their growing apart. Mary's handling of this situation also clues the viewer in to the beginning of a new phase of her own complex relationship with Lou. A must-see episode.

EPISODE 22

"A Friend in Deed"

Writer: Susan Silver
Director: Jay Sandrich
Cast
Twinks McFarland: Pat Finley

Twinks, the new WJM receptionist, is living proof that Mary makes friends wherever she goes, even when she doesn't know it. Twinks swears she met Mary at summer camp in her youth, and Mary's too embarrassed to admit she doesn't remember her. Before you know it, Mary's a member of her new best friend's wedding party.

EPISODE 23

"Smokey the Bear Wants You"

Writer: Steve Pritzker
Director: Jay Sandrich
Cast
Chuck Pelligrini: Michael Callan

Rhoda begins to think that Chuck, the gentleman she's been seeing, could be Mr. Right. But he keeps strange hours, and this gives Rhoda pause. When she finds out he's planning to become a forest ranger, she passes on an opportunity to join him.

Award: In this episode, Rhoda demonstrates that her strong desire to find a man doesn't prevent her from knowing what's best for here. We witness growth in her character as she decides she doesn't need a man to define her as a person. Performances like this one earned Valerie Harper her first Emmy Award as Best Supporting Actress in a Comedy Series at season's end.

EPISODE 24

"The Forty-Five-Year-Old Man"

Writer: George Kirgo
Director: Herbert Kenwith
Cast
Wild Jack Monroe: Slim Pickens
Big Chicken: Richard Libertini
Everett Edwards: Sidney Clute

Like any other TV station, WJM gets pressure from management. The newscast ratings are terrible, so Wild Jack Monroe, the station's owner, makes Lou the scapegoat and fires him. Guess who intervenes and gets Mr. Grant his job back?

Classic Guest Star: This season-ending segment is loaded with familiar faces. Slim Pickens brings his one-of-a-kind cornpone insanity to his portrayal of Wild Jack Monroe. Sidney Clute is best known for playing Detective Paul La Guardia on *Cagney and Lacey*. Richard Libertini has logged in performances in a wide variety of projects, from series like *Soap* to popular movies like *Nell*.

Awards: Edward Asner won his first Emmy for Best Supporting Actor in a Comedy Series for his work in this episode. In all, the series picked up four Emmys in its first year.

EPISODE 25

"The Birds . . . and . . . Um, Bees"

Writer: Treva Silverman
Director: Jay Sandrich

Move over, Dr. Ruth. That noted sex expert Mary Richards produces a documentary called "What's Your Sexual IQ?" and suddenly sex is on everyone's mind, from the perverts who make obscene calls to the station to Bess, who must know the facts of life . . . now.

EPISODE 26

"I Am Curious Cooper"

Writers: David Davis and Lorenzo Music
Director: Jay Sandrich
Cast
Mike Cooper: Michael Constantine

It's Lou's turn to play matchmaker, and he thinks Mary and his good friend Mike Cooper can make beautiful music together. But Lou watches in horror as the two become (gasp) platonic friends! Lou will not be deterred, for when he makes a match, he's determined to make it stick.

Classic Guest Star: At the time of this guest appearance, Michael Constantine was costarring as Principal Seymour Kaufman on *Room 222*.

EPISODE 27

"He's No Heavy, He's My Brother"

Writer: Allan Burns
Director: Jerry Paris
Cast
Gustavo: Frank Ramirez

Mare and Rho plan yet another vacation together, this time to Mexico. Of course, their plans are complicated—hey, if things were simple, there wouldn't be a show, would there?—by the owner of a Mexican restaurant and his waiter.

For the Record: In this episode, Jerry Paris, the principal director of *The Dick Van Dyke Show*, is reunited with Mary Tyler Moore for the first of three stints as guest director. Paris went on to become principal director for other classic series, including *The Odd Couple* and *Happy Days*.

Parallel Plot: Bob and Emily also had trouble getting their Mexico vacation off the ground in episode 27 of *The Bob Newhart Show*.

EPISODE 28

"Room 223"

Writer: Susan Silver
Director: Jay Sandrich
Cast
Dan Whitfield: Michael Tolan
DeForest: Val Bisoglio
Mrs. Marshall: Florida Friebus

Mary decides to sharpen her reporting skills by taking a journalism class. Sure enough, she becomes involved with her professor, handsome Dan Whitfield. They're consenting adults, so there's no problem, right? Well, there *is* the little matter of her grade. What will she get, now that she appears to be the teacher's pet?

For the Record: Michael Tolan makes the first of his three appearances as teacher Dan Whitfield. He'll return in episodes 63 and 134.

Classic Guest Star: Florida Friebus played Dobie's mother and Mrs. Bakerman in Dr. Hartley's regular group.

EPISODE 29

"A Girl's Best Friend Is Not Her Mother"

Writers: David Davis and Lorenzo Music
Director: Jay Sandrich
Cast
Ida Morgenstern: Nancy Walker

She's Baaack! Just when Rhoda has nearly forgotten her overbearing mother's last visit, Ida returns. This time, she longs to be close to her daughter, but Rho doesn't *wanna* be that close. After seeing Ida in action, who can blame her?

EPISODE 30

"Cover Boy"

Writer: Treva Silverman
Director: Jay Sandrich
Cast
Hal Baxter: Jack Cassidy

You think Ted's obnoxious? His brother Hal *invented* the word. Having achieved fame as the Clear Bag TV pitchman, Hal considers himself the Olivier of commercials. This sibling rivalry so intimidates Ted that he blurts out that Mary is his girlfriend. A blubbering Ted has to beg Mary to go along with this shocking ruse.

Classic Quote
MARY: You must be Ted's brother.
HAL: No, no, no . . . Ted is *my* brother.

Classic Guest Star: The late, great Jack Cassidy made his living playing creeps filled with bluster and overinflated ego run amok. Notably, he played actor Oscar North, a character who bore a startling similarity to Ted Baxter, on the critically acclaimed but short-lived series *He and She*. Cassidy, of course, was the father of teen idols David and Shaun Cassidy and was once married to Shirley Jones.

For the Record: This was a key early episode that dared to humanize the Ted Baxter character, showing that his outsized ego masked deepseated insecurities.

EPISODE 31

"Didn't You Used to Be . . . Wait . . . Don't Tell Me"

Writer: Allan Burns
Director: Jay Sandrich
Cast
Howard: Richard Schaal
Eldon Colfax: Jack Riley
Ed Mims: Ron Masak
Vandermast: Kermit Murdock
Estelle: Pippa Scott

Mary is eager to go to her high school reunion, but as everyone knows, it's virtually impossible to have a good time at those events. Mary, being Mary, has an even worse time than most.

Classic Guest Stars: Jack Riley, who played the bitter neurotic, Elliot Carlin, on *The Bob Newhart Show*, is one of the all-time great TV characters. He puts his usual spin on Eldon Colfax, one of Mary's ex-classmates.

Ron Masak is a TV staple in many series and in commercials. His most recent role is that of Sheriff Mort Metzger in *Murder, She Wrote.*

Richard Schaal makes yet another appearance on the series, this time as Howard, another ex-classmate of Mary's.

EPISODE 32

"Thoroughly Unmilitant Mary"

Writer: Martin Cohan
Director: Jay Sandrich
Cast
Herb: Larry Gelman
Al: Dick Balduzzi
Waiter: Paul Micale

Some of WJM's staff members go on strike, Murray and Ted among them. Mary replaces Murray, but she proves that she's no writer. As for "newscaster" Lou . . . well, let's just say that he manages the dubious achievement of making viewers pray for Ted's safe return to the airwaves.

For the Record: Though the episode titles were for internal reference only, the writers always had fun with them. The title of this segment parodies that of the Mary Tyler Moore–Julie Andrews movie *Thoroughly Modern Millie.*

EPISODE 33

"And Now, Sitting in for Ted Baxter"

Writer: Steve Pritzker
Director: Jerry Paris
Cast
Rod Porter: Jed Allan
Bill Woodson

Ted is forced, kicking and screaming, to take a vacation. Replacing him while he's gone is handsome, affable Rod Porter, who is—horrors!—a competent news anchor. As Minneapolis experiences Portermania, Ted's worst fears may come true—he may lose his job!

EPISODE 34

"Don't Break the Chain"

Writers: David Davis and Lorenzo Music
Director: Jerry Paris
Cast
Armand: Jack DeMare
Roy Martoni: Gino Conforti

Gruff realist Lou doesn't seem like the type to believe in superstitions, but he has sent a chain letter to his friends, warning them not to break the chain. Against her better judgment—*that* problem again—Mary continues the chain and gets involved, to her chagrin, with an unwanted suitor and an aggressive cookware salesman.

EPISODE 35

"The Six-and-a-Half Year Itch"

Writer: Treva Silverman
Director: Jay Sandrich
Cast
Bill: Lawrence Pressman
Elizabeth Berger

Who Lou sees his son-in-law, Bill, out on the town with a woman who's not his wife, he jumps to the obvious conclusion. Mary tries to be the voice of reason, but Lou will have none of that. A good thing, too, because Lou's instincts are right on the money. Bill has made Lou angry, and Bill won't like Lou when he's angry.

Classic Guest Star: Lawrence Pressman most recently played the chief hospital administrator on *Doogie Howser, M.D.*

EPISODE 36

" . . . is a Friend in Need"

Writer: Susan Silver
Director: Jay Sandrich
Cast
Waitress: Beverly Sanders

Rhoda gets fired from her window-dressing gig just as a job opens up at WJM. Rhoda's qualified for the position, so it's a perfect fit, right? Not to Mary, who lies—yes *lies*—to her best friend, telling Rho the job has already been filled. Guess the thought of having Rhoda constantly underfoot at home and at work is too much for Mare.

EPISODE 37

"The Square-Shaped Room"

Writer: Susan Silver
Director: Jay Sandrich

Lou's living room could stand some redecorating. He asks aspiring decorator Rhoda to help but soon wishes he hadn't, when he sees the results—not to mention her bill. Watch Lou's classic response when he gets a load of her masterpiece.

EPISODE 38

"Ted over Heels"

Writers: David Davis and Lorenzo Music
Director: Peter Baldwin
Cast
Betty: Arlene Golonka

To his surprise, but no one else's, Ted's love life is decidedly less than exciting. That may change soon for he develops a crush on Betty, the pretty daughter of WJM ratings champ Chuckles the Clown. Alas, the course of true love never did run smooth, and when Ted's involved, the course is rockier still.

Classic Guest Star: Arlene Golonka has graced many a sitcom episode with her cute, slightly ditzy sexiness. Most notably, she played Millie Swanson, the love interest of Howard Sprague (Jack Dodson) on *The Andy Griffith Show* and, later, of Sam (Ken Berry) on the spin-off series *Mayberry, R.F.D.*

EPISODE 39

"The Five-Minute Dress"

Writers: Pat Nardo and Gloria Banta
Director: Jay Sandrich

Mary thought her career kept her hopping, but it's nothing compared to her latest boyfriend's. He's a handsome government official whose schedule is so hectic that he can hardly fit her in. Mary's developing a complex as this new beau keeps backing out of dates.

For the Record: MTM staff members Pat Nardo and Gloria Banta have written and produced television comedy for years, but they will always have a special place in Classic TV history as the sources for the names of *The Bob Newhart Show*'s Michelle Nardo and *Taxi*'s Elaine Nardo and Tony Banta.

EPISODE 40

"Feeb"

Writers: Dick Clair and Jenna McMahon
Director: Peter Baldwin
Cast
Waitress: Barbara Sharma

Dear, sweet Mary gamely tries to endure bad service from an incompetent waitress, but she eventually cracks and complains to the management, getting the waitress fired. Of course, Mary's guilt gets the better of her, and she gets the klutzy woman a job at the station. Naturally, she's just as ineffectual there. When, oh, when will Mary learn to trust those instincts of hers?

Classic Guest Star: Barbara Sharma's quirky nervousness, her stock in trade, was perfect for her role here. She was a regular on *Rowan & Martin's Laugh-In* and also played Myrna Morgenstein on *Rhoda*.

EPISODE 41

"The Slaughter Affair"

Writer: Rick Mittleman
Director: Peter Baldwin

Old reliable Murray has been acting strangely loopy lately, and he's keeping odd hours, to boot. Marie thinks he's cheating on her . . . with Mary. Mary sets out to clear her name and learns that Murray's been moonlighting as a cabby so he can buy his beloved (uh, that would be Marie) a car of her own.

For the Record: There's something to be said about woman's intuition. Marie's suspicions about Murray's interest in Mary aren't totally groundless, as we'll see in episode 124, "Murray in Love."

EPISODE 42

"Baby Sitcom"

Writer: Treva Silverman
Director: Jay Sandrich
Cast
Sandy: Joshua Bryant
Dee-Dee: Leslie Graves

After having agreed to baby-sit with Bess, Mary has to back out because she has a very important date. Enter Lou, that noted child-care expert. He pinch-hits for Mary, providing the classic comedy formula: gruff old guy plus cute little girl.

Classic Quote
LOU: Do anything you want, kid. Just don't play with matches.

For the Record: The same classic comedy formula was the basis of Edward Asner's most recent series, *Thunder Alley*.

EPISODE 43

"More Than Neighbors"

Writer: Steve Pritzker
Director: Jay Sandrich
Cast
Michael Lee: Jack Bender

Ted's on the lookout for a new pad. He learns that there may be an available apartment in Mary's building and considers moving in. Mary and Rhoda desperately go to great lengths to prevent Ted's trademark greeting, "Hi, guys," from turning into "Hi, neighbors"!

EPISODE 44

"The Care and Feeding of Parents"

Writers: Dick Clark and Jenna McMahon
Director: Jay Sandrich
Cast
Turner: Jon Locke
Mitchell: Brad Trumbull

When Mary reads an essay that Bess has written for school, she makes the mistake of praising Bess's writing talent in front of Phyllis. Now Phyllis is plaguing Mary to get the essay published. How Mary became the route to publication is a little hard to explain.

EPISODE 45

"When There's Smoke, There's Rhoda"

Writer: Martin Cohan
Driector: Peter Baldwin
Cast
Fireman: Michael Bell

On February 12, Rhoda's apartment catches fire, and she must vacate the premises. With no place else to go, she appears at the door of her friend Mary, with whom she must stay for a couple of days. Can these best friends share an apartment without driving each other crazy?

Classic Quote
RHODA (*trying on Mary's dress*): Last time I wore a seven, it was on my softball uniform.

For the Record: This episode is reminiscent of the classic tone established in *The Odd Couple*. In fact, the episode's writer, Martin Cohan, wrote several episodes of *The Odd Couple* around the same time he wrote for *The Mary Tyler Moore Show*.

EPISODE 46

"You Certainly Are a Big Boy"

Writer: Martin Cohan
Director: Jay Sandrich
Cast
Matt: Bradford Dillman
Matt Junior: John Rubinstein

Mary's dating Matt, a great new man. There is a catch, unfortunately: she discovers that Matt's son, Matt Junior, isn't all that junior. In fact, the son is just about the same age as Mary. You know, sometimes it seems the dating scene just isn't cut out for Mary.

Classic Guest Stars: Bradford Dillman did dozens of guest shots during the seventies. It seemed that every time he turned around, he was on some Quinn Martin show. John Rubenstein, son of the famed pianist Arthur Rubenstein, had regular roles on *Family* and *Crazy like a Fox*. He is also a talented composer.

EPISODE 47

"Some of My Best Friends are Rhoda"

Writer: Steve Pritzker
Director: Peter Baldwin
Cast
Joanne: Mary Frann

Mary becomes fast friends with WASPy Joanne, whom she meets after a minor traffic accident. Rhoda feels left out as Mary and Joanne indulge in common pursuits. But Mary's faux friend turns out to be an anti-Semite who wants nothing to do with Rhoda, who's Jewish. As we always suspected, Joanne, who's been slow in paying for damages in the accident, was never really a threat to Rhoda and Mary's friendship.

Classic Guest Star: Mary Frann plays an unsympathetic character in this episode, but she had a long run as the good-natured Joanna, wife of Dick Loudon, on *Newhart*.

EPISODE 48

"His Two Right Arms"

Writers: Jim Parker and Arnold Margolin
Director: Jay Sandrich
Cast
Pete Peterson: Bill Daily
Mrs. Wilson: Isabel Sanford
Jennifer Riley: Carol Androsky
Sherry Wilson: Janet MacLachlan
Walter Ellis: Wally Taylor
Woman in Audience: Phillipa Harris
Man in Audience: Davis Roberts

Mary's planning a new talk show, and her guest will be Pete Peterson, a klutzy politician who knows little about the issues of his own campaign. What can Mary do to make him look good on the air? Well, of course, she'll pair him with the consummate professional himself, Ted Baxter.

Classic Guest Stars: Two well-known actors appear in this final episode of the second season, Bill Daily is hilarious as Pete Peterson. Fresh off his run on *I Dream of Jeannie*, Bill would begin work on *The Bob Newhart Show* at the beginning of the 1972–1973 season.

Isabel Sanford would soon have a long-running hit series of her own, *The Jeffersons*.

Awards: The Emmy Awards were kind to Ed Asner and Valerie Harper once again; they won for Best Supporting Actor and Actress. (Valerie Harper shared her award with Sally Struthers, of *All in the Family*.)

EPISODE 49

"The Good-Time News"

Writers: James L. Brooks and Allan Burns
Director: Hal Cooper
Cast
Robert Hogan
Jack Stoneham

Happy-talk news with forced banter is all the rage. Mary is assigned to develop WJM's version of this format, although Lou's unhappy about it. As you can well imagine, Ted's on-air style is ill-suited to the changes, resulting in some pioneering television broadcasting.

EPISODE 50

"What Is Mary Richards Really Like?"

Writer: Susan Silver
Director: Jerry Belson
Cast
Mark Williams: Peter Haskell

Mark Williams, a Minneapolis columnist, wants to interview Mary about her career as the only woman who works in local broadcast news. Lou, who thinks the journalist's intentions are self-serving, barges into the interview, roaring about Williams's womanizing and about his reputation as a hatchet man—and thoroughly embarrassing Mary.

EPISODE 51

"Who's in Charge Here?"

Writer: Martin Cohan
Director: Jay Sandrich
Cast
Mrs. Thorn: Joan Tompkins

Lou's promotion to news program director leaves Murray as senior person in charge of the newsroom. Unfortunately, as a producer Murray makes a great newswriter. Of course, chaos reigns in the newsroom until Murray is mercifully relieved of his duties.

For the Record: In Lou's executive office, while he explains his plan to move the six o'clock news to five-thirty, we get a rare glimpse at the WJM program schedule. That lineup is as follows:

> Morning movie
> Cartoons/self-defense
> Matinee movie
> *Bet Your Bottom Dollar*
> *Homemaking with Mimi*
> *Gilligan's Island*
> *Coast to Coast*
> *My Mother the Car*
> *Chuckles the Clown*
> Six o'clock news
> *The Sporting Scene*
> Variety hour
> *Edge of Evening*
> *Your City at Night*
> *Backstage, Little Theatre*
> *Thirty Minutes with . . .*

The rest of the list is obscured. *The Happy Homemaker* must have replaced Mimi's show. Also, the choice of *My Mother the Car* was a nod to MTM creator Allan Burns, who had also created that much-maligned series, which starred Jerry Van Dyke.

EPISODE 52

"Enter Rhoda's Parents"

Writer: Martin Cohan
Director: Jay Sandrich
Cast
Martin Morgenstern: Harold Gould
Ida Morganstern: Nancy Walker

Hurricane Ida makes another appearance in Minneapolis. This time she hits Rhoda with the news that her husband, Rhoda's father, Martin is cheating on her after thirty-five years of marriage. Misery loves company, and if you look in the dictionary, you just might see Ida's picture under "misery" and Rhoda's under "company."

Classic Guest Star: Wisecracking Martin Morgenstern's first appearance is made memorable by the fine character actor Harold Gould, whose shrewd underplaying complemented Nancy Walker's over-the-top characterization.

For the Record: Series co-creator James Brooks—thin and bearded—can be seen as an extra late in the episode, as Mary catches a bouquet.

EPISODE 53

"It's Whether You Win or Lose"

Writer: Martin Donovan
Director: Jay Sandrich

Murray, once a compulsive gambler, has for years been able to resist the urge to wager. Unfortunately, all it takes is one innocent, friendly poker game, planned by Mary, to start the cycle again. Soon Murray's betting on everything, and he's wagered a lot of money on a "sure thing"—

Ted's inability to read the script correctly on the news.

Awards: Jay Sandrich's expert direction of this episode earned him another Best Director Emmy in the Comedy Series category.

EPISODE 54

"Rhoda the Beautiful"

Writer: Treva Silverman
Director: Jay Sandrich

Thanks to a strict diet club that Rhoda and Murray have joined, Rhoda's lost a lot of weight and looks like a million bucks, but she still feels like a buck ninety-eight. Unfortunately she's immune to the compliments of her friends, and even an invitation to appear in her company's beauty contest doesn't move her. It's up to Mare to practice her own version of tough love and make her friend appreciate the new Rhoda.

For the Record: This episode used Valerie Harper's real-life weight-loss to great advantage, advancing the character of Rhoda Morganstern to a new level.

EPISODE 55

"Just around the Corner"

Writer: Steve Pritzker
Director: Jay Sandrich
Cast
Mrs. Richards: Nanette Fabray
Mr. Walter Richards: Bill Quinn

Lest you think that Rhoda is the only one with parent problems, Mary's parents make their first appearance in this episode. Mary's mother starts sticking her nose in where it doesn't belong, and Mare has to gently but firmly set her straight.

Classic Guest Stars: The musical comedy star Nanette Fabray made her mark as Mary's sweet-natured mother. Along with her many movie roles, she became a frequent guest star on the situation comedy *One Day at a Time*, playing Grandma Romano.

Bill Quinn's many television credits include a regular stint as Mr. Van Ranseleer, the blind bar patron on *Archie Bunker's Place*.

EPISODE 56

"But Seriously, Folks"

Writer: Ed. Weinberger
Director: Peter Baldwin
Cast
Wes Callison: Jerry Van Dyke
Bowler: John Fox
Stage Manager: Bob Duggan
Nightclub Manager: Rudy DeLuca
Woman: Reda Leopold

Wes Callison, a sweet, bumbling writer for Chuckles the Clown, has a desire to be a newscaster. His nervous nature makes him an odd candidate for that job, but leave it to Mary to give him the encouragement he doesn't need. After an unsuccessful tryout, he does a comedy routine at a bowling alley—talk about your tough rooms!

Classic Guest Star: This episode reunited Mary Tyler Moore with Jerry Van Dyke, Dick's younger brother, who played Stacey Petrie on four classic episodes of *The Dick Van Dyke Show* (28, 29, 111, 112). Here, Jerry plays a character remarkably similar to Stacey Petrie, whose goal was to have a career in show biz. The younger Van Dyke is often teased about having starred in one of TV's most notorious series, *My Mother The Car*. He made other unsuccessful series attempts before landing the role of Luther Van Dam on the long-running hit *Coach*.

EPISODE 57

"Farmer Ted and the News"

Writer: Martin Donovan
Director: Jay Sandrich
Cast
Bella Swann: Lurene Tuttle
Announcer: Patrick Campbell

Before the days of high-salaried newscasters, Ted had to make ends meet any way he could. His agent gets Lou to approve a clause in Ted's contract allowing him to do commercials. Lou lives to regret his decision when these commercials made Ted look like a buffoon. Well, even more like a buffoon than before.

EPISODE 58

"Have I Found a Guy for You"

Writer: Charlotte Brown
Director: Hal Cooper
Cast
Jack Foster: Bert Convy
Linda Foster: Beth Howland
Arthur Price: Dan Keough

Mary thinks her new friends, Jack and Linda Foster, are happily married, but she's wrong. When they separate, Mary is caught in the middle, as only she can be. Jack wants to date her, but Linda's against the idea.

Classic Quote
RHODA: I like Pat and Dick Nixon's marriage. You know he can't fool around.

Classic Guest Stars: Both of this episode's guests later became important TV stars. Bert Convy brought his amiable presence to many TV shows, but is best known for his stints as the host of *Win, Lose, or Draw* and *Password*.

Beth Howland brought laughter to millions of viewers as Vera, the loopy waitress on the long-running comedy series *Alice*.

EPISODE 59

"You've Got a Friend"

Writer: Steve Pritzker
Director: Jerry Belson
Cast
Mrs. Richards: Nanette Fabray
Mr. Walter Richards: Bill Quinn
Waitress: Beverly Sanders

Mary's father has just retired and has too much free time on his hands. Thinking that her dad needs a friend, or maybe trying to score some brownie points with her boss, she offers Lou as a volunteer companion. Not a good idea, but Mary's determined to make this odd friendship work, even if it kills both men.

EPISODE 60

"It Was Fascination, I Know"

Writer: Ed. Weinberger
Director: Jay Sandrich
Cast
William: Gerald Michenaud
Maître D': Jack Manning
Violinist: Murray Korda

There seems to be no one Mary can't turn on with her smile. The latest convert? Bess's fifteen-year-old boyfriend, William, who takes one look at Mary and decides that they are destined to be together. Mary must find a way to let William down easy and not shatter Bess's self-esteem at the same time.

For the Record: This episode marked the first but certainly not the last time Ted Baxter regaled anyone who would listen with his story of the origins of his legendary career: "It all started at a five-thousand-watt station in Fresno. . . ."

EPISODE 61

"Operation: Lou"

Writers: Elias Davis and David Pollock
Director: Jay Sandrich
Cast
The Nun: Florida Friebus
Nurse: Linda Sublette

Can't a guy even get some World War II shrapnel removed without all hell breaking loose? That question is on Lou's mind while he's stuck in the hospital getting rid of his souvenir of the war. Meanwhile, Mary and Murray are engaged in a power struggle for control of the office. And where is Ted? Being a real pain in Lou's rear, as usual.

EPISODE 62

"Rhoda Morgenstern: Minneapolis to New York"

Writer: Treva Silverman
Director: Jay Sandrich
Cast
Barry Barlow: Jack Riley
Rob: Robert Casper

Rhoda makes plans to move back to New York and turn its citizens on with her sneer. Mary can't bear the thought of her beloved friend leaving the nest, but she keeps a stiff upper lip, even at the farewell party. After all, Rhoda wouldn't really leave, would she?

For the Record: This third-season episode marks the first appearance of one of *The Mary Tyler Moore Show*'s best-loved characters, the kind-hearted, ditsy Georgette. In seasons to come she would enrich Ted Baxter's life in side-splittingly wonderful ways. This segment also foreshadowed Rhoda's real move to New York, and to her own series, after the fourth season.

EPISODE 63

"The Courtship of Mary's Father's Daughter"

Writer: David Pollock and Elias Davis
Director: Jay Sandrich
Cast
Jonas Lasser: Steve Franken
Judy's Father: Gordon Jump
Dan Whitfield: Michael Tolan
Walter Richards: Bill Quinn
Judy Conrad: Barra Grant
Man in Elevator: Arthur Abelson
Woman at Party: Molly Dodd

Mary learns that teacher Dan Whitfield, her former boyfriend, is getting married to a woman named Judy. Mary is invited to the engagement party, where her presence unsettles Judy, but Mary finds that there isn't any way for her to leave gracefully.

Classic Guest Stars: Steve Franken played Chatsworth Osbourne Jr. on *Dobie Gillis.* Gordon Jump went on to a memorable portrayal of bumbling station manager Arthur Carlson on *WKRP in Cincinnati.*

EPISODE 64

"Lou's Place"

Writer: Ed. Weinberger
Director: Jay Sandrich
Cast
Alice: Rhoda Gemignani
Philly: Dick Balduzzi
Al: Jack Spritt
Tim: Arthur Abelson
Rick: Lew Horn
Henry: Russ Grieve
Betty: Kathleen O'Malley

Lou realizes a dream when he buys his favorite watering hole and becomes a barkeep. His dream turns into a nightmare, though, when the regular customers stop frequenting the establishment. Could it be that Lou's demands that they have fun make their experience anything but?

Classic Guest Star: Rhoda Gemignani has made countless appearances on shows and commercials. She was a semi-regular on *Who's the Boss?* as Tony's beloved Mrs. Rossini.

EPISODE 65

"My Brother's Keeper"

Writers: Dick Clair and Jenna McMahon
Director: Jay Sandrich
Cast
Ben Sutherland: Robert Moore

It's Phyllis's turn to play matchmaker. The victims: Mary and Phyllis's brother, Ben. The scene: a party given by Mary. But to Phyllis's genuine horror, Ben shows an interest in Rhoda instead! Phyllis reacts with a tantrum that ruins the party. However, it is revealed that Ben is homosexual, and all is right in Phyllis's world once again, now that she knows she won't become a Morgenstern-in-law.

Bad party!
Mary's party is a rousing failure, a trend that would continue in future episodes.

Our Television Heritage: This episode is typical of the refreshing, natural way *The Mary Tyler Moore Show* deals with controversial topics, not as big events, but as simple matters of fact. This story, for example, is more about Phyllis's feelings regarding Rhoda than it is about Ben's sexual orientation.

EPISODE 66

"The Georgette Story"

Writer: Ed. Weinberger
Director: Peter Baldwin

Georgette is now dating Ted—that is, if you define dating as doing Ted's shopping and laundry. Not surprisingly, Ted likes things the way they are. Leave it to Mare and Rho to "ruin" things by teaching human doormat Georgette to stand up for herself.

For the Record: This episode firmly establishes Georgette as Ted's girlfriend and sets the tone for their subsequent complicated but loving relationship. It's here that Ted learns for the first time not to take Georgette's naïveté for granted.

EPISODE 67

"Romeo and Mary"

Writers: Jim Mulholland and Mike Barrie
Director: Peter Baldwin
Cast
Warren Sturges: Stuart Margolin
Lowell: Bo Kaprall
Peter: Joe Warfield
Peggy: Barbara Brownell

It's Rhoda's turn to play matchmaker. (Among all of the shows characters, only Gordy never tries to fix Mary up.) Rhoda sets up her best friend with Warren, a boorish oaf who tries very hard to win Mary over, even after she's made it clear she's not interested in him.

Classic Guest Star: Stuart Margolin, who has made persistent obnoxiousness an art form, was a regular on *Love, American Style* and served as the perfect foil for James Garner as Angel Martin on *The Rockford Files.*

EPISODE 68

"What Do You When the Boss Says 'I Love You'?"

Writers: David Pollock and Elias Davis
Director: Jay Sandrich
Cast
Barbara Coleman: Lois Nettleton
Philly: Dick Balduzzi
Doris: Carol Worthington

Mary is uncharacteristically gleeful over Lou's discomfort when they learn that the new station manager, Barbara Coleman, is an attractive woman. Lou has enough trouble accepting her as his new boss, but when she puts the moves on him, will he have trouble remembering his wedding vows?

Classic Guest Star: Dependable character actress Lois Nettleton is perfect as the predatory Barbara Coleman. Man-hungry characterizations served her well in dozens of guest appearances and in a regular role on the comic soap opera *All That Glitters.* Regardless of that stereotype, however, she did effectively play Carroll O'Connor's girlfriend on the first few seasons of *In the Heat of the Night.*

EPISODE 69

"Murray Faces Life"

Writer: Martin Cohan
Director: Jay Sandrich

Murray is down in the dumps. He feels that he's stuck in a personal and professional rut with no growth potential. In other words, he's having a midlife crisis. When his depression spreads to other WJM staff members, they set out to restore his confidence.

EPISODE 70

"Remembrance of Things Past"

Writers: Dick Clair and Jenna McMahon
Director: Jay Sandrich
Cast
Tom Vernon: Joseph Campanella

Tom Vernon, yet another of Mary's former boyfriends, resurfaces to make one more try with her. There is the same old spark in their rekindled romance, but alas, there's also the same old problem as well: he wants a trophy girlfriend, and that attitude clashes with Mary's need for independence. Tom Vernon hates spunk, too.

Classic Guest Star: Joseph Campanella has graced TV shows with his ramrod-straight professional presence for years. He played regular roles on several series, including *Mannix*, *The Bold Ones*, and *One Day at a Time.*

EPISODE 71

"Put On a Happy Face"

Writers: Marilyn Suzanne Miller and Monica Magowan
Director: Jay Sandrich
Cast
Jonas Lasser: Steve Franken
Norman: Art Gilmore
Cleaning Man: Herbie Faye
Emcee: Eddy Carroll

This is the famous "hair bump" episode. Mary has once again been nominated for a Teddy Award, but Murphy's Law rears its ugly head for our favorite lady. You don't even *want* to know how she ends up wearing one shoe and one fuzzy slipper to the awards dinner.

For the Record: Writer Marilyn Suzanne Miller was a staff writer for the original *Saturday Night Live.* Her partner Monica Magowan later collaborated, as Monica Johnson, with Albert Brooks on his various feature films.

Note that in this episode, instead of the kitten in the MTM logo, Mary appears, saying "That's All Folks."

EPISODE 72

"Mary Richards and the Incredible Plant Lady"

Writer: Martin Cohan
Director: John Chulay
Cast
Anne Adams: Louise Lasser
Bob: Robert Karvelas
Harry: Henry Corden
Charlie: Craig T. Nelson
Salesman: Bob Ross

Only Mary would borrow money so that she could lend it to a friend. She takes out a bank loan for Rhoda, who's opening a plant store. When the business thrives, Mary waits for Rhoda to repay her, and waits . . . and waits. . . .

Classic Guest Stars: Louise Lasser, who plays the loan officer at the bank, will forever be known to scores of fans as the star of *Mary Hartman, Mary Hartman.*
Robert Karvelas played Larabee, the kooky agent on *Get Smart.* Craig T. Nelson went on to star as Hayden Fox of *Coach.*

Awards: This was the final episode of the third season. By now the series was collecting Emmys in buckets. Valerie Harper earned her third in a row, Ted Knight won his first Supporting Actor award, and the star herself took home her first Best Actress Emmy.

EPISODE 73

"The Lars Affair"

Writer: Ed. Weinberger
Director: Jay Sandrich

It seems that Phyllis's husband, Lars, is cooking in someone else's kitchen. Whose kitchen, pray tell? Why, none other than that of the "Happy Homemaker" herself, Sue Ann Nivens. As Phyllis prepares to confront Sue Ann, all of Minneapolis is braced for the collision of two forces of nature that may rock the city to its core.

For the Record: Enter the Happy Homemaker. Sue Anne's first appearance on *The Mary Tyler Moore Show* makes "The Lars Affair" a classic must-see episode. Betty White's brilliant performance ensured that the series would have another beloved character for the remainder of its run.

EPISODE 74

"Angels in the Snow"

Writers: Marilyn Suzanne Miller and Monica Magowan Johnson
Director: Jay Sandrich
Cast
Stephen: Peter Strauss
Salesgirl: Elayne Heilveil
Girl at party: Carole Ita White
Beck Wilson: Jon Korkes

Mary, you cradle robber! She's beginning a relationship with groovy young Stephen, a man in his twenties. The gang cautions Mary about the pitfalls of such a relationship, but it takes a party given by Stephen's friends to show just how little Mary has in common with him.

Classic Guest Star: A young Peter Strauss makes one of his first TV appearances in this episode. Strauss would later make his mark in distinguished TV dramas such as *Rich Man, Poor Man* and would win an Emmy for his role in the notable TV movie *The Jericho Mile.*

EPISODE 75

"Rhoda's Sister Gets Married"

Writer: Karyl Geld
Director: Jerry Belson
Cast
Martin Morgenstern: Harold Gould
Debbie Morgenstern: Liberty Williams
Aunt Rose: Brett Somers
Ida Morgenstern: Nancy Walker

Rhoda's sister Debbie is getting married, and leave it to Ida to cast her own brand of gloom on the happy occasion. She's so sure that Rhoda is jealous of Debbie that she baits Rho into another mother-daughter skirmish. Mary takes on her usual peacekeeping role to set things in their proper place.

Classic Guest Star: Brett Somers, who was Mrs. Jack Klugman at the time, made several appearances as Oscar Madison's ex-wife, Blanche, on *The Odd Couple.* She was also a regular panelist on *Match Game* throughout the 1970s.

For the Record: We get another glimpse at the Morgenstern family, with the second appearance of Martin Morgenstern. Rhoda's other sister, Brenda, is nowhere to be found and will not appear until the start of *Rhoda*, still a year away.

EPISODE 76

"The Lou and Edie Story"

Writer: Treva Silverman
Director: Jay Sandrich
Cast
Mr. Charney: Darrel Zwerling

This is the beginning of the end of Lou Grant's marriage. He and his wife, Edie, have had prob-lems in the past, but this time there will be no quick fix. Edie, who wants to see what life has to offer her as an individual, is leaving Lou, moving out. After the decision is made, she will only promise to stay until Lou comes home that night, so he won't face an empty house.

Classic Performance: The late Priscilla Morrill brought grace and dignity to the difficult role of Edie Grant, allowing fans of the series to sympa-thize with Lou's wife instead of resenting her for leaving him.

Our Television Heritage: This episode is a highlight of the series, reaching a then-unprece-dented level of poignancy. Ed Asner's perfor-mance is absolutely heartbreaking, and we really feel this middle-aged man's pain and subsequent loneliness as he faces a turning point in his life.

Priscilla Morrill will make several more ap-pearances as Edie as the dissolution of the Grants' marriage is played out over the course of the season.

Awards: Treva Silverman's sensitive and witty treatment of Lou and Edie's broken marriage won her a well-deserved Emmy Award for Best Writing in a Comedy Series.

EPISODE 77

"Hi There, Sports Fans"

Writer: Jerry Mayer
Director: Jay Sandrich
Cast
Ed Cavanaugh: Dick Gautier
Hank Morton: Gordon Jump

Mary learns to be careful what she wishes for in this episode. After she nags Lou to give her more responsibility at the station, he does just that: he tells her to fire the sportscaster. Can she do it?

Classic Guest Stars: Dick Gautier played Maxwell Smart's robotic partner, Hymie, on *Get Smart* and appeared as a comic Robin Hood on *When Things Were Rotten*, among many other roles.

EPISODE 78

"Father's Day"

Writers: Ed. Weinberger and Stan Daniels
Director: Jay Sandrich
Cast
Mr. Baxter: Liam Dunn
Caldwell: John Holland

This episode provides more information about the events that have shaped Ted Baxter's life. It seems that Ted's never gotten over the fact that his father abandoned him as a baby. Now the elder Baxter reenters Ted's world, hoping to make amends, but as expected, Ted isn't very happy to see him.

EPISODE 79

"Son of 'But Seriously, Folks'"

Writer: Phil Mishkin
Director: Jay Sandrich
Cast
Wes Callison: Jerry Van Dyke

The bumbling Wes Callison returns, this time to work in the newsroom. It turns out that he is in love with Mary (what guy *isn't*, really?) and cannot keep his feelings to himself. Unfortunately, Wes's emotions get in the way of his job performance; thus, he makes even more of a mess of things than he would have in normal circumstances.

EPISODE 80

"Lou's First Date"

Writers: Ed. Weinberger and Stan Daniels
Director: Jay Sandrich
Cast
Edie Grant: Priscilla Morrill
Martha: Florence Lake
Mike Montgomery: Jeff Thompson

Edie Grant is moving on with her life, but Lou needs more time for his wounds to heal. Mary helps him get a date for an awards dinner. The problem? The woman is, ahem, slightly older than Lou. If he'd wanted to date someone old enough to be his mother, he probably would have brought his own mother to the dinner.

For the Record: This is the first episode to deal with Lou's newly single status. Starting with his eighty-year-old date, Lou will embark on a series of romantic situations that, in true *MTM* fashion, will take many comic twists and turns, all leading to the inevitable encounter with Mary in the penultimate episode of the series, "Lou Dates Mary."

EPISODE 81

"Love Blooms at Hempel's"

Writers: Sybil Adelman and Barbara Gallagher
Director: Jay Sandrich
Cast
Doug Hempel: William Burns
Margaret Kellogg: Barbara Barrett
Eve Bayless: Meg Wylie

Rhoda falls for her boss, Doug Hempel, and she's anxious to tell him how she feels. Mare, not wanting Rho to blow this potential romance, warns her to take things slowly. Does Rhoda listen to Mare's sensible advice? If your answer is yes, go back to episode number one and start reading again.

EPISODE 82

"The Dinner Party"

Writer: Ed. Weinberger
Director: Jay Sandrich
Cast
Steve Waldman: Henry Winkler
Mrs. Geddes: Irene Tedrow

Mary is coaxed into giving a dinner party for Mrs. Geddes, a congresswoman. The coaxers must be crazy. Don't they know that Mary is famous for throwing the worst parties in Minneapolis? What were they thinking? They'll be sorry . . .

Bad Party!
Do you have any idea what happens to Veal Prince Orloff if you leave it in the oven too long?

Classic Moment: The incredibly, delightfully awkward moment when Lou takes two servings.

Classic Guest Stars: Fresh from the Yale School of Drama, a young Henry Winkler appears as Steve Waldman, but he would soon carve out a classic TV character of his own—Arthur "Fonzie" Fonzarelli on *Happy Days*.

EPISODE 83

"Just Friends"

Writer: William Wood
Director: Nancy Walker

Ever since Edie walked out on him, morose Lou has been spending his free time at Mary's apartment. Desperate to regain her lost space,

Mary attempts the impossible: she tries to get the estranged Grants back together. Her efforts are all for naught, though, as Lou and Edie are truly through.

For the Record: The Edie Grant character makes her third appearance in another show focusing on the irreversible state of Lou's marriage. Whatever last, lingering heartbeats the Grant marriage had are slowing to a halt. Nancy Walker makes her first mark as a director, helming this fine episode.

EPISODE 84

"We Want Baxter"

Writer: David Lloyd
Director: Jay Sandrich

Ted Baxter for city council? If Phyllis has her way, that scary thought just might become a reality. Despite Phyllis's best efforts, though, clearer heads prevail, and Ted leaves the political arena to return to the newscasting world, where he belongs.

For the Record: This is the first script written by David Lloyd. He eventually wrote thirty episodes—more than any other writer for *The Mary Tyler Moore Show*—and he contributed to the series finale.

EPISODE 85

"I Gave at the Office"

Writers: Don Reo and Allan Katz
Director: Jay Sandrich
Cast
Bonnie Slaughter: Tammi Bula
Man: Bruce Boxleitner

Murray gets his daughter Bonnie a job at the station, but instead of letting her learn at her own pace, he makes her (and everyone else) tense with his constant hovering. Take Our Daughters to Work Day was never so much fun.

Classic Guest Star: Bruce Boxleitner who appears here in a brief cameo later became a stalwart TV leading man on such series as *Scarecrow and Mrs. King* and *Babylon 5*.

EPISODE 86

"Almost a Nun's Story"

Writers: Ed. Weinberger and Stan Daniels
Director: Jay Sandrich
Cast
Sister Anne: Gail Strickland

The course of true love never did run smoothly, and with Ted and Georgette bringing their own peculiar logic to the relationship, the course is strewn with land mines. In this episode, Ted's inability to be faithful gets Georgette to a nunnery.

Classic Guest Star: Gail Strickland made many guest shots in her lengthy career. She recently co-starred as the lesbian head nurse on the drama series *Heartbeats.*

EPISODE 87

"Happy Birthday, Lou"

Writer: David Lloyd
Director: George Tyne

It's Lou's birthday. Now, pretend you're Mary. What would you do to celebrate the birthday of a middle-aged man who's depressed over the breakup of his marriage, and who hates surprises and public displays of affection?

Bad Party!
Mary's efforts to wheedle Lou into accepting one guest at a time at his party result in a truly classic performance.

Our Television Heritage: Lou's reaction to his surprise party in this episode is based on a real-life experience of writer-producer Ed. Weinberger. When a friend tried to surprise him with a party—the last thing Weinberger expected or wanted—he refused to let the partygoers enter his home. Finally he relented and proceeded to have a completely miserable time.

EPISODE 88

"WJM Tries Harder"

Writer: Karyl Geld
Director: Jay Sandrich
Cast
Anthony Eisley
Ned Wertimer
Regis Cordic

Mary fraternizes with the enemy when she begins dating the anchor of WJM's rival newscast. Unfortunately, her new relationship has a bad side effect: all of a sudden Mary casts a more critical eye on the quality of her station's newscasts, and finds it lacking.

EPISODE 89

"Cottage for Sale"

Writer: George Atkins
Director: Jay Sandrich
Cast
Rena: Michele Nichols
David: David Haskell

Watch out, world! Phyllis is getting into the real estate game, and no potential homebuyer is safe. Neither, it appears, are homeowners. She tries to get Lou to sell his lonely house, but she may be barking up the wrong tree.

EPISODE 90

"The Co-Producers"

Writers: David Pollock and Elias Davis
Director: Jay Sandrich

A recipe for a disastrous new talk show: take one experienced, sensible producer (Mary), one not-so-experienced but oh-so-opinionated producer (Rhoda), add two temperamental co-hosts (Ted and Sue Ann) and stir well. Serves no one very well.

EPISODE 91

"Best of Enemies"

Writers: Marilyn Suzanne Miller and
Monica Johnson
Director: Jay Sandrich

Mare and Rho have had their share of spats over the years, but this time it's serious. Rhoda betrays Mary's confidence by revealing a secret on her job application, and Mary responds harshly. The resulting rift is so severe that the whole gang gets involved in a desperate attempt to reconcile the two.

Classic Quote
GEORGETTE: You, Mary and Rhoda, are a lot like Pittsburgh.

EPISODE 92

"Better Late . . . That's a Pun . . . Than Never"

Writer: Treva Silverman
Director: John Chulay
Cast
Erica: Jennifer Leak

Those two wacky gals Mary and Rhoda are having fun writing comic obituaries late at night, making the obits zanier as the clock ticks on into the wee hours. Fate, being the powerful thing that it is, finds Ted reading one of the obits on-air, leading Lou to fire Mary. All because of Wee Willy Williams and his little hobby of breathing.

For the Record: With this episode, John Chulay steps up from his usual job as assistant director. He and his children play an important role in Our Television Heritage; see *Dick Van Dyke*, episode 78, for details.

EPISODE 93

"Ted Baxter Meets Walter Cronkite"

Writer: Ed. Weinberger
Director: Jay Sandrich

Cast

Walter Cronkite: Himself
Andy: John Gabriel

Teddy Alert! After years of being nominated but never winning, Ted finally bags the elusive Teddy Award, and in his hilarious acceptance speech, he's as humble as ever. What a coincidence, then, when the dean of all broadcasting, Walter Cronkite, arrives in Minneapolis to visit Lou. Imagine—Ted and Walter Cronkite talking shop. Can Minneapolis stand it? Can Walter Cronkite stand it?

Classic Cameos: Walter Cronkite acquits himself quite nicely in this episode, assuring Lou that he'll get revenge for exposing him to Ted.

For the Record: Walter Cronkite's appearance sets a precedent of sorts that *Murphy Brown* would emulate years later—having real news personalities interact with fictional characters.

EPISODE 94

"Lou's Second Date"

Writer: Ed. Weinberger
Director: Jerry London

Lou goes out on his second date since his breakup with Edie. This date is with, of all people, Rhoda! Fortunately, the comfort level the two have had with each other over the years helps, and after a second date, everyone assumes they're an item. Of course, their relationship can't last.

Rhoda will soon have her own series to worry about, after all.

Our Television Heritage: By the fall of 1974, Valerie Harper was due to begin *Rhoda*. This episode marks her last appearance as a regular character, and the other characters say their good-byes in appropriate fashion. *Rhoda*, of course, was a successful series, lasting four and a half years, but her departure from *The Mary Tyler Moore Show* definitely marks the end of an era for many fans.

EPISODE 95

"Two Wrongs Don't Make a Writer"

Writer: David Lloyd
Director: Nancy Walker

Cast

Mrs. Malone: Shirley O'Hara

Ted's boorish behavior continues as he barges in on a creative writing class that Mary is taking. Ted steals Mary's idea for their writing assignment, claiming it as his own.

Parallel Plot: There is a hint of a parallel plot in episode 164, "Murray Ghosts for Ted." Ted's sheer inability to be creative always leads him to hurt his friends. Also, this is not the first time Mary Tyler Moore has taken up writing classes: as Laura Petrie, she took up the quill in *Dick Van Dyke* episodes 94 and 138.

EPISODE 96

"I Was a Single for WJM"

Writer: Treva Silverman
Director: Mel Ferber

Cast

Dino: Richard Schaal
Toni: Penny Marshall
Alice: Arlene Golonka
Bartender: Robert Riesel
Stage Manager: Randy Kirby

The staff decides to do a live segment inside a singles bar to capture the essence of that scene. Unfortunately, the customers are scared off by the cameras, and Mary, Lou, and Murray have to fill the airtime any way they can. As we've seen before, that's a dicey proposition at best.

Classic Guest Star: Penny Marshall, at the time a co-star on *The Odd Couple*, soon left that series for a bigger role on the MTM vehicle *Paul Sand in Friends and Lovers*. After that came an even bigger role on a little series called *Laverne and Shirley*. And after that, of course, Penny Marshall became an A-list movie director.

EPISODE 97

"Will Mary Richards Go to Jail?"

Writers: Ed. Weinberger and Stan Daniels
Director: Jay Sandrich

Cast

Sherry: Barbara Colby
Harrison: James Randolph
Kim: Mary Ann Chinn
Matron: Darlene Conley
Reporter: Don Macon
Mr. Everett: Charles Wolfe

When Mary refuses to reveal a news source she is sent to jail. Lou urges her to hang tough, but Mary begins to waver. Luckily she meets some prostitutes in the slammer who see her through.

For the Record: This, the first episode in the fifth season, is one of the best in the series. The scenes with Mary in jail are classic. The plot threads from this story will be picked up again in episodes 117 and 152.

EPISODE 98

"Not Just Another Pretty Face"

Writers: Ed. Weinberger and Stan Daniels
Director: Jay Sandrich

Cast

Paul Van Dillen: Robert Wolders
Nice Little Man: Lou Cutell
Waitress: Julie Rogers
Waitress: Cathy Baco

Mary is dating Paul Van Dillen, a handsome ski instructor. Paul has not one thing in common with sophisticated career woman Mary, but you don't think she would date him only because he's an

Adonis, do you? Mary wouldn't do that, would she? You bet she would!

For the Record: This episode rather honestly explores Mary's pursuit of a strictly physical relationship. Director Jay Sandrich bluntly stated that Mary Richards would date someone like Paul for only one reason: because he's good in bed. But Mary is simply being honest, and the result is the revelation of another facet of her personality.

EPISODE 99

"You Sometimes Hurt the One You Hate"

Writer: David Lloyd
Director: Jackie Cooper

We always knew that Ted's incompetence would push Lou too far one day. That day finally comes when Ted messes up on the air. This time Lou pushes Ted back, literally. Ted suffers slight injuries, but Lou suffers more in terms of remorse—so much, in fact, that he begins to cater to the anchorman's every whim. Big mistake.

For the Record: This episode was directed by Jackie Cooper, former child star of countless *Our Gang* comedies and the feature film *The Champ*. He hated this directing stint; he was apparently annoyed by the constant suggestions from the regular writers and producers. Nevertheless, Cooper has had a successful second career as a TV director, listing M*A*S*H and *The White Shadow* among his many credits.

EPISODE 100

"Lou and That Woman"

Writer: David Lloyd
Director: Jay Sandrich
Cast
Charlene: Sheree North
Drunk: Fred Festinger

Still reeling from his busted marriage, Lou develops a crush on Charlene, a faded lounge singer. Soon they are dating, but how can the gang really find her acceptable for Lou after they find out how many men she's been with over the years?

Classic Guest Star: Sheree North brought a warmth and earthy sexiness to her role in this episode. She started her career as a starlet in the 1950s, and in 1980 she played Diana Canova's mother on *I'm a Big Girl Now.*

EPISODE 101

"The Outsider"

Writer: Jack Winter
Director: Peter Bonerz
Cast
Consultant: Richard Masur

WJM has suffered through five years of bad ratings, and *now* they decide to bring in a consultant? Well, the consultant they pick is a young, brash, arrogant jerk who is overly critical of everything and everyone. The staff hates him—until they see the rise in the ratings under his command. Okay, so it's only a one-point increase, but it's the direction that counts, right?

For the Record: This was the first episode directed by Peter Bonerz, a costar on *The Bob Newhart Show.* Bonerz later became a full-time director, most notably helming many *Murphy Brown* episodes.

EPISODE 102

"I Love a Piano"

Writer: Treva Silverman
Director: Jay Sandrich
Cast
Judith: Barbara Barrie

Will Murray's midlife crisis ever end? This time, feeling somewhat unattractive, he's tempted by Judith, an attractive elementary school teacher and musician who's willing to tinkle Murray's ivories. Will good ol' Murr cross over the line and give in to his dark side, or will he remember the vow he took to stay faithful to his beloved Marie? He's thinking, he's thinking. . . .

Classic Performance: Murray suavely sings "Strangers in the Night" with Judith, but he gets stuck after the first line, because he doesn't know the rest of the lyrics.

Classic Guest Star: The lovely Barbara Barrie's delicate beauty and superior acting ability helped her turn in a winning performance as Murray's almost lover. Ms. Barrie was a welcome presence on countless TV series, but she is perhaps best known for her role as Elizabeth, Captain Miller's understanding wife on *Barney Miller*.

EPISODE 103

"A New Sue Ann"

Writer: David Lloyd
Director: Jay Sandrich
Cast
Gloria: Linda Kelsey
Station Manager: Ron Rifkin

Sue Anne's future as the Happy Homemaker is in jeopardy: the new WJM station manager is toying with the idea of replacing Ms. Nivens—a woman of a certain age—with Gloria, a younger woman whose sweet demeanor masks a calculating nature. Where's Mary when Sue Ann needs her? Getting prepared for Rhoda's wedding. Fairweather friends indeed!

Classic Guest Stars: Linda Kelsey, as the scheming Gloria, would later make a better impression as the intrepid reporter Billie Newman on *Lou Grant*.

Ron Rifkin costarred on a number of short-lived series, including *Husbands, Wives & Lovers*.

EPISODE 104

"Menage à Phyllis"

Writer: Treva Silverman
Director: Jay Sandrich
Cast
Phyllis's Friend: John Saxon

Phyllis starts a "relationship" with a handsome young man . . . but her interest in him is purely intellectual. When the man gets a look at Mary, though, we know he has more on his mind than reading Plato. When the two start dating, the passive-aggressive Phyllis meddles as only she can.

Classic Guest Star: Tall, dark, and handsome leading man John Saxon has made many TV and movie appearances over the years and has played regular roles on *The Bold Ones* and *Falcon Crest*.

EPISODE 105

"Not a Christmas Story"

Writers: Ed. Weinberger and Stan Daniels
Director: John Chulay

Snow, the nemesis of Minneapolis, rears its ugly head once again. The city is hit with a major snowstorm, trapping the WJM staff in the office like rats. This time Sue Ann is the cat who stalks them by deciding that they should have a Christmas party . . . in November! It's almost enough to make them want to brave the storm to escape.

Parallel Plots: This episode draws upon elements from two earlier episodes. "The Snow Must Go On" (episode 8) and "Christmas and the Hard-Luck Kid" (14), for its inspiration. Humor is sure to follow from situations in which the regulars are stuck together.

EPISODE 106

"What Are Friends For"

Writer: David Lloyd
Director: Alan Rafkin
Cast
Hal: Noble Willingham
Freddy: David Huddleston
Waiter: Robert Karvelas
Bellhop: Dan Barrows

Mary's pride at having been chosen as the station's representative at a broadcasting convention turns sour when she learns that Sue Ann will be going with her. Soon Mary and Sue Ann arrive in Chicago, where they date two morticians (Sue Ann's idea). But both men ending up liking Mary more than Sue Ann (not Sue Ann's idea).

EPISODE 107

"A Boy's Best Friend"

Writer: David Lloyd
Director: Mary Tyler Moore
Cast
George Tewksbury: Nolan Leary

Ted learns that his mother is shacking up with George Tewksbury, a man who's—gasp—not his father. According to Ted's logic, this makes him a b- b- b- . . . illegitimate child. Of course, we know that Ted's father abandoned him and his mother when he was a baby, so this new man couldn't be Ted's father, could he? That doesn't stop Ted from letting his insecurities show.

For the Record: This is the only episode directed by series star Mary Tyler Moore.

EPISODE 108

"A Son for Murray"

Writers: Ed. Weinberger and Stan Daniels
Director: Jay Sandrich
Cast
Le Chan: Michael Higa
Andy Rivers: John Gabriel
Phil Kramer: David Frescoe

Murray is devoted to his three daughters, but he still has a desire to have a son. After Marie tells him she's retired from baby-making, they have a fight, and Murray storms out to stay at Ted's. Fate, of course, steps in when Murray becomes attached to Le Chan, a young Vietnamese boy. So Murray gets a son after all, while an elated Marie stays in retirement.

EPISODE 109

"Neighbors"

Writer: Ziggy Steinberg
Directors: James Burrows and John Chulay
Cast
David: Clifford David

After nearly letting Phyllis talk him into selling his house, in episode 89, Lou finally decides to sell it and find a smaller place. There's just one slight problem: he's got his eye on Rhoda's vacated apartment. Again, Mary must find a way to delicately but firmly dissuade her boss from becoming her new neighbor.

For the Record: As in episode 43, "More Than Neighbors," Mary must defend her home from being invaded by a friend.

This episode is the first one directed by James Burrows, son of the legendary Broadway writer-director Abe Burrows. The younger Burrows wrote to the series producers about his interest in TV direction and was paired with John Chulay, the principal assistant director, who had directed several segments himself. The rest, as they say, is history. Burrows went on to be the principal director for *Taxi* and *Cheers*, winning truckloads of Emmys in the process.

EPISODE 110

"A Girl like Mary"

Writers: Ann Gibbs and Joel Kimmel
Director: Jay Sandrich
Cast
Enid: Rosalind Cash
First Auditioner: Judie Stein

Lou, perhaps tired of having Ted as the sole anchor of the news, decides to hire a female co-anchor. Aspirants to the position include Sue Ann and Mary, those two Barbara Walters wanna-bes. Just watching the two compete for the job makes Lou look at Ted in a whole new light.

EPISODE 111

"An Affair to Forget"

Writers: Ed. Weinberger and Stan Daniels
Director: Jay Sandrich

For reasons that only he understands, Ted spreads a rumor that he's having an affair with Mary. Her sheer horror at such a thought becomes more acute when it appears that the others give some credence to Ted's claims.

EPISODE 112

"Mary Richards, Producer"

Writer: David Lloyd
Director: Norman Campbell
Cast
Mel Peters: Anthony Holland
Gus Brubaker: Phillip R. Allen
Drunk: Fred Festinger
Bartender: Joe Scott

At last, after five long, hard years of struggling to prove herself, Mary finally asks Lou to let her produce the news (and here we thought she was already the news producer). Once again Mary fails to be careful what she wishes for as Lou grants her the opportunity.

For the Record: With this episode, Mary becomes producer, and Lou gets bumped up to news director.

EPISODE 113

"The System"

Writers: Ed. Weinberger and Stan Daniels
Director: Jay Sandrich

Lou likes to gamble on football games, but he isn't very successful at it. After losing a sizable amount of money, he stumbles onto a system that so-called football expert Ted has devised. Against all logic, he becomes Ted's partner. But Lou and his money are soon destined to part.

Our Television Heritage: This is another example of art imitating life for an *MTM* writer. Scriptwriter Stan Daniels had innocently stumbled onto a system for betting on football games, even though he was not much of a fan. When his more football-savvy colleagues saw dollar signs, they incorporated his system into their bets. Naturally, the results were less than impressive.

This show originally aired the night before the 1976 Super Bowl that saw the Minnesota Vikings lose again, this time to the Pittsburgh Steelers. Listen for Mary's topical voice-over during the end credits.

EPISODE 114

"Phyllis Whips Inflation"

Writers: Ed. Weinberger and Stan Daniels
Director: Jay Sandrich
Cast
Helen Farrell: Doris Roberts
Brewster: George Memmol

When Phyllis's husband, Lars, puts his foot down and takes away her credit cards, she has to think about . . . getting a job. Is Phyllis ready to enter the workforce? Is the workforce ready for Phyllis?

Classic Guest Star: Doris Roberts makes one of her delightful TV guest shots in this episode. Among her many roles were regular stints as Angie's mom on *Angie* and a memorable turn as Mildred, the doting secretary, on *Remington Steele.*

For the Record: This episode marks the end of Cloris Leachman's regular run on *The Mary Tyler Moore Show*, but her character lived on in *Phyllis*, which debuted in the fall of 1975. Although not without its moments, that series wasn't quite as successful as Valerie Harper's spin-off, *Rhoda. Phyllis* struggled through two low-rated seasons before going off the air.

Awards: Cloris Leachman won an Emmy for Best Single Performance by a Supporting Actress in a Comedy or Drama for this episode. A nice way to leave the series.

EPISODE 115

"The Shame of the Cities"

Writers: Michael Elias and Arnie Kogen
Director: Jay Sandrich
Cast
Charlene: Sheree North
Man: Robert Embardt
Bartender: Chuck Bergansky
Customer: James Jeter

After regaling Charlene and others with tales of his glory days as a serious journalist, Lou decides to relive those muckraking days of yore. He targets a local politician whose sterling reputation he feels must mask corruption. Lou digs and digs, and sure enough, he finds that the man really is as clean as he appears to be. Lou does deserve an A for effort, though.

For the Record: This episode poked fun at Lou's journalistic instincts, but he'll find himself back in the serious arena after the end of this series. The last *MTM* spin-off series, *Lou Grant*, was an hour-long dramatic series that tackled many controversial issues, and Ed Asner easily proved himself capable of carrying the dramatic load.

EPISODE 116

"Marriage: Minneapolis Style"

Writer: Pamela Russell
Director: Jay Sandrich
Cast
Ellen: Eileen McDonough

Murray and Marie's celebration of twenty years as a happily married couple has a profound effect on Ted. Despite his bravado over the years, he was pretty lonely until Georgette entered his life. After a lot of thought, Ted does the smartest thing he's ever done: he proposes to Georgette on the air. Then, in a typical Ted act, he develops cold feet. Luckily, his feet warm up by episode's end and the engagement is on.

EPISODE 117

"You Try to Be a Nice Guy"

Writer: Michael Leeson
Director: Jay Sandrich
Cast
Sherry: Barbara Colby

Sherry, the hooker with a heart of gold whom Mary met in jail in episode 97, resurfaces here as an ex-hooker in search of a job. She asks "Miss Responsibility" to be her sponsor so she won't have to go back to the big house. Mary agrees and even persuades Sherry to try her hand at designing clothes. Only when she actually tries on one of Sherry's creations does Mary realize that having an ex-hooker design her clothes is not the best idea she's ever had.

EPISODE 118

"You Can't Lose Them All"

Writer: David Lloyd
Director: Majorie Mullen

It's the Teddys! This time Lou learns he will receive an award he deserves but doesn't want. At the same time, Ted is devastated by the fact he wasn't even nominated for the award he probably doesn't deserve to win. Lou then becomes a reluctant confidence booster for his fallen anchorman.

EPISODE 119

"Ted Baxter's Famous Broadcasters School"

Writer: Michael Zinberg
Director: Jay Sandrich
Cast
Tony: Bernie Kopell
Lawrence Hannon: Leonard Frey
Alan Marsh: Norman Bartold

Ted's raging egomania and incredible gullibility are a potent combination. This time he lends his name to a bogus broadcasting school, much like the ones that are advertised on matchbook covers—only worse. When he's stuck with actually having to teach a class, you know that Mary, Lou, and Murray will get stuck as well.

Classic Performance: The entire ensemble gives a bravura performance during the class.

Classic Guest Stars: Bernie Kopell played Maxwell Smart's evil archenemy, Seigfried, on *Get Smart* before costarring as Dr. Adam Bricker with Gavin MacLeod on *The Love Boat.*

The late Leonard Frey was a familiar TV presence. He played regular roles on such sitcoms as *Best of the West* and *Mr. Smith.*

EPISODE 120

"Anyone Who Hates Kids and Dogs"

Writer: Jerry Mayer
Director: Jay Sandrich
Cast
Ken: Laurence Luckinbill
Stevie: Lee Montgomery
Ethel: Mabel Albertson
Grandfather: Ian Wolfe
Aunt Helen: Carole King Larkey

Mary's involvement with otherwise-perfect boyfriend Ken is hampered by Ken's bratty son, Stevie, apparently one of the few people Mary *can't* turn on with her smile. The feeling, unfortunately, is mutual.

Classic Guest Stars: Laurence Luckinbill, a frequent TV leading man during the 1970s, starred in the short-lived adventure series *The Delphi Bureau.* He later married Lucie Arnaz, daughter of TV icon Lucille Ball.

Lee Montgomery, a busy child actor, will forever be remembered as the kid who befriended Ben, the rodent who starred in the movie of the same name.

Mabel Albertson, sister of *Chico and the Man* star Jack Albertson, had a recurring role as Darrin Stephen's mother on *Bewitched.*

Awards: This was the final episode of the fifth season. On top of all the Emmys won by its performers and writers, *The Mary Tyler Moore Show* finally landed the biggie—an Emmy for Outstanding Comedy Series.

EPISODE 121

"Edie Gets Married"

Writer: Bob Ellison
Director: Jay Sandrich
Cast
Janey: Nora Heflin

It had to happen someday: Lou's ex-wife plans to remarry. Lou's conflicting emotions make it difficult for him to come to terms with this event, and once again Mary and the gang join forces to help him in his time of need. He's finally able to accept the inevitable and even wishes Edie well in her new life.

For the Record: A fitting coda to the Lou and Edie story, with Ed Asner yet again delivering big-time. Priscilla Morrill makes her last *Mary Tyler Moore Show* appearance in this episode.

EPISODE 122

"Mary Moves Out"

Writer: David Lloyd
Director: Jay Sandrich

Mary's apartment just isn't the same since Rhoda and Phyllis moved away (those darn spin-offs!) so she decides it's time for a change. She trades up to a new high-rise pad, but not everything has changed. Like a shadow, that big wall-hanging "M" survives the move, resurfacing in her new apartment.

For the Record: Series director Jay Sandrich is the one primarily responsible for Mary's move to a new apartment; he felt that the old set was stale after five years. The producers picked up on Sandrich's idea, even hoping, perhaps, to create new characters for Mary to interact with. That plan didn't bear any fruit, but this episode is a turning point at any rate, allowing viewers to identify episodes from the later seasons at a glance.

EPISODE 123

"Mary's Father"

Writer: Earl Pomerantz
Director: Jay Sandrich
Cast
Father Brian: Ed Flanders

We know that Mary can turn the world on with her smile, but a *priest*? Come on! Yet Mary believes that the good-natured Father Brian is in love with her and plans to leave the priesthood because of her. When Mary realizes she's made a big mistake, her embarrassment is true penance.

Classic Guest Star: Character actor Ed Flanders was well cast in this episode as Father Brian. In addition to winning an Emmy for playing the lead in *Harry S Truman: Plain Speaking*, Mr. Flanders would embark on his best-known (Emmy-winning) role a few years later as kindhearted Dr. Donald Westphall on *St. Elsewhere*.

EPISODE 124

"Murray in Love"

Writer: David Lloyd
Director: Jay Sandrich
Cast
Paula Kovacks: Penny Marshall
Sally Jo Hotchkiss: Mary Kay Place
Steve: Barry Coe
Bartender: Peter Hobbs

It all starts with Murray presenting his long-time co-worker Mary with a goldfish. But this time the look in Murray's eyes is different. The guy's got it bad for Mary. What about Marie? Murray still loves her . . . he thinks. But all he knows for sure is that he must tell Mary how he feels, and he must hear her response.

Classic Guest Stars: Penny Marshall made another guest appearance before stardom found her in *Laverne and Shirley*.

Mary Kay Place would soon segue onto the satire *Mary Hartman, Mary Hartman* as Loretta Haggers.

Our Television Heritage: The seeds of this episode were planted in an earlier show ("The Slaughter Affair," episode 41), in which Murray's wife, Marie, suspected Murray and Mary of having an affair. Marie never knew how on the mark she was. In any event, the performances by Mary Tyler Moore and Gavin MacLeod (who, by the way, was the only original regular never to win an Emmy, just as Murray was the only newsroom regular never to win a Teddy) make this episode a high point in the series.

M

The Mary Tyler Moore Show

EPISODE 125

"Ted's Moment of Glory"

Writers: Charles Lee and Gig Henry
Director: Jay Sandrich

Ted gets an audition for a job as the emcee of a new game show, *The Fifty Thousand Dollar Steeplechase*, a program so moronic that even an idiot could host it. He aces the audition and is offered the job, but we ask you, how could Ted possibly want national fame and fortune when he has everything he needs in Minneapolis? Of course, he turns down the job.

EPISODE 126

"Mary's Aunt"

Writer: David Lloyd
Director: Jay Sandrich
Cast
Aunt Flo: Eileen Heckart

Mary's aunt Flo is a famous journalist and a whirling dervish. For a change, Lou is impressed. But over a dinner welcoming her into town, Lou and Flo clash like two hurricanes battling for a chance to destroy a town, leaving Mary to run for shelter.

Classic Guest Star: Eileen Heckart's first appearance as Aunt Flo perfectly sets up her love-hate relationship with Lou. She would make two more appearances on this show and one on Ed Asner's *Lou Grant*. Ms. Heckart's most recent series role was as the domineering Mother Buchanan on *The Five Mrs. Buchanans*.

EPISODE 127

"Chuckles Bites the Dust"

Writer: David Lloyd
Director: Jay Sandrich
Cast
Reverend Burns: John Hawkins

After years of laughter, beloved WJM superstar Chuckles the Clown meets his Maker in a tragic mishap: dressed as a peanut, he is shelled by a rogue elephant. The gang can't help poking fun at the macabre nature of Chuckles's demise, but Mary admonishes them for their irreverence. Then, at the clown's solemn funeral, the tables are turned, and Mary makes a spectacle of herself by laughing uncontrollably.

Our Television Heritage: For many fans of this series, "Chuckles Bites the Dust" is *the* best episode ever, and, without a doubt the ludicrous circumstances surrounding Chuckles's death make it one of the most memorable.

EPISODE 128

"Mary's Delinquent"

Writers: Mary Kay Place and Valerie Curtin
Director: Jay Sandrich
Cast
Mackenzie Phillips
Tamu

Mary and Sue Ann couldn't be less alike. It's fitting, then, that they are lumped together in awkward situations. This time they become big sisters to two streetwise kids. Needless to say, their sisterly approaches both surprise and confuse the urchins.

Classic Guest Stars: Mackenzie Phillips's ease at playing troubled youngsters stemmed from real life. The daughter of Mamas and Papas singer John Phillips led a drug-infested lifestyle that got her fired several times from her long-running sitcom *One Day at a Time*. Today Mackenzie is cleaned up and reviving her acting career.

Tamu, the other little sister, played streetwise characters on many 1970s series, including *Good Times* and *Sanford and Son*.

EPISODE 129

"Ted's Wedding"

Writer: David Lloyd
Director: Jay Sandrich
Cast
The Minister: John Ritter

It has taken thirteen episodes for Ted to come to his senses, but he finally proposes to Georgette in a serious fashion. This time she throws him a curve: either Ted marries her within a half hour or she's outta here. Now it's a comic race against time as Ted's future happiness is placed in the hands of a swinging young minister who's dressed for tennis.

Classic Guest Star: This episode marks an early comedy guest appearance by John Ritter, who was then playing a recurring role on *The Waltons* as another young minister. Less than two years after this appearance, Ritter would land his signature role on *Three's Company*.

For the Record: The long, wacky courtship of Ted and Georgette culminates in a hilariously sweet marriage. Ted Knight and Georgia Engel shine.

EPISODE 130

"Lou Douses an Old Flame"

Writer: David Lloyd
Director: Jay Sandrich
Cast
Veronica: Beverly Garland

Lou's love life takes another twist when Veronica, an old girlfriend who dumped him with a Dear John letter thirty years ago, makes contact with him. When Lou finally learns what Veronica wants after all these years—money—he lets her have it, along with a sticky dessert poured over her head. It's the best money he ever spent.

Classic Guest Star: Beverly Garland has had a long career in TV. Among her highlights was a two-year stint as Fred MacMurray's love interest on *My Three Sons* and a role as Kate Jackson's feisty mom on *Scarecrow and Mrs. King*.

EPISODE 131

"Mary Richards Falls in Love"

Writers: Ed. Weinberger and Stan Daniels
Director: Jay Sandrich
Cast
Joe Warner: Ted Bessell
Joe Gerard: David Groh

Mary's got a boyfriend . . . really! Mary falls for Joe Warner, a fun-loving guy who's perfect for her in every way—except that he has this habit of being overly affectionate in public, something that the prim and proper Mary has trouble getting used to.

Classic Guest Star: Ted Bessell has had a long and varied career as an actor and director, with an Emmy to his credit for directing *The Tracey Ullman Show*, but he will forever be known as Donald, Marlo Thomas's boyfriend on *That Girl*.

Crossover Appearances: Valerie Harper reprises her role as Rhoda, flush with the success of her own series. *Rhoda* costar David Groh tags along for the ride.

For the Record: The producers toyed with the idea of bringing back the Joe Warner character as a steady love interest for Mary, but Ted Bessell's busy schedule made that impossible. He did make another appearance, however, in episode 134, "One Boyfriend Too Many."

EPISODE 132

"Ted's Tax Refund"

Writer: Bob Ellison
Director: Marjorie Mullen
Cast
Irv Gevins: Paul Lichman

Ted mistakenly receives a $6,000 tax refund. He knows he's not entitled to the money, but he spends it anyway. Just then the dreaded IRS realizes its error and demands its money back. Don't you hate when that happens? Ted does.

EPISODE 133

"The Happy Homemaker Takes Lou Home"

Writer: David Lloyd
Director: James Burrows
Cast
Lazlo Kralic: Titos Vandis
Wynn Irwin

The first time Sue Ann laid eyes on Lou, she knew she wanted him. When her own unique charms fail to lure Lou, she calls in Mary as a reinforcement. Mary reluctantly tricks Lou into accepting a dinner date with Sue Ann. When Sue Ann makes her intentions known, Lou desperately tries to make the dinner part of the evening last forever.

Our Television Heritage: This first of two serious Lou–Sue Ann encounters reveals more about Sue Ann than Lou wants to know, but having faced down the demons of his own loneliness, he's able to relate to her as a real person and help her, if only temporarily, to be better to herself. Thus Lou escapes Sue Ann's mantrap—for now. She does get another shot at him, though, in episode 138.

EPISODE 134

"One Boyfriend Too Many"

Writer: David Lloyd
Director: Jay Sandrich
Cast
Joe Warner: Ted Bessell
Dan Whitfield: Michael Tolan

Torn between two lovers . . . Mary's current love, Joe Warner, watches as Dan Whitfield, Mary's old boyfriend, comes back into her life.

When she agrees to go out with Dan for old times' sake, Joe doesn't take it very well.

For the Record: The two actors who lasted the longest as love interests for Mary, Michael Tolan and Ted Bessell, are paired off against each other in this episode. No one could really win Mary's heart, however, and she remained free and single for the duration of the series.

EPISODE 135

"What Do You Want to Do When You Produce?"

Writers: Shelley Nelbert and Craig Allen Hafner
Director: Jay Sandrich

For Murray, there's good news and bad news on the career front. The good news is that he's getting a raise and a promotion. The bad news is that he's now the producer of *The Happy Homemaker Show*—in other words, he's Sue Ann's indentured servant. After a short time, he settles for returning to the newsroom where he's poorer but safer.

EPISODE 136

"Not with My Wife, I Don't"

Writer: Bob Ellison
Director: Jay Sandrich

With Ted, it's always something. This time, it seems that Mr. Baxter isn't performing his husbandly duties. An unfulfilled Georgette is thinking of leaving him. All of this leads Ted to the destination he should have headed for a long time ago—a psychiatrist's couch—to seek the root of his problem.

EPISODE 137

"The Seminar"

Writers: James MacDonald and Robert Gerlach
Director: Stuart Margolin
Cast
Betty Ford: Herself
Dabney Coleman

Mary and Lou are attending a political seminar in Washington, D.C., and she wants to explore the city. Lou declines, waiting for invitations from some old friends to come through. When it appears that the invitations won't come, Mary leaves without him. When she returns, Lou tells her she missed the party of the year, with Betty Ford as one of the guests. Mary doesn't believe him, even when the First Lady calls back to thank Lou for a good time.

Classic Cameo: Getting Betty Ford for a guest shot, even if it was only a phone call, was a major coup for *The Mary Tyler Moore Show*, and, true to form, the series used the former First Lady to good comic effect.

EPISODE 138

"Once I Had a Secret Love"

Writers: Pat Nardo and Gloria Banta
Director: Jay Sandrich

One look at a disheveled, unshaven Lou, and we know the inevitable had occurred: Sue Ann has bagged the big one. Lou makes Mary promise not to tell anyone, but hey, this is a sitcom, and of course, she betrays his trust. An angry Lou severs his friendship with Mary, leaving two situations to be resolved.

For the Record: In the most adult episode to date, Sue Ann's conquest of a drunken Lou is dealt with hilariously and then sensitively. As a testament to the quality of the series, this episode gives equal weight to the rift between Lou and Mary, adding an element of poignancy to their increasingly complex relationship.

EPISODE 139

"Ménage à Lou"

Writer: Bob Ellison
Director: Jay Sandrich
Cast
Charlene: Janis Paige
Paula: Penny Marshall

Lou's sometime girlfriend Charlene has started seeing a younger man. First Lou gets mad, then he gets even—by going out with a younger woman of his own—Mary's nasal-voiced neighbor, Paula.

Classic Guest Star: Sheree North's sudden unavailability forced the producers to recast the role of Charlene, and Janis Paige, an actress with experience playing roles similar to those played by Ms. North, took over the part. Ms. Paige also played the woman whom Archie Bunker almost had an affair with on *All in the Family.*

For the Record: Penny Marshall makes another appearance as Mary's nutty neighbor, Paula. Perhaps the producers hoped to recapture the magic of having strong characters at home for Mary to interact with, but that never panned out. The WJM regulars would remain Mary's only foils for the rest of the run.

EPISODE 140

"Murray Takes a Stand"

Writer: David Lloyd
Director: Jay Sandrich

Murray protests the station owner's new policies, but his stand, while admirable, is ill-advised. For his actions, Murray gets fired, and it's up to the gang to get the family man his job back.

Parallel Plot: Watch a different gang try to get Mel Cooley's job back in episode 146 of *The Dick Van Dyke Show.*

EPISODE 141

"Mary's Aunt Returns"

Writer: David Lloyd
Director: Jay Sandrich
Cast
Aunt Flo: Eileen Heckart

Aunt Flo is back for round two of her battle with Lou. Their second encounter starts peacefully enough: Flo wants to work with Lou on a special PBS project, but once they begin, they do what comes naturally to them—clash. They detest each other's ideas, so Flo recruits Murray and Lou grabs Mary. The race is on to see which proposal will win.

EPISODE 142

"A Reliable Source"

Writer: Richard M. Powell
Director: Jay Sandrich
Cast
Politician: Edward Winter

The muckraker in Lou rears its ugly head again. The consummate newsman targets another local political figure. The problem is, the politician is a man whom Mary greatly admires. The two are at odds over him.

EPISODE 143

"Sue Ann Falls in Love"

Writer: Bob Ellison
Director: Doug Rogers
Cast
Doug Kellem: James Luisi

Once the predatory Sue Ann lets her guard down, she can be very vulnerable. Here she falls for Doug Kellem, a scoundrel who's hoping to use her to make money off her show. On top of that, Kellem's making a play for Mary right under Sue Ann's nose. The cad!

EPISODE 144

"Ted and the Kid"

Writer: Bob Ellison
Director: Marjorie Mullen

Ted and Georgette are having trouble conceiving. To Ted's shame, his shooter is filled with blanks. Then fate steps in and brings the couple David, an eight-year-old genius, whom they decide to adopt. And then a true miracle occurs: Georgette gets pregnant!

Classic Guest Star: The blond, bespectacled Robbie Rist was rivaled only by Rodney Allen Rippy for the most constant presence on TV commercials and shows in the mid-1970s. He landed a regular role as Oliver on the last half season of *The Brady Bunch.*

For the Record: This was the final episode of the sixth season.

EPISODE 145

"Mary Midwife"

Writer: David Lloyd
Director: Jay Sandrich
Cast
Dr. Rainey: Ford Rainey

At an éclair-tasting party at Mary's apartment, Georgette announces that her baby's on the way. The usual hilarity ensues, and when all is said and done, Lou and Mary successfully deliver Georgette's baby girl.

Bad Party!
Yes, but a blessed event.

Our Television Heritage: The story line that the producers chose for Ted and Georgette culminates in a frenzied, spirited, and touching season-opening episode. From their not-so-promising beginning in the third season, the Baxters have truly grown into a loving, if unconventional, family of four. Before this season started, it was decided that *The Mary Tyler Moore Show* would gracefully exit after year seven. This episode and quite a few others from this season would subtly bring a sense of closure to the characters' story lines.

EPISODE 146

"Mary the Writer"

Writer: Burt Prelutsky
Director: James Burrows

Mary's excited about an article she's written. She's hurt when Lou gives it a negative review, and she immaturely pretends that she's sold the article to *Reader's Digest*. At the same time, Lou gives Ted encouragement on a book *he's* written, which is absolutely unreadable. As Mary seethes with resentment, Lou finally explains that he respects her too much to lie to her. Ted, of course, gets no respect from Lou.

EPISODE 147

"Sue Ann's Sister"

Writer: David Lloyd
Director: Jay Sandrich
Cast
Lila Nivens: Pat Priest

What's younger than Sue Ann, cooks more delicious dishes, and chases men with even more zeal? Why, Sue Ann's little sister Lila, of course. Lila blows into Minneapolis and stakes her claim on Sue Ann's turf as she weighs an offer to do her own homemaking show. She also has her eye on the big prize: Lou. If Sue Ann's not careful, both her show and the object of her desire will be swept away with yesterday's news.

Classic Scene: The peek into Sue Ann's love nest, with its hilariously kinky vibrating bed, elicited delightful, uproarious laughter, perhaps the most sustained audience response in the history of *The Mary Tyler Moore Show.*

Classic Guest Star: Pat Priest who played Lila, is known as the "ugly" relative Marilyn Munster on *The Munsters.*

EPISODE 148

"What's Wrong with Swimming?"

Writer: David Lloyd
Director: Marjorie Mullen
Cast
B.J. Smathers: Caren Kaye

Mary hires B.J. Smathers, an Olympic swimming medalist, as WJM's newest sportscaster. When the male staff objects, Mary things they're sexists, but they're really protesting B.J.'s refusal to report on any major spectator sport—a major faux pas when the Vikings are doing well. Reluctantly Mary must summon all of her toughness and fire B.J.

Classic Guest Star: Caryn Kaye was a genial TV leading lady in the late 1970s and early 1980s, costarring with Nancy Walker on *Blansky's Beauties.*

EPISODE 149

"Ted's Change of Heart"

Writer: Earl Pomerantz
Director: Jay Sandrich
Cast
Harvey Vornun
Jerry Fogel

Ted suffers a mild heart attack, which he interprets as a wake-up call from the big newscaster in the sky to change his ways. However, Ted's new *carpe diem* attitude drives his fellow staffers up the wall, making them wish something they never thought they would—that the old Ted would return.

EPISODE 150

"One Producer Too Many"

Writer: Bob Ellison
Director: Jay Sandrich
Cast
Richard Self
Murray Korda

Even WJM isn't immune to office politics. To keep Murray from taking another job offer, Lou promises him a promotion to co-producer with Mary. But Lou hasn't told Mary of his intentions. Stepping totally out of character, Lou wines and dines Mary instead of telling her directly. Needless to say, the whole thing blows up in his face, and he must fix things before he has an outright mutiny on his hands.

EPISODE 151

"My Son the Genius"

Writer: Bob Ellison
Director: Jay Sandrich
Cast
Morris Bender: Ned Glass
William Bogart

Ted and Georgette's adopted son, David, shocks his parents when he does poorly in school. Could it be that David is a chip off the old block after all, even if he is adopted? It turns out that David's IQ is at the genius level, but he's bored with his studies. Now Ted has another problem. . . .

EPISODE 152

"Mary Gets a Lawyer"

Writer: Burt Prelutsky
Director: Jay Sandrich
Cast
John McMartin

At last, after two years in limbo (see episode 97), Mary finally goes to court to fight her contempt charge for refusing to reveal a news source. However, her lawyer is so turned on by her smile that he cannot concentrate on his job. After all she's been through, will Mary Richards really go back to jail?

EPISODE 153

"Lou Proposes"

Writer: David Lloyd
Director: Jay Sandrich
Cast
Aunt Flo: Eileen Heckart

Lou's love-hate relationship with Mary's aunt reaches the boiling point. Mr. Conservative himself is so confounded by Flo, a bleeding-heart liberal, that he has no choice but to propose—just so he can get a word in edgewise. Things cool down, though, and they both agree—for the first time—that marriage is not such a great idea for them.

For the Record: Eileen Heckart would be reunited with Mary Tyler Moore when she played Mary's mother on the short-lived sitcom *Annie McGuire* in the mid-1980s.

EPISODE 154

"Murray Can't Lose"

Writer: David Lloyd
Director: Jay Sandrich
Cast
Emcee: Larry Wilde
Presenter: Lisa Parkes

Teddy Alert! This time out, Lou gets a tip from an inside source that perennial also-ran Murray will finally win the elusive Teddy Award. He tells the others not to tell Murray, but of course they can't keep the secret. Even so, Lou's not worried, because Murray can't lose. Lou's forgetting one thing, though, this is *Murray* we're talking about. But even in defeat, Murray basks in the love of family and friends, who declare him a winner.

EPISODE 155

"Mary's Insomnia"

Writer: David Lloyd
Director: James Burrows
Cast
Bonnie Slaughter: Sherry Hursey
Janitor: Ted Lehman

Mary can't sleep, so she starts taking sleeping pills to aid her. Unfortunately, they become a habit she can't break, and the guys take turns trying to help her quit cold turkey, even if they have to watch Mary take a bubble bath to do it. Jeez, what torture!

For the Record: This is one of the few episodes to deal with a serious issue up front, yet it's done in the style that fans of the series have grown accustomed to. The scenes in which Mary's in the tub and Murray, Ted, and Lou visit her are standouts.

EPISODE 156

"Ted's Temptation"

Writer: Bob Ellison
Director: Harry Mastrogeorge
Cast
Whitney Lewis: Trisha Noble

At a broadcaster's convention in Hollywood, Mary and Ted encounter Whitney Lewis, an attractive young woman who takes more than a friendly interest in the anchorman. What she sees in Ted we'll never know, but want him she does. Ted manages to fight temptation and resist Whitney's charms.

EPISODE 157

"Look at Us, We're Walking"

Writer: Bob Ellison
Director: Jay Sandrich
Cast
Mel Price: David Ogden Stiers

Uh-oh, there's a new station manager in town, and his name is Mel Price. His presence immediately antagonizes Mary and Lou, whose requests for pay raises are a bone of contention. Playing hardball, Price deliberately lowballs them, and the battle of wills and paychecks is on.

Classic Guest Star: David Ogden Stiers, forever known as Major Winchester of *M*A*S*H*, makes the first of several guest appearances as station manager Mel Price.

For the Record: The strong-willed, assertive Mel Price's introduction is a harbinger of things to come, as his desire to reverse the low ratings tide leads him to a critical decision in the final episode.

EPISODE 158

"The Critic"

Writer: David Lloyd
Director: Martin Cohan
Cast
Karl Heller: Eric Braeden
Mel Price: David Ogden Stiers

Mel Price once again puts his stamp on the newscast, this time by hiring Karl Heller, a pompous, self-important critic who hates everything in Minneapolis, or so it seems. Mary actually braves an evening out on the town with Karl—then watches gleefully as he gets the comeuppance he so richly deserves.

Classic Guest Star: Foreign-born Eric Braeden began his acting career under his given name, Hans Gudaguest, when he costarred on the war drama *Rat Patrol*. After changing his name to Eric Braeden, he made many TV guest appearances, and of course he played the devious Victor Newman on *The Young and the Restless* for over twenty years.

EPISODE 159

"Lou's Army Reunion"

Writer: Bob Ellison
Director: Jay Sandrich
Cast
Ben: Alex Rocco

At his army reunion, Lou renews his acquaintance with Ben, an old buddy. Ben takes one look at Mary and tries to make a move on her. Before she can respond, Lou handles the situation in typical macho fashion. Mary is hurt that Lou doesn't think she can handle these things, but Lou's explanation that he considers her just like his own daughter is all she needs to hear.

Classic Guest Star: Alex Rocco has played gravelly-voiced bad guys, and a few good guys as well, for years. He won an Emmy for playing the slimy agent Al Foss on *The Famous Teddy Z.*

EPISODE 160

"The Ted and Georgette Show"

Writer: David Lloyd
Director: Jay Sandrich
Cast
Mel Price: David Ogden Stiers
Elliot: Alex Hentelhoff

Jeez, in Minneapolis, they'll give *anyone* a show, as evidenced by the new variety program that's all the local rage, even though it's hosted by Georgette and Ted! There's soon trouble in paradise, however. Georgette quickly tires of show biz, but Ted doesn't want the ride to end.

EPISODE 161

"Sue Ann Gets the Ax"

Writer: Bob Ellison
Director: Jay Sandrich
Cast
Sam: Louis Guss
Gelson: Linden Chiles

The ratings for *The Happy Homemaker* are at an all-time low, so the management cancels it. Just when you think it's the end of Sue Ann's reign, she informs the station that she has two years left on her contract and she intends to make the station honor it. Yes, even if she has to humiliate herself by dressing as a giant daisy for a puppet show.

EPISODE 162

"Hail, the Conquering Gordy"

Writer: Earl Pomerantz
Director: Jay Sandrich

WJM's most successful alumnus to date returns to Minneapolis for a visit. Gordy the weatherman is now Gordy the talk show host, based out of New York. No one is happier to see him than Ted, and how he's angling to become Gordy's Ed McMahon. Being nobody's fool, Gordy graciously declines Ted's overture.

EPISODE 163

"Mary and the Sexagenarian"

Writers: Les Charles and Glen Charles
Director: Jay Sandrich
Cast
Doug Slaughter: Lew Ayres

In the seven years Mary's been in Minneapolis, she's dated virtually all of the men in her age range, with no lasting success. Now she decides to give Doug, a man in his sixties, a shot. Did we mention that he's Murray's father?

Classic Guest Star: Lew Ayres is a longtime Hollywood star who was the first to play Dr. Kildare in the movies.

For the Record: This show was written by Glen and Les Charles, a talented duo whose future career would include writing for *Taxi* and co-creating *Cheers*.

EPISODE 164

"Murray Ghosts for Ted"

Writer: David Lloyd
Director: Jay Sandrich
Cast
Laurie Slaughter: Helen Hunt

Murray agrees to ghostwrite an article for Ted. It turns out so well that it's picked up nationally. Ted takes all the credit, of course, and Murray's dying inside because he promised Ted not to tell anyone he wrote it, not even his family. Finally, Mary and Lou, who have guessed the truth, force Ted to come clean, making Murray a hero to his family at last.

Classic Guest Star: Child actress Helen Hunt made tons of guest appearances on television. She grew up quite nicely, too, and became a costar in the hit series *Mad about You.*

EPISODE 165

"Mary's Three Husbands"

Writer: Bob Ellison
Director: Jay Sandrich

Murray, Lou, and Ted sit around thinking, "What if . . . ?" as they imagine what it would be like to be married to Mary. Murray keeps her devoted, barefoot, and pregnant, while Lou's fantasy still has Mary and him working side by side in the newsroom. As for Ted's dream, well . . . does the phrase "Stepford wife" mean anything to you?

For the Record: This was a late-season episode that effectively dealt with the lingering romantic feelings the three male characters had for Mary. This was also the only episode to use extensive makeup effects, and it took longer to film than any other.

EPISODE 166

"Mary's Big Party"

Writer: Bob Ellison
Director: Jay Sandrich
Cast
Johnny Carson: Himself

Why shouldn't Mary's last party be as bad as all the others? Her earlier parties all sucked, but this one is the worst. This time she nails a really cool guest, Johnny Carson, but the partygoers can't see him because of a power failure.

Bad Party!
You said it. The party itself is just a setup for clips from memorable past episodes. This, by the way, is the only time *The Mary Tyler Moore Show* ever used this conceit.

Classic Cameo: Johnny Carson's cameo was heard but not seen by the viewers; nevertheless, his distinctive voice made his presence felt.

EPISODE 167

"Lou Dates Mary"

Writer: David Lloyd
Director: Jay Sandrich

When Mary's latest date makes his intentions crystal clear—let's face it, just how many men take off their clothes without being asked?—she's at the end of her rope. Georgette sweetly suggests that Mary date Lou, and just like that, the moment we've been waiting for for seven years is about to occur. There it is . . . they're gonna . . . kiss—and then crack up in laughter.

For the Record: This next-to-last episode wrapped up the Mary-and-Lou relationship, arguably the most important and most eagerly antic-ipated ongoing story line of the series. And it's not predictable or a cop-out—just one more episode that marks the end of an era.

EPISODE 168

"The Last Show"

Writers: Allan Burns, James L. Brooks, Ed. Weinberger, Stan Daniels, David Lloyd, and Bob Ellison
Director: Jay Sandrich
Cast
Frank Coleman: Vincent Gardenia

Seven years of consistently bad ratings has finally taken its toll on WJM management, and they decide to totally overhaul the news operation. That means everyone must go—except Ted, who obviously had nothing to do with the sorry ratings in the first place, right? In any event, they all leave after hugging, saying good-bye, and singing "It's a Long Long Way to Tipperary" in unison. Mary is the last person out the door. She takes a last wistful look at the place where her life was shaped over the past seven years, then turns out the lights.

For the Record: There was not a dry eye in the house after the end of "The Last Show." After seven years and 168 episodes, *The Mary Tyler Moore Show* left the airwaves in the fashion hundreds of other series only wish they could—on top of the game and with nary a dip in quality, attesting to the show's stature as a true class act.

Awards: The six writers who made "The Last Show" a success were rewarded with the Comedy Writing Emmy award.

The Munsters

But it is Mr. Gwynne who walks off with the show and makes palatable even the extremes of broad slapstick to which the program is not immune. His gift for underplaying adds enormously to the hilarious image of a heart of gold beneath the forbidding facial exterior.

—*The New York Times*, September 25, 1964

As for the acting, the cast handed in some of the best—and most outrageous—character portrayals in sitcom stardom. All of them deserve a hand.

—Stephen Cox, *The Munsters: Television's First Family of Fright*

Gwynne's Herman had all the charm of a puppy dog, and he looked at the world with loving eyes, embracing all with his gentle and innocent warmth. And like a puppy, though he didn't seem to understand everything, and often not much of anything, he exuded loyalty to family.

—David Story, *America on the Rerun*

In comparing *The Munsters* to *The Addams Family* the edge must go to *The Munsters* for, as "unnatural" shows go, this one is more natural, more credible, it's less frenzied, and doesn't shove its "way out" quality down the viewer's throat. . . . It isn't easy to achieve a sort of restraint in such epics, but "cool ghoul" is applicable both to Gwynne and Yvonne De Carlo as Herman's wife.

—*Variety*, September 30, 1964

There was a message of mid-sixties tolerance behind the affectionate characterization of the gentle giant and his weird but happy family.

—John E. Lewis and Penny Stemple, *Cult TV*

Turning the TV dial to *The Munsters* is a defensive reaction to the insecurities and threats of a real world. . . . The viewer comes away refreshed.

> —George Horsley Smith, Department of Psychology, Rutgers University

Fred Gwynne is the most engaging and amusing monster ever to reach TV. . . . *The Munsters* is inspired offbeat nonsense that will disarm everyone who thought an era of horror might be descending on TV.

> —Jack Gould, *The New York Times*, October 25, 1964

The Munsters is sort of a Donna Reed monster show where everybody is lovable.

> —*Look*, September 8, 1964

The Munsters

on Nick at Nite

The Munsters first aired on the final evening of Nick at Nite's Tenth Anniversary Week, in June 1995. The episode chosen to lead off the series was number 50, "Will Success Spoil Herman Munster?"

Then—thanks to VertiVision, the modern programming miracle—six episodes of *The Munsters* aired every Monday during Block Party Summer. This was not, however, the first time that Al Lewis and Fred Gwynne worked together on Nick at Nite: *Car 54, Where Are You?* had aired on the network from July 1987 to March 1990.

And, naturally, on Halloween 1995, the Munsters were featured in a special event. Yes, sir, that's the kind of thinking that earns us the title "Classic TV experts."

Cast

Herman Munster: Fred Gwynne
Lily Munster: Yvonne De Carlo
Grandpa: Al Lewis
Marilyn (episodes 1–13): Beverly Owen
Marilyn (episodes 13–70): Pat Priest
Edward "Eddie" Wolfgang Munster: Butch Patrick
The Raven (voice): Mel Blanc, Bob Hastings

EPISODE 1

"Munster Masquerade"

Writers: Joe Connelly and Bob Mosher
Director: Lawrence Dobkin
Cast
Mrs. Agnes Daly: Mabel Albertson
Frank Wilcox
Linden Chiles

A boyfriend has invited Marilyn and her family to a masquerade party. Marilyn is dressed as Priscilla, and her boyfriend goes as John Alden, while Lily is Little Bo Peep, Grandpa is Napoleon, and Herman is King Arthur in a suit of shining armor. The boyfriend's father, who is dressed up like Frankenstein's monster, is insulted when Herman suggests that he's attending without a costume. But Lily is just as insulted when Herman wins the prize for wearing a costume under his costume.

Classic Guest Star: Mabel Albertson is best known to supernatural sitcom fans as Darrin's mother on *Bewitched*.

Classic Fear Take: Watch the boyfriend's hair fly up, as if blown by unseen winds.

EPISODE 2

"My Fair Munster"

Writers: Norm Liebmann and Ed Haas
Director: David Alexander
Cast
Mailman: John Fiedler
Claire Carleton
Edward Mallory

Concerned over Marilyn's difficulty in keeping boyfriends, Grandpa concocts a love potion designed to make members of the opposite sex fall madly in love with the person who ingests it. Grandpa secretly slips the potion into Marilyn's oatmeal, but since she has no time to eat breakfast, Lily stirs Marilyn's serving back into the pot and serves it to the rest of the family. In due course, Lily attracts the affections of the mailman, the next door neighbor suddenly has eyes for Herman, and Eddie is chased home by a flock of hysterically amorous schoolgirls.

Classic Quote

LILY (*to Eddie*): Now, you go on up to bed. And don't forget to close the lid.

For the Record: This was the first *Munsters* episode to be filmed.

Classic Guest Star: John Fiedler has made countless guest appearances on sitcoms for three decades, capitalizing on his quintessential meek looks and high-register voice. He might be best remembered as Mr. Peterson, Dr. Hartley's patient for five seasons on *The Bob Newhart Show*.

EPISODE 3
"A Walk on the Mild Side"

Writers: Norm Liebmann and Ed Haas
Director: Norman Abbott
Cast
Cliff Norton
Roy Roberts

The only thing that will cure Herman's insomnia is a late night walk in the park. But Lily wants him to stay at home because a fiendish monster has been sighted in that vicinity. Naturally, the only monster is a Munster.

Classic Quote

GRANDPA: Lots of people have insomnia. You don't find *them* losing any sleep over it.

Classic Sight Gag: Grandpa's enlarging machine makes all the appliances in the Munster house go haywire. He accidentally uses it in reverse on Eddie, causing him to shrink to the size of a table lamp.

EPISODE 4
"Rock-a-Bye, Munster"

Writers: Joe Connelly and Bob Mosher
Director: Norman Abbott
Cast
Dr. Dudley: Paul Lynde
Diamond Jim: Sid Melton
Marilyn Lovell
Peter Robbins

When Herman and Grandpa eavesdrop on Lily and Marilyn, they get the false impression that Lily is pregnant. The truth is that the playmate she's expecting for Eddie is Dr. Dudley's son, Elmer, who will be staying with the Munsters while the Dudleys are on vacation.

Munster Musical Moment: Herman plays the Brahms "Lullaby" on the organ.

Classic Guest Stars: This is Paul Lynde's first appearance as Dr. Dudley. Lynde, of course, later became well known as Uncle Arthur on *Bewitched*, but he also made numerous visits to other 1960s sitcom favorites, including *I Dream of Jeannie*.

Sid Melton played Alf Monroe on *Green Acres*. He was also Bert Monker, the delicatessen owner who falls for Sally (in episode 101) of *The Dick Van Dyke Show*.

For the Record: This episode includes the first appearance of the Munster Koach, the car specially designed for *The Munsters* by Kustom Kar King George Barris, who also designed the Bat-mobile and the Monkeemobile, among others. Lily buys two cars from a used-car dealer (Melton)—an antique hearse and a snazzy hot-rod dragster. She has a custom car shop meld the two together into this unique vehicle, which she gives to Herman as a birthday gift.

EPISODE 5
"Pikes Pique"

Writers: Norm Liebmann and Ed Haas
Director: Seymour Berns
Cast
Borden T. Pike: Richard Deacon
Sonny Harkness: Pat Harrington
Jane Withers

The city's gas department attempts to run a pipeline twenty-five feet under the Munsters' house. Unfortunately, at that level, it runs straight into Grandpa's dungeon laboratory. When the workers are freaked by Herman and Grandpa's appearance, the head of the department, Mr. Pike, thinks the Munsters are using scare tactics to drive up the price of doing construction on their property. He decides to pay the family a visit to negotiate.

Classic Quote

LILY: I think we should take Herman's advice. After all, he's always been the level-headed one in the family.

Classic Guest Stars: Richard Deacon played two unforgettable TV Land characters simultaneously in the early 1960s: Mel Cooley on *The Dick Van Dyke Show* and Fred Rutherford on *Leave it to Beaver.*
Pat Harrington was a regular for one season on *Make Room for Daddy.* In 1975 he landed the role of Schneider in the long-running sitcom *One Day at a Time.*

EPISODE 6
"Lo-Cal Munster"

Writers: Norm Liebmann and Ed Haas
Director: Norman Abbott
Cast
Dr. Dudley: Paul Lynde
Dick Winslow
Monty Margetts
Elsie Baker
Diane Cortney
Scott McCarter
Caryl Rowe

Herman wants to attend a reunion of his army buddies, but he can't fit into his old uniform. Lily doesn't want him to go, so she strikes a deal: if Herman can lose enough weight to fit into the uniform, she'll let him go. Herman immediately goes on a starvation diet, but a TV commercial about food makes him lose control.

Our Television Heritage: This episode made use of a TV Land device known as *framing.* In this case, the program opens by showing the last scene, then proceeding as a flashback to the events that lead up to this scene, and finally showing the original scene again. This technique sometimes requires the services of a narrator to explain to the audience that they're about to see a flashback. Here the narration is provided by Herman.

Classic Quote

HERMAN: That's my hand.
DR. DUDLEY: You mean you were born with this?
HERMAN: No, someone else was. And I'll always be grateful. Not everyone will give you a hand when you need one.

EPISODE 7

"Tin Can Man"

Writers: Norm Liebmann and Ed Haas
Director: Earl Bellamy
Cast
Arch Johnson
Richard Simmons

Eddie is in danger of being expelled from school, thanks to the recommendation of an investigator from the board of education. His only chance to prevent this from happening is to make a great project for the school's science fair. Grandpa helps him to construct a robot, and when Herman is mistaken for the robot, Eddie wins first prize and gets to stay in school.

For the Record: The Richard Simmons who is credited as an actor in this episode is not the frizzy-haired exercise guru of the same name, unless he has changed a great deal.

In this episode it is revealed that the funeral parlor where Herman works has a layaway plan.

EPISODE 8

"Herman the Great"

Writers: Joe Connelly and Bob Mosher
Director: Earl Bellamy
Cast
John Hubbard
Johnny Silver
Joe Mell
Teddy Eccles
Jimmy Lennon
Tiger Joe Marsh

Herman becomes a professional wrestler, the Masked Marvel, after he demonstrates his superhuman strength to the son of a pro wrestling manager. Herman figures he could use the extra cash from his bouts to pay for Eddie's college education; however, Herman's kind nature and gullibility allow his opponents to take advantage of him.

For the Record: This episode also featured real-life wrestlers Count Billy Varga, Gene LeBell, Jay York, the Great John L., and Matt Murphy.

EPISODE 9

"Knock Wood, Here Comes Charlie"

Writers: Norm Liebmann and Ed Haas
Director: Lawrence Dobkin
Cast
Knuckles: Mike Mazurki

It's evil twin time, and we get an acting tour de force as Fred Gwynne portrays Herman's twin brother, Charlie. When this fast-talking con artist comes to town and ends up staying at the Munster home, Herman wishes he would leave. Charlie claims to have an invention that extracts uranium from seawater, and he's looking for an investor. Herman's fear that this is a crooked scheme to get at Lily's inheritance of $5,000 turns out to be right on target.

Classic Sight Gag: Herman slips on a skateboard and falls flat on his back.

Classic Quote
GRANDPA: A breath of fresh dirt.

EPISODE 10

"Autumn Croakus"

Writers: James Allardice and Tom Adair
Director: Lawrence Dobkin

Cast

Malcolm: Neil Hamilton
Linda Watkins
Richard Reeves
Jerry Mann

Grandpa, feeling lonely and depressed, contacts an agency that promises to find him a mate. The agency sends over an attractive elderly woman who finds the old man charming. It turns out, however, that she's the Black Widow, a parasite who makes her living by marrying her suitors, getting them to sign a life insurance policy naming her as beneficiary, and then murdering them.

Our Television Heritage: Look for a studio technician in a white T-shirt walking in the background in the Munster house in the opening scene.

Classic Guest Star: Neil Hamilton is best remembered for playing Commissioner Gordon on the TV series *Batman.*

EPISODE 11

"The Midnight Ride of Herman Munster"

Writers: Joe Connelly and Bob Mosher
Director: Ezra Stone

Cast

Big Louis: Slapsie Maxie Rosenbloom
Lennie Weinrib
Lee Krieger
Joe Devlin
Val Avery
Joel Donte
Pat McCaffrie
Vince Williams
Mike Ross

Herman falls asleep in the back of his car, leaving the keys in the ignition. A pair of bank robbers steal the car, unaware that Herman is lying in the back seat. When Herman awakens, he wanders into their hideout, is mistaken for Big Louie, a gang member who has taken twenty years of beatings in the boxing ring, and winds up as an accomplice in a heist.

EPISODE 12

"Sleeping Cutie"

Writers: James Allardice and Tom Adair
Director: Norman Abbott

Cast

Paul Newmar: Gavin MacLeod
Grant Williams
Walter Woolf King
John Hoyt

Grandpa intends to give Marilyn a magic elixir to cure her insomnia, but—oops!—he accidentally gives her the Sleeping Beauty potion. Now Marilyn won't be able to wake up unless she is kissed by a prince. Lily and Herman advertise for a prince in the classified section of the newspaper, but their ad only attracts a couple of out-of-work actors. Meanwhile, Grandpa is negotiating with an oil company for the rights to a magic pill he's invented that turns water into gasoline.

Classic Guest Star: Gavin MacLeod, who satirizes Method actors in this episode, playing a character whose name resembles that of a famous Actors Studio graduate, was featured in three long-running TV series: *McHale's Navy*, *The Love Boat*, and *The Mary Tyler Moore Show*, on which he played Murray Slaughter.

Classic Sight Gag: Herman kicks a swivel chair, sending the cushion spinning so fast it becomes airborne.

Classic Guest Star: Harvey Korman, in addition to making many guest spots on classic sitcoms over the years, is best remembered as a regular on *The Carol Burnett Show*.

For the Record: This episode marked the last appearance by Beverly Owen, the first Marilyn Munster. She left to get married and move to New York.

EPISODE 13

"Family Portrait"

Writers: James Allardice and Tom Adair
Director: Lawrence Dobkin
Cast
Lennie Bates: Harvey Korman
Roy Roberts
Fred Beir
Bill Daniels

Event magazine chooses the Munsters as the average American family. How? Not surprisingly, the choice was made by the magazine's computer. Grandpa, insulted at being labeled average, disappears, jeopardizing the family's photo opportunity and the substantial prize money that accompanies it. When a journalist and photographer arrive at the Munster home, Herman and Lily mistake them for burglars, causing a madcap climax.

The Message in the Munsters
The subtext of this episode might be that computerization is dehumanizing American society.

Classic Quote
LILY: I could just lay down and die. Again.

EPISODE 14

"Grandpa Leaves Home"

Writers: Dick Conway and Roland MacLane
Director: Norman Abbott
Cast
Robert Strauss
Iris Adrian
Sarah Ross
Bill Duncan
Bill Couch
Nicky Blair

Grandpa feels neglected and unwanted and decides to depart the Munster clan. At first, Lily and Herman believe this is just a ploy to get attention, and they let the old man leave, expecting he'll come slinking back very soon. Shortly afterward, however, they begin to miss him badly and try to track him down. They discover he's doing a magic act at a local nightclub.

Classic Quote
GRANDPA: You just can't wait to see me in my grave.
LILY: Oh, Grandpa. We've seen you there lots of times before.

Our Television Heritage: This is the first episode to feature Pat Priest as the second Marilyn. Is there a difference? Discuss amongst yourselves.

EPISODE 15

"Herman's Rival"

Writers: Dick Conway and Roland MacLane
Director: Joseph Pevney
Cast
The Wolf Man: Irwin Charone
Lee Bergere
Karen Glynn
Chet Stratton
Tommy Farrell

Lily is under the impression that Herman has lost all his savings through a bad investment, when in fact he lent it to her brother, the Wolf Man. She decides to replenish the family's funds by taking a job reading palms in a tearoom. In a plot twist that recalls a classic episode of *The Honeymooners*, Grandpa and Herman suspect that Lily is sneaking out of the house to have an affair.

Classic Quote
LILY: Every silver cloud has a dark lining.

EPISODE 16

"Grandpa's Call of the Wild"

Writers: Joe Connelly and Bob Mosher
Director: Earl Bellamy
Cast
Mike Ragan
Bing Russell
Don Haggerty
Ed Peck
Curt Barrett

Herman takes the family on a camping trip in a national park. After dinner by the campfire, Grandpa hears the howls of the wolves and reminisces about his days in the old country. The next morning, Grandpa is missing and Lily surmises that he changed himself into a wolf to roam the woods with his canine friends. When she hears a news report about the capture of a rare Transylvanian wolf, Lily goes to the authorities to reclaim her grandfather.

Classic Sight Gag: Herman rearranges the park's trees to provide Lily with adequate shade.

Classic Quote
GRANDPA (*to Herman, as he sets up a tent*): Herman, I asked you not to pound stakes when I'm around. You know it gives me heartburn.

EPISODE 17

"All-Star Munster"

Writers: Joe Connelly and Bob Mosher
Director: Earl Bellamy
Cast
Coach: Pat Buttram
Robert Easton
Frank Maxwell

Herman goes to the dean's office of Marilyn's college to straighten out a matter about her tuition. In searching for the office, he accidentally wanders into the gym, where he is mistaken for a student basketball star who is expected for a tryout. Herman demonstrates his shooting skills and astounds the coach with his superhuman abilities. The coach offers Herman a contract to play for the college team.

Classic Sight Gags: Herman's basketball tryout features several memorable and impossible shots. In another scene, Grandpa breathes on the fireplace to ignite the flames.

Classic Guest Star: Pat Buttram's trademark squeaky voice is familiar to fans of *Green Acres*, in which he played Mr. Haney.

EPISODE 18

"If a Martian Answers, Hang Up"

Writers: Joe Connelly and Bob Mosher
Director: Norman Abbott
Cast
Captain Halbert: Herbert Rudley
Ray Montgomery
Larry Thor
Ronnie Dapo
Pat Rosson
Dort Clark
John Stenner

Herman fools around with a ham radio in Grandpa's dungeon and thinks he's contacted Martians, when in fact he's speaking to two kids who are fooling around with walkie-talkies. The kids think Herman is also a kid, and a stupid one at that.

Classic Quote
HERMAN: Grandpa, we're making history. We're Galileo, Columbus, and David Susskind all rolled into one.

Classic Guest Star: Herbert Rudley is best known for playing Herb Hubbard on *The Mothers-in-Law.*

EPISODE 19

"Eddie's Nickname"

Writer: Richard Baer
Director: Joseph Pevney
Cast
Dr. Dudley: Paul Lynde
Alice Backes

Eddie wants to quit school because all the kids there call him Shorty. Grandpa comes to the rescue by fixing him a frog-leg-filled potion guaranteed to make Eddie grow six inches overnight. But rather than accomplishing this, the potion causes the young Munster to grow a full beard and mustache.

The Message in the Munsters

HERMAN: All that matters is the size of your heart and the strength of your character, not what you look like.

EPISODE 20

"Bats of a Feather"

Writer: Dick Conway
Director: Jerry Paris
Cast
Laboratory Scientist: Alvy Moore
Barbara Babcock
Tom McBride
Ronnie Dapo
Jimmy Mathers
Gilbert Green
Sally Mills
Frank Gardner
Alan Hunt

Eddie needs an impressive pet to take to the school pet fair, but Spot, the fire-breathing monster, is too shy to come out of hiding. The family decides that Eddie will take Igor the bat, but Igor gets insulted by one of Herman's wisecracks and flies away. Without Eddie's knowledge, Grandpa changes himself into a bat to impersonate Igor, causing trouble when Eddie trades Grandpa to another student, whose father wants to send him on a scientific mission to outer space. This episode packs plenty of plot into a half hour.

Classic Guest Star: One year after this episode, Alvy Moore was cast as Hank Kimball, the confused agricultural official on *Green Acres*. (The

Hooterville connection: Alvy Moore, Sid Melton, and Pat Buttram all appear in this series.)

Jerry Paris, this episode's director, got his first directing job on *The Dick Van Dyke Show*, on which he also played the featured role of Jerry Helper. He later went on to direct numerous episodes of *Happy Days*.

EPISODE 21

"Don't Bank on Herman"

Writer: Douglas Tibbles
Director: Ezra Stone
Cast
Mousie Garner
Maurice Manson
Pitt Herbert
Audrey Swanson
Jack Bernardi

When Herman and Grandpa go to the bank to make a withdrawal, they are mistaken for armed and dangerous bank robbers and are handed $18,000 in cash. When Herman gets home and realizes the wrong he's committed, he can't rest until he returns the money. When he and Grandpa try to bring it back in the middle of the night, they wind up locked in the bank's vault.

Classic Quote

MARILYN: If there's one thing those two dig, it's graveyards.

EPISODE 22

"Dance with Me, Herman"

Writers: James Allardice, Tom Adair, Joe Connelly, and Bob Mosher
Director: Joseph Pevney

Cast

Happy Havemeyer: Don Rickles
Joyce Jameson

In order to accompany Marilyn to her school dance, Herman decides to take up dancing lessons. He goes to Happy Havemeyer's Dancing School, where he is suckered into signing a ten-year contract for 1,500 lessons at $7.50 a lesson. Herman is under the misguided impression that he is going to become a dancing instructor for the school.

Munster Musical Moment
Herman performs a rendition of "Singin' in the Rain."

Classic Sight Gag: Twice in this episode Herman falls backwards on the sofa and his head crashes into the harp.

Classic Quote
HERMAN: Dancing has never been one of my strong points. I guess you can say I have two left feet.
GRANDPA: Well, that's what happens when you put someone together in the dark.

Classic Guest Star: Before Don Rickles starred in his own sitcoms in the 1970s, he made frequent TV Land appearances on such classic shows as *Get Smart*, *F Troop*, *The Dick Van Dyke Show*, *I Dream of Jeannie*, and *Gilligan's Island*. Ironically, Rickles in private life is best friends with Bob Newhart, on whose show he never appeared!

EPISODE 23

"Follow That Munster"

Writers: Joe Connelly and Bob Mosher
Director: Joseph Pevney

Cast

Ken Lynch
Herb Armstrong
Doris Singleton
Mike Winkelman
Miss Ronnie Haran

Herman sneaks out each night to practice being a detective. Lily, however, suspects he's having an affair and hires the detective agency Herman is working for to have Herman followed. In an existential plot twist worthy of Camus, Herman gets the assignment to follow himself.

Classic Quote
LILY: I'd hate to lose Herman. He's one in a million.
DETECTIVE: One in a million? From the description, I'd say the odds are much higher.

Parallel Plot: This episode is the opposite-sex version of episode 15.

Classic Sight Gag: Grandpa uses his mouth as a pencil sharpener.

For the Record: The sketch of the suspect Herman is assigned to follow was actually drawn by Fred Gwynne.

EPISODE 24

"Love Locked Out"

Writers: James Allardice and Tom Adair
Director: Charles Barton
Cast
Elliot Reid
Norman Grabowski
Bryan O'Byrne

After Herman attends an office party that goes on until the wee hours of the morning, Lily locks Herman out of their bedroom and makes him sleep on the sofa. When they are unable to reconcile, Lily and Herman independently see a marriage counselor.

Munster Musical Moment: Herman sings "The Camptown Races."

Our Television Heritage: Charles Barton was highly qualified to direct *The Munsters*, since he was also the director of the films *Abbott and Costello Meet Frankenstein* and *Abbott and Costello Meet the Killer Boris Karloff*.

EPISODE 25

"Come Back, Little Googie"

Writers: Joe Connelly and Bob Mosher
Director: Joseph Pevney
Cast
Googie: Billy Mumy
Russ Conway

Grandpa is under the impression that he's turned Eddie's friend Googie into a monkey. The truth is that the little boy is hiding to fool the Munsters.

Classic Guest Star: Billy Mumy made many memorable TV Land appearances as a child actor. But his most famous role was as Will Robinson on *Lost in Space.*

For the Record: Billy Mumy was originally up for the role of Eddie Munster, but his parents objected to the severe makeup requirements.

EPISODE 26

"Far Out Munsters"

Writers: Joe Connelly, Bob Mosher, and Richard Conway
Director: Joseph Pevney
Cast
The Standells: Themselves
Man with Beard: Zalman King
Alex Gerry
Kelton Garwood
Sue Winton
Tom Curtis
Frank Killmond

The Standells, a rock group from Hollywood, are in town for a club appearance and want a secluded place to stay to escape from their screaming teenage fans. Their manager pays an exorbitant fee to the Munsters to use their house for the weekend. Needing the cash, the Munsters pack up and relocate to a hotel, but they can't get adjusted to its cleanliness and normality. When they arrive home prematurely, they find the Standells singing "I Want to Hold Your Hand" and throwing a wild party with far-out beatniks and hipsters. The Munsters are initially shocked but soon find that they fit in with these freaky people, who never once question their unusual appearance. The family happily participates in the festivities.

The Message in the Munsters

This episode contains the clearest expression of the message that underlies the entire series: it's okay to be a nonconformist.

Munster Musical Moment: Lily entertains the guests by accompanying herself on the harp while singing an old Negro spiritual.

Our Television Heritage: Here is the poem that the beat poet recites at the party:

> In the vortex of the future of that cool tomorrow-land
> We'll all wig there, play a gig there, in that great non-union band.
> Scuba-doo and scuba-dabber,
> Life's a gas and life's a grabber,
> Hip is hip and groove is groovy,
> Life's a wild Fellini movie.
> When that hairy fist of silence slugs us, bugs us, puts us down,
> We'll all wing it, we'll all sing it, Guy Lombardo's back in town.

And this is the poem that Herman recites at the party:

> Ibbidy bibbidy sibbidy Sam
> ibbidy bibbidy canal boat
> Dictionary down the ferry
> Mary Mary quite contrary
> Life is real, life is earnest
> If you're cold turn up the furnace.

For the Record: When this episode was filmed, the Standells—Larry Tamblyn, Gary Lane, Tony Valentino, and Dick Dodd—were a nondescript rock band trying to cash in on the success of the Beatles. But by the time this show originally aired in March of 1965, they had just recorded what would prove to be their biggest hit, "Dirty Water," for their new label, Tower Records. This song, plus "Sometimes Good Guys Don't Wear White," "Riot on Sunset Strip," and "Try It," would turn them into 1960s garage-punk-psychedelic rock legends.

Zalman King, who plays the bearded beatnik, was later the producer of the film *9½ Weeks* and the director of the film *Wild Orchid*.

EPISODE 27

"Munsters on the Move"

Writers: George Tibbles, Joe Connelly, and Bob Mosher
Director: Joseph Pevney

Cast

Bert Freed
Eddie Hanley
Lenore Shanewice
Alma Murphy
Jan Arvan
Bella Bruck
Charles Seel
Joey Scott
Hydia Westman

So he can accept a promotion, Herman has to shuffle his family off to Buffalo. No one has a problem with moving, except Eddie, who happens to be doing real swell on the baseball team. He throws a temper tantrum in an attempt to avoid departing from Mockingbird Heights. But since Grandpa has already sold the house to a wrecking company, the Munsters have no choice but to wage war, French Revolution style.

Munster Musical Moment: Herman sings "Shuffle Off to Buffalo" as he shuffles to the right and crashes through the wall.

The Message in the Munsters

HERMAN: You can't just go around aiming a cannon at everybody without having anarchy. And anarchy is violence. And violence is . . . very naughty.

EPISODE 28

"Movie Star Munster"

Writers: Joe Connelly and Bob Mosher
Story: James Allardice and Tom Adair
Director: Jerry Paris
Cast
J. R. Finlatter: Jesse White
Walter Burke

A pair of con artists want to stage a phony accident as an insurance scam. All they need is someone to play the part of the victim, preferably a big stupid guy with a face that looks as if it's been in an accident. Luckily for them, they stumble upon Herman. Posing as a couple of movie producers, they get him to sign an accident policy, telling him it's a contract for him to star in their motion picture, a remake of *Double Indemnity*. As the crooks devise various ways to kill off their leading man, Herman becomes a prima donna.

Classic Sight Gag: When the driver of a sports car smashes into Herman, he goes flying out of his car and lands inside a mailbox.

Classic Quote
HERMAN: One must dig deep to come up with the right character.
GRANDPA: You're telling me. That's how I found my first ten wives.

Classic Guest Star: Jesse White, known to contemporary TV Land fans as the first Maytag Repairman, was a regular on the Ann Sothern show *Private Secretary* and on *Make Room for Daddy*, which starred Danny Thomas.

EPISODE 29

"Herman the Rookie"

Writers: Joe Connelly and Bob Mosher
Director: Jerry Paris
Cast
Leo Durocher: Himself
Elroy "Crazy Legs" Hirsch
Gene Darfler
Ken Hunt

Leo Durocher, manager of the Los Angeles Dodgers, needs a power hitter for his team. When he gets conked on the head by one of Herman's line drives from seven blocks away, he believes he has found his man. After Herman demonstrates his power as a batter, Durocher comments, in a sign of the times, "I don't know whether to sign him with the Dodgers or send him to Vietnam."

For the Record: Since trying out for the Dodgers does not require a road trip for Herman, we get a strong clue that Mockingbird Heights is probably in the Los Angeles vicinity.

Classic Sight Gag: One of Herman's ground balls burns a neat round hole through a fielder's mitt.

EPISODE 30

"Country Club Munster"

Writer: Douglas Tibbles
Director: Joseph Pevney
Cast
Woodrow Parfrey
J. Edward McKinley
Dan Tobin
Johnny Jacobs
Janet Dey
Sally Ross
Al Checco

The Munsters win a membership in the highly exclusive Mockingbird Heights Country Club. The membership board wants to get a close look at the family to see if they measure up to club standards, so they invite Lily and Grandpa to a fashion show, and they ask Herman to play golf. While Lily and Grandpa stand out like a couple of freaks, Herman sends golf balls soaring like missiles, wreaking havoc on the putting green. Afterward the Munsters decide that the club doesn't meet their high standards.

Classic Quote
LILY: This place is depressingly cheerful.

For the Record: In this episode we get some insight into Lily's fashion ensemble. We discover that her cape is made of tufted coffin lining in a lovely shade of cemetery green, the dress is made of black-widow webs, and the underslip is woven from pure unborn centipede.

EPISODE 31

"Love Comes to Mockingbird Heights"

Writers: Joe Connelly and Bob Mosher
Director: Joseph Pevney
Cast
Charles Robinson

The Munsters receive $180,000 in gold doubloons from Uncle Gilbert. When their bank's assistant manager arrives to pick up the money for deposit, he instantly falls in love with Marilyn. Grandpa and Lily do their best to enhance the romance, not realizing that this gentleman is after Marilyn only for her doubloons.

Classic Quote
GRANDPA: I wouldn't mind having a banker in the family. After all, a guy who works in a vault can't be all bad.

Classic Fear Take: When the banker tries to elope with Marilyn and finds Herman in her bed instead, he jumps out the window, slides down the ladder head first, and burrows through the ground to escape.

For the Record: Uncle Gilbert turns out to be the Creature from the Black Lagoon.

EPISODE 32

"Mummy Munster"

Writers: Joe Connelly and Bob Mosher
Director: Ezra Stone

Cast

Dr. Wilkerson: Philip Ober
Mr. Thatcher: Pat Harrington
Diana Frothingham
Dennis Cross
Pat McCaffrie
Ralph Smiley

Herman arranges to meet Marilyn at the natural history museum, but he accidentally gets locked inside an Egyptian sarcophagus, whereupon a sleeping pill he swallowed earlier takes effect. A pair of museum curators open the box the next day, and they naturally mistake the sleeping Herman for an ancient mummy. When Lily reads about their supposed scientific discovery in the newspaper, she goes to the museum and asks the curators to put Herman in a cab and send him home as soon as he wakes up.

The Message in the Munsters
HERMAN: We shouldn't be too hasty to retaliate when someone treats us ill. In other words, one who fights fire with fire only gets in trouble with Smokey the Bear.

Classic Guest Star: Philip Ober, once married to actress Vivian Vance, has appeared on *I Love Lucy*, but his TV Land claim to fame is his portrayal of General Wingard Stone during the first season of *I Dream of Jeannie*.

EPISODE 33

"Lily Munster, Girl Model"

Writers: Joe Connelly and Bob Mosher
Story: Dick Conway
Director: Earl Bellamy

Cast

Laszlo Brastoff: Roger C. Carmel
Lois Roberts
Sally Morris
Sondra Matesky
Nina Shipman
Susan Wedell
Tracey Butler
Kimberly Beck

Realizing that she is not useful around the house, Lily searches for a job. She eventually lands a position as a fashion model, causing Herman to become wildly jealous as he entertains fantasies about the suave men she's likely to mingle with. With Grandpa's help, he transforms himself into a swinging playboy. Grandpa, also in disguise, poses as his beautiful blond girlfriend.

Classic Guest Star: Roger C. Carmel portrayed Roger Buell in the late 1960s comedy series *The Mothers-In-Law*.

EPISODE 34

"Munster the Magnificent"

Writers: James Allardice and Tom Adair
Director: Norman Abbott

Cast

Master of Ceremonies: Dave Ketchum
Eddie Ryder
Stuart Nisbet

Eddie volunteers Herman as a performer for his school's talent night. Since Herman has no discernible talent, Grandpa conjures up a pair of magic ballet shoes that will transform their wearer into a gifted dancer. But Herman is uneasy about strapping on this footwear. He tells Lily, "I don't want to do the ballet at Eddie's school. People might get the wrong impression . . . that I was a Communist or something." Fortunately, Eddie already has him billed as the world's greatest magician.

Classic Quote

HERMAN: As that great philosopher Steve Allen once said, "Jealousy is the stinkweed in the garden of life."

Classic Guest Star: Dave Ketchum played the guy who was always hidden in a drawer, a locker, a sofa, or a mailbox as Agent 13 on *Get Smart*. He also starred in the series *Camp Runamuck*.

EPISODE 35
"Herman's Happy Valley"

Writer: Dick Conway
Director: Ezra Stone
Cast
John Hoyt
Richard Reeves
Bartlett Robinson

Herman purchases ten acres in Happy Holiday Valley through a magazine ad. It turns out to be a patch of wasteland in a broken-down ghost town, so of course the Munsters absolutely adore it. This makes things difficult for the fly-by-night salespeople, who get a better offer for the property and want to buy it back.

Classic Quote

LILY: It's so hard to find a good vacation spot since they closed down Devil's Island.

EPISODE 36
"Hot Rod Herman"

Writers: Joe Connelly and Bob Mosher
Director: Norman Abbott
Cast
Henry Beckman
Brian Corcoran
Ray Montgomery
Gavin MacLeod
Eddie Donno

Eddie, who thinks his father is the greatest driver in the world, enters Herman in a drag-strip competition. After souping up the Munster Koach and dressing up like Marlon Brando in his *Wild One* getup, Herman loses his car in a drag race. In a rematch, Grandpa races in the Dragula, a motorized coffin on wheels.

Classic Quote

LILY: Herman, this is the worst thing you've done since you bought us that mausoleum at the cemetery and we couldn't move in because there were no kitchen privileges.

For the Record: This episode offers a rare opportunity to see Herman actually enter the Munster Koach. Due to Herman's lift-boot-enhanced size, it was difficult for him to squeeze behind the steering wheel, making it awkward to film such scenes.

EPISODE 37

"Herman's Raise"

Writers: Joe Connelly, Bob Mosher, and
Douglas Tibbles
Story: Douglas Tibbles
Director: Ezra Stone
Cast
Mr. Gateman: John Carradine
Tom Fong: Benny Rubin

Egged on by Lily, Herman demands a raise
from his boss Mr. Gateman, and is promptly fired.
Apparently, at the funeral parlor, they're not used
to "raising" people. Herman is afraid of Lily's reaction, so he pretends he's still going to work
when in fact he is searching for employment.
Herman gets fired from a number of blue-collar
jobs, including one at a Chinese laundry, where
he wreaks total slapstick chaos. Eventually,
Herman returns to his original job.

For the Record: Celebrated film actor John
Carradine makes the first of two appearances on
this series as Herman's boss.

Munster Musical Moment: Herman sings
"This Is the Way We Wash Our Clothes" while
ironing a shirt.

Our Television Heritage: Notice the decidedly
politically incorrect impersonation of a Chinese
laundry owner by Caucasian actor Benny Rubin.

Classic Quote
MARILYN: Aunt Lily, what happened? All the color
has rushed into your face.

EPISODE 38

"Yes, Galen, There Is a Herman"

Writers: Joe Connelly and Bob Mosher
Director: Norman Abbott
Cast
Galen Livingston Stewart: Brian Nash
Dr. Leinbach: Harvey Korman
Walter Brooke
Marge Redmond

Herman saves the life of young Galen
Livingston Stewart by bending the bars between
which his head is stuck, and they immediately become close friends. The problem is, Galen's parents think that "Uncle Herman" is a figment of
the boy's imagination. They take him to a psychiatrist, played by Harvey Korman, who speaks with
a thick German accent.

Classic Guest Star: Brian Nash played Joel
Nash on the mid-1960s series *Please Don't Eat
the Daisies.*

For the Record: This is the last episode of the
first season.

EPISODE 39

"Herman's Child Psychology"

Writers: Joe Connelly and Bob Mosher
Director: Ezra Stone
Cast
Michael Petit
Bill Quinn
Gene Blakely
Lee Henry

Eddie is upset because his family does not
treat him badly. He thinks their kindness means
they don't care about him. When he decides to

run away from home, Herman employs a little child psychology, which naturally backfires. Circumstances eventually lead to Herman getting involved with a dancing bear.

Leave it to Herman

HERMAN: I just don't understand what went wrong with my child psychology. It always worked on *Leave It to Beaver.*

Joe Connelly and Bob Mosher, the writing-producing team of *The Munsters*, were previously the writing-producing team for *Leave It to Beaver.* The above dialogue is one of several references to that show scattered within this series.

EPISODE 40

"Herman the Master Spy"

Writer: Douglas Tibbles
Director: Ezra Stone
Cast
Leonard Yorr
John Lawrence
Bella Bruck
John Zaremba
Robert Millar
Howard Wendell
Val Avery
Ed Reimers
John Silo
Edward Mallory
Henry Hunter

In this cold war episode, a Russian trawler picks up a scuba-diving Herman in its haul of fish, and the fisherman mistake him for the missing link. They report their discovery to Moscow, claiming it puts the Soviets ahead in the missing-link race. The response from the commissar is that Herman is, in fact, an American spy.

TV Land Reference: These Russian fishermen learned to speak English by watching reruns of *Dobie Gillis.*

EPISODE 41

"Bronco Bustin' Munster"

Writers: Joe Connelly and Bob Mosher
Story: Dick Conway
Director: Ezra Stone
Cast
Don "Red" Barry
William Phipps
Leonard P. Greer
Dick Lane

In yet another example of Eddie's exaggerated regard for his father's abilities, the young Munster enters Herman's name in the bucking bronco contest at the local rodeo. Lily is unable to talk Herman out of this dangerous enterprise; he's intent on being a hero to his son even though he's scared stiff. Meanwhile, the promoters have scheduled Herman to ride a horse that is guaranteed to break every bone in his body.

Classic Fear Take: A bronco-busting cowboy is thrown sky high and into the rodeo audience. After catching a glimpse of Lily, he is so terrified that he leaps into the air in reverse and lands back on his horse.

For the Record: This episode features the first appearance of the tail of Eddie's pet dragon-dinosaur-monster, Spot.

EPISODE 42

"Herman Munster, Shutterbug"

Writer: Dick Conway
Director: Earl Bellamy

Cast

Herbie Faye
Joe DeSantis
Alma Murphy
Jesse Kirkpatrick
Robert Morgan

Herman takes up amateur photography and accidentally snaps a picture of two men making their escape from a bank robbery. While he has visions of getting a big reward for his evidence, the robbers track him down and decide to hole up with the Munsters until the heat is off.

The Message in the Munsters

This episode revisits the recurring theme of criminality that runs rampant throughout this series, with a particular emphasis on banks. Perhaps this is intended as a comment on how wealth in a capitalist society is controlled by a relative few. Maybe this story also reflects a distrust of the international monetary system.

Classic Fear Take:
A statue of Daniel Boone springs to life and flees in horror when Herman takes a picture of it.

EPISODE 43

"Herman, Coach of the Year"

Writers: James Allardice and Tom Adair
Director: Norman Abbott

Cast

The Wife: Emmaline Henry
Henry Beckman

When Eddie is called Lead Foot by the other kids on his track team, Herman offers to become his coach. While demonstrating his out-of-this-world prowess in shot put, discus, and pole-vaulting, Herman causes untold destruction and makes a fool of himself. Grandpa decides to come to the rescue by creating a magic speed pill that will make Eddie a champion runner.

The Message in the Munsters

This could be considered, in today's TV parlance, a Very Special Munsters episode, as it features a blatant anti-drug message: Grandpa's magic pill is clearly an amphetamine.

Classic Fear Take:
When Herman offers to give advice to a member of the track team, the boy takes one look at him and breaks the record for the hundred-yard dash.

Classic Guest Star:
Emmaline Henry became a semi-regular in the later seasons of *I Dream of Jeannie* as Amanda Bellows, the wife of NASA psychiatrist Dr. Bellows.

EPISODE 44

"Happy 100th Anniversary"

Writer: Douglas Tibbles
Director: Ezra Stone
Cast
Bank Manager: Vinton Hayworth
The Admiral: Foster Brooks
William O'Connell
Robert Cornthwaite
Jack Grinnage
Noam Pitlik

Herman and Lily want to buy each other expensive gifts for their one hundredth anniversary. Without telling each other, they both take nightshift positions as ship welders. Since this job requires them to wear protective helmets that conceal their faces, they don't recognize each other until they start to flirt.

Classic Guest Star: Vinton Hayworth became General Winfield Schaeffer in the fourth season of *I Dream of Jeannie.*

EPISODE 45

"Operation Herman"

Writers: Joe Connelly and Bob Mosher
Story: Dick Conway
Director: Norman Abbott
Cast
Dayton Allen
Marge Redmond
Don Keefer
Bill Quinn
Justin Smith

When Herman visits the hospital to see Eddie, who is having his tonsils out, he is mistaken for an accident victim and is immediately given a dose of nitrous oxide, otherwise known as laughing gas.

Grandpa rescues him and brings him home, but Lily presumes that Herman has been drinking.

TV Land References
LILY: Herman, as head of the house I think you should get to the bottom of this. Now, you go right on upstairs and have a father-and-son talk with your boy.
HERMAN: Well, gosh, Lily. I'm not very good at that. You're his mother. Why don't you go up and have a father-and-son talk with him?
LILY: No. A thing like this is up to the father. Anyone who's watched *Father Knows Best* for nine years ought to know that.
HERMAN: All right. But Donna Reed always handles these things on *her* show.

EPISODE 46

"Lily's Star Boarder"

Writer: Douglas Tibbles
Director: Ezra Stone
Cast
Charles Bateman
Buddy Lewis
Chet Stratton

Herman becomes insanely jealous of Chester, a mysterious boarder whom Lily brings into the household in yet another of her schemes to raise a little extra cash. After searching Chester's room, Herman concludes that he's a gangster, when in fact he's a lieutenant in the police department.

Classic Sight Gag: Grandpa sets a booby trap that catapults Chester into the air and sends him plunging down into the dungeon, where he lands in Herman's arms.

EPISODE 47

"John Doe Munster"

Writer: Richard Baer
Director: Earl Bellamy
Cast
Frank Maxwell
Joe Quinn
Willis Bouchey
Olan Soule
Vince Williams
Michael Blake
Monica Rush
Barry O'Hara
Peter Dawson

It's amnesia time! This case is caused when a 300-pound safe drops on Herman's head. In order to get him released into her custody, Lily petitions the court to allow her to adopt Herman as her son. Until he regains his memory, he is treated as Eddie's infantile brother, John.

Classic Quote
LILY: Eddie, your father wouldn't let you down. Even if he were lying dead somewhere, he'd be thoughtful enough to phone.

For the Record: Grandpa reads *The Vault Street Journal.*

TV Land Reference: Grandpa turns on his favorite TV program about that "crazy, mixed-up family that's always having weird, fantastic adventures"—*My Three Sons.*

EPISODE 48

"A Man for Marilyn"

Writers: James Allardice and Tom Adair
Director: Ezra Stone
Cast
Roger Perry
Don Edmonds
Dick Wilson
Dave Willock
Jan Barthel
Jackie Coogan, Jr.

To provide poor, unfortunate Marilyn with a future husband, Grandpa tries to turn a frog into a prince. Conveniently, he chooses a nearsighted frog who won't be put off by Marilyn's hideous looks. Not realizing that the potion has failed, Grandpa and Herman mistake a passing stranger for their princely frog.

EPISODE 49

"Herman's Driving Test"

Writer: Dick Conway
Director: Ezra Stone
Cast
Charlie Ruggles
Francis DeSales
Irwin Charone
Will J. White

Herman gets promoted to hearse driver and has to renew his driver's license. This requires him to take a road test, which he fails. Grandpa convinces him that he'd have better luck taking the test in a one-horse town. He turns out to be consummately correct.

For the Record: In this episode we learn that Herman started out at the funeral parlor as a lowly box boy.

EPISODE 50

"Will Success Spoil Herman Munster?"

Writers: Lou Shaw, Joe Connelly, and Bob Mosher
Director: Ezra Stone

Cast

Disc Jockey: Gary Owens
Penny Kunard
Frank Evans
Don Dillaway
Nolan Leary
Debbie Butler
Sandra Ferra
Gail Ganley

Eddie borrows a tape recorder that belongs to the disc-jockey father of one of his friends. When Herman is by himself, he records a version of "Dry Bones," accompanying himself on the guitar. The following day the disc jockey plays the taped song on his radio show, and it becomes an instant hit. Herman identifies himself as the mystery singer and quickly turns into an egomaniacal would-be celebrity. Grandpa comes to the rescue with his nuthin' muffins.

Munster Musical Moment: Herman's performance of this old song is unforgettable, especially with the lyrics altered to reflect his personal history as Frankenstein's monster.

For the Record: That's actually Fred Gwynne playing the guitar on the audio track.

Classic Sight Gag: Grandpa gets Herman to eat a nuthin' muffin by launching it into his mouth with a cannon.

Classic Guest Star: Gary Owens became a regular on *Laugh-in* in the late 1960s and was one of the very few performers to appear on that show every season. (Dan Rowan, Dick Martin, and Ruth Buzzi were the others.)

EPISODE 51

"Underground Munster"

Writers: Joe Connelly and Bob Mosher
Director: Don Richardson

Cast

J. Edward McKinley
Warren Parker
Jimmy Joyce
Hoke Howell
Bob Harvey
David Azar
John Mitchum
Buck Kartalian
Helen Kleeb
Elsie Baker

The Munsters' pet, Spot, runs away from home and is mistaken for a dangerous monster when he is sighted in the sewer. When Herman goes down the manhole to search for Spot, he too is mistaken for a dangerous monster. The mayor vows to rid the city of these menaces by using TNT.

EPISODE 52

"The Treasure of Mockingbird Heights"

Writer: George Tibbles
Director: Charles Rondeau

While searching for a fuse box in the dungeon, Herman and Grandpa discover a secret chamber and a clue to a treasure hidden by a pirate on the Munsters' property.

Munster Musical Moment: The Munster family sings "Here We Go 'round the Treasure Chest."

For the Record: This is the only episode to have absolutely no supporting cast, not even unbilled extras.

EPISODE 53

"Herman's Peace Offensive"

> Writer: Douglas Tibbles
> Director: Ezra Stone
> #### Cast
> Jackie Minty
> Chet Stratton
> Bryan O'Byrne

Herman advises Eddie to turn the other cheek when he gets pushed around by a bully. Shortly thereafter, Herman is the victim of a practical joke at work. Grandpa takes the situation in hand by teaching both Eddie and Herman how to box.

EPISODE 54

"Herman Picks a Winner"

> Writer: Dick Conway
> Director: Ezra Stone
> #### Cast
> Lefty: Charlie Callas
> Big Roy: Barton MacLane
> Joyce James
> Sammy Shore

Herman tries to teach Eddie a lesson about the folly of gambling by betting his piggy-bank money on a long shot at the racetrack. But his horse wins, ruining the point of Herman's lesson and leading to his entanglement with organized crime.

Classic Guest Star: Barton MacLane played General Martin Peterson on *I Dream of Jeannie.*

EPISODE 55

"Just Another Pretty Face"

> Writer: Richard Baer
> Director: Gene Reynolds
> #### Cast
> Dr. Dudley: Dom DeLuise
> Joan Swift
> Jackie Joseph
> Lenore Kingston

Herman is struck in the head by a bolt of lightning from one of Grandpa's experiments. It causes him to become so disfigured that he resembles Officer Francis Muldoon from *Car 54, Where are You?* Lily hopes to restore Herman's face with plastic surgery.

EPISODE 56

"Big Heap Herman"

> Writers: Joe Connelly and Bob Mosher
> Director: Ezra Stone
> #### Cast
> Ned Romero
> Len Lesser
> Felix Locher
> Sally Frei
> Richard Jury

The Munsters are heading for a vacation in Buffalo Valley when Herman gets off the train for a rest stop at Indian Flats, gets left behind, and wanders into the village of an Indian tribe that caters to the tourist trade. Herman is mistaken for an ancient spirit leader by the tribe's eldest member.

Classic Sight Gag: Herman leaps up to the upper berth of the train and smashes his head through the ceiling.

EPISODE 57

"The Most Beautiful Ghoul in the World"

Writer: Ted Bergman
Director: Ezra Stone
Cast
Elvia Allman
Mary Mitchel
Charles Lane
Adele Claire

With inheritance money from Cousin Wolverine, Grandpa and Herman develop an invention for transporting electrical current without wires. Lily and Marilyn use the rest of the money to operate their own beauty salon. Both endeavors are a disaster, causing various parties to take legal action.

EPISODE 58

"Grandpa's Lost Wife"

Writer: Douglas Tibbles
Director: Ezra Stone
Cast
Jane Withers
Douglas Evans

A lady in Sioux City, Iowa, has placed an illustrated advertisement offering a reward for the return of her lost husband, who looks exactly like Grandpa. Grandpa claims never to have seen this woman in his life, but when he discovers that she's filthy rich, he's ready to sign an affidavit stating that she is his spouse.

EPISODE 59

"The Fregosi Emerald"

Writer: Richard Baer
Director: Ezra Stone
Cast
Paul Reed
Louise Glenn
Joan Swift
Leslie Connors

As a birthday present, Eddie gives Marilyn a ring he found in the attic. Grandpa recognizes it as the Fregosi Emerald, a centuries-old ring that carries a Transylvanian curse. Herman, who doesn't believe in such a silly superstition, is intent on proving that the ring does not bring bad luck. He soon comes to regret the attempt.

EPISODE 60

"Zombo"

Writer: Dennis Whitcomb
Director: Ezra Stone
Cast
Zombo: Louis Nye
Digby Wolfe
Mike Barton
Jimmy Stiles
Jackie Minty

Eddie, an avid fan of ghoulish TV host Zombo, wins the Why-I-Like-Zombo Contest and gets to be on the Zombo show. Herman becomes jealous of Eddie's new hero and wants to appear equally outlandish, but his efforts fail to impress his son. Eddie eventually learns that Zombo is not a real person but a phony character played by an actor.

Munster Fact: Grandpa likes to read *Playghoul* magazine.

Classic Guest Star: Louis Nye was briefly a regular on *The Ann Sothern Show, The Beverly Hillbillies,* and *The Steve Allen Show.*

TV Land Reference
ZOMBO: I am made for much better things: *Hamlet, Macbeth, My Mother the Car. . . .*

EPISODE 61

"Cyrano de Munster"

Writer: Douglas Tibbles
Director: Joseph Pevney
Cast
Chet Stratton
Joan Staley
Eileen O'Neill

After Herman has his poetry published in *The Mortician Monthly,* a shy co-worker named Clyde asks him to compose love letters to help him attract the attention of a young lady he's fallen for. Herman obliges, but soon Lily discovers samples of this mushy writing and, not surprisingly, becomes suspicious. After a reenactment of the hiding-in-the-bushes scene from *Cyrano de Bergerac,* the object of Clyde's desire falls for Herman, while Herman mistakenly suspects that the object of Clyde's desire is Lily.

For the Record: Six years after this show aired, an episode of *The Brady Bunch* was entitled "Cyrano de Brady."

EPISODE 62

"The Musician"

Writer: Richard Baer
Director: Ezra Stone
Cast
Mr. Gateman: John Carradine

Grandpa's magic transforms Eddie from a rotten trumpet player into a classical virtuoso. But when he needs to duplicate the potion for a command performance for Herman's boss, Grandpa can't remember the exact formula, and Eddie is accidentally turned into a jazz-playing, jive-talking hipster.

EPISODE 63

"Prehistoric Munster"

Writer: Douglas Tibbles
Director: Joseph Pevney
Cast
Professor Gearhart von Fagenspahen:
Harvey Korman
Professor Hansen: George Petrie
Richard Poston

Herman has his ego inflated twice by his family. First, Eddie wants to enter him in the Father of the Year Contest. Next, Marilyn wants to sculpt a clay bust in his likeness. When her art professor is told that the sculpture represents a living person, he has plans to make a bundle from his discovery of a missing link. Herman is summoned to his office for an examination, but he's under the impression he's about to receive an award and a bunch of neat prizes.

Classic Guest Stars: Harvey Korman appears—with his Teutonic accent—for yet another memorable guest appearance, his third on this series.

(An episode of *F Troop* features more Germanic Korman.)

George Petrie is familiar to fans of *The Honeymooners*, on which he played a wide variety of supporting parts over several seasons.

For the Record: The bust of Herman created for this episode was on display for many years afterward on the Universal Studios tour.

EPISODE 64
"A Visit from Johann"

Writers: Joe Connelly and Bob Mosher
Director: Gene Reynolds
Cast

John Abbott
Forrest Lewis
Helen Kleeb
Jefferson County

In this semi-evil twin episode, Fred Gwynne once again does double duty. Dr. Victor Frankenstein IV from Germany visits Mockingbird Heights and brings with him Johann, Herman's lookalike cousin, who is quite primitive and behaves like the Frankenstein monster from the movies. Johann was a reject of the original Dr. Frankenstein, and it's up to Herman to try to civilize him and teach him to speak English. Lily, who is not informed of this plan, mistakes Johann for Herman and takes him away for a romantic weekend. Never let it be said that *The Munsters* doesn't deliver a full complement of plot turns per episode.

EPISODE 65
"Eddie's Brother"

Writer: Dick Conway
Director: Ezra Stone
Cast

Wendy Cutler

Eddie longs for the companionship of a younger brother, so Grandpa builds him a robot named Boris. Yet Eddie comes to resent this silent mechanical boy—who is so considerate and well behaved that he garners all of Herman's attention and admiration.

Classic Quote
GRANDPA: Herman, what's the matter? You look like a zombie.
HERMAN: Thank you, but flattery is not going to cheer me up.

EPISODE 66
"Herman the Tire Kicker"

Writers: James Allardice and Tom Adair
Director: Ezra Stone
Cast
Fair Deal Dan: Frank Gorshin
Johnny Silver
Pat McCaffrie
Jimmy Cross
Jack Perkins
Rian Garrick
Dennis Cross
Saul Gorse
Fred Carson

Herman purchases a convertible for Marilyn from a fly-by-day used car dealer named Fair Deal Dan. When he starts the engine, the car disintegrates into a pile of scrap metal. Herman later finds out that it is a stolen piece of junk, and he's placed under arrest.

Classic Guest Star: Frank Gorshin's most famous TV Land character is the Riddler on *Batman*, a part in which he appeared on the first episode of that classic series.

EPISODE 67

"A House Divided"

Writer: Dick Conway
Director: Ezra Stone

A massive argument erupts between Grandpa and Herman after Herman accidentally destroys a go-cart the two of them constructed for Eddie. Since Grandpa claims to own half of the house, Herman draws a white line down its center and insists that Grandpa remain on his side of the line.

Our Television Heritage: This white-line-down-the-middle plot has proven its durability by being used on such later series as *The Brady Bunch* and *Happy Days*, to name but two.

Classic Sight Gag: Herman drives a go-cart down Mockingbird Lane while Grandpa tries to stop him. He has near-misses with a car, a truck, and a baby carriage before squarely hitting a fire hydrant.

EPISODE 68

"Herman's Sorority Caper"

Writer: Douglas Tibbles
Director: Ezra Stone
Cast
Janice: Bonnie Franklin
John: Ken Osmond
Michael Blodgett
Frank Gardner
David Macklin
Vicki Draves
Vicki Fee
Hedy Scott
William Fawcett
Michael Ross

To cure Herman of hiccups, Grandpa puts him in a trance by using the Transylvanian brain freeze. Meanwhile, a couple of fraternity pledges are sent to spend a night in the Munster house as part of their initiation. Thinking that the sleeping Herman is a dummy, they take him to a sorority house, where he awakens from his trance.

Classic Quote
LILY: Herman has a very mechanical brain. In fact, I believe it used to belong to an old mechanic.

Classic Sight Gag: Herman's hiccups cause Grandpa to keel over backwards into his steaming cauldron.

Leave it to Herman
Ken Osmond is best known as Eddie Haskell on *Leave It to Beaver*.

Classic Guest Star: Bonnie Franklin later starred in the long-running series *One Day at a Time*.

EPISODE 69

"Herman's Lawsuit"

Writers: Douglas Tibbles, Joe Connelly,
and Bob Mosher
Director: Ezra Stone

Cast

Simon Scott
Dorothy Green
Jerome Cowan
Fabian Dean
Eddie Marr
Bob Harvey
Than Wyenn
Monroe Arnold

Herman is struck by a car, resulting in no physical harm to him but total damage to the automobile. The uninjured driver, however, assumes she has disfigured Herman, and her attorney suggests that she try to settle with him for $10,000. When Herman receives the offer, he wrongly assumes that this is the amount he's required to pay for the damage he caused to the car. Since he has no hope of raising that much cash, he runs away from home to escape bringing financial ruin to his family.

EPISODE 70

"A Visit from the Teacher"

Writers: Joe Connelly and Bob Mosher
Director: Ezra Stone

Cast

Pat Woodell
Willis Bouchey

When Eddie reads a school composition entitled "My Parents: An Average American Family" the his class, his teacher believes the boy is exhibiting symptoms of an overactive imagination. The school principal suggests that Eddie's wild exaggerations might be motivated by an underprivileged home life. It is decided that a visit to the Munster home is in order.

Drawing from a wide palette of inspiration, the creators have taken the intelligent humanism they'd perfected on *Mary Tyler Moore,* added a dollop of the surreal wackiness that Dave Davis favored on *The Bob Newhart Show,* and then dropped the strange brew into a blue-collar setting that could easily have been stomping grounds for Ralph Kramden. The potent blend that resulted fused the hip sophistication of MTM-style humor with the broad physical comedy of more traditional shows like *The Honeymooners.*

—Vince Waldron, *Classic Sitcoms*

Taxi is an enormously promising new series. . . . The quality of the dialogue on the premiere is particularly good—not just rapid-fire gags or exchanges but lines that delineate characters and states of mind.

—*The Washington Post*

What makes this series something special is the on-screen and off-screen talent executing the setup. The actors come with impressive credentials, and for the most part the product is superb. . . . This vehicle helped put Danny DeVito's patented selfish son-of-a-bitch character on the map.

—Castleman and Podrazik, *Harry and Wally's Favorite TV Shows*

It's different. Not just fast-flying gags, great sight jokes, or insult exchanges—although they're all there—but the fact that each word of each episode shows us what's going on inside the character's heart as well as his mouth.

—Rick Mitz, *The Great TV Sitcom Book*

The relative complexity of *Taxi*'s ironic plotlines, the allusive, plugged-in tone of its dialogue, and the not overly sweetened taste of its moral position are all definitive traits of Brooks's work.

—David Marc and Robert J. Thompson, *Prime Time Prime Movers*

Dave Davis and I were having coffee with New York's only charismatic cabdriver, who came in and dropped off his cab. Two girls were waiting for him, and all the other cabdrivers wanted to be with him. Everybody was saying how they intended to become actors and singers, and we said to him, "What about you?" And he said, "Me, I'm just a cabdriver." That gave us the key to Judd's character.

—Co-creator James Brooks

There are people I don't wish to thank at all tonight. . . . They should really put the show back on the air.

—Judd Hirsch, knocking NBC while accepting an Emmy in 1983

Without each other, these dreamers would be alone in life. So they tolerate each other's quirks, soothe each other's wounds, and celebrate each other's victories together. *Taxi* is a comedy about friendship—about people helping and needing each other. That's something that everyone can understand.

—John Javna, *Cult TV*

Taxi

on Nick at Nite

T*axi* was launched on Nick at Nite in November 1994 with a week-long marathon that included every episode of the show. Taxi Appreciation Week not only encouraged our viewers to appreciate this TV classic but also sent Nick at Nite into the streets of Manhattan to show our appreciation for the real taxi drivers of today. Our on-air host gave out toasters, shoes, flowers, candy, free phone calls, big tips, and free eye exams by an actual optometrist, as well as blood pressure tests by a registered nurse.

On the day of the launch, Nick at Nite offered a taxi drivers' comfort station where New York's cabbies could stop in for a free car wash, coffee, and doughnuts while being regaled by the Nick at Nite Taxi Drivers' Chorus, a singing group composed of genuine cabdrivers, who sang such songs as "Everything's Coming Up Roses" and "My Way."

On the air, Talking Taxi spots featured the stars and creators of the series reflecting on the show's longevity and sharing backstage stories. Carol Kane, Christopher Lloyd, Jim Burrows, James L. Brooks, Marilu Henner, Jeff Conaway, and Judd Hirsch all participated.

Nick at Nite also presented the Taxi Merit Badge to viewers who answered *Taxi* trivia questions correctly. Seven thousand badges were awarded.

Cast

Alex Reiger: Judd Hirsch
Louie De Palma: Danny DeVito
"Reverend" Jim Ignatowski: Christopher Lloyd
Latka Gravas: Andy Kaufman
Tony Banta: Tony Danza
Bobby Wheeler: Jeff Conaway
Elaine O'Connor Nardo: Marilu Henner
John Burns: Randall Carver
Simka Dahblitz Gravas: Carol Kane
Jeff Bennett: J. Alan Thomas

SERIES REGULARS
Tommy: T. J. Castronova
Rudy: Rusdi Lane

EPISODE 1

"Like Father, Like Daughter"

Writers: James L. Brooks, Stan Daniels,
David Davis, and Ed. Weinberger
Director: James Burrows
Cast
Cathy Consuelos: Talia Balsam
Airline Attendant: Jill Jaress

In this ambitious premiere episode, we are introduced to the world of cabdrivers. We meet nearly a dozen characters and take an all-night ride from New York to Miami.

At the center is Alex Reiger, a career cabdriver who's been around the block a few times. He's jaded, complacent, mellow, pessimistic. Even gruff Louie De Palma's insults roll off Alex's back. As old and new faces pass in and out of the garage, Alex observes comfortably from the sidelines. In a telling speech to Elaine, he sums up the melting pot of characters around him: "You see that guy over there? Now, he's an actor. The guy on the phone? He's a prizefighter. This lady over here? She's a beautician. The man behind her? He's a writer. Me? I'm a cabdriver. I'm the only cabdriver in this place."

As this episode begins, the cabbies discover that the garage pay phone is broken, and each one in turn uses it to make free long-distance calls. Finally, it's Alex's turn, and he decides to call his estranged daughter, Cathy. He learns that Cathy is on her way to Portugal, but her plane will be stopping in Miami the next morning. Impulsively, Alex decides to go for it. He takes Latka, Bobby, and John along for the ride. When he meets his daughter at the airport in Miami, their reunion is emotional and ultimately uplifting; Alex is revitalized, happy, and perhaps a little hopeful.

Classic Quote
ALEX (*describing Louie*): He's really a fine person. He'd give you the scales off his back.

Our Television Heritage: Judd Hirsch also starred in the mystery series *Delvecchio*.

Classic Guest Star: Talia Balsam, who is the daughter of Martin Balsam and Joyce Van Patten, appears as Alex's daughter, reprising her role in episode 48.

For the Record: In this episode, which first aired October 12, 1978, we learn that Alex's ex-wife's name is Phyllis Bornstein Consuelos; we will meet her in episode 48.

EPISODE 2
"Blind Date"

Writer: Michael Leeson
Director: James Burrows
Cast
Angela: Suzanne Kent

After speaking to her on the phone, Alex makes a date with sweet-voiced Angela, who works at Bobby's telephone answering service. When Angela turns out to be hostile and resentful about her obesity, Alex selflessly resolves to help turn her frown (and her double chin) upside down.

Our Television Heritage: The opening theme music for *Taxi* was written and performed by jazzman Bob James, who titled the tune "Angela (Theme from Taxi)" after the character in this episode. This memorable TV theme earned a 1979 Grammy Award nomination for best instrumental composition.

Parallel Plot: In a classic episode (number 77) of *The Bob Newhart Show*, a similar story involves

the unselfish, kind efforts of Carol Kester to soothe the fat ogre Mr. DePaolo.

Awards: This episode won both a Humanitas Award and a 1979 Emmy Nomination for Outstanding Writing in a Comedy Series.

EPISODE 3
"The Great Line"

Writer: Earl Pomerantz
Director: James Burrows
Cast
Suzanne Caruthers: Ellen Regan
Mr. Caruthers: Dolph Sweet
Beer Chugger: William Foster

Cabdriver John Burns falls for Suzanne, a cute girl at Mario's bar, but his pickup line works a little too well. Within forty-eight hours, they're married. With Alex's help, John tracks down his wife Suzanne and tries to prevent the annulment of the marriage he didn't *not* want in the first place.

Classic Performance: Actor Randall Carver, whose character was eventually written out of the series, brought realism and charm to the pleasant midwestern simpleton John Burns, who can be viewed as a forerunner to Woody on *Cheers*.

Our Television Heritage: Dolph Sweet played the gruff but lovable father on *Gimme a Break*.

Parallel Plot: Weddings are a surprisingly frequent plot device in *Taxi*. They're featured in episodes 8, 74, 87, and 100.

Favorite: Of writer Earl Pomerantz—whose name, by the way, is eligible for inclusion in Rob's army buddies list (see *Dick Van Dyke* episode 8)—calls this, his first *Taxi* script, his favorite. "I thought it was very funny: the notion of a pickup line so good the guy gets married!" Pomerantz also worked on *The Mary Tyler Moore Show* and *The Cosby Show.*

EPISODE 4

"Come As You Aren't"

Writers: Glen Charles and Les Charles
Director: James Burrows
Cast
James Broderick: William Bogert
Rita: Andra Akers
Mrs. Hazeltine: Paula Victor
Paul: Clyde Kusatsu
Woman: Treva Silverman

In Elaine's first showcase episode, she throws a cocktail party to impress the muckety mucks at the art gallery where she works. But when she tries to get Alex to lie about their occupation as cabdrivers, their friendship is strained.

Classic Quote
LATKA *(succeeding with Alex's pickup line):* Isn't this place full of a bunch of phonies? Let's get out of here.

EPISODE 5

"One-Punch Banta"

Writer: Earl Pomerantz
Director: James Burrows
Cast
Jerry Martin: Allan Arbus
Carlos Palomino: Carlos Navarone
Attendant: Ron Rich
Frankie Wallace: Dwight Woody

While sparring at the gym, Tony knocks out the champ and earns a shot at a big fight. Problem is,

the champ took a dive in his round with Tony to stir up some publicity, and Tony soon realizes his iron fists are merely kid gloves.

Classic Scene: Louie lectures Latka on love versus lust.

Classic Performance: While the cabbies are away at Tony's fight, Louie belts out "From This Moment On" over the garage P.A.

For the Record: Allan Arbus is better known as Dr. Sidney Freedman, the army psychiatrist often featured on *M*A*S*H.*

Our Television Heritage: When Tony Danza gets knocked down in the locker room scene, the punch looks amazingly real—because it was. WBC Welterweight Champion Carlos Navarone's punch accidentally connected, and you can tell by his astonished reaction that he was just as surprised as Tony. Tony Danza quickly recovered and finished the scene without missing a beat.

EPISODE 6

"Bobby's Acting Career"

Writers: Ed. Weinberger and Stan Daniels
Director: James Burrows
Cast
Hamlet's Owner: John Lehne
Peter Nicholson: Michael Mann
Director's Assistant: Robert Phalen
Policeman: Taurean Blacque

Time is running out for Bobby. No, he's not gonna die or anything, it's just that he set a time limit for himself to get a real acting job, and the deadline is midnight. As Bobby waits for the phone to ring, the cabbies wait with him for what could be Bobby's final chance.

B-Plot: Alex rescues a Great Dane named Hamlet from an abusive owner.

Classic Guest: Taurean Blacque's portrayal of a cop prefigured his role as Detective Neal Washington in the Classic TV series *Hill Street Blues*.

Classic Scene: When Bobby pretends to be angry to show Alex what a good actor he is, we see just how talented Jeff Conaway really is. After all, he's an actor acting like an actor who's acting angry to show that as an actor he can actually act. Bravo!

For the Record: Bobby lives in apartment A, as does Elaine.

EPISODE 7
"High School Reunion"

Writer: Sy Rosen
Director: James Burrows
Cast
Beverly: Joanna Cassidy
Sheila Martin: Arlene Golonka
Stanley Tarses: Pierrino Mascarino
George Wilson: Angelo Gnazzo
Woman: Sandy Holt

Louie is ashamed to face his former classmates at his twentieth high school reunion. But Bobby comes to the rescue by taking on the greatest challenge of his acting career—inpersonating Louie De Palma.

Classic Performance: The elaborate dance scene in this episode was choreographed by Jeff Conaway, who actually pulled an inner thigh muscle while rehearsing, but persevered through pain to perform the scene you see.

Classic Scene: Bobby convinces Louie he can do Louie by doing Louie.

Our Television Heritage: Louie's rival, Stanley Tarses, is named after Jay Tarses, co-executive producer of *The Bob Newhart Show*.

EPISODE 8
"Paper Marriage"

Writers: Barton Dean, Glen Charles, and Les Charles
Director: James Burrows
Cast
Vivian Harow: Rita Taggart
INS Agent Richards: James Randolph
Second INS Agent: Woody Eny
Woman in Cab: Michele Bernath

Latka's visa has expired, so the cabbies set up a marriage of convenience to keep him in the United States. Who's the lucky bride? A call girl, of course.

Classic Performance: This episode serves as our introduction to one of Classic TV's most wonderfully inventive characters, Reverend Jim, whose last name—Ignatowski—is not revealed until episode 27. Brought to the garage by Bobby to perform the nuptials, Reverend Jim claims he was ordained in 1968 by the Church of the Peaceful, which "was investigated and cleared completely."

Our Television Heritage: Christopher Lloyd's appearance is all the more memorable because of his appearance. Who can forget his mangy haircut, his ragged whiskers, and his trademark denim clothing? In fact, when Nick at Nite asked Lloyd the story behind the jacket, he told us it was a genuine relic. A friend of his had found it in some bushes in Laurel Canyon, a woodsy area of Los Angeles. Lloyd wore it when he auditioned for

Taxi and continued to wear it nonstop during shoots. It was never washed or mended throughout the run of the show. Where is the legendary coat now? Someone stole it from the Paramount prop closet.

Parallel Plot: Latka will get married again—to Simka—in episode 87.

EPISODE 9

"Money Troubles"

Writer: Earl Pomerantz
Director: James Burrows

Cast

Suzanne: Ellen Regan

Newlyweds John and Suzanne are strapped for cash, and Alex must wrestle with the concept of loaning money to friends.

B-Plot: Latka cooks dinner.

Classic Quote

LATKA: I'm so hungry, I could eat a dog.

EPISODE 10

"A Full House for Christmas"

Writer: Barry Kemp
Director: James Burrows

Cast

Nick: Richard Foronjy
Caroler: Darren Milton
Other Carolers: The Benny Powell Singers

Louie's little brother, Nicky, is in from Las Vegas for the holidays. But instead of visiting their mother as he promised, Nicky gets everyone to play the mother of all poker games. After the other cabbies lose their shirts, Louie turns to poker expert Alex, and the showdown begins.

Our Television Heritage: The role of Louie's slimy brother Nick was originally to be played by Andy Kaufman in a bizarre dual-role multiple-personality arrangement. Kaufman's off-camera alter ego, Tony Clifton, had actually been contracted *separately from Kaufman* to act on the show. Everyone got really annoyed and confused by Kaufman's elaborate charade, however, and *Taxi*'s brass eventually fired Clifton. The spirit of Clifton will surface in episode 64, though, when Latka becomes Vic Ferrari.

EPISODE 11

"Sugar Mama"

Writers: Glen Charles and Les Charles
Director: James Burrows

Cast

Dee Wilcox: Ruth Gordon
Weldon Manning: Herb Vigran
Ramon: Aharon Ipale

Alex's night is made when a spunky old lady beats his tip record. She turns out to be a wealthy widow, and she shares that wealth with Alex in big tips and lavish gifts. Their innocent friendship blossoms—until Alex realizes he's just a gigolo.

B-Plot: John walks around stoned.

Classic Guest Star: You may recognize Herb Vigran from his numerous turns as the bad guy on the Classic TV series *Superman.*

Awards: Veteran actress Ruth Gordon won an Emmy for her sensitive yet uproarious portrayal of Dee Wilcox.

EPISODE 12

"Men Are Such Beasts"

Writers: Ed. Weinberger and Stan Daniels
Director: James Burrows
Cast
Denise: Gail Edwards
Cabdriver: George Reynolds

Tony can't shake his obsessive girlfriend. How obsessive is she? Well, did you ever see the movie *Fatal Attraction?* Tony's the rabbit.

B-Plot: Alex pops an upper.

Classic Scene: As a last resort, Tony explains that the other person in his life is . . . Louie.

Classic Guest Star: Actress Gail Edwards portrayed Dot Higgins on ABC's waitress comedy *It's a Living.*

Our Television Heritage: *Taxi* was one of the first TV shows to feature alternative lifestyles by incorporating gay characters into its stories, and this is the first of several *Taxi* episodes (including number 50) that refer to homosexuality. Other shows of the era that offered pioneering gay story lines were *Soap, Three's Company,* and *Barney Miller.*

EPISODE 13

"Elaine and the Lame Duck"

Writers: Glen Charles and Les Charles
Director: James Burrows
Cast
Congressman Walter Griswald: Jeffrey Tambor

Alex picks up a total dork in his cab, then fixes him up with Elaine. What a pal!

Classic Guest Star: Actor Jeffrey Tambor was considered for the role of Alex Reiger when initial casting auditions for *Taxi* were held. Tambor lost out to Judd Hirsch, but went on to become a popular character actor, portraying such memorable characters as the wacky neighbor on the *Three's Company* spin off, *The Ropers,* and starring as sidekick Hank Kingsley on *The Larry Sanders Show.*

EPISODE 14

"Bobby's Big Break"

Writer: Barry Kemp
Director: James Burrows
Cast
Olivia: Amanda McBroom
Actress: Michele Conaway

Bobby gets his first big acting gig, playing a long-lost boyfriend on a soap opera. The cabbies gather to watch his small-screen debut, but Bobby's scenes have been cut. Now the only scene to watch is Louie's, as he prepares to ridicule Bobby's failure.

Classic Quote
ALEX: You think you're pretty cute, don't you?
LOUIE: I *am* cute!

Classic Scene: Alex tells Louie to leave Bobby alone, but when Louie refuses, Alex peels open the cage and lifts Louie out like a squirming sardine.

For the Record: The name of the soap opera is *For Better, For Worse,* and it's mentioned again in episode 34.

Our Television Nepotism: Michele Conaway is Jeff Conaway's sister. Originally Jeff asked if his sister could be considered for the role of Olivia—

without knowing that Bobby and Olivia would be required to kiss romantically. Michele was instead cast as the "Actress."

EPISODE 15

"Friends"

Writer: Earl Pomerantz
Director: James Burrows
Cast
Dominique: Liz Miller

When Tony goes out of town for a boxing match, he leaves his two beloved goldfish with Bobby, who neglects the fish as he pursues a beautiful woman. The fish die—and so does his friendship with Tony.

B-Plot: Latka doesn't want to go to the dentist.

For the Record: It took him fifteen episodes, but actor Jeff Bennett finally delivers his first big line when he says, "Hey, Banta, telephone!" As the series progressed, Jeff would be given more and more dialogue, and eventually his own story lines in episodes 78 and 102.

Our Television Heritage: The classic dead pet switcheroo plot device is used in this episode when Bobby tries to replace Tony's dear departed fish with lookalikes. Of course, Tony can tell the difference; to this day, this trick hasn't worked once.

Parallel Plot: "It's a goldfish show," according to writer Earl Pomerantz as quoted in the book *Hailing Taxi.* "I went out of town once, and I gave my goldfish to [*Taxi* co-creator] Les Charles and his wife to take care of. And when I came back, one of them was dead—the fish, not Les or his wife." Pomerantz used this pet-loss tragedy as inspiration for this episode of *Taxi* and for the

"goldfish funeral" episode of *The Cosby Show,* which he also wrote.

By the way, the names of the fish in this episode are George and Wanda. And in the 1980s, there was a movie titled *A Fish Called Wanda.* Coincidence? Someday, researchers will uncover the truth.

EPISODE 16

"Louie Sees the Light"

Writer: Ruth Bennett
Director: James Burrows
Cast
Goodwin: John Dukakis
Nurse: Fay Hauser

After a brush with death, or at least with a serious surgical procedure, a reverent Louie begins to smile, laugh, and look on the bright side of life. He becomes a completely new man . . . for a few hours.

Classic Scene: Latka tells (in his native language) a hilarious, albeit incomprehensible, joke.

Parallel Plot: Ted Baxter undergoes a similar transformation in episode 149 of *The Mary Tyler Moore Show.*

For the Record: This episode features the first mention of Latka's cousin Baschi, who appears in episode 35.

Our Television Heritage: When Louie's suppressed rage boils over, he hangs poor Bobby from a winch hook and harangues him. During this scene of vengeful anger, the camera angle is unusually high, allowing us to watch Louie from Bobby's perspective. Cinematic techniques like this are often used in film to invest additional emotional weight to a troubled character; however, the high camera angle is rarely used in sitcoms.

EPISODE 17

"Substitute Father"

Writer: Barry Kemp
Director: James Burrows
Cast
Spelling Bee Moderator: David Knapp
Marilu Hartman: Suzanne Carney
Christa Fowler: Tan Adams
Boyd Fowler: Carl Byrd
Jason: Michael Hershewe

Elaine must visit her ailing aunt, so she leaves her son, Jason, in the cabbies' care. But instead of helping him study for a spelling bee, the guys surround him with distractions.

For the Record: During the spelling bee, Jason misspells the word "vermeil."

Classic Cameo: The little girl who plays Marilu in this episode is Marilu Henner's real-life niece.

Parallel Plot: The cabbies' sing-a-long of "Sonny Boy" is a conspicuous re-creation of a similar scene on *The Bob Newhart Show,* in which Bob and Jerry sit on the lap of the Peeper (Tom Poston) and all three croon the same tune. And if you think this is just a coincidence, check out episode 78.

EPISODE 18

"Mama Gravas"

Writers: Glen Charles and Les Charles
Director: James Burrows
Cast
Greta Gravas: Susan Kellerman

Latka's mother comes to visit her son, but spends a lot of time visiting with Alex, if you know what I mean.

B-Plot: John and Tony discuss the dilemma of obtaining fresh fruit from the vending machine.

Classic Quote
And speaking of fruit, Latka mangles the local idiom by referring to New York as "the Big Banana." He later demands to have a conversation with Alex "man to face."

Classic Scene: When Latka asks his mother about their relatives, we hear hilarious tales of Grishmael, Schmopsi, and Lurrgid.

For the Record: In this episode, Mama Gravas reveals that Alex's name, in Latka's language, means "one who makes nik-nik during harvest." Mrs. Gravas will return in episodes 18, 87, and 90.

EPISODE 19

"Alex Tastes Death and Finds a Nice Restaurant"

Writer: Michael Leeson
Director: James Burrows

Cast

Priest: James Staley
Maître d': Byron Webster
Waiter: John Petlock
Patrons: Charles Thomas Murphy, Mavis Palmer

After a close call with a carjacker leaves Alex resembling Vincent van Gogh, he hangs up his beaded car-seat cover and quits. But when the cabbies come visit him at his new job at a posh restaurant, they make a scene and persuade him to come back.

Classic Scene: The cabbies' dining experience at Genevieve's rivals Jake and Elwood's restaurant scene in *The Blues Brothers.*

Parellel Plot: The show ends with a still-wary Alex guardedly letting a harmless Girl Scout get into his cab. In episode 65, Jim predicts that death is waiting for Alex behind his front door, and sure enough, the evil that lurks there is none other than a Girl Scout. *Aaahh!*

For the Record: In this episode, Tony reveals that he has a "Keep on truckin'" tattoo.

EPISODE 20

"Hollywood Calling"

Writers: Glen Charles and Les Charles
Director: James Burrows

Cast

Roger Chapman: Martin Mull
Michael Patrese: Joey Aresco
Lea: Christine Dickinson
Richard: Gary Imhoff
Cook: Rik Colitti

A smooth-talking Hollywood director is making a movie about cab drivers, and everyone wants to be in the limelight—except Alex.

Classic Guest: Actor Martin Mull is a familiar face to Classic TV viewers. He starred in *Mary Hartman, Mary Hartman,* hosted the talk-show parody shows *America 2-Nite* and *Fernwood 2-Night,* and became a featured player on *Roseanne.*

Our Television Heritage: The names of the director's secretary and the producer's assistant, Lea and Richard, came from real-life *Taxi* assistants Lea Goldbaum and Richard Sakai. Similarly, Bobby Wheeler, Elaine Nardo, and Tony Banta were named after actual staff members Donna Wheeler, Patricia Nardo, and Gloria Banta. Note also that on *The Bob Newhart Show,* one of his regular patients, Renée, is played by Michelle Nardo. Relatives? We honestly don't know.

For the Record: In this episode, Alex demands to file a grievance with the shop steward, Ben Garetsky, but the cabbies remind him that Garetsky died two years ago. In episode 42, the cabbies again require the services of a shop steward, making no reference to Ben. But in the very next episode, number 43, we actually see Ben Garetsky in the garage during Latka's fantasy sequence. Spooky.

EPISODE 21

"Memories of Cab 804," Part One

Writer: Barry Kemp
Director: James Burrows
Cast
Robber: Scoey Mitchlll
Kid: Chris Barnes
Father: Rod Browning
Suicidal Man: Ed. Weinberger

When the cabbies hear that John has had an accident with cab number 804, their favorite, they begin to reminisce. Bobby tells of the robbery he thwarted, Tony brags about the life he saved, and Louie remembers how he swindled a snotty rich brat, all in cab 804.

Classic Quote
LOUIE: All dispatchers are scum. Remember that.

Classic Cameo: *Taxi* co-creator Ed. Weinberger makes a cameo as the man Tony talks out of jumping off a bridge. This scene was filmed on the same day—and on the same bridge—on which the opening sequence of the series was shot. And yes, Tony Danza *is* the driver in the cab in the *Taxi* opening, although you can't see him. Weinberger makes other *Taxi* cameos in episodes 56 and 85.

Classic Scenes: Both Bobby's and Louie's memories of cab 804 are classic television scenes. Scoey Mitchlll (why he spells his name that way is a mystery) is hilarious as the intelligent thief who is bewildered and ultimately outsmarted by Bobby's desperate bravery. The gun farce alone is priceless. And Louie's heartless hustle of the poor little rich kid is a character-defining display for Louie. In this cutthroat contest, Louie demonstrates that it's a dog-eat-kid world.

For the Record: This is the first of a two-part story, the first of seven two-parters, and the first of five flashback episode pairs.

The flashback scene in which John knocks down the glass safety shield in Alex's cab was originally shot for use in an earlier episode.

Our Television Heritage: The footage of Alex's cab pulling over to pick up John was shot on location in Times Square. In the background, you might catch a glimpse of Lindy's, a landmark Manhattan restaurant, which shares an address with Nick at Nite's New York headquarters.

Parallel Plot: Much of this episode is assembled from unused scenes and extra footage from previous *Taxi* episodes. The flashback–dream sequence storytelling device is used several more times on *Taxi*, specifically in episodes 43, 67, 89, and 113.

EPISODE 22

"Memories of Cab 804," Part Two

Writer: Barry Kemp
Director: James Burrows
Cast
Man: Mandy Patinkin
Pregnant Woman: Regi Baff
Mike Beldon: Tom Selleck

In the second of two parts, Latka tries to repair the wreck of cab 804, while Alex and Elaine recall their experiences in it: Alex helped deliver a baby, and Elaine met Mr. Right.

Classic Guest Stars: Actor Mandy Patinkin appears as the helpless father of the baby delivered in the cab. He would go on to play a doctor on the drama series *Chicago Hope*. And who can forget actor Tom Selleck's appearance as the hunky fare who drives Elaine wild? Selleck's successful series *Magnum, P.I.* would eventually air opposite *Taxi*, driving the nail into the sitcom's coffin.

Parallel Plot: TV Land babies are rarely born in hospitals, as demonstrated in virtually every sitcom, from *All in the Family* (a pay phone booth) to *Night Court* (a jury box).

EPISODE 23
"Honor Thy Father"

Writers: Glen Charles and Les Charles
Director: James Burrows
Cast
Charlotte: Joan Hackett
Alex's Father, Joe: Jack Gilford
Old Man: Ian Wolfe
Lady: Margaret Ladd
Cabby: Richard Beauchamp

Alex's sister Charlotte visits the garage with some bad news: Alex's father is in the hospital. But Alex has some worse news: he won't go visit him.

B-Plot: Latka and a Puerto Rican cabbie face a language barrier.

Classic Scene: The multilingual Charlotte engages Latka in a conversation—*in Latka's language.*

Classic Guest Star: You may recognize veteran character actor Jack Gilford from his classic commercials for Cracker Jacks.

Favorite: Of series co-creator James L. Brooks, who based this and other episodes of *Taxi* (and *The Mary Tyler Moore Show,* for which he also wrote) in part on his own troubled relationship with his father.

EPISODE 24
"The Reluctant Fighter"

Writer: Ken Estin
Director: James Burrows
Cast
Brian Sims: Marc Anthony Danza
Benny Foster: Armando Muniz
Vince: Michael V. Gazzo
Referee: Gene LeBell
Maintenance Man: John Dennis

In this corner, wearing blue trunks: former boxing champ Benny Foster, who's coming out of retirement to raise the spirits of a wheelchair-bound kid. In the other corner, wearing red trunks: Tony Banta, the challenger, agonizing over the moral no-win situation of the fight.

Classic Quote
TONY (*talking about Benny Foster*): Not only was he a great fighter, but he was one of the nicest guys ever to wear a cup.
BRIAN (*complaining about Benny's defeat*): You know how hard it is to get boxers to come to the hospital? We keep getting singers!

Classic Cameo: Marc Anthony Danza, who plays Brian, the handicapped boy, is Tony Danza's son. He will return in episode 37.

Classic Scene: Tough-kid Brian pulls a fast one on Louie by stealing a hug—along with his wallet.

EPISODE 25

"Louie and the Nice Girl"

Writer: Earl Pomerantz
Director: James Burrows
Cast
Zena Sherman: Rhea Perlman

Why would any woman fall in love with Louie De Palma? That's what Elaine, Alex, and even Louie can't figure out when candy-machine lady Zena goes sweet on Louie.

Classic Quote
LOUIE (*savoring a Baby Ruth*): Why does the first one always taste the best?
LOUIE (*whenever he thinks of Zena*): Heh-heh-heh!

Classic Scene: When Zena plants a farewell kiss on Louie, it sweeps him off his feet—literally.

Our Television Heritage: Rhea Perlman, who is married to Danny DeVito in real life, went on to play Carla on the Classic TV series *Cheers*. Zena will return in episodes 36, 47, 72, and 100. Two other future *Cheers* stars also made early appearances on *Taxi:* George Wendt, who played barfly Norm, portrayed an exterminator in episode 64, and Ted Danson who went on to play bartender Sam Malone, played a flamboyant hairdresser in episode 84. It's no wonder that Rhea, Ted, and George took a *Taxi* to *Cheers:* both shows were created by the same guys. By the way, the names Zena Sherman and Rhea Perlman almost rhyme.

For the Record: This is the first time we see Louie shirtless; the second is in episode 83.

EPISODE 26

"Wherefore Art Thou, Bobby?"

Writer: Barry Kemp
Director: James Burrows
Cast
Steven Jensen: Michael Horton

Bobby befriends Steve Jensen, a young actor who's new in town and needs a break. But when Steve gets a break that Bobby thinks he should have gotten, Bobby wants to break Steve's leg—er, neck.

Classic Performance: Bobby and Steve perform Act V, Scene III, of *Romeo and Juliet.*

EPISODE 27

"Reverend Jim: Space Odyssey"

Writers: Glen Charles and Les Charles
Director: James Burrows

At Mario's, the cabbies run into Reverend Jim and decide to help him get a job at the garage. After they dispatch dispatcher Louie with a mickey, only one obstacle remains between Jim and a cab-driving job: he has to pass his driving test.

Classic Quote
JIM: Whaattt doooeess aaa yellooow liiight meeeaan?

Classic Performance: A wasted Louie serenades the empty garage with "Moonlight Bay."

Classic Scene: From the very moment Jim arrives at the Department of Motor Vehicles, the laughs are nonstop. Helping Jim answer the questions on the written test, Bobby asks, "Mental illness or narcotic addiction?" Jim's responds, "That's a tough choice." Of course, one of the most memorable moments in *Taxi* history occurs when Jim takes Bobby's hint of "slow down" literally.

Favorite: Of director Jim Burrows, who knew that Jim's test scene was going to get big laughs. He warned the cast that he wasn't going to call "cut" until the studio audience quit laughing, no matter how many times Jim and Bobby repeated their exchange. And indeed, it was one of the show's longest laughs.

EPISODE 28
"Nardo Loses Her Marbles"

Writer: Earl Pomerantz
Director: James Burrows
Cast
Dr. Bernard Collins: Tom Ewell
Fran Strickland: Mary Woronov
Philip: Robert Picardo
Gallery owner: William Callaway

When Elaine tries to juggle an opening at her art gallery, her cab-driving job, and her two kids, Alex convinces her that only a therapist can help her keep all those balls in the air.

Classic Quote
ELAINE (*to Alex*): I love it when a man accuses me of unconsciously avoiding therapy!

Classic Scene: The distraught Elaine seeks tenderness from Alex—and her version of solace is a big wet kiss. This is Alex and Elaine's first on-screen kiss, which plants the seed, so to speak, for further exploration of their on-again, off-again attraction.

Classic Guest: Tom Ewell may be best known for his starring role opposite Marilyn Monroe in the classic movie *The Seven Year Itch.*

EPISODE 29
"A Woman between Friends"

Writer: Ken Estin
Director: James Burrows
Cast
Janet: Constance Forslund

Tony and Bobby both pursue the same beautiful girl, and the resulting rivalry threatens to ruin their friendship.

B-Plot: Alex doesn't want to go to the dentist.

Classic Scene: To avoid a beating from Tony, Bobby volunteers to hit himself.

Classic Quote
ALEX: What am I doing, breaking up a fight between one guy?

Classic Guest: Constance Forslund went on to portray Ginger Grant in the 1981 TV Movie *The Harlem Globetrotters on Gilligan's Island.*

EPISODE 30

"The Lighter Side of Angela Matusa"

Writer: Earl Pomerantz
Director: James Burrows
Cast
Angela Matusa: Suzanne Kent
Wayne Hubbard: Phil Rubenstein
Waiter: Dick Miller

Alex's friend Angela returns to the garage with a big surprise—she's not big anymore. But although she's lost a lot of excess weight, she still hasn't lost her excess self-pity.

B-Plot: Tony is putting together a softball game.

For the Record: The character of Angela Matusa first appeared in episode 2.

EPISODE 31

"The Great Race"

Writer: Glenn Gordon Caron
Director: James Burrows
Cast
Nuns: Kres Mersky, Julie Payne
Taxi Inspector: Scott Brady
Businessman: James Hong
Lady: Jean Owens Hayworth
Blind Man: Fred Stuthman

Louie gets behind the wheel of a cab and competes with Alex to see who can book the most money. The stakes are particularly high for Elaine, because if Alex loses, she has to go on a date with Louie. Although he is tempted to cheat, honest Alex eventually wins fair and square.

For the Record: Writer Glenn Gordon Caron went on to create the TV series *Moonlighting*.

EPISODE 32

"The Apartment"

Writer: Barry Rubinowitz
Director: James Burrows
Cast
Maid: Nancy Steen
Party Guy: Dick Butkus

Latka, who needs a new place to live, spends all of his savings on a $3,000 luxury penthouse apartment. But when the cabbies explain that he has to pay $3,000 every month, Alex volunteers to become Latka's roommate.

Classic Quote: Latka *(when asked why his old apartment building had to be torn down):* Because it could not be burned.

Classic Guest: Pro Football Hall of Famer Dick Butkus appears as a rowdy party crasher.

Parallel Plot: Sharing an apartment with a co-worker is a common plot development on *Taxi*. It happens with Bobby and Elaine in Episode 51 and with Jim and Louie in episode 88.

EPISODE 33

"Elaine's Secret Admirer"

Writer: Barry Kemp
Director: James Burrows
Cast
Don Reavy: Michael DeLano

Someone is sending love poems to Elaine, and she and the rest of the cabbies can't figure out who it is. Later, when Elaine finds out that it's Jim, she thinks her romantic dream of "magic castles" will never come true—until Jim builds her a castle from van parts.

B-Plot: The guys repaint Elaine's apartment in this episode.

Classic Quote
LOUIE's poem for Elaine:

> Cascading. Cascading.
> Cascading water.
> A waterfall.
> Clouds.
> Lots of them, light and puffy.
> You know, clouds!
> And flowers, covered with dew.
> And trees hangin' over.
> And you and me, naked on a rock!

Classic Scene: When Elaine talks to handsome cabby Don Reavy to see if he wrote the poems, he answers her questions with just the word "yeah"—nine times.

For the Record: When Elaine lists the people in the garage she thinks may be her secret admirer, actress Marilu Henner is actually naming old friends and relatives.

Classic Guest: Actor Michael DeLano portrayed Johnny Venture on *Rhoda*.

EPISODE 34

"Alex's Romance"

Writers: Ian Praiser and Howard Gerwitz
Director: Ed. Weinberger
Cast
Joyce Rogers: Dee Wallace

Bobby unloads a hysterical, crying, just-fired actress on Alex, but their spontaneous date turns into a successful whirlwind romance. When she is offered a job in Hollywood, Alex decides to pro-

pose marriage. Unfortunately, those wedding bells aren't ringing in stereo.

Classic Performance: A trio of violinists play "As Time Goes By."

Classic Guest: You may recognize actress Dee Wallace as the mother from the blockbuster motion picture *E.T. The Extra-Terrestrial*.

Classic Scene: Alex's proposal plans are ridiculously elaborate—and touchingly romantic.

For the Record: Joyce has just been fired from *For Better, For Worse*, the soap opera Bobby worked on in episode 14.

EPISODE 35

"Latka's Revolting"

Writers: Glen Charles and Les Charles
Director: James Burrows
Cast
Baschi: Lenny Baker

A revolution has broken out in Latka's homeland, and he decides to return to join the fight. But when the cabbies throw a going-away party for him, Latka has doubts about leaving his beloved America.

Classic Quote
LATKA (*to Baschi*): Kiss my yaktabe!

Classic Performance: Latka and Baschi sing their homeland's gibberishy national anthem, written and composed by Stan Daniels, while, in a tribute to the film *Casablanca*, the cabbies sing "Yankee Doodle Dandy" to drown out Baschi's patriotic call to arms.

For the Record: The voice of the foreign announcer on Latka's transistor radio was provided by Judd Hirsch.

EPISODE 36

"Louie Meets the Folks"

Writer: Barry Kemp
Director: James Burrows
Cast
Zena Sherman: Rhea Perlman
Zena's Father: John C. Becher
Zena's Mother: Camila Ashland

Louie reluctantly agrees to meet his girlfriend's parents, but only if Alex goes along to regulate Louie's behavior. But when Louie's obnoxious personality surfaces, Zena's father is mortified—and Zena's mother is murderous.

B-Plot: Tony's preparing for a big fight.

Classic Scene: Louie is apparently too much for Zena's mother, and she actually threatens to have him killed in a kitchen scene that makes Norman Bates's mother look like the Little Mermaid.

EPISODE 37

"Tony and Brian"

Writer: Ken Estin
Director: James Burrows
Cast
Brian: Marc Anthony Danza
John Brennan: Michael Fairman
Mrs. Brennan: Barbara Stuart
Tommy: Shane Butterworth
Maid: Mary Betten

When little orphan Brian returns to the garage, he's working every angle so he can get adopted by some rich parents. But the cabbies, in that dependable TV Land way, realize that Brian should be adopted by someone else: Tony.

B-Plot: Bobby reads the critics' reviews of his latest acting role.

Classic Quote
TONY (*accepting a snifter of brandy*): You know, if you're short on brandy, I could have a beer.

EPISODE 38

"Jim Gets a Pet"

Writer: David Lloyd
Director: James Burrows

After the guys take Jim to the racetrack, he gets gambling fever. Then, when one of his bets pays him $10,000, he uses his winnings to buy the racehorse.

Classic Quote
LOUIE: Get that ugly, smelly, dirty creature out of my garage, and tell him to take his horse with him!

Classic Scene: In his lecture to Jim about the hazards of gambling, Alex impersonates mobsters, loan sharks, and even a mother, in an impressive display of actor Judd Hirsch's versatility and range.

Parallel Plot: Alex tries to talk Jim out of gambling in this episode, but in episode 92, Jim tries to talk Alex out of gambling. It's like an eerie full-circle thing, man.

EPISODE 39

"What Price Bobby?"

Writer: Ken Estin
Director: James Burrows
Cast
Nora: Susan Sullivan

Bobby's latest big break comes in the form of a powerful theatrical manager who gets into his cab. She eventually agrees to represent him, and Bobby eventually agrees to sleep with her. But soon Bobby struggles with his self-respect—and he comes close to losing his shoes.

Classic Quote
BOBBY: I still have my *shoes!*

For the Record: Judd Hirsch appears only in the last scene of this episode, when he calls Bobby from a ski lodge. At this time Hirsch was busy working on the movie *Ordinary People*, in which he costarred with Mary Tyler Moore and for which he was nominated for an Oscar.

Classic Guest Star: Actress Susan Sullivan starred in ABC's waitress-comedy *It's a Living* and the nighttime soap *Falcon Crest*. More recently she has appeared in commercials for Tylenol.

EPISODE 40

"Guess Who's Coming to Brefnish?"

Writer: Barry Kemp
Director: James Burrows
Cast
John Hannon: Frank Ashmore

Simka Dahblitz, a cute girl from Latka's homeland, walks into the garage and into his heart. But when Latka learns that she is one of the loathsome "mountain people" he literally cannot face her.

B-Plot: Louie hires a new secretary.

Classic Quote
LATKA (*to Simka*): I think you are a wonderful girl, and I am proud to be the man whose life you have totally wrecked.

Classic Performance: The rendition of "Summer Lovers" that Latka plays on the jukebox was sung by Marilu Henner and Jeff Conaway, who starred in *Grease* on Broadway.

Classic Scene: After Simka tells Latka that she is a mountain person, Latka can't look her in the eye. But when he tries—even to move his head in her direction—it's hilarious.

Parallel Plot: This is our first meeting with Simka, who returns in episodes 40, 81, and 87. By the beginning of the fifth season, Simka was so popular that Carol Kane joined the regular cast.

EPISODE 41

"Shut It Down," Part One

Writers: Mark Jacobson, Michael Tolkin, Howard Gewirtz, and Ian Praiser
Director: James Burrows

The cabbies are fed up with driving unsafe cabs, and newly elected shop steward Elaine calls for a strike. But when Alex tells Louie he's facing eternal damnation for putting the drivers' lives at risk, Louie agrees to negotiate with Elaine. In exchange for needed repairs, Elaine must go on a date with Louie.

Classic Scene: To escape the angry garage mob, Louie sneaks through a secret passageway.

For the Record: For more information about the Sunshine Cab Company's bizarre shop steward history, see episode 20.

EPISODE 42

"Shut It Down," Part Two

Writers: Howard Gewirtz and Ian Praiser
Director: James Burrows
Cast
Maître d': Lee DeLano

In the second of two parts, Elaine must fulfill her end of the strike-settlement bargain by going on a date with Louie.

Classic Scene: Louie's good night kiss with Elaine is one of the most memorable scenes in *Taxi* history.

For the Record: Elaine's apartment number is now 5B.

Favorite: Of Marilu Henner.

EPISODE 43

"Fantasy Borough," Part One

Writer: Barry Kemp
Director: James Burrows
Cast
Eric Sevareid: Himself
Herve Villechaize: Himself
Customers: Warren Munson, Carl Lumbly

After Tony meets actor Herve Villechaize from *Fantasy Island,* it prompts the cabbies to envision their own fantasies. Tony imagines being invited to an elitist conference; Latka dreams of turning the dispatcher tables on Louie. Bobby has visions of being a rock star, and Jim's fantasy involves a close encounter with aliens.

Classic Quotes
ERIC SEVAREID: I just want you to come and be on my side in the debate.
TONY: Who are we debatin'?
ERIC: Bill Buckley, Henry Kissinger, John Kenneth Galbraith.
TONY: We'll kick their butt.

HERVE VILLECHAIZE (*talking about Louie's impression of Tattoo*): Will somebody tell the big guy that he stinks?

Classic Guests: Diminutive actor Herve Villechaize and ABC newscaster Eric Sevareid appeared in the same television episode for the first—and last—time.

Our Television Heritage: Latka mentions two popular TV shows in his country: *The Dorfnickys,* a variation on *The Honeymooners,* and *I Nik-Nik Lucy.*

For the Record: This is the first of a two-part episode, the third two-parter of seven, and the second in a row.

The voice emanating from the alien spaceship is provided by Danny DeVito.

EPISODE 44

"Fantasy Borough," Part Two

Writer: Barry Kemp
Director: James Burrows
Cast
Tawny: Priscilla Barnes
Lassie: Lassie

In the second of two parts, the cabbies continue to indulge in fantasy. Alex tries to imagine the taxi driver's ultimate fantasy: the beautiful girl passenger. Louie dreams of being nouveau riche during the Depression. And Elaine's fantasy turns garage life into a Broadway musical number.

Classic Performance: Marilu Henner's dancing background came in handy for Elaine's "Lullaby of Broadway" fantasy. And that's her singing it, too.

Classic Guest Star: Classic TV's Lassie, owned and trained by Rudd Weatherwax, appears in this episode.

Classic Scene: Alex the realist can't seem to get the hang of fantasizing; something goes wrong in each of his scenarios.

EPISODE 45

"Art Work"

Writers: Glen Charles and Les Charles
Director: James Burrows
Cast
Auctioneer: Marvin Newman
Buyers: Richard Derr, Peg Stewart

Elaine encourages the guys to invest their money in art, and they try to buy a soon-to-be valuable painting at an art auction.

B-Plot: Tony has a gambling tip for an upcoming boxing match.

Classic Quote
LOUIE: You know, if you guys were at Normandy, we'd all be eating strudel right now.

Classic Scene: To clear the auction room of the bidding competition, Louie clears his throat—a lot.

EPISODE 46

"Alex Jumps Out of an Airplane"

Writer: Ken Estin
Director: James Burrows
Cast
Jump Master: Beverly Ross

A skiing adventure inspires Alex to take more risks with his life. The risks include singing in public, boxing a pro fighter, and skydiving.

B-Plot: Louie tries to take out a life insurance policy on Alex.

Classic Performance: At the piano in Mario's, and again during his skydiving descent, Alex sings the Broadway tune "Being Alive."

Classic Scene: Alex gets knocked for a loop during his sparring bout with a tough boxer.

EPISODE 47

"Louie's Rival"

Writer: Ken Estin
Director: James Burrows
Cast
Zena Sherman: Rhea Perlman
Dwight: Richard Minchenberg

Louie suspects that something's wrong with his relationship with Zena, and he's right—she's dumping him for someone else. Even when the other man dumps Zena, she doesn't exactly welcome Louie back with open arms.

B-Plot: Bobby tries to get out of baby-sitting with Elaine's kids.

Classic Quote
LOUIE: You know somethin', Zena? Someday you're gonna come back to me, crawlin' on your knees, beggin' me to take you back, and when you do, you know what I'll say? I'll say "Thank God."

EPISODE 48

"Fathers of the Bride"

Writer: Barry Kemp
Director: James Burrows
Cast
Cathy Consuelos: Talia Balsam
Phyllis Bornstein Consuelos: Louise Lasser
Carlo Consuelos: Carlo Quinterio
Attendant: Harvey Skolnick

When Alex finds out that his ex-wife didn't invite him to his daughter's impending wedding, he crashes the reception to confront his ex. But when they get together, the sparks fly—and rekindle her fire.

Classic Guest Stars: Offbeat actress Louise Lasser starred in the acclaimed Norman Lear series *Mary Hartman, Mary Hartman.* Lasser will return to *Taxi* in episodes 83 and 103.

Carlo Consuelos is played by *Taxi's* second assistant director, Carlo Quinterio.

EPISODE 49

"Going Home"

Writers: Glen Charles and Les Charles
Director: James Burrows
Cast
Mr. Caldwell: Victor Buono
Tom: Walter Olkewicz
Spencer: Dick Yarmy
Lila: Barbara Deutsch
Butler: John Eames

A private investigator tracks down Jim, whose estranged father has been looking for him. Jim and Alex journey to Boston, where they attend a reunion dinner with Jim's family. But when Jim's rich dad asks his favorite son to come home and

live a "decent, normal life," Jim bids his father a fond and oddly loud farewell.

Classic Guest: The late Victor Buono may have been best known as King Tut from the 1960s Classic TV series *Batman.*

Dick Yarmy, who played the private investigator, is in real-life the brother of *Get Smart*'s Agent 86, Don Adams.

For the Record: We learn that in the 1960s, Jim changed his last name from Caldwell to Ignatowski because when said backward, Ignatowski is supposed to sound like "star child." (It actually sounds more like "Ix-wah-tangy.")

EPISODE 50
"Elaine's Strange Triangle"

Writer: David Lloyd
Director: James Burrows
Cast
Kirk: John David Carson
Dancing Man: Michael Pritchard

Just as Elaine is complaining to her friends that she can't meet the right man, a nice-looking guy named Kirk approaches their table at Mario's. Tony fixes him up with Elaine, but her heart gets broken again—because Kirk was really hoping for a date with Tony.

Classic Scene: While at a gay bar to talk with Kirk, Alex gets pulled onto the dance floor where he shakes his bootie and creates one of the most outrageously funny moments in *Taxi* history.

Awards: David Lloyd won an Emmy for Outstanding Writing in a Comedy Series for this episode.

EPISODE 51
"Bobby's Roommate"

Writer: Earl Pomerantz
Director: James Burrows

Elaine faces every New Yorker's worst nightmare: she has to find a new apartment. Fortunately, Bobby is going on the road with a touring company, so Elaine has a temporary place to stay. But when Bobby comes home three weeks early, Alex and Tony fear their two friends may be at risk of living in sin.

Classic Scene: When Alex responds to Bobby's alarm, he runs twenty-six blocks—barefoot and in his pajamas—and bursts into Bobby's apartment, breaking down the door and bringing down the house with laughter. Alex's crash through the door was even more realistic than expected: the breakaway door didn't break away as easily as it should have, and both the door *and the door frame* came tumbling down.

EPISODE 52
"Tony's Sister and Jim"

Writer: Michael Leeson
Director: James Burrows
Cast
Monica Banta Douglas: Julie Kavner
Waiter: Andrew Bloch

When Tony's sister Monica comes to New York, he fixes her up with Alex. But to Tony's chagrin, Monica's more interested in another cabbie—Jim.

Classic Quote
JIM: Oh, I'm sorry . . . I forgot to shave. My face grows hair very fast. I shave, and it seems like only a matter of days . . .

Classic Performances: Jim and Monica take turns humming passages from Vivaldi's classical masterpiece "The Four Seasons." Later in the show, Jim blows a mean jug while Monica plays the flute—and that's actually Julie Kavner playing.

Classic Scene: When an angry Tony confronts Jim and Monica, Tony lifts Jim and holds him up in the air throughout the scene.

Classic Guest Star: Emmy-winning actress Julie Kavner portrayed Rhoda's sister Brenda Morgenstern on *Rhoda,* and she'll always be remembered as the voice of Marge on *The Simpsons.*

EPISODE 53

"Call of the Mild"

Writer: Katherine Green
Director: James Burrows
Cast
Guide: Harry Vernon

Alex, Bobby, Tony, and Jim trek to an isolated cabin in the wilderness "to stand face to face with nature." But when they get there, they realize there's no place like home.

Classic Quote
ALEX: It's so quiet here you can actually hear yourself think.
JIM: I can't hear anything.

Parallel Plot: In episode 134 of *The Bob Newhart Show,* Emily, Howard, Jerry, and Herb go into the wilderness to fish. When Herb says, "Isn't it nice to get up here where you can hear yourself think?" Howard replies, "I don't hear anything."

Classic Scene: Tony, Alex, and Bobby try to take the bags of groceries outside for cold storage—while Jim keeps bringing them back in.

For the Record: The beer for which Bobby does a commercial is Brickhauser.

The wild turkey in this episode was somewhat difficult to direct, so the producers had to lead it around on a thin, relatively invisible leash.

EPISODE 54

"Thy Boss's Wife"

Writer: Ken Estin
Director: James Burrows
Cast
Mrs. McKenzie: Eileen Brennan
Ed McKenzie: Stephen Elliott

Louie gets an ominous warning: the boss, Mr. McKenzie, and his wife are fighting, which means that Mrs. McKenzie will choose a cabbie to sleep with, after which that cabbie will never be heard from again. The game is a little different this time, though, as Mrs. McKenzie selects Louie.

B-Plot: Bobby demonstrates the art of mime to a bewildered Jim.

Classic Quote
JIM (*when told of Mrs. McKenzie's Revenge*): I caught that in Mexico once.

Classic Scene: Watch for Louie's aerial leap onto the bed, which was aided by an off-screen mini-trampoline.

Awards: Actress Eileen Brennan received a Best Actress Emmy nomination for her sultry portrayal of Mrs. McKenzie. She has had regular roles on series as diverse as *Rowan & Martin's Laugh-In* and *Private Benjamin.*

EPISODE 55

"Latka's Cookies"

Writers: Glen Charles and Les Charles
Director: James Burrows
Cast
Wally: Famous Amos

Latka quits the Sunshine Cab Company to sell cookies made with his late grandmother's secret ingredients, and the cabbies start eating them like candy. But when Jim takes a bite, he realizes why the cookies are so addictive: they're laced with drugs.

B-Plot: Louie trains Jeff as Mechanic Latka's replacement.

Classic Quote
LATKA (*after dreaming of Famous Amos*): Bye-bye, Famous Amos. Thank you for the hallucination.

Classic Cameo: Cookie entrepreneur Famous Amos appears to Latka in a drug-induced dream sequence.

Classic Scene: Jim, the drug connoisseur, makes a hilarious on-the-spot chemical analysis of the cookies, declaring them "poignant but not overbearing."

Parallel Plot: On a classic episode of *Barney Miller*, Wojo's girlfriend baked a batch of hash-laced brownies for the men of the Twelfth Precinct, with similarly high-octane results.

EPISODE 56

"The Ten Percent Solution"

Writer: Pat Allee
Director: James Burrows
Cast
Casting Assistant: Sabrina Grant
First Producer: Jim Staskel
Second Producer: Ed. Weinberger

Bobby loses an acting job because he doesn't have the right look—a look, it turns out, that Tony does have. Soon Bobby is theatrically representing Tony the actor. The problem is, Tony can't act.

B-Plot: Louie and Jeff combat a colossal cockroach.

Classic Scene: Tony's acting audition is indescribably terrible.

Classic Cameo: Producer Ed. Weinberger makes a brief appearance as—what else?—a producer.

EPISODE 57

"Zen and the Art of Cab Driving"

Writers: Glen Charles and Les Charles
Director: Will Mackenzie
Cast
Jim's Passengers: Nicholas Hormann, Michael Mann, Jim McKrell

Inspired by one of them newfangled self-help philosophies, Jim becomes a new man. First he becomes the greatest cabdriver he can be, serving snacks and singing to his fares, but then he spends his hard-earned money on something not-so-great—a home entertainment center.

For the Record: Director Will Mackenzie spent some time in front of the camera on *The Bob Newhart Show* as secretary Carol Kester's ditzy husband, Larry Bondurant.

EPISODE 58

"Elaine's Old Friend"

Writers: Susan Jane Lindner and Nancy Lane
Director: Jeff Chambers
Cast
Mary Parker: Martha Smith
Michael: John Considine
Maître d': Myron Natwick
Pilot: John Yates

This episode is based on a classic sitcom premise: Elaine tries to impress an old high school friend by pretending to be happier, wealthier, and more successful romantically than she really is. But instead of backfiring, her pretense works great, thanks to Alex's amazing job of pretending to be Elaine's loving boyfriend, Bill Board. But is Alex pretending?

For the Record: In this episode Elaine lives in apartment 5B, just as she did in episode 42. But in episode 51, she moved out of apartment 5B, so we can only presume she took the 5B door with her.

We also learn that Elaine's maiden name is O'Connor.

EPISODE 59

"The Costume Party"

Writer: David Lloyd
Director: James Burrows
Cast
Maxie Melcher: Louis Guss
Gus Bates: Hector Britt

One of Bobby's Theater District passengers leaves behind a locked briefcase, and Bobby hopes it will lead to an encounter with a powerful Broadway contact. And sure enough, the contents of the briefcase lead to a celebrity costume party, which the cabbies decide to crash.

Classic Costume: Tony, Alex, and Latka show up at the costume party in drag, dressed as the Andrews Sisters, and Jim goes dressed as a burned-out sixties derelict. But then, he always looks like that.

Classic Scene: Louie, master of all sleaze, opens the locked briefcase the way Fonzie turned on the jukebox—by giving it a good whack.

EPISODE 60

"Out of Commission"

Writer: Sam Simon
Director: James Burrows
Cast
Dr. Webster: Al Ruscio
Lou-Lou Pantusso: Carmine Caridi
Shotgun: Jessie Goins
El Gato: Mauricio Aldana
Referee: Vince Delgado
Mean Boxer: Jon St. Elwood
Jimmy Lennon: Himself

A doctor advises Tony that it's unsafe for him to continue fighting, and Tony's boxing license is revoked. Undaunted, Tony ignores the doctor's orders and continues under the name of Kid Rodriguez. Can Alex and the cabbies talk him out of the ring?

Classic Quote
ALEX: I'm not really a cabdriver. I'm just waiting for something better to come along. You know. Like death.

EPISODE 61

"Bobby and the Critic"

Writer: Barry Kemp
Director: James Burrows
Cast
John Bowman: John Harkins

Bobby gets fed up and writes an angry letter to a powerful New York theater critic. He chickens out before sending it, but Louie fishes it out of the trash can and mails it. When it hits the papers, you-know-what hits the fan. Now the critic is coming to see Bobby's play. . . .

B-Plot: Latka wins a complete wardrobe.

Classic Quote
JIM (*reading a newspaper*): Did you read the story about a woman who got her cat's head stuck in her mouth?

Classic Scene: Watch as Louie unsuccessfully tries to throw Bobby's crumpled note back into the garbage can. His evil hand just can't let an opportunity for cruelty slip away.

For the Record: The play Bobby performs in is titled *Charles Darwin Tonight*. We also learn that Bobby's middle initial is *L*.

EPISODE 62

"Louie's Mother"

Writer: Katherine Green
Director: James Burrows
Cast
Gabriella De Palma: Julia DeVito

Louie's mother moves into a rest home, leaving Louie finally free to live the life of a bachelor. Make that a lonely bachelor.

Classic Guest: Danny DeVito's real-life mother plays the role of Louie's mom.

Classic Scene: Watch as Louie and his Italian-speaking mother converse through a door.

EPISODE 63

"Louie Bumps into an Old Lady"

Writer: David Lloyd
Director: James Burrows
Cast
Edith Tremayne: Iris Korn
Edith's Attorney: Joe Medalis
Louie's Attorney: Sam De Fazio
Janine: Lane Brody
The Judge: Jay Flash Riley

Louie takes a cab out and accidentally hits a sweet old lady. His attempts to butter her up fail, and she sues him for a million dollars. When Alex remembers that the old lady is a scam artist, Louie seeks his revenge in court. Although Louie ends up in jail, Alex is authorized to get him out on bail. However, when Alex realizes that Louie's fate is in his hands, he takes his sweet time.

EPISODE 64

"Latka the Playboy"

Writers: Glen Charles and Les Charles
Director: James Burrows
Cast
Karen: Robin Klein
Exterminator: George Wendt

When Latka strikes out with a beautiful girl in Mario's bar, he decides it's because he's just too darn cute. After a quick study of FM disc jockey lingo and *Playboy* magazine, Latka transforms himself into the smooth-talking, suave-walking Vic Ferrari. Oh, yes, he's slick, but to Alex, he seems slimy.

B-Plot: Louie again combats a colossal cockroach.

Classic Performance: Andy Kaufman demonstrates his acting range—and introduces Latka's internal personality struggle—with this impressive dual-personality role. Vic Ferrari will return in episodes 70, 74, 77, and 80 before he's exorcised from Latka in episode 81.

Classic Guest: George Wendt, of course, later played Norm on *Cheers.*

For the Record: This episode marks Jeff Conaway's last one he would film as a regular cast member on *Taxi.* (His part of episode 68 was shot earlier.) He will return one more time, as a guest star in episode 79.

EPISODE 65

"Jim the Psychic"

Writers: Holly Holmberg Brooks and Barry Kemp
Director: James Burrows
Cast
Bar Brawlers: Bob Larkin, J. P. Bumpstead
Girl Scout: Kiva Dawson

Jim has had an ominous dream—that Alex will die at seven o'clock after a series of bizarre events. Of course, Alex doesn't believe in that kind of thing . . . until, one by one, Jim's ridiculous predictions start coming true.

For the Record: Alex's apartment number is again A2.

Writer Holly Holmberg Brooks is *Taxi* writer Jim Brooks's wife.

EPISODE 66

"Fledgling"

Writer: Ken Estin
Director: James Burrows
Cast
Craig Eagen: Paul Sand

Elaine befriends a reclusive artist and, after a long and sappy period of persuasion, coaxing, and cajoling, gets him to come out of his shell and—inexplicably—into the garage.

For the Record: Elaine works at the Hazeltine art gallery.

Classic Guest Star: Character actor Paul Sand appeared as an amorous IRS Agent on *The Mary Tyler Moore Show.*

EPISODE 67

"On the Job," Part One

Writers: Dennis Danziger and Ellen Sandler
Director: James Burrows
Cast
Father: John O'Leary
Lou-Lou: Carmine Caridi
George Givens: Bill Wiley
Board Chairman: John Petlock
Barrett: Robert Balderson
Housewife: Alice Hirson

When the Sunshine Cab Company goes broke, the cabbies must find new jobs. One month later, the gang gathers and through a series of flashbacks, we see that Tony gets a job as a bookie's collector, Elaine works as a secretary, Jim sells door-to-door, and Latka works at Mario's.

Classic Scene: To demonstrate the Magic Carpet Wizard vacuum cleaner, Jim creates a giant stain on an unsuspecting housewife's rug. But then he remembers that he's not selling vacuum cleaners—he's selling encyclopedias.

EPISODE 68

"On the Job," Part Two

Writers: Dennis Danziger and Ellen Sandler
Director: James Burrows
Cast
Mr. Gray: Michael McGuire
Ms. Lang: Dana Halsted
Night Watchman: Al Lewis
Security Guard: Clint Young
Director: Cynthia Beck
Children: Howie Allen, Heather Hobbs

The cabbies are still reminiscing about the jobs they've taken since the garage shut down. In flashbacks over beers at Mario's, Louie tells of his Wall Street experience, Bobby describes his job in the "entertainment field" (he plays the Easter Bunny at children's parties), and Alex recounts his lonely stint as a night watchman. In the end, the Sunshine Cab Company re-opens for business, and they all return to their jobs.

Classic Guest Stars: Actor Michael McGuire portrayed Sumner Sloane, Diane's boyfriend on *Cheers.*

Alex's night watchman compadre is played here by none other than Al (Grandpa) Lewis from *The Munsters.*

EPISODE 69

"Vienna Waits"

Writer: Ken Estin
Director: Howard Storm
Cast
Todd Bentley: Gary Phillips
James: Warwick Sims
Oumas: Reuven Bar-Yotam
Desiree: Cassandra Gava
Waiter: Rob Hughes
Woman on Plane: Patch Mackenzie

Elaine invites Alex to join her on a whirlwind trip to Europe. But instead of romance and excitement, wallflower Alex jealously watches as Elaine has fun without him. But then, in Vienna, Alex finally finds romance—with Elaine.

Classic Scene: In a London pub, a depressed Alex lethargically plays darts—and accidentally throws one into a bar patron's back.

For the Record: Billy Joel's song "Vienna" is used as a musical background for Alex and Elaine's European escapades. The song used in the show is not the original version from *The Stranger,* but an incredible simulation.

Alex and Elaine walk off hand in hand at the end of this episode, preparing for a "night of love." We can only assume that the answer to "Will they or won't they?" is finally yes.

EPISODE 70

"Mr. Personalities"

Writers: Ian Praiser and Howard Gewirtz
Director: Howard Storm
Cast
Dr. Jeffries: Barry Nelson
Woman Patient: Bernadette Birkett
Secretary: Wendy Goldman

Latka's alter ego, Vic Ferrari, gets some schizophrenic company as Latka develops multiple personalities. But after Alex encourages him to visit a psychiatrist, Latka takes on yet another identity: Alex Reiger.

B-Plot: Tony is thinking about going to college.

Classic Performance: Andy Kaufman's performance as Latka Gravas portraying Alex Reiger as played by Judd Hirsch is a masterful acting achievement.

For the Record: Vic Ferrari first appeared in episode 64; Latka's multiple personality problems will continue in episode 81.

EPISODE 71

"Jim Joins the Network"

Writer: David Lloyd
Director: Noam Pitlik
Cast
Janine: Melendy Britt
Mitch Harris: Martin Short

Jim gives a ride—and some advice—to a television executive, who promptly hires him to consult for the network. But when the weasely programmer takes advantage of Jim's talent, Alex persuades Jim to stand up for himself.

Classic Scene: Louie tries to catch a mouse in this episode, but he ultimately releases it while singing "Born Free."

Classic Guest Star: Martin Short starred in the comedy ensemble series *SCTV* and *Saturday Night Live*.

Our Television Heritage: The wacky TV shows mentioned on the fictional network's schedule include *Brooke Shields Turns Seventeen*, *The Pittsburgh Steelers at Marineland* and a game show featuring Paul Lynde getting slimed by a vat of cheese.

EPISODE 72
"Louie's Fling"

Writer: Sam Simon
Director: James Burrows
Cast
Zena Sherman: Rhea Perlman
Emily: Andrea Marcovicci

Zena tries to cheer up her friend Emily, who's just broken up with her boyfriend. But when Louie drives the distraught Emily home, they end up sleeping together, with dire consequences for Zena, Louie, and their relationship.

Favorite: Of Rhea Perlman, who said, in *Hailing Taxi*, "I got to scream my head off in the last scene, when I kicked him out and told him he was garbage. I really liked doing that."

EPISODE 73
"Like Father, like Son"

Writer: David Lloyd
Director: James Burrows
Cast
Joe Reiger: Jack Gilford
Karen: Barbara Babcock

Alex reluctantly goes to lunch at Mario's with his estranged father, Joe, a notorious womanizer. And sure enough, Joe charms a woman dining nearby into a date with Alex—and eventually makes a date with her for himself.

B-Plot: Tony is called for jury duty.

Classic Quote
LOUIE (*after Joe Reiger asks out Alex's new girl*): Reiger's on thin ice, and I'm a blowtorch!

Classic Guest Stars: You may recognize character actress Barbara Babcock from her frequent appearances on Classic TV. She has played everything from aliens on *Star Trek* to Sergeant Esterhaus's lover on *Hill Street Blues*, a role for which she won an Emmy.

Jack Gilford's only other appearance as Alex's father on *Taxi* was in episode 23.

EPISODE 74
"Louie's Mom Remarries"

Writer: Earl Pomerantz
Director: James Burrows
Cast
Gabriella De Palma: Julia DeVito
Itsumi Fujimoto: Jerry Fujikawa

Louie's mother is getting married again, and Louie can't stand it.

B-Plot: Vic Ferrari plans a swinging ski trip.

Classic Quote
JIM *(comparing Vic to a doughnut):* Charisma does not have jelly in the middle.

Classic Scene: After Louie spends the night in the garage cage, Alex and Jim witness his sickening wake-up ritual like Marlon Perkins and Jim Fowler on *Wild Kingdom.*

EPISODE 75
"Of Mice and Tony"

Writers: Glen Charles and Les Charles
Director: James Burrows
Cast
Terry Carver: Ernie Hudson
Doctors: John Christy Ewing, Nat Bernstein, Andrew Winner, Howard Gewirtz, Ian Praiser
Jimmy Lennon: Himself
Gene LeBell: Himself

Tony gets back into the ring—sort of—by managing a young boxing hopeful.

B-Plot: Louie makes a football wager and places a bet against Tony's fighter.

Classic Guest Stars: Look for *Taxi* writer-producers Ian Praiser and Howard Gewirtz, who play Drs. Baker and Hardin of "the syndicate." And of course you may recognize Ernie Hudson, who starred in the *Ghostbusters* movies and, more recently, in *Congo.*

EPISODE 76
"Nina Loves Alex"

Writer: David Lloyd
Director: Jim Darling
Cast
Nina Chambers: Charlaine Woodard
Prom Kids: John Mengatti, Audrey Berindi

A happy-go-lucky, free-spirited young girl bounces into the garage and Alex's life. She's in love with Alex, but he won't have anything to do with a girl who is his polar opposite. Of course, Alex's polar ice soon begins to melt.

Classic Scene: Alex and Nina share a then-controversial interracial kiss. The first such buss on TV occurred between Captain Kirk (William Shatner) and Lieutenant Uhura (Nichelle Nichols) on *Star Trek* in 1968.

EPISODE 77
"Louie Goes Too Far"

Writer: Danny Kallis
Director: Michael Lessac
Cast
Andrea Stewart: Noni White
Robert: Allen Williams

Elaine catches Louie peeping at her as she changes her clothes, and her formal complaint gets Louie fired.

B-Plot: Vic Ferrari lectures Jim on the merits of Jazzercise.

Classic Quote
LOUIE *(as he bids farewell):* Good-bye, cockroach . . . good-bye, mouse . . . good-bye, Jeff.

Classic Scene: Louie's plea for Elaine's forgiveness is at once pathetic, heartbreaking, and touching—but mostly pathetic.

EPISODE 78

"I Wanna Be Around"

Writers: Glen Charles and Les Charles
Director: James Burrows

A doomsday discussion on *Donahue* prompts Louie to convert the toolroom into a four-person bomb shelter. But when he faces the consequences of selecting his survival team, Louie is morally doomed.

Classic Quote
LOUIE (*on the merits of spending money on the shelter*): What good is money in the bank when you're a radioactive pretzel?

Parallel Plot: Jim enters the garage singing "The Java Jive," a song also briefly performed in episode 83 of *The Bob Newhart Show.* Episode 17 of *Taxi* contained a similar parallel.

EPISODE 79

"Bobby Doesn't Live Here Anymore"

Writers: Glen Charles and Les Charles
Director: James Burrows
Cast
Waiter: Tony Gaetano

Bobby, who's been away from the garage for six months, returns from Hollywood to visit. He's up for a big role in a big TV series in Hollywood, and, as usual, his career hangs in the balance.

B-Plot: Latka keeps having to change his going-away gift for Bobby.

Classic Quote
LATKA (*hinting about his surprise present*): It keep you warm and it rhyme with "zearmuffs."

Classic Scene: As they say good-bye for the last time, Alex wishes Bobby good luck: "Y'know, Bob, if you become a star, there's a good chance we'll never see each other again. . . . Here's hoping we never see each other again."

Our Television Heritage: This is actor Jeff Conaway's final appearance on *Taxi.*

EPISODE 80

"Tony's Lady"

Writer: Ken Estin
Director: Michael Zinberg
Cast
Christina Longworth: Rebecca Holden
Doug Blakely: John Calvin
Nick: Joel Brooks

Tony takes a part-time job as a chauffeur, and the beautiful woman for whom he drives is driving him crazy. Should Tony propose marriage to his dream girl, or will he be too late?

B-Plot: Vic Ferrari returns to torture Latka.

Classic Guest Star: Rebecca Holden went on to play April Curtis, the beautiful technician who works on Kitt, the talking car on *Knight Rider.*

EPISODE 81

"Simka Returns"

Writers: Howard Gewirtz and Ian Praiser
Director: Michael Zinberg

Simka Dahblitz, the love of Latka's life, returns to visit. She is single, and Latka vows to tell her that he loves her—that is, unless Vic Ferrari makes a move on her first.

Classic Quotes
LATKA (*to Simka after she has confessed to having slept with Vic*): You have shamed me, degraded yourself, disgraced your family, cheapened your people, and blemished your planet!

SIMKA: Latka, I hate you, I never want to see you again, and thanks for a wonderful night.

Classic Performance: The mood music Latka selects for his dinner date with Simka is a record from his homeland of the Elvis classic "Love Me Tender," sung in Latka's native language. The song was actually recorded by Elvis fanatic Andy Kaufman.

For the Record: In this episode, when Simka kicks Vic Ferrari out of her life, Vic says, "If I walk out that door, I'm never coming back." And sure enough, this is Vic's last appearance on the show, perhaps explaining why actor Andy Kaufman spoke the line so slowly and deliberately.

Awards: Carol Kane won her first of two *Taxi* Emmys for her performance in this episode.

EPISODE 82

"Jim and the Kid"

Writer: David Lloyd
Director: Michael Zinberg
Cast
Terry: Tony La Torre
Mr. Booth: Mark Harrison
Mrs. Booth: Rebecca Clemons
Policeman: Wendall W. Wright

Jim befriends a young runaway who stiffed him for a cab fare. But just as Jim is becoming attached to the son he never had, the boy's parents come to take him home. Now Alex must help surrogate-father Jim deal with the surrogate loss of a surrogate son.

Classic Quote
POLICE OFFICER (*to Louie*): You prod me one more time, I'm gonna show you eight places you can beat a man and leave no marks.

Classic Guest Star: Tony La Torre went on to play Mary Beth Cagney's son, Harvey Junior, on *Cagney & Lacey.*

EPISODE 83

"Take My Ex-Wife, Please"

Writers: Howard Gewirtz and Ian Praiser
Director: Noam Pitlik
Cast
Phyllis Bornstein Consuelos: Louise Lasser
Randi and Candi Brough: Randi and Candi Moratta
Maître d': Alex Rodine

Tony and Alex are on a double date with beautiful twins, along with Jim, who is under the incorrect impression that he was invited. Then Alex runs into his clinging ex-wife. Alex blows her off, but when she becomes Louie's latest love target, Alex blows his top.

Classic Quotes

PHYLLIS: I mean, I'll admit, [Louie] won't make anybody forget Paul Newman . . . or Edwin Newman . . . or Alfred E.

LOUIE (*to Alex*): The answer's right under your nose, but then again, what isn't?

Classic Scene: Louie forces Jeff to make spontaneous conversation—by reading from a prepared script.

For the Record: This is the second time we've seen Louie shirtless; the first time was in episode 25.

Classic Guests: Twins Randi and Candi Moratta portrayed Teri and Geri Garrison on *B.J. and the Bear.*

EPISODE 84

"The Unkindest Cut"

Writers: Barbara Duncan, Holly Holmberg Brooks, and Sam Simon
Director: Noam Pitlik
Cast
Vincenzo Senaca: Ted Danson
Receptionist: Gela Jacobson

Elaine, who's going to a big museum party, decides to splurge on an elegant new hairdo from a trendy New York salon. The high-priced hairstylist is haughty and hostile, however, and his hideous haircut humiliates her. But with Alex and Louie's help, Elaine gets her revenge.

B-Plot: To the delight of greedy Louie, Jim pumps quarters into the garage's new Pac-Man video game.

Classic Quote

LOUIE (*dumping goop on Vincenzo*): She may be better than you, but I ain't!

Classic Guest Star: A pre-*Cheers* Ted Danson turns in a memorable performance as the flamboyant hairdresser.

EPISODE 85

"Tony's Comeback"

Writer: Sam Simon
Director: Michael Lessac
Cast
Lucius Franklin: Bubba Smith
Aunt Lucia: Naomi Stevens
Jimmy Lennon: Himself
Referee: Gene LeBell
Eddie Burke: John Steve
Boxing Fans: Ed. Weinberger and Jim Brooks

Tony finds inspiration in former athlete Lucius Franklin, who motivates him to make a boxing comeback.

Classic Quote

LUCIUS (*after telling Tony an inspirational parable*): C'mon, Tony, do it for the duck!

Classic Guest: National Football League Hall of Famer Bubba Smith appears as the gentle athlete Lucius.

EPISODE 86

"Elegant Iggy"

Writer: Ken Estin
Director: Noam Pitlik
Cast
Mrs. Weber: Fran Ryan
Rich Woman: Nina Van Pallandt

Jim invites Elaine to a classical music concert, where they bump into an influential art gallery patron. To Elaine's delight, the woman invites her to a posh private recital; to Elaine's dismay, she also invites Jim.

Classic Quote
JIM: A Yoda doll, for a beautiful woman.

Classic Performance: Although Jim appeared to be playing the piano, Chopin's "Fantasy Impromptu" was actually played off-camera by *Taxi* musical director Stan Daniels.

Classic Guest Star: Fran Ryan played Mrs. Ziffel on several episodes of *Green Acres.*

Favorite: Of writer Ken Estin who came up with the general idea for this plot as a sequel to episode 33, about Jim's infatuation with Elaine. Estin wrote the script when he was asked to come up with a show that could be the season's Emmy submission. And sure enough . . .

Awards: This episode earned writer Ken Estin an Emmy for Outstanding Writing in a Comedy Series.

EPISODE 87

"The Wedding of Latka and Simka"

Writers: Howard Gewirtz and Ian Praiser
Director: James Burrows
Cast
Latka's Mother Greta: Susan Kellerman
Mascha: Peter Elbling
Reverend Gorky: Vincent Schiavelli
Dr. Joyce Brothers: Herself

In this riotous mockery of wedding rites, Latka and Simka must pass tests, participate in bizarre rituals, and prove their love before they can tie the knot and make nik-nik.

Classic Quote
LATKA: The only things that separate us from the animals are mindless superstition and pointless rituals. [For a similar quote from Jim, see episode 105].

Classic Cameo: Veteran character actor Vincent Schiavelli is known to links lovers from his appearance with Tim Conway in *Dorf on Golf.*

Our Television Heritage: One of the words in Latka's language is "gewirtzal," a nod to scriptwriter Howard Gewirtz. And "mertzig" sounds like a tribute to Classic TV's most famous next-door neighbors, Fred and Ethel Mertz of *I Love Lucy.*

For the Record: This is technically Latka's second marriage; he married a call girl to gain U.S. residency in episode 8. Also, writer Stan Daniels, who created the word "nik-nik," was later informed by a philologist that "nik-nik" actually did mean "lovemaking" in the language of ancient Egypt.

EPISODE 88

"Cooking for Two"

Writers: Ken Estin and Sam Simon
Director: James Burrows

After Jim's apartment is condemned and destroyed, he moves into—and promptly sets fire to—Louie's apartment. An apologetic Jim offers financial restitution by means of a blank check from his rich father, and greedy Louie must decide how to fill in the blank.

Classic Quote
LOUIE (*describing life with Jim*): We went to sleep, Jim screamed, we went back to sleep.

Classic Scene: Look out! It's a giant wrecking ball!

For the Record: Marilu Henner provides the voice of the soap opera actress on Jim's TV.

EPISODE 89

"The Road Not Taken," Part One

Writers: Ken Estin and Sam Simon
Director: James Burrows
Cast
Jack: Eugene Roche
Frank: Charles Cioffi
Referee: Gene LeBell
Wilkes: Jim Echollas
Tom: Pat O'Malley
Felipe Rodriguez: Michael A. Salcido
Heather: Wendy Phillips
Boy in Dorm: Tony Eldridge
Gordon: Tom Hanks

To help Elaine decide whether or not to change her life and move to Seattle, the cabbies discuss the significant decisions they've made in their own lives. In flashback, Tony recalls the fight he almost threw, Louie tells of his ascension to cab dispatcher, and Jim recounts his first drug-taking experience.

Classic Quote
LOUIE (*to the Irish dispatcher*): Cram it up your bagpipe.

Classic Guest Star: In a Gumpesque flashback to the sixties, Tom Hanks appears as Jim's pot-addled roommate, Gordon. Hanks, sporting a frizzy *Bosom Buddies*–era perm, demonstrates his gift for physical comedy as he carries a hot lava lamp and executes an impressive face-first pratfall.

J. Pat O'Malley was one of the actors who played Rob's father on *The Dick Van Dyke Show*.

EPISODE 90

"The Road Not Taken," Part Two

Writers: Ian Praiser and Howard Gewirtz
Director: James Burrows
Cast
Latka's Mother: Susan Kellerman
Jennifer: Melanie Gaffin
Jason: David Mendenhall
Sally: Jill Jaress
Mr. Ambrose: Max Wright
Mr. Thompson: Matthew Faison

Elaine is still considering a move to Seattle, and Latka tells how he left his homeland to come to America (the story is hilariously told with English subtitles). Alex then describes his experience in the world of corporate bootlicking. After receiving some adorable encouragement from her loving children, Elaine finally faces her decision—and punches her future boss in the stomach!

Classic Quotes

LATKA: In America, a man can become another O.J. Simpson!

LATKA'S MOTHER: Who?

LATKA: The Juice!

ALEX (to Mr. Ambrose): I was wrong, I'm very sorry, and it will never happen again, you miserable stupid rotten jackass!

Classic Scene: Latka's farewell scene with his Mother is a sensitive and touching Classic TV moment.

For the Record: We are introduced to Elaine's children, Jennifer and Jason, who also appear in episodes 105, 111, and 112.

Classic Guest Star: Max Wright portrayed the father on *ALF*.

EPISODE 91
"The Schloogel Show"

Writers: Ken Estin and Sam Simon
Director: Noam Pitlik
Cast
Vicki DeStefano: Anne De Salvo
Arnie Ross: Wallace Shawn
Marcia Wallace: Herself
Judy Griffith: Murphy Cross
Susan McDaniel: Carlene Watkins

Simka and Latka announce that they are having a "schloogel," a sort of matchmaking party for friends. They fix up each cabbie with a mate, and we watch the couples as they chat at Mario's.

Classic Quote

JIM: Why, you're Carol, as played by Marcia Wallace!

Classic Guest Star: Marcia Wallace played Carol Kester Bondurant on *The Bob Newhart Show*.

Carlene Watkins later married *Taxi* writer Ed. Weinberger.

For the Record: In this episode we hear the theme song from "The Love Boat"—but not the version sung by Jack Jones for the ABC series. This rendition is by a singer whose identity remains shrouded in mystery, controversy, and superstition to this day.

Alex's phone number is 555-2437. The last four digits spell C-H-E-R!

EPISODE 92
"Alex Goes Off the Wagon"

Writer: Danny Kallis
Director: Noam Pitlik
Cast
Japanese Gambler: Keone Young
Craps Table Stickman: Anthony Charnota
Lady Gambler: Carolyn DeMirjian

After ex-gambler Alex wins $2,000 on a fluke bet in Atlantic City, greedy Louie pushes him to take advantage of his good luck at a craps table. Unfortunately, Alex's luck is crappy, and he slides back into compulsive gambling.

Classic Scene: Fortunately, this serious subject matter is balanced with the lightness of Reverend Jim's being. Alex and Jim's trust and friendship are tested in the poignant closing scene. In a none-too-subtle metaphor for enlightenment, Alex and Jim stare at a light fixture in the bathroom.

Parallel Plot: Episode 38 also deals with a gambling problem, in that case Jim's.

EPISODE 93

"Jim's Inheritance"

Writer: Ken Estin
Director: Noam Pitlik
Cast
Attorney John Bickers: Dick Sargent
Judge: F. William Parker
Perez: Santos Morales
Winslow: Richard Monahan

Jim's father has died and left Jim a huge fortune, but Jim's brothers and sisters go to court to have Jim declared incompetent. Although Alex and Louie make sincere pleas on his behalf, Jim loses his fight—and the money. (Jim will still get a hefty allowance, spent in various ways in later episodes.) But when Jim plays a cassette tape that he finds in his father's old suit, he hears an encouraging musical message from his dear departed dad: "You Are the Sunshine of My Life."

B-Plot: Tony's George Steinbrenner theory.

Classic Quote
JIM: I'm gonna get my three and a half million! Or fail to do so.

Classic Performance: Christopher Lloyd, who earned an Emmy for Outstanding Acting in a Comedy Series for this season, again puts in a brilliant performance. His heartfelt monologue is moving yet hilarious, clearly Emmy bait.

Classic Guest Star: Need we remind you that Dick Sargent was the second Darrin Stephens on *Bewitched?*

Classic Scene: When Louie hears that Jim's inheritance is $3.5 million, he knocks the window screens off his dispatcher cage.

For the Record: Christopher Lloyd claims that the scene in which he is going through his father's belongings was enhanced by a freak staging accident. When Jim drapes his father's enormous suit over a nearby chair, it reclines under the weight. Apparently this was not planned, but it certainly added to the gravity of the scene.

For the Record 2: What's up with Elaine's hairdo?

Awards: This episode was nominated for an Emmy for Outstanding Writing in a Comedy Series.

EPISODE 94

"Scenskees from a Marriage," Part One

Writers: Howard Gewirtz and Ian Praiser
Director: Noam Pitlik
Cast
Reverend Gorky: Vincent Schiavelli
Mascha: Peter Elbling
Cindy Bates: Allyce Beasley

Latka goes to the rescue of a blizzard-stranded female cabdriver, and in order to keep warm and save their lives, they resort to having sex. Latka and Simka then go to their church to seek guidance in their marital crisis. There they learn that, since Latka has been unfaithful to Simka, she must now be unfaithful to him—with one of his co-workers.

Classic Quote
SIMKA (*the instant she sees Latka*): You did it with another woman!

Classic Scene: As Reverend Gorky speaks in his native tongue, Mascha translates—with comical results.

Classic Guest Star: Allyce Beasley is known to TV viewers as Agnes Dipesto of *Moonlighting* and as Coach's daughter on *Cheers.* Allyce met her future husband, Vincent Schiavelli, during the filming of this *Taxi* episode.

Favorite: Of James L. Brooks.

EPISODE 95

"Scenskees from a Marriage," Part Two

Writers: Howard Gewirtz and Ian Praiser
Director: Noam Pitlik

Simka must now sleep with one of Latka's coworkers. But which one?

Classic Quote
SIMKA (*as she seduces Alex*): Now peel me like a grape so I can get outta here!

Classic Scene: Latka tearfully invites the male cabbies to a party at which he will choose one man for Simka to sleep with. Later, Simka tries every trick in the seduction book in her vain attempt to woo Alex into bed.

EPISODE 96

"Alex the Gofer"

Writer: David Lloyd
Director: Michael Lessac
Cast
Producer: Matthew Laurence
Director: David Paymer
Actress: Caren Kaye

On Broadway, a gofer performs menial tasks such as "go for coffee" in order to get a whiff of the greasepaint. And when theater-lover Alex gets a chance to moonlight near the limelight, he says "Down in front!" to his self-respect and enters from stage left.

B-Plot: Latka has a cold.

Classic Guest Stars: David Paymer played the weaselly TV producer J. J. Enright in the film *Quiz Show*, and Matthew Laurence starred in the short-lived Fox sitcom *Duet.*

Classic Scene: As Alex inflates an air cushion—one of his many demeaning theatrical duties—Louie tries to sneak past him to the rhythm of each breath.

EPISODE 97

"Louie's Revenge"

Writer: Sam Simon
Director: Stan Daniels
Cast
Emily: Andrea Marcovicci
Bartender: Charlie Stavola

When a girl from Louie's past comes back into his life, he at first enjoys the relationship. But soon he realizes he's become an obedient weenie, and he schemes to spring himself out of the girlfriend trap.

B-Plot: Jim and Alex discuss the movie *E.T.*

Classic Scene: After a triumphant night with the drunken Emily, Louie uses a handy camera and tripod to snap a quick conquest photo of the two of them in bed.

For the Record: We first met Emily in episode 72.

EPISODE 98

"Travels with My Dad"

Writer: Barton Dean
Director: Michael Zinberg
Cast
Angie Banta: Donnelly Rhodes
Seaman Fergie: Dick Miller
Seaman: Wendall W. Wright

Tony's father, Angie, invites him to become a merchant seaman and sail the high seas like his ol' dad. But, on board the ship, Tony spends time catching up with his father—and throwing up.

B-Plot: Louie asks Jim to *not* answer the phone.

Classic Scene: Only a merchant marine and his prizefighter son could have a sensitive, loving father-son talk while brawling with drunks in a Singapore bar.

Classic Guest Star: Donnelly Rhodes played the ex-con, Dutch, on the TV series *Soap*.

Parallel Plot: Angie's story about a tarantula crawling on his face is reminiscent of Peter Brady's encounter with a crawling creature on *The Brady Bunch*.

EPISODE 99

"Elaine and the Monk"

Writer: David Lloyd
Director: Danny DeVito
Cast
Zifka: Mark Blankfield

Latka introduces the cabbies to Simka's cousin Zifka, a charming, handsome young man who happens to be a monk—on the monastic version of shore leave. Zifka's monastery allows each monk one week of pleasure every ten years, and this week Elaine is available.

B-Plot: Tony farms chinchillas.

Classic Quote
ELAINE (*defending her actions*): I don't toy with monks.

Classic Scene: Elaine and the monk dance to the classic Fred Astaire number "Cheek to Cheek."

For the Record: Elaine's latest apartment number is 3A.

This episode marks Danny DeVito's debut as a director on *Taxi*.

Classic Guest Star: Comic actor Mark Blankfield was a cast member on the late night variety show *Fridays*.

EPISODE 100

"Zena's Honeymoon"

Writer: David Lloyd
Director: Richard Sakai
Cast
Tom Pelton: Peter Jurasik
Waiter: Robert Woberly
Man: Jim Pollack

Zena is getting married, and she returns to the garage to share the good news with everyone. But her good news is the worst news of Louie's life.

Classic Scene: Louie eats a leftover piece of cheese from a sprung mousetrap. Later, when Zena tells him she's getting married, he chugs glass after glass of wine, finishing off an entire bottle in a matter of seconds.

For the Record: If Rhea Perlman looks a little bigger than usual in this episode, it's because she was pregnant with her and Danny DeVito's first child.

Classic Guest Star: Peter Jurasik played Sid the Snitch on *Hill Street Blues.*

EPISODE 101

"Louie Moves Uptown"

Writer: David Lloyd
Director: Michael Zinberg
Cast
Board Members: Lois DeBanzie, Gayle Hunnicutt, Nelson Welch
Penny Marshall: Herself

Louie wants to buy a Manhattan co-op apartment, but he must first be approved by the co-op's arrogant board. While Alex is turned off by their blatantly bigoted screening process, Louie feels right at home.

B-Plot: Jim isn't cashing his inheritance checks.

Classic Cameo: Penny Marshall made this cameo appearance when she was at the height of her *Laverne and Shirley* success. Not only does she sing a few lines from her show's theme song here, but she also moons the co-op board.

Classic Scene: Louie shows his delight in his new apartment as only he can—he makes angels in the shag rug, spits a loogie over the balcony ledge, and pats the posterior of the board's chairwoman.

EPISODE 102

"Crime and Punishment"

Writer: Katherine Green
Director: Stan Daniels
Cast
Ben Ratledge: Allen Goorwitz
Cabbie: Martin Garner
Policeman: Thom Koutsoukos

To save his job, Louie makes Jeff the scapegoat in a car-part-selling scam, then fires him. But when the big boss presses charges and sends Jeff to jail, Alex talks Louie into confessing his crime—with hilarious results.

Classic Performance: Actor Jeff Thomas once again steps out of the shadows of Louie's cage to turn in a stirring performance.

Classic Scene: Because the concept of an honest Louie is such a joke, we all get to laugh with Boss Ratledge at Louie's outrageous, ridiculous, unbelievable—yet truthful—confession.

For the Record: In all previous *Taxi* episodes, the Sunshine Cab Company's boss was a Mr. McKenzie. Perhaps there was a political power play in the garage boardroom.

EPISODE 103

"Get Me through the Holidays"

Writers: Ken Estin and Sam Simon
Director: Michael Zinberg
Cast
Phyllis Bornstein Consuelos: Louise Lasser
Singing Messengers: Joseph Brennan, Hillary Carlip

Alex's ex-wife, Phyllis, knocks on his door on Christmas Eve. She's lonely, alone, desperate, depressed, pathetic—the perfect holiday companion!

B-Plot: Generous Jim makes it a very green Christmas.

Classic Quote
ALEX (*when Phyllis complains even in her prayers*): Phyllis, you're noodging God!

Classic Scene: When Simka pays Louie off so Latka can have the night off, she makes a check out to "the blood-sucking jackal."

For the Record: We find out that Elaine was born on February 4, 1952. By the way, Marilu Henner's real birthday is *April 6, 1952*, a difference of sixty-two days, which corresponds numerologically to—nothing significant.

EPISODE 104

"Alex's Old Buddy"

Writers: Ken Estin and Sam Simon
Director: Richard Sakai
Cast
Shawn: Judith-Marie Bergan
Veterinarian: John Hancock
Buddy the Dog: Tucker the Dog

Alex is reunited with his dog, Buddy, but he soon learns that the old gray dog just ain't what he used to be.

B-Plot: Jim has written a script for *M*A*S*H*.

Classic Quote
ALEX (*on Buddy's bladder-control problem*): Sometimes when I come home, there's a rainbow in here.

Classic Scene: Alex lavishes love and affection on his dying dog, along with gourmet dog food, which Alex's girlfriend inadvertently eats—not once, but twice.

For the Record: Buddy is nineteen years old (that's 133 in dog years).

Parallel Plot: Alex also experienced puppy problems in episode 6.

EPISODE 105

"Sugar Ray Nardo"

Writer: Katherine Green
Director: Danny DeVito
Cast
Jason: David Mendenhall
Benny's mother: Elizabeth Hill
Bulldog Greg: Brad Kesten
Johnny DeCeo: Michael Saucedo

To Elaine's dismay, her son Jason gets bitten by the boxing bug and takes lessons from Tony. But when Jason "The Butcher" Nardo steps into the ring, he busts some heads—and gets his nose broken.

B-Plot: Louie thinks a picture of Jeff's mother is hideous.

Classic Quote
JIM: The ability of two men to put on gloves, stand toe-to-toe in the spirit of sportsmanship, and pummel each other into insensibility is what separates us from the animals.

For the Record: This is the second episode of *Taxi* directed by Danny DeVito.

Parallel Plot: I'm thinkin' *The Karate Kid.*

EPISODE 106

"Alex Gets Burned by an Old Flame"

Writer: Barton Dean
Director: Harvey Miller
Cast
Diane McKenna: Cathie Shirriff
Arm-wrestling Cabbie: Martin Azarow
Waiter: Robert Woberly

Alex falls for a beautiful woman from Jim's hippie past. But when he mocks Jim in front of her, Jim questions Alex's friendship.

B-Plot: Garage arm-wrestling champ Tony has a new foe: Elaine.

Classic Scene: When Alex asks Jim to leave him and Diane alone at dinner, Jim loudly fakes a gastrointestinal attack and embarrasses everyone in the restaurant.

EPISODE 107

"Tony's Baby"

Writer: Dari Daniels
Director: Richard Sakai
Cast
Vicki: Anne De Salvo
Leo Goodman: Keenan Wynn
Referee Gene LeBell: Himself
Announcer Jimmy Lennon: Himself

Tony is preparing for a big fight when his new girlfriend, Vicki, gives him some unexpected news—she's pregnant with his child. Honorable Tony proposes marriage, but when Vicki turns him down, his whole life hits the canvas.

Classic Quote
JIM (*entering Tony's locker room*): You know, I really like your apartment . . . elegant without being pretentious.

Classic Scene: Just as his boxing opponent is declared the winner of the fight, Tony jumps in the air, victorious, as Vicki finally accepts his marriage proposal.

Classic Guest Star: Keenan Wynn, who portrays Tony's manager, also played a boxing manager in Rod Serling's classic teleplay *Requiem for a Heavyweight.*

EPISODE 108
"Jim's Mario's"

Writers: Ken Estin and Sam Simon
Director: Danny DeVito
Cast
Tom: Walter Olkewicz
Inspector Donovan: Peter Iacangelo
Liquor Authority Agent: William Hootkins
Customers: Thomas Murphy, Charles Bouvier
Nun: Sharon Madden
Blonde: Ro Kendall

To his brother Tom's dismay, Jim uses some of his inheritance allowance to buy Mario's. But when Tom gives Jim a one-week ultimatum to make the investment successful, the cabbies must help "Jim's Mario's" turn a profit—and keep its liquor license.

B-Plot: Simka is now selling Sheeshkaflu brand cosmetics.

Classic Quote
JIM (*lovingly justifying Tom's negativity*): That's okay, you don't know my brother Tom . . . he's a pompous ass.

Classic Performance: Alex plays and sings "Ebb Tide" and "Lazy River" at the piano bar.

Classic Scene: Jim buys a cup of coffee from the vending machine—with a rare coin valued at $5,000.

EPISODE 109
"Louie and the Blind Girl"

Writers: Larry Scott Anderson, Ken Estin, Sam Simon, and Al Aidekman
Director: Noam Pitlik
Cast
Judy Griffith: Murphy Cross
Dr. Gordon: David Young

Louie is dating Judy Griffith, a blind girl he met on a blind date arranged by Latka and Simka (see episode 91), and now he wants to marry her. But when Judy announces that an impending operation may restore her vision, Louie worries that she'll hate what she sees.

Classic Quote
When Jim offers to officiate at Louie's wedding, Louie says he'd rather have a baboon do it, to which Jim replies, "I don't blame you. I've seen that. It's lovely."

Classic Scene: To settle a decision, Louie suggests that he and Judy play odds-or-evens. Of course, the blind girl cannot see the outcome of the contest, so Louie cheats to get his way.

EPISODE 110

"Simka's Monthlies"

Writer: Holly Holmberg Brooks
Director: Harvey Miller
Cast
Immigration Officer: Howard Witt

Simka is just one interview away from getting her green card, but her *krimkapoosh* is preventing her from going through with it. Translation: she's suffering from premenstrual syndrome.

Classic Quote
ALEX: Simka's having her . . . monthly problem.
JIM (*knowingly*): Bills, bills, bills.

LATKA (*about Simka*): She's one hot fidgety mama.

Classic Scenes: Louie ridicules Alex and calls him "Reiger the Good," making fun of Alex's constant habit of helping everybody with their problems. Also, Simka's "Bride of Frankenstein" transformation is a hoot.

Our Television Heritage: No TV comedy series had ever dealt with the sensitive issue of PMS before this "Very Special" episode of *Taxi*, and this show's tender treatment of the subject matter earned critical praise and helped raise public awareness.

EPISODE 111

"Arnie Meets the Kids"

Writer: John Markus
Director: Richard Sakai
Cast
Arnie Ross: Wallace Shawn

Elaine's relationship with her boyfriend, Arnie, is going well, but she's a little concerned about taking that inevitable big step—introducing him to her kids.

B-Plot: Latka doesn't want Simka to become ambassador to France. (Now *that's* a B-Plot!)

Classic Quote
ARNIE: As long as there's ice cream to scoop or a riddle to tell or a toy on the shelf, those kids are *mine!*

Classic Guest: Wallace Shawn's films include *The Princess Bride, Manhattan,* and *My Dinner with André.*

For the Record: Elaine's apartment is now 6A. Man, that chick sure moves around a lot.

EPISODE 112

"A Grand Gesture"

Writers: Ken Estin and Sam Simon
Director: Noam Pitlik
Cast
Panhandler: Tracey Walter
Reverend Gorky: Vincent Schiavelli
Cartoonist: Tom Villard
Walt: Benjamin Sherman "Scatman" Crothers

Generous Iggy gives each of the cabbies $1,000 so they can experience how good it feels to give money to the needy. But when Jeff refuses to accept Louie's grand, he's hurt: after all these years, Jeff still doesn't trust Louie. This is the final straight-narrative episode of *Taxi.*

Classic Scene: The tradition in Latka and Simka's country is to staunchly refuse money before accepting it, and when they try to donate their $1,000 to their church, the cavalcade of refusals is hilarious.

Classic Guest Stars: Tom Villard starred in the wacky ABC sitcom *We've Got It Made.* And veteran character actor Scatman Crothers has appeared in a zillion series, including *Chico and the Man.*

EPISODE 113

"Retrospective," Part One

In this first half of a one-hour compilation show, Danny DeVito hosts some highlights from *Taxi*'s five years. Included are Elaine's first appearance (episode 1); Jim and his driver's test (27); Alex and Angela (2); various Latka and Simka stories (87, 94, 95); a Bobby vs. Louie story (14); and Tony and Alex at a gay bar (50).

EPISODE 114

"Retrospective," Part Two

In the second half of this retrospective special, Danny DeVito presents these highlights: Elaine's encounter with Mr. Right (episode 22); Louie's encounter with Zena (25); Jim's psychic warning to Alex (65); Elaine's Broadway number in the garage (44). In the final shot of this episode, a lone cab rides into the sunset, and we hear Louie's voice echoing through the garage: "We got a lot of cabs here, let's hit the streets! Banta, 472! Nardo, 218! Latka, get your butt to work! Iggy, 714! Reiger, 421!"

Welcome Back, Kotter

The *Dobie Gillis* of the 1970s, *Welcome Back, Kotter,* deftly combines touches of reality with slapstick humor, winding up as a funny 1970s ensemble comedy . . . it is a sprightly schoolroom stand-up routine, with ex-stand-up comic Gabe Kaplan acting as a Groucho Marx–type straightman to the punch lines tossed in by the Sweathogs.

—Castleman and Podrazik, *Harry and Wally's Favorite TV Shows*

The appeal of *Welcome Back, Kotter* may be in the smart-aleck one-liners and anti-establishment attitude of the Sweathogs rather than in the show's moral lessons.

—Megan Rosenfield, *The Washington Post,* April 27, 1976

Welcome Back, Kotter is the real thing, the way a poor school is now. The language isn't pretty, but it's honest.

—James Komack, 1975

Kotter is not a show, it is my life. Kotter is the make-believe teacher I wanted to have in Brooklyn.

—Gabe Kaplan, *People,* 1978

Barbarino is the kid of guy you can't help but have a crush on, and your mom can't help but forbid you to date.

—*Seventeen,* October 1977

A sweathog is somebody who perspires a lot and acts like a pig.

—John Travolta, *Celebrity,* October 1976

Like *Chico [and the Man]*, it used the real-seeming tone and style of Norman Lear. But the use of an ensemble cast of eccentrics, a familial emotional support group created not by the family but by a public institution, owed more to Mary Tyler Moore. In many cases, in fact, the families of the Sweathogs were shown to be broken or dysfunctional. High school was family for them, as WJM-TV was family for Mary.

—Gerard Jones, *Honey, I'm Home*

Welcome Back, Kotter made a lot of people stars . . . but the biggest of them all was the swaggering Sweathog, Vinnie Barbarino, played by John Travolta. Right from the start, viewers knew they were in for something special. There had been speculation that Travolta's character would merely be a seventies version of Henry Winkler's fifties Fonzie. Not so. Travolta had an energy, a glow, that permeated his character. There was a star bursting and beaming beneath the character of Vinnie.

—Rick Mitz, *The Great TV Sitcom Book*

Welcome Back, Kotter

on Nick at Nite

The newest show in Nick at Nite's Classic TV lineup, as of this publication, *Welcome Back, Kotter,* was welcomed back with a week devoted to the very best episodes. Each weeknight was devoted to a different catchphrase, and every episode that night contained the phrase. "Up Your Nose Monday" began with the very first episode. "Ooh, Ooh Tuesday" naturally featured the patented hand-raising Horshack. "What? Where? Wednesday" was a very special evening of Vinnie Barbarino at his dumbest and most sensitive. "Hi, There Thursday" was Freddie "Boom Boom" Washington's turn in the spotlight, and "Very Impressive Friday" collected Mr. Kotter's classroom antics, the ones that Horshack judged "very impressive." After that, the show was featured every Friday during Nick at Nite's Block Party Summer, and then it entered the regular schedule.

And don't worry. Juan Luis Pedro Philippo de Huevos Epstein will have his day in the sun before we're through.

MR. KOTTER

Cast

Gabe Kotter: Gabriel Kaplan
Julie Kotter: Marcia Strassman
Vinnie Barbarino: John Travolta
Freddie "Boom Boom" Washington: Lawrence Hilton Jacobs
Juan Luis Pedro Philippo de Huevos Epstein: Robert Hegyes
Arnold Horshack: Ron Palillo
Michael Woodman: John Sylvester White

SERIES REGULARS

Judy Borden: Helaine Lembeck
Todd Ludlow: Dennis Bowen
Rosalie "Hotsy" Totsy: Debralee Scott
Carvelli: Charles Fleischer
Murray: Robert Harcum
Verna Jean: Vernée Watson
Beau De LaBarre: Stephen Shortridge
Mary Johnson: Irene Arranga

EPISODE 1

"Pilot"

Writer: Peter Meyerson
Director: James Komack

In this very first episode of *Welcome Back, Kotter*, cleverly titled "Pilot," Gabe Kotter returns to his alma mater, James Buchanan High School, to teach a group of bell-bottomed remedial students known as Sweathogs. These juvenile delinquents don't want to be taught—until, that is, they discover Mr. Kotter was once a sweathog himself. Oddly enough, even though Kotter is teaching in a Brooklyn public high school, his classroom consists of only nine or so students. With that impressive faculty-to-student ratio, it's a wonder these Sweathogs aren't academic scholars.

Classic Quote
The line "Up your nose with a rubber hose" is first uttered by Vinnie Barbarino. It becomes the Sweathog battle cry.

For the Record: "Pilot" was the only episode directed by James Komack, the executive producer of *Welcome Back, Kotter*. Komack was also the creative force behind *Chico and the Man* and *The Courtship of Eddie's Father*, in which he also portrayed the nutty best friend with the high-powered-TV-executives-hybrid name Norman Tinker.

EPISODE 2

"The Election"

Writers: Eric Cohen and Tiffany York
Director: Bob LaHendro
Cast
Scott: Jeff Martin

It's election time at James Buchanan High, and for the first time, a Sweathog has a chance to become student body president. But Vinnie, suffering under the intense pressure that so often surrounds a high school campaign, considers dropping out of the race. But with Kotter's help, Vinnie and the other Sweathogs learn a little about the election system and a little about themselves.

Classic Quote
KOTTER: It's okay, Mr. Woodman, you can use the word. "Sweathog" is a term of affection and endearment.

Classic Performance: Kotter teaches the Sweathogs all about presidential conventions with his one-man rendition of a rowdy convention floor.

For the Record: Freddie "Boom Boom" Washington delivers his signature "Hi, there" greeting for the first time in this episode. Notice, though, that Kotter is first to say "Hi, there," and Washington merely repeats it. This simple salutation went on to become a "Boom Boom" catchphrase.

EPISODE 3

"Basket Case"

Writer: Jerry Ross
Director: Bob LaHendro
Cast
Coach: Jess Nadelman

Freddie "Boom Boom" Washington makes the varsity basketball team and decides that, as a star athlete, he doesn't need to take Kotter's exam. Not surprisingly, Kotter is unhappy and spends the rest of the episode showing Washington the importance of an education.

Classic Quote
WASHINGTON: If you got it, flaunt it.
EPSTEIN: And if you ain't got it, you're Horshack.

For the Record: Barbarino first thrills the TV audience with his "What? Where?" routine in this episode. That expression becomes the pompadoured Sweathog's catchphrase and an instant TV Classic.

Also in this episode, Epstein brandishes the first of many notes signed "Epstein's Mother," excusing him for being absent, from taking exams, and even from participating in gang rumbles.

EPISODE 4

"Whodunit"

Writers: Jerry Rannow and Jewel Jaffe Rannow
Director: Bob LaHendro

Rosalie "Hotsie" Totzi tells Kotter she's pregnant and that one of his Sweathogs is responsible. Kotter systematically cross-examines the Sweathogs, and eventually Horshack takes responsibility. Obviously, however he's only playing the martyr. Rosalie drops another bomb when she confesses that she's not really pregnant: she made the whole story up to stop the Sweathogs from spreading the rumor that she was promiscuous.

Classic Quotes
KOTTER: Boy what an honor. In my class, all four Marx Brothers: Wacko, Stupo, Jerko, and Dummo.

HORSHACK: You know, Horshack is a very old and respected name. It means "the cattle are dying."

EPISODE 5

"The Great Debate"

Writer: Rick Mittleman
Director: Bob LaHendro
Cast
Alex Welles: James Woods

In the spirit of such great debates as Lincoln vs. Douglas and Kennedy vs. Nixon, the Sweathogs take on the brainy Turkeys in a showdown of verbal fisticuffs. The topic: Humans Are Naturally Aggressive.

Classic Guest Star: Yes, that's acclaimed film actor James Woods appearing as the ascot-wearing debate teacher, Alex Welles, a short-lived character who never quite takes off.

Classic Performance: While commanding the debate podium, Washington acts like an overly charismatic preacher. It's a bit he will return to in future episodes.

Classic Quote
WOODMAN: This debate is canceled on account of dumbness.

For the Record: When Welles refers to Kotter's students as Sweathogs, Kotter takes offense and

tells him that "no enlightened educator would call a child a Sweathog." But earlier, in episode 2, Kotter defended the use of that term. (The air is thick with inconsistency.)

This is the first episode in which Arnold Horshack pleads for attention by raising his hand and calling "ooh, ooh," perhaps the most renowned of all Sweathog trademarks. As a young student, actor Ron Palillo actually cried "ooh, ooh" before shouting out answers to teachers' questions. Once again, art imitates life.

EPISODE 6

"No More Mr. Nice Guy"

Writer: George Yanok
Director: Bob LaHendro

It's a case of trading places, when Vice Principal Woodman becomes the Sweathogs' pal while Mr. Kotter acts as the school disciplinarian. But when Woodman discovers it was the Sweathogs who hid his beloved yellow chalk, he flips out, and things go back to normal at James Buchanan High.

For the Record: In a rare vocal cameo, the voice of the elusive principal, Mr. Lazarus, is heard on the school intercom.

EPISODE 7

"One of Our Sweathogs Is Missing"

Writer: Marilyn Miller
Director: Bob LaHendro

Juan Epstein, Buchanan High's toughest kid, the kid who was voted "most likely to take a life," runs away after getting beaten up by the nerdy Todd Ludlow. The rest of the Sweathogs conduct an all-out dragnet to find their lost pal. In the end, Kotter teaches the guys that brains are more important than brawn. He also explains how his nose got so big.

Classic Quote

KOTTER: Arnold, you can't trust a knish.

EPISODE 8

"Classroom Marriage

Writers: William Raynor and Myles Wilder
Director: Bob LaHendro

When Washington and his girlfriend Verna Jean threaten to run off and get married, Mr. Kotter uses valuable class time to convince the couple that marriage might be a mistake. Be sure to catch Kotter's wide-collared, leaf-print dress shirt in the opening scene—a distressing reminder of seventies fashions.

Classic Quote

WOODMAN (to Kotter): The world is divided into two parts: us and them. And they're them. And, come to think of it, you're them, too.

EPISODE 9

"Mr. Kotter, Teacher"

Writers: Jerry Rannow and Jewel Jaffe Rannow
Director: Bob LaHendro
Cast
Charlie Piper: Arnold Soboloff
Ms. Riley: Hope Summers

Kotter argues that although his teaching methods may be unorthodox, they are effective. But crusty old Woodman is fed up with all the classroom shenanigans and brings Kotter up on charges for failing to use the required textbooks, for not following the prescribed curriculum, and for doing his Groucho Marx impression in the classroom.

For the Record: In this episode we learn that Woodman's first name is Michael.

Classic Performance: In a classic entrance, the Sweathogs strut into Kotter's classroom in unison. The strut is not quite the hustle, not quite the freak, but definitely a behavioral relic from an earlier era.

Classic Quote

MS. RILEY (imitating Groucho Marx): I was a teacher myself for forty-odd years, and they were forty of the oddest years I've ever known.

EPISODE 10

"Barbarino's Girl"

Writer: Eric Cohen
Director: Bob LaHendro

The shroud of despair has draped itself around Buchanan High's classroom 11 in the form of midterm report cards. It goes without saying that the Sweathogs' grades are less than stellar, but Barbarino's report card seems to be the worst. To get his grades up, Barbarino enlists the brainy Judy Borden as his tutor, then suffers humiliation from his fellow classmates. But it's pure sensitive Vinnie in the end, when he actually asks Judy out on a date.

Classic Quote

BARBARINO (explaining to Kotter how his saintly mother will react to his report card): You probably got no idea what it feels like to get hit with beads.

Classic Scene: In a classic scene featuring the art of insults—"ranking" or "the dozens," as they are commonly known—Judy, Barbarino, and Kotter exchange barbs. Some of the more memorable insults: "You're so low, you could crawl under a pregnant ant," "I understand there are three kids in your family—one of each," and "When you were born, they took one look at your face, then turned you over and said, 'Hey look, twins.'"

EPISODE 11

"The Reunion"

Writer: George Yanok
Director: Bob LaHendro
Cast
Lyle Flannagan: Michael Taylor
Mary Francis: Bridget Hanley

Envy rears its ugly head when Kotter's old high school chum, Lyle Flannagan, drops in for dinner. Not only is Lyle rich and successful, but he never had a pimple in high school. Who wouldn't envy him? In the end, it's the Sweathogs who show Kotter just how lucky he really is.

Classic Quote
KOTTER: Lyle Flannagan was the nicest boy who ever went to Buchanan. He was so nice he would help old ladies cross their legs.

EPISODE 12

"California Dreamin'"

Writer: Michael Weinberger
Director: Bob LaHendro
Cast
Bambi: Susan Lanier

The Sweathogs go ga-ga for the sexy new student, Bambi, but she has the hots for Mr. Kotter. With some understanding, some reasoning, and some strong urging from Julie, Kotter finds out the real reason Bambi is starved for attention.

Classic Line
BAMBI (*describing Epstein*): Wow, he's magic!
KOTTER: Yeah, maybe one day he'll disappear.

Classic Performance: Barbarino tries to gain the attention of Bambi with his trademark "Ba-Ba-Barbarino" song-and-dance routine. Notice the now legendary disco pose Barbarino assumes, foreshadowing John Travolta's *Saturday Night Fever* performance.

For the Record: Though Susan Lanier made only this one appearance on *Welcome Back, Kotter*, fans of 1970s TV may recognize her from the short-lived *Tony Orlando and Dawn Rainbow Hour* and the even shorter lived sitcom *Szysznyk*.

Parallel Plot: Kotter gets in hot water in episode 68, in which he is suspected of having a fling with another female student.

EPISODE 13

"Arrividerci, Arnold"

Writers: Jerry Rannow and Jewel Jaffe Rannow
Director: Bob LaHendro

Horshack's improved grades makes him eligible to leave the remedial class and join "the real world." After discovering that life away from the Sweathogs is difficult, Horshack yearns to return to the old gang. Without even making an effort to fit in with the new class or to live up to his potential, Horshack is reunited with Kotter's Sweathogs, and once again everyone is happy. The lesson here: when the going gets tough, whine a little until they send you back to where you can easily coast through life.

Classic Scene: In a version of the classic Harpo Marx mirror routine, Horshack and Kotter do a bit dressed as identical Horshacks, complete with matching striped scarves, oversized olive jackets, and lunch boxes.

Classic Quote

KOTTER: Am I crazy or do I see Arnold Horshack nestled to my wife's bosom?

For the Record: Barbarino tells Horshack he has to go meet Bonzo Maretti. Bonzo Maretti, of course, is a former Sweathog whom Kotter keeps talking about. Two other episodes in which he's mentioned include 34 and 37.

EPISODE 14
"The Sit-in"

Writers: William Bickley and Michael Warren
Director: Bob LaHendro

Teen angst is the focus when the Sweathogs rebel against liver being served in the high school cafeteria. Kotter and the Sweathogs organize a protest sit-in, then wind up spending the entire night in the classroom. As hunger sets in, Julie Kotter comes to the rescue with her infamous tuna casserole—the subject of a running joke throughout the entire series.

For the Record: Is it more than a coincidence that Epstein walks and talks like Chico Marx? Not really. Actor Robert Hegyes based the Epstein character on a combination of his podiatrist brother and the legendary Marx Brother.

Could the writer of this episode be the actor who went on to play Officer Bobby Hill on *Hill Street Blues?*

EPISODE 15
"The Longest Weekend"

Writer: Carl Kleinschmitt
Director: Bob LaHendro

When Julie goes away for an innocent ski weekend, the Sweathogs are convinced she's up to no good. A jealous Kotter tries to while away the time by inviting the Sweathogs over for a Friday night poker game. Dig those crazy sunglasses Epstein wears throughout this episode.

Classic Performance: While alone in his classroom, Gabe Kaplan showcases his natural gift for mimicry by impersonating a German ski instructor trying to woo Julie—though it could also be an impression of Colonel Klink.

Classic Quote

JULIE: I'm an intelligent person. I'm a college graduate. What am I doing? I'm watching meat loaf.

For the Record: With his partner, Dale McRaven, Carl Kleinschmitt wrote numerous episodes of *The Dick Van Dyke Show,* including number 125, "Br-room, Br-room."

EPISODE 16

"Dr. Epstein, I Presume"

Teleplay: George Yanok
Story: Ann Gibbs, Joel Kimmel, and
George Yanok
Director: Bob LaHendro
Cast
Ms. Helms: Laura Zucker

Epstein disrupts social studies class with his pet hamster, so Kotter encourages him to become a veterinarian. Epstein wants to get into medical school, but his aptitude tests suggest he won't even make it out of the remedial class. On that sour note, the doomed Sweathog gives all of his pets to Kotter, then delivers a pair of baby hamsters.

Classic Scene: While Epstein's hamster, Florence, goes into delivery, the Sweathogs don emergency medical outfits. Where did a group of high school ruffians get the doctor uniforms and equipment? Nobody knows.

Parallel Plot: In *The Patridge Family*, the birth of hamsters serves to remind the assembled rock-and-roll family of the miracle of life.

EPISODE 17

"Follow the Leader," Part One

Writers: Jerry Rannow and Jewel Jaffe
Rannow
Director: Bob LaHendro

When Barbarino, like many other dictators, is overthrown as leader in a Sweathog revolution, he winds up quitting school. At the same time, Kotter experiences his own problems when Julie walks out on him for spending too much time with the Sweathogs.

For the Record: Be sure to catch Barbarino's priest disguise, complete with bald wig and eyeglasses.

Classic Quote
JULIE *(to Kotter):* They're not students, they're inmates. And you're the head cuckoo.

EPISODE 18

"Follow the Leader," Part Two

Writers: Jerry Rannow and Jewel Jaffe
Rannow
Director: Bob LaHendro

Kotter's life is turned upside down when Julie leaves him. Barbarino sleeps on his couch, and Washington abuses his power as the newly appointed Sweathog leader.

Classic Quote
BARBARINO: You don't need brains to get a job, and I'm gonna prove it.

For the Record: In this episode we learn that Julie's college major was anthropology.

EPISODE 19

"One Flu over the Cuckoo's Nest"

Writer: Eric Cohen
Director: Bob LaHendro

A flu epidemic has run rampant through James Buchanan High, and the absent teaching staff has forced the academically enriched class to join Kotter and the Sweathogs. This is the first and only episode in which Juan Epstein, the Buchanan con artist, presents a legitimate excuse for being absent from school.

Classic Quote
JUDY: You don't know who Amerigo Vespucci was?
BARBARINO: Of course I know who he was. It was Chef Boyardee's maiden name.

Classic Performance: Kotter does a song-and-dance impersonation of James Cagney, with the Sweathogs backing him up as the chorus.

For the Record: In episode 5, James Woods played Alex Welles, the teacher of the academically enriched class. Mysteriously, there was never any mention of Welles after that episode, and apparently Ms. Fishbeck became their teacher.

EPISODE 20
"The Telethon"

Writers: Pat Proft and Bo Kapral
Director: Bob LaHendro
Cast
Oliver Niles: Jerry Rannow

In a move that sounds unconstitutional, Woodman announces that he will drop the remedial program unless someone raises $700 for the school budget, so Kotter and the gang put on a telethon to save the Sweathog class. Not surprisingly, the anonymous Sweathogs who sit in class like lifeless slugs also spend the telethon silently in the background.

Classic Performance: This episode is chock-full of great and not so great performances.

Among the better acts is Kotter and the Sweathogs' stirring rendition of "Me and My Shadow." Also, John Travolta demonstrates his flair for disco, performing the "Ba-Ba-Barbarino" song and dance outfitted in a shiny gold disco suit.

Favorite: Of Gabe Kaplan . . . at least it's *one* of his favorites. As he explained, there was just more comedy improv on this particular episode, and everyone went nuts and had a good time. It shows.

Classic Cameo: He may not look familiar, but the actor who played cheesy TV director Oliver Niles was Jerry Rannow, a regular writer for *Welcome Back, Kotter.* Before *Kotter,* he was a writer for the popular early seventies series *Love, American Style*—another TV comedy with a comma in the title.

EPISODE 21
"Mr. Kotter Makes Good"

Writer: George Yanok
Director: Bob LaHendro

School records indicate that Kotter never took his high school finals, and now Vice Principal Woodman insists he make them up. So, with the help of his Sweathogs, Kotter spends the weekend boning up for finals. To get into the role of teacher, Horshack dresses up as Mr. Kotter, though he could also pass for defense attorney Alan Dershowitz.

Classic Quote
KOTTER: I don't have to know anything. I'm a teacher.

For the Record: This is the final episode of the first season.

EPISODE 22

"Father Vinnie"

Writer: Eric Cohen
Director: Bob LaHendro

What! Vinnie a priest? When Barbarino's dying grandmother requests that her well-coiffed grandson becomes a man of the cloth, Vinnie goes overboard with his newfound religious calling. Luckily his buddies are there to pull this heavenly Sweathog back down to earth.

Classic Quote
EPSTEIN: Roses are red, violets are blue, I've been home two days with the Asian flu.

EPISODE 23

"Sweatside Story"

Writer: Eric Cohen
Director: Bill Persky

In spite of their pretty pink satin jackets, the Sweathogs have evolved into a tough new street gang. When Freddie gets roughed up by a group of New Utrecht students, the Sweathogs seek revenge by declaring a full-scale schoolyard rumble. However, they quickly realize that they are completely chicken and don't want to get hurt. Feeling pressure to join the gang, Horshack dresses up in what looks like a Fonzie outfit and tries to inspire fear. The night of the rumble arrives, and Kotter, Horshack, and Woodman all show up decked out as gang members. When the other gang comes to understand that the Sweathogs' gang includes a teacher and the vice principal, they're impressed. They decide that maybe they can settle their misunderstanding later, without knives.

Classic Quotes
KOTTER: In Nebraska, a rumble is when your cow has a gas attack.

WOODMAN: Barbarino, the only reason you've got a head is to separate your ears.

Classic Performance: If you think you've seen John Travolta move weird, check out the gang rumble scene, in which he struts forward, exaggerating his tough guy walk so much that he appears to be convulsing.

Classic Guest Star: After playing the annoying punk Carvelli on *Welcome Back, Kotter*, comic-actor Charles Fleischer provided the voice of the cartoon bunny in the hit film *Who Framed Roger Rabbit?* This episode marked the first of many Carvelli appearances on *Welcome Back, Kotter*.

For the Record: Director Bill Persky was a regular writer for Sid Caesar's *Your Show of Shows* as well as *The Dick Van Dyke Show*.

EPISODE 24

"A Love Story"

Writers: Jerry Rannow and Jewel Jaffe Rannow
Directors: James Komack and Gary Shimokawa
Cast
Carmen Epstein: Lisa Mordente

Hormones run amok after Juan Epstein's younger sister, Carmen, joins the remedial class. While Barbarino and Horshack compete for the hand of the young lady, Juan is chained to the lockers. All this romance incites Kotter to lecture on the mysteries of love.

Classic Guest Star: Lisa Mordente is the daughter of musical theater legend Chita Rivera.

For the Record: Don't get too attached to Carmen Epstein. Like so many of the female Sweathogs, after only one episode she is never heard from again.

EPISODE 25

"Gabe under Pressure"

Writer: George Yanouk
Director: Bob LaHendro

Buchanan's students are being given free physical examinations, and Gabe—who feels just fine, thanks—is pressured to submit to a long-overdue checkup along with all the others.

EPISODE 26

"The Museum"

Writer: Bob Shayne
Director: Bill Davis
Cast
Museum Curator: John Astin

Kotter and the Sweathogs get the wits scared out of them when they are locked in a mummy's tomb with a weird museum curator and an ancient corpse. Abbott and Costello, move over.

Classic Guest Star: John Astin, is, of course, best known for his TV portrayal of the creepy and eccentric Gomez on *The Addams Family*.

Favorite: Of Ron Palillo and Robert Hegyes. Both actors enjoyed working with John Astin so much that they consider this episode one of their favorites.

For the Record: Barbarino debuts his latest catchphrase, the frantic "I'm so confuse!" cry, in this episode.

EPISODE 27

"Career Day"

Writer: Eric Cohen
Director: Bill Hobin
Cast
Mr. Takahashi: Pat Morita
Mr. Ferguson: George Yanok

All the Asian stereotypes are pulled out when a Japanese inventor, Mr. Takahashi, visits the Sweathog class on Career Day. Takahashi decides he likes the cut of Kotter's jib and offers him a lucrative job at his Chicago-based company. Now Kotter must make a big decision: go for the gold or stay with the Sweathogs.

Classic Quote
MR. TAKAHASHI: I never forget the time I sitting in subway and the lady next to me hear Wolfman Jack howling in my pants.

Classic Guest Star: Pat Morita, one of the most versatile actors in TV and films, flipped hamburgers as Arnold on *Happy Days*, then went on to beat up punks as Mr. Miyagi in the Karate Kid movies.

Classic Cameo: No, that isn't Bob Keeshan playing the arrogant disc jockey, Mr. Ferguson. It's one of the regular writers for this series, George Yanok, in a rare cameo.

EPISODE 28

"Inherit the Halibut"

Writers: George Tricker and Neil Rosen
Director: Bill Hoben

Someone has stolen the Sweathogs' treasury money—and coincidentally, Freddie just bought a new bike. Kotter and the Sweathogs put Freddie on trial to unravel this mysterious case of the vanishing eight dollars. Notice that Verna Jean, who agreed to marry Freddie in episode number eight, is the first to accuse her former fiancé of embezzlement.

For the Record: Usually the students enter and leave Kotter's social studies class any time they please. This is conveniently the only episode in which Kotter fines them for tardiness. The money goes to the class treasury.

The title of this episode is a takeoff on *Inherit the Wind,* a play about the famous Scopes trail of 1925. The 1960 movie version, directed by Stanley Kramer, starred Spencer Tracy and featured Classic TV stars Dick York, Harry Morgan, and Claude Akins. The film was in many ways superior to this episode—but didn't have as many jokes.

Classic Quote
KOTTER: You can't pardon someone unless you first establish that they're guilty. This is a court, not the White House.

EPISODE 29

"The Sweathog Clinic for Smoking"

Writers: Eric Cohen and Steve Hayden
Director: Bob LaHendro

Like many reckless youths, Epstein jeopardizes his health for the momentary pleasure of a cigarette. And even though we've never seen him light up in any previous episodes, Epstein claims he's been smoking on and off since age twelve. To rid him of his nicotine habit, Kotter and the other Sweathogs go all out and create a zany smoking-aversion clinic.

Classic Scene: Horshack and Kotter ham it up as bumbling doctors as they try to break Epstein's smoking habit. The scene is reminiscent of vaudeville comedy, and the jokes illustrate why vaudeville is no longer around.

Classic Quote
BARBARINO (*combing his hair*): You see, when you're the Sweathog heartthrob, you've got a responsibility to look perfect.

EPISODE 30

"Chicken à la Kotter"

Writer: Raymond Siller
Director: Bob LaHendro

In an episode reflecting the tough economic struggles of the seventies, Kotter takes on a part-time job to pay for his $1,200 root-canal procedure. With no other job prospects in sight, he's forced to dress up like a giant chicken for the Mr. Chicken restaurant chain.

Classic Quote

KOTTER (*in chicken outfit*): There are a lot of people in this town worse off than I am.

HORSHACK: Oh, I know. There's a man down the block in the hot dog stand dressed as a weenie . . . and he doesn't even work there.

Classic Performance: Gabe Kotter, in chicken costume and yellow leotards, performs a cabaret rendition of "Everything's Coming Up Roses."

Favorite: Of Gabe Kotter—*not*. He hated the chicken suit.

EPISODE 31

"The Fight"

Writers: Jerry Rannow and Jewel Jaffe Rannow
Director: Bob LaHendro

All because Vinnie forgot to do Washington's homework, there's an all-out, every-Sweathog-for-himself fight in which they all stop speaking to one another. Watch for the long-building pratfall when Epstein precariously sets his delicate home-crafted model boat on a chair, and Horshack accidentally sits on it. Did *you* see it coming?

Classic Quote

Putting a clever spin on the "Up your nose" bit, Barbarino hurls a new insult: "In your pants with a bag of ants."

EPISODE 32

"Sweathog, Nebraska Style"

Writer: George Yanok
Director: Bob LaHendro
Cast
Jenny: Susan Pratt

Romance blooms in Bensonhurst when Julie Kotter's younger sister, Jenny, comes for a visit and is charmed by the Brillo-haired Epstein. But situation comedy means doomed romance, and their whirlwind courtship lasts only thirty minutes. Then Jenny heads back to Nebraska.

Classic Quote

KOTTER: You lead a really exciting life, Mr. Woodman. What do you do for fun at home? Sit there and watch your suits go out of style?

For the Record: In this episode we learn that Julie's maiden name is Hansen.

Our Television Heritage: This is rarity: an episode title that includes a comma in a series whose title includes a comma. Overall, very few television show titles carry a comma. A few of these are *Love, American Style*, *Mary Hartman, Mary Hartman* and *Magnum, P.I.* In any case, *Welcome Back, Kotter* may not have invented title punctuation—the hyphens of *The A-Team* and *Laugh-in* leap to mind, as do the asterisks of *M*A*S*H*, *Kate & Allie's* ampersand, and, of course, the periods in *The Man from U.N.C.L.E.*— but none used punctuation any more effectively. One might even say that they paved the way for such groundbreaking choices as the dollar sign in *Vega$* and the unusual capitalization of *CHiPs*.

EPISODE 33

"Sadie Hawkins Day"

Teleplay: Eric Cohen
Story: Steven Clements and Joyce Cittlin
Director: Bob LaHendro

No girl has asked Barbarino to the Sadie Hawkins dance, and now the hunky Sweathog is feeling mighty low. Even crusty Vice Principal Woodman has a date. Fans of the disco craze—and who isn't, really?—will especially love this episode, complete with hustle lessons from Freddie "Boom Boom" Washington.

Classic Quote
KOTTER (*to Barbarino*): I think your pants are under arrest.

EPISODE 34

"Hello, Ms. Chips"

Writers: Royce D. Applegate and Ira Miller
Director: Bob LaHendro

The new student teacher has a hard time connecting with the Sweathogs, so she decides to quit teaching. But the Sweathogs prove their hearts are as big as their hair by advising Ms. Wright not to give up and to just be herself. Apparently Ms. Wright does quit, though, because she is never seen or heard from in any future episodes.

Classic Quote
KOTTER: This is a very famous classroom here, Ms. Wright. Some of the best teachers in the city have passed through these windows.

For the Record: James Buchanan, for whom the high school was named, was the fifteenth U.S. president. He was the only president who never married, was considered very dull, and was in some ways responsible for the Civil War.

EPISODE 35

"Whatever Happened to Arnold?" Part One

Writers: Peter Meyerson and Nick Arnold
Director: Bob LaHendro

The good natured barbs are carried a little too far, and Horshack runs away after the guys tease him for joining the school theater group. In a surprisingly insensitive display, Kotter's main concern is to fill Horshack's role as Cyrano de Bergerac instead of searching for the ungainly and emotional Sweathog. After the performance, Kotter's instincts tell him something may be seriously wrong with the still-missing Horshack.

Classic Performance: Barbarino gives new meaning to the word "ham" with his reckless portrayal of Cyrano de Bergerac.

EPISODE 36

"Whatever Happened to Arnold?" Part Two

Writers: Jerry Rannow and Jewel Jaffe Rannow
Directors: James Komack and Bob LaHendro

Arnold was lost, but now is found. Ron Palillo was making a pilot for another series! The story? Well, Arnold's fifth father passed away, leaving the "ooh, ooh" Sweathog to become the head of the whole Horshack clan. Very impressive!

Our Television Heritage: This episode was written and produced as a pilot for a sitcom that would feature the whole Horshack family. Though it is a fine episode, misguided Hollywood executives passed on it.

EPISODE 37

"Horshack vs. Carvelli"

Writer: Garry Shandling
Director: Bob LaHendro

The delinquent Carvelli challenges Horshack to a Silver Gloves boxing match. In order to save face, Horshack accepts—and winds up getting his face punched in.

Parallel Plot: This episode pays homage to one of the classic TV comedy situations: the mismatched boxing challenge. This plot device was used in many other TV sitcoms, including *The Honeymooners, Happy Days, M*A*S*H, Taxi,* and *Three's Company.*

Classic Quote
WOODMAN: We're going to need a real powerhouse against Carvelli.
WASHINGTON (*looking at Horshack*): Would you settle for a power failure?

For the Record: Garry Shandling has become a big star through *The Tonight Show, It's the Garry Shandling Show,* and *The Larry Sanders Show.* But back in the seventies, the struggling comedian used his talents behind the camera writing for many sitcoms, including this one.

EPISODE 38

"Hark, the Sweat Kings"

Writers: Peter Meyerson and Nick Arnold
Director: Bob LaHendro
Cast
Angelo: Michael V. Gazzo

The Sweathogs are touched by the Christmas spirit after giving their homeless pal, Angelo, a second chance in life.

Classic Guest Star: Character actor Michael V. Gazzo portrayed the weaselly Frankie "Five Angels" Pantangalli in *The Godfather, Part II.*

Classic Line: ANGELO (*to the Sweathogs*): You guys are as funny as a pork chop at a bar mitzvah.

EPISODE 39

"Sweatgate Scandal"

Teleplay: Eric Cohen
Story: Paul Wayne and Gabriel Grunfield
Director: Bob LaHendro

In a Sweathog version of *All the President's Men,* Barbarino and Epstein become investigative reporters to unmask the faculty member who replaced the cafeteria liver with a meat substitute. Truth has a price, but Kotter and the Sweathogs are willing to pay it, in the name of virtue, justice, and fresh liver.

For the Record: Look for Kotter's felt-collared tuxedo and peach-colored three-piece suit.

Classic Quote
HORSHACK (*to Judy*): I hear there's a very fancy Park Avenue plastic surgeon who's using your old nose as his waiting room.

EPISODE 40

"Caruso's Way"

Writer: Jim Parker
Director: Bob LaHendro
Cast
Caruso: Scott Brady

Vinnie wants revenge after Coach Caruso hits him in front of the girls. Kotter warns Barbarino to keep his cool, but the wavy-haired stud doesn't want to look bad in front of the other Sweathogs. He and Caruso finally settle the score in an impromptu arm-wrestling match held in Kotter's classroom. Corporal punishment has never been so funny!

For the Record: Watch for the two blatant Pepsi product placement shots.

Parallel Plot: A classic episode of *The White Shadow* explores these same issues when Coach Reeves loses his temper and smacks a delinquent.

Classic Quote
WOODMAN (*to Caruso*): You know, Lou, in the twenty-odd years that I've known you, I never once tried to imagine you in your underwear.

EPISODE 41

"Kotter and Son"

Writers: Peter Meyerson and Nick Arnold
Director: Bob LaHendro
Cast
Mr. Kotter Sr.: Harold J. Stone

Kotter's grouchy father drops in for a visit, driving Gabe crazy in the apartment and in the classroom.

For the Record: In this episode we learn that Gabe has a brother (never seen in the show) who makes $100,000 a year as a doctor.

Classic Performance: To teach the Sweathogs about the Great Depression, Kotter performs a one-man floor show featuring impressions of Walter Winchell and President Herbert Hoover.

Classic Guest Star: Character actor Harold J. Stone can be seen in two Jerry Lewis films: *The Big Mouth* and *Hardly Working*.

EPISODE 42

"The Littlest Sweathog"

Writer: Eric Cohen
Director: Bob LaHendro

There another little sweathog on the way! Julie reveals to Gabe that there's a bun in the oven, and he's delighted . . . while she is overcome with anxiety. They are still living in a studio apartment, after all.

EPISODE 43

"I'm Having Their Baby"

Writers: George Tricker and Neil Rosen
Director: Bob LaHendro
Cast
Nervous Substitute Teacher Number Two: Ned Wertimer

While Kotter is away at a teachers' conference, the Sweathogs keep a watchful eye on the pregnant Julie, but their good intentions create more problems than Julie bargained for. Be sure to catch Epstein's gross overacting as he wrestles with an out-of-control vacuum cleaner.

Did I Ever Tell You About . . .

We've heard so many stories about Gabe Kotter's family, it's surprising that the only family member we ever meet is his father. It is, on the other hand, not surprising that Kotter's pater is grouchy. It is undoubtedly difficult growing up in a family of at least forty-seven brothers and a handful of sisters. Here is just a short branch of the Kotter family tree:

Aunt Bernice, very rich (episode 13)

Aunt Esther, movie house matron (15 and 28)

Cousin Howard, very rich (13)

Great Ancestor Caveman Zorg Kotter, invented the chicken (2)

Uncle Buzz Kotter, the astronaut (8)

Uncle Cecil, highway patrolman (23)

Uncle Eddie, the thief (49)

Uncle George, resourceful urbanite (65)

Uncle Habib Kotter, the salesman (43)

Uncle Harry Kotter (23)

Uncle Hawkeye Kotter, the famous frontiersman (29)

Uncle Joe, the drunk (62)

Uncles Jonas, the doctor (29)

Uncle Julian, raised by wild dogs, became a mailman (67)

Uncle Luther, a dietician and inventor (65)

Uncle Malcolm, a salesman (13)

Uncle Moreau, the biologist (62)

Uncle Sanford, the lumberjack (15)

Uncle Sidney, reincarnated, now a bull in Montana (49)

Uncle Sky Kotter, the paratrooper (44)

Uncle Slapsy Maxy Kotter, the boxer (41)

Uncle Socrates Kotter, the tailor (6)

Uncle Wilfred Kotter, engaged to an elephant (34)

Uncle William, a pharmacist (67)

Classic Quote

BARBARINO: Pregnant people ain't supposed to travel. I think it's against the law or something.

Classic Guest Star: The seventies were a fat time for some actors, including Ned Wertimer. Wertimer is best known for his role as the groveling doorman, Ralph Hart, on *The Jeffersons*, but you can also spot him as Nervous Substitute Teacher Number Two in this episode of *Welcome Back, Kotter*.

EPISODE 44

"Radio Free Freddie"

Story: Mark Evanier, Dennis Palumbo, and George Yanok
Teleplay: George Yanok, Peter Meyerson, and Nick Arnold
Director: Bob LaHendro
Cast
Wally: George Carlin
Andy: Fred Grandy

Fame and fortune nearly rip the gang apart after Freddie Washington becomes an overnight radio sensation. In an unusual episode, the students are able to work out their differences *outside* Kotter's classroom, where Freddie decides he'd rather be a Sweathog than a radio star.

Classic Guests: Comedy icon George Carlin guest stars as former Sweathog and WBAD radio DJ Wally the Wow. And Fred Grandy, prior to becoming a congressman, played the lovable Gopher on *The Love Boat*.

Classic Quote
HORSHACK (*on the phone*): Hey, Ma, it's me, it's little Arnold. Did you see me on the radio?

For the Record: In this episode, Juan Epstein claims his mother had nine children, but in episode 27, he said he had nine brothers and sisters, for a total of ten children in the family. The fate of Epstein's other sibling remains one of the deepest mysteries surrounding this series.

EPISODE 45

"I Wonder Who's Kissing Gabe Now?"

Writers: Peter Meyerson and Nick Arnold
Director: Bob LaHendro
Cast
Paula Hotlzgang: Denise Galik

Potential scandal emerges in the schoolhouse when the sexy art teacher becomes smitten with Kotter and kisses him on the lips. Epstein witnesses the interlude and assumes that Kotter is having an affair. What he didn't see is Kotter gently telling Ms. Holtzgang that he's happily married. For the remainder of the episode, Epstein and the other Sweathogs prepare to tell Julie about Kotter's infidelity.

Classic Quote
WASHINGTON: If the Kott-airs broke up, who'd get custody of us? (For an interesting parallel quote, see episode 139 of *The Bob Newhart Show* in which Howard worries about the Hartleys' divorcing: "What a terrible thought. Who's gonna get custody of me?")

Parallel Plot: Watch episodes 12 and 68, in which Julie and the Sweathogs assume Kotter is involved with other attractive young blondes.

EPISODE 46

"And Baby Makes Four," Part One

Writer: Eric Cohen
Director: Bob Claver

Wow! After months of not showing her pregnancy, Julie has gotten really big, so it comes as no surprise when delivery day arrives. At the same time, the Sweathogs are gearing up for a new school year—all except Barbarino, that is. He never took the makeup final exam and has to repeat the tenth grade. Be sure to catch his bizarre reaction shot, which elicited spontaneous audience applause.

For the Record: This is the first of a special three-part episode.

Classic Quote

KOTTER: If your water breaks, don't touch the toaster.

EPISODE 47

"And Baby Makes Four," Part Two

Writer: Eric Cohen
Director: Bob Claver
Cast
Dr. Melmann: Alan Oppenheimer
Nurse: Kathleen Doyle
Expectant Father: Ken Samson

The big day comes when Julie heads off to the delivery room, leaving Kotter and Sweathogs to panic in the waiting room. When the big moment arrives, the Kotters become parents to unnamed twin baby girls. Barbarino's dilemma of failing the tenth grade, however, has not been resolved.

EPISODE 48

"And Baby Makes Four," Part Three

Writer: Gabriel Kaplan
Director: Bob Claver
Cast
Mr. Hansen: Jack Dodson
Mrs. Hansen: Alice Backes

With Julie's parents visiting from Nebraska, there's not a moment's peace as the Kotters try to adjust to the new twin girls (though the babies do provide a convenient excuse for Gabe to mug at the camera), whom they name Robin and Rachel. Meanwhile, Woodman has agreed to let Barbarino take a makeup exam to get into the eleventh grade.

Classic Quote

HORSHACK (*to Julie's farmer father*): Have you ever been to a locust plague?

Classic Guest Star: Jack Dodson is perhaps best known for his role as Mayberry's Howard Sprague on *The Andy Griffith Show*.

For the Record: This is the last episode in a very special three-part series. This is also the only occasion on which Gabriel Kaplan was credited as a script writer, although as co-creator of the show he oversaw every script during the first three seasons of the series.

MR. KOTTER

EPISODE 49

"Brother, Can You Spare a Million?"

Writers: Peter Meyerson and Nick Arnold
Director: Bob Claver
Cast
Sexy Nurse: Robin Riker
Wendy: Wendy Rastatter

Kotter donates a quarter for the absent Barbarino toward the Sweathogs' collective lottery ticket. This generous deed goes unappreciated, though, when the ticket proves a winner to the tune of a thousand dollars. Despite all of Kotter's past and present contributions, the gang won't include him in the payout.

Classic Quote
HORSHACK: This may come to a shock to you, Mr. Kotter, but I am slightly irregular.

Our Television Heritage: Spontaneous star-induced applause is a blight on situation comedies. The phenomenon has occurred on many shows, including *Here's Lucy*, *The Lucy Show*, and *The Carol Burnett Show*. *Welcome Back, Kotter* began to be affected by it when Travolta's fame began to grow, and in this episode the phenomenon reaches a strange new level: there is actually audience applause when Kotter mentions that Vinnie is in the hospital getting his tonsils removed.

Classic Guest Star: Wendy Rastatter played Epstein's girlfriend, Wendy, and later portrayed David Cassidy's wife in the very short-lived crime drama *David Cassidy—Man Undercover*.

EPISODE 50

"Just Testing"

Writers: George Bloom and Beverly Bloomberg
Director: Bob Claver

The twins have the Kotter residence spinning out of control, and at the same time Barbarino needs help studying for his makeup exam. So while the Sweathogs assist Julie with the housework, Kotter can help Vinnie study.

Classic Quote
BARBARINO: I had to study by myself, and now my head hurts.

Parallel Plots: This is not the first time the Sweathogs have helped Julie with the housework. In episode 43 their efforts had disastrous results.

For the Record: The name Bob Claver is a familiar one at the home of Classic TV. Claver not only wrote and directed many episodes of *Welcome Back, Kotter*, but was also the executive producer of that fun-loving show, *The Partridge Family*.

EPISODE 51

"The Deprogramming of Arnold Horshack"

Writers: Mike Barrie and Jim Mulholland
Director: Bob Claver
Cast
Mrs. O'Hara: Ellen Travolta

The seventies were a decade of weird religious cults, so this episode was not just entertainment but also trenchant social commentary. After joining a cult, Arnold Horshack prances around Buchanan High wearing nothing but a yellow sheet. Only the love of his fellow Sweathogs can bring Arnold back to his old self. There's a treat in this episode for constitutional history buffs, as Kotter reminds the Sweathogs that people in the United States have a right to the religion of their choice, even one that requires them to shave their heads.

Classic Guest: The actress who plays Horshack's mom is in real life John Travolta's sister. Ellen Travolta made quite a career playing TV moms. See if you can match Ellen Travolta's motherly role with the following TV shows:

A. Chachi's mom   1. *Makin' It*
B. Greg and Tony's mom   2. *Charles in Charge*
C. Charles's mom   3. *Joanie Loves Chachi*

Answers: A-3, B-1, C-2

For the Record: John Travolta later became a member of L. Ron Hubbard's Church of Scientology.

EPISODE 52

"What a Move"

Writers: Peter Meyerson and Nick Arnold
Director: Bob Claver
Cast
Moe Epstein: Herb Edelman

In this sentimental episode, the Kotters leave their tiny studio for roomier digs. Trouble begins when their new landlord, Juan's uncle Moe, discovers the twins and threatens to evict the Kotters. Moe only talks a mean game, however. Deep down he's as soft and cuddly as his delinquent nephew.

Classic Quote
HORSHACK (*describing Woodman*): There is only one thing that could make a man that crabby: he buys his underwear too small.

Classic Guest Star: The role of Epstein's leisure suit–clad Uncle Moe was played by Herb Edelman, who went on to portray Bea Arthur's ex-husband in the hit show *The Golden Girls*. Notice that he was bald way back in this episode, too.

For the Record: It is against the law for New York City landlords to prohibit children from living in any premises. This whole episode might have been avoided if the Kotters had been familiar with the law.

EPISODE 53

"A Novel Idea"

Writers: George Bloom and Beverly Bloomberg
Director: Nick Havinga

Literature takes an ugly turn when Woodman pens a scathing Civil War epic based on Kotter and the Sweathogs. In retaliation, the gang members write their own book, depicting Woodman as an evil intergalactic tyrant. Of course, the argument could be made that if the Sweathogs didn't waste so much time writing drivel, they might be able to work their way out of the remedial class.

Classic Scene: The Sweathogs do their own version of *Gone With the Wind*.

Classic Quote
WOODMAN: Barbarino, I've met cabbage deeper than you.

EPISODE 54

"Barbarino in Love," Part One

Writers: Peter Meyerson and Nick Arnold
Director: Bob Claver
Cast
Cassy: Amy Johnston
Lou: Martin Garner

In a story that alludes to the Beatles' clash with Yoko Ono, Barbarino decides to quit the Sweathogs' singing group for true love. Even though the Sweathogs never had a singing group until this episode, they manage to win the talent show semifinals. Before they head for the state finals, however, Vinnie must decide what's more important, the group or his girlfriend.

Classic Performance: In a cultural marriage of fifties doo-wop and seventies disco, the Sweathogs perform a rousing song-and-dance rendition of "Jeepers, Creepers," complete with blue-and-gold glitter jumpsuits. Some of the recognizable dance steps in this routine include the hustle and the robot.

EPISODE 55

"Barbarino in Love," Part Two

Writers: Peter Meyerson and Nick Arnold
Director: Bob Claver
Cast
Cassy: Amy Johnston
Lou: Martin Garner

Barbarino quits the Sweathogs' singing group so that his new girlfriend can have a better chance to win the state talent championship, but this act of chivalry makes her furious. And without Barbarino's lead, the Sweathogs' singing group is sure to lose the finals. As usual, Kotter steps in and shames Barbarino into doing what's right.

Classic Performance: The Sweathogs perform again. Though it's a different song, the routine is pretty much the same as in the preceding episode. So if you didn't feel thoroughly entertained by the last one, you probably won't be thrilled by this one, either.

EPISODE 56

"Kotter for Vice Principal"

Writers: Steve Clements and Joyce Gittlin
Director: Bob Claver
Cast
Mr. Jan: Ernest Harada
Kotter's Grown-up Twins: Beth and Kay Kearney

The winds of change stir when Woodman's contract as vice principal runs out and Kotter considers taking the job. This episodes employs a classic weird dream sequence in which Kotter envisions Buchanan High in the year 2050. He is king, Arnold is teacher, Washington is bald, and Barbarino resembles Albert Einstein. Woodman fans take heart: after much consideration, the school board decides to renew the crusty vice principal's contract.

For the Record: Kotter actually does become Buchanan's vice principal in episode 73. Also, when Marcia Strassman broke her arm in real life, the writers incorporated her condition into the script.

Favorite: Of Gabe Kaplan. The dream sequence was mostly improvised, through some of the funniest bits were axed by the networks for being too tasteless.

Classic Quote

WOODMAN: Okay, Kotter, maybe you have the guts. But you haven't got the pom-poms.

EPISODE 57

"Swine and Punishment"

Writers: Nick Rosner and Bob Silberg
Director: Bob Claver

Would Boom Boom cheat on a test? The Sweathogs rally to Freddie's defense in the face of Woodman's accusation.

Our Television Heritage: One of the most important issues underlying this show was this burning question: how were we supposed to believe that the Sweathogs were genuine juvenile delinquents when in fact they were just as moral as Richie Cunningham (*Happy Days*) almost as moral as Jeff Stone (*Donna Reed*) and twice as moral as Eddie Haskell (*Leave It to Beaver*)? Sure, they claim to steal cars, but let's look at their actual behavior. They wimp out of their gang rumble, Epstein smokes for half an episode, and they sometimes don't do their schoolwork. Perhaps it was reassuring to America to think that inner-city gang members were deeply concerned about such issues as lying to a friend and letting others down if you quit the school play.

EPISODE 58

"Epstein's Madonna"

Teleplay: Eric Cohen
Story: Earle Doud
Director: Bob Claver
Cast
Mrs. Holtzgang: Denise Galik
Jerry Cronkite: Frank O'Brien
Weirdo in School Yard: Stan Ross

Epstein's mural of a nude woman sparks a heated debate on the difference between art and sleaze. Naturally, the controversial parts of the mural remain unseen.

Classic Quote

WOODMAN: If God wanted us to be naked, why would there be leisure suits?

For the Record: Epstein's flair for painting nudes was foreshadowed in episode 45, "I Wonder Who's Kissing Gabe Now."

EPISODE 59

"Angie"

Teleplay: George Bloom and Beverly Bloomberg
Story: James Komack and Paul Mason
Director: Bob Claver
Cast
Angie Globagoski: Melonie Haller

Angie wants to become a Sweathog, but the boys, who just aren't hip to the women's rights movement, deny her membership. In order to prove herself, Buchanan's newest student dumps water on Vice Principal Woodman and gets everyone expelled. Through understanding, compassion, and a broken fire alarm, Angie is forgiven and anointed a Sweathog.

Classic Quote

BARBARINO (*to Angie*): Go gargle with glue.

For the Record: In this episode, Barbarino, Washington, Horshack, and Epstein claimed that women couldn't make it as Sweathogs. But there were, in fact, many women who had been honored by inclusion as full-fledged Sweathogs, including Verna Jean, Rosalie "Hotsie" Totzi, and Julie's sister, Jenny.

EPISODE 60

"Sweatwork"

Writer: Eric Cohen
Director: Alan Myerson

This episode finds the Sweathogs running the new school radio station. In this takeoff of the hit film *Network*, low ratings cause Arnold to beef up his news program with bombastic accusations about the conduct of the Buchanan faculty, leaving Woodman and Kotter in his verbose wake.

Classic Quote

HORSHACK (*shouting out the window*): I'm fed-up Arnold, and I don't care who knows it!

Parallel Plot: Episode 44, "Radio Free Freddie," also deals with a Sweathog's inability to cope with broadcasting success.

EPISODE 61

"Meet Your New Teacher"

Teleplay: Garry Ferrier and Aubrey Tadman
Story: Judy Skelton and Tony Schnurer
Director: Bob Claver
Cast
Mr. Jan: Ernest Harada
Computer Voice: Sonny Melendez

The Sweathogs leap into the computer age when Kotter is replaced by an electronic teacher. Typical of most electronic gizmos, the new computer teacher isn't as much fun as Kotter, so the Sweathogs engage in a little classroom sabotage. Through vandalism of school property, the Sweathogs get Kotter his job back.

Classic Quote

KOTTER (*teaching about Eric the Red*): That was twelve hundred years before James the Brown, Slappy the White, and Schecky the Greene.

EPISODE 62

"Epstein's Term Paper"

Writer: Eric Cohen
Director: Bob Claver

Epstein and the other Sweathogs buy term papers from a couple of local hoods, but Kotter realizes Epstein's paper on FDR is the very same one that he handed in eleven years earlier.

Classic Quote

WASHINGTON: I can't stand out in this cold much longer, you know. My Afro is liable to freeze and snap off.

Classic Guest Star: Speaking of Afros, guest star Charles Fleischer, who provided the voice of

Roger Rabbit, also sported an impressive Afro in this episode.

For the Record: In addition to Freddie Washington and Carvelli, many of the Sweathogs favored haircuts that could be loosely described as Afros—Kotter, Epstein, and, at times, Horshack, for example.

EPISODE 63

"There's No Business like Show Business," Part One

Teleplay: Gabriel Kaplan
Story: Richard Eckhaus
Director: Bob Claver
Cast
Pete the Agent: Sam Weisman
Eddie Mincer: Michael Preminger

"Being a comedian has sort of been like a secret dream," Kotter admits to his Sweathogs, and so starts this episode. After bombing on his debut comedy night, Kotter changes his act and becomes an instant comedy sensation.

For the Record: Before he became Gabe Kotter, Gabe Kaplan was a stand-up comedian. In fact, this series and its characters were based on his original comedy routines. He also wrote the teleplay for this episode.

EPISODE 64

"There's No Business like Show Business," Part Two

Teleplay: Beverly Bloomberg and George Bloom
Story: Richard Eckhaus
Director: Bob Claver
Cast
Pete the Agent: Sam Weisman

Kotter makes the big time as a stand-up comedian, but success puts a strain on his friendship with the Sweathogs and on his marriage with Julie.

Parallel Plot: See episode 44, "Radio Free Freddie," in which Freddie's success as a disc jockey also puts a strain on the Sweathogs—though not so much on Julie.

Classic Quote
KOTTER: My wife is so skinny she's gotta run around the shower to get wet.

EPISODE 65

"What Goes Up"

Teleplay: Nick Arnold
Story: George Tricker and Neil Rosen
Director: Jeff Bleckner

The Sweathogs declare their own personal war on drugs after Washington becomes addicted to painkillers. By acting as if they're goofy on dope, the gang shows Washington the error of his drug-ingesting ways. Watch for John Travolta's hilarious scene-stealing turn as a "confused" drug addict.

Classic Quote

BARBARINO (*to a naive Horshack*): You don't know nothing about medicine. I bet you don't even know how to bleed right.

Parallel Plot: In episode 92 the gang helps cure Arnold of alcohol addiction.

In a classic Mary Tyler Moore episode (number 155), Lou, Ted, and Murray help Mary kick her addiction to sleeping pills. Apparently sleeping pills and painkillers were "acceptable" TV addictions. As of this writing, no sitcom character has ever had to kick a heroin habit.

EPISODE 66

"Good-bye, Mr. Kripps"

Writers: Aubrey Tadman and Garry Ferrier
Director: Bob Claver

Cast

Norman Alden
Jack Fletcher
Bryan O'Byrne

Typical Sweathog shenanigans cause the crusty old shop teacher to drop dead of heart attack, leaving Barbarino with a guilty conscience. With nowhere else to turn, Vinnie turns himself in to the police for murder.

Classic Quote

KOTTER: Vinnie, you do not use an electric saw to slice a salami.

Parallel Plot: See *The Bob Newhart Show*, episode 75, "Death of a Fruitman."

For the Record: The roles of Mr. Kripps, lieutenant Ed Lasky, and the Bald Cop were played by actors Norman Alden, Jack Fletcher, and Bryan O'Byrne, but not necessarily in that order.

If you can successfully match each actor with the right character, consider yourself a classic TV expert, and reward yourself with a delicious milk shake. Oh, and let us know, okay?

EPISODE 67

"Horshack and Madame X"

Writer: Peter Meyerson
Director: Al Schwartz

Horshack's love life needs a lift, so Julie gives him some advice on wooing the opposite sex. Naturally, the schlemielish Sweathog falls in love with Mrs. Kotter. It's a classic May-September romance. (Actually, because Ron Palillo and Marcia Strassman are really approximately the same age, it's more like a July-July romance.)

Classic Quote

JULIE *(to Horshack):* Arnold, no one but Mr. Kotter's allowed to grab my gusto.

Our Television Heritage: While this series was on the air, Golden Press published a series of comic book–sized novellas of *Welcome Back, Kotter.* One of these featured roughly the same plot as this episode, except that it was Barbarino who fell for Julie after taking her advice on how to romance women. That story, written by Arnold Drake, includes a scene in which Vinnie reads Shakespeare's eighteenth sonnet, "Shall I Compare Thee to a Summer's Day," to Julie. Here is an excerpt from the novella: "For an hour, Julie talked and read from John Donne, Bobby Burns, and Robert Frost. So intent was she on her new role that she did not notice Barbarino's eyes riveted upon her and growing wider with each second. She was not even aware of the unrelenting stare when the coffee that he poured missed the cup and wound up in her African violet plant."

EPISODE 68

"The Kiss"

Story: Peter Meyerson and Max Wynne Goldenson
Teleplay: Peter Meyerson
Director: Bob Claver
Cast
Laura: Sally Hightower
Mr. Jan: Ernest Harada
Baby: Demetre Phillips

If we learn anything in this episode, it's that eating too many bean sprouts can make you faint. And that's exactly what happens to Kotter's sexy student, Laura. So when Kotter tries to revive her with artificial respiration, Woodman walks in and jumps to the most clichéd of conclusions.

Classic Quote
EPSTEIN: My socks don't cry. They're men.

Classic Scene: The Sweathogs do their impression of male hairdressers. Ask yourself if they could get away with that today.

Parallel Plot: A kiss leads to suspicion when Kotter is accused of having a fling in episode 45, "I Wonder Who's Kissing Gabe Now."

EPISODE 69

"Class Encounter of the Carvelli Kind"

Writers: George Bloom and Beverly Bloomberg
Director: Robert Hegyes

Kotter daydreams that Carvelli contacts beings from the planet Yorxyl and Woodman is chosen to travel through space.

Classic Quote
KOTTER *(to Woodman):* You believe in UFOs, Mr. Woodman? You, who thought electricity was just a fad?

For the Record: It goes without saying that this episode is one of the weirdest offerings in the series.

Epstein fans may notice that the Brillo-haired Sweathog is absent from this episode. Actually, actor Robert Hegyes was on the other side of the camera, making his directorial debut. In order to get his director's credit, Hegyes had to spend this episode in the control room, calling the shots.

EPISODE 70

"The Return of Hotsy Totsy"

Writer: Gabriel Kaplan
Director: Bob Claver
Cast
Olga the Stripper: Marlise Peiratt

Her stage name at the strip club is Honey Pie, but we all remember her as Rosalie "Hotsy" Totsy from previous episodes. That's right, the female Sweathog has turned to a life of nudity and glitter in order to support her six-month-old baby. But with the gang's help, Hotsy Totsy gets a respectable job at Brooklyn College, and we never hear from her again.

Classic Performance: Barbarino and Washington explode into an improvised dance routine that can only be described as groovy.

For the Record: We know why Hotsy Totsy dropped out of Buchanan High, but why did actress Debralee Scott leave the series? Perhaps it had to do with her involvement in two other successful TV ventures. In 1976 and 1977, Scott was featured in the cult hit *Mary Hartman, Mary Hartman,* and later she played a pivotal role in the sitcom *Angie.*

EPISODE 71

"Sweathog Christmas Special"

Writers: Eric Cohen and Mel Stuart
Director: Mel Stuart

In the inevitable retrospective clip show, Kotter, Julie, and the Sweathogs spend Christmas Eve reminiscing about their favorite moments from episodes past. Among the highlights are an "up your nose with a rubber hose" montage.

Classic Quote
KOTTER (*describing Woodman in a Santa suit*): Oh, look who it is—it's Santa Fraud.

EPISODE 72

"Sweathog Back-to-School Special"

Teleplay: Peter Meyerson and Nick Arnold
Story: Paul Mason
Director: Dick King
Cast
Female Sweathogs: Melody Anderson, Deloreese Daniels, and Rebecca York

The gang looks back over classic highlights from the series in this "best of" clip show. More importantly, a *Welcome Back, Kotter* milestone is achieved when three of the usually anonymous female Sweathogs actually talk with Kotter.

EPISODE 73

"The Drop-Ins" Part One

Writers: Bill Richmond and Gene Perret
Director: Norman Abbot

It's a brand-new school year at Buchanan, and changes are in the air. Carvelli has joined the Sweathog class, Woodman's been promoted to principal, and Kotter has become Buchanan's new vice principal. Feeling betrayed that Kotter has deserted to "the other side," the Sweathogs quit school and search for jobs.

Classic Quote
HORSHACK (*to Woodman*): I'm happy to see success has not gone to your head. In fact, I don't see it in any part of your body.

For the Record: If you watch closely, you'll notice that the classroom door mysteriously closes in the first scene.

Our Television Heritage: After three successful seasons on prime-time television, Gabe Kaplan decided it was time for the Sweathogs to graduate, but the network bosses disagreed and kept the gang in high school for one more year. Kaplan then decided that Kotter should move on as vice principal and play a smaller role in the program. A whole new stable of writers—most of them from *The Carol Burnett Show*—was brought in for the show's final season.

The show's opening and closing montages also went through slight revisions. Historians may note that Howard Golden is listed as Brooklyn borough president on the new opening's "Welcome to Brooklyn" sign; in the earlier episodes, Sebastian Leone reigned as borough president. The theme song however, remained the same—speaking of which, *Welcome Back, Kotter*'s theme, which was composed and sung by the Lovin' Spoonful's John

Sebastian, reached number one on the *Billboard* list in 1976.

EPISODE 74

"The Drop-Ins," Part Two

Writers: Bill Richmond and Gene Perret
Director: Norman Abbot
Cast
Nurse Baker: Marian Collier

Barbarino becomes a hospital orderly, and the other Sweathogs ask him to fix them up with jobs. But the guys soon discover that life in the real world is tougher than they bargained for.

For the Record: In this episode, we learn that Freddie Washington's middle name is not "Boom Boom"—it's Percy.

EPISODE 75

"Frog Day Afternoon"

Writers: George Bloom and Earl Barrett
Director: Nick Arnold

Giving us another indication that the Sweathogs are juvenile delinquents with ultra-refined moral sensibilities, Horshack refuses to dissect a frog, then leads a Save the Frogs campaign.

For the Record: Today there are genuine protest groups organized for this very purpose: to eliminate dissection from high school biology curricula.

EPISODE 76

"Beau's Jest"

Writers: Earl Barret and George Bloom
Director: Norman Abbot
Cast
Big Thug: Richard Moll

The newest Sweathog, Beau De Labarre, joins the ranks, and he and Epstein erupt into a war of practical jokes. The hilarity begins when Beau sets up Epstein on a date with a woman, then tells him she's married and that her husband is out for blood.

Classic Guest Star: Do you recognize the giant thug who's looking to beat up Epstein? Well, if you take away his long hair and muttonchops, you'll see Richard Moll, better known as Bull from *Night Court*.

For the Record: After the success of *Saturday Night Fever*, John Travolta made fewer appearances on *Welcome Back, Kotter*. The hunky Italian Sweathog was replaced by a hunky southern Sweathog named Beau De Labarre.

EPISODE 77

"The Sweatmobile"

Writers: Rick Hawkins and Liz Sage
Director: Norman Abbot

The Sweathogs pool $158 to buy a car from Barbarino's uncle Louie. The car turns out to be a lemon, Uncle Louie ends up in the hospital, and the Sweathogs get dates with four gorgeous cheerleaders.

Classic Quote
EPSTEIN: Never buy nothing from a Barbarino.

EPISODE 78

"Don't Come Up and See Me Sometime"

Writers: Liz Sage and Rich Hawkins
Director: Nick Arnold

The Sweathogs learn a lesson in true friendship—as if they need one. It all starts when Vinnie gets his own pad but doesn't want the other perspiring porkers to visit.

EPISODE 79

"Once upon a Ledge"

Writers: Rick Hawkins and Liz Sage
Director: Norman Abbot

In an episode dealing with teen suicide, Mary, the new girl, has a hard time making friends, so she threatens to jump off the school ledge. If Mary had only watched episode 59, she would have known that the easiest way to get the Sweathogs' attention is to dump water on Woodman and get everyone expelled.

For the Record: Keep your eye on Mary. She'll become a vital character in the last *Welcome Back, Kotter* episodes.

Favorite: Of Ron Palillo. Watch as Horshack dramatically coaxes the new girl back into safety, and you'll see why this is one of the actor's personal favorites.

EPISODE 80

"Barbarino's Boo-boo"

Writers: Linda Morris and Vic Rauseo
Director: Norman Abbott
Cast
Nurse Bonnie: Jane Dulo
Impatient Spanish Woman: Jeannie Linero
Bobby: Patrick Collins

It's mayhem at the hospital when Principal Woodman checks in for a routine bunion removal and Barbarino loses him. Watch John Travolta try his hand at physical comedy as he helps an incapacitated man out of his hospital room.

Classic Guest Star: Playing nurse was second nature to Jane Dulo. *McHale's Navy* fans might recognize Dulo for her role as Nurse Molly Turner in the 1962 sitcom.

EPISODE 81

"Washington's Clone"

Writers: Julie Kirgo and Diane Kirgo
Director: Norman Abbott
Cast
Arthur: Ron Dennis

Hero worship turns ugly when an impish young student tries to emulate Freddie "Boom Boom" Washington and ends up becoming a delinquent. The Sweathogs set the boy back on the right track with their own personal "scared straight" program. This episode also offers more physical humor with Barbarino and the incapacitated patient. It's times like this when Gabe Kaplan is really missed.

Our Television Heritage: You might have noticed that Kotter is missing from this and many of the other fourth-season episodes. Because of creative differences with the networks, Gabe Kaplan opted to appear in many fewer episodes during the show's final season. With so little Kotter, is it right to keep his name in the series title? Here are a few title options the series could have tried:

You'd Be Welcome Back, Kotter
Mr. Kotter, Car 54 Wants to Know Where Are You?
In Search of Kotter
Welcome Back, humm-hum-hum
What Ever Happened to Gabey K.?
The Misadventures of a Bunch of Guys with Really Big Hair Who Can't Get Out of the Remedial Class
Six Characters in Search of a Kotter

EPISODE 82

"X-Rated Education"

Writers: Kathy Greer and Bill Greer
Director: Norman Abbott
Cast
Mrs. Zugler: Jenna McMahon
Mr. Finch: Stanley Brooks
Ms. Jones: Bebe Drake Brooks

In yet another case of the old switcheroo, Carvelli brings an X-rated movie to school and gets it mixed up with a sex education film. Not only does this episode employ one of the oldest and most widely used comedy situations, the accidental switch, but it also presents a compelling, intelligent argument for in-school sex education.

Classic Quote
HORSHACK: Oooohhhhh! An X-rated movie—where they really show the *X*'s!

EPISODE 83

"The Barbarino Blues"

Writers: Vic Rauseo and Linda Morris
Director: Norman Abbott
Cast
Sally: Linda McCullough

Vinnie's afraid he's lost his magic with women, so he pretends to get drunk, then wrestles with the Sweathogs. Draw you own conclusions. This episode showcases the many facets of Barbarino: thug, dimwit, sensitive guy with needs, seventies superstar.

Classic Quote
DE LABARRE: Your concern for Sally's well-being is mighty chivalrous.
BARBARINO: Yeah, well, when babies were given chival in heaven, I got an extra scoop.

Classic Guest Star: Linda McCullough broke Barbarino's heart in this episode, and daytime drama fans might best remember her heartbreaking role as Hilary Kincaid Bauer in *The Guiding Light*.

EPISODE 84

"A Little Fright Music"

Writers: Earl Barret and George Bloom
Director: Norman Abbott

Woodman's school anthem may be traditional, but it's dull and lifeless, so Washington gives it a funky new beat with a little disco flair. Now J. Bubba Hampton, a big-time recording executive, wants to make the song a Top 40 hit. Will a big-time recording contract make Woodman and Washington unlikely business partners?

Classic Performance: In past episodes, Washington showed he could carry a tune, but in this episode, Woodman proves himself a strong baritone, singing the school anthem, "O Buchanan."

For the Record: Woodman pays tribute to John Travolta's film success by singing a few bars of "Stayin' Alive."

EPISODE 85

"Bride and Gloom"

Writers: Earl Barrett and George Bloom
Director: Norman Abbott

Wha'? Wedding bells. Where? In a church. When? Real soon. Who? America's teen heartthrob, Vinnie Barbarino. Does he actually go through with the marriage? Naahh.

EPISODE 86

"The Good-bye Guy"

Teleplay: Susanne Gayle Harris, Rick Hawkins, and Liz Sage
Story: Susanne Gayle Harris
Director: Norman Abbott
Cast
Kelly: Georganne LaPiere
Emily: Alston Ahern
Waiter: Corey Fischer

Principal Woodman stumbles upon his intellectual niece, Kelly, making out with Epstein on the Kotters' living room floor, and, brother, do the sparks ever fly! Inevitably, the hot and sweaty love affair cools, as Epstein's brashness clashes with Kelly's gentility. Of course, we knew the romance was doomed when Epstein innocently said Kelly's friend was fat.

Parallel Plot: Epstein chooses another unlikely mate when he dates Julie's younger sister in episode 32 "Sweathog, Nebraska Style."

EPISODE 87

"A Winter's Coat Tail"

Writers: Earl Barret and George Bloom
Director: Norman Abbott
Cast
Punks: Adam Hollander, John Hollander

Barbarino is looking particularly stylish in his new camel-hair coat. So it is indeed a tragedy when a couple of hoods steal the coat from him on the street. This Christmas episode concludes with a warm, fuzzy ending as the punks return the jacket to Barbarino.

Classic Quote
BARBARINO (*to Epstein, who is about to clean the eraser crumbs from his test paper*): What do you do—do you blow or do you brush?

EPISODE 88

"Barbarino's Baby"

Writers: Linda Morris and Vic Rauseo
Director: Norman Abbott
Cast
Nurse Bonney: Jane Dulo
Mrs. Fishbein: Mary Jo Catlett
Mr. Fishbein: Henry Corden

It's a classic TV situation: Barbarino must deliver a baby when he, a pregnant woman, and (for comedic reasons) the rest of the Sweathogs get stuck in a hospital elevator.

Classic Quote

BARBARINO (*after learning that the father will name the baby Reggie*): See that, I deliver the guy's baby and he names him after a candy bar.

Parallel Plot: Rob, a pregnant Laura, and guest star Don Rickles are trapped in an elevator in episode 102 of *The Dick Van Dyke Show.* Alex delivers a baby in *Taxi,* episode 22.

EPISODE 89

"The Sweat Smell of Success"

Writers: Earl Barret and George Bloom
Director: Norman Abbott

In a plot that parallels the life and times of Charles Foster Kane, Juan Epstein transforms the dreary school newspaper into a hot gossipy tabloid. His half-truths and innuendos make Epstein this episode's least popular Sweathog.

Classic Quote

EPSTEIN (*to Mary, the editor*): With my ideas and your spelling, we're going to set this school on its ear.

For the Record: This isn't the first episode in which Juan Epstein reported for the *Buchanan Bugle.* In episode 39 Epstein became a hard-edged reporter uncovering a scandal within the Buchanan faculty. Sadly, his journalistic ethics had been lost and forgotten by the time he returned to the paper in this episode.

EPISODE 90

"I'm Okay, but You're Not"

Writers: Rick Hawkins and Liz Sage
Director: Norman Abbott

To prove he's not a suck-up, De Labarre goes beyond the call of Sweathogdom to steal Woodman's pants and then sound the fire alarm. For the remainder of the episode, Woodman employs a classic sight gag; he wears a dress.

For the Record: Keep a close watch for the camera lens that accidentally dips into the left side of the picture at the end of the show. Or don't bother—but it's there, trust us.

Classic Quote

WOODMAN (*in dress*): What's wrong with you people? Didn't you ever see a man with a skirt before?

EPISODE 91

"The Gang Show"

Writers: Bill Richmond and Gene Perret
Director: Norman Abbott
Cast
Mrs. Tremaine: Della Reese

Once again the Sweathogs and Carvelli go head to head in a showdown. Only this time it's with talent, not fists, at Buchanan's annual talent show. Washington and Epstein do a lame rendition of an old comedy routine, and the audience justifiably showers them with the traditional rotten produce.

Classic Guest Star: Singer and entertainer Della Reese is no stranger to TV comedy. She played the sassy landlady in *Chico and the Man,* and she was a sassy host on her own short-lived talk show, *Della.*

Classic Performance: This episode focused on the comedy stylings of Charles Fleischer. Before lending Roger Rabbit his voice, Fleischer was a leading stand-up comic. His performance in this episode shows he wasn't too bad at it, either.

EPISODE 92

"Come Back, Little Arnold"

Writers: Bill Richmond and Gene Perret
Director: Norman Abbott

It's time for a Very Special episode, which means heavy moralizing to match a heavy-duty topic. Horshack find his courage in a bottle of booze, in a wrong-headed effort to gain enough confidence to impress Mary. Luckily, a Sweathog intervention saves him from a lost weekend.

EPISODE 93

"Ooh, Ooh, I Do," Part One

Writers: Bill Richmond and Gene Perret
Director: Norman Abbott

"So the little guy's growin' up, huh?" Epstein says, speaking of Horshack. While Horshack and Mary's affection for one another grows, Mrs. Horshack demands that her son move to Atlantic City with her and her new husband. In order to stay in Brooklyn with his girlfriend and the Sweathogs, Horshack gets engaged to Mary.

Classic Quote
WOODMAN *(to Julie):* Sweathogs are hard to get rid of—they're like warts.

EPISODE 94

"Ooh, Ooh, I Do," Part Two

Writers: Bill Richmond and Gene Perret
Director: Norman Abbott

Just before his wedding day, Horshack gets scared and disappears without a trace. His fiancée and the Sweathogs scour the streets in search of him before finding him in a darkened movie theater. Happily, the two lovebirds tie the knot in a Sweathog-style wedding.

Classic Performance: Epstein tops Woodman's skirt by dressing as a female stripper at Horshack's bachelor party.

For the Record: Running from adversity is a typical Sweathog reaction. Other episodes that featured Sweathogs scurrying from trouble include number 35, "Whatever Happened to Arnold"; episode 7, "One of Our Sweathogs Is Missing"; and number 17, "Follow the Leader." Among other things, these story lines give one actor most of the production week off.

A bearded Kotter makes a rare fourth-season appearance at Horshack's wedding, which would have made a fitting finale for the series. But wait—there's one more episode. . . .

EPISODE 95

"The Breadwinners"

Writers: Linda Morris and Vic Rauseo
Director: Norman Abbott
Cast
Kelly Woodman: Georganne LaPiere
Mrs. Trevor Smite: Priscilla Morrill
Samson Malone: Henry Beckman

After four years of solid friendship, Epstein and Washington stop speaking to each other after arguing over an after-school job. The two decide to settle their differences in a round of fisticuffs. Before the first punch is thrown, however, both injure themselves with weights, then dissolve into uncontrollable laughter.

Classic Guest Stars: Two TV sitcom pioneers appeared in this episode. Henry Beckman played Colonel Harrigan on *McHale's Navy,* and Priscilla Morrill was featured on *In the Beginning,* one of the numerous doomed McLean Stevenson sitcoms.

For the Record: "The Breadwinners" was the final *Welcome Back, Kotter* episode. But don't think the Sweathogs spent their final half hour in a sickly sweet sentimental farewell. On the contrary, it was business as usual when ABC unceremoniously pulled the program from the airwaves. The last *Welcome Back, Kotter* shot was a freeze-frame showing Epstein and Washington in a cheerful fists-up pose.

Afterword

Phew! That's a lot of Classic TV. We really thought we'd seen it all—until we actually tried to catalog every episode. We've made every effort to get our facts straight, but we take full responsibility for any mistakes. For future editions, and just for our own edification, we would love to hear from you if you find any errors or omissions.

We would also like to know if you disagree with us. Did we give short shrift to your favorite episode? Did we fail to highlight a truly classic performance? Is there a Classic Quote out there that we missed?

Drop us a note at Nick at Nite Books, 1515 Broadway, New York, NY 10036. Or find us on America Online (see below.) We can't guarantee an answer to everyone, but we'll try.

Nick at Nite On-Line is available through America Online. It's a great place to get more information about Classic TV, chat with fellow fans, and get the latest programming updates. It's easy to get there: Keyword: Nick at Nite.

Bibliography

We are greatly indebted to the TV scholars who have gone before us. The following selected bibliography includes the many books that were vital in compiling the information, and are heartily recommended for further reading. Among them, Bart Andrews's *The I Love Lucy Book* and Frank Lovece and Jules Franco's *Hailing Taxi* are especially detailed in their episode-by-episode descriptions.

Andrews, Bart. *The I Love Lucy Book*. Doubleday, 1985.

Alley, Robert S. and Irby B. Brown. *Love is All Around: The Making of the Mary Tyler Moore Show*. Delta, 1989.

Brooks, Tim. *The Complete Directory to Prime Time TV Stars*. Ballantine Books, 1987.

Brooks, Tim and Earle Marsh. *The Complete Directory to Prime Time Network TV Shows*. Ballantine Books, 1985.

Castleman, Harry and Walter J. Podrazik. *Harry and Wally's Favorite TV Shows*. Prentice Hall Press, 1989.

Cox, Stephen. *The Munsters: Television's First Family of Fright*. Contemporary Books, 1989.

Denison, D. C. *As Seen on TV: An Inside Look at the Television Industry*. Simon & Schuster, 1992.

Eisner, Joel and David Krinsky. *Television Comedy Series: An Episode Guide to 153 TV Sitcoms in Syndication*. McFarland, 1984.

Fireman, Judy, Ed. *TV Book: The Ultimate Television Book*. Workman, 1977.

Freud, Sigmund. *Jokes and Their Relation to the Unconscious*. W. W. Norton, 1963.

Green, Joey. *The Partridge Family Album*. HarperCollins, 1994.

Javna, John. *Cult TV*. St. Martin's Press, 1985.

Javna, John. *The TV Theme Song Sing-Along Song Book*. St. Martin's, 1984.

Javna, John. *The TV Theme Song Sing-Along Song Book, Volume 2*. St. Martin's, 1985.

Jones, Gerard. *Honey I'm Home! Sitcoms: Selling the American Dream*. Grove Weidenfeld, 1992.

Lovece, Frank with Jules Franco. *Hailing Taxi: The Official Book of the Show*. Prentice Hall Press, 1988.

MacLeod, Gavin and Patti MacLeod with Marie Chapian. *Back on Course*. Fleming H. Revell, 1987.

Marc, David and Robert J. Thompson. *Prime Time, Prime Movers*. Little, Brown, 1992.

McKibben, Bill. *The Age of Missing Information*. Random House, 1992.

McNeil, Alex. *Total Television*. Penguin, 1991.

Mitz, Rick. *The Great TV Sitcom Book*. Richard Marek Publishers, 1980.

Parish, James Robert. *Actor's Television Credits*. The Scarecrow Press, 1973. Supplemental volumes, 1978, 1982.

Pilato, Herbie J. *The Bewitched Book*. Delta, 1992.

Stempel, Tom. *Storytellers to the Nation: A History of American Television Writing*. Continuum, 1992.

Story, David. *America on the Rerun*. Citadel Press, 1993.

Waldron, Vince. *The Official Dick Van Dyke Show Book*. Hyperion, 1994.

Waldron, Vince. *Classic Sitcoms: A Celebration of the Best in Prime-Time Comedy*. Macmillan, 1987.

Weissman, Ginny and Coyne Steven Sanders. *The Dick Van Dyke Show: Anatomy of a Classic*. St. Martin's Press, 1983.

Winship, Michael. *Television*. Random House, 1988.

About the Writers

LAURA BELGRAY feels that *Bewitched* is not sexist, but in fact "proto-feminist." She began her TV career at age three when she appeared in the opening to *Sesame Street* in her little red snow suit. She has written for Nick at Nite and VH1, where she found every possible rhyme for "Hootie."

BRUCE BERNSTEIN is a noted scholar of classic television, as well as an expert in avante-garde cinema of the fifties and the sixties, modern jazz, and the music of the Ventures. He has written Nick at Nite promos, advertising, and on-line material since 1991, including the classic "Mod Joe Friday" spot, the "Major Nelson Howl," the 1994 Block Party Summer promotion, as well as the half-hour Nick at Nite specials *Isaac Mizrahi: A Frockumentary* and *Nick at Nite Time.*

GENNIFER BIRNBACH works in the Nick at Nite Programming department where her vast knowledge of TV Land is put to constant use. She has almost sixty lunchboxes, knows every word of every Flintstones episode, and can identify any Brady Bunch episode within twenty seconds of the opening. Her family greets her visits home with *The Dick Van Dyke Show* theme song, because it's guaranteed she will trip over something soon.

DALE CUNNINGHAM works as a writer-researcher for Nick at Nite On-Air Promotions and Marketing, where his greatest thrill so far was meeting Bill Daily in person. While watching every episode of *I Dream of Jeannie,* Dale felt himself slowly transforming into a younger, shorter version of Bill Daily, and to this day will unconsciously put his hands flat against his upper chest and drum his fingers.

MARK DAVIS is a man about town, sometime radio personality, writer and producer. He wrote the "Jeannie's Diner," Bob Newhart, and Dick Van Dyke song parodies for Nick at Nite, (his "singing" can be heard on the latter two pieces) along with other promos. He also does an excellent Vin Scully impression, collects Fossil watches, and if you throw a handful of M&Ms in the air while calling out a color, he can catch that color M&M in his mouth.

TOM HILL is the Associate Creative Director of On-Air Promotion for Nick at Nite, where he has worked writing promos since 1989. He also wrote the 1995 Nick at Nite special *Brady: An American Chronicle*. Tom is known as the Frank Adamo of Nick at Nite because of his frequent on-air cameo appearances. He is also author of six young-adult novels and several humor books, most recently the parody guide for father-to-be *What to Expect When Your Wife is Expanding*.

BOB HOGAN credits his mother for being the classic TV connoisseur who urged him to think about what he was watching and is also proud that her son has counted every "Hi Bob" in the *The Bob Newhart Show*. Of course it was only natural for the chapter on Dr. Robert Anthony Hartley (of the Midwest) to be written by Robert Anthony Hogan (also of the Midwest). Bob currently works as a Writer-Producer at WNEM-TV5 in Saginaw, Michigan.

JOHN MILLER would like to be recognized as "the boy genius," but since he is no longer a boy, and hardly a genius, that wish looks to be dead. As a TV producer, John has contributed to such shows as *The Dick Cavett Show* and *Politically Incorrect*—as well as such Nick at Nite promotional events as "Shirley It Must Be Mother's Day" featuring the Partridge Family—before writing about *Welcome Back, Kotter*. John would like to thank his imaginary friend, Reggie, for his help with the spelling.

PETER RISAFI was a proud member of the Nick at Nite on-air promotions team for many years, writing and producing spots like "Gladys: The Neighbor Who Knew Too Much," the "1991 Classic TV Countdown," and the "Nick at Nite Loves Lucy" marathon. Growing up watching *I Love Lucy* he knew life would be better if he adopted a thick Cuban accent and learned to play the congo drums. Failing these, he decided simply to watch too much TV. As fate would have it, he wandered into TV promotion where watching too much TV is a job requirement, and it all paid off. He can now be found watching too much TV at f/X Networks as Executive Producer of On-Air Promotion.

CHRISTOPHER SIMMONS is a television trivia expert. He was a writer and researcher on the nationally syndicated TV trivia game show *Couch Potatoes* and is the author of the *1997 TV Trivia Desk Calendar* that will be available in bookstores in mid-1996. He has also written scripts for Nickelodeon's animated series. In the best Ted Baxter Tradition, Chris extends to all readers a hearty "Hi, Guys."